MW01632973

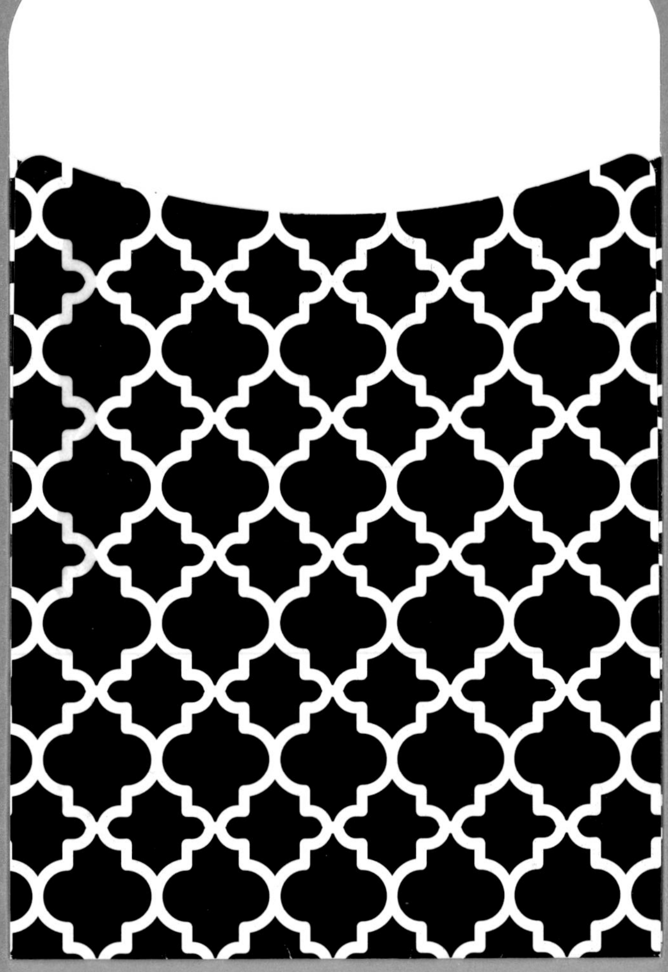

illus-trative **Brand-ing™**

Smashing illustrations for brands

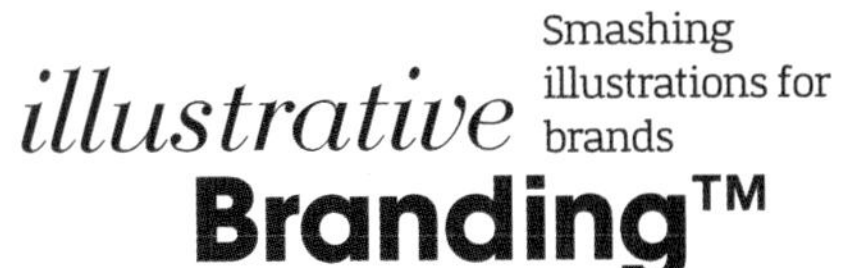

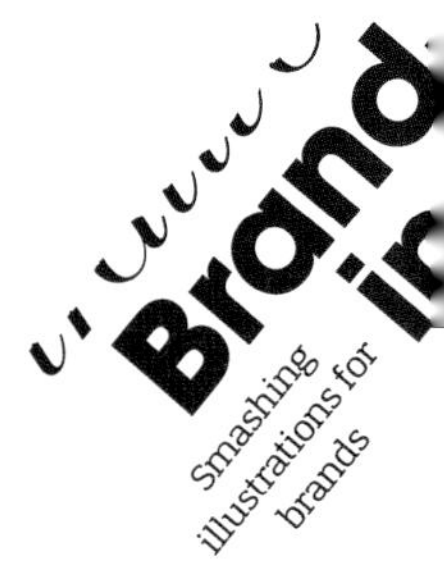

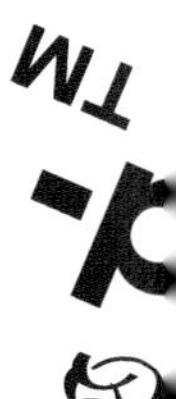

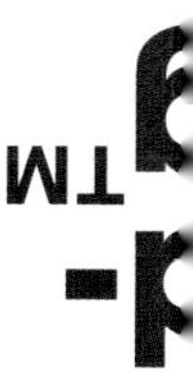

First published and distributed by
viction workshop ltd

viction:ary

viction workshop ltd
Unit C, 7/F, Seabright Plaza, 9-23 Shell Street,
North Point, Hong Kong
Url: www.victionary.com
Email: we@victionary.com
www.facebook.com/victionworkshop
www.twitter.com/victionary_
www.weibo.com/victionary

Edited and produced by viction:ary
Preface by Katee Hui

Concept & art direction by Victor Cheung
Book design by viction workshop ltd

ISBN 978-988-12228-5-5
Printed and bound in China

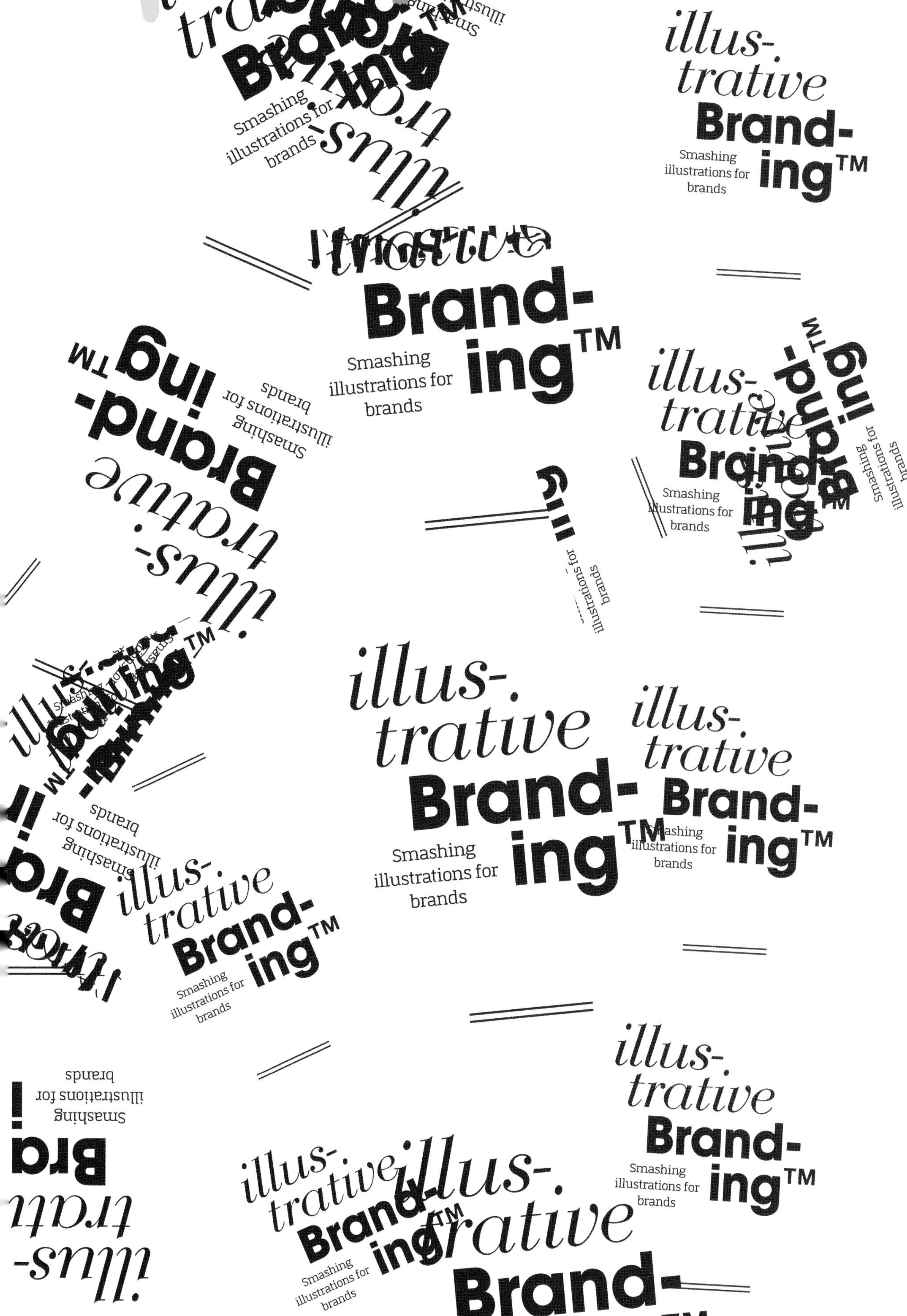
illus-
trative
Brand-
ing™
Smashing
illustrations for
brands

people
Remember.

Illustrations tell stories. It's what people Remember.

Preface

Illustrations tell stories. It's what people Remember.

In an increasingly interconnected world, where markets are saturated with a growing number of products, brands must explore ways of distinguishing themselves. A shift towards all things digital makes it harder for people to relate to brands as there's a lack of personal interaction. Brands need to work harder to create an identity and visual language that is unique and can create a meaningful connection with consumers.

It is important for a brand to be memorable and desirable. Brands want to communicate to consumers what they stand for and the value they can add to a person's life. Through a visual identity, brands reveal the quality of their product or service. From the very first point of contact for consumers, a brand will be judged on its look and feel. Bad visual language can lower consumer engagement. If language is confusing or not distinctive, it won't endure in peoples mind. It will be lost in a competitive marketplace. Good graphic language, however, can lead to more sales and a greater loyalty base. Creating a recognisable brand territory reminds consumers of a brand's presence. A strong visual language can provide a holistic brand experience, engaging consumers in the narrative of what it means to buy into a brand.

Illustration offers brands the ability to be memorable and desirable. Through crafted visuals, like hand-rendered typography and linocut print patterns, illustration has the ability to solve problems where other mediums may fall short. Photography for example, can be limited by the camera's ability to story tell. Whilst photos can be compelling, they show specific situations. Illustration is capable of storytelling and showing abstract concepts. It's more fantastical and not bound to reality in the same way photography is.

Hand crafted visuals add value because they straddle the art realm. Art is a desired commodity and consumers may have an appreciation for brands that embrace artistic qualities in their branding. Beautifully coloured shapes adorning wrapping paper in a shop represent part of the brand experience, where the illustrated shapes on something tactile can lead to consumers collecting visual elements of the brand, the same way that people collect art. It's unique and can represent something meaningful. It also shows a brand's creative ambitions to develop a propriety personality.

It's often the smallest of details that show the level of consideration and thought in the design. The slightest of brush strokes on a business card or a stray drop of sealing wax on an envelope shows authenticity and craft. It's these details that can have the biggest impact. It's what people remember. The bespoke nature of hand rendered designs invites a meaningful connection through the care put into the details.

Illustration has the ability to be flexible. From personified animals to alternative realities to labyrinths of rich textures, these worlds are made possible through illustrated. Brands become memorable through the stories told through illustrations. To be positioned as fun and playful, a brand may use humour and hand rendered quirky characters to show this. These characters may have names and always appear in a similar place on products. For brands wishing to convey luxury, a highly detailed approach to artwork that covets heritage and tradition may be employed. Regardless of market, illustration can cater to a range of branding requirements because of its flexibility.

Take a restaurant space as an example. Illustration can create a theatric experience, one that takes the customer on a journey in a setting that transports them into a different world. Restaurant spaces need to have a sense of occasion and an environment that is different to the everyday. Through large environmental murals the brand language drives the experience and invites the diner to a place that's out of the ordinary. This canvas allows visual language to play out in the space through each customisable touchpoints.

On a smaller scale, illustrated packaging can be a unique touchpoint experience for a consumer. The graphic language on a package may reveal part of the design on the outside and as it's unwrapped there could be a world of overlapping patterns lining the inside or a hidden handwritten massage. The packaging could also be an imaginative version the object that's wrapped up. A hand drawn depiction of the contents contained within a package could tempt curiosity. The flexible nature of illustration allows a dynamic approach, applicable on any scale and on a variety of touchpoints.

When developing a visual language, great results are achieved through collaboration. Illustrators learn and understand the brand that designers have established and then they work together to express this in a way. This collaboration can involve reinvigorating brand assets, such as a redrawn identity or adding more colours to the palette. Illustrators and designers may also work together to evolve a brand by creating new brand assets to express the overall graphic language.

Illustrative Branding features work that captivates the imagination through carefully crafted visual languages for brands. Each example in this book demonstrates how illustration has strengthened brands through well-executed solutions and ideas. When an illustrator's work compliments a brand's objectives the result is a powerful story told through stunning visuals. From delightful packaging exploding with bold colours, to serene naturescapes full of fauna and flora, this books takes you on a journey through some of the finest illustrative branding projects.

Powerful
Stories

The Powerful Stories

The Powerful Stories

The Powerful Stories

Illustration has the ability to transport people's minds. In its mix of fantasy and realism, these personalised objects captivate imagination and connect stories. From household brands to international art shows, these case studies ask eight brand builders what constitute a holistic brand experience.

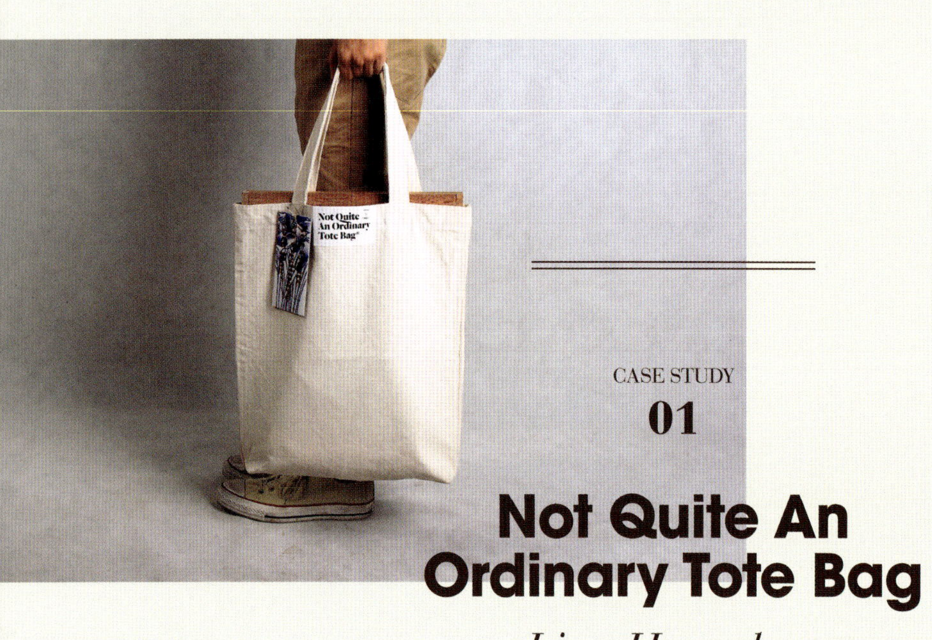

CASE STUDY

01

Not Quite An Ordinary Tote Bag

Liow Heng-chun

Not Quite An Ordinary Tote Bag is the collaborative effort between young fashion brand, Bershka and designer Liow Heng-chun. As a school assignment, the brief challenges the students' ability in incorporating their personal styles into a brand's essence where the designer and the assigned fashion brand complement each other across a myriad of communication mediums.

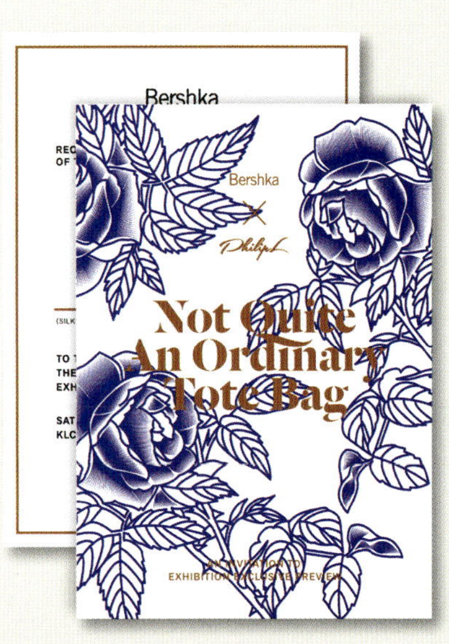

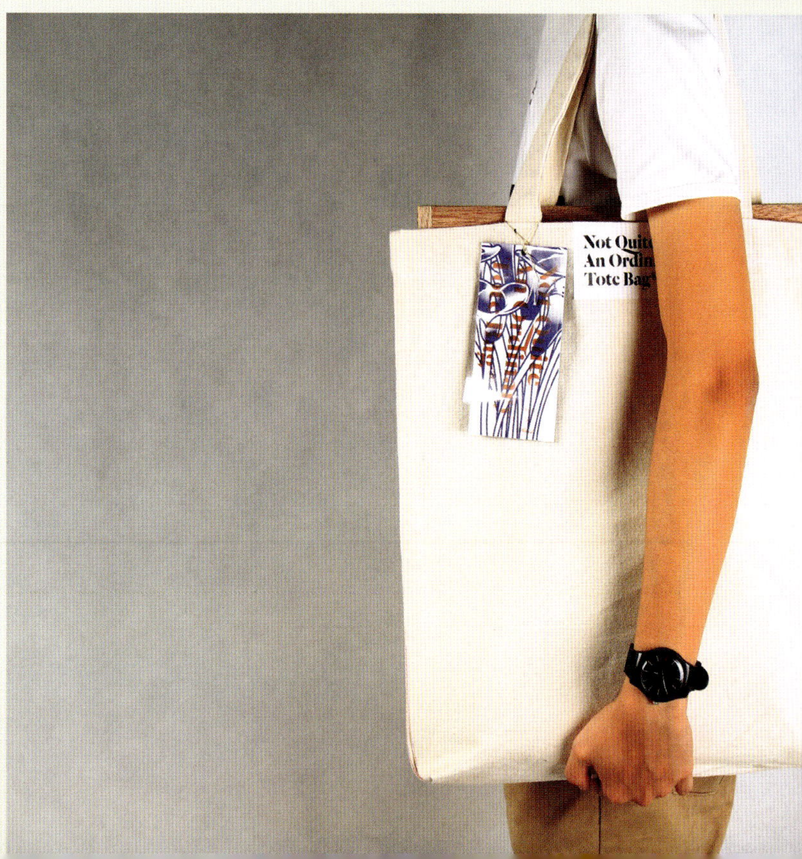

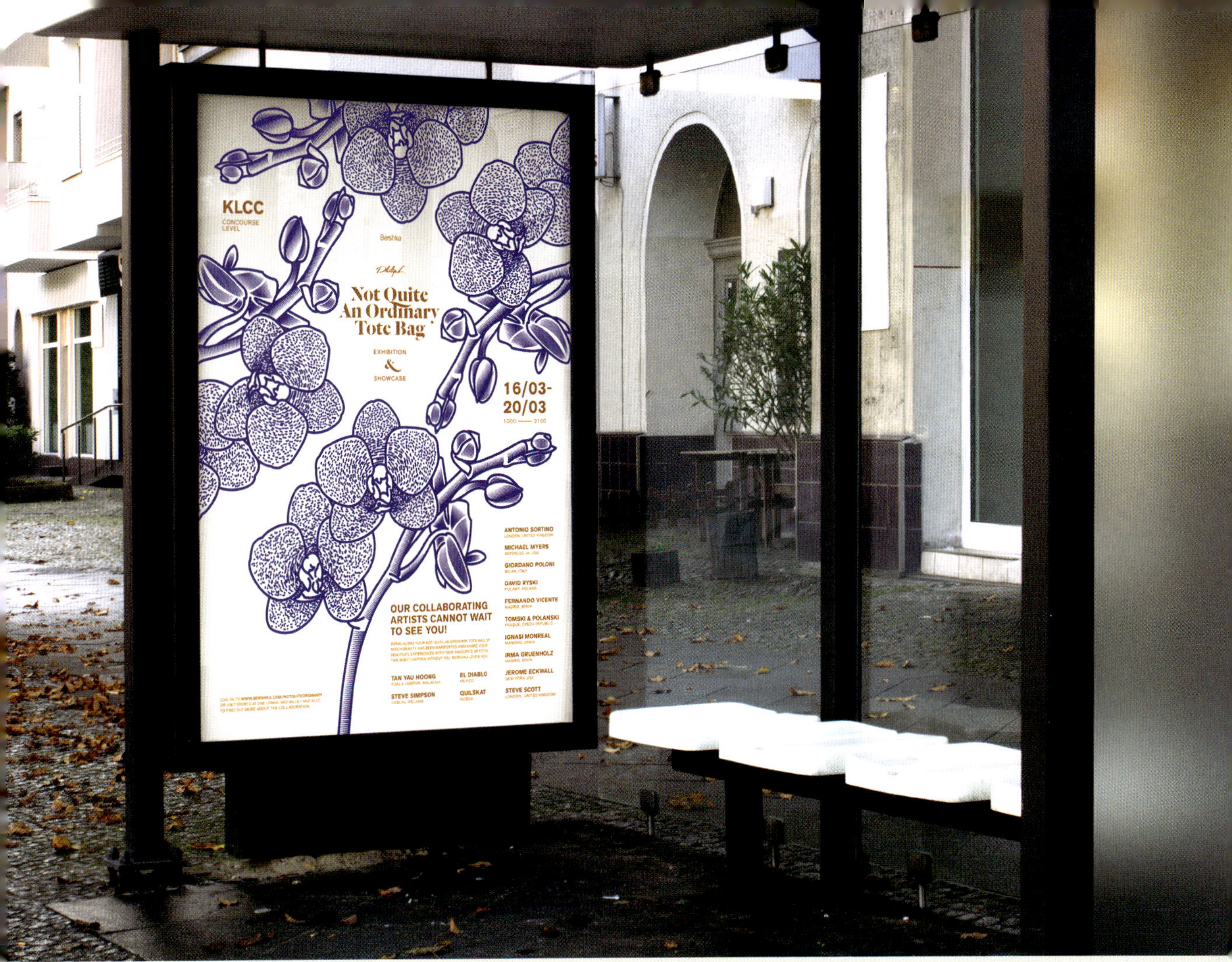

Conception

Bershka not only puts emphasis on the slightest details, but also youthful expression with marked individuality. A loather of fast fashion, Liow envisioned a platform which directly facilitates creative exchange and impassions engagement between the fashion brand and its consumers.

Conceptually a blank canvas, Not Quite An Ordinary Tote Bag is designed to be an experience instead of a product. The branding approach was assumably a bold statement that would appeal to people who are rebelliously fashionable and flamboyant in nature. Liow also reckoned that on top of a typographic approach with witty lines, personal touches could make for a more effective branding strategy. Although he was especially inspired by Amelia Earhart, the first female aviator to fly solo across the Atlantic Ocean, his first attempts featuring American aviation-inspired patterns and geometric designs turned out overly monotonous – not eye-catching enough.

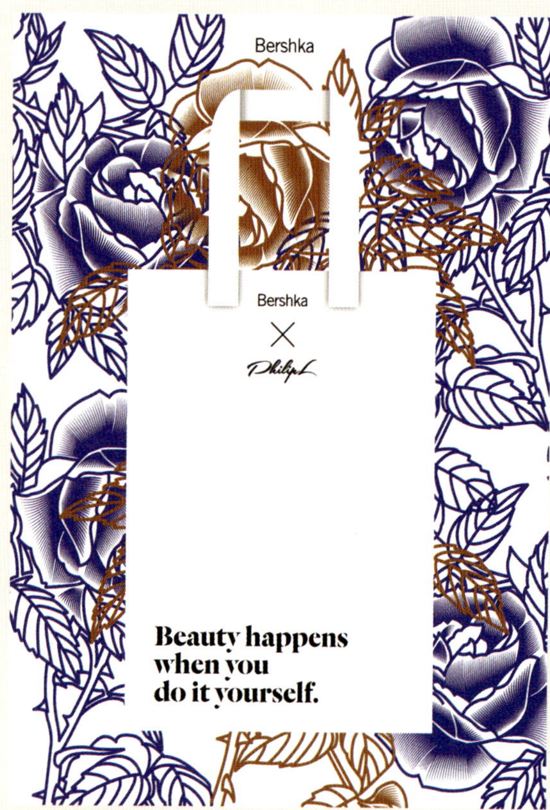

Bershka

×

In Beauty
We Trust

Manifesting beauty like never before, Not Quite An Ordinary Tote Bag® by Bershka is more than just an experience.

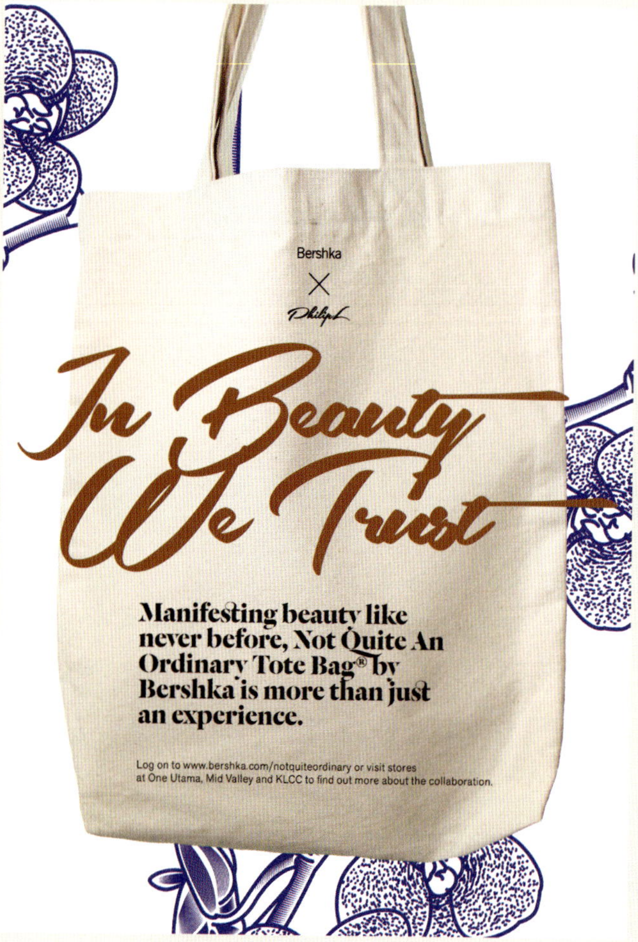

Log on to www.bershka.com/notquiteordinary or visit stores at One Utama, Mid Valley and KLCC to find out more about the collaboration.

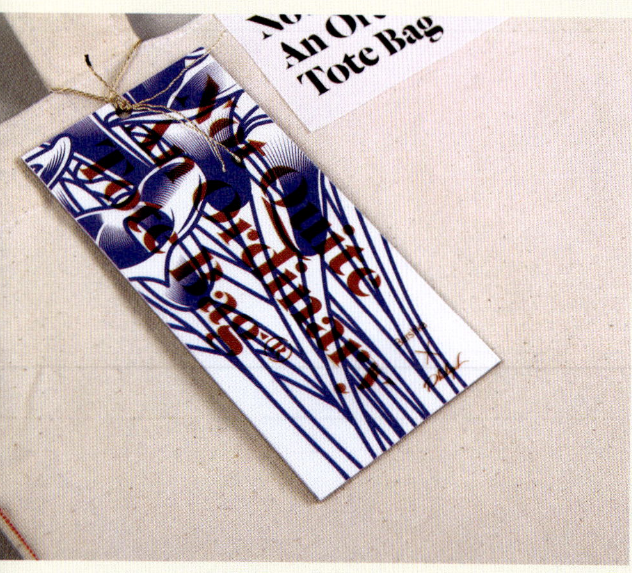

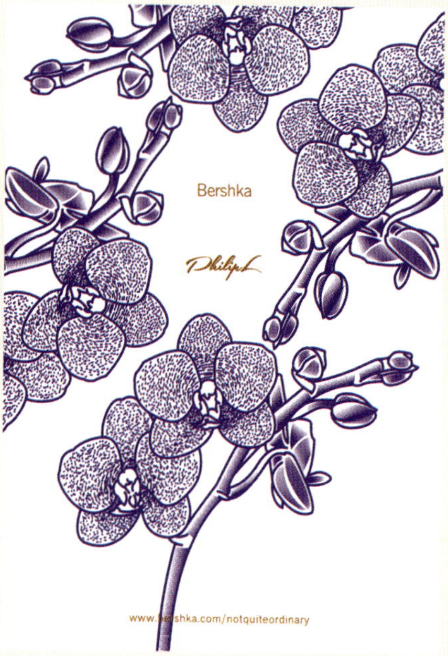

Bershka

www.bershka.com/notquiteordinary

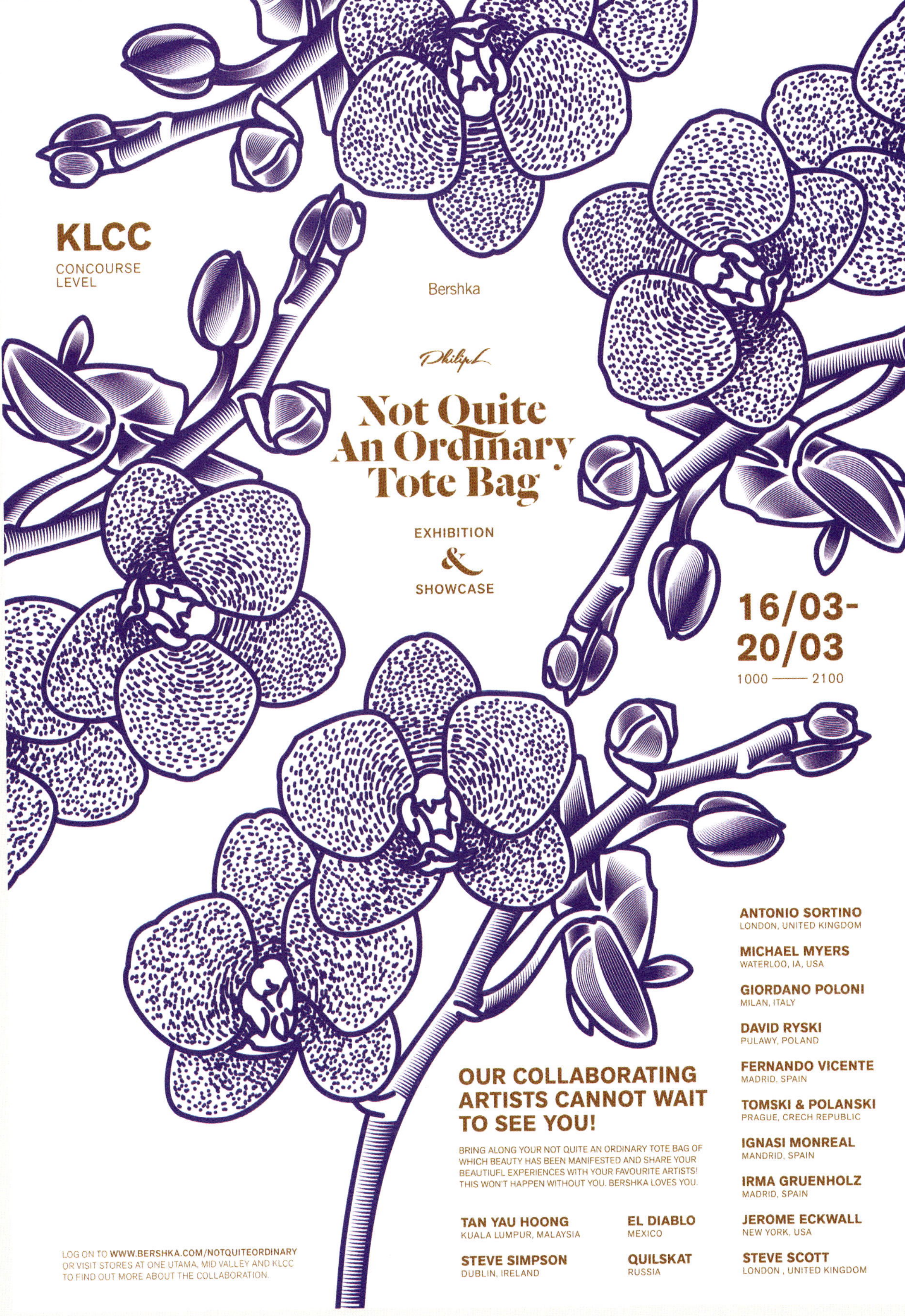
KLCC
CONCOURSE LEVEL
Bershka
Philip
Not Quite An Ordinary Tote Bag
EXHIBITION
&
SHOWCASE
16/03-
20/03
1000 —— 2100
ANTONIO SORTINO
LONDON, UNITED KINGDOM
MICHAEL MYERS
WATERLOO, IA, USA
GIORDANO POLONI
MILAN, ITALY
DAVID RYSKI
PULAWY, POLAND
FERNANDO VICENTE
MADRID, SPAIN
TOMSKI & POLANSKI
PRAGUE, CRECH REPUBLIC
IGNASI MONREAL
MANDRID, SPAIN
IRMA GRUENHOLZ
MADRID, SPAIN
JEROME ECKWALL
NEW YORK, USA
STEVE SCOTT
LONDON , UNITED KINGDOM
OUR COLLABORATING ARTISTS CANNOT WAIT TO SEE YOU!
BRING ALONG YOUR NOT QUITE AN ORDINARY TOTE BAG OF WHICH BEAUTY HAS BEEN MANIFESTED AND SHARE YOUR BEAUTIUFL EXPERIENCES WITH YOUR FAVOURITE ARTISTS! THIS WON'T HAPPEN WITHOUT YOU. BERSHKA LOVES YOU.
TAN YAU HOONG
KUALA LUMPUR, MALAYSIA
EL DIABLO
MEXICO
STEVE SIMPSON
DUBLIN, IRELAND
QUILSKAT
RUSSIA
LOG ON TO WWW.BERSHKA.COM/NOTQUITEORDINARY OR VISIT STORES AT ONE UTAMA, MID VALLEY AND KLCC TO FIND OUT MORE ABOUT THE COLLABORATION.

Solution

Since Bershka targets mostly the ladies, flowers was thought to be a more intuitive choice for effective communication. Rose that signifies passion and timelessness, orchid that denotes beauty and strength, and a slightly unusual choice, calla lily that symbolises youth were taken as the core visual elements, and illustrated in a way that subtly suggested rebellious charm of which the target audience takes pride.

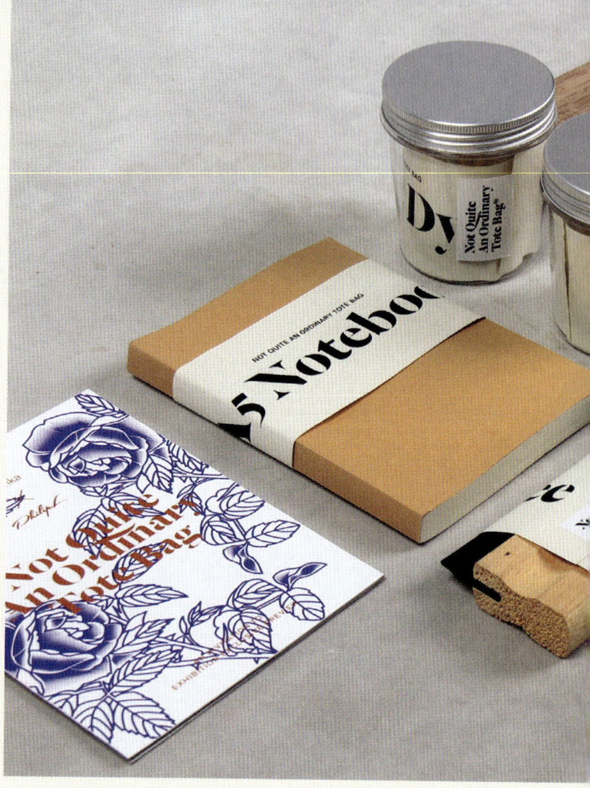

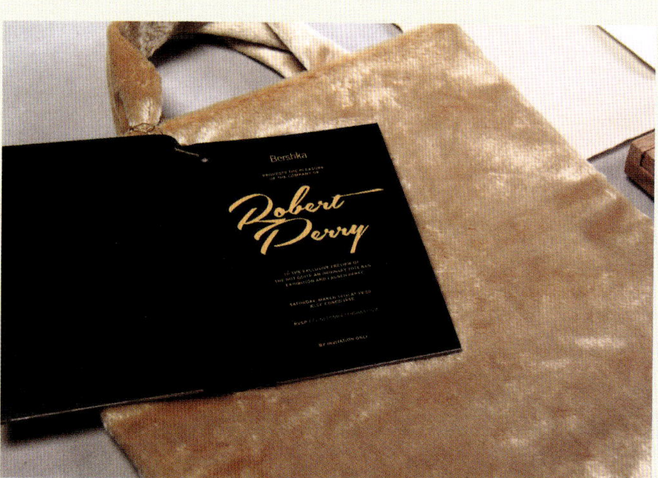

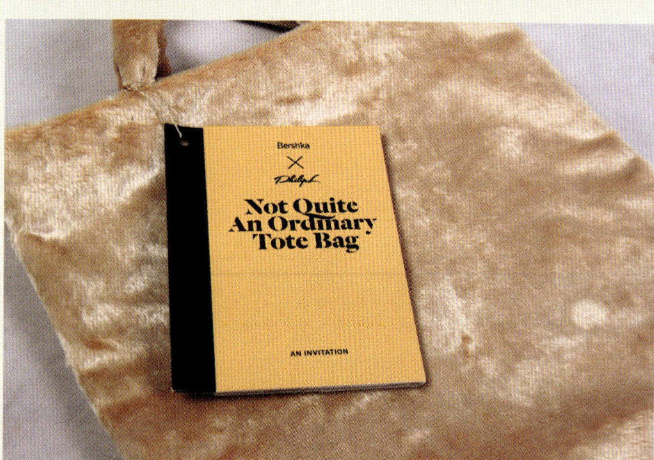

The resulting visual identity features patterns on Bershka's price tag and invitations that admits guests to an exclusive exhibition where artists' contribution to Not Quite An Ordinary Tote Bag were displayed. Liow himself had also made a custom tote bag using golden pleuche and an invitation card attached to one of its handles. In stores, the flowers grew oversize, looking exceptionally magical and majestic.

Not Quite An Ordinary Bag contained an instruction manual, a 12"x18" screen, a squeegee, fabric paint colour at user's choice, photo emulsion, a notebook, a blank T-shirt and an invitation card that encourages individual artistic expression and reconnects its owners to their innate creativity.

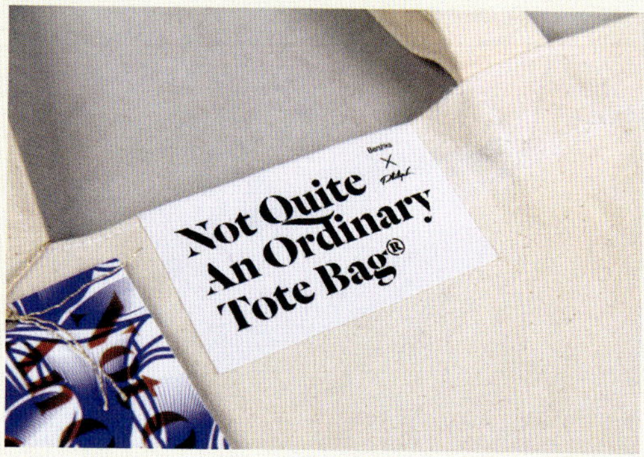

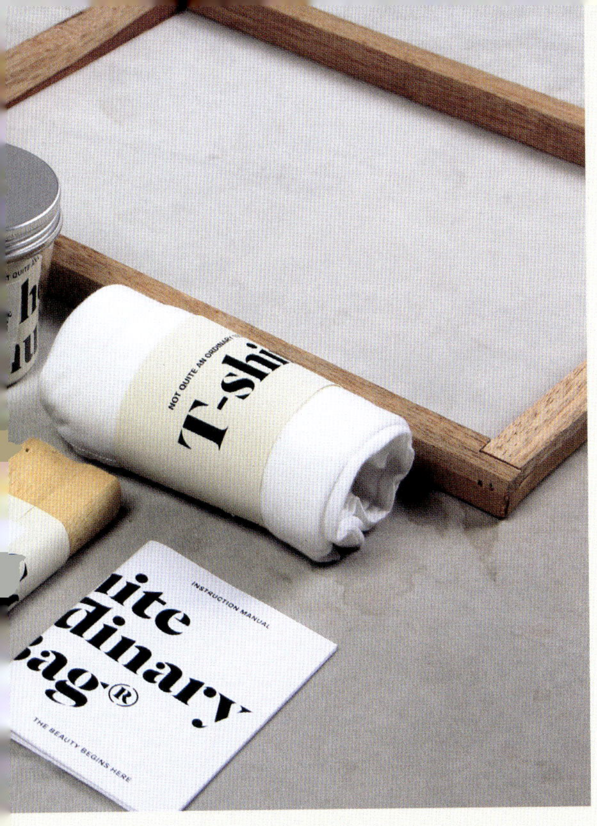

Review

To Liow, working with illustrations had been a lot of fun, but it would have been less effective without the beautiful typeface (Dala Floda by Commercial Type) to complete the visual identity. As for future brand development, it was the designer's wish to see how these floral illustrations could be further expanded to materialise into a full garden and perhaps be incorporated into Bershka's upcoming collection.

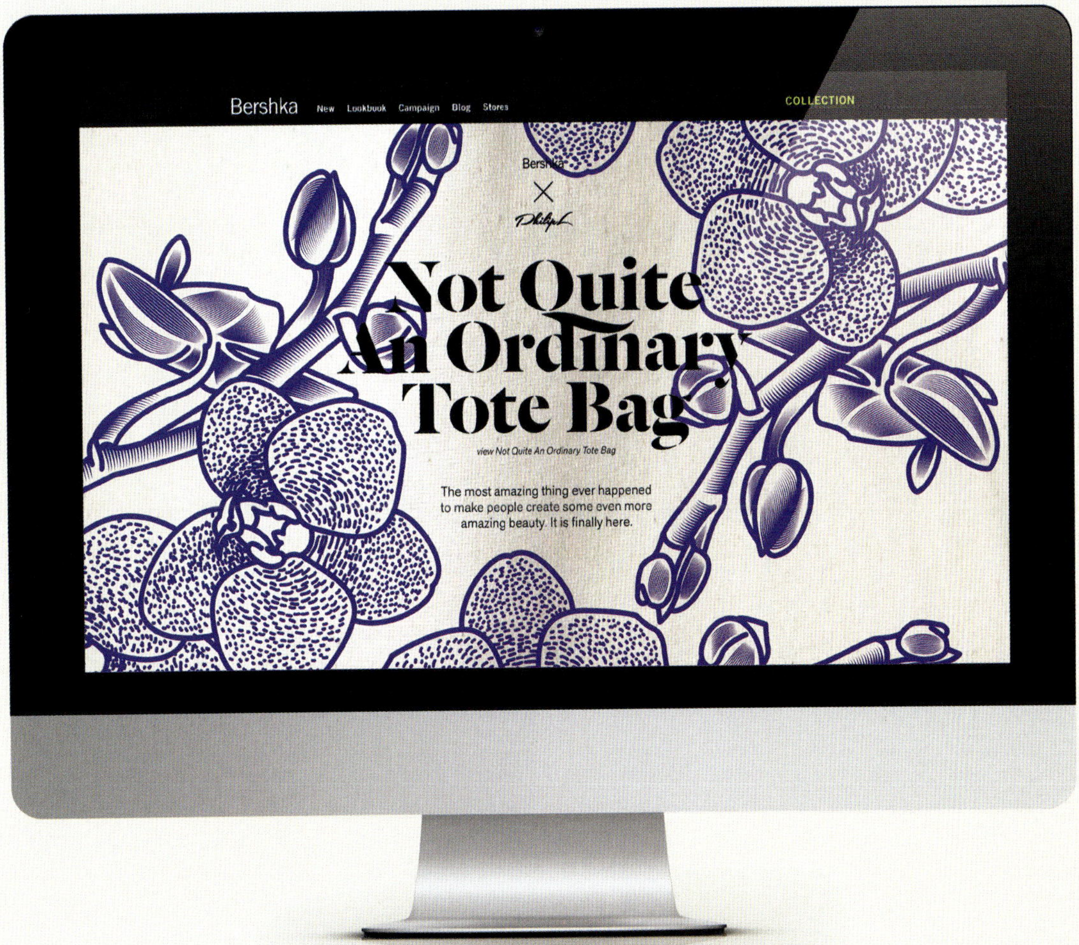

Conception

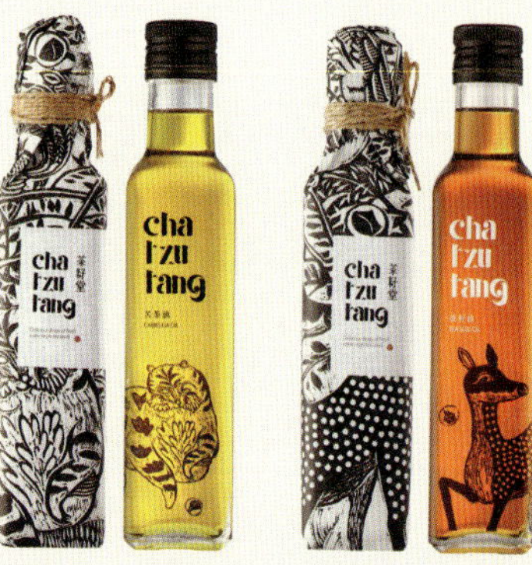

The project was originated from a second generation's resolution to rebrand his family business. Targeting those aspired to live a natural lifestyle, Cha Tzu Tang upholds the core values of harmony between man and nature, sustainable development as well as reinforcing Taiwanese artisan and cultural heritage. Despite carrying products with a competitive edge and cultural connotation, they couldn't shake off the daunting episodes of being mistaken as another brand. The company is in need of a distinctive image that delivers their core values when brought to international spotlight.

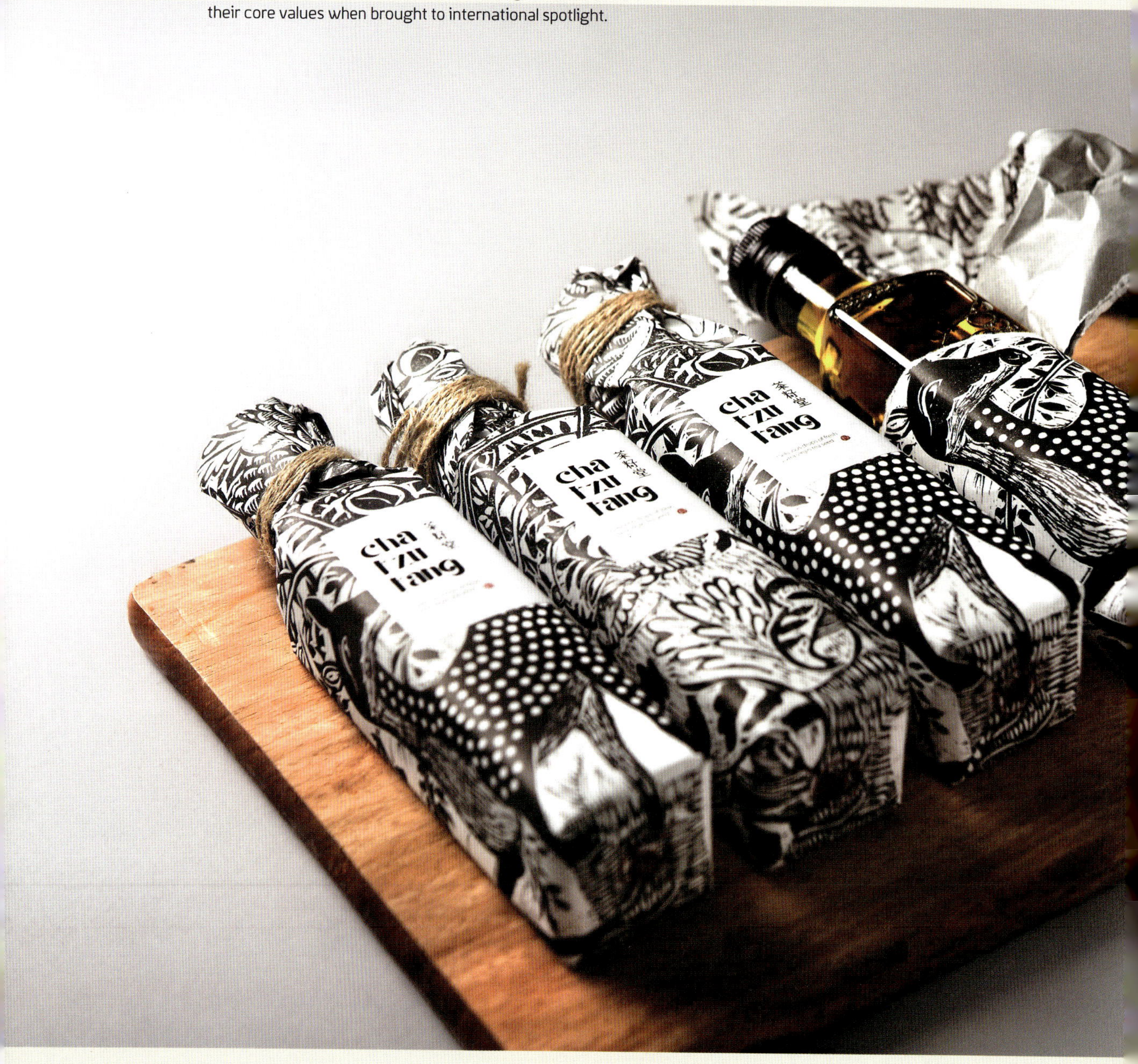

CASE STUDY

02

Cha Tzu Tang

Victor Branding Design Corp.,

With roots planted deep in Taiwan, Cha Tzu Tang is a manufacturer of health-and-environmentally conscious household items with the essence of local tea seeds (Cha Tzu). To support local farmers, Cha Tzu Tang not only practises direct trade but also helps innovating age-old techniques to sustain the growth of this botanic treasure only harvesting once a year.

Illustration: Shiu Ruei-jr

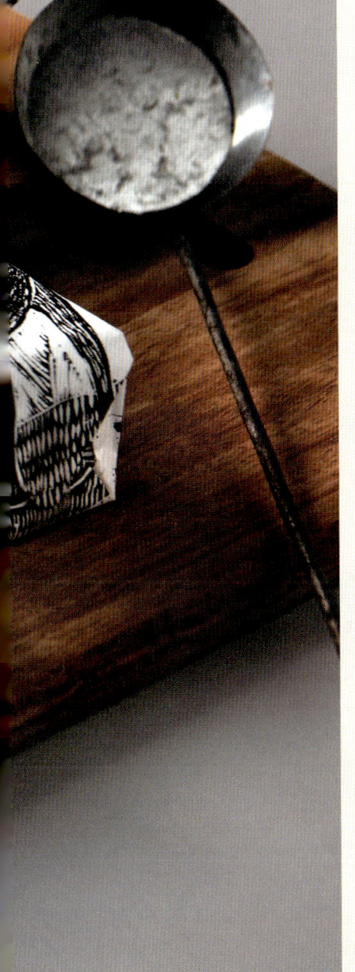

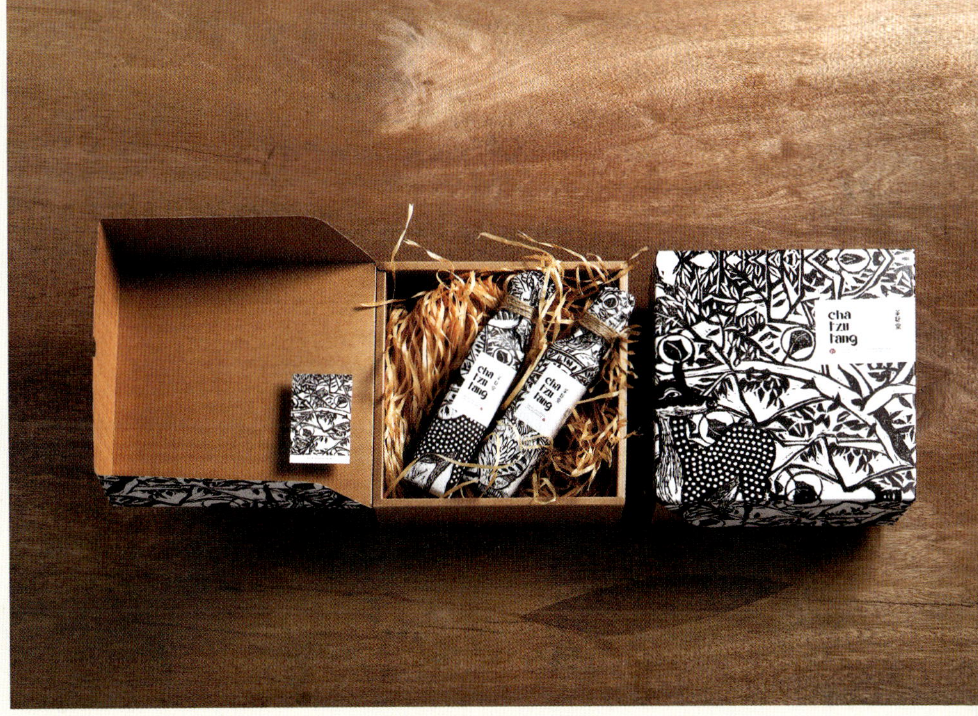

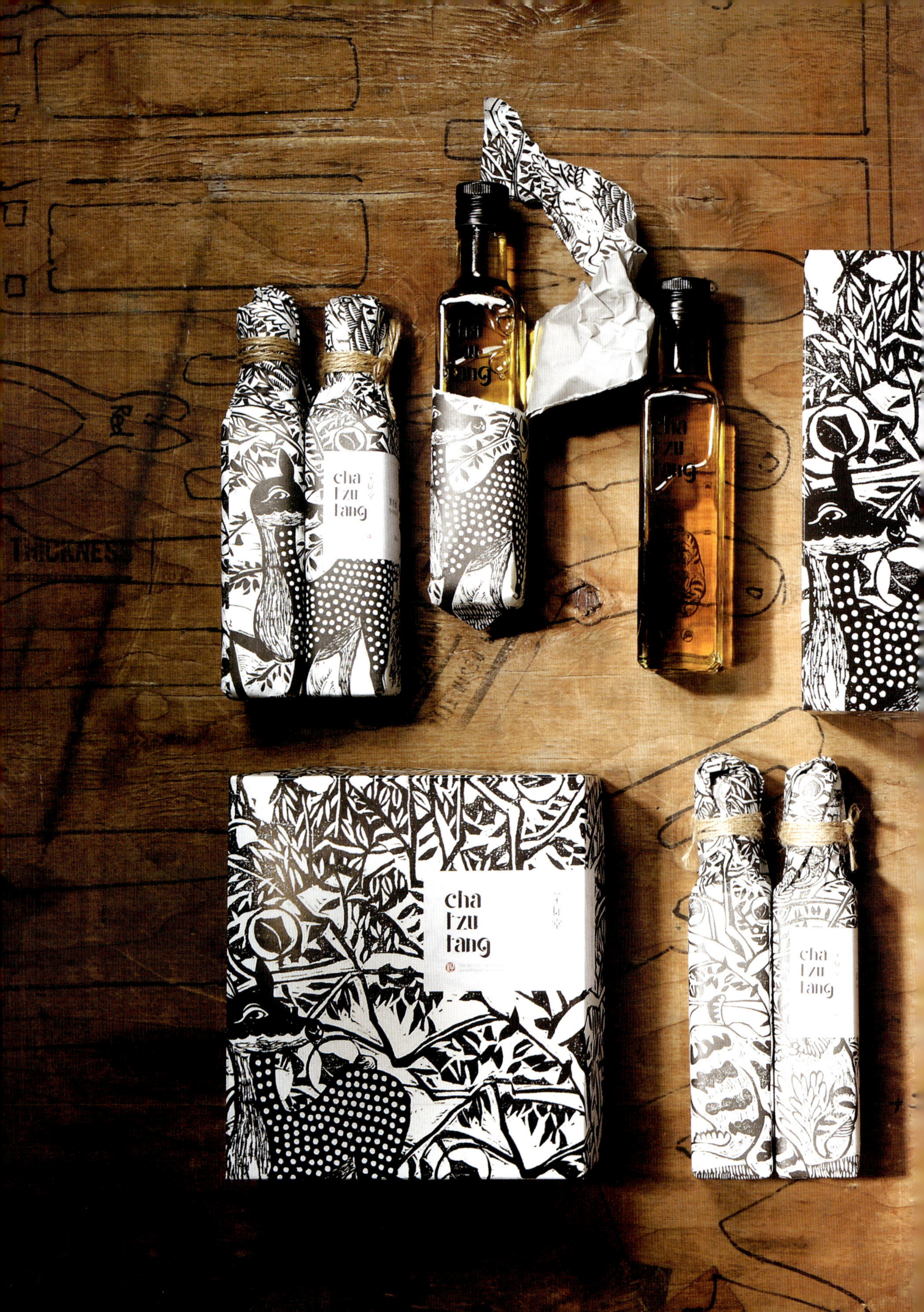
cha
tzu
tang
THICKNESS
Red

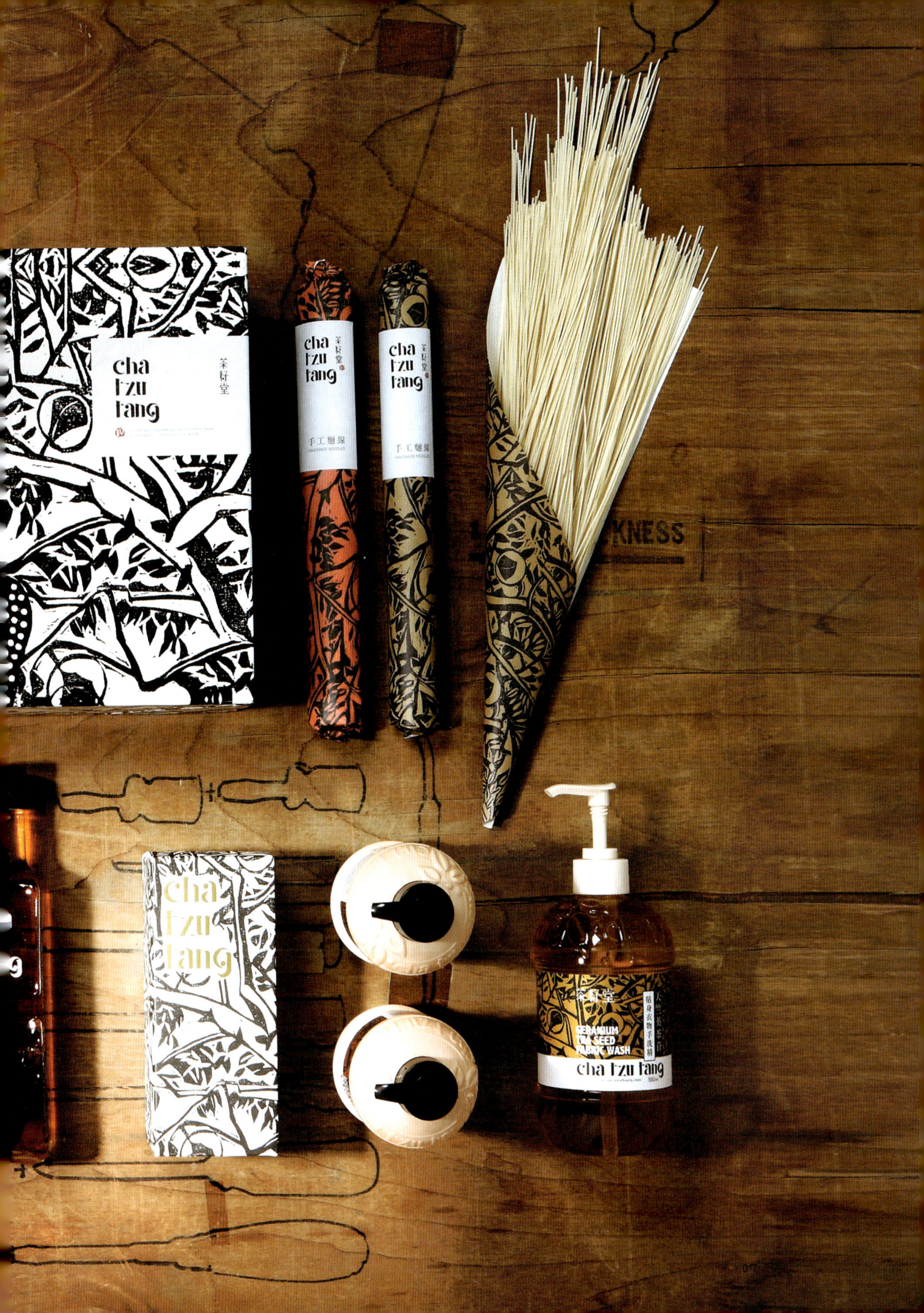
cha
tzu
tang
茶籽堂
cha
tzu
tang
茶籽堂
手工麵線
HANDMADE NOODLES
cha
tzu
tang
茶籽堂
手工麵線
HANDMADE NOODLES
cha
tzu
tang
茶籽堂
GERANIUM
TEA SEED
FABRIC WASH
貼身衣物手洗精
cha tzu tang
550ml

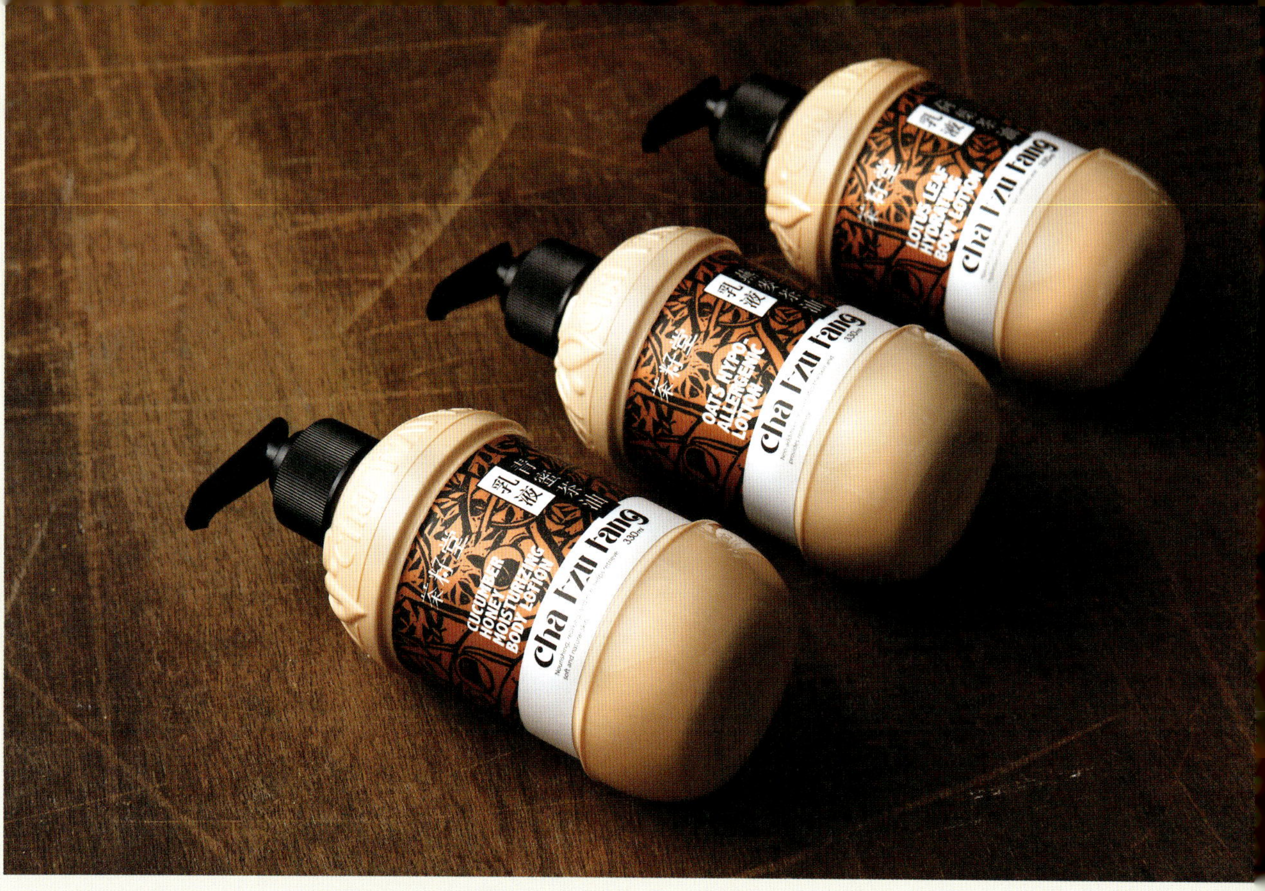

Solution

Bold and spirited, traditional monochrome prints by Taiwanese print artist Shiu Ruei-jr portrays the local tea seed habitat with tension, emphasising the presence of nature cohesively throughout the brand system. The logo was also reworked. Adhering to the style of prints, the English logotype carries equal weight as its Chinese counterpart to cater for an international market.

Born in Kaohsiung in 1982, Shiu is a MFA graduate at Taipei National University of the Arts. This collaboration was realised to match Cha Tzu Tang's vision to carry forward Taiwanese art and artisan excellence. It was hoped that the land's flourishing creativity and profuse cultural energy are let known around the globe along with their own products.

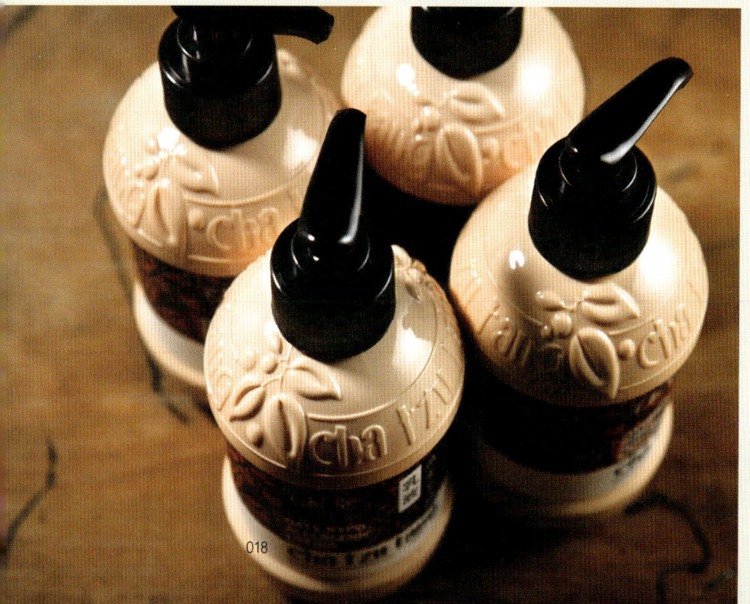

Review

Cha Tzu Tang carries quality products with a vision to better the lives of users – these are what Victor Design looks for in a client. It was a valued collaboration with a trusting counterpart under the agency's partners-oriented service – succeeded in a total make-over for their brand image, which has become more refined and grandeur.

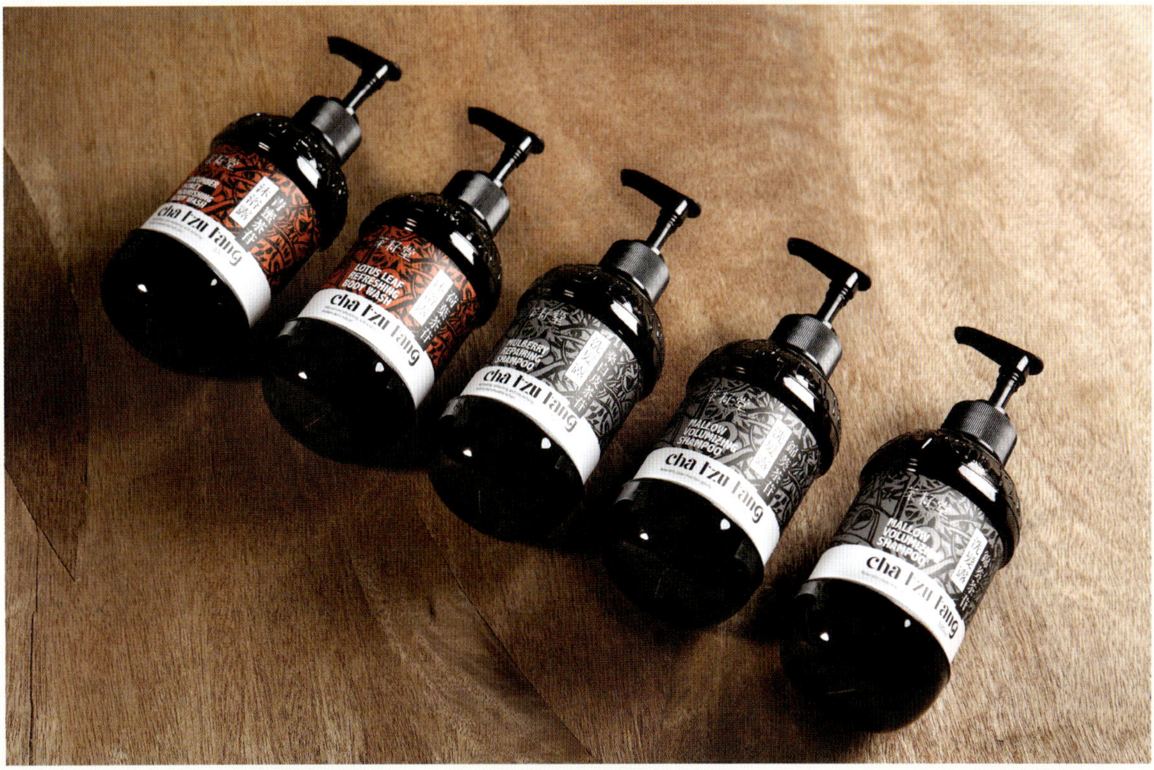

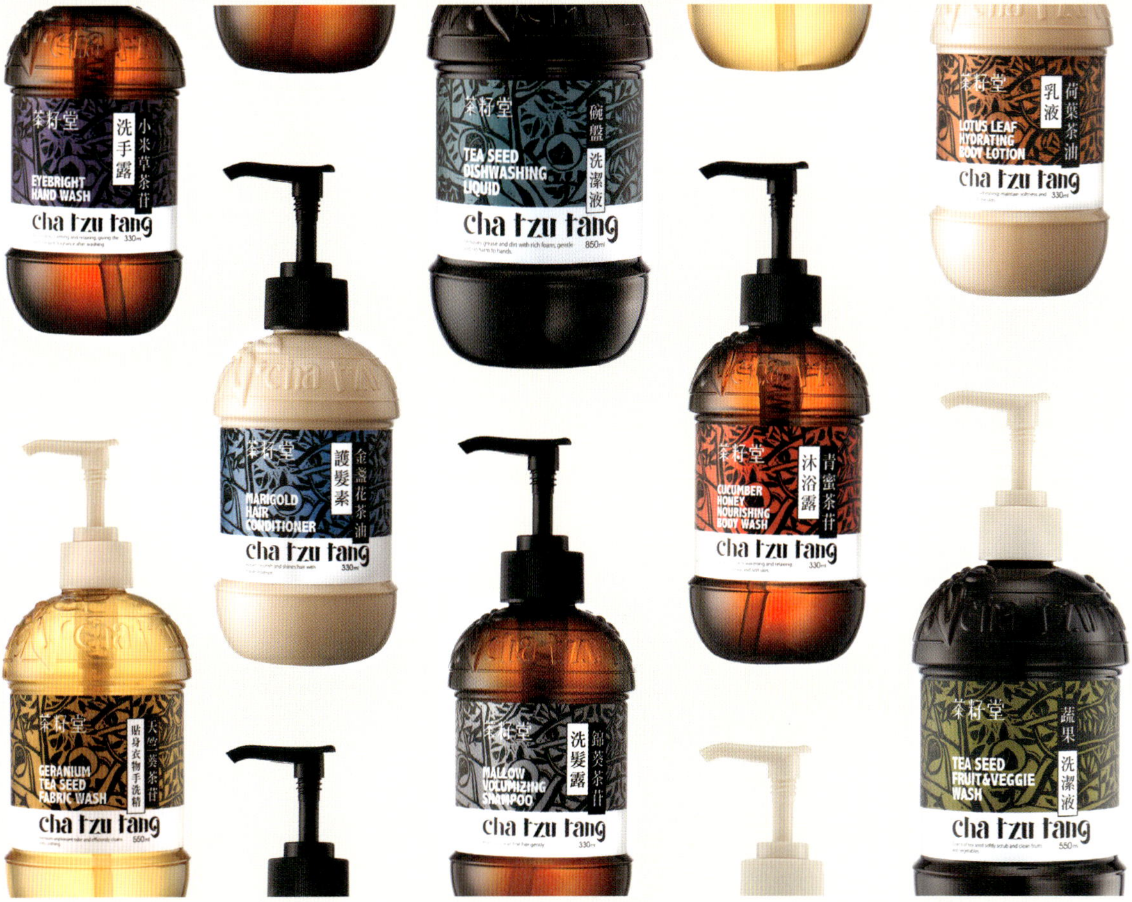

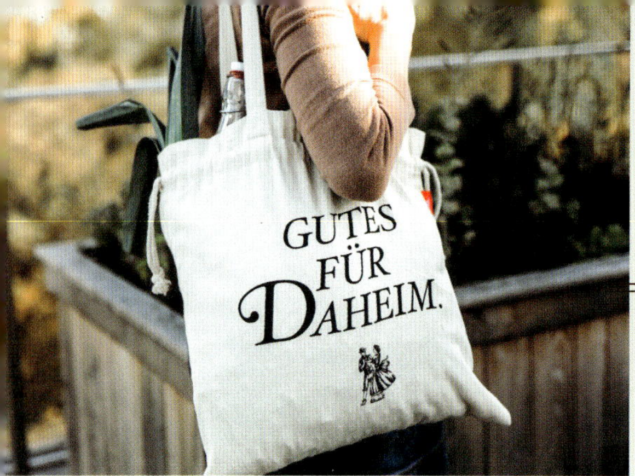

CASE STUDY

03

Servus am Marktplatz

moodley brand identity

The Red Bull Media House is the creator of the Austrian brand "Servus". They produce several magazines, even stream their own TV channel and offer lovely regional goods in their online shop. The "Servus am Marktplatz" online store is the centre of attention and moodley brand identity was asked to create a new packaging concept, suitable for everything they have to offer – from delicious treats to wooden garden rakes and felt slippers. The wrapping of the handmade products should reflect the value of all Servus projects: love of one's homeland, traditions of rural life and the quality of regional goods.

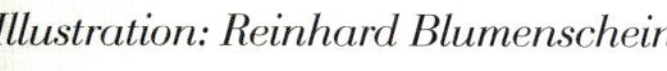

Illustration: Reinhard Blumenschein

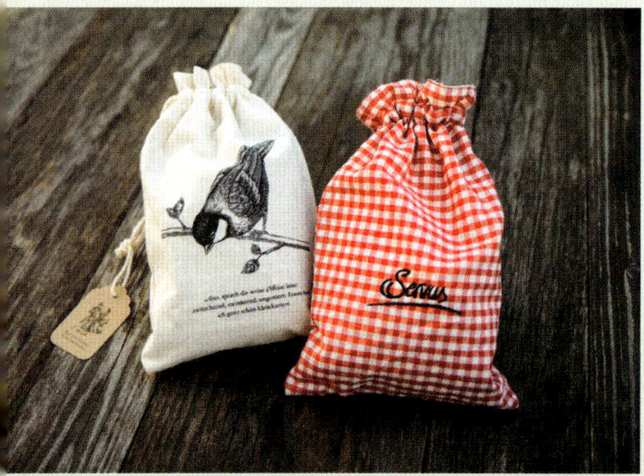

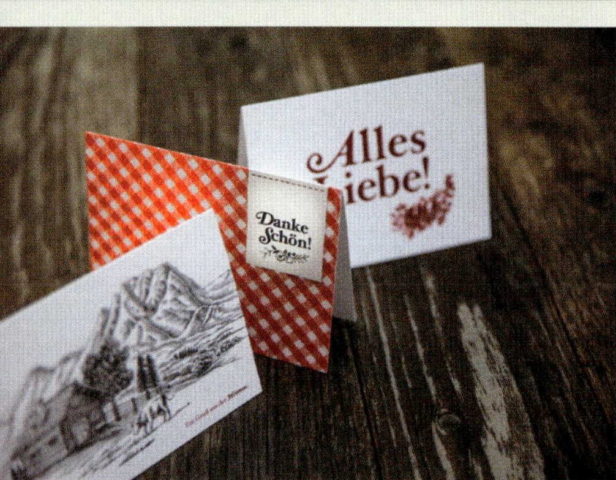

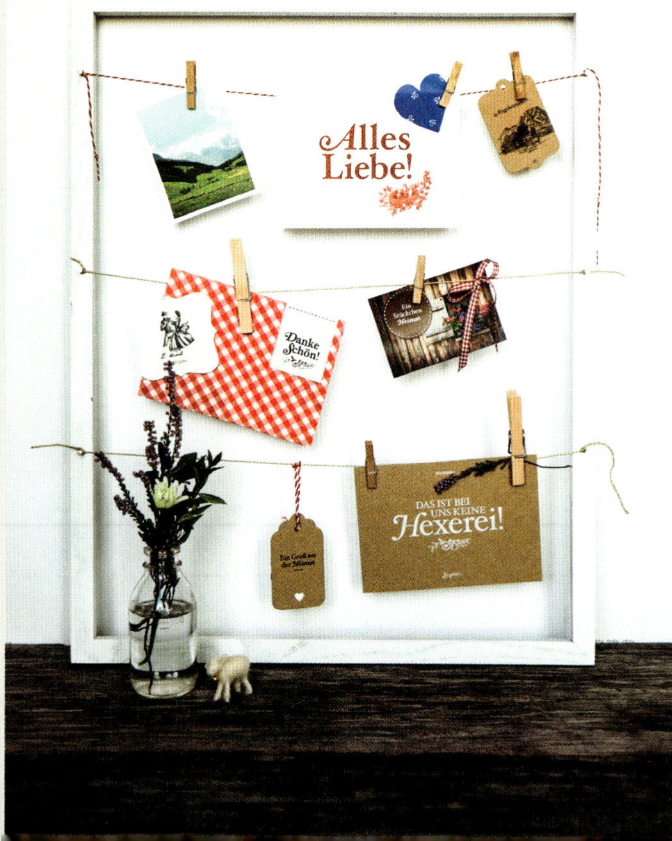

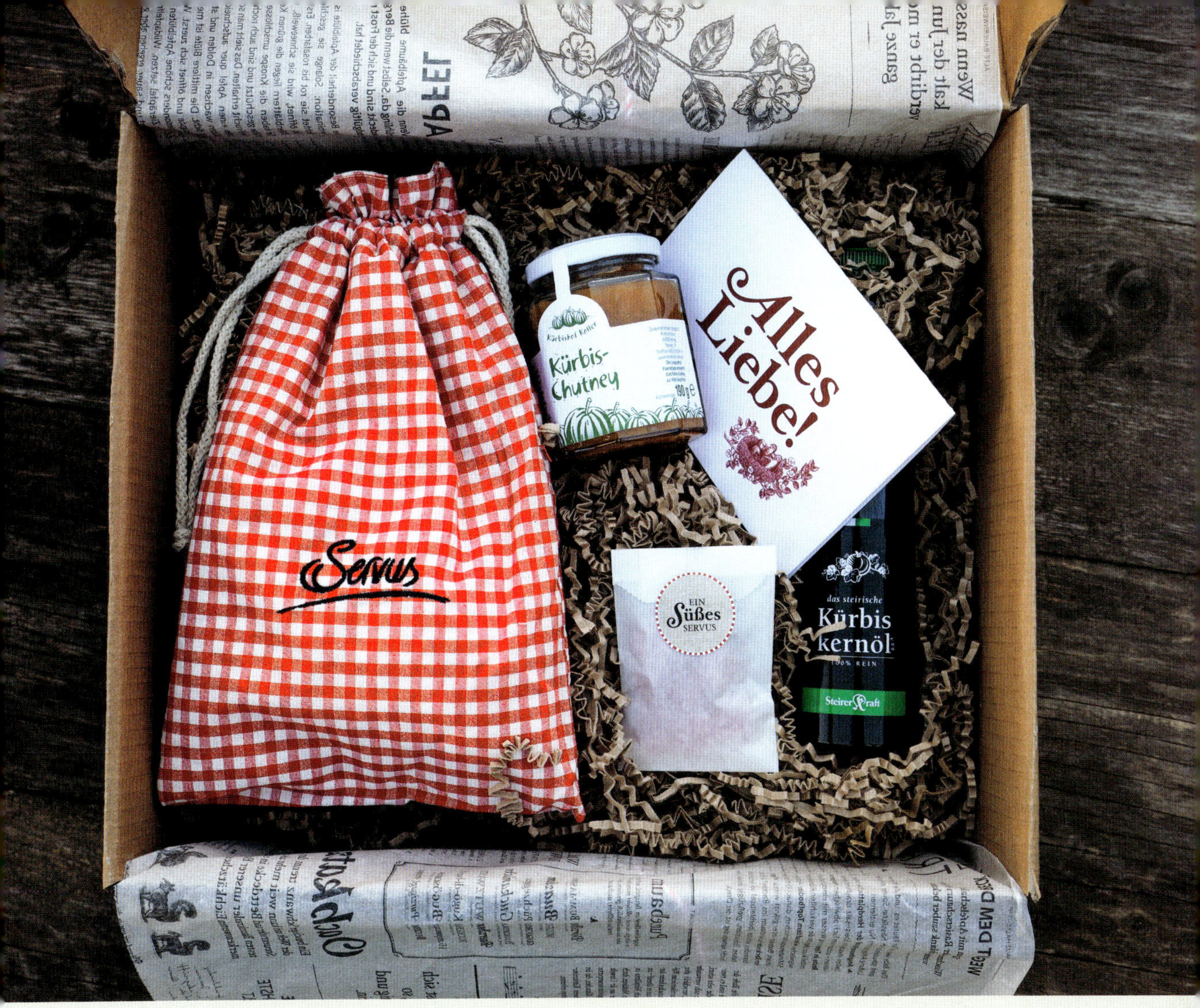

Conception

Who does not like to be surprised? Receiving something beautiful that you were not expecting and being able to hold it in your hands so that you can see and feel its quality, is something extremely valuable in our increasingly digital world. It was important for the designers to create customer proximity and to uphold the personal touch of regional goods, although you are buying them in a web shop.

It is well-known that a picture is worth a thousand words – and that was exactly what the designers had in mind. A beautiful illustration can be noticed in a second and can convey a sense of one's own cultural roots and home with only a few well-placed lines. The designers aimed to make customers see and feel the love, care and skill with which every product was crafted, wrapped and sent. By choosing illustrations as the core element of the design and with a passion for detail, they were able to send their message as soon as the customer first glanced at their delivered parcel – raising their joyful expectations.

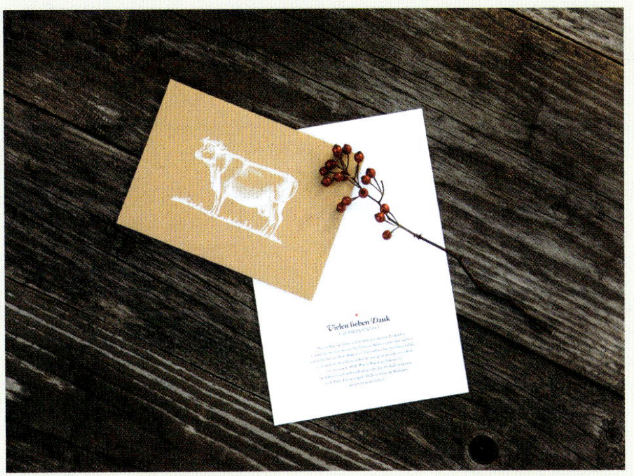

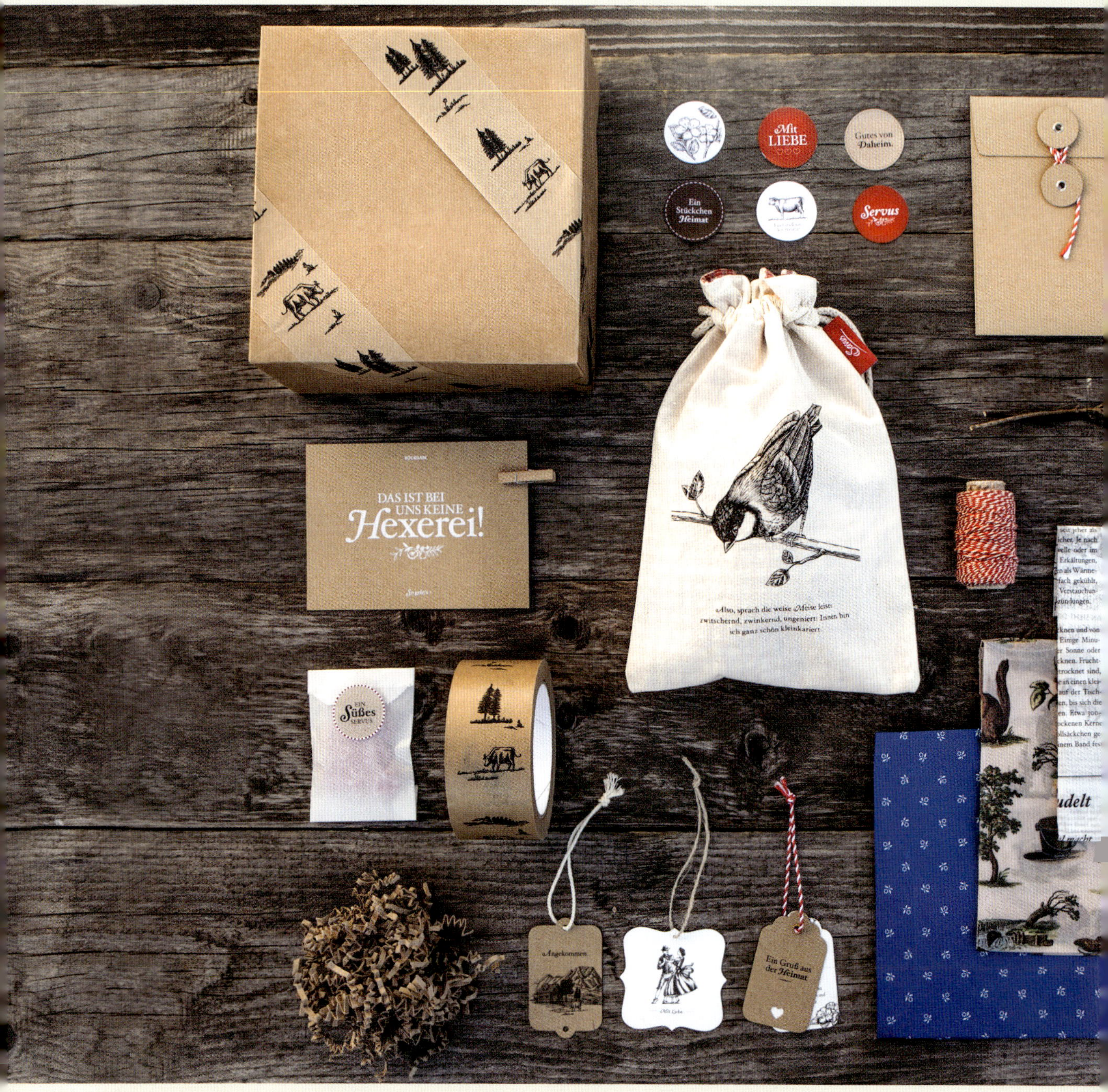

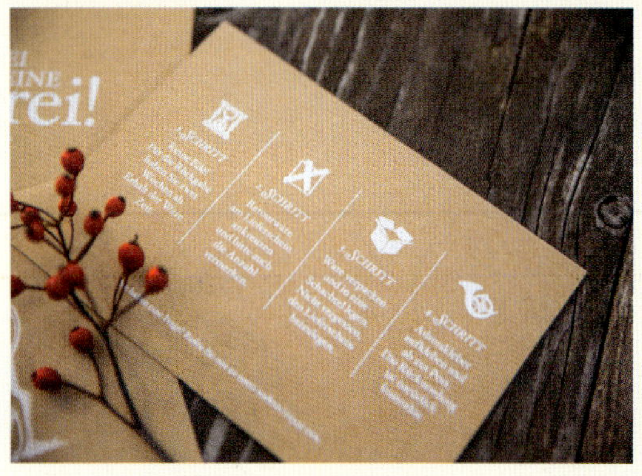

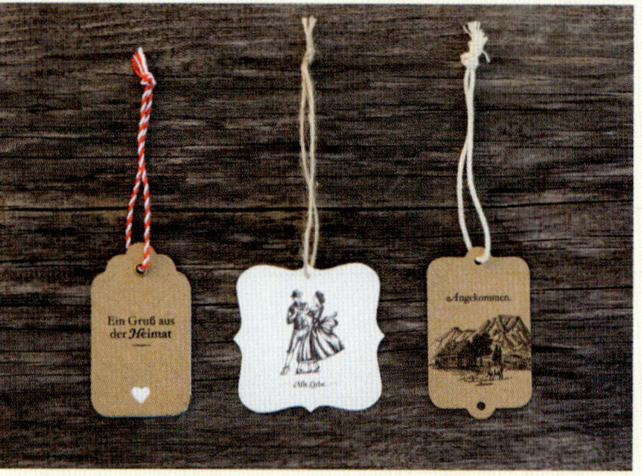
Ein Gruß aus der Heimat
Angekommen

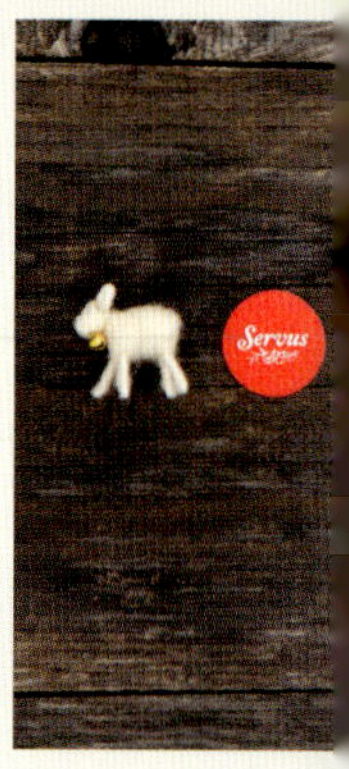
Servus

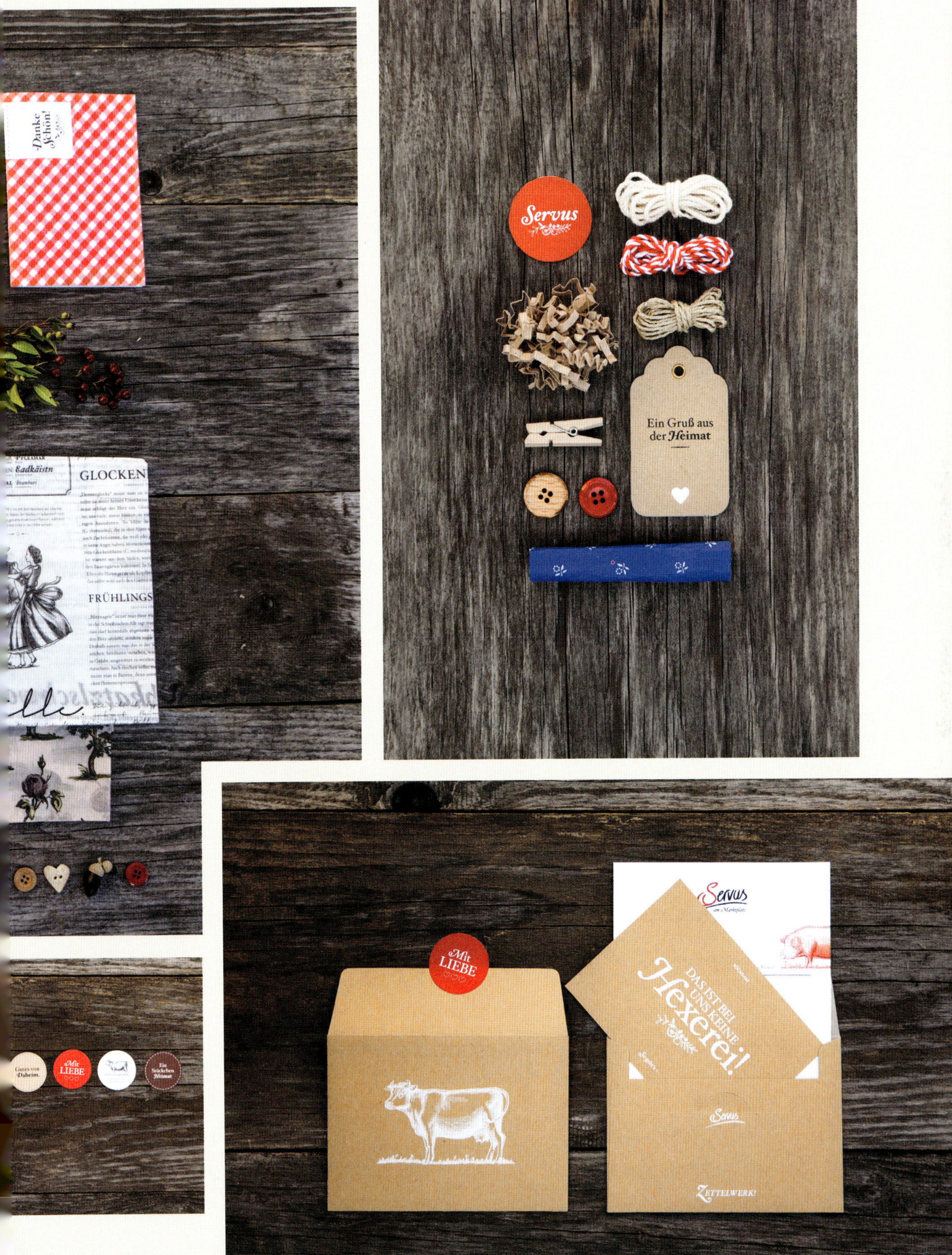

Danke Schön!
GLOCKEN
FRÜHLINGS
Servus
Ein Gruß aus der Heimat
Mit LIEBE
Servus
DAS IST BEI UNS KEINE Hexerei!
Servus
ZETTELWERK!

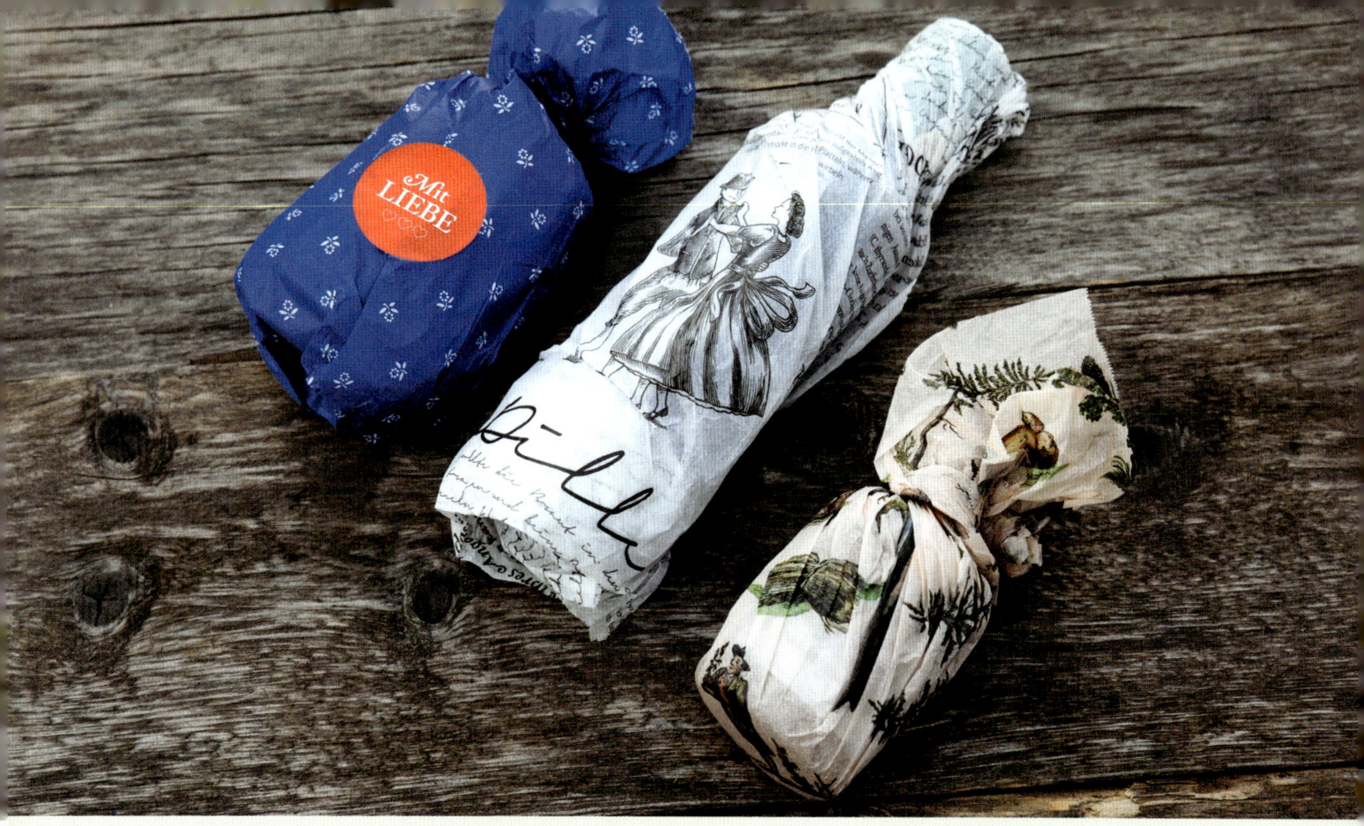

Solution

Illustrator Reinhard Blumenschein happened to be the perfect choice for the "Servus am Marktplatz" project. Not only is he a genuine, friendly and patient person and partner, but also a great illustrator, who convinced with his impressive previous works. His style fits the Servus philosophy perfectly and resembles the down-to-earth art of woodblock print – clear and strong lines arranged cautiously to create a lovely and detailed overall image.

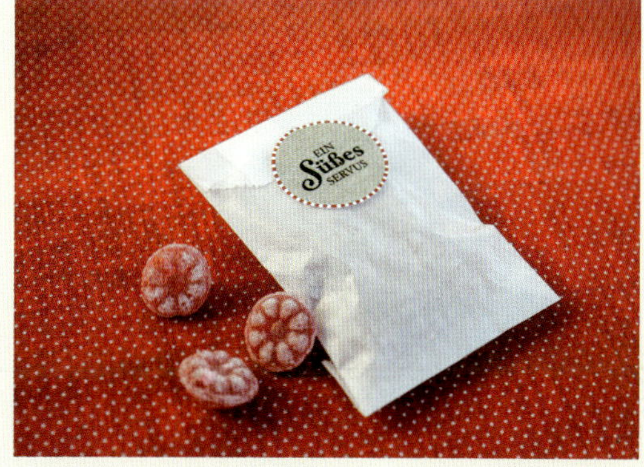

The little black and white pictures illustrate rural subjects ranging from birds and pigs to landscapes and dancing couples. The whole packaging concept was based on the idea of not to merely sending the ordered product, but surprising the customer with a gift. The illustrations can be rediscovered in different variations while the gift is being unpacked: on the cardboard boxes, tape, cloth bags, gift tags, cards, stickers and the delicate tissue paper in which the lovely goods are wrapped. Other than that, the typography and illustrations characteristic of Servus were maintained but interpreted in a fresh and new way.

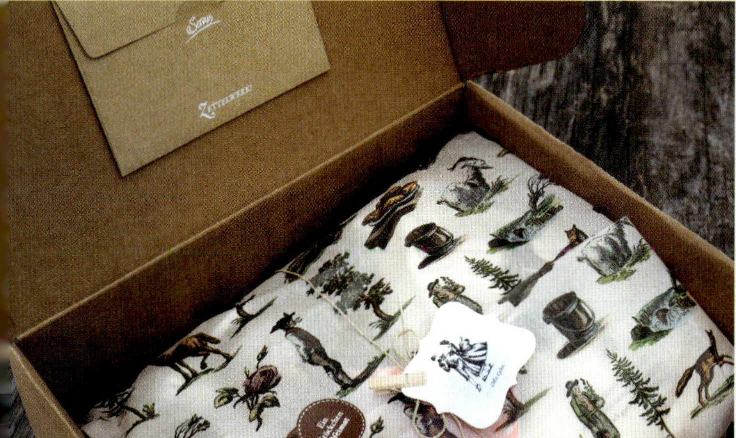

Review

All the separate pieces of the newly-designed packaging material can be combined with each other so that it never gets boring. No parcel is like another and the customers can be surprised once more. This forward-looking concept is easily extendible and remains outstanding, no matter if you are simply adding another tissue paper design or if you are planning on producing a Christmas special. Fruitful collaboration with the client and also with the illustrator enabled moodley brand identity to put such a thoughtful and refreshing idea into action.

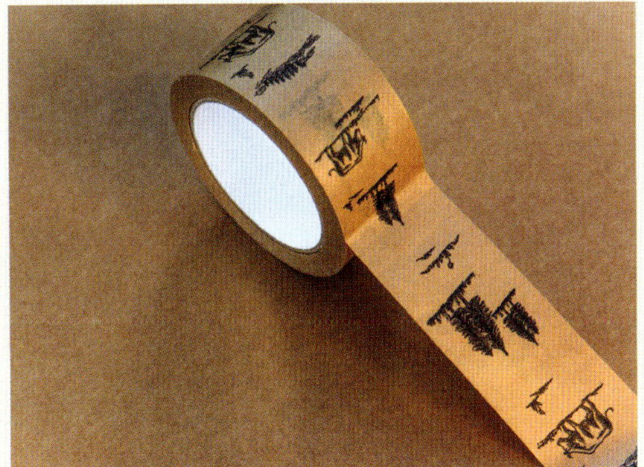

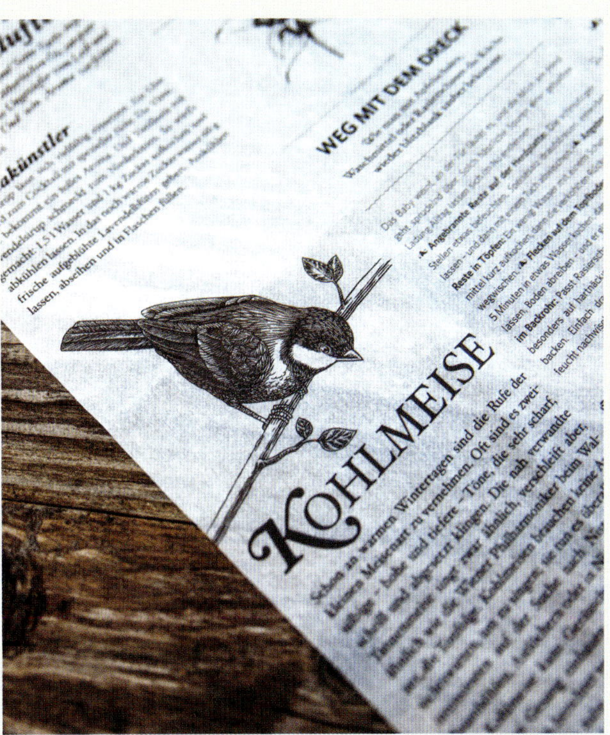

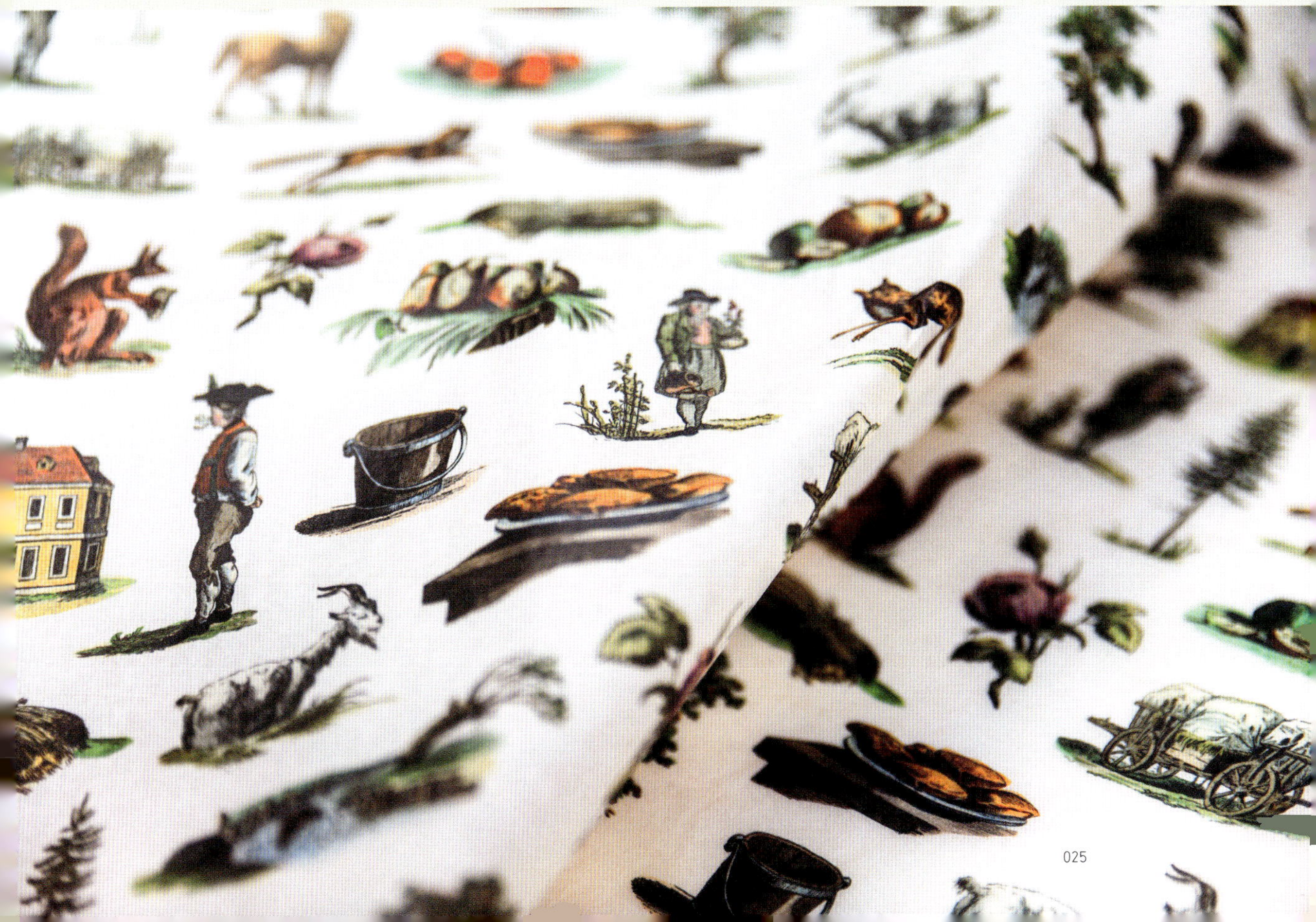

CASE STUDY

04

Forest Design Week

Anastasia Kolesnikova

Forest Design Week is an international design festival where young professionals gather at a forest to discuss eco-designs. The festival will appeal to both young designers and potential investors. Forest Design Week was a school project which the designer conceived during her study at Kuban State University. The assignment asked for a graphic identity that would allow the festival to stand out against other events alike.

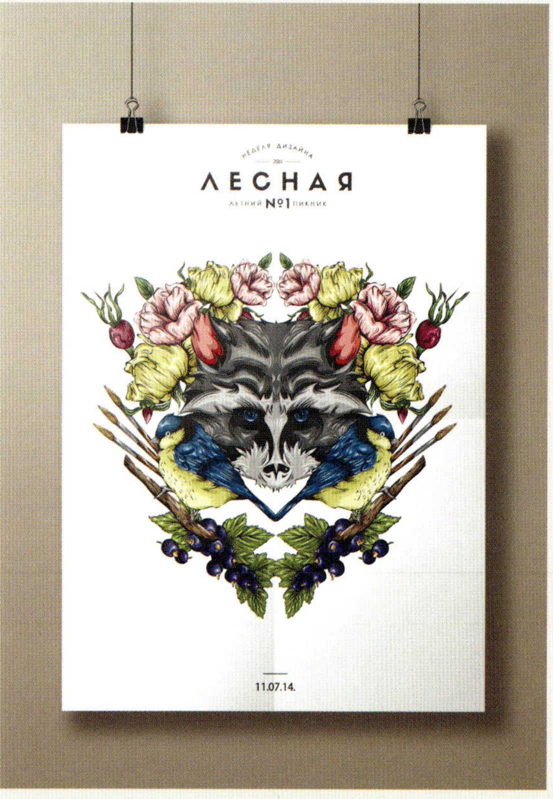

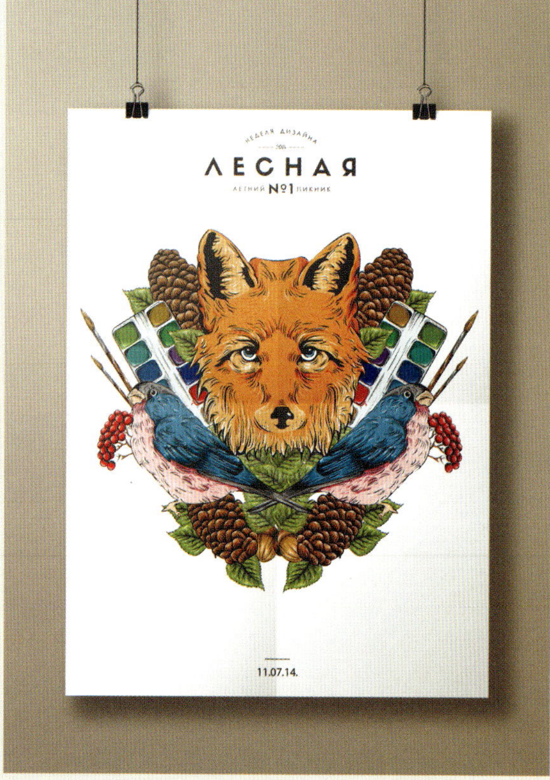

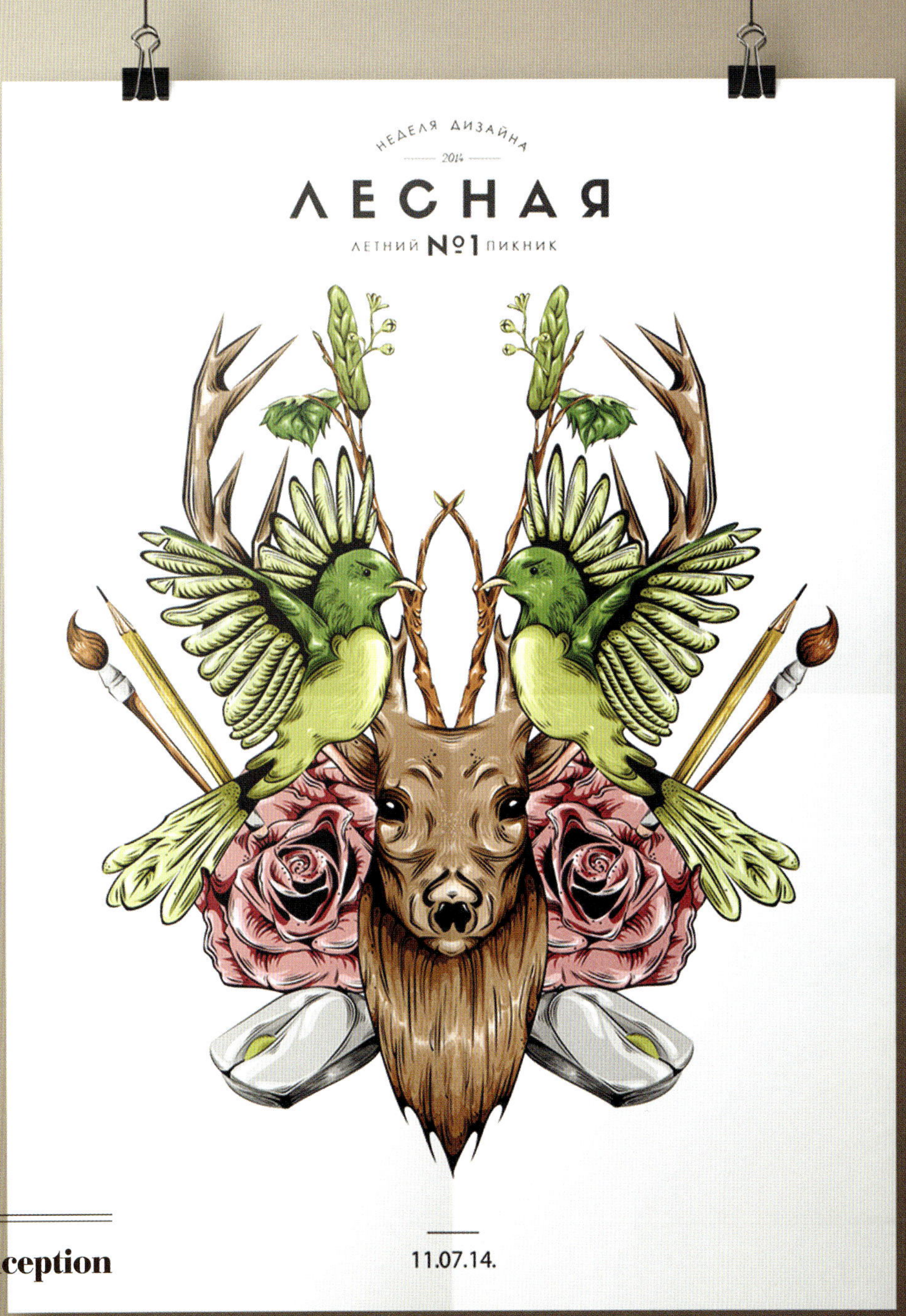

Conception

While the festival promotes the creation and advancement of eco-friendly design, Anastasia Kolesnikova took the festival's ultimate objective as to foster a sense of unity between man as designers and the nature. Since the festival aligns itself with events like London Design Festival, and orients to the entire industry on an international basis, Kolesnikova adopted a visual language that is fun, attractive, professional, expressive yet able to effectively communicate the event's fundamental values to a diverse audience. The resulting design should also appear in tune with the natural environment, where the event would take place.

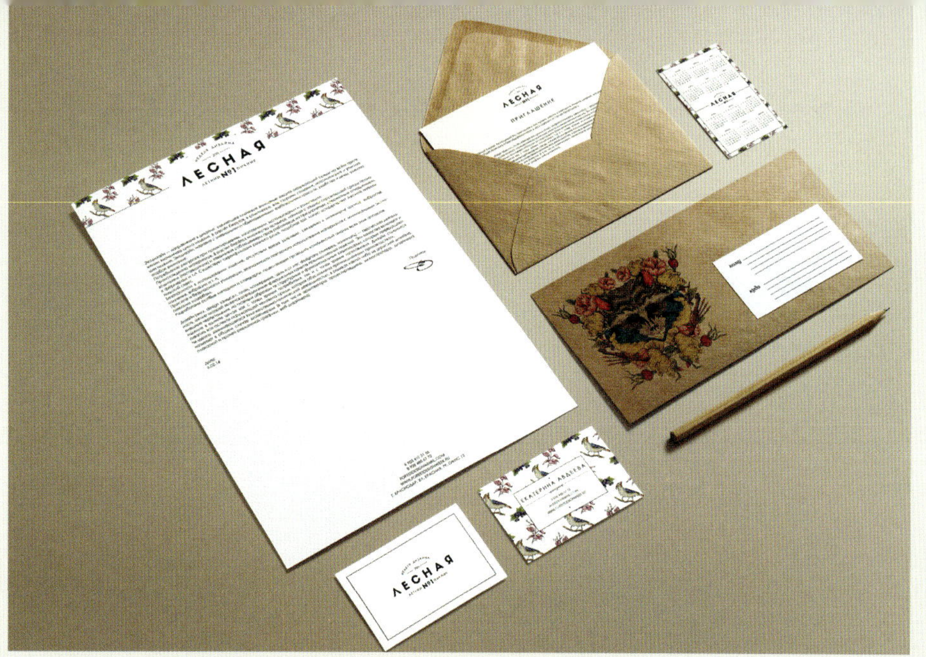
ЛЕСНАЯ
ПРИГЛАШЕНИЕ

ЛЕСНАЯ
НЕДЕЛЯ ДИЗАЙНА
2014
ЛЕСНАЯ
ЛЕТНИЙ №1 ПИКНИК

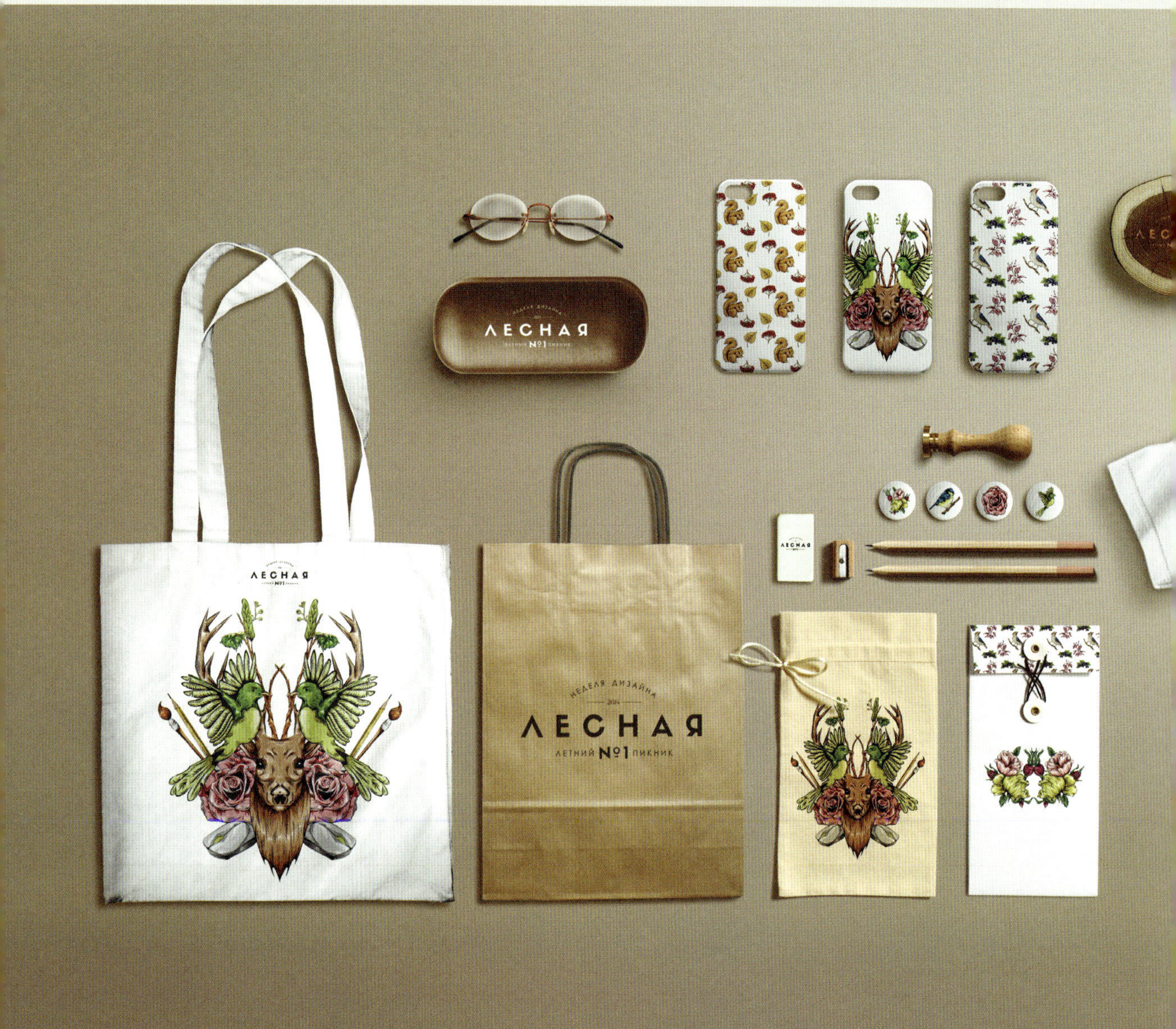

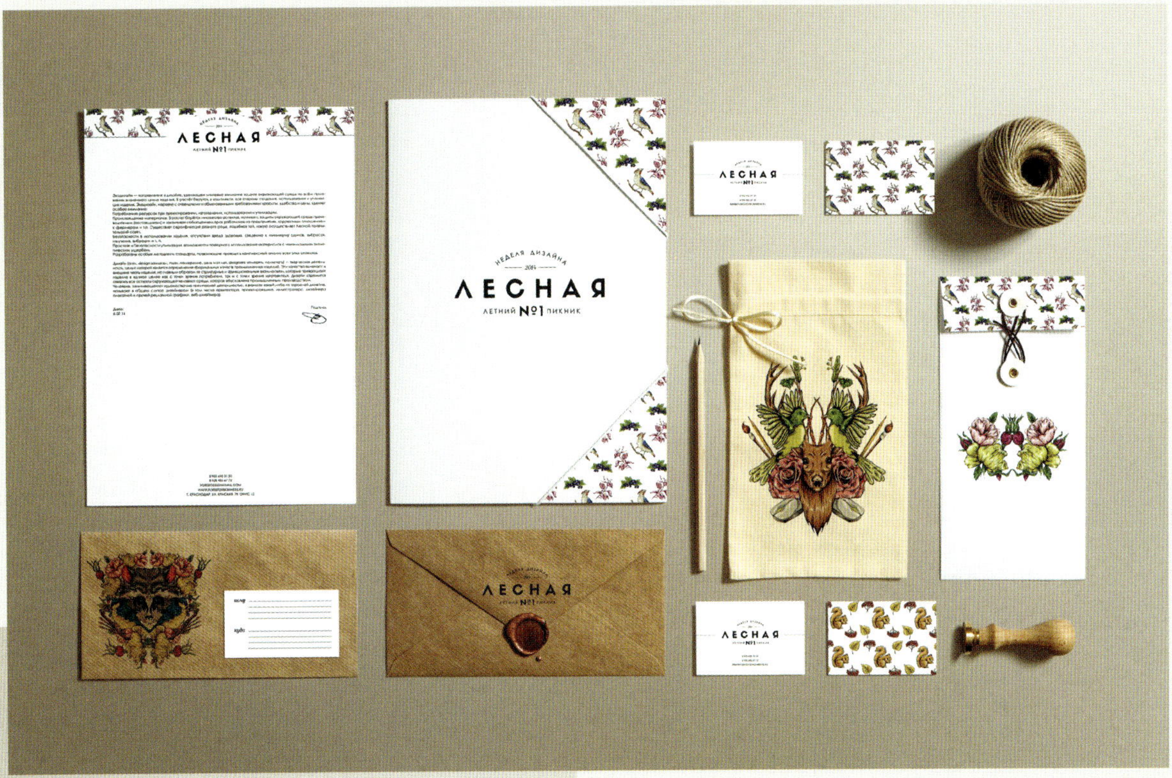

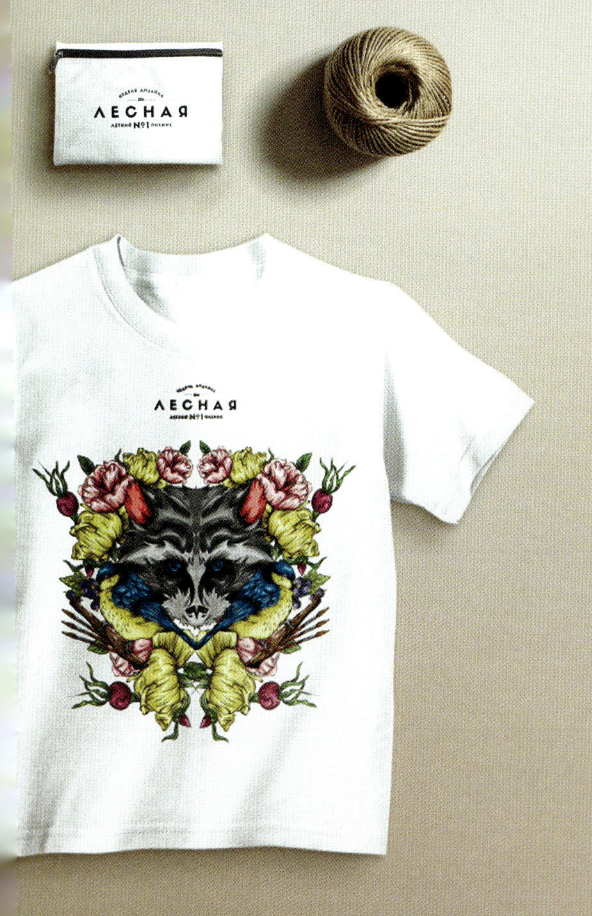
ЛЕСНАЯ
ЛЕТНИЙ №1 ПИКНИК
ЛЕСНАЯ

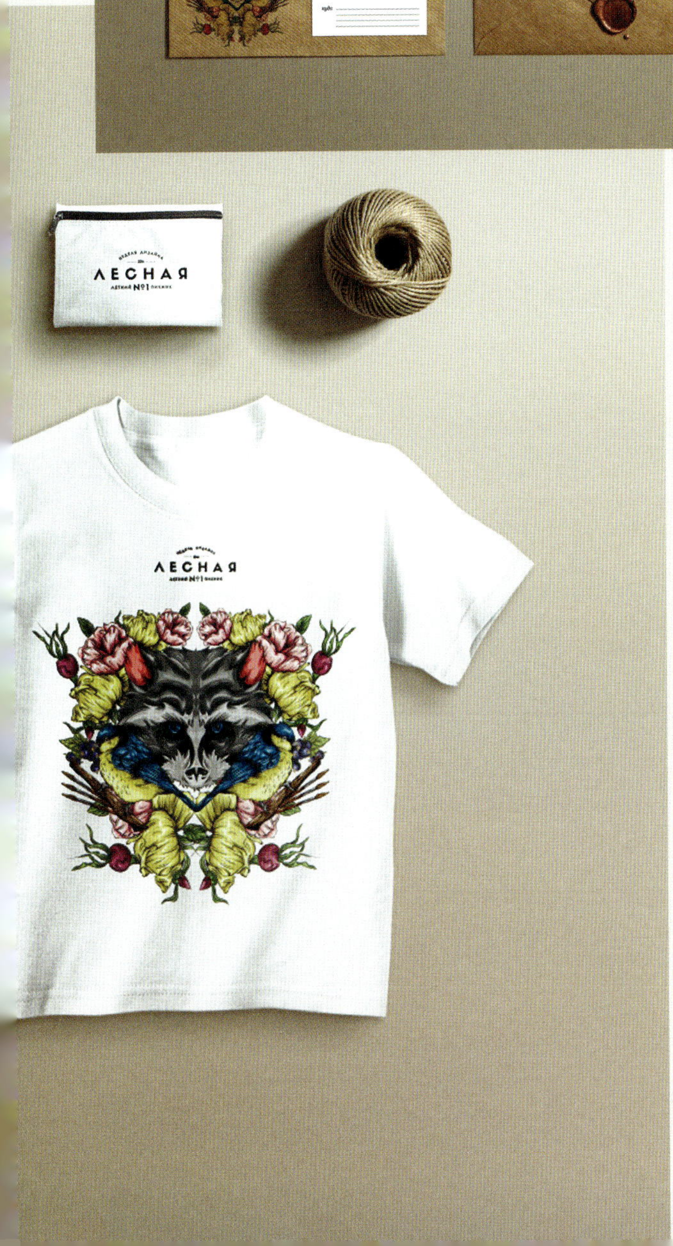

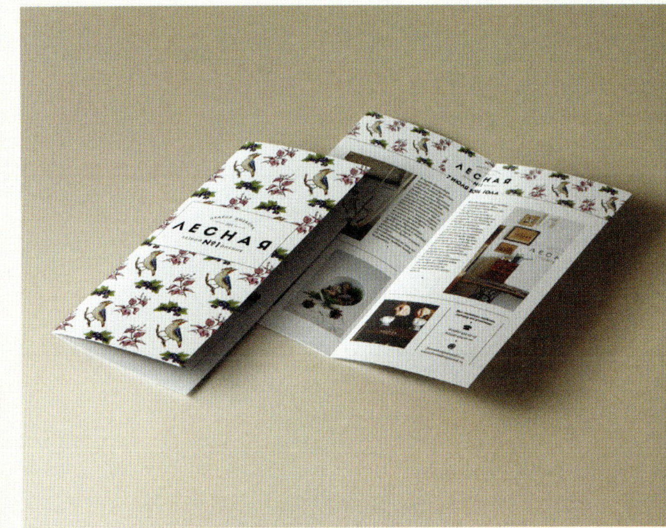
ЛЕСНАЯ

Solution

The final design contained a variety of vector artwork and patterns fit for applications ranging from stationery for daily communications as well as tote bags and printed shirts to be taken away by participants, honourable guests and the press as mementos. To evoke the grace of the beautiful nature amid mankind, human made a subtle presence among flora and fauna, straightforwardly as designer tools like brushes, paints and pencils, and understatedly as artificial colouring and symmetry. Eschewing green as the most direct and common colour to suggest the nature, a light and fresh tone was adopted as the corporate colours, primarily composed of white and pale pink.

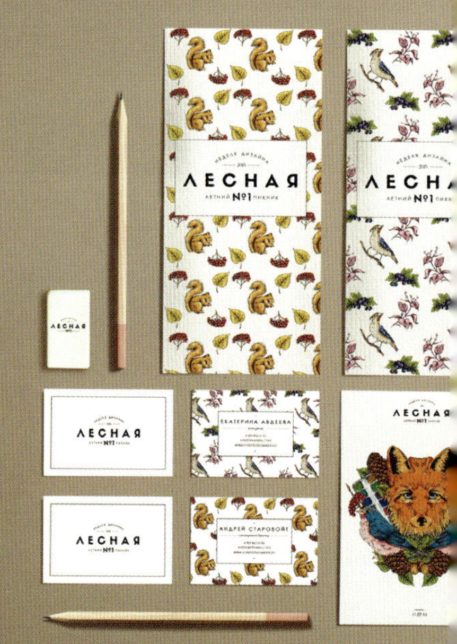

Review

Illustrations have successfully conveyed the intended idea and appealed to its target audience because they give a vivid description of the event's ideologies and that strengthens memories. There were a lot of small parts that together conjured up a powerful, narrative picture. All in all, designers' eyes go for details.

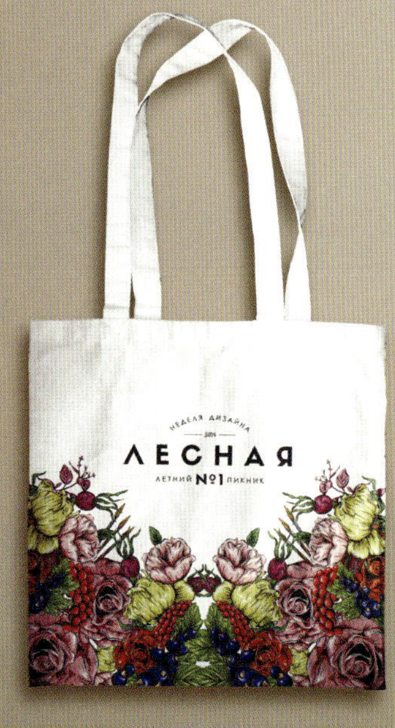

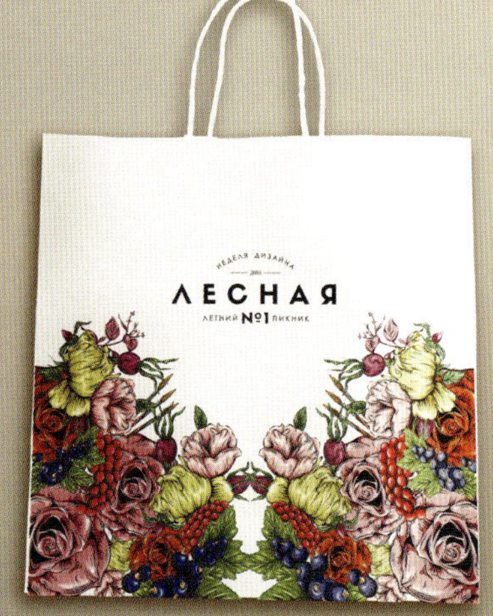

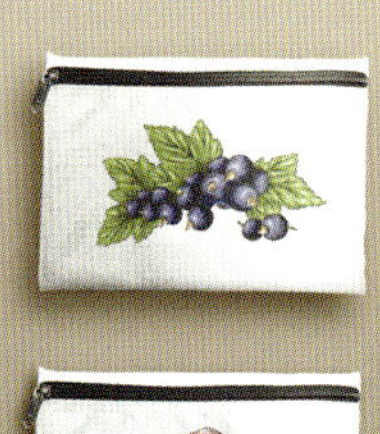

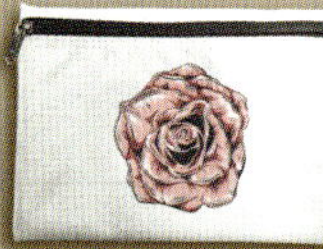

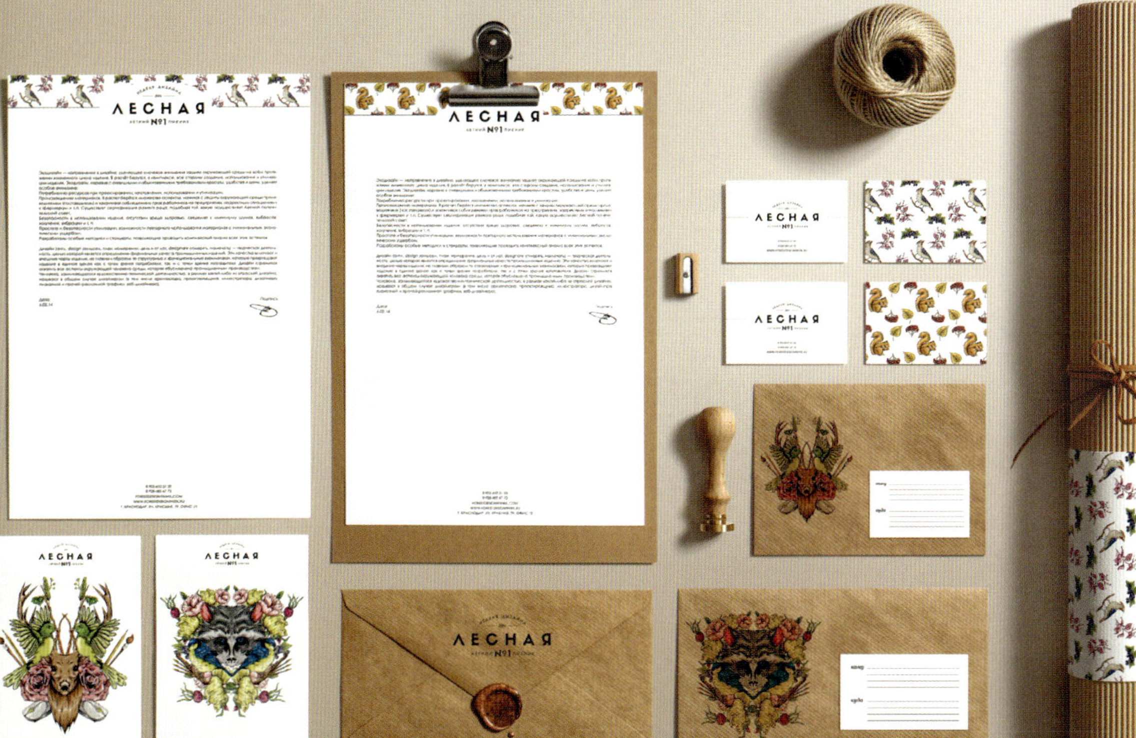
ЛЕСНАЯ

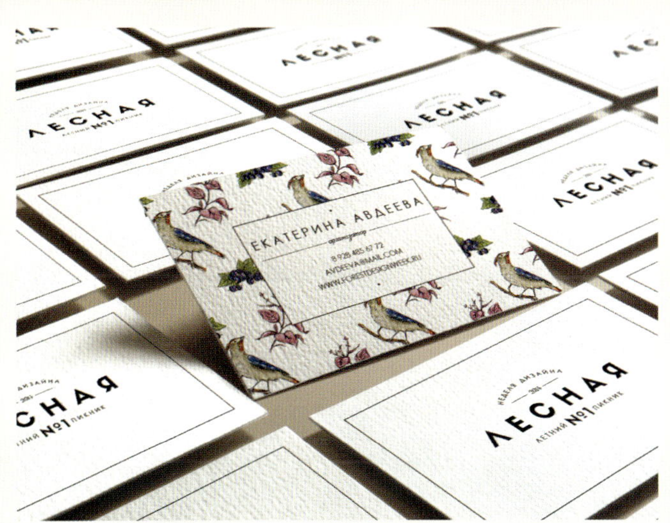
НЕДЕЛЯ ДИЗАЙНА
ЛЕСНАЯ
ЛЕТНИЙ №1 ПИКНИК
ЕКАТЕРИНА АВДЕЕВА
8 926 485 67 72
AVDEEVA@MAIL.COM
WWW.FORESTDESIGNWEEK.RU

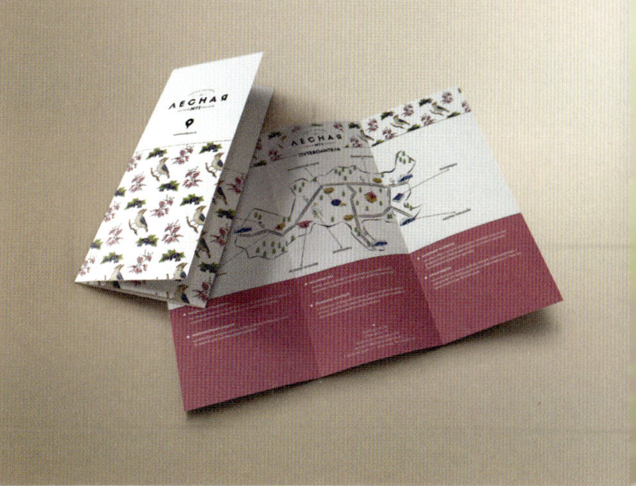
ЛЕСНАЯ

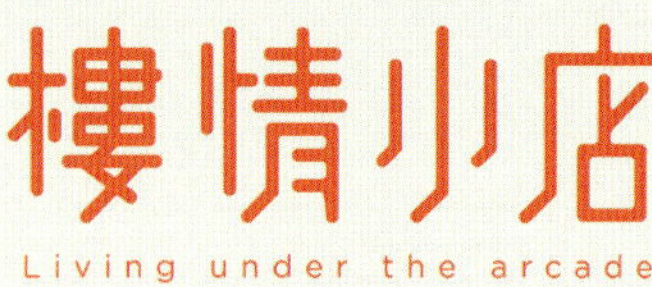

樓情小店
Living under the arcade

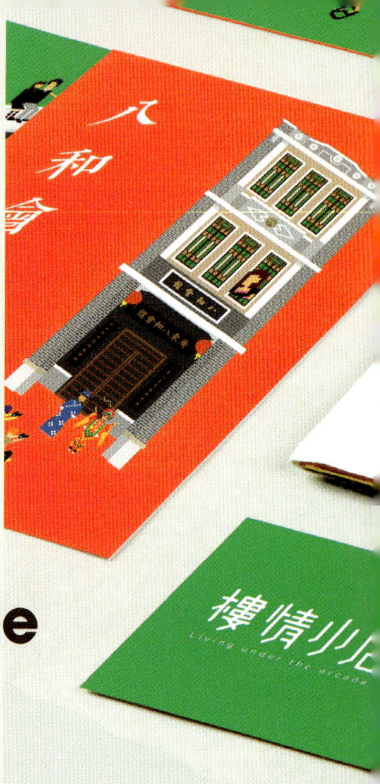

CASE STUDY

05

Living Under the Arcade

Kay Dung

Living Under the Arcade is established to boost public interest in Guangzhou's arcades. As a shop the initiative invites locals and tourists to contemplate the architecture as they visit the place for local and arcade-themed products. The subject was a fictional client in Kay Dung's graduation project.

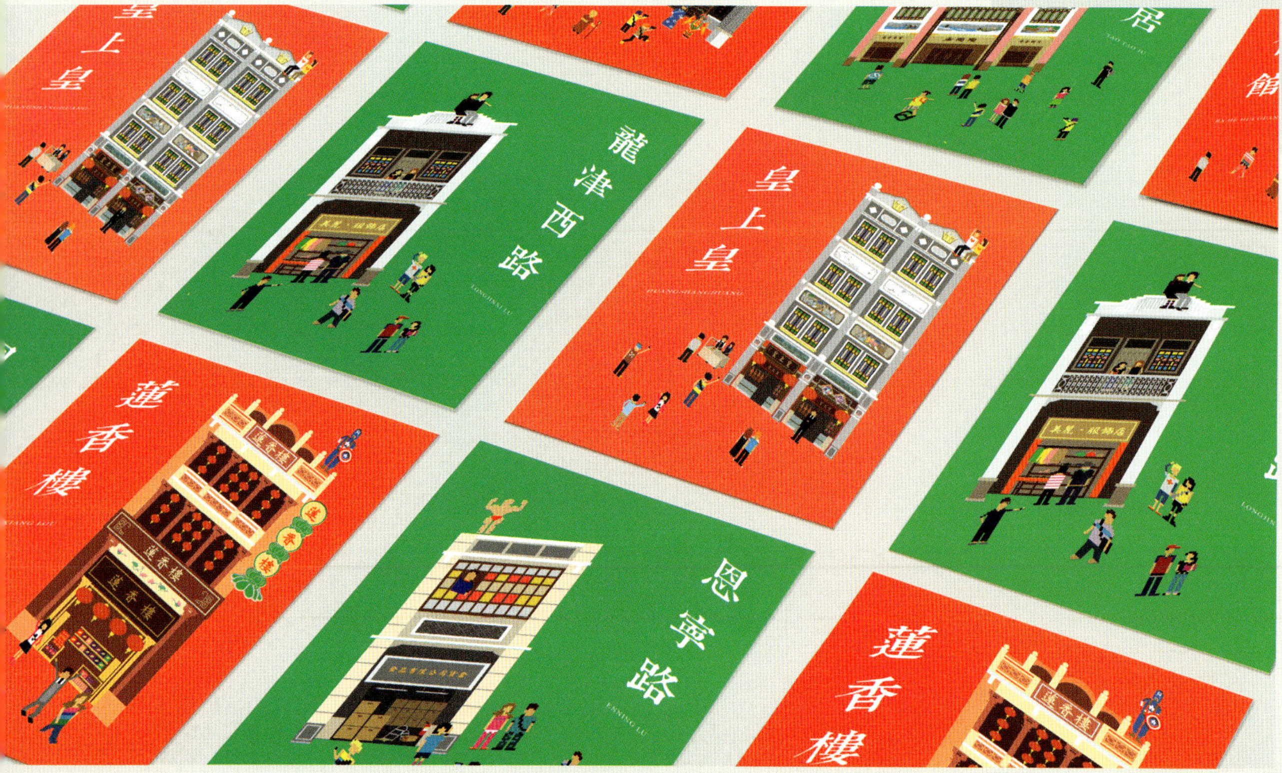

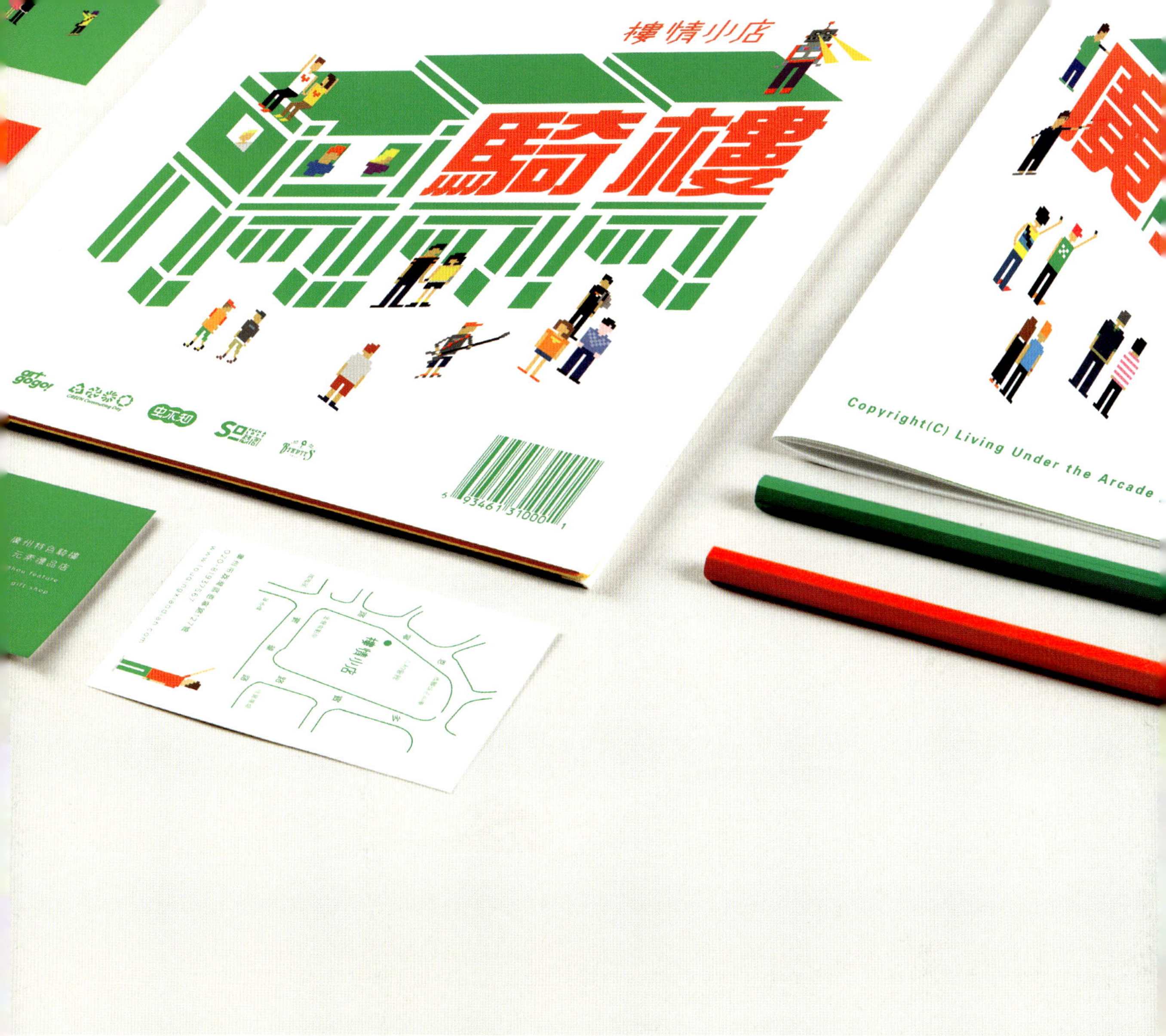

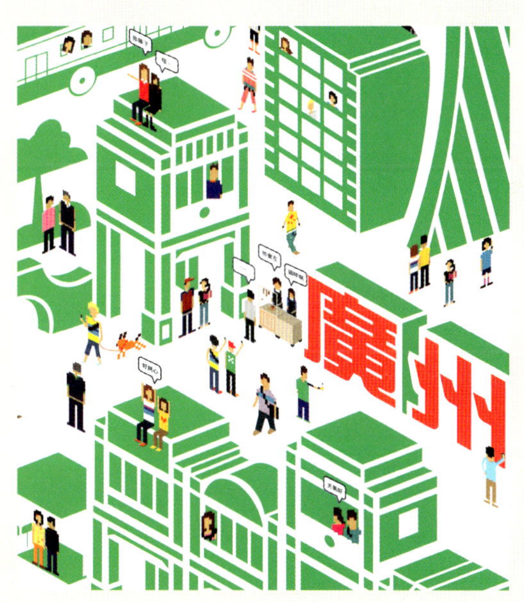

Conception

A native of Guangzhou and a design student in Macau, Kay Dung researched the historical development of Guangzhou's arcades and felt a strong calling to promote them to the public. Dung's experiences in promoting with illustrations has proved that rich graphic details and colours can make a product look attractive and easier to take in. The notion to present this age-old artefact afresh led Dung to accentuate arcades' features and charisma with illustrations, alongside pixellated characters and conversations to evoke a lively neighbourhood scene. All these interesting elements were effectively used to draw and direct attention and leave a mark on the visitors.

Solution

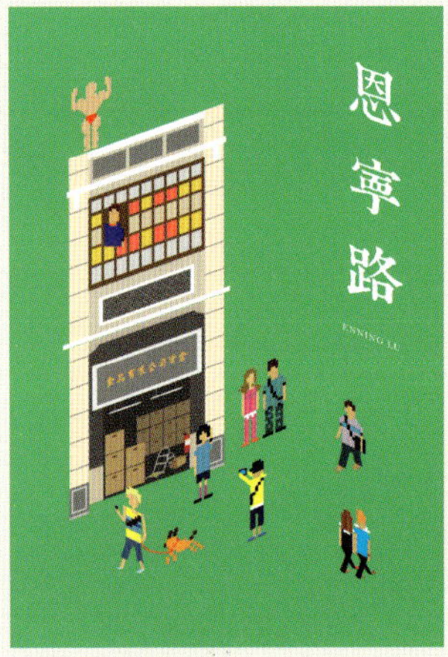

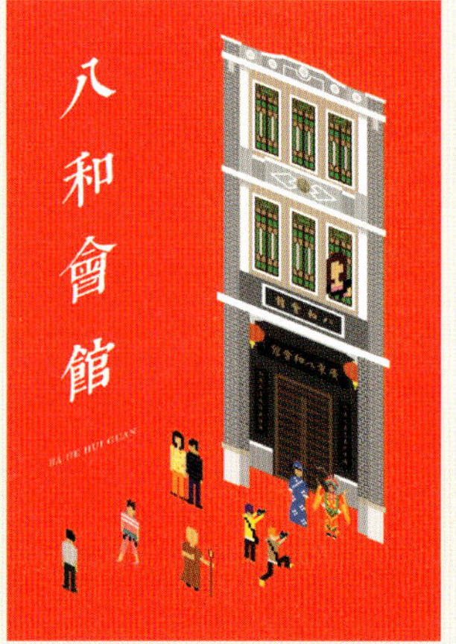

As when illustrations produce visual experience and text informs, the two were combined to highlight 'arcades' and unlock viewers' imagination. Visual elements were taken from movie tickets and bus tickets from the 60s and 70s for its interesting qualities and its subordinate connection with arcades, under which many cinemas and bus stops were lodged back then. Colours were consciously boosted to catch the eyes and an isometric view was used to present Guangzhou's interlocking structure which passers-by can rarely acquire from the street. The logotype with greater height and thinner lines resembles arcades' standing rectangular forms, and sometimes tilted for a refreshing look.

Review

For Dung, if he is really to turn Living Under the Arcade into a feasible and successful venture, careful thoughts on actual implementations and additional original elements will be critical. He also believes that it is time for the new generation of designers' to contribute to the society with their specialty and skills.

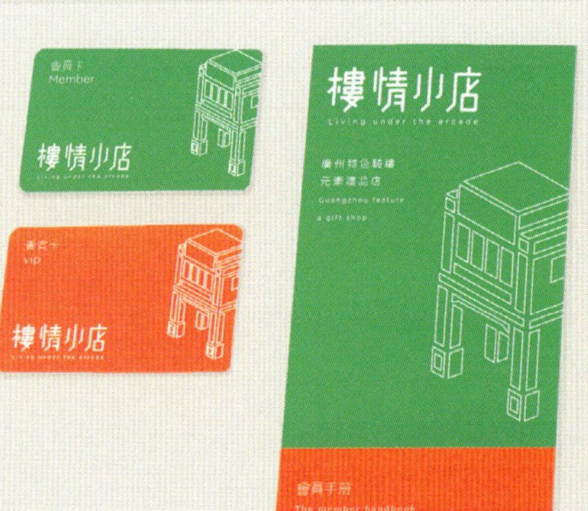

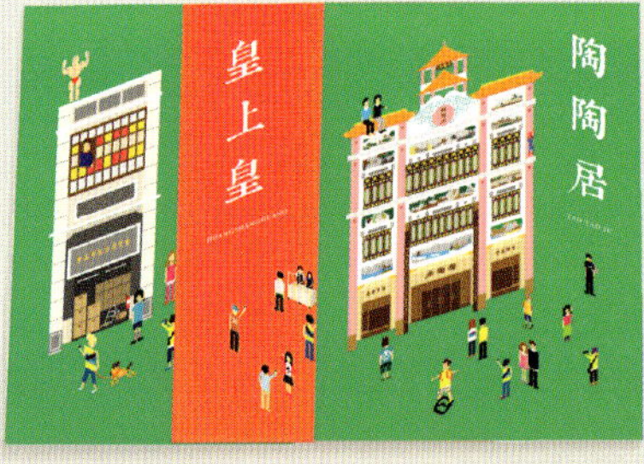

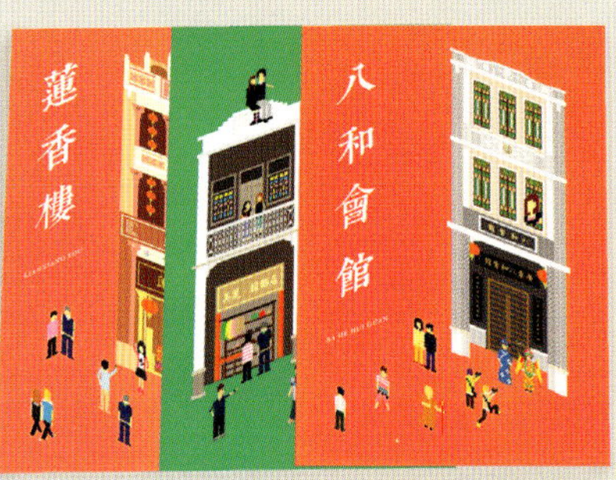

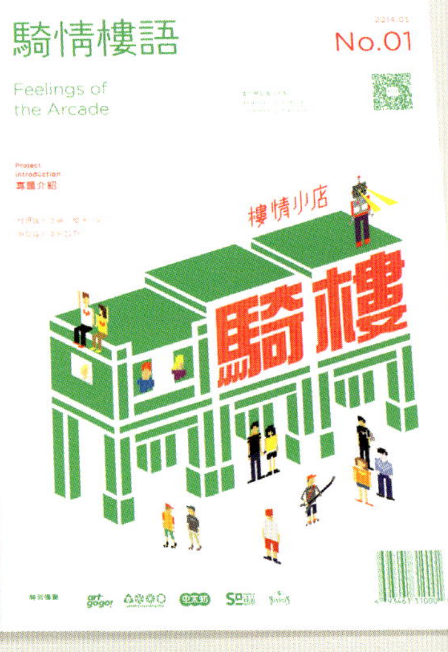

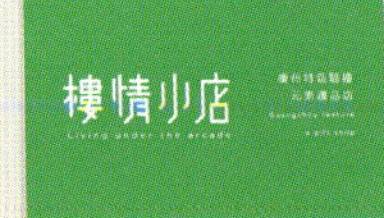

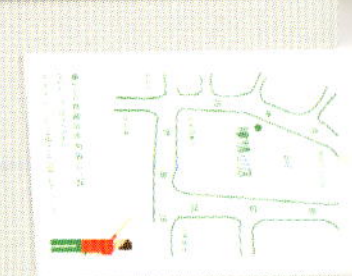

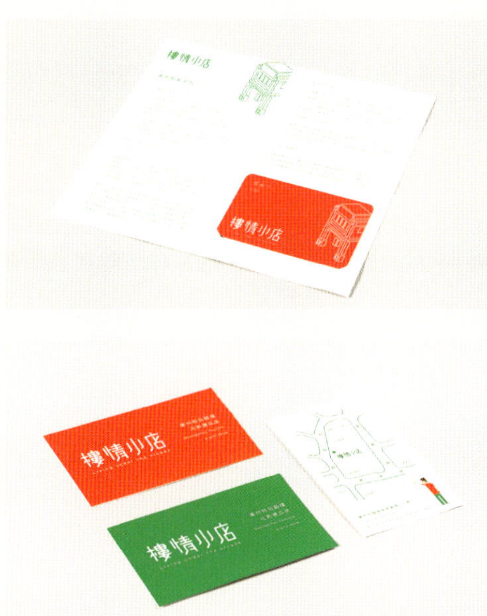
樓情小店

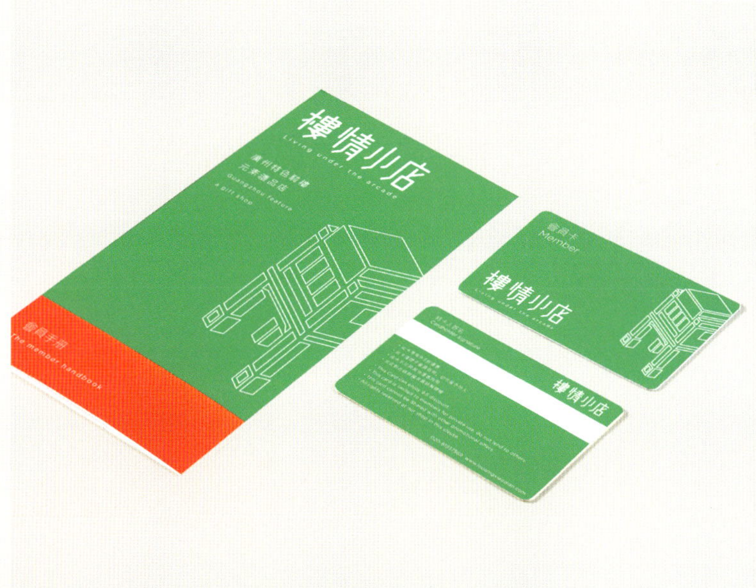
樓情小店
Living under the arcade
廣州特色騎樓
元素禮品店
Guangzhou feature
a gift shop
會員手冊
the member handbook
會員卡
Member

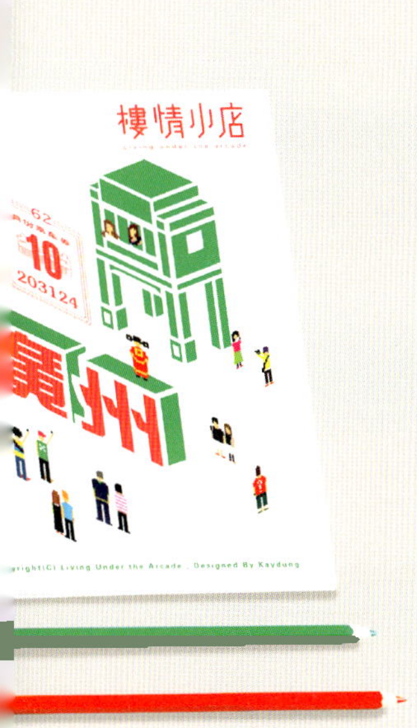
樓情小店
living under the arcade
廣州

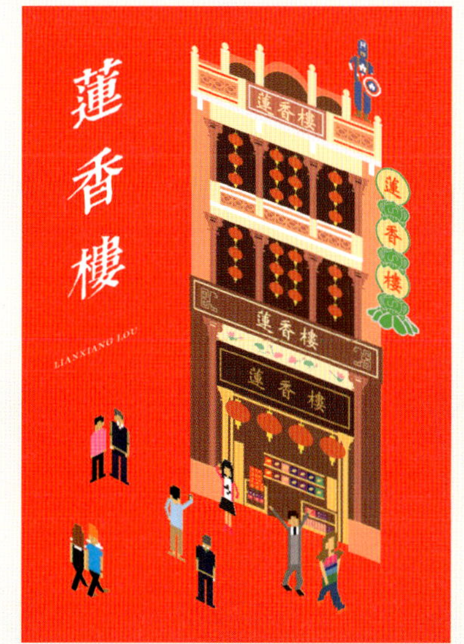
蓮香樓
LIANXIANG LOU

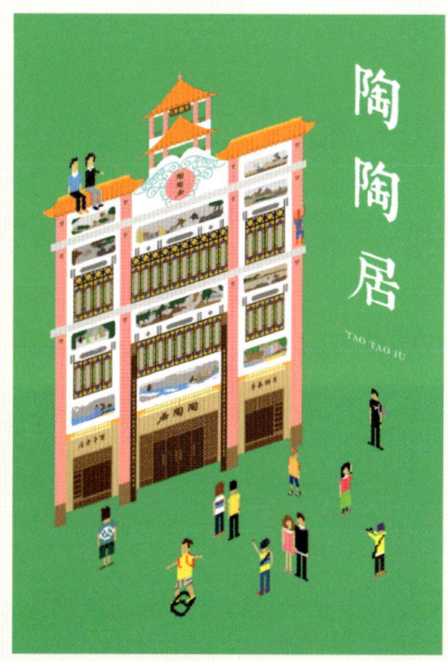
陶陶居
TAO TAO JU

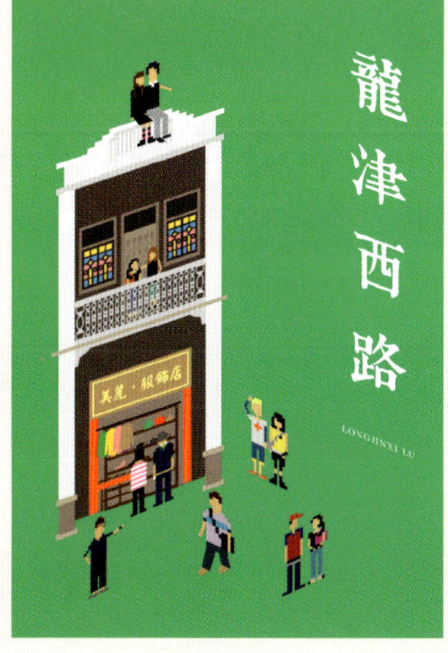
龍津西路
LONGJINXI LU

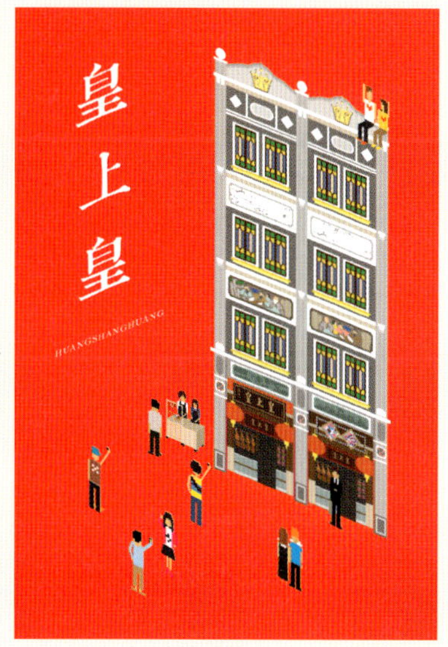
皇上皇
HUANGSHANGHUANG

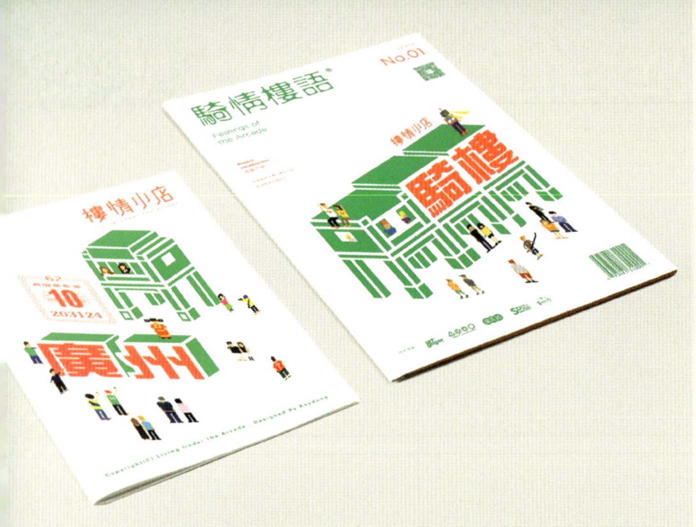
騎情樓語
No.01
Feelings of the Arcade
樓情小店
騎樓
62
10
203124
廣州

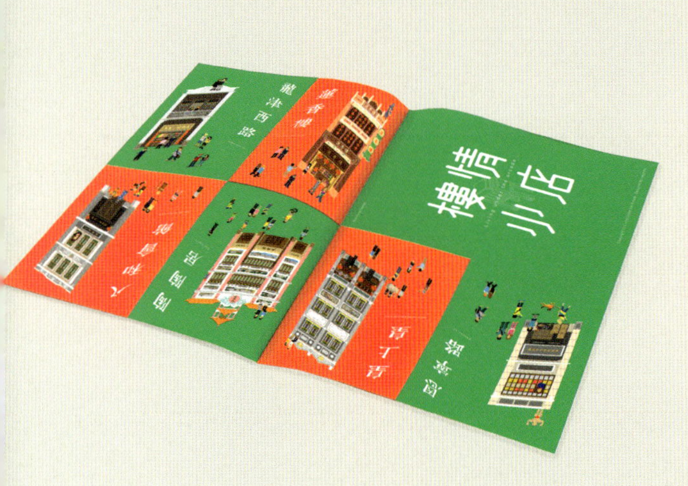
樓情
小店

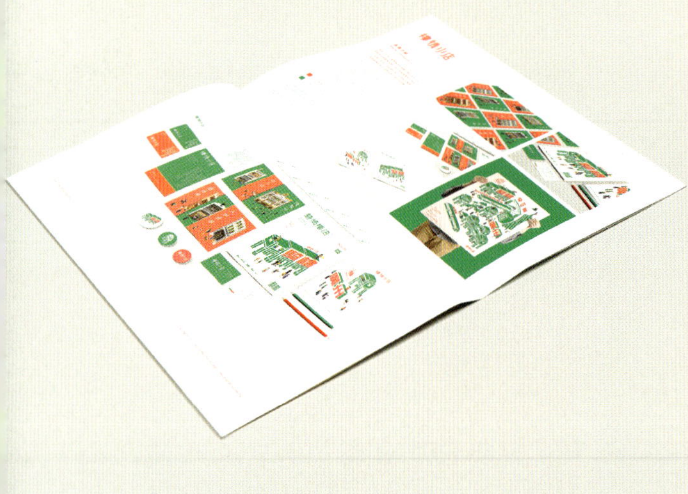

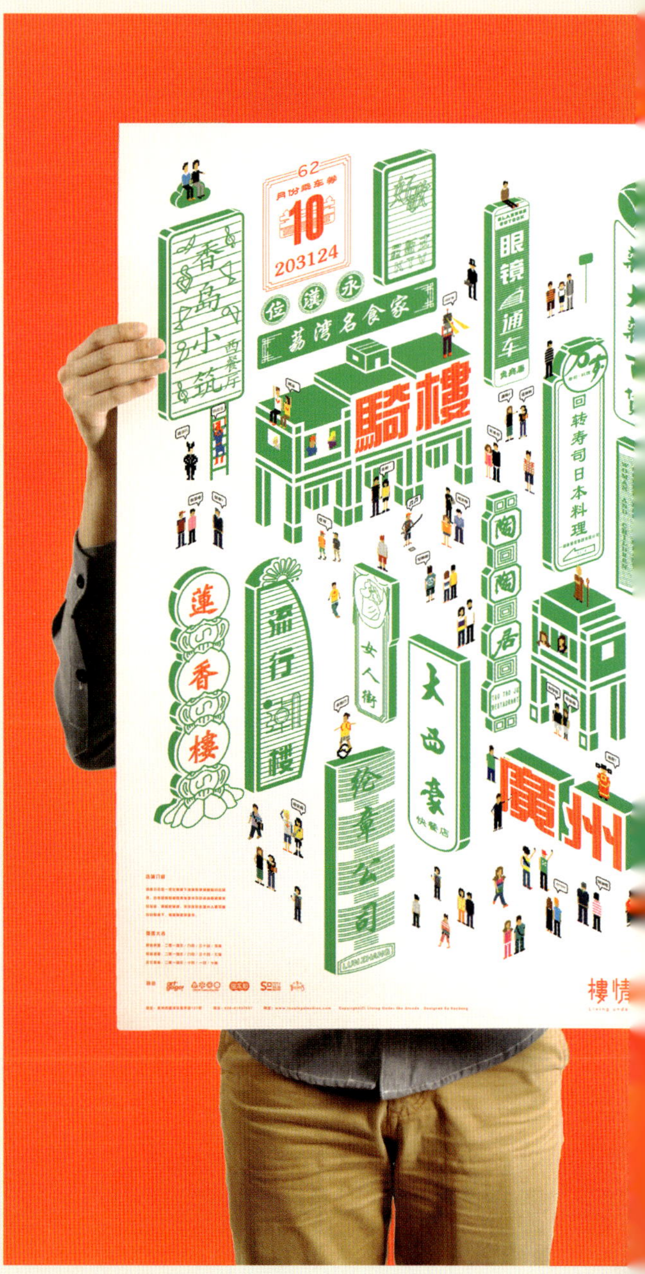
62
10
203124
香島小筑
西餐厅
眼镜
通车
荔湾名食家
騎樓
回转寿司日本料理
蓮香樓
陶陶居
女人街
大西豪
快餐店
廣州
樓情

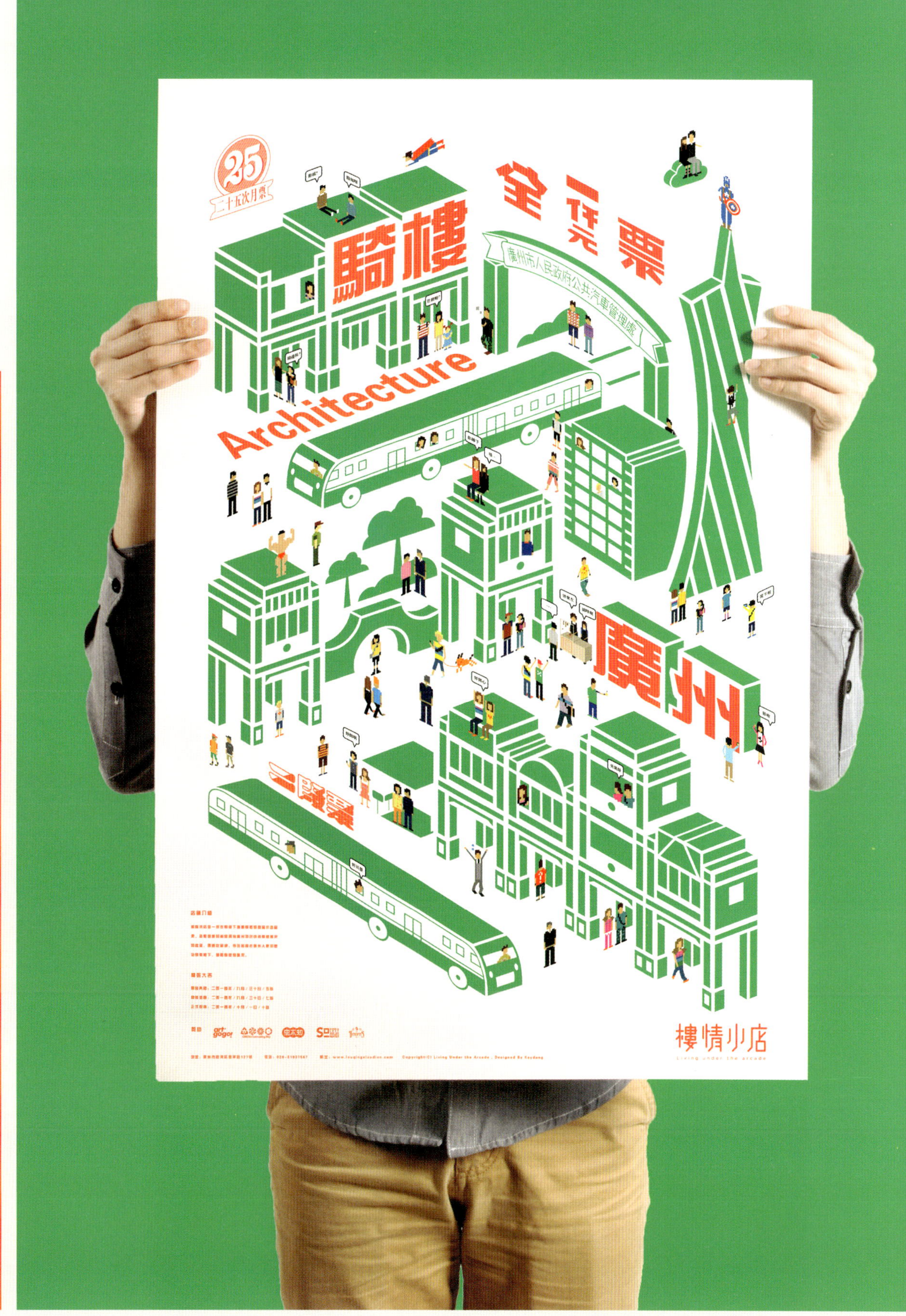
25
二十五次月票
騎樓
全一年票
廣州市人民政府公共汽車管理處
Architecture
廣州
樓情小店
Living under the arcade

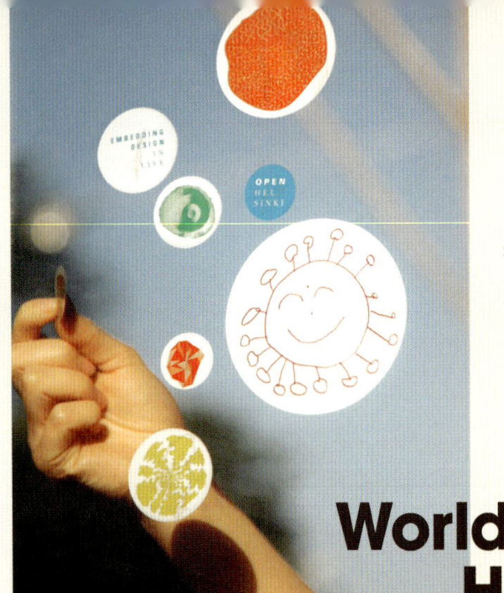

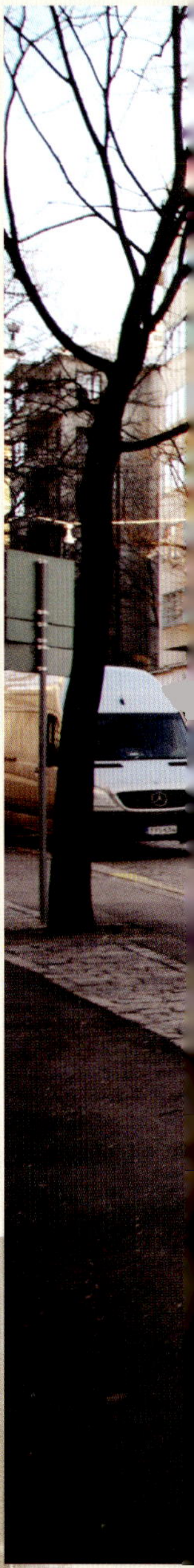

CASE STUDY

06

World Design Capital Helsinki 2012

Kokoro & Moi

The World Design Capital is a city promotion project celebrating the merits of design. Held biennially, it seeks to highlight the accomplishments of cities that are truly leveraging design as a tool to improve their social, cultural and economic climate throughout a year-long programme of design-related events. After successfully completing the application phase in 2009, Kokoro & Moi was brought in to develop the identity concept, visual identity, communication design, advertising, and several design projects from product to spatial and interactive design for World Design Capital Helsinki in 2012.

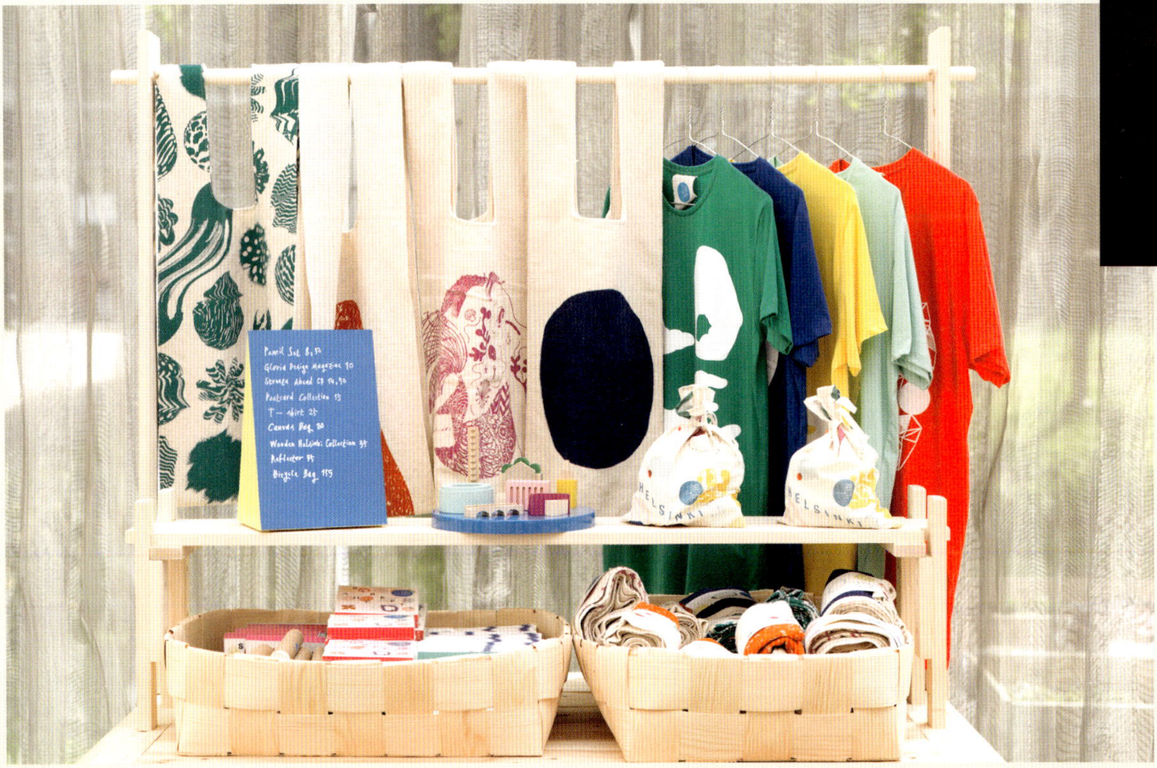

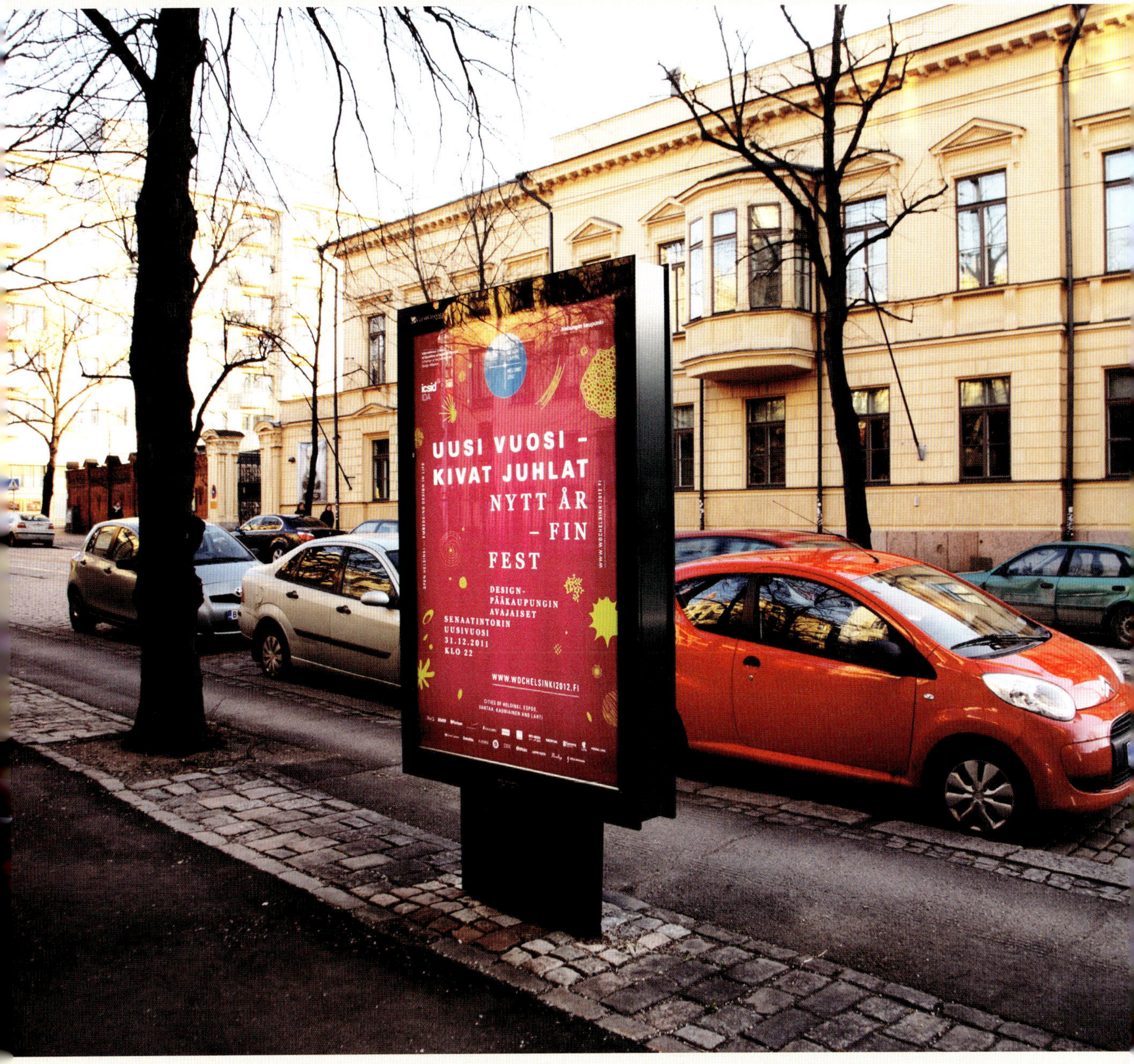

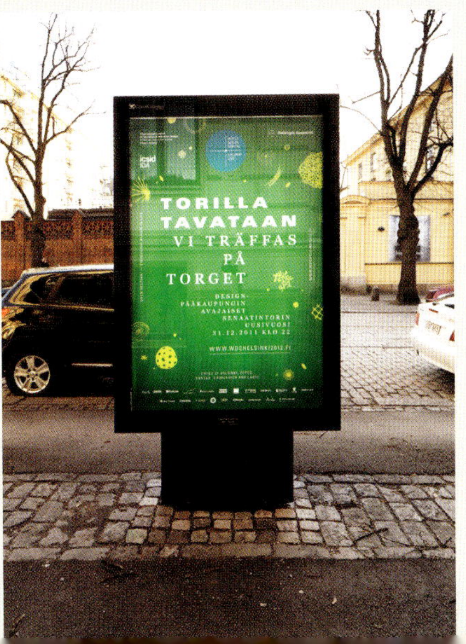

Conception

The main themes for the WDC Helsinki 2012 edition were Open City, Global Responsibility, and Roots for New Growth. The visual identity for the project played a very important role, bringing it to life and making it visible to citizens and guests who visited Helsinki during 2012. Kokoro & Moi imagined an identity based on the core messages in the WDC Helsinki 2012 strategy, which highlighted the idea of openness and encouraged people to get involved in the development of their city.

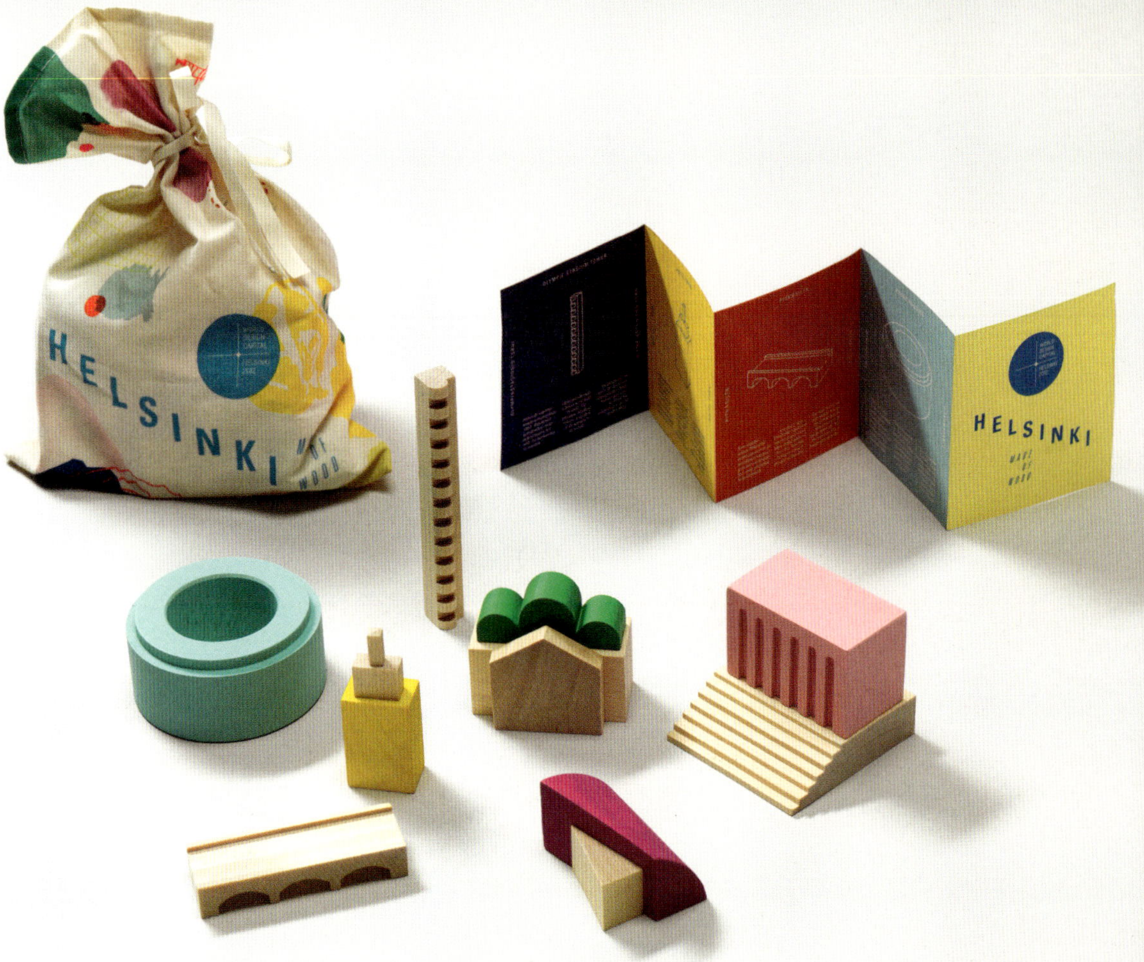

Solution

Kokoro & Moi created the "Open Identity Workshop" concept where anybody could come to draw and give their input to the identity. In parallel with this non-professional approach, established designers were invited to join in the creation of official WDC Helsinki 2012 products. The same brief that was given to people at the Open Identity workshops was presented to a group of Finnish designers – including architects, graphic designers, industrial designers and textile designers such as Vuokko Nurmesniemi, Kustaa Saksi, Oiva Toikka and Tuomas Toivonen. A collection of products ranging from clothing to various accessories featured the final artworks of group members. Alongside this 'pro collection' a series of products were created celebrating the general public's work as well. These included various collectibles for the home – and especially for childrens' rooms.

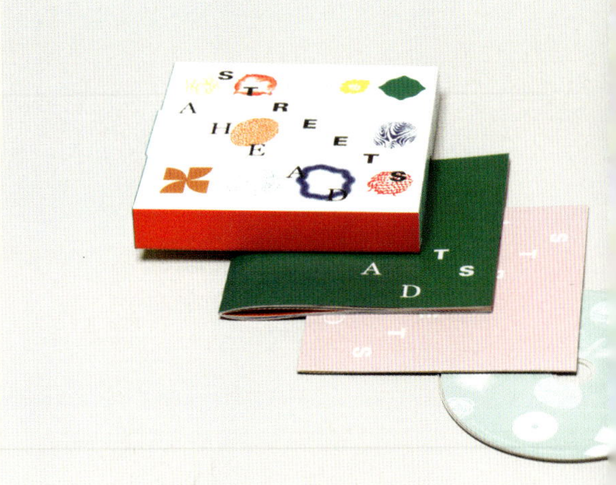

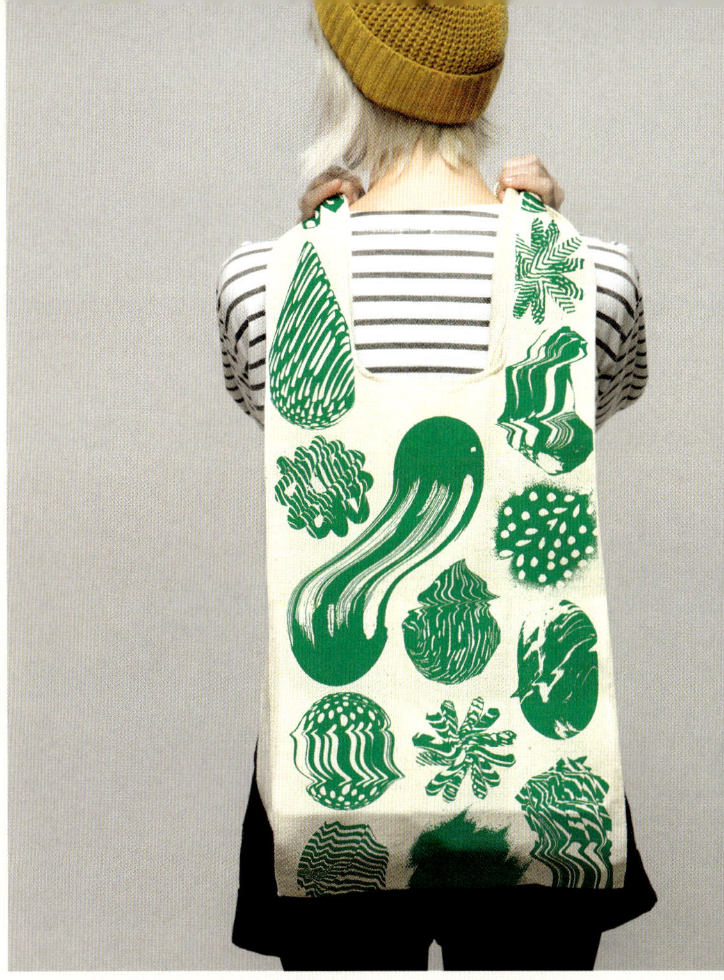

Review

The identity succeeded with its vivid, colourful, fresh look and attitude, being something different to the clear and minimalistic language of form that Finnish design is usually known for. The concepts were a huge success with hundreds of people attending and contributing to the identity development. They were also a great way to tell people about the design capital project, its strategy, and the goals. The identity changed its look across mediums and events as more graphics were fed in, representing the open source idea in the form of an identity system, as well as a concept of an ever-developing urban habitat.

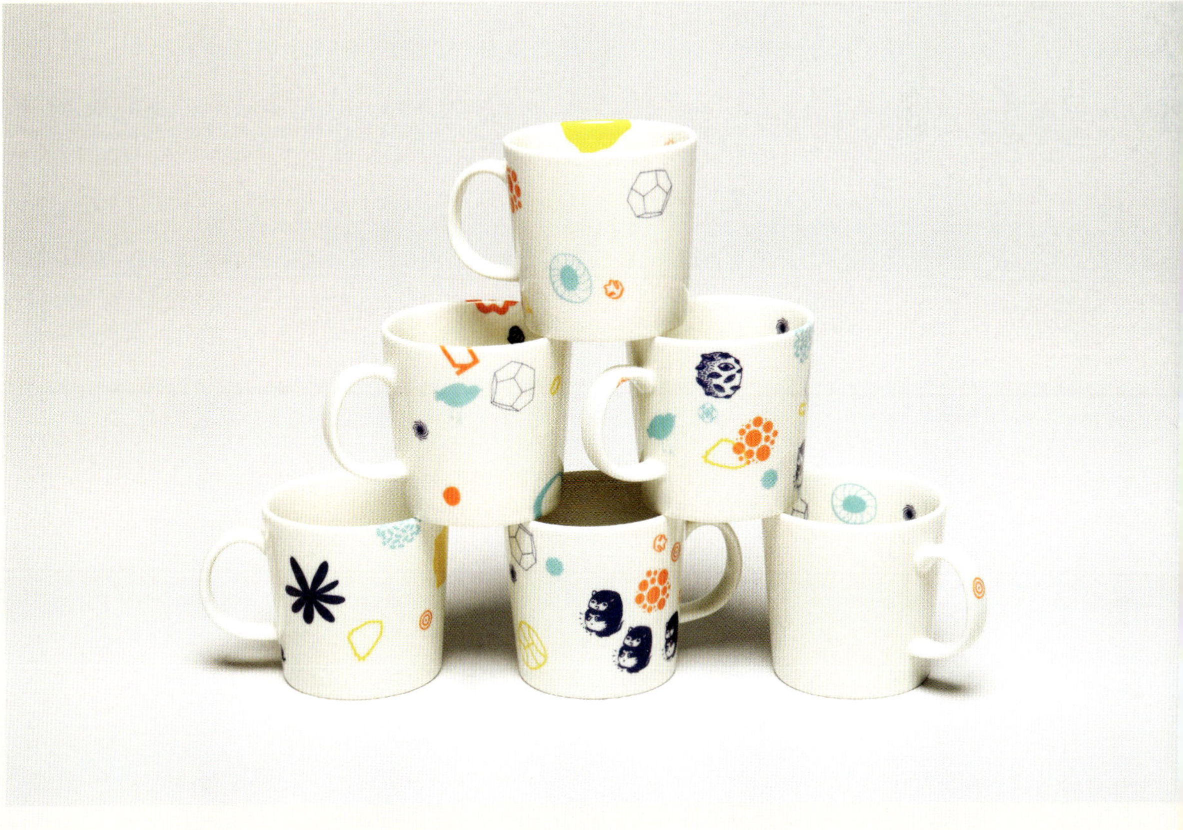

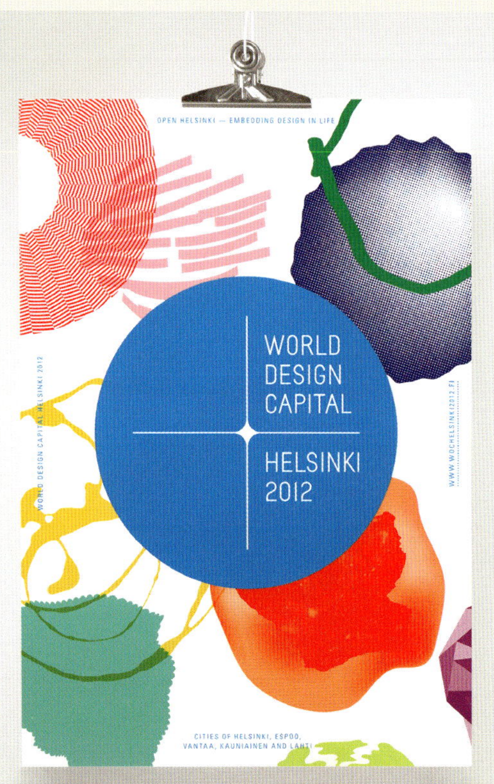
OPEN HELSINKI — EMBEDDING DESIGN IN LIFE
WORLD DESIGN CAPITAL
HELSINKI 2012
WORLD DESIGN CAPITAL HELSINKI 2012
WWW.WDCHELSINKI2012.FI
CITIES OF HELSINKI, ESPOO, VANTAA, KAUNIAINEN AND LAHTI

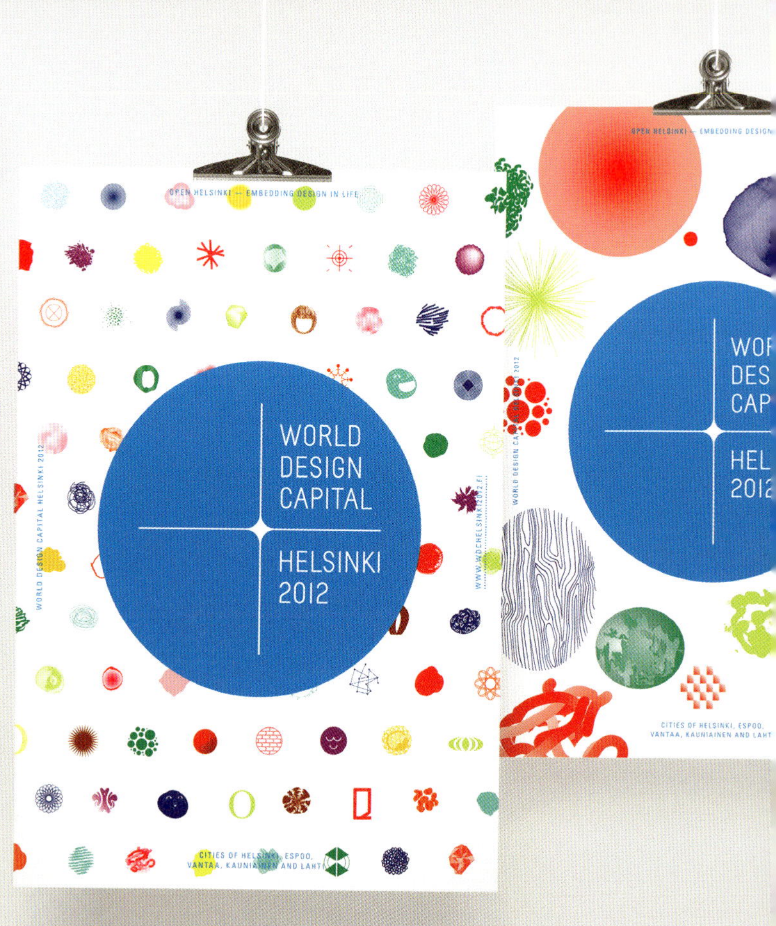
OPEN HELSINKI — EMBEDDING DESIGN IN LIFE
WORLD DESIGN CAPITAL
HELSINKI 2012
WORLD DESIGN CAPITAL HELSINKI 2012
WWW.WDCHELSINKI2012.FI
CITIES OF HELSINKI, ESPOO, VANTAA, KAUNIAINEN AND LAHTI

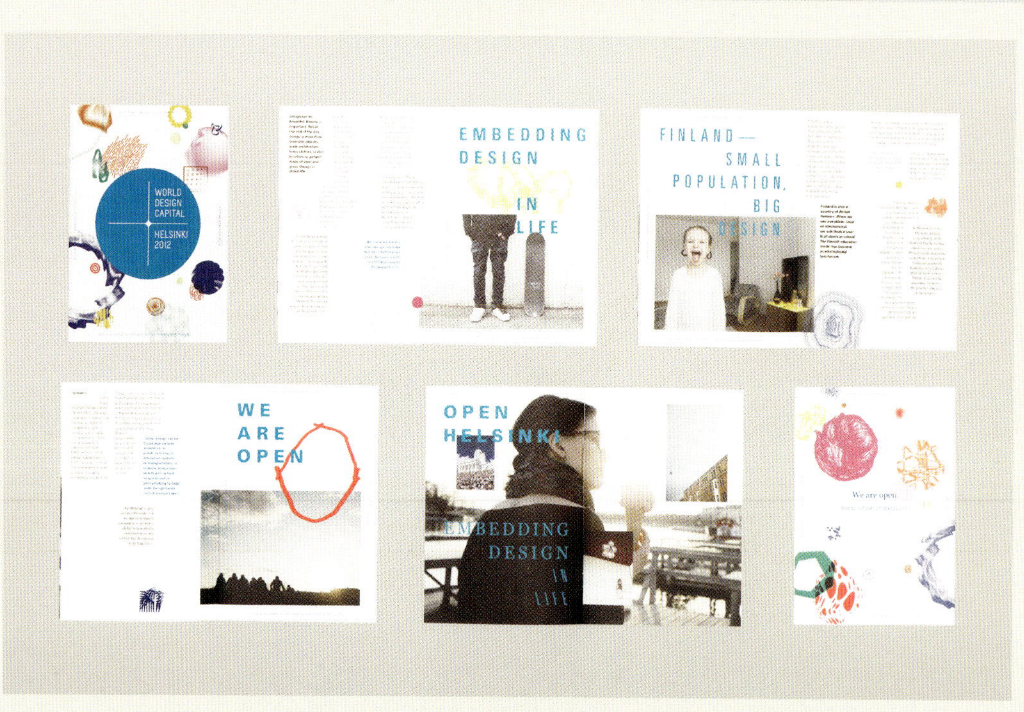
WORLD DESIGN CAPITAL
HELSINKI 2012
EMBEDDING DESIGN IN LIFE
FINLAND — SMALL POPULATION, BIG DESIGN
WE ARE OPEN
OPEN HELSINKI
EMBEDDING DESIGN IN LIFE
We are open

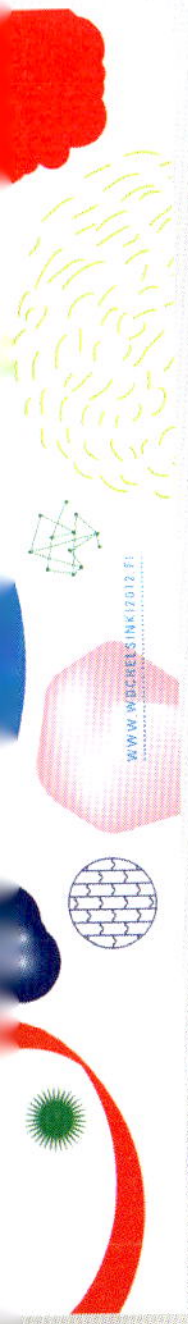

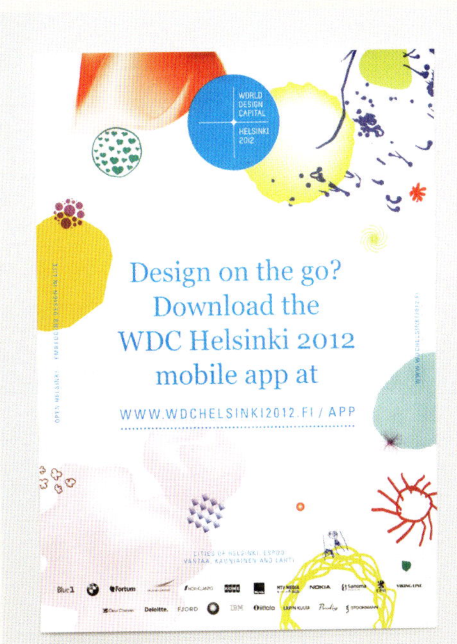
WORLD DESIGN CAPITAL HELSINKI 2012
Design on the go?
Download the
WDC Helsinki 2012
mobile app at
WWW.WDCHELSINKI2012.FI / APP

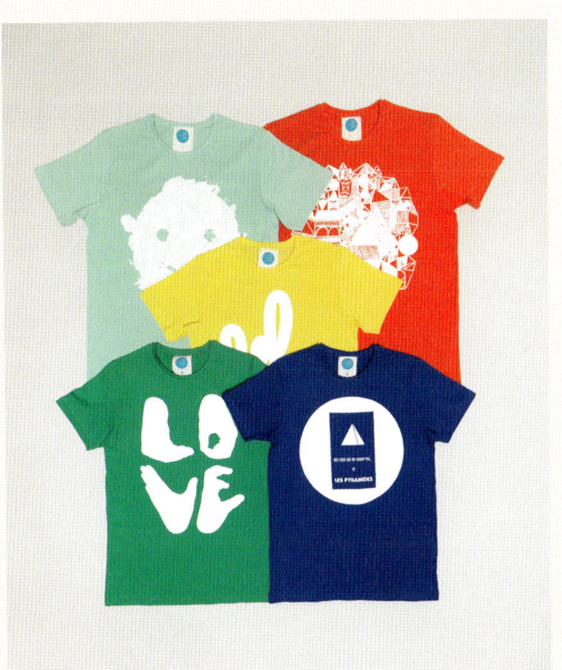

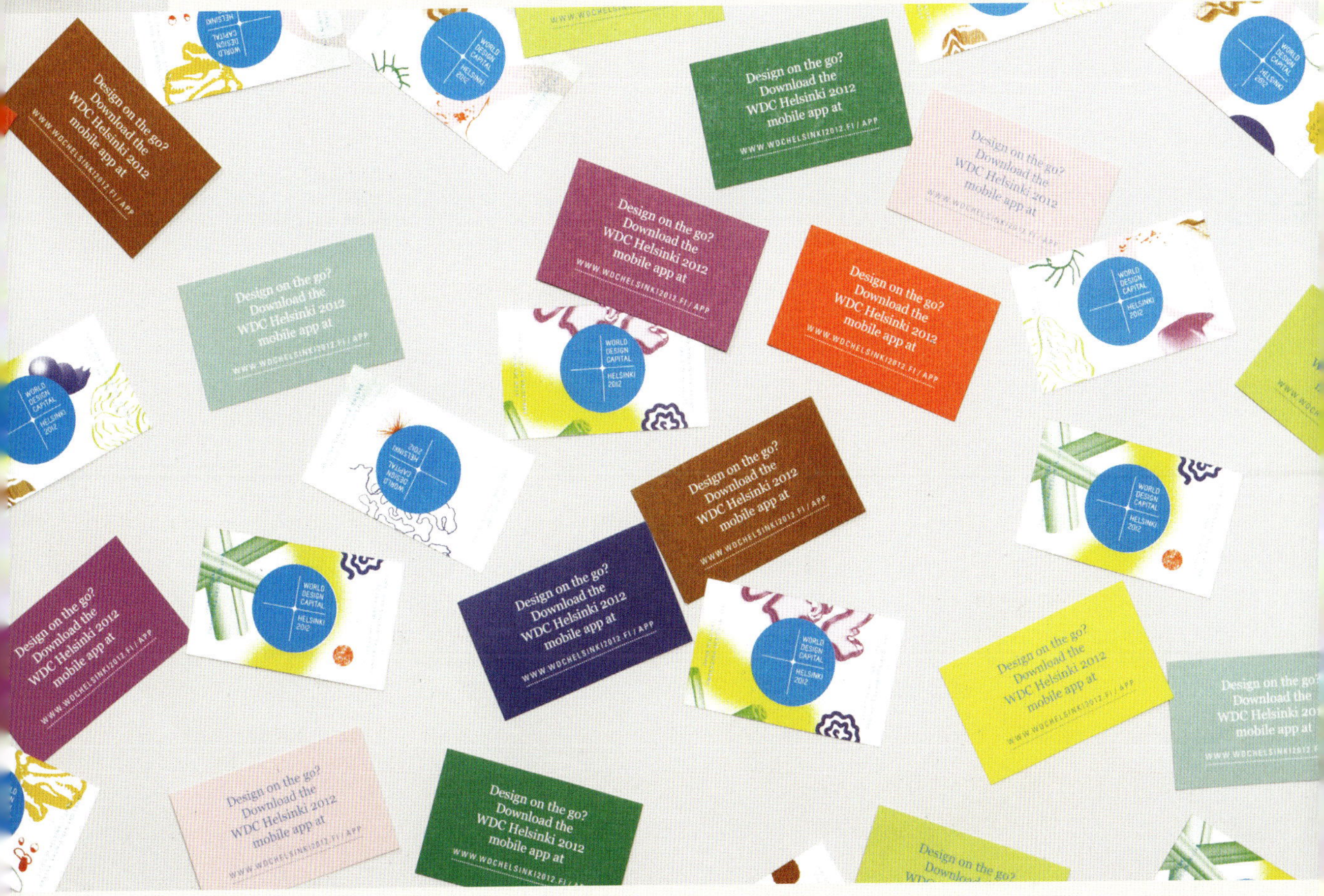

CASE STUDY

07

Fika Bar & Kitchen

Designers Anonymous

Based in Brick Lane, East London Fika Bar & Kitchen has built up a loyal following since its 2008 launch. In recent years, however, the venue's weekday trade has suffered from an influx of new bars, restaurants and cafés into the increasingly trendy Brick Lane area. To combat this threat, Fika asked Designers Anonymous to devise a flexible, easy-to-implement, multifaceted identity that would be effective across multiple touchpoints.

Illustration: Danijela Dobric

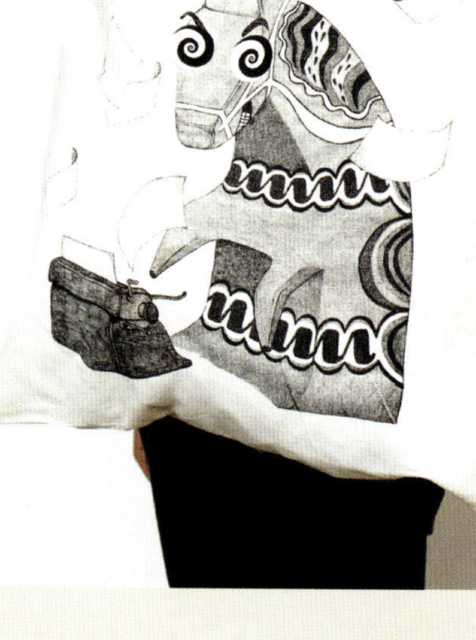

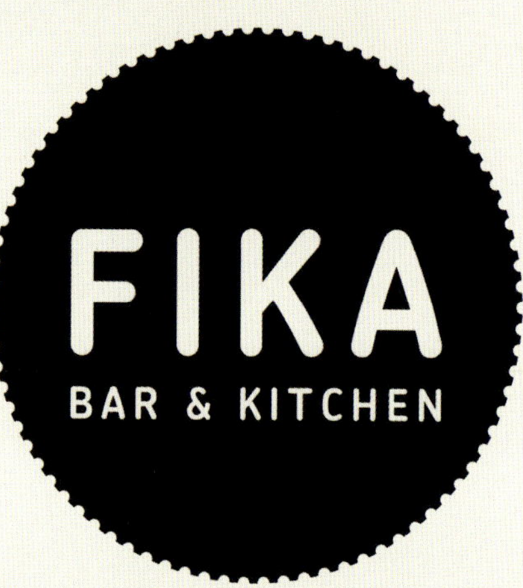

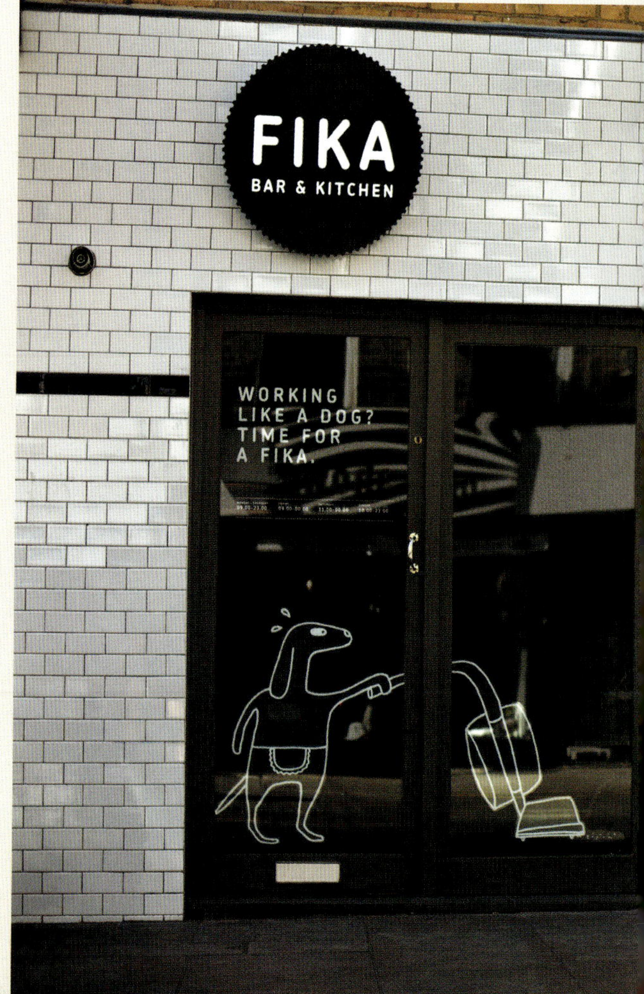

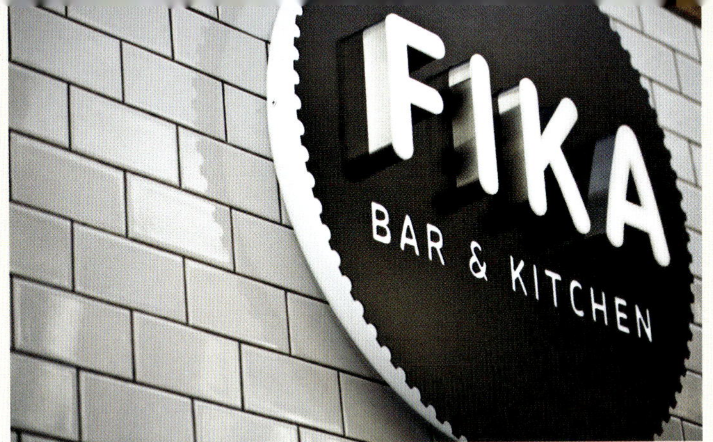

Conception

All that Fika needed was to freshen up its brand image to re-engage with its audience, encourage customer loyalty and re-establish its credentials as a fun, quirky place to visit. Named after the Swedish word for coffee break, Designers Anonymous felt that they needed no encouragement to express its 'Take a Break' proposition in a way that matches the brand's quirky personality and cosmopolitan location. The branding solution is based on the notion of literally a 'break' from the dull routine of daily life.

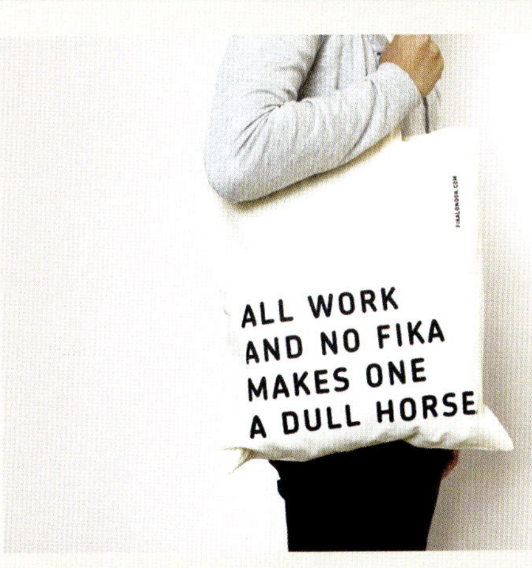

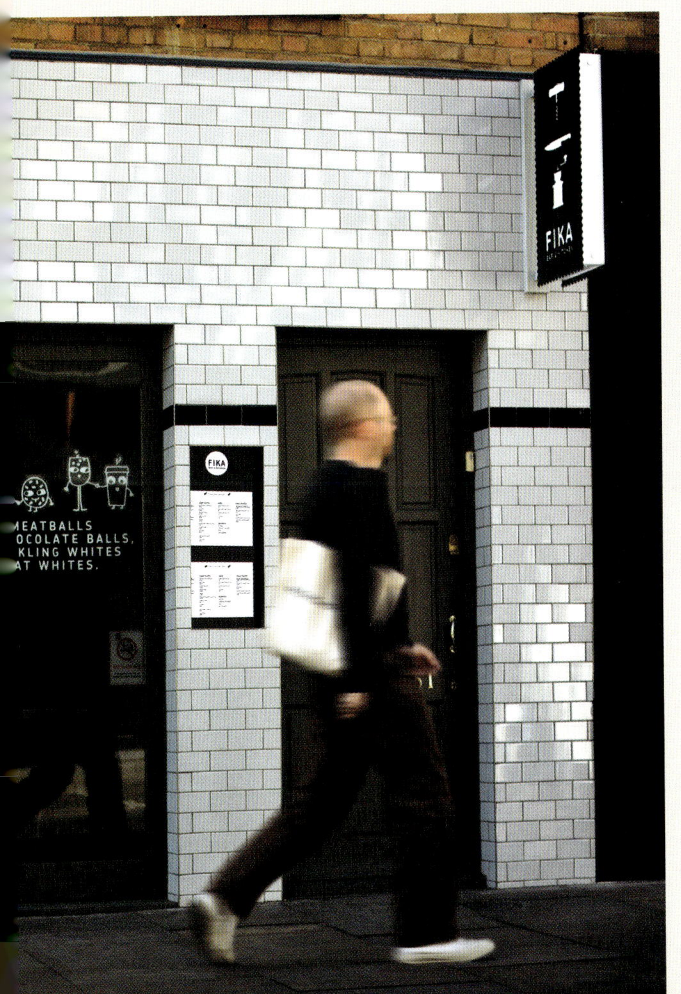

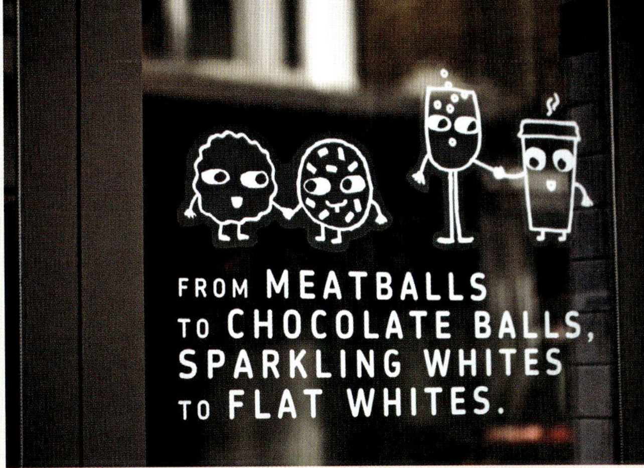

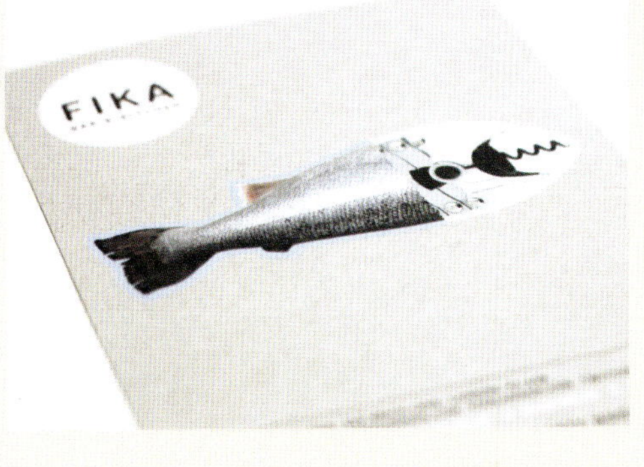

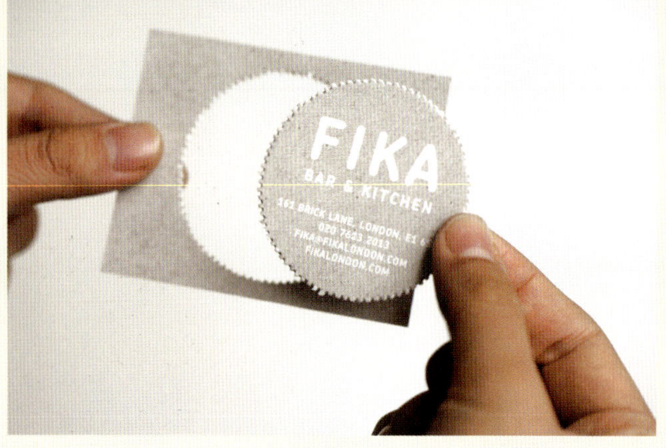

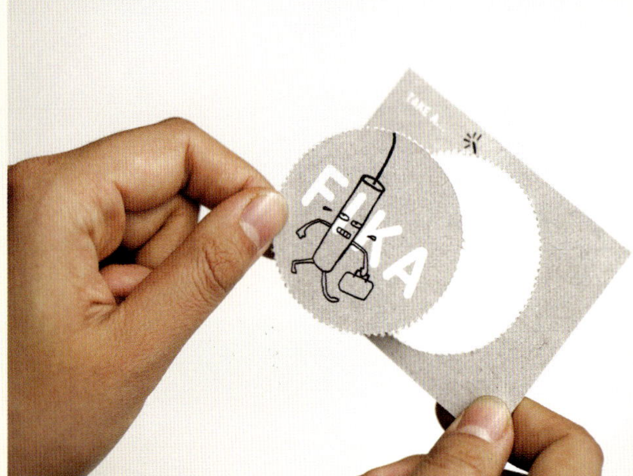

Solution

Altogether, Fika branding is a feat of joined-up, broken-up thinking. This was subtly expressed by perforating sections around and within a mix of photographs and illustrations. They were either assembled as collage or used individually to express a variety of messages. The perforated edging detail links each image back to Fika and the theme of 'Take a Break'.

The website photo gallery, for instance, is illustrated by a cardigan-wearing lady with a Polaroid camera head and the catering section features a casserole dish walking with the aid of cow's legs to communicate 'Fika away from Fika'.

For the window signage, Designers Anonymous featured monotonous situations that 'break' when the café door is opened. Branded bookmarks were also placed in classic novels to help find food and drink menus and provide a break from the story. The branding concept extended to many other situations, including a loyalty scheme and Fika's takeaway offer. A bespoke bottle opener was also created based on a Swedish Dala horse.

Review

The concept of the perforated edge that links an eclectic set of illustrations allowed the brand identity to develop and would unify any illustration style used in the future. The brand refresh has been implemented in stages and further positive results are expected.

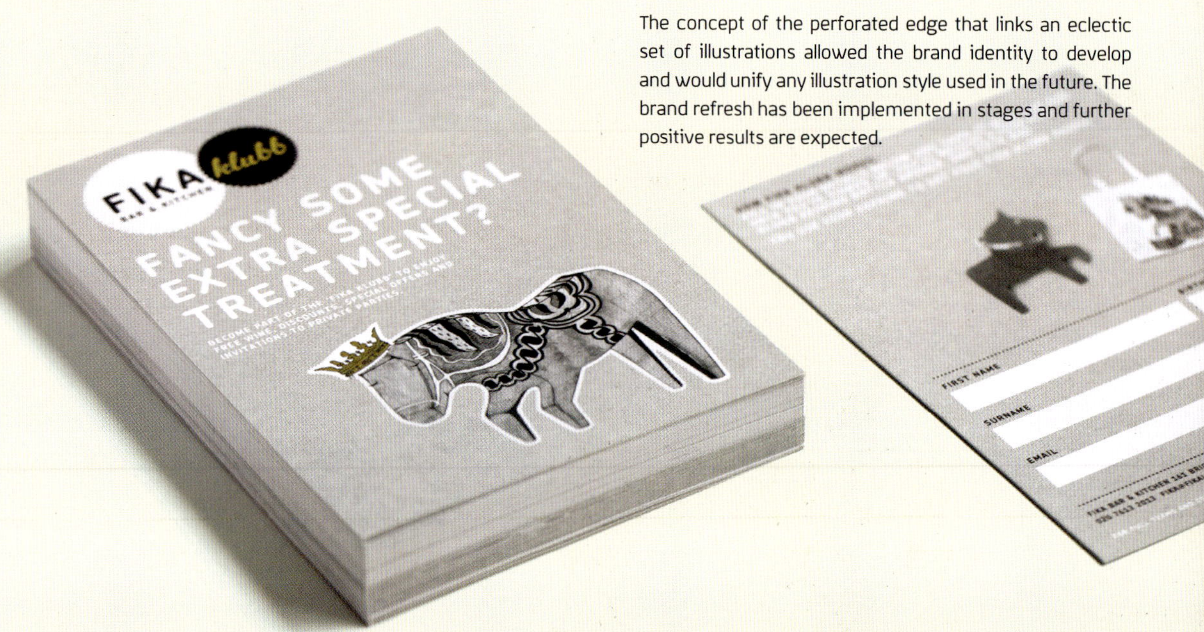

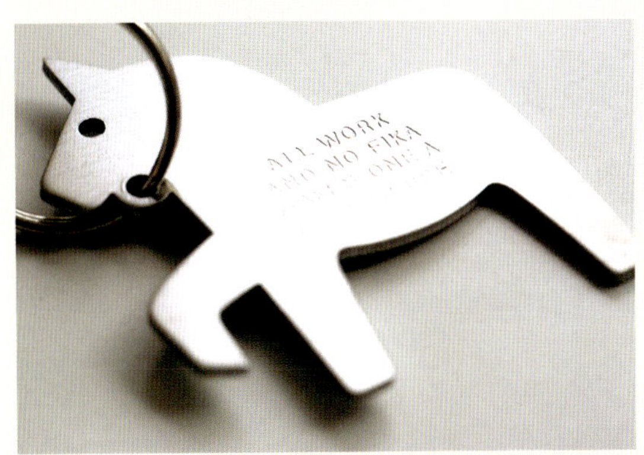

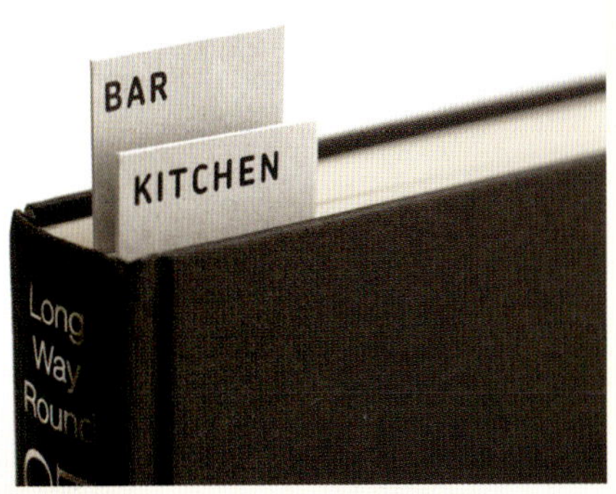

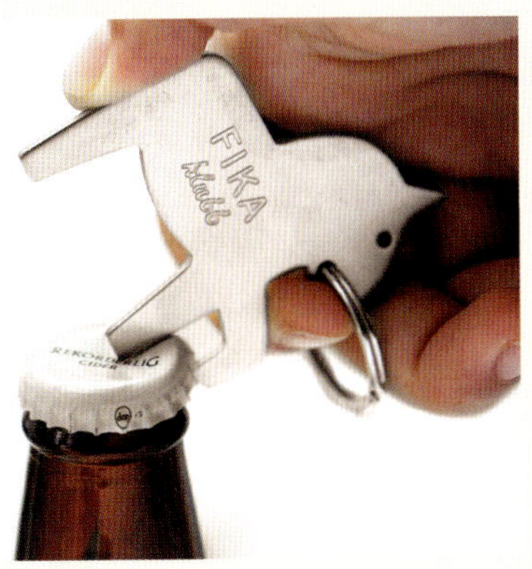

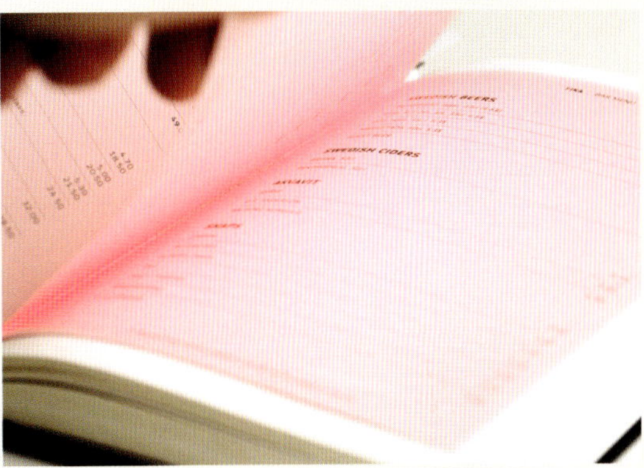

FIKA BAR & KITCHEN To Go

FIKA BAR & KITCHEN To Go

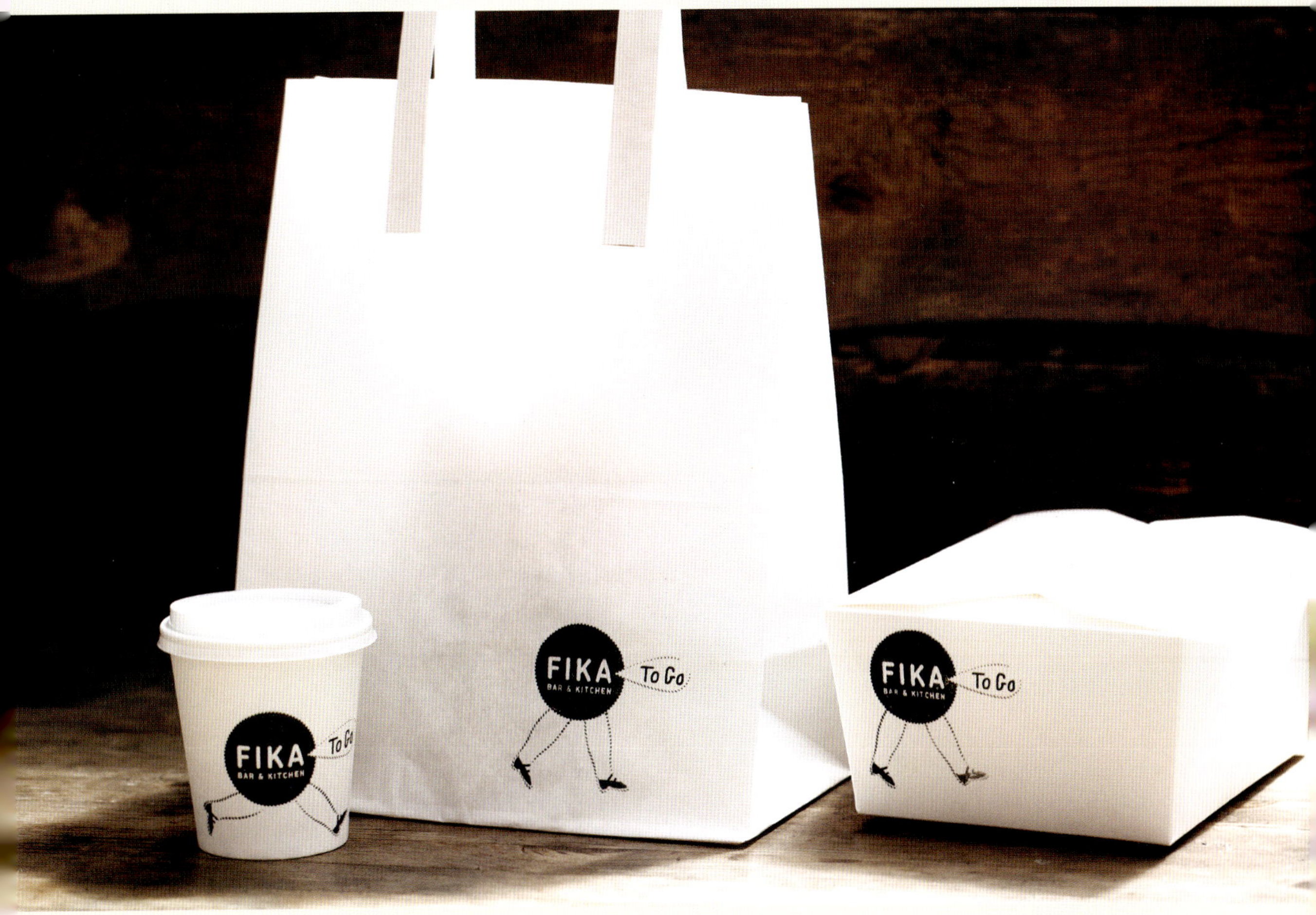

FIKA BAR & KITCHEN To Go

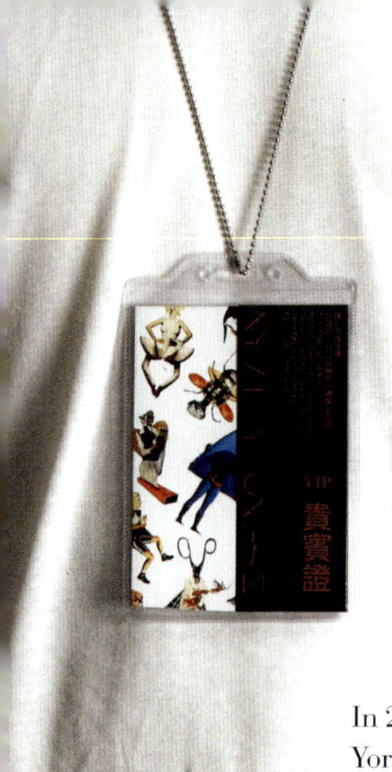

CASE STUDY

08

ADC Young Guns 8

Lee Ken-tsai

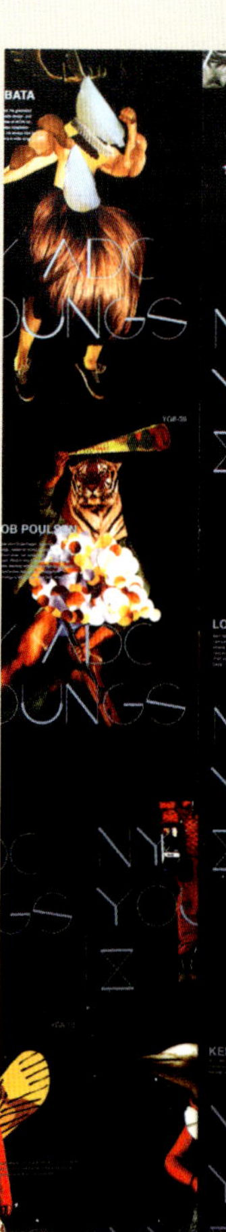

In 2011, Cheng Chung-yi from Kun Shan University (KSU) asked the New York's Art Directors Club representative Lee Ken-tsai in Taiwan to hold an ADC Young Guns show at KSU. The show aimed to expose design students and young designers to high quality designs while, on the other hand, introducing Taiwan's quality design to the Club.

Illustration: Zhan Yu-shu

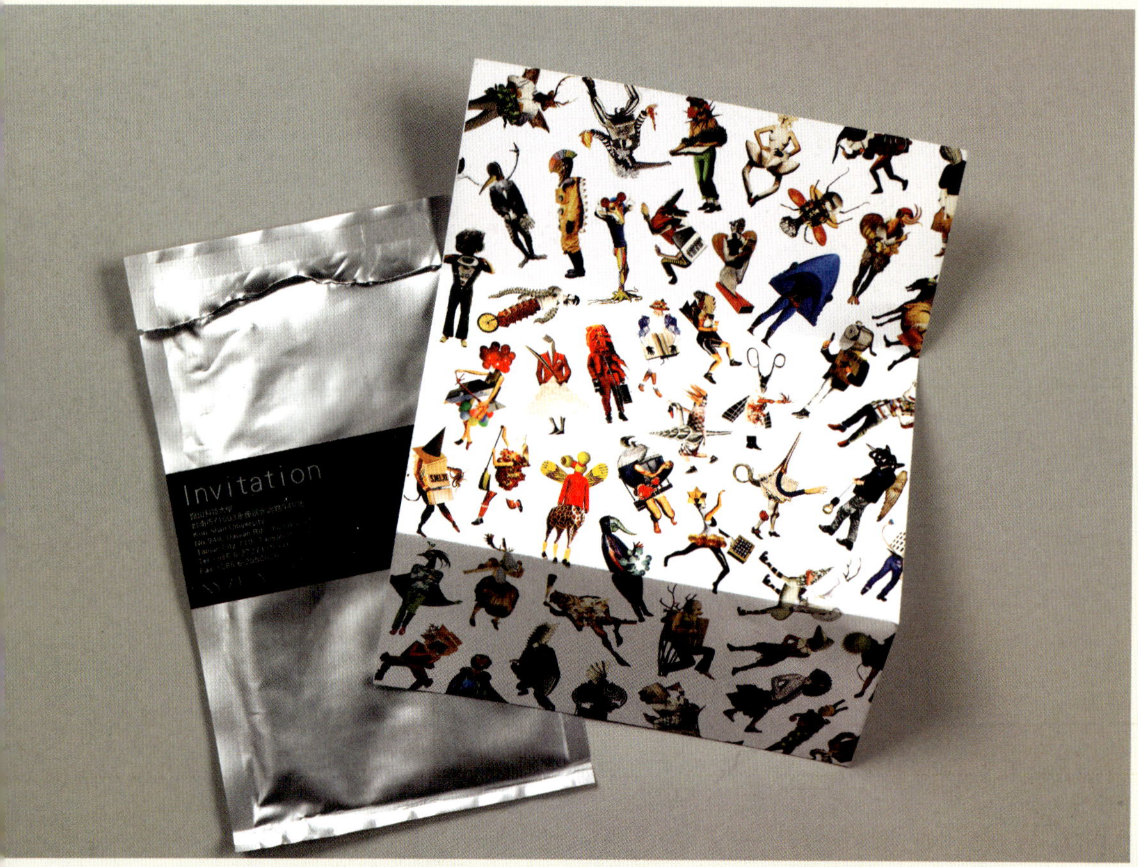

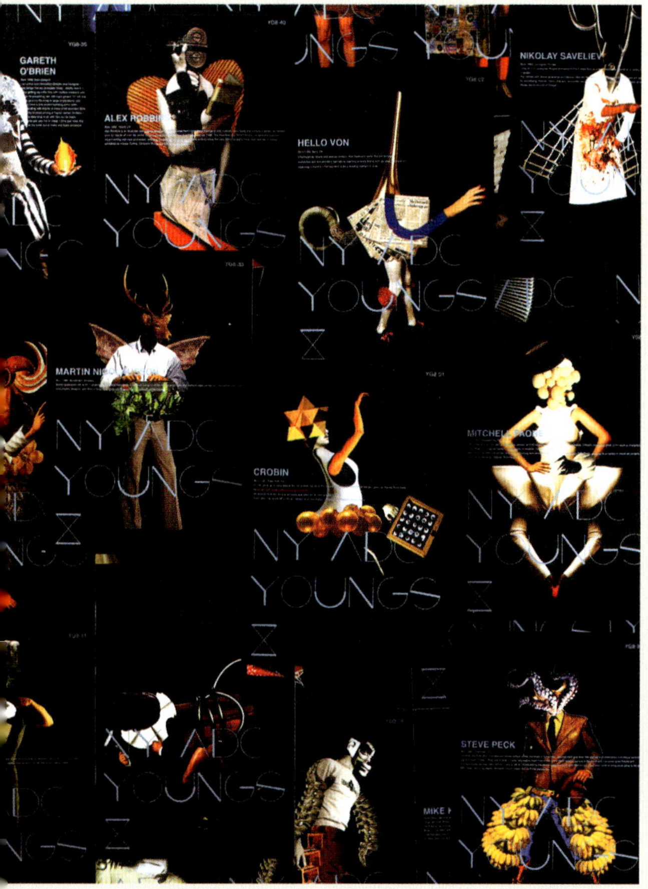

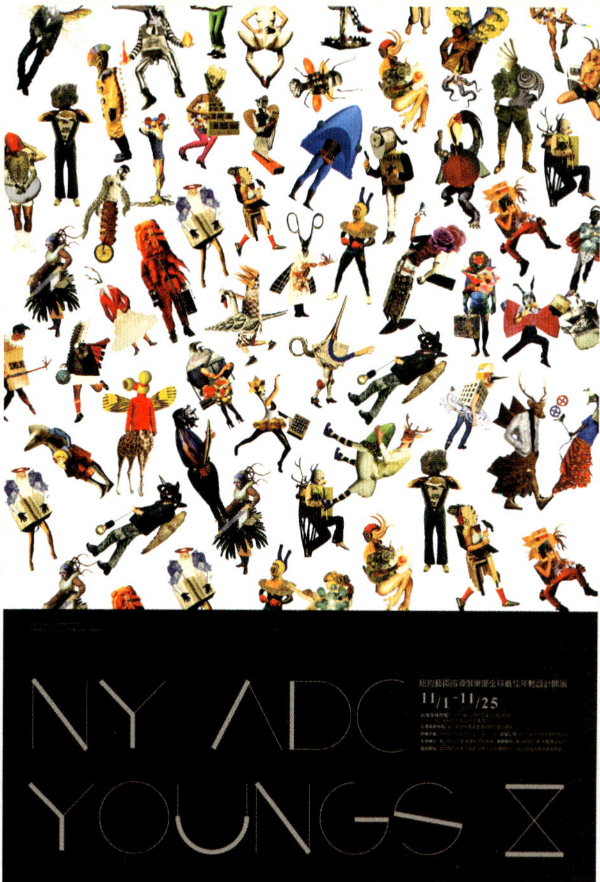

Conception

Lee was personally responsible for the exhibition's visual identity while Cheng helped with the settings and installation.

Only 50 top young creative professionals would be selected to partake with their work in the international exhibition Young Guns 8. As Chinese old saying describes multitalented people as 'monsters' with six arms and three heads, Lee consciously drew on this concept to add a local flair to the identity design.

Seeing the Young Guns show as a rare opportunity to bring local names to global attention, Lee deliberately looked for young Taiwanese talents with untapped potential to join the project.

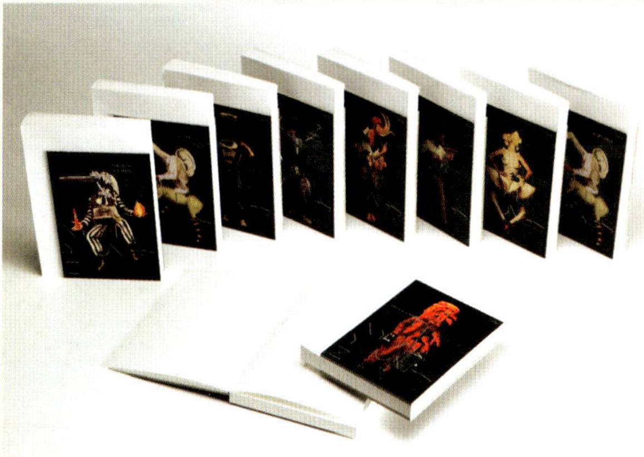

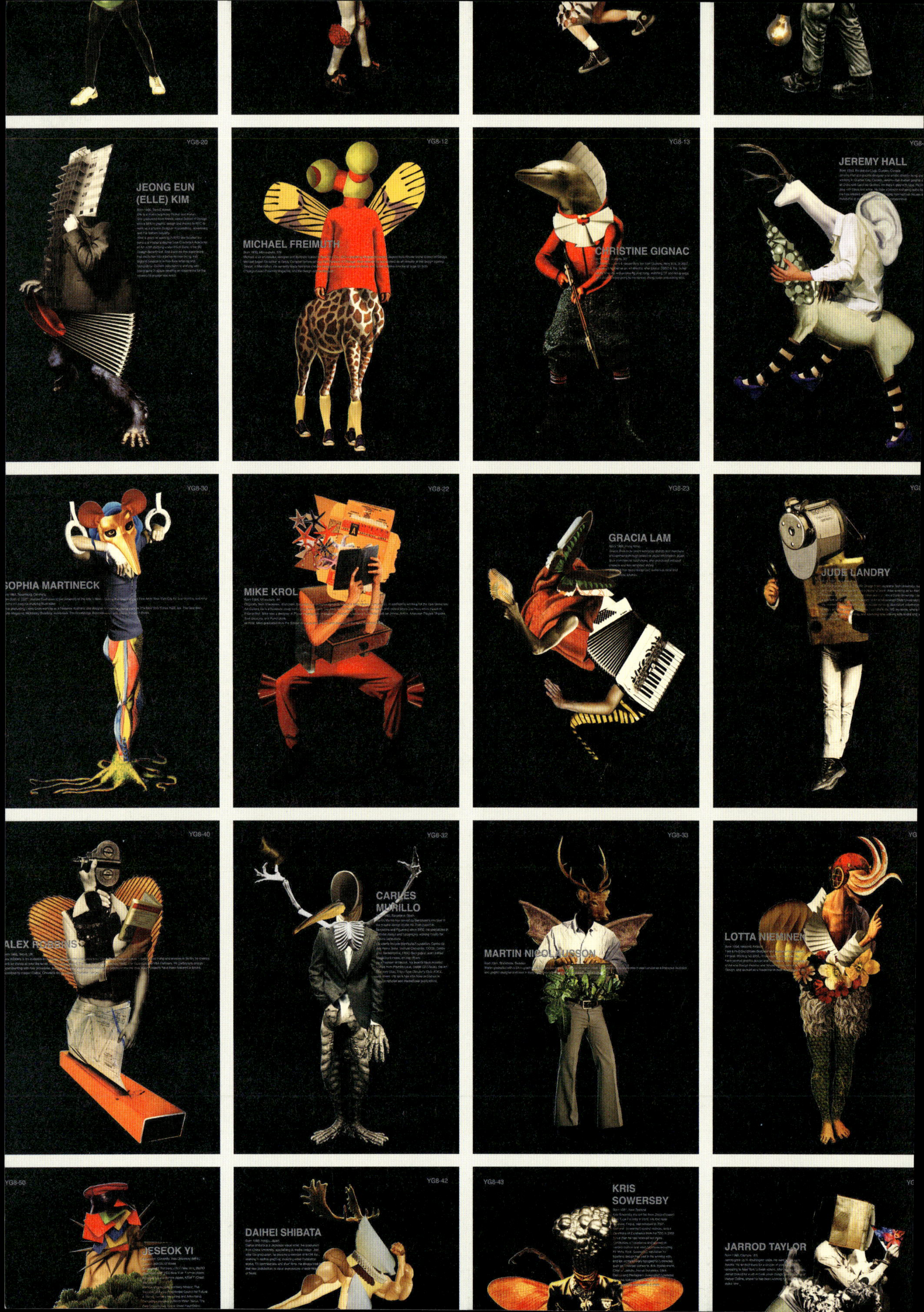
YG8-20
JEONG EUN (ELLE) KIM
YG8-12
MICHAEL FREIMUTH
YG8-13
CHRISTINE GIGNAC
JEREMY HALL
YG8-30
SOPHIA MARTINECK
YG8-22
MIKE KROL
YG8-23
GRACIA LAM
JUDE LANDRY
YG8-40
ALEX ROBBINS
YG8-32
CARLES MURILLO
YG8-33
MARTIN NICOLAUSSON
LOTTA NIEMINEN
YG8-50
JESEOK YI
YG8-42
DAIHEI SHIBATA
YG8-43
KRIS SOWERSBY
JARROD TAYLOR

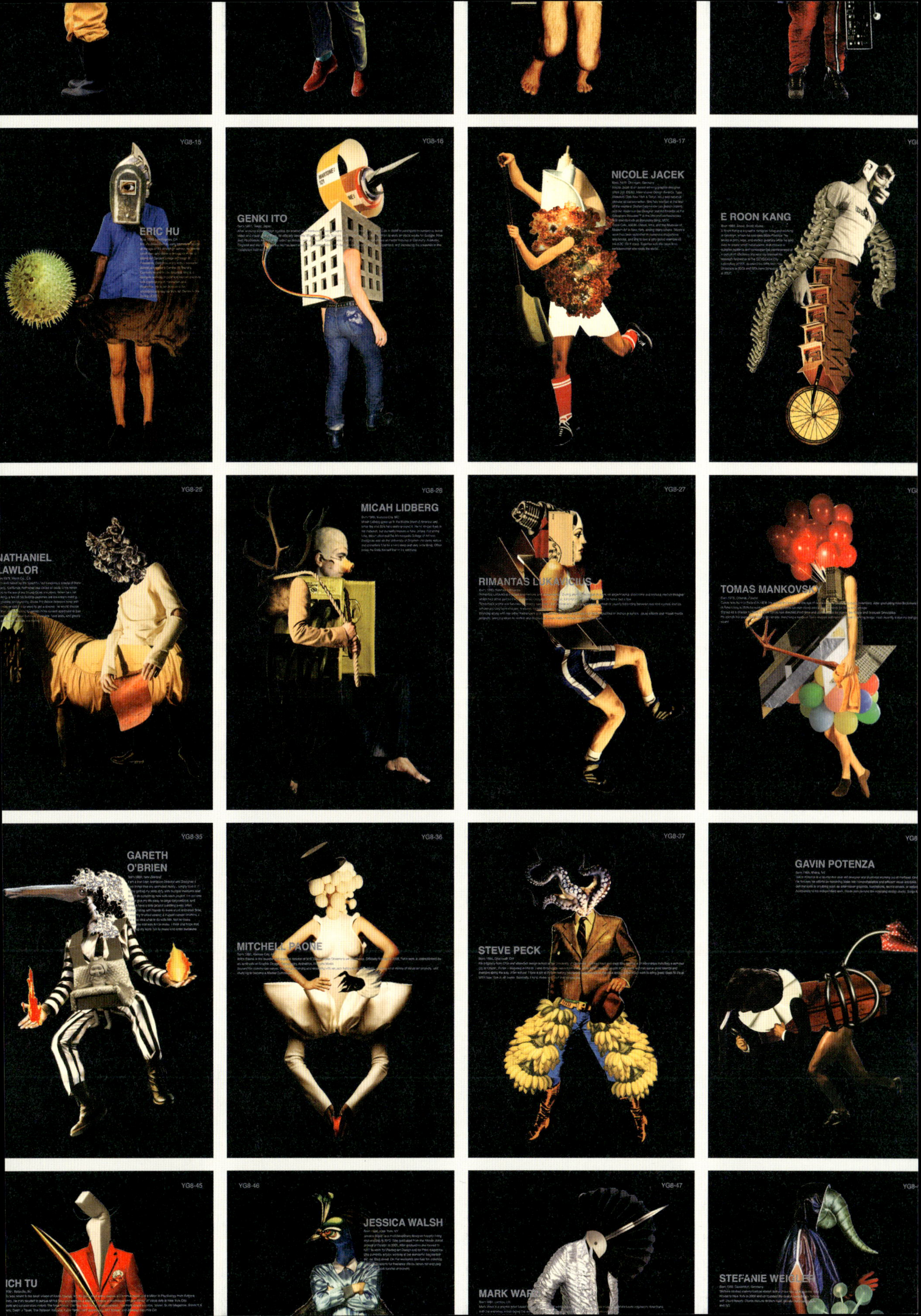

YG8-15
ERIC HU
YG8-16
GENKI ITO
YG8-17
NICOLE JACEK
E ROON KANG
YG8-25
ATHANIEL
AWLOR
YG8-26
MICAH LIDBERG
YG8-27
RIMANTAS LUKAVICIUS
TOMAS MANKOVSK
YG8-35
GARETH
O'BRIEN
YG8-36
MITCHELL PAONE
YG8-37
STEVE PECK
GAVIN POTENZA
YG8-45
ICH TU
YG8-46
JESSICA WALSH
YG8-47
MARK WAR
STEFANIE WEIGLER

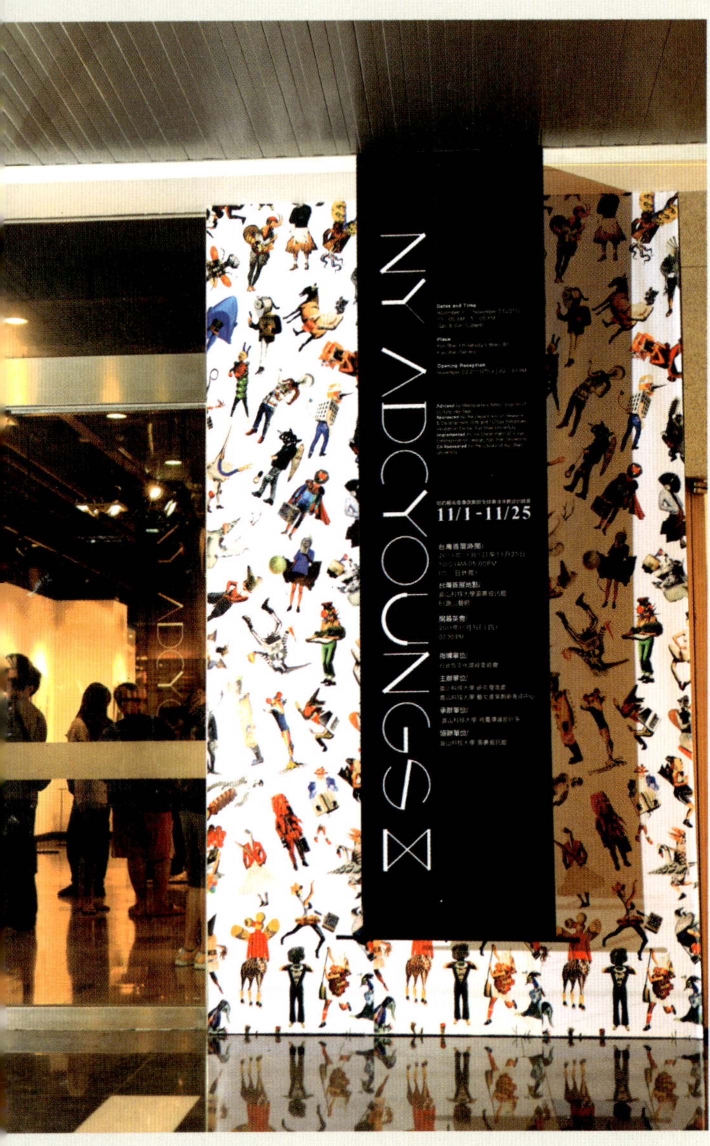
NY ADCYOUNGS X
11/1-11/25

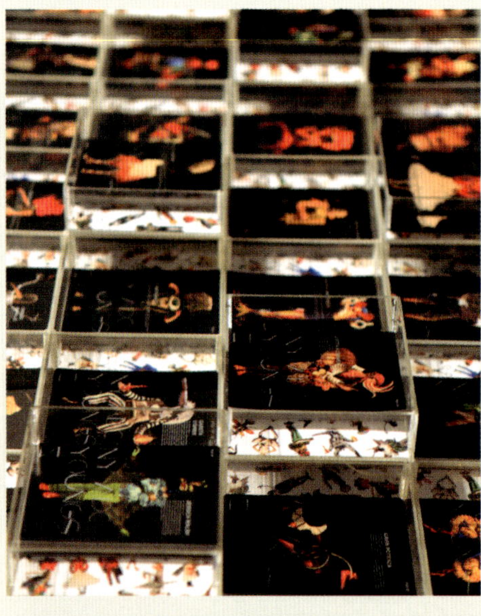

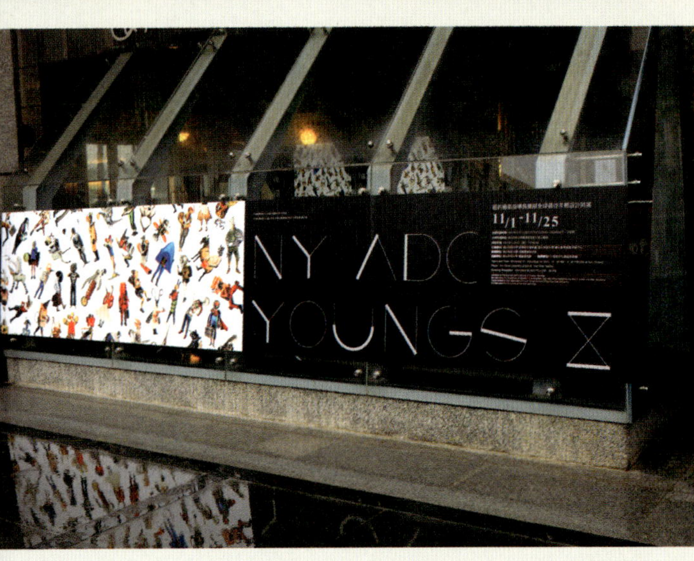
11/1-11/25
NY ADC
YOUNGS X

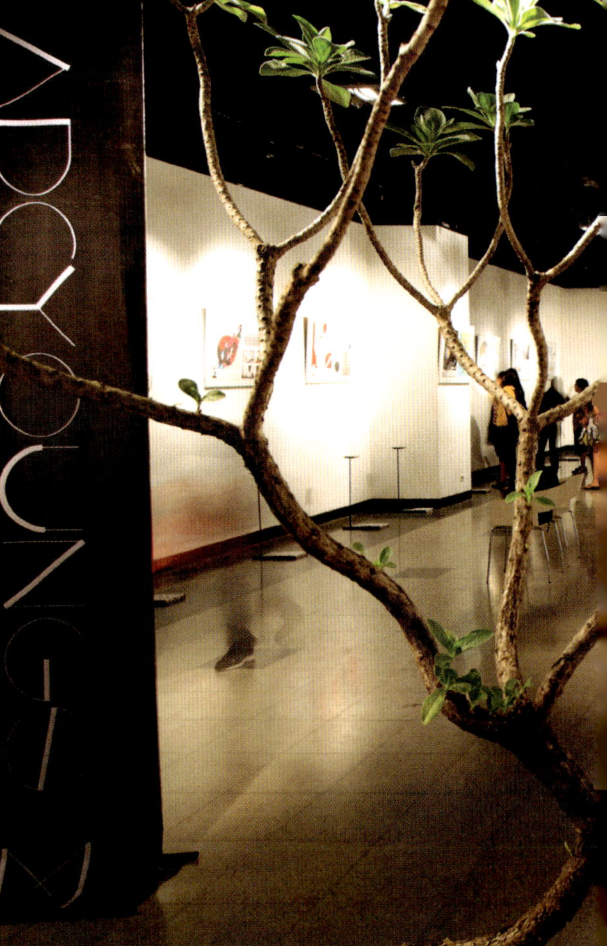
ADCYOUNGS

Solution

Zhan Yu-shu is a self-taught illustrator with over ten years of experience creating collage images. Lee found his retrospective collage illustrations a good fit for his identity concept and thus, commissioned Zhan to picture the selected young designers as 50 monsters.

Zhan eventually created 50 quirky characters on his own with a blend of (random) objects such as scissors, buildings, animals, insects, exotic plants and humans. Each of them had an exceptional look and was occupied in some tasks or actions and hence their varied poses. The characters were made into a pattern, applied across the exhibition site and collateral, such as brochures (and postcards). Lee set off the pattern with a comparatively sensible typeface and dark panels to highlight the subject and practical details of the show.

Review

The resulting design created out of the many distinctive characters offered rich and colourful attractions that metaphorically stressed the unparalleled talents that guests and visitors should expect to discover at the show. The success of the show also prompted Lee to continue bringing new blood from Taiwan to the sight of the western world.

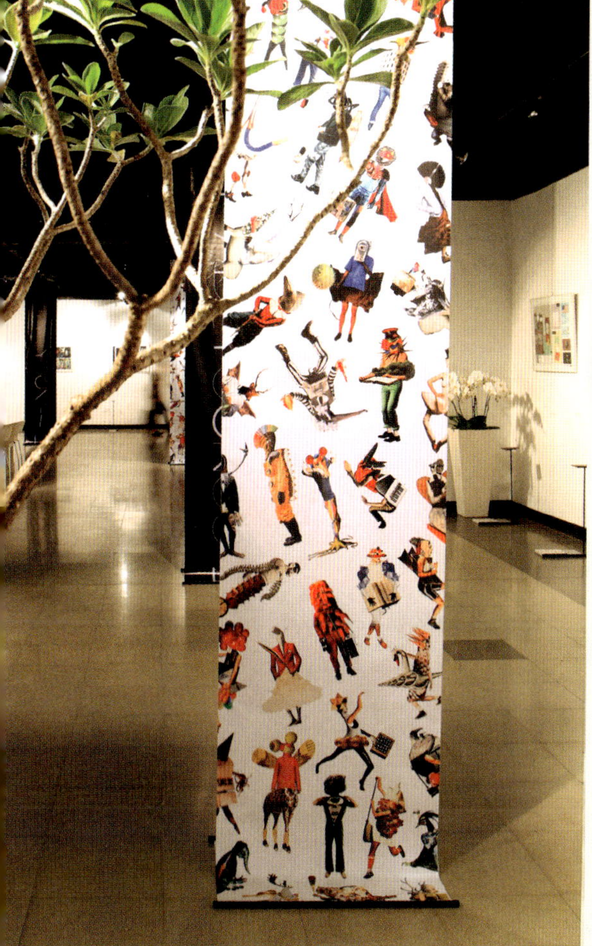

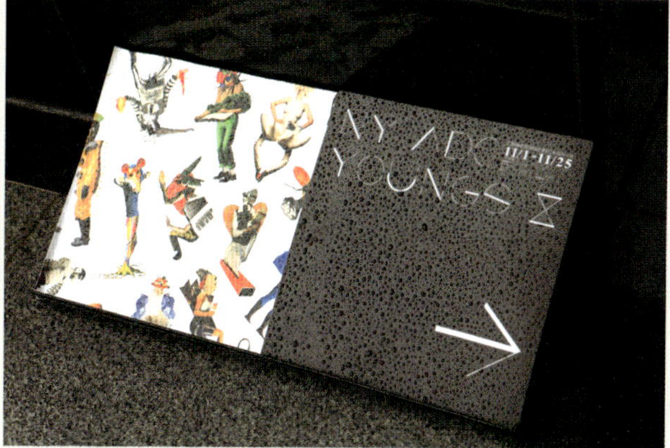

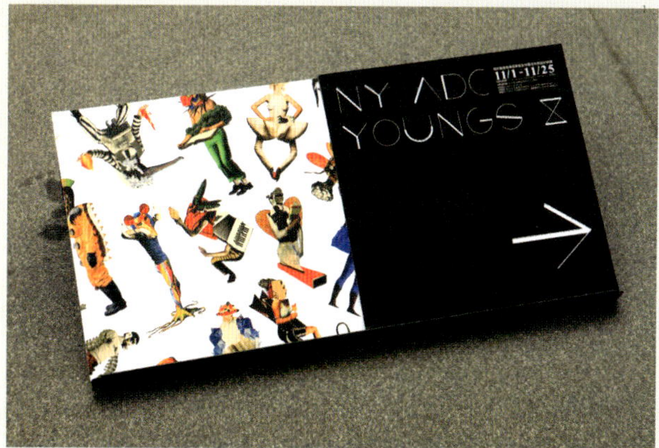

Illustra-
tion

Beyond
Illustra-
tion

Beyond Illustra-tion

Beyond
Illustra-
tion

Hand-rendered typography or linocut print patterns, exquisitely crafted patterns or childlike characters — be fascinated by compelling brand messages delivered by variegated illustrative elements. This section gathers around 90 outstanding projects that exemplify how meanings can be put in illustrations.

1983 ASIA, SUSU & YAO
Abraham Lule & Kuro Strada
Andrea Ferrandis (Kinton)
Anya Aleksandrova
Bardo
Bielke+Yang
Big Horror Athens
Bob Studio
Booth
Büro Destruct
Calvin Tan
Coton Design
Crosspoint New York, Inc.
CROWD STUDIO
dn&co.
dolphins// communication design
EIGA Design
Enrique Larios
Eskimo Design Studio
Estudio Yeyé
Foxall Studio
FullFill Artplication
Gal Sevi Karniel @ Studio OPEN.Total Brand Experience
Gustavo Emilio Quintana
Happycentro
Hara Design Institute
Huang Zhong-xing (Park Lane by Splendor)
Il-Ho Jung design, interactive & motion
Jean Jullien
Jefferson Cheng
Jonathan Calugi, Federico Landini
Judit Besze
Kinetic Singapore
Kinga Offert
Ko. Machiyama
Lo Siento
Mara Vissers
Marta Spendowska
Mind Design
Mucca Design
MURA
NHOMADA
Oh Babushka
ONE & ONE DESIGN
oraviva! designers
P.A.R
Perky Bros llc
Polyester Studio
Robot Food
RONCHAM DESIGN OFFICE
Rosie Gopaul
Rossoamaranto
Ryoji Nakajima
Sasha Vinogradova
Sciencewerk
SeventhDesign™
Shinsegae Graphic Design
SHISHKI branding agency
Sidney Lim
Sleep Projects
Stockholm Design Lab
Studio AH — HA
Studio Brave
Studioahamed
Substance
Tofu
TYMOTE
Vicki Turner
viction workshop ltd
Victor Branding Design Corp.,
village®
Warren Tey

Fruits Block is a line of memo pads as a stack of sliced fruit, launched under the label, Paperable. Jointly developed by printing company Yamakoshi and art initiative Kapo, Paperable seeks to delight conversations through paper and prints in the digital era.

Client: YKP (Yamakoshi + Kapo Project)

Ko. Machiyama

Fruits Block

Fruits Block is a line of memo pads as a stack of sliced fruit, launched under the label, Paperable. Jointly developed by printing company Yamakoshi and art initiative Kapo, Paperable seeks to delight conversations through paper and prints in the digital era.

Client: YKP (Yamakoshi + Kapo Project)

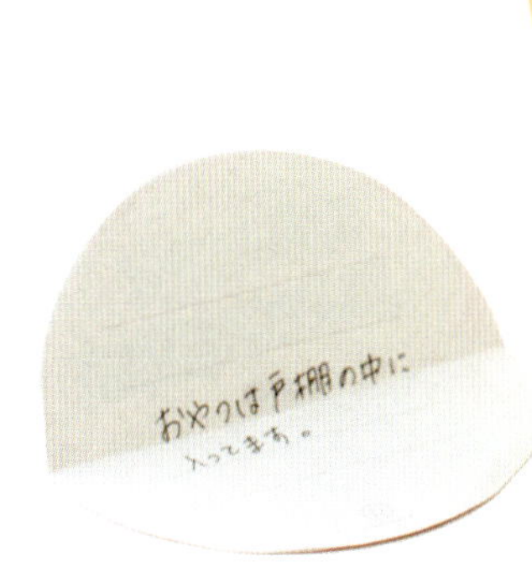

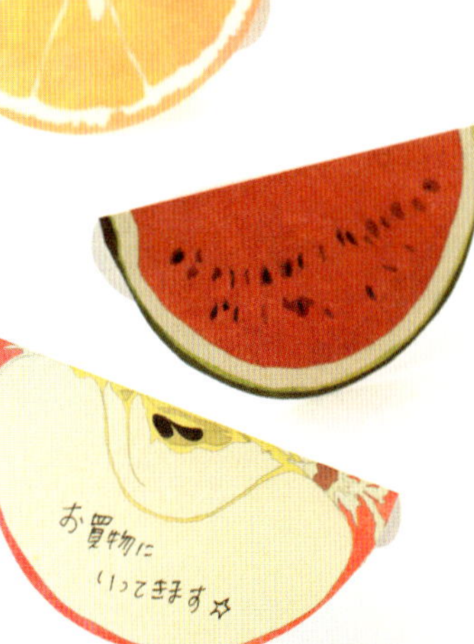

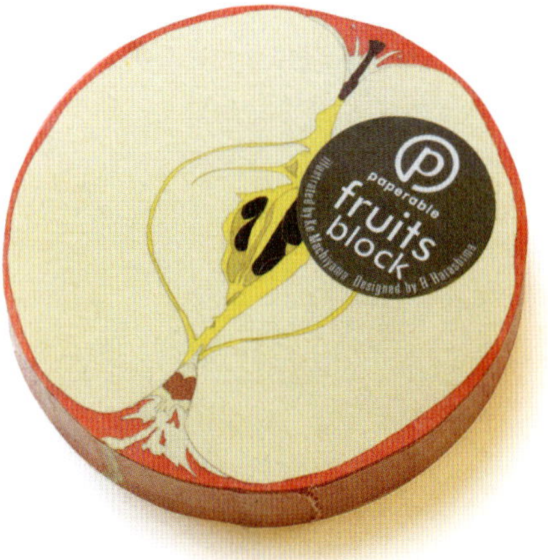

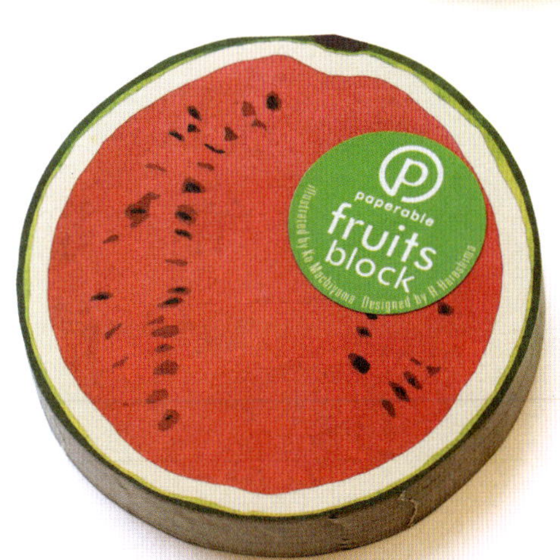

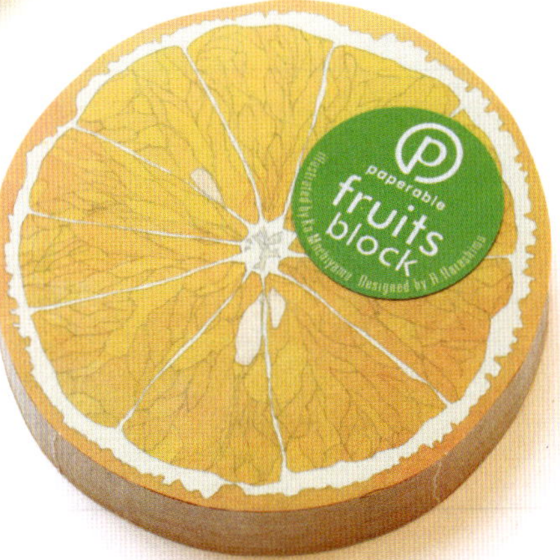

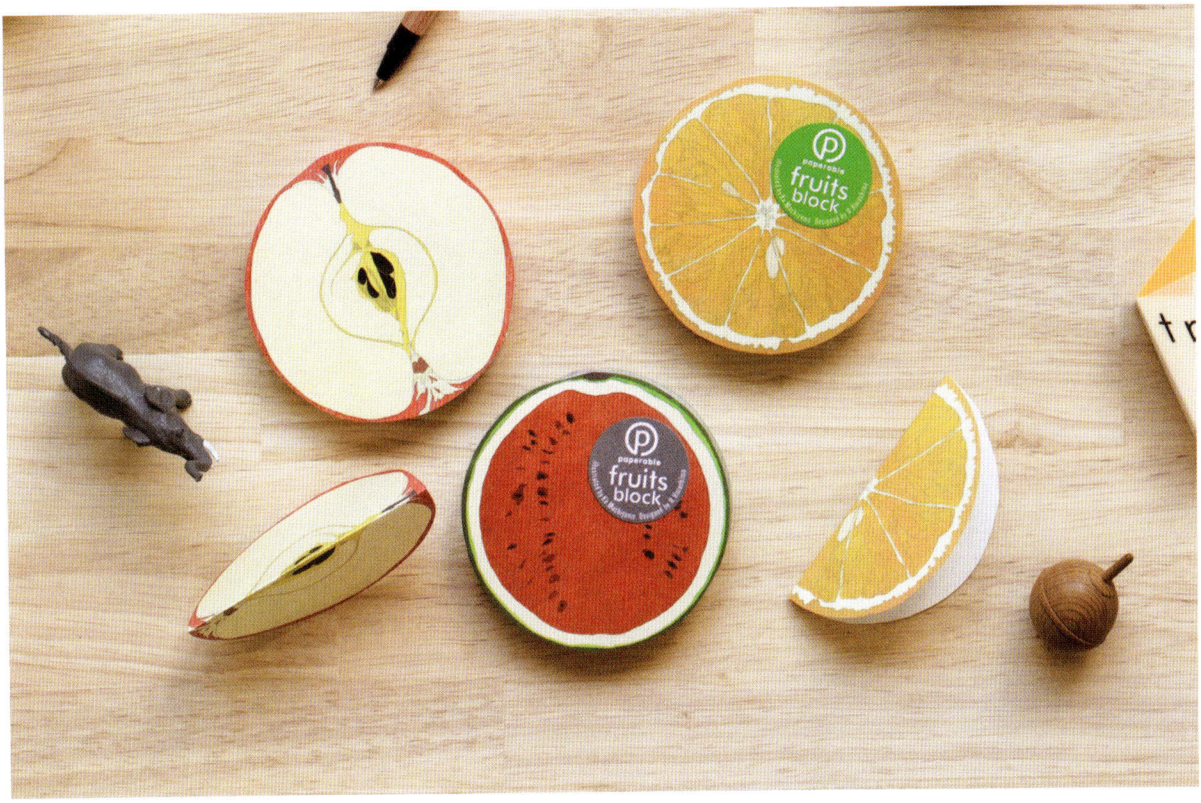

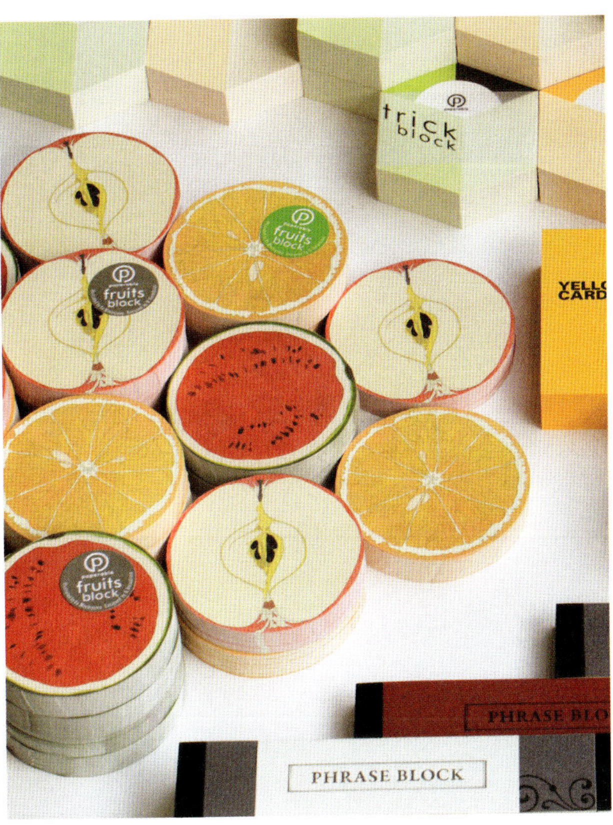
trick
block
PHRASE BLOCK

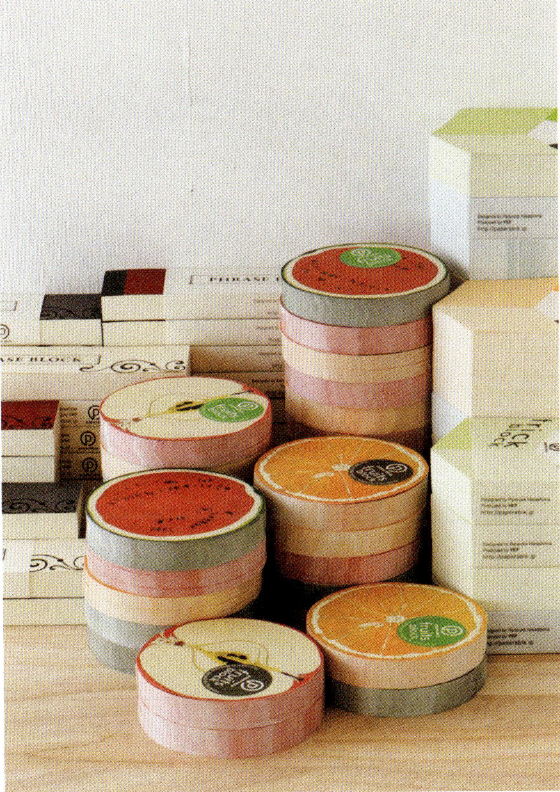

Developed under stationery brand Paperable, this set of notepad lets birds and hippos be the messengers and speak on the users' behalf. Enlivened by the pens of Ko. Machiyama, all that mews, howls, tweets, and roars will do whatever they can to spread the words.

Client: YKP (Yamakoshi + Kapo Project)

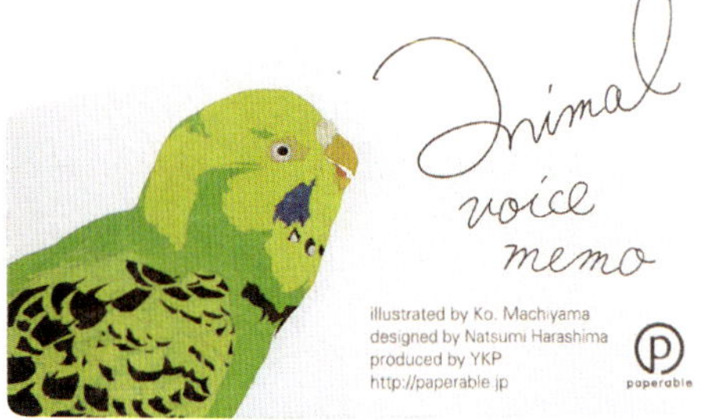

Ko. Machiyama

Animal Voice Memo

Developed under stationery brand Paperable, this set of notepad lets birds and hippos be the messengers and speak on the users' behalf. Enlivened by the pens of Ko. Machiyama, all that mews, howls, tweets, and roars will do whatever they can to spread the words.

Client: YKP (Yamakoshi + Kapo Project)

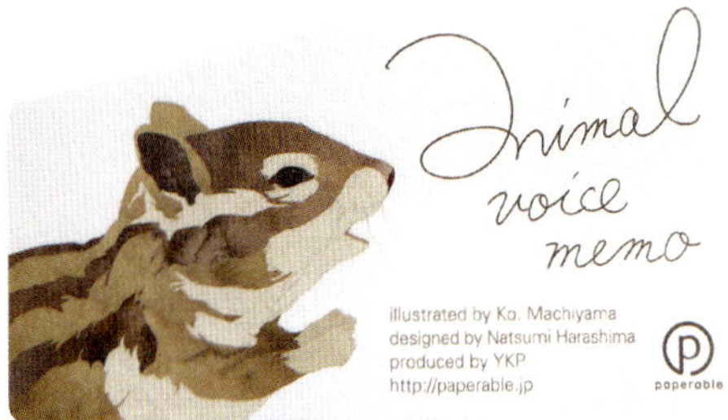

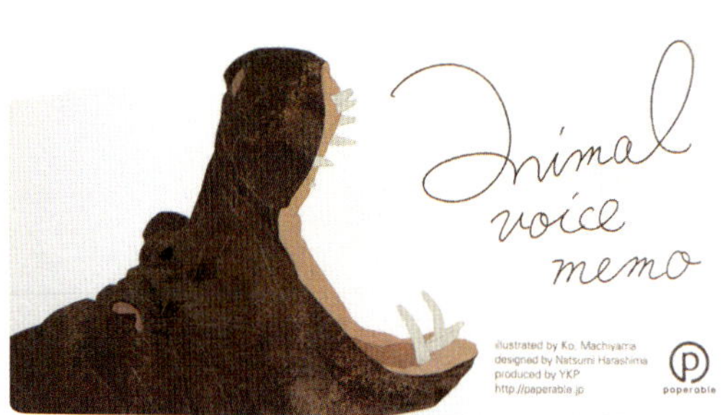

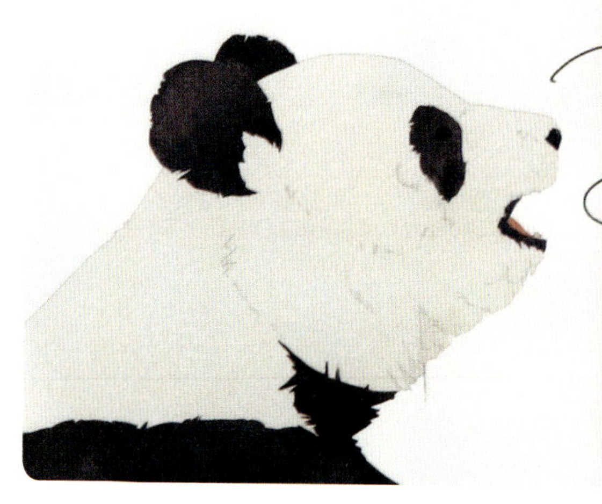

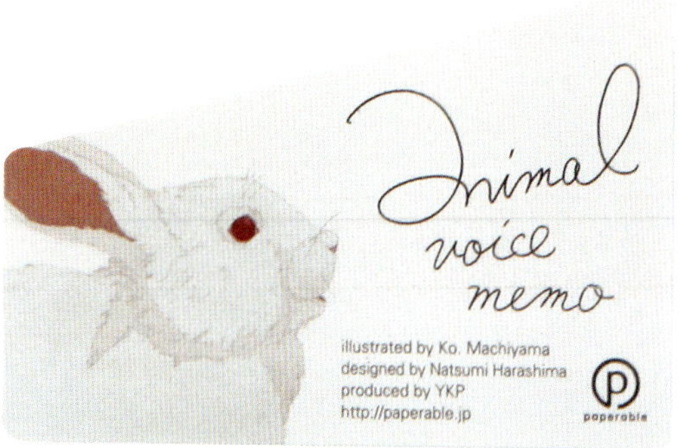

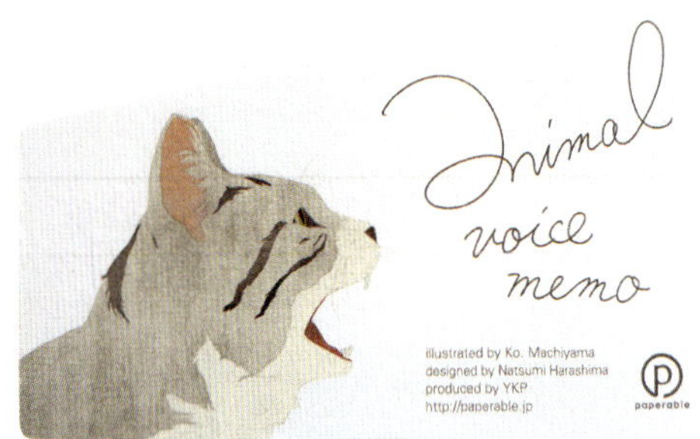

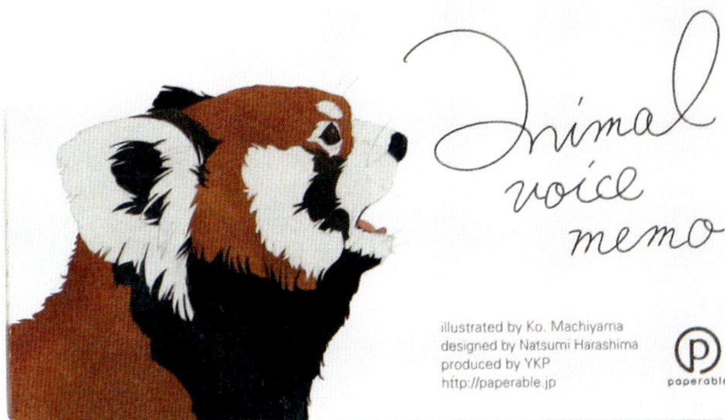
Animal
voice
memo
illustrated by Ko. Machiyama
designed by Natsumi Harashima
produced by YKP
http://paperable.jp
paperable

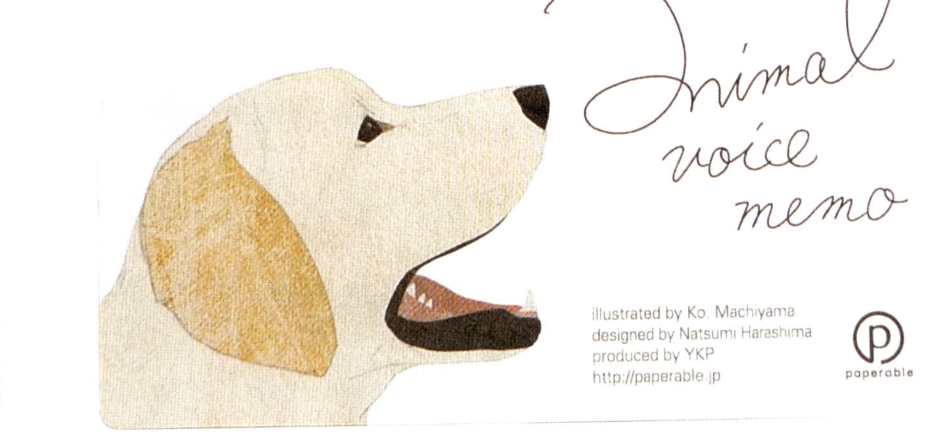
Animal
voice
memo
illustrated by Ko. Machiyama
designed by Natsumi Harashima
produced by YKP
http://paperable.jp
paperable

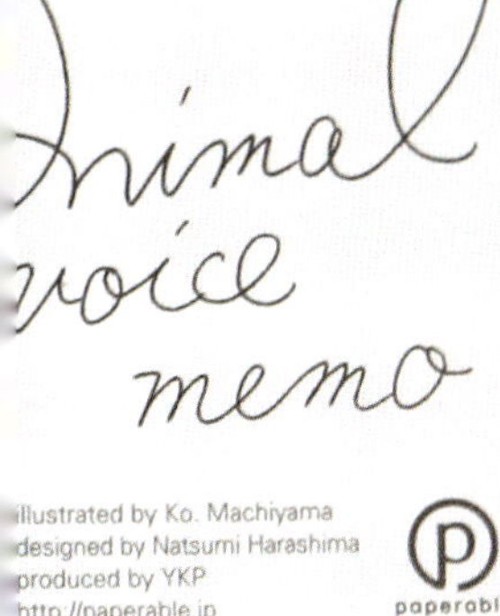
voice
memo

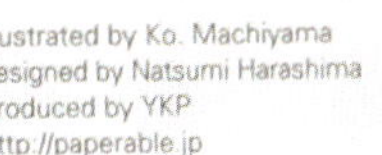
illustrated by Ko. Machiyama
designed by Natsumi Harashima
produced by YKP
http://paperable.jp

paperable

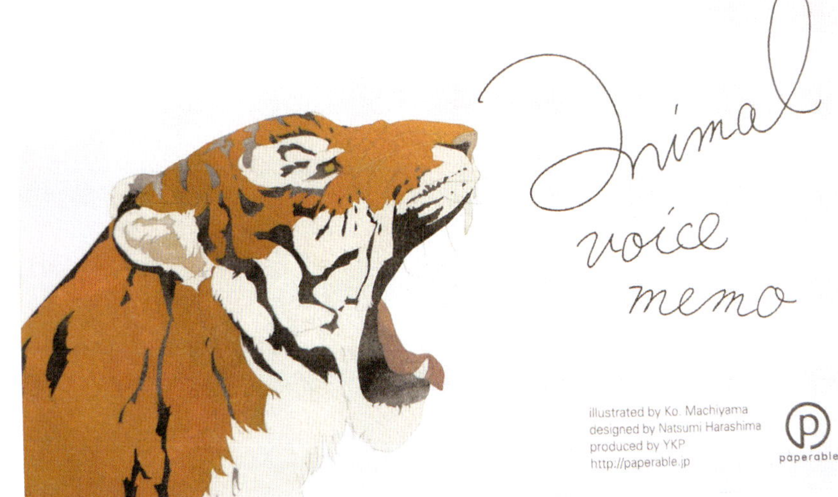
Animal
voice
memo
illustrated by Ko. Machiyama
designed by Natsumi Harashima
produced by YKP
http://paperable.jp
paperable

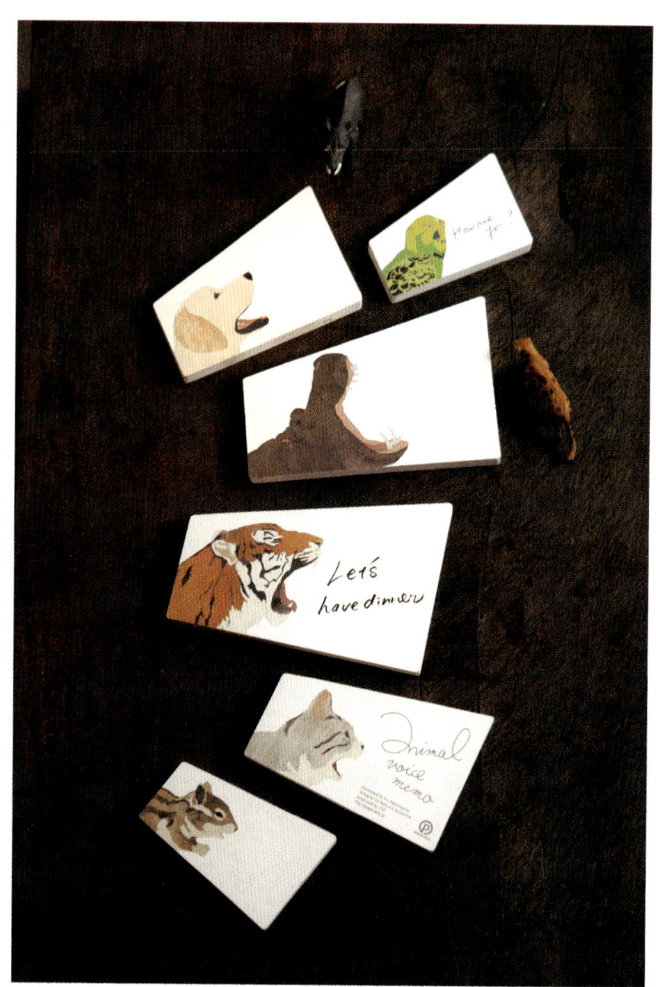
How are you?
Let's have dinner
Animal voice memo

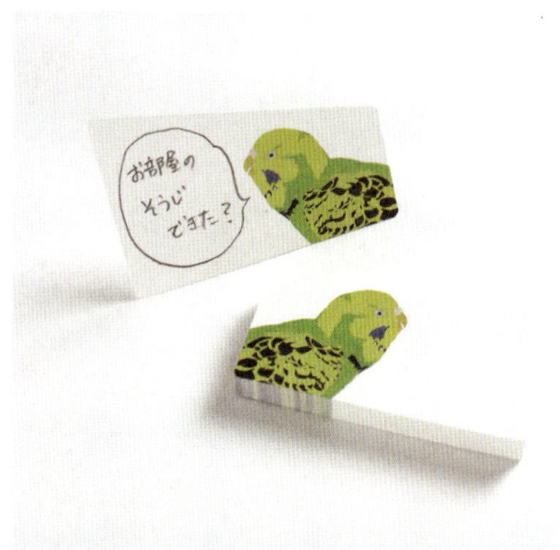
お部屋の
そうじ
できた？

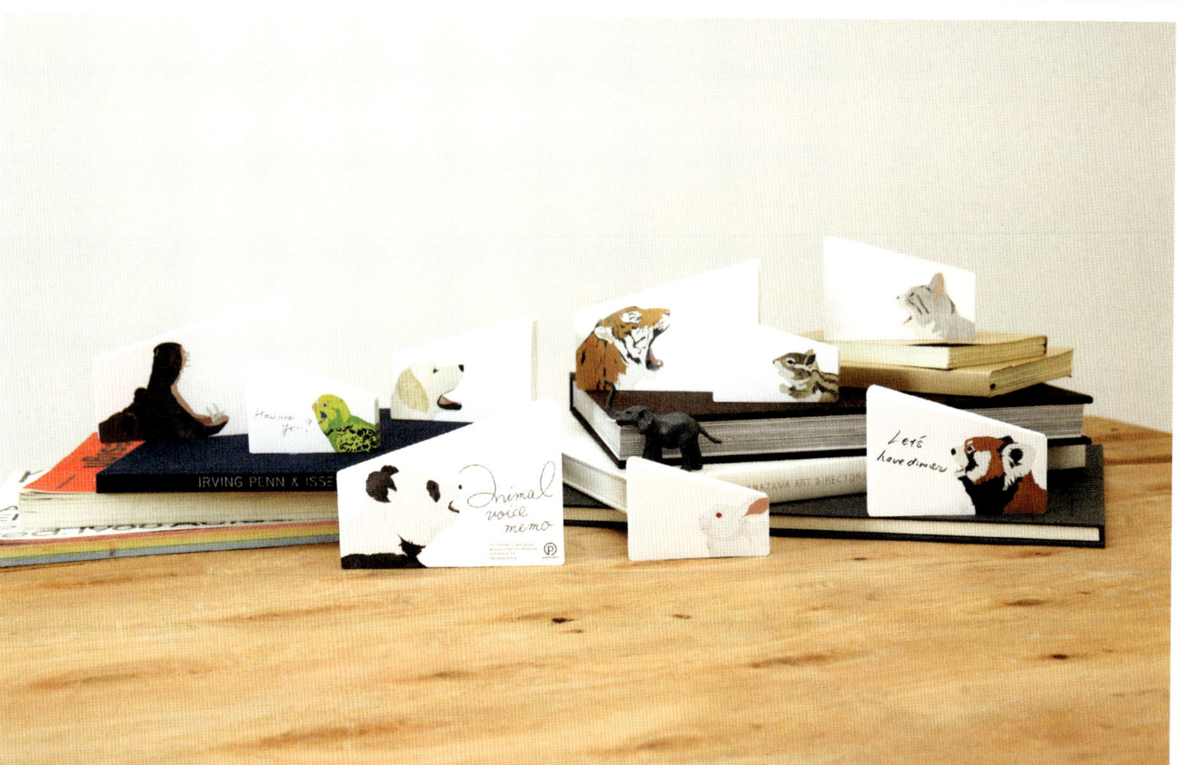
How are you?
IRVING PENN & ISSE
Animal voice memo
Let's have dinner

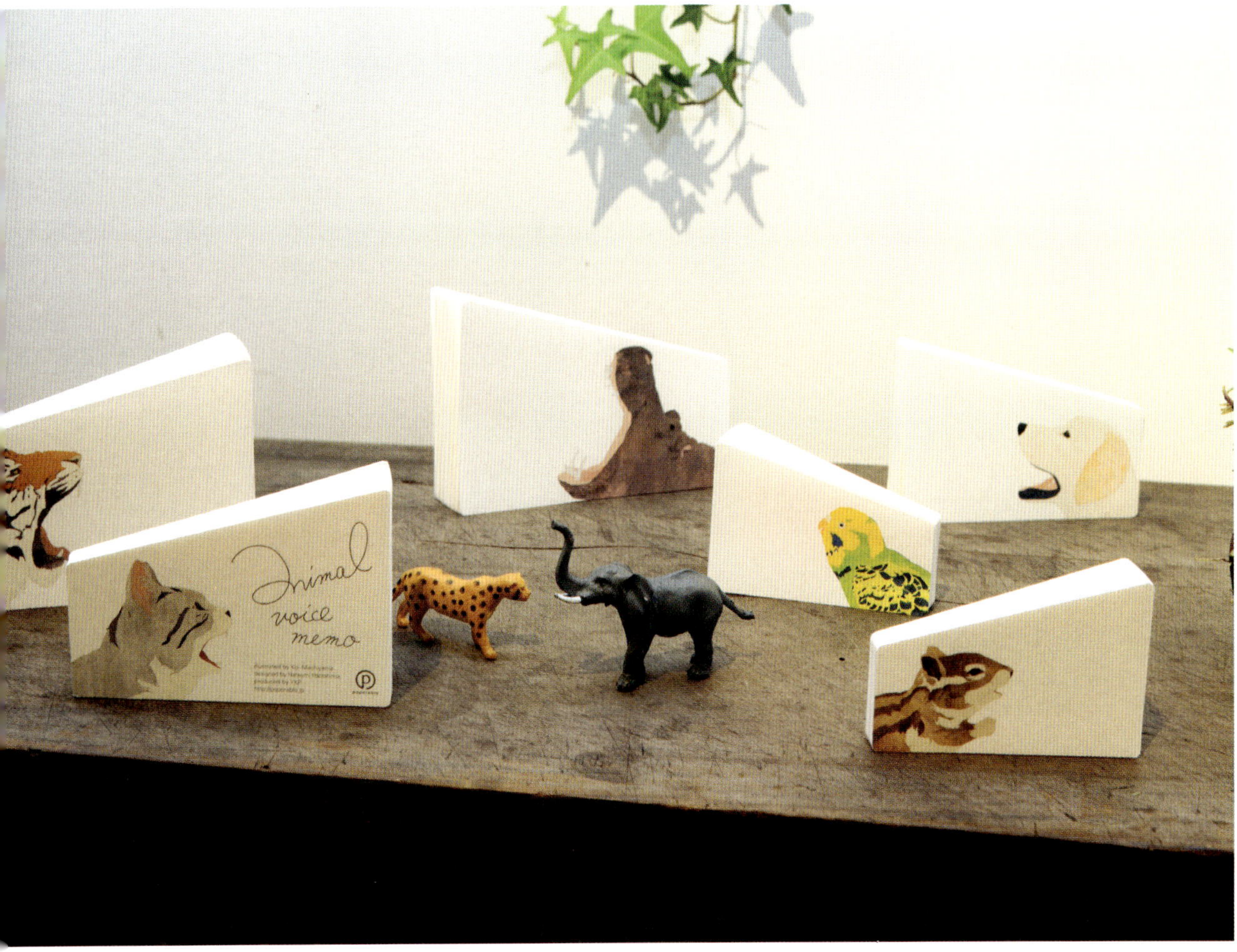

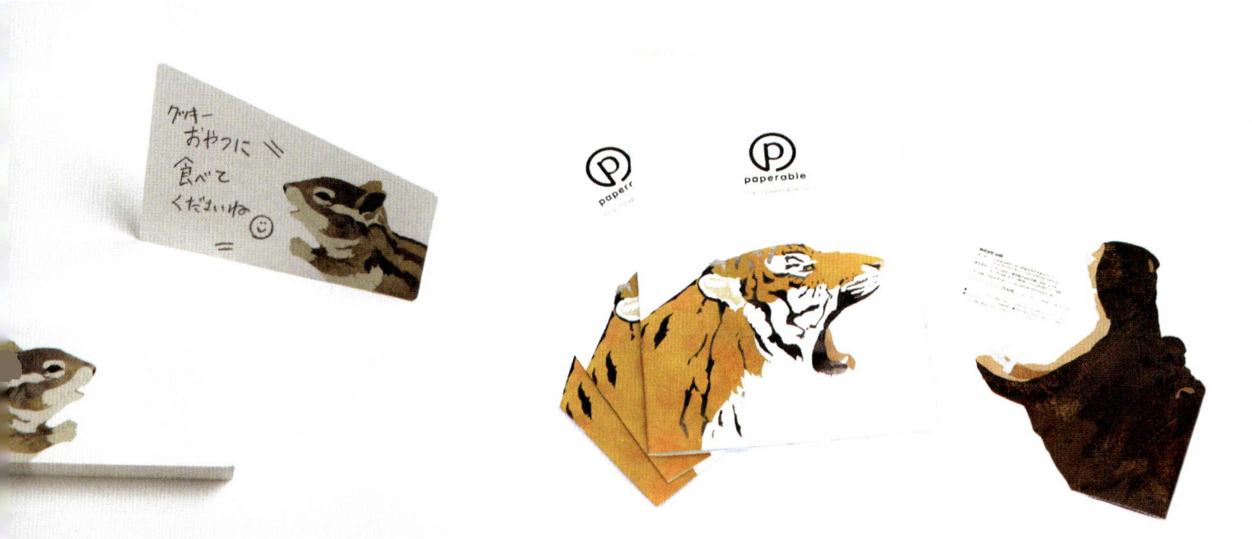
グッキー
おやつに
食べて
くださいね
paperable

of Mooncake Festival

"Why do we do what we do every Mid-Autumn?" The relevant ancient contradictions that Tofu discovered were melded with the packaging of their home-made moon cakes. Gift boxes are designed, illustrated, scored, folded and bound by hand.

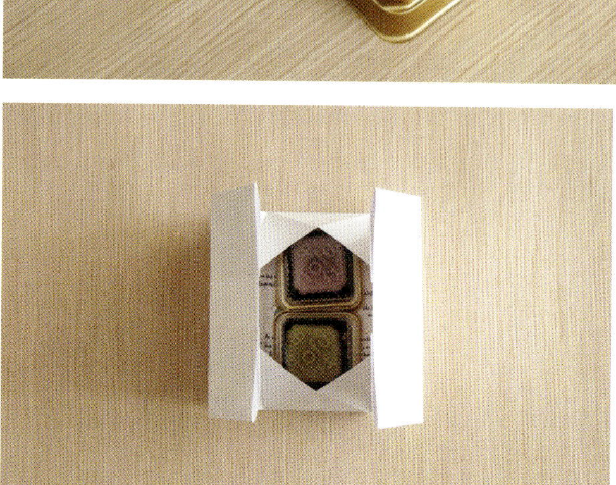

Tofu

The Unclear Origins of Mooncake Festival

"Why do we do what we do every Mid-Autumn?" The relevant ancient contradictions that Tofu discovered were melded with the packaging of their home-made moon cakes. Gift boxes are designed, illustrated, scored, folded and bound by hand.

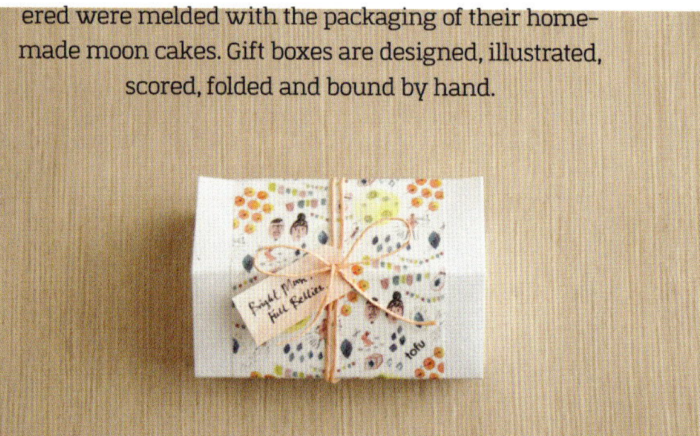

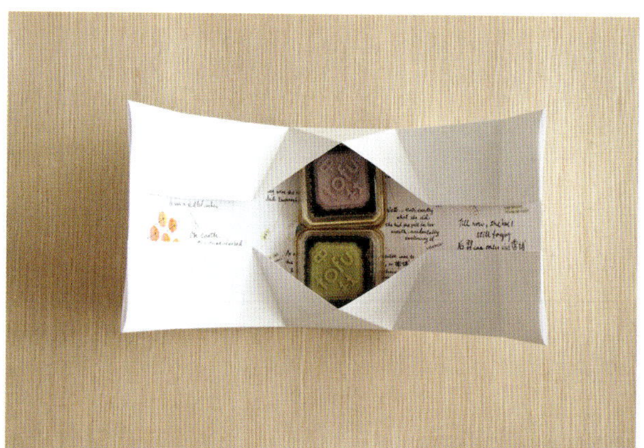

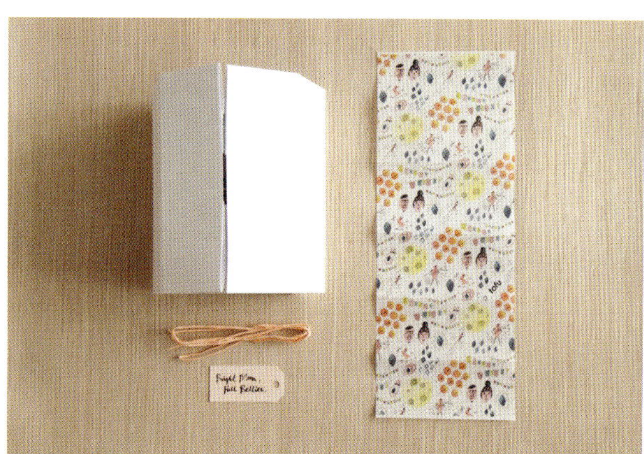

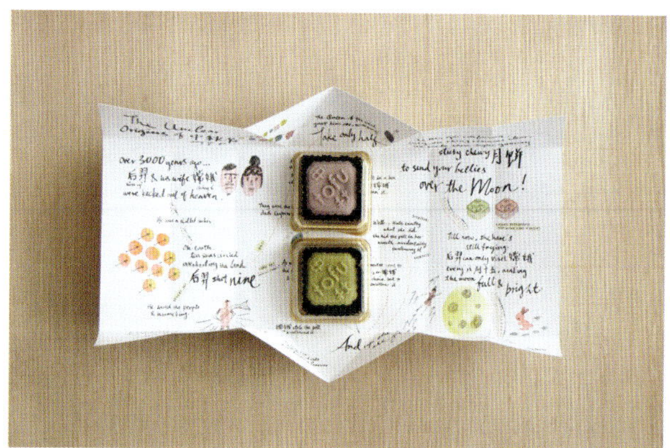

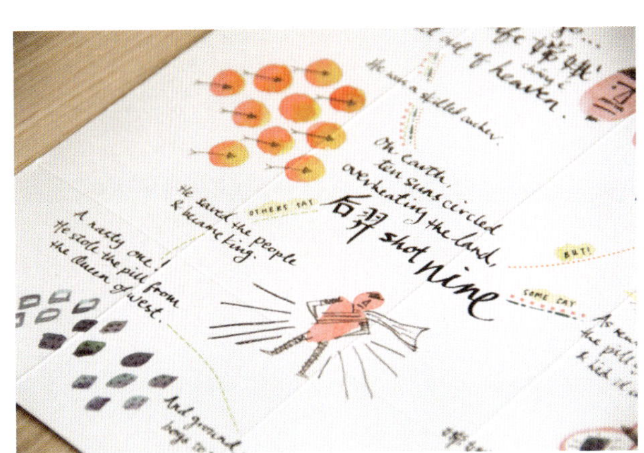

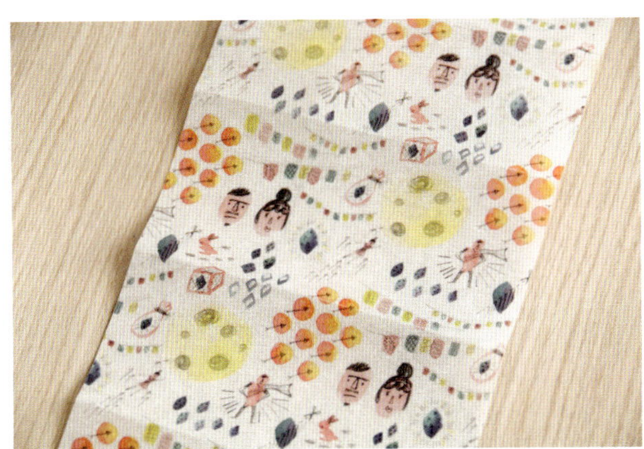

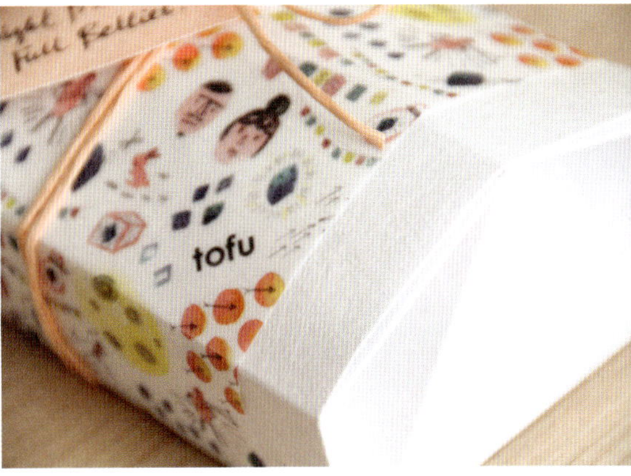
tofu

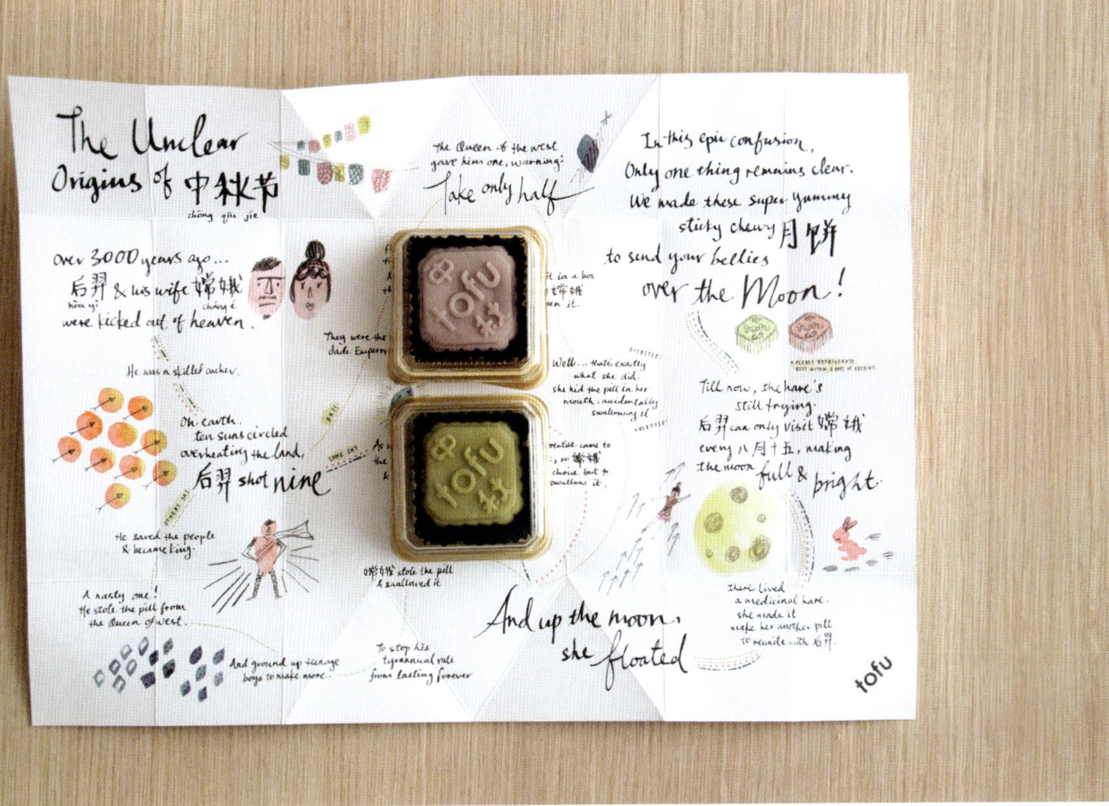
The Unclear Origins of 中秋节
zhōng qiū jié
over 3000 years ago...
后羿 & his wife 嫦娥
were kicked out of heaven.
He was a skilled archer.
On earth, ten suns circled overheating the land.
后羿 shot nine
He saved the people & became king.
A nasty one! He stole the pill from the Queen of west.
And ground up teenage boys to make more.
The Queen of the west gave him one, warning:
Take only half
To stop his tyrannical rule from lasting forever
嫦娥 stole the pill & swallowed it.
And up the moon, she floated
In this epic confusion, Only one thing remains clear.
We made these super yummy sticky chewy 月饼
to send your bellies over the Moon!
Till now, the hare's still trying.
后羿 can only visit 嫦娥 every 八月十五, making the moon full & bright.
There lived a medicinal hare. She made it make her another pill to reunite with 后羿.
tofu

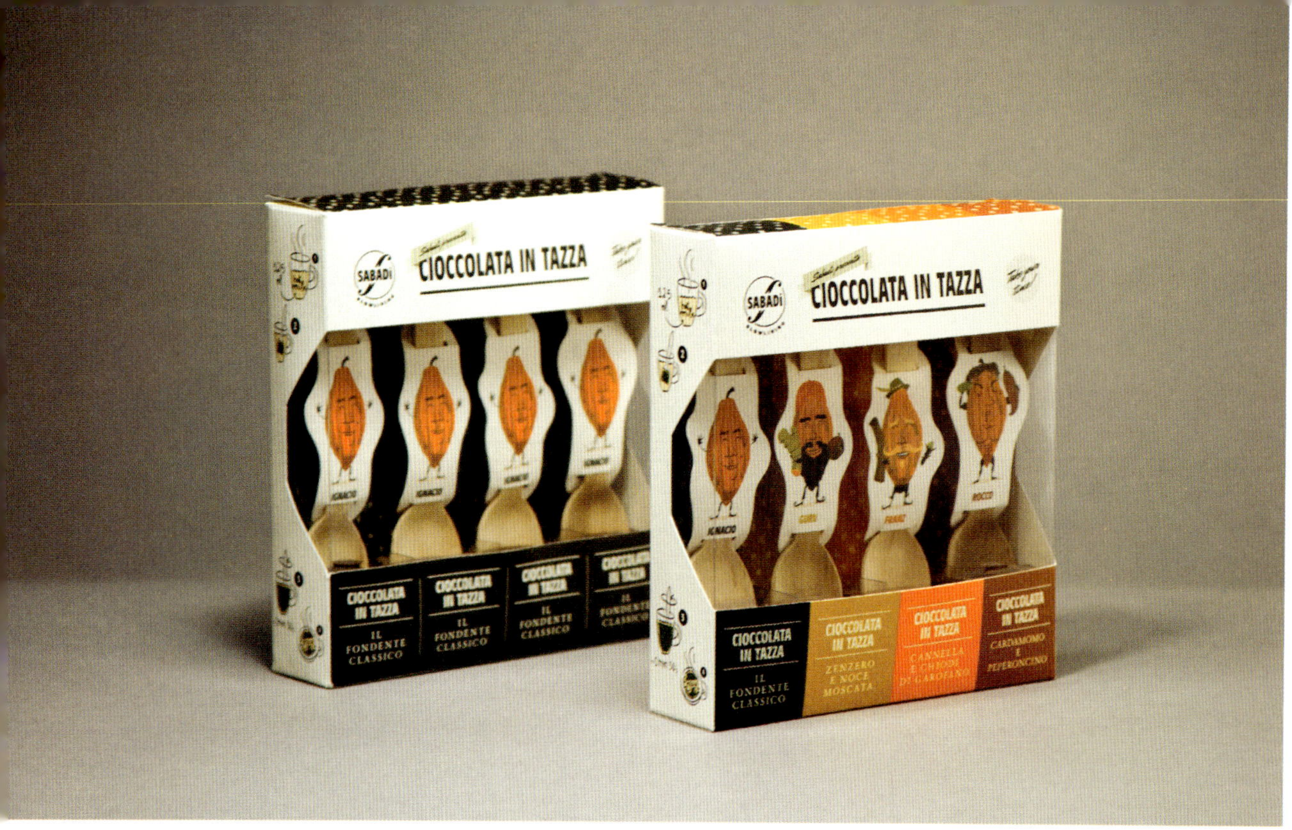

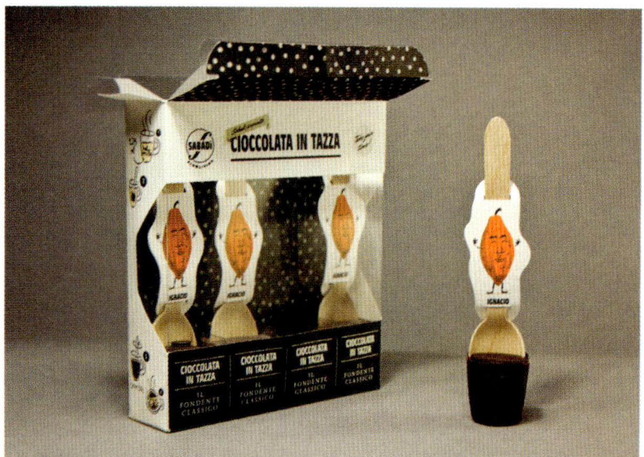

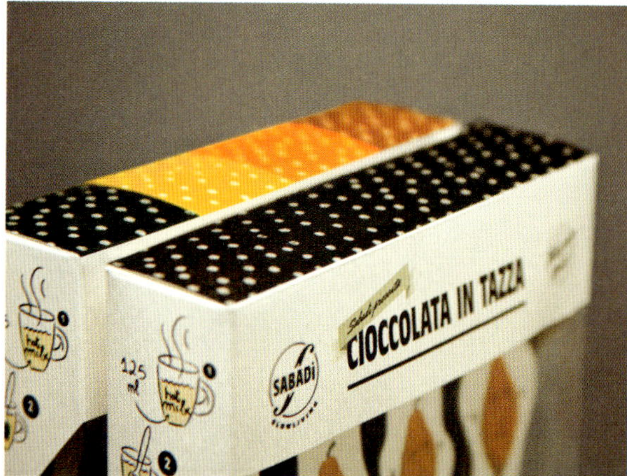

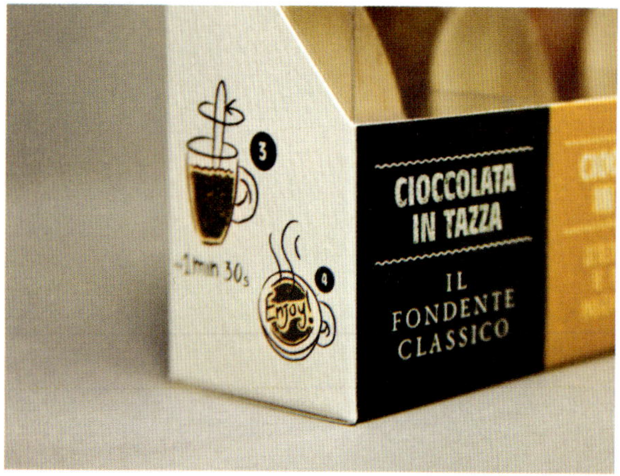

Happycentro

Sabadì — Cioccolata in Tazza

Cioccolata in Tazza caters for a convenient way of making gourmet hot chocolate drinks. Cocoa beans are personified to indicate different flavours with preparation instructions delightfully illustrated on the packaging box.

Packaging design: Roberto Solieri
Illustration: Andrea Manzati, Federico Galvani
Client: Sabadì

Happycentro

Saba —

Cioccolato di Modica

Sabadì's first chocolate collection, Cioccolato di Modica comes in six flavours, each with strong personality represented by the six characters created. An overall earthy tone is set for the packaging to convey the Sicilian brand's preference for fair trade and slow living.

Design: Andrea Manzati
Illustration: Federico Galvani, Andrea Donà
Client: Sabadì

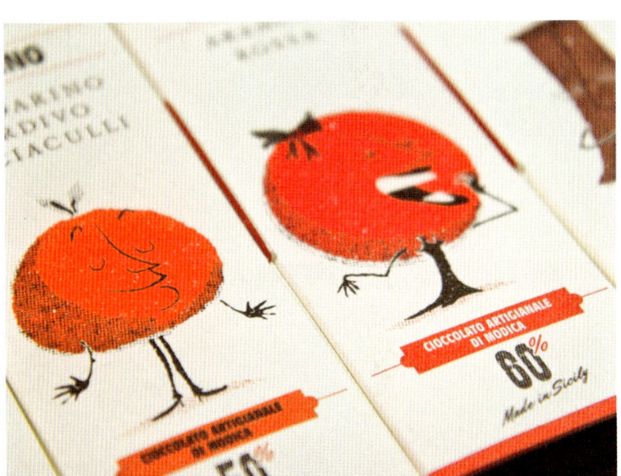

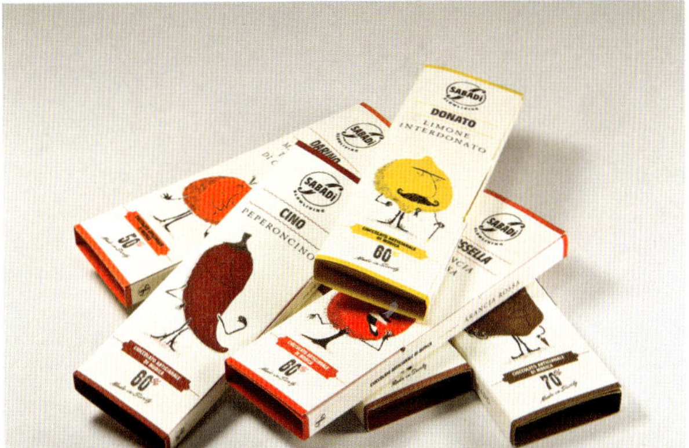

Happycentro

Sabadì — Cioccolato di Modica

Sabadì's first chocolate collection, Cioccolato di Modica comes in six flavours, each with strong personality represented by the six characters created. An overall earthy tone is set for the packaging to convey the Sicilian brand's preference for fair trade and slow living.

Design: Andrea Manzati
Illustration: Federico Galvani, Andrea Donà
Client: Sabadì

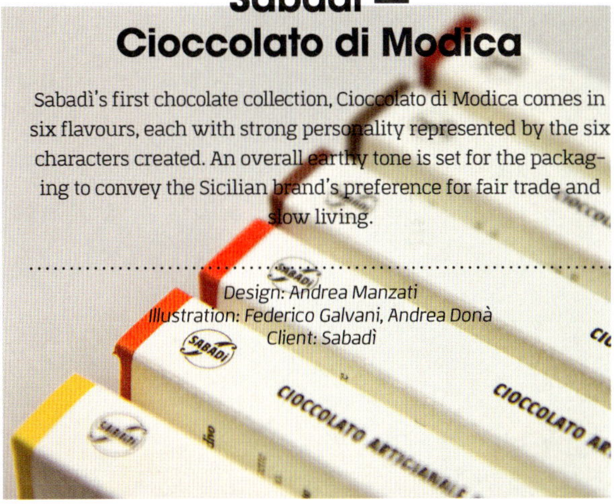

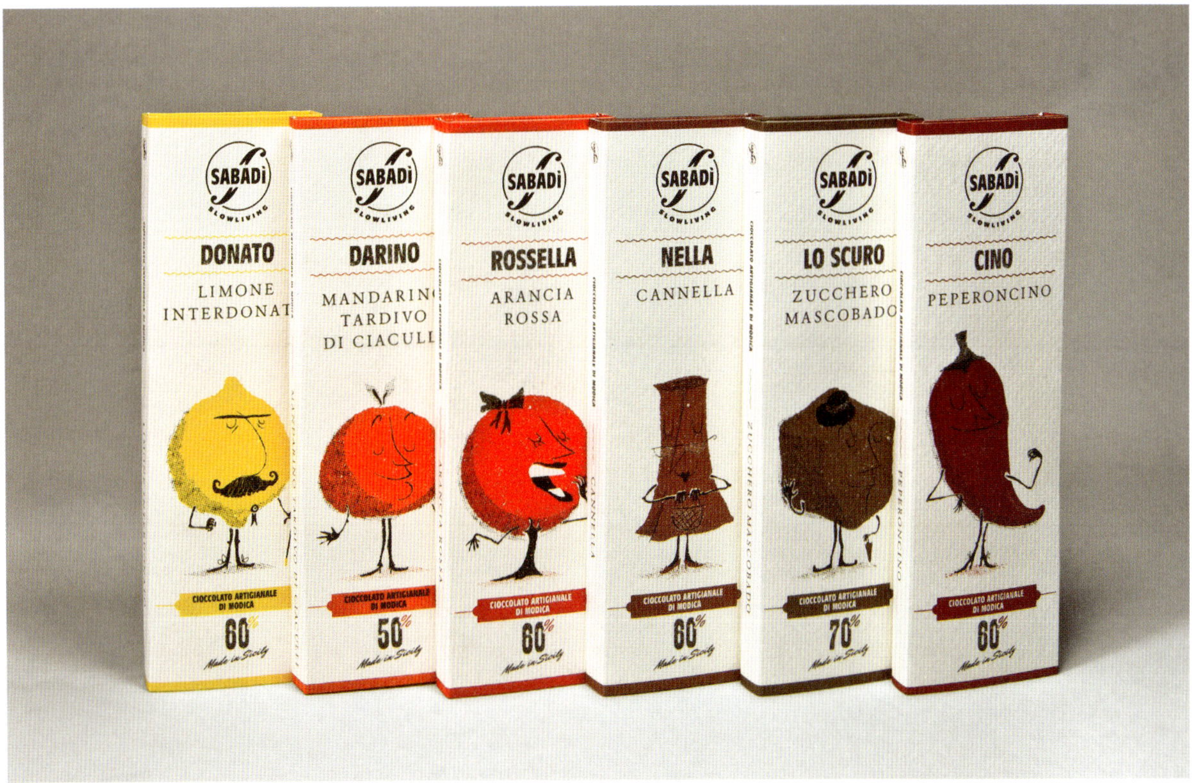

Sugar High Open

All members of Sugar High Films gathered on posters and cups as a much of characterful ice-cream men to promote this ice-cream-and-foosball tournament, as well as its new team comprised of experts from various creative fields. A bespoke typeface "Anna Fontanna" was also created to fulfill all application needs.

Mobile app: Thodoris Katsimanis (Web Productions)
Client: Sugar High Films

Bob Studio

Sugar High Open

All members of Sugar High Films gathered on posters and cups as a much of characterful ice-cream men to promote this ice-cream-and-foosball tournament, as well as its new team comprised of experts from various creative fields. A bespoke typeface "Anna Fontanna" was also created to fulfill all application needs.

Mobile app: Thodoris Katsimanis (Web Productions)
Client: Sugar High Films

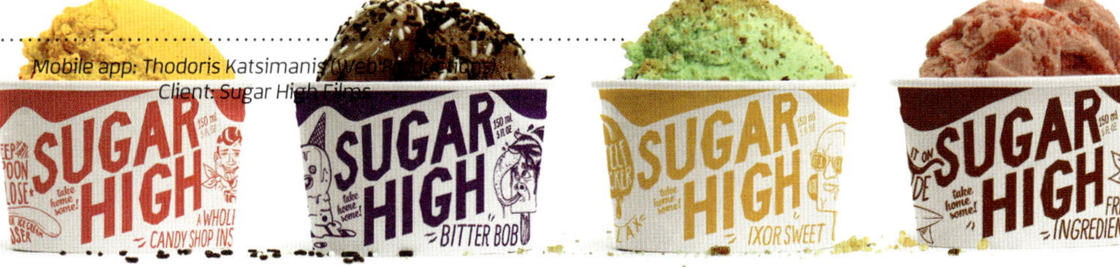

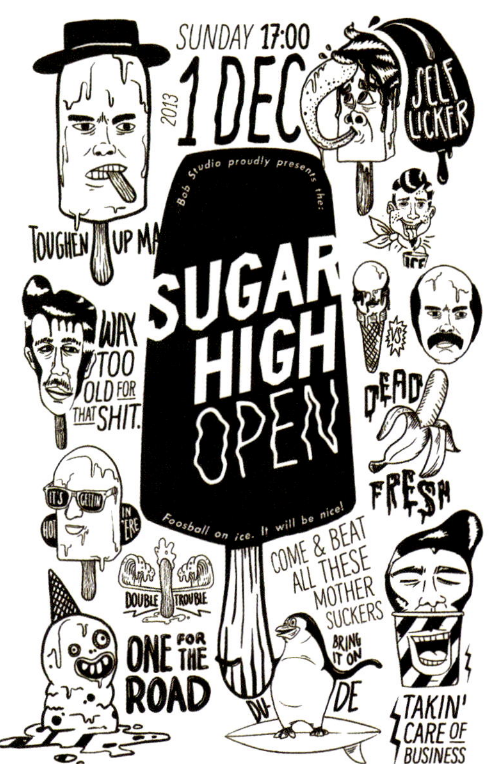

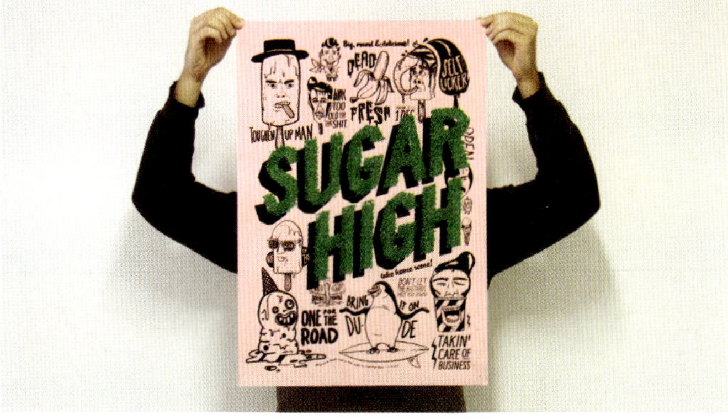

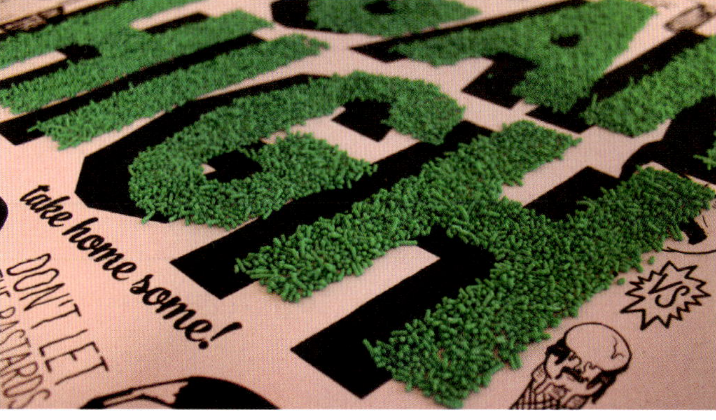

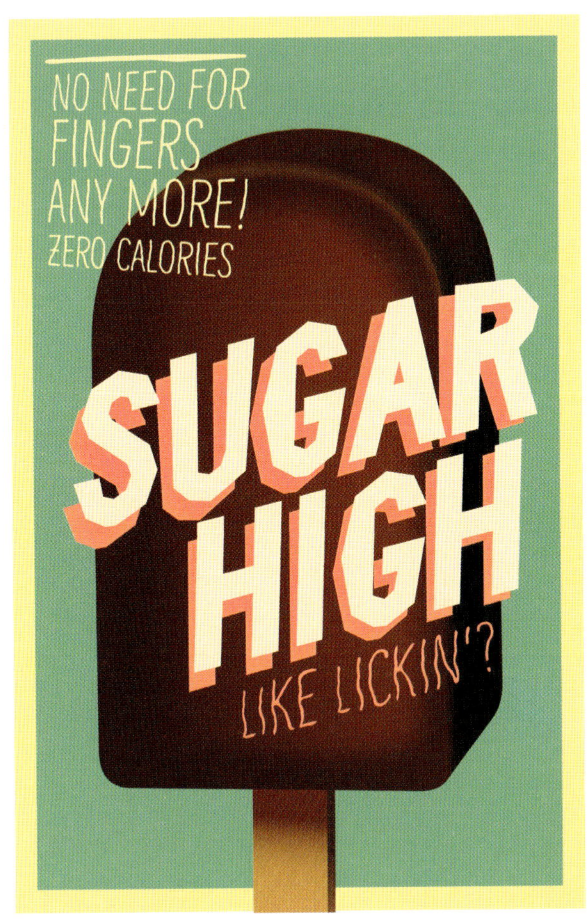
NO NEED FOR
FINGERS
ANY MORE!
ZERO CALORIES
SUGAR
HIGH
LIKE LICKIN'?

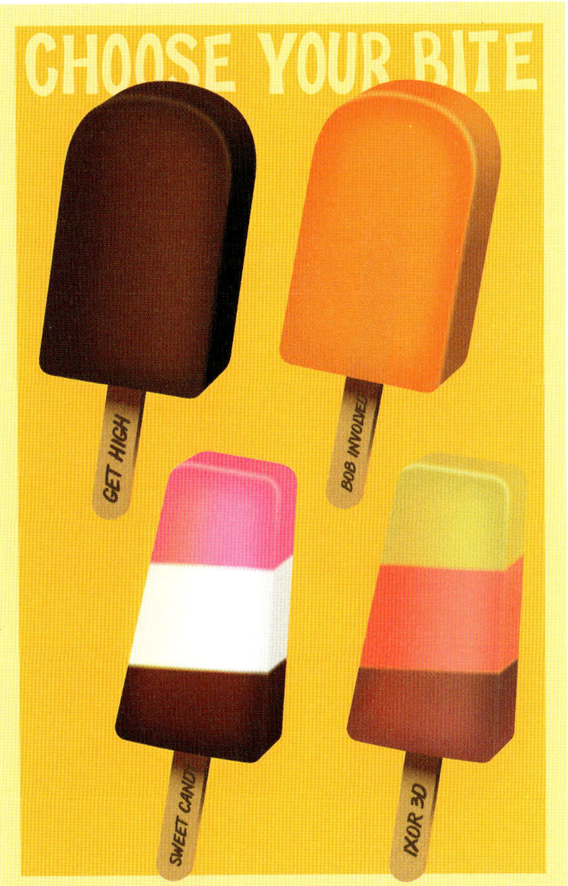
CHOOSE YOUR BITE
GET HIGH
BOB INVOLVED

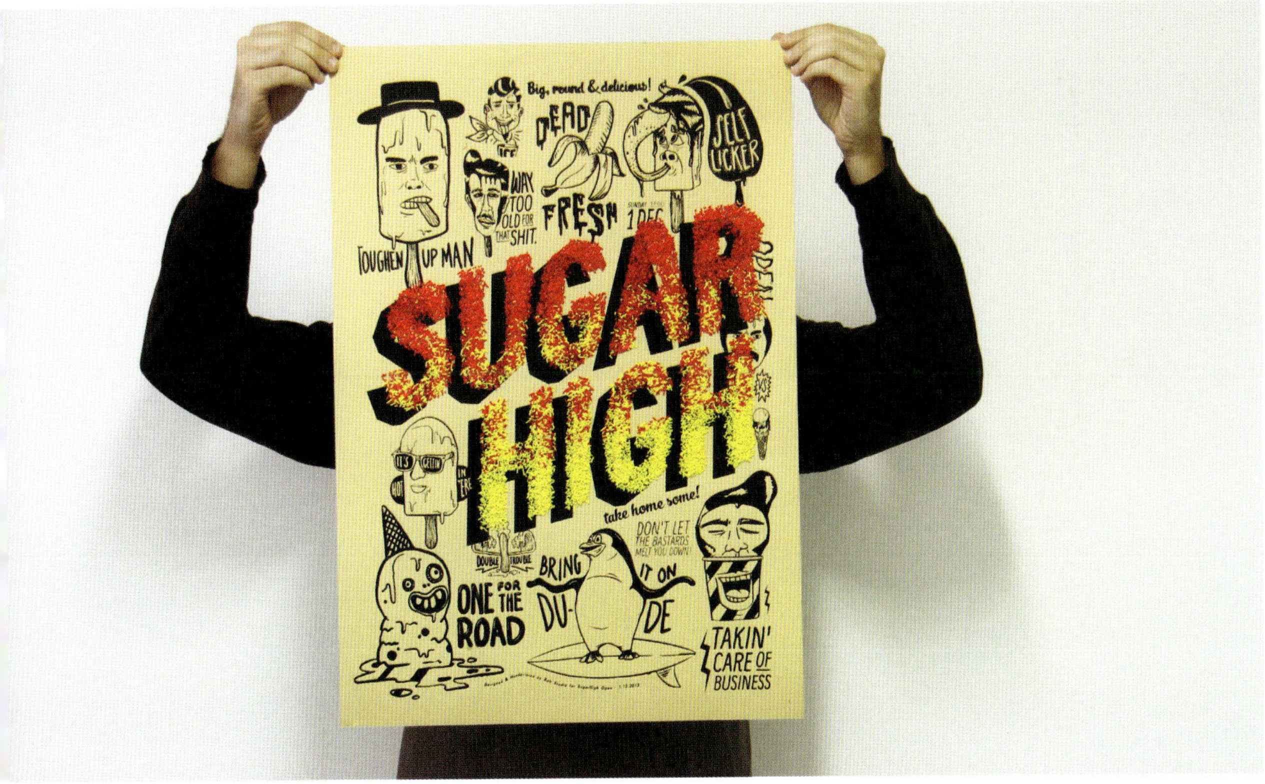

Dee and Cheng's wedding invitation was set to unfold a delightful string of surprises. With the couple's memorable moments beautifully illustrated, the envelope unveiled their story bit by bit once unfurled, and progressed to a happy wedding as the invitation and cards indicated.

Special credits: Jaeson Printing Press

Jefferson Cheng

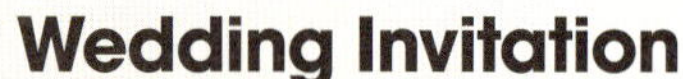

Dee and Cheng's wedding invitation was set to unfold a delightful string of surprises. With the couple's memorable moments beautifully illustrated, the envelope unveiled their story bit by bit once unfurled, and progressed to a happy wedding as the invitation and cards indicated.

Special credits: Jaeson Printing Press

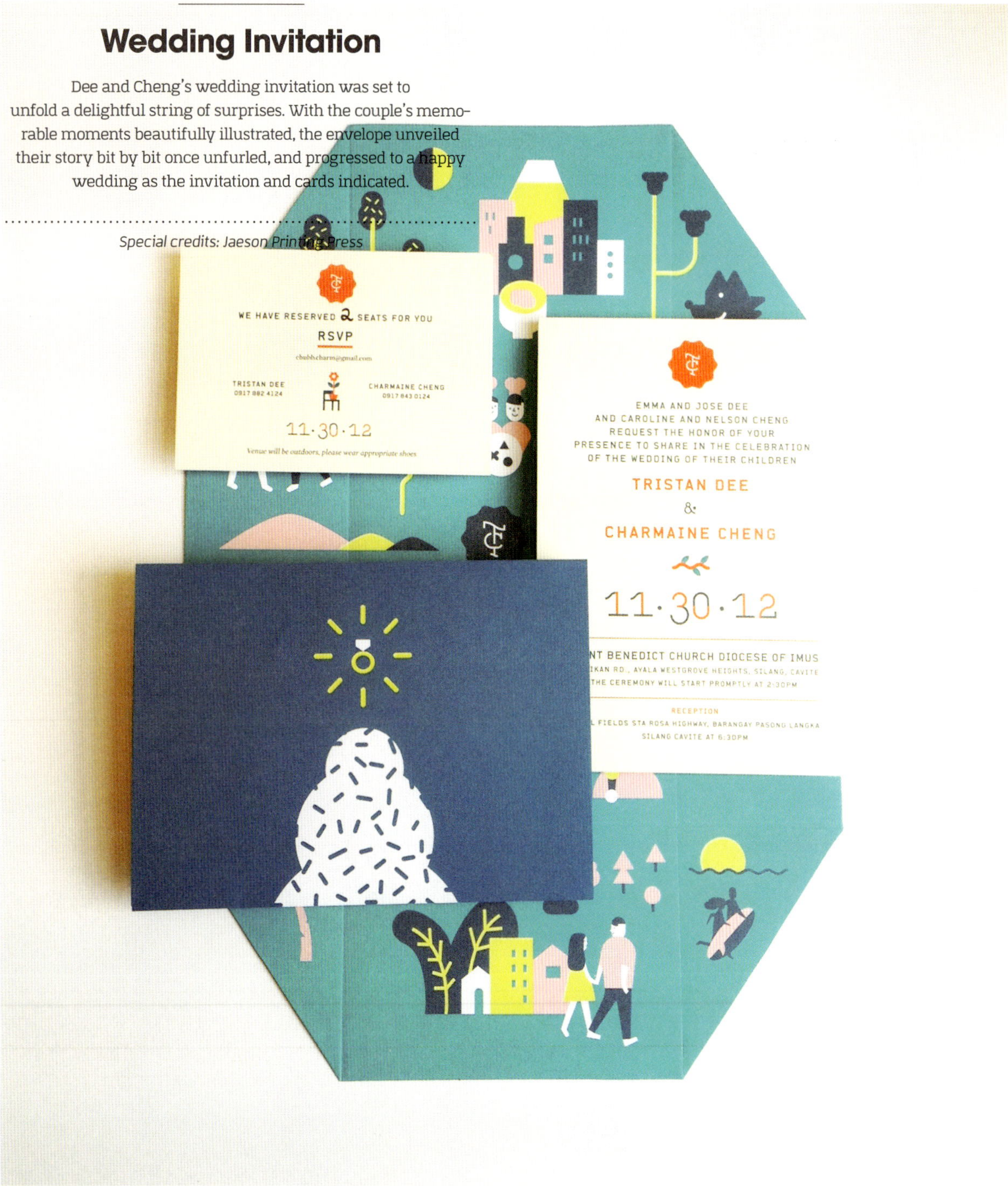

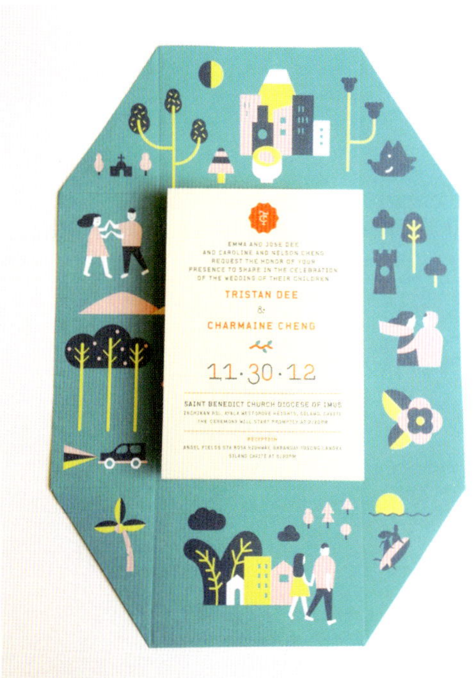
EMMA AND JOSE DEE
AND CAROLINE AND NELSON CHENG
REQUEST THE HONOR OF YOUR
PRESENCE TO SHARE IN THE CELEBRATION
OF THE WEDDING OF THEIR CHILDREN
TRISTAN DEE
&
CHARMAINE CHENG
11·30·12
SAINT BENEDICT CHURCH DIOCESE OF IMUS

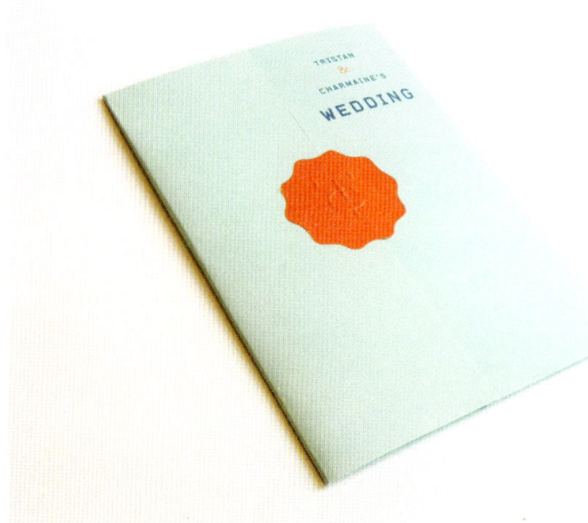
TRISTAN
&
CHARMAINE'S
WEDDING

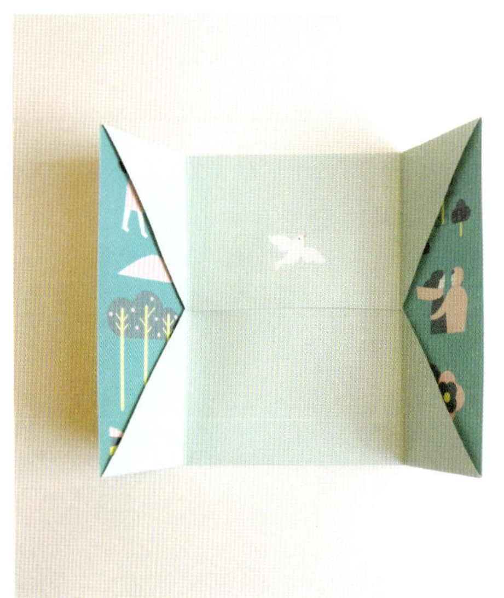

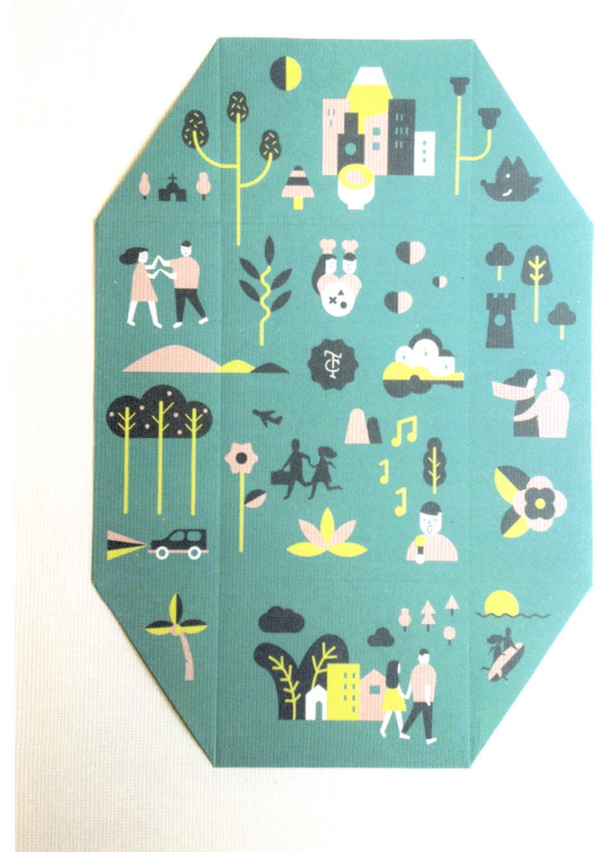

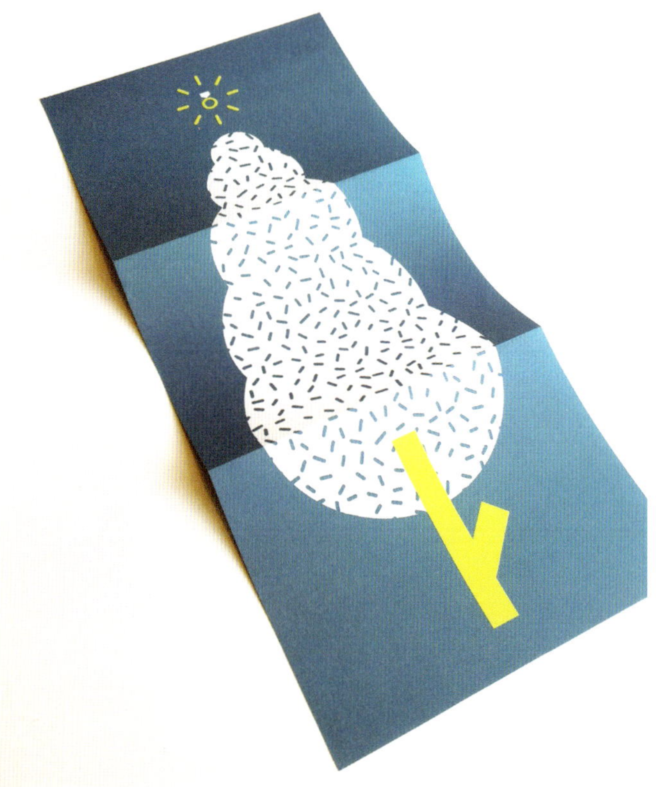

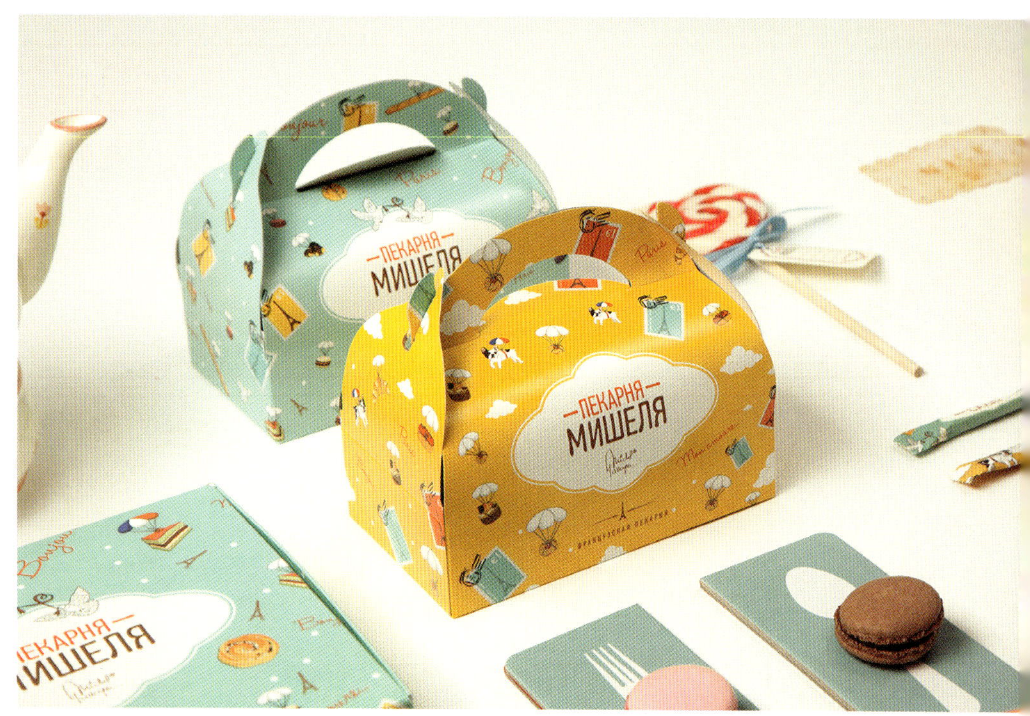
ПЕКАРНЯ
МИШЕЛЯ
Paris
Bonjour
ФРАНЦУЗСКАЯ ПЕКАРНЯ

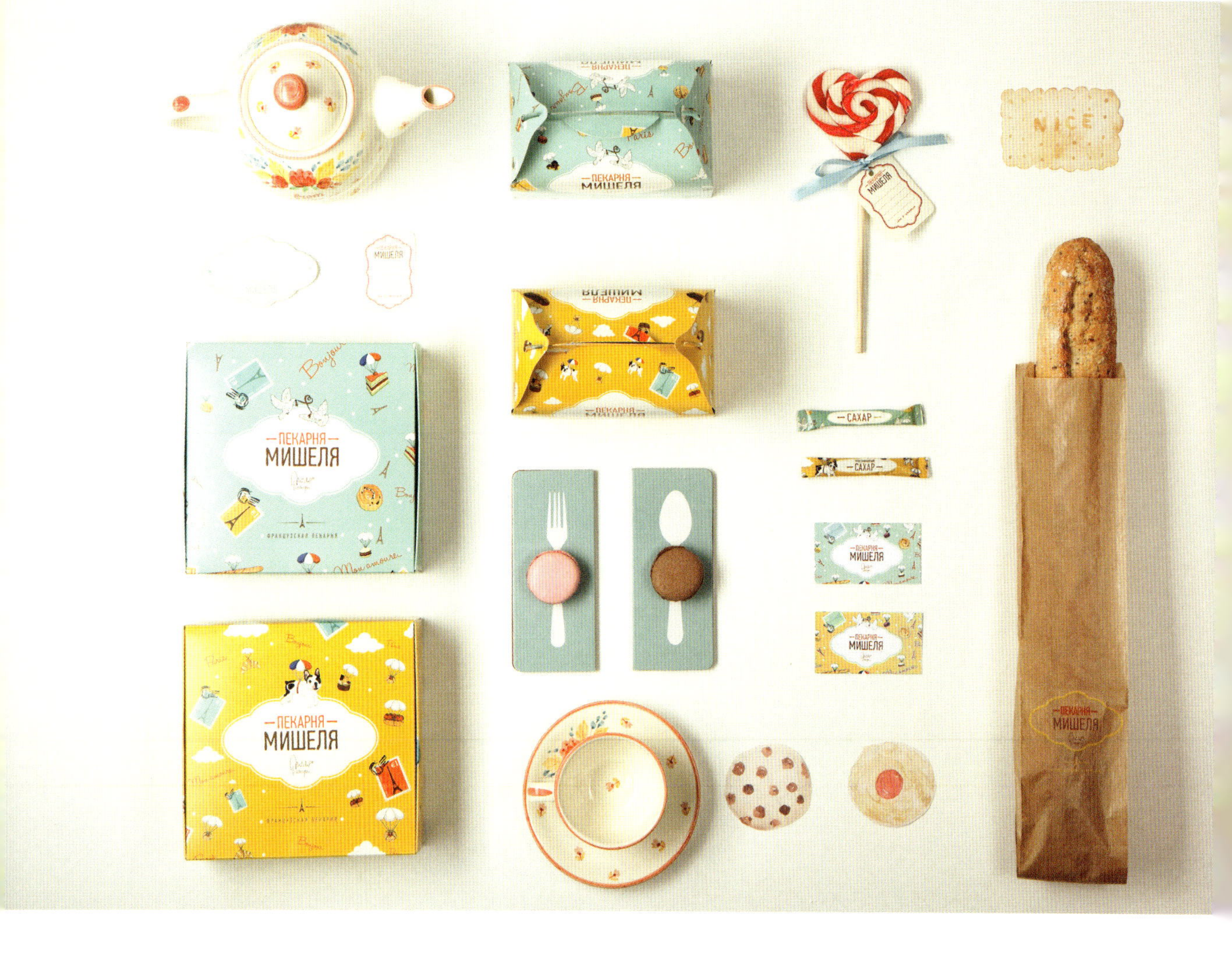

Michelle's Bakery residing at the heart of Moscow is a French style delicatessen frequented by children and young families. Iconic elements suggestive of Parisian leisure lifestyle dangle across the bakery's business applications with a striking tone to give it a twist.

Client: G.Sign, Michelle's Bakery

Anya Aleksandrova

Michelle's Bakery

Michelle's Bakery residing at the heart of Moscow is a French style delicatessen frequented by children and young families. Iconic elements suggestive of Parisian leisure lifestyle dangle across the bakery's business applications with a striking tone to give it a twist.

Client: G.Sign, Michelle's Bakery

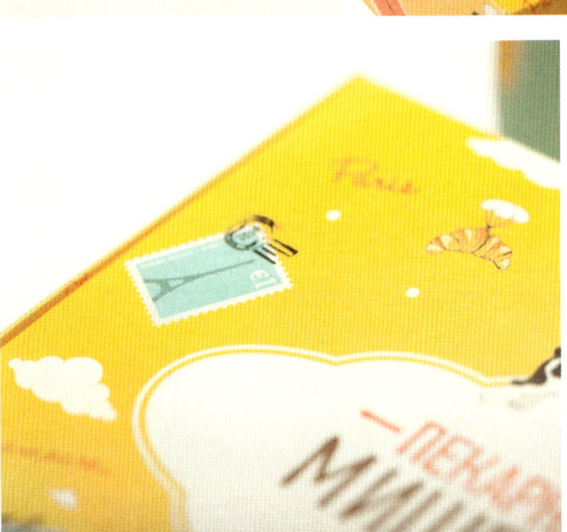

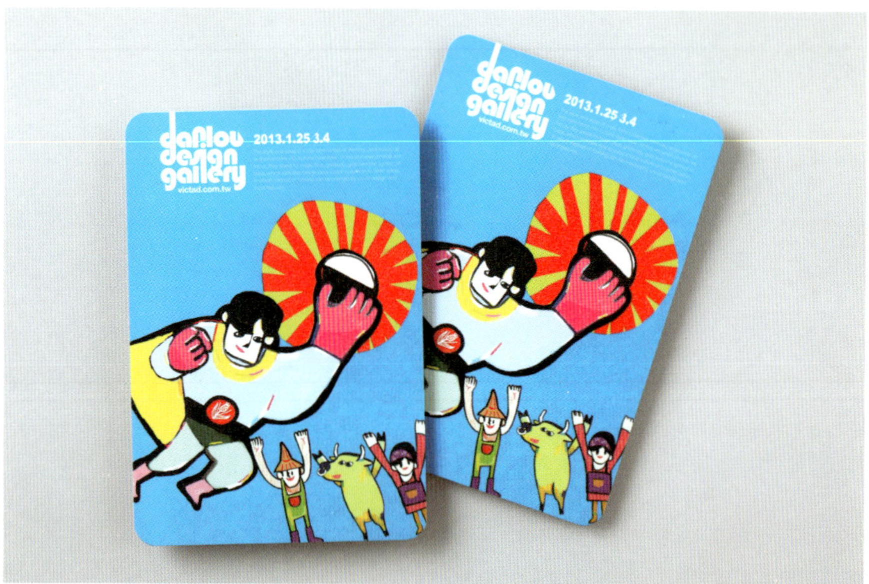

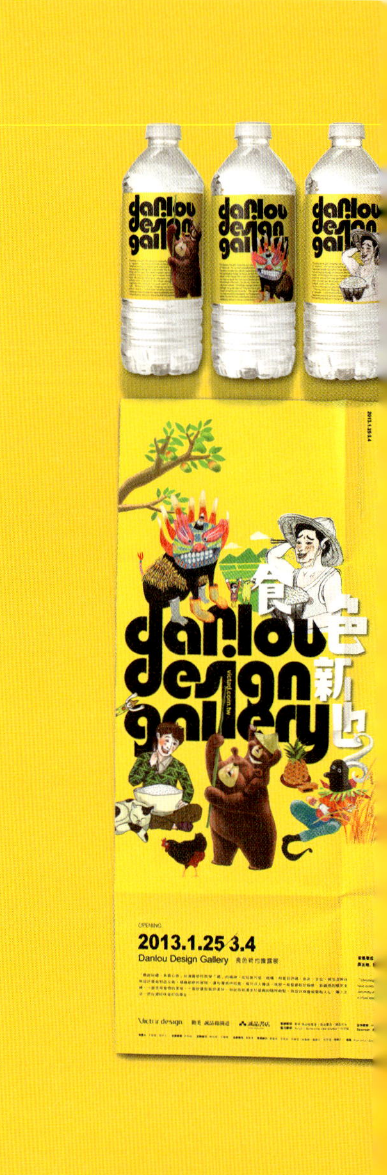

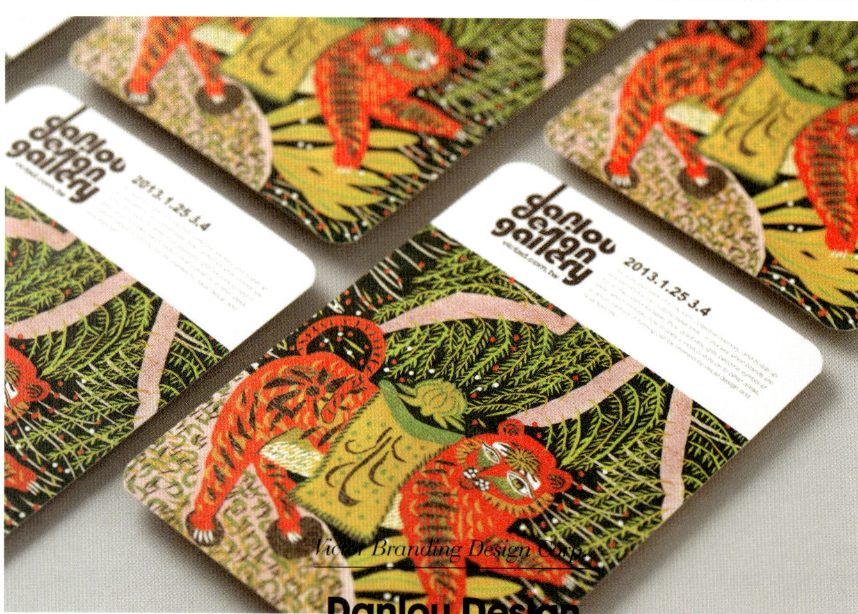

Victor Branding Design Corp.

Danlou Design Gallery

Co-organised with Park Lane by CMP and Eslite, Victor Branding curated and presented a showcase of exceptional packaging designs that summed up Taiwanese flavours and gifting culture. The distinctive characters in the visual identity provided a quick view of the show, and a piece of memory to take away.

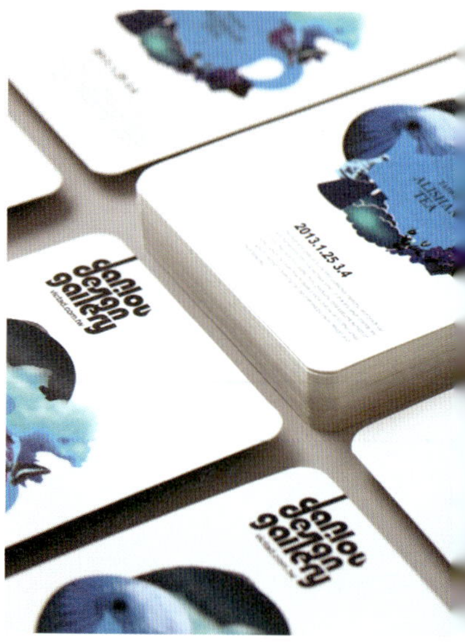

Victor Branding Design Corp.,

Danlou Design Gallery

Co-organised with Park Lane by CMP and Eslite, Victor Branding curated and presented a showcase of exceptional packaging designs that summed up Taiwanese flavours and gifting culture. The distinctive characters in the visual identity provided a quick view of the show, and a piece of memory to take away.

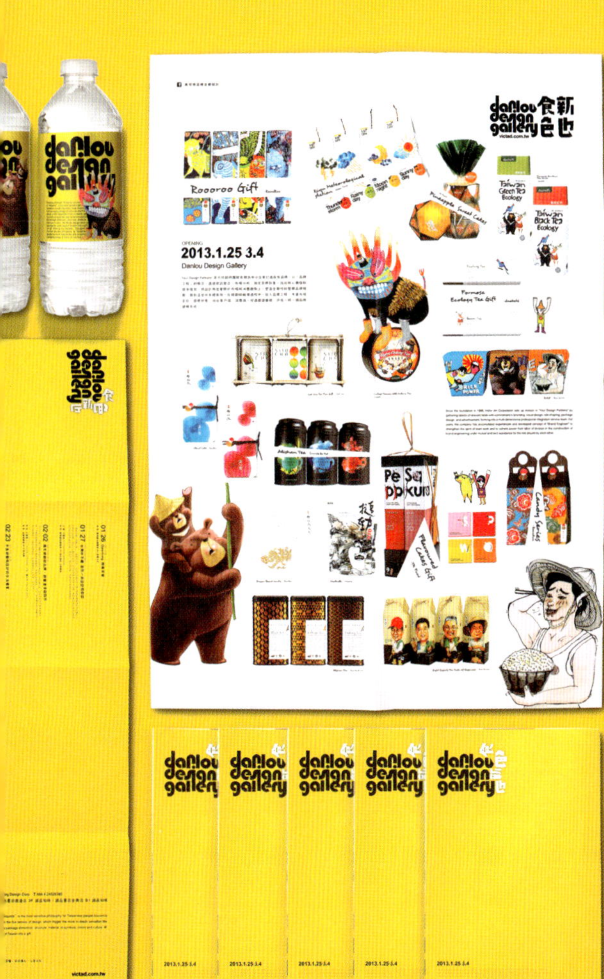
danlou design gallery
食色新也
victad.com.tw
2013.1.25 3.4
Danlou Design Gallery

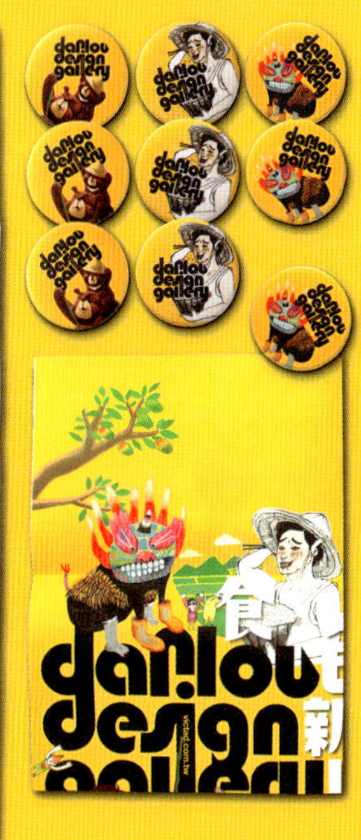
danlou design gallery
victad.com.tw

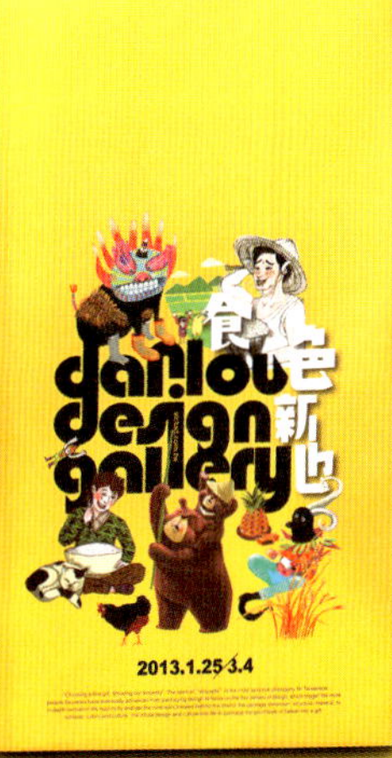
danlou design gallery

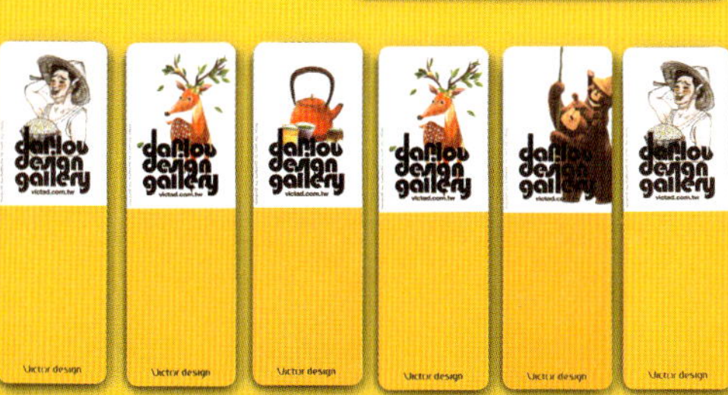
danlou design gallery
victad.com.tw
Victor design

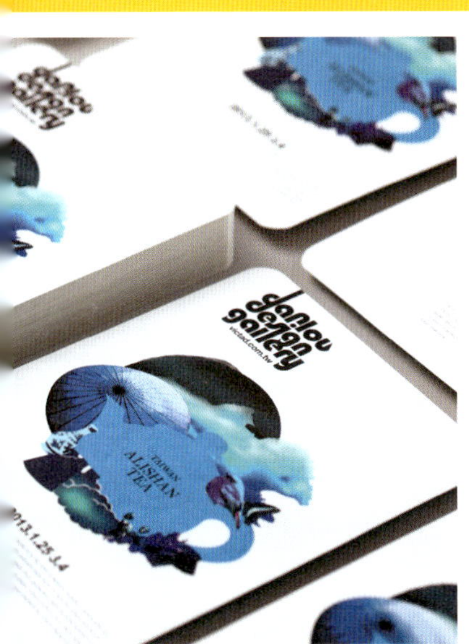
danlou design gallery
victad.com.tw
TAIWAN
ALISHAN
TEA
2013.1.25 3.4

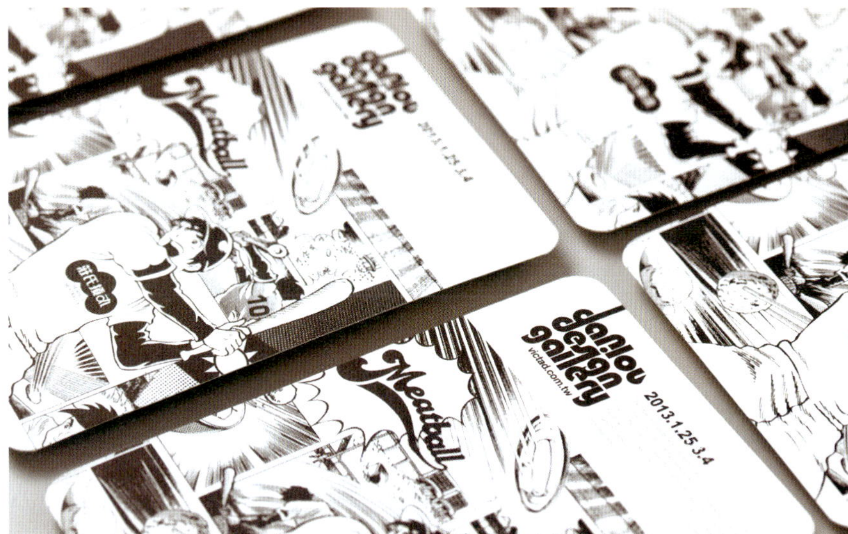
Meatball
danlou design gallery
victad.com.tw
2013.1.25 3.4

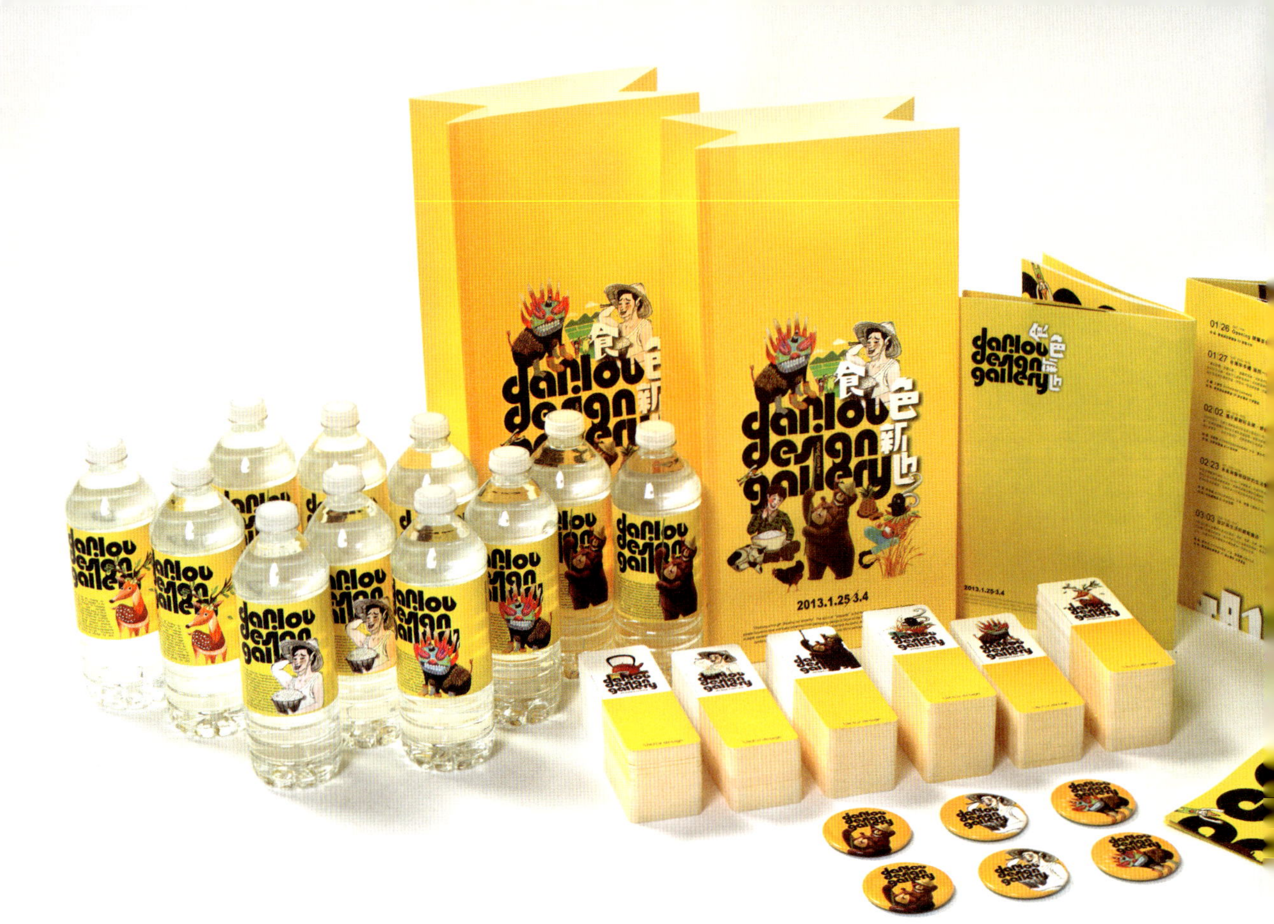

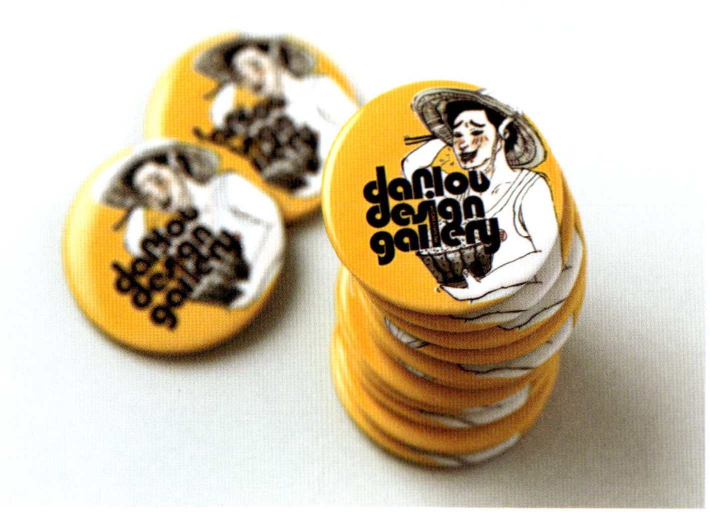

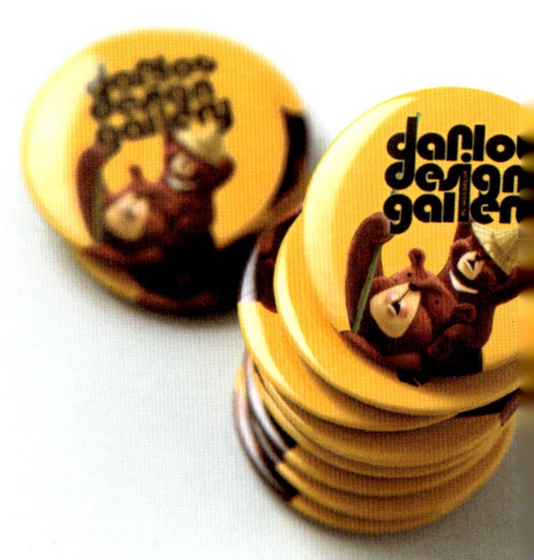

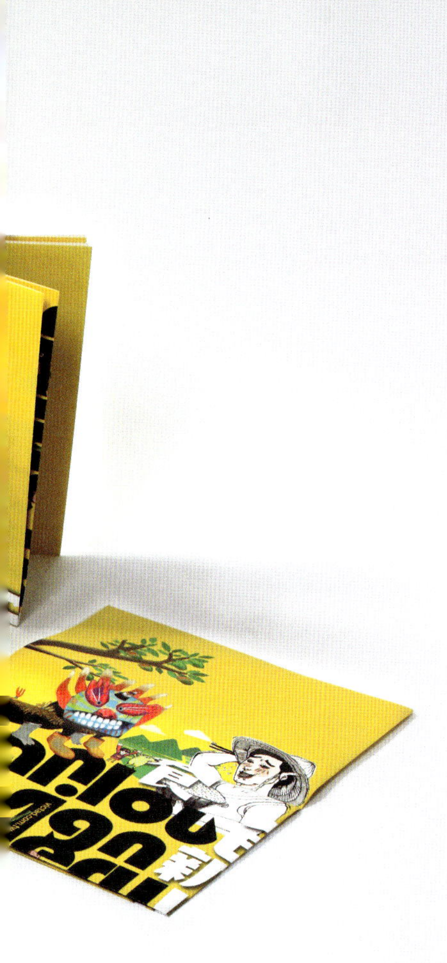

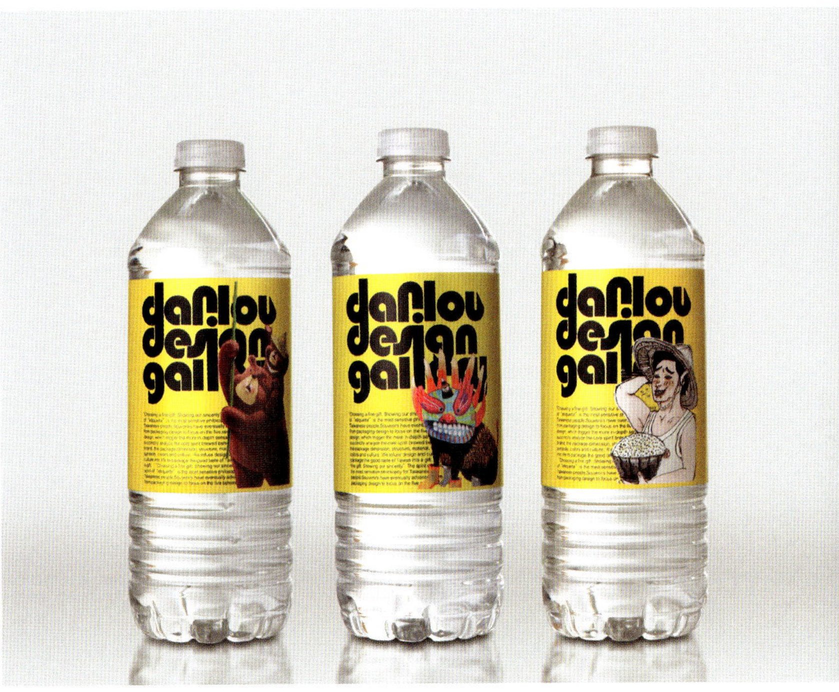

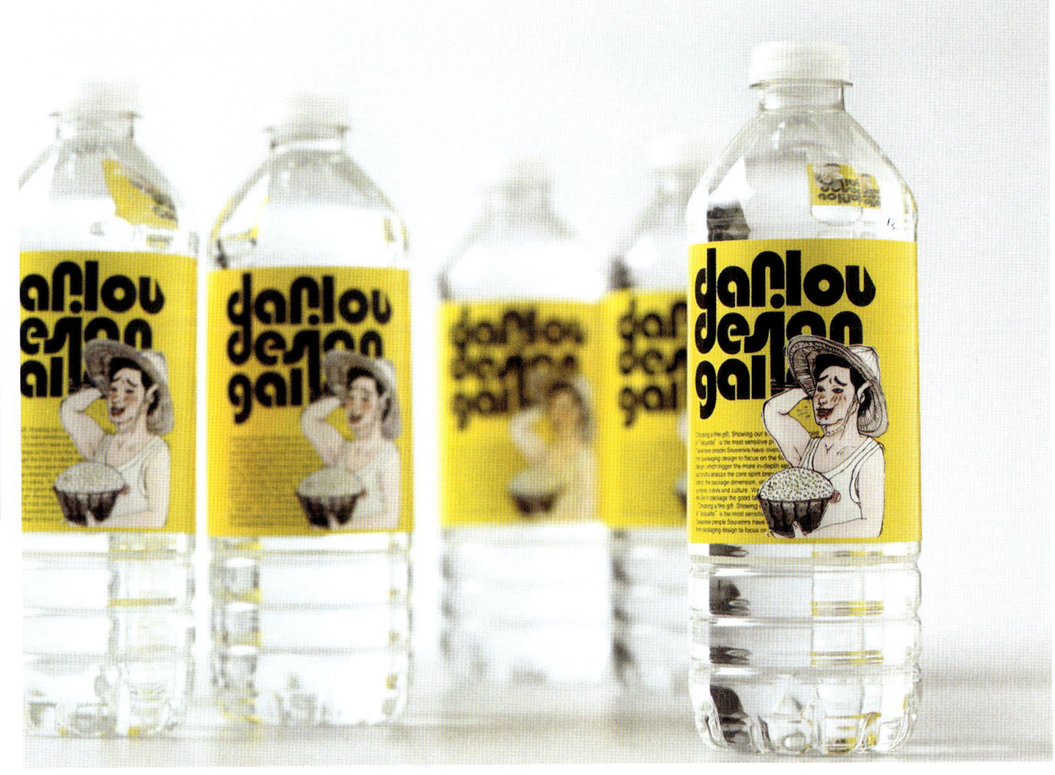

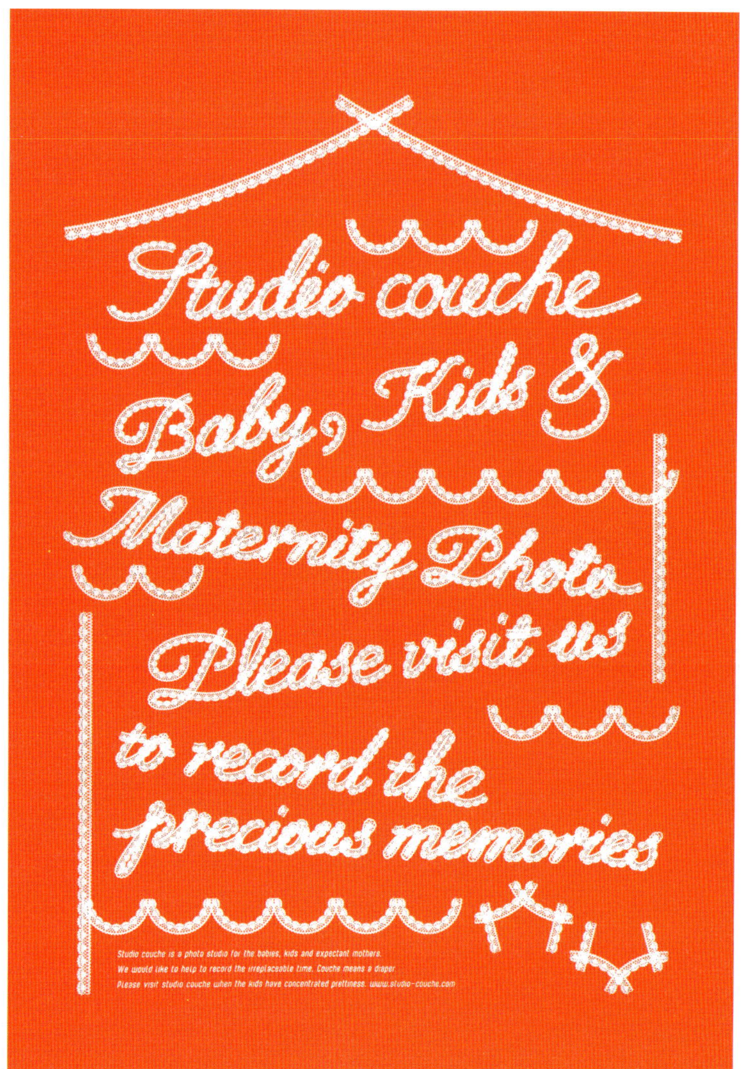

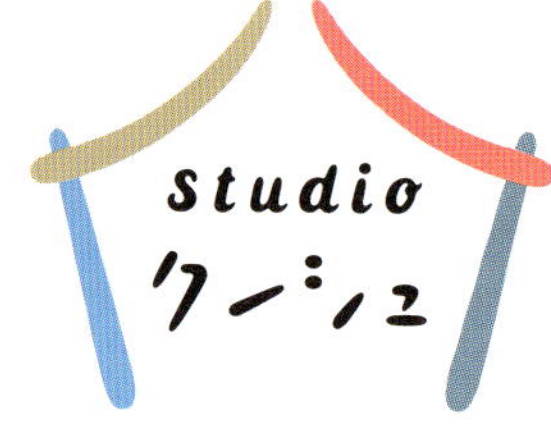

Coton Design

studio couche

A studio specialising in baby, kids and maternity photography, studio couche's visual identity evokes pleasant moments of being an imaginative child. Interactive elements were incorporated into its bags where rope handles were considered part of the illustration element per se.

Client: studio couche

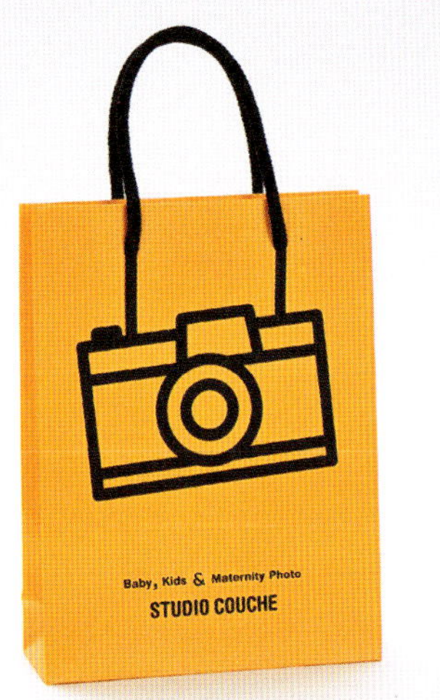

Coton Design

studio couche

A studio specialising in baby, kids and maternity photography, studio couche's visual identity evokes pleasant moments of being an imaginative child. Interactive elements were incorporated into its bags where rope handles were considered

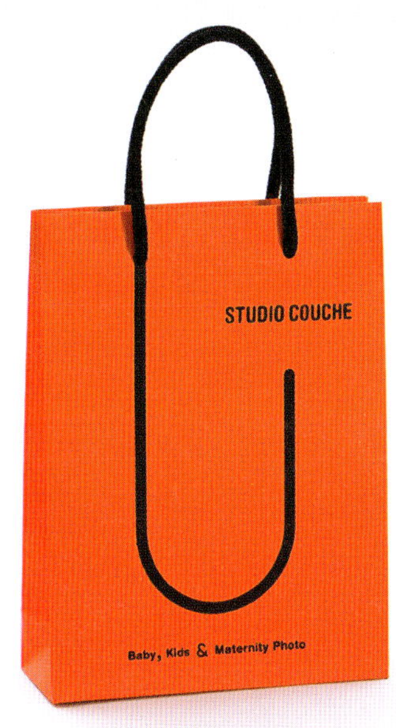
STUDIO COUCHE
Baby, Kids & Maternity Photo

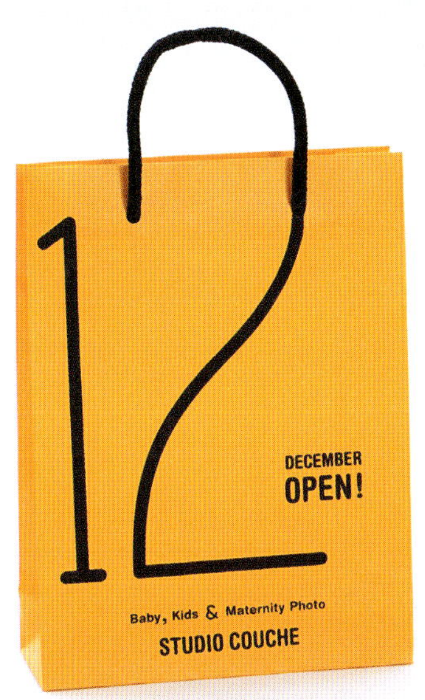
DECEMBER
OPEN!
Baby, Kids & Maternity Photo
STUDIO COUCHE

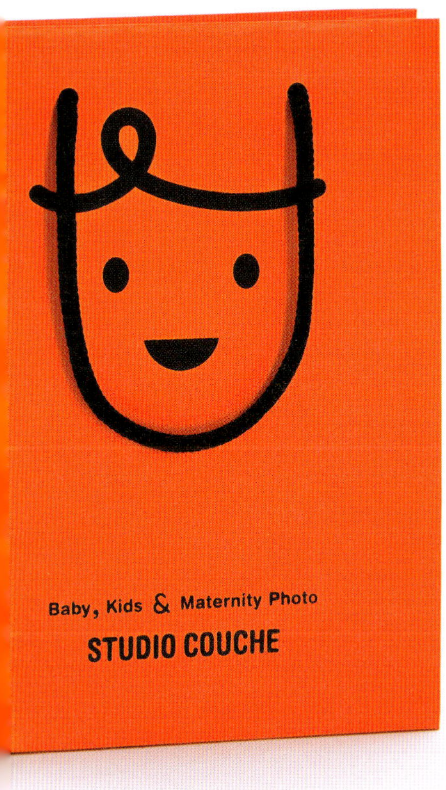
Baby, Kids & Maternity Photo
STUDIO COUCHE

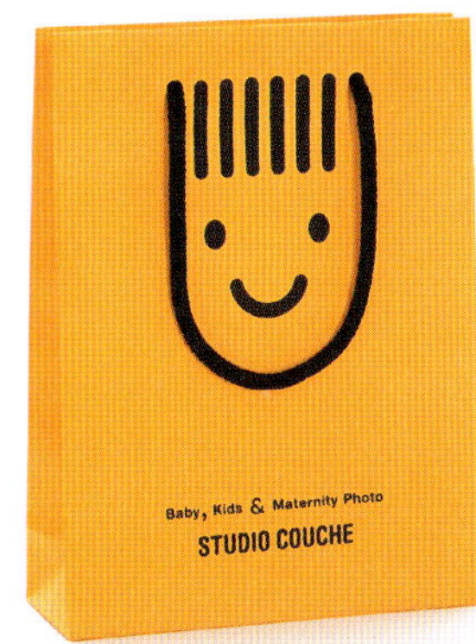
Baby, Kids & Maternity Photo
STUDIO COUCHE

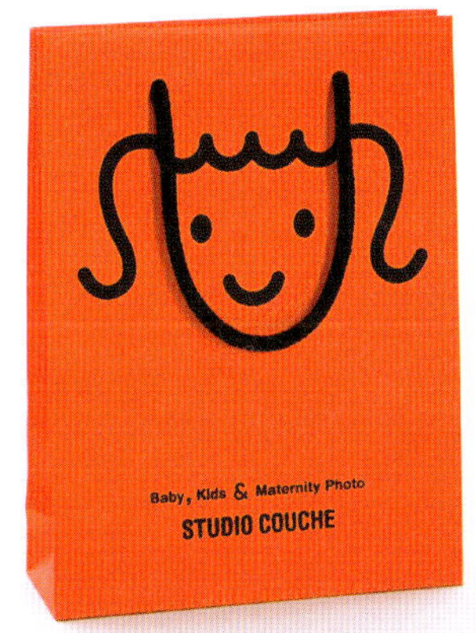
Baby, Kids & Maternity Photo
STUDIO COUCHE

Lifeboats Institution

RNLI is a charity that provides 24-hour lifeboat search and rescue services in the UK. Packaging of their confectionery range is refreshed with peaceful scenarios and nostalgic elements of the British seaside, engaging visitors across the country with memories of the beautiful days by the sea.

Client: Royal National Lifeboats Institution (RNLI)
Special credits: James Champion, Katie Steel

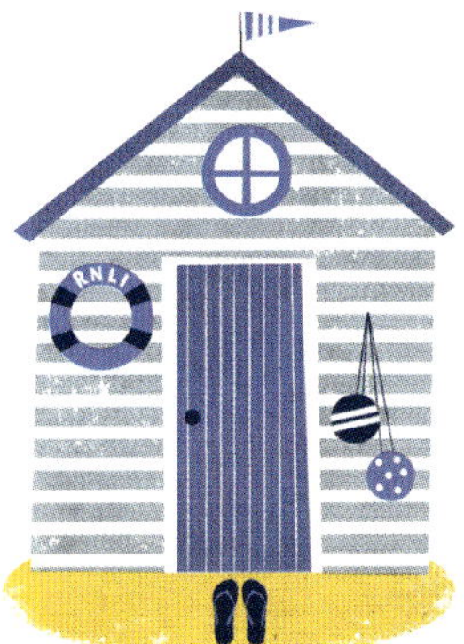

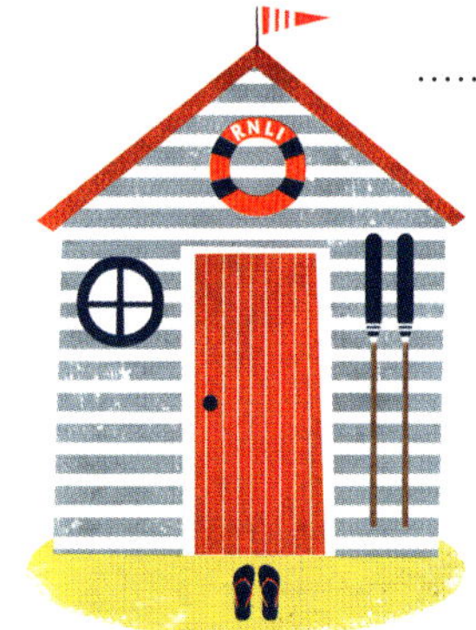

Vicki Turner

Royal National Lifeboats Institution

RNLI is a charity that provides 24-hour lifeboat search and rescue services in the UK. Packaging of their confectionery range is refreshed with peaceful scenarios and nostalgic elements of the British seaside, engaging visitors across the country with memories of the beautiful days by the sea.

Client: Royal National Lifeboats Institution (RNLI)
Special credits: James Champion, Katie Steel

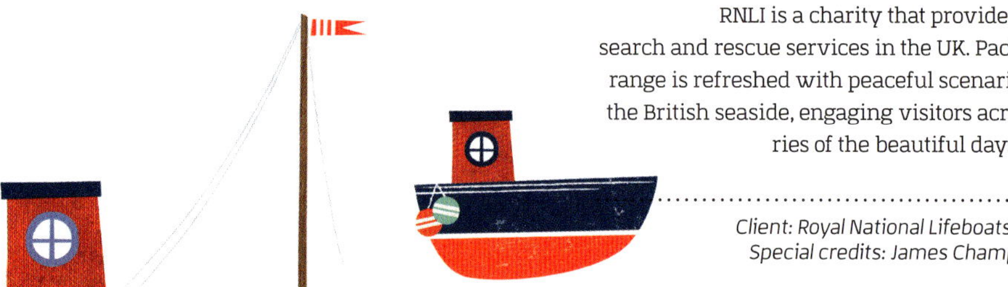

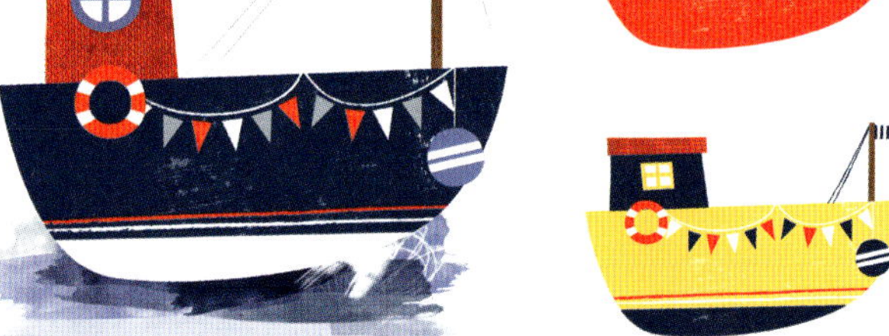

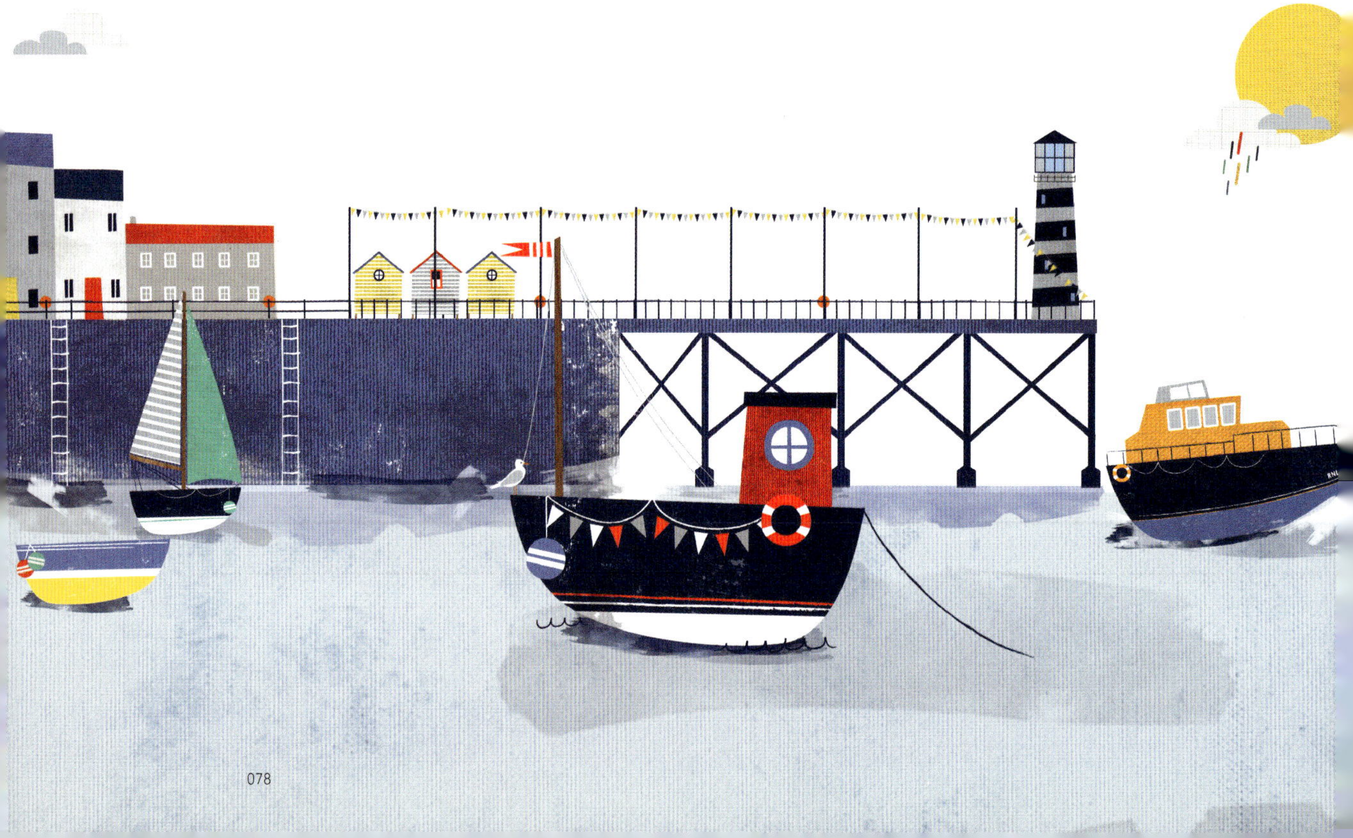

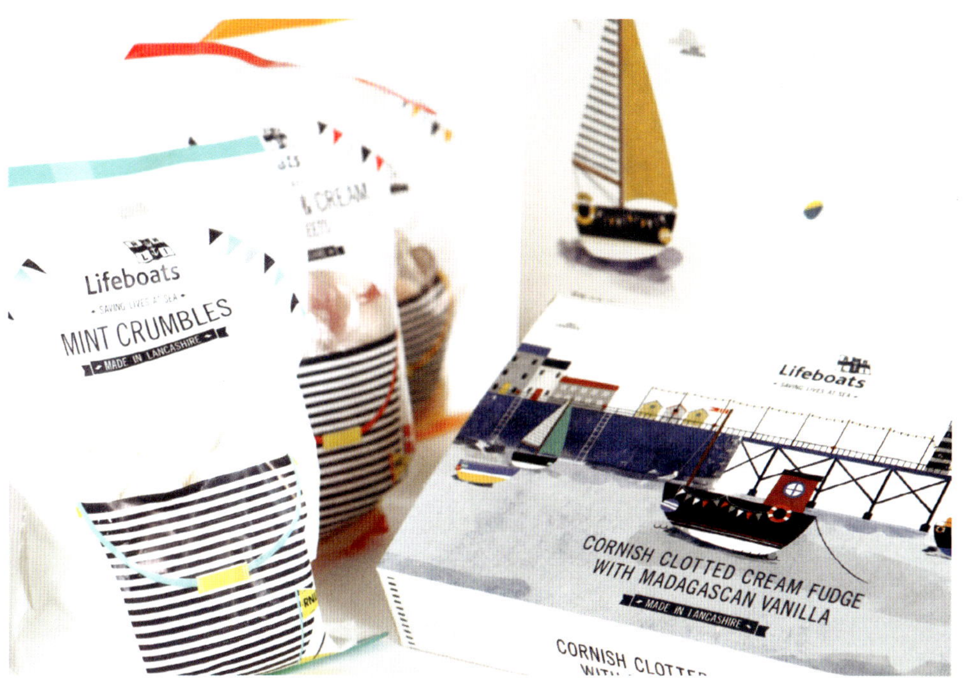
Lifeboats
MINT CRUMBLES
MADE IN LANCASHIRE
CORNISH CLOTTED CREAM FUDGE
WITH MADAGASCAN VANILLA
MADE IN LANCASHIRE

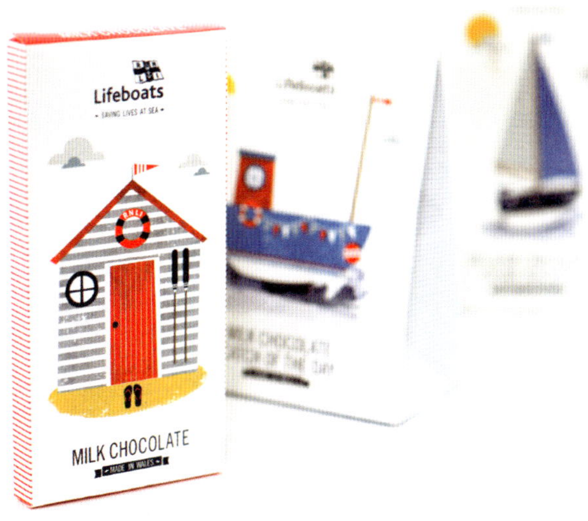
Lifeboats
SAVING LIVES AT SEA
MILK CHOCOLATE
MADE IN WALES

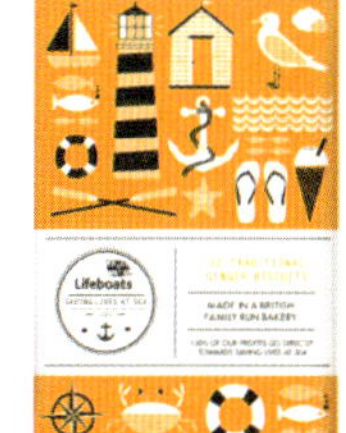

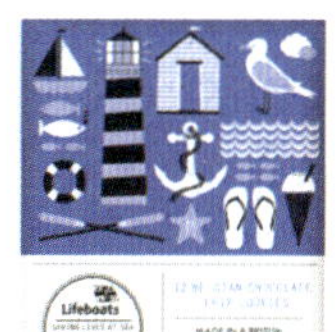

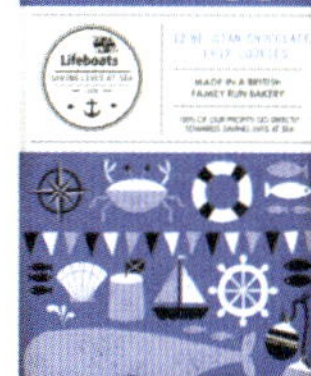

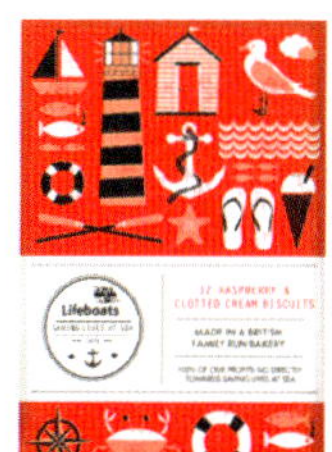

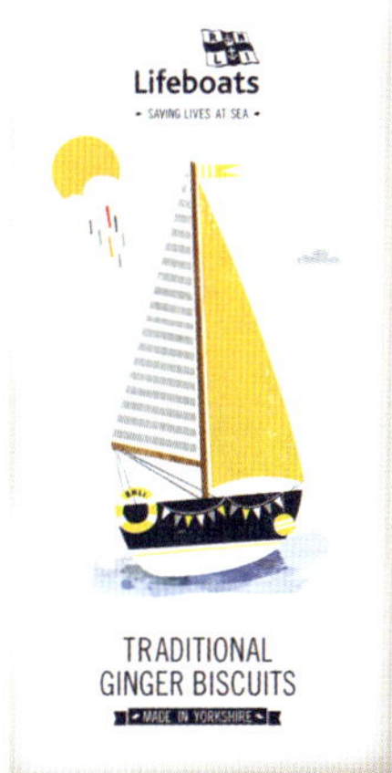
Lifeboats
SAVING LIVES AT SEA
TRADITIONAL
GINGER BISCUITS
MADE IN YORKSHIRE

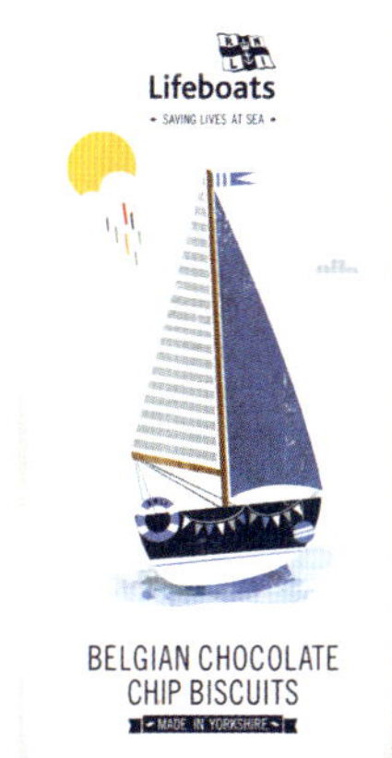
Lifeboats
SAVING LIVES AT SEA
BELGIAN CHOCOLATE
CHIP BISCUITS
MADE IN YORKSHIRE

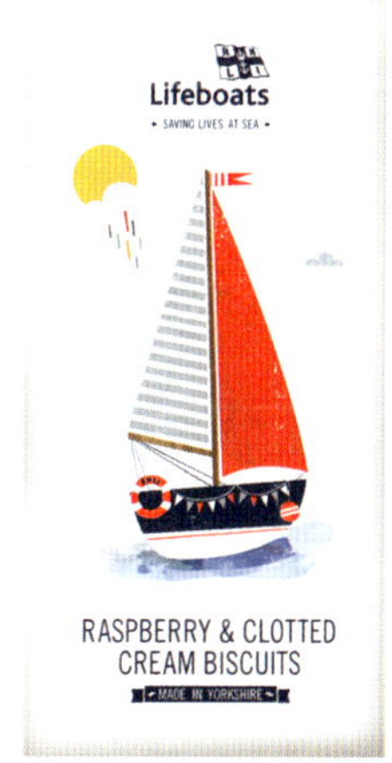
Lifeboats
SAVING LIVES AT SEA
RASPBERRY & CLOTTED
CREAM BISCUITS
MADE IN YORKSHIRE

colette Candle

Packaging design for colette's new candle Air du Parisien was a lighthearted view of people's obsession with smell in their daily life. These favourites include the aroma of a freshly-baked croissant, ink on newspapers, bird and shoes – for puppies.

Client: colette

Jean Jullien

colette Candle

Packaging design for colette's new candle Air du Parisien was a lighthearted view of people's obsession with smell in their daily life. These favourites include the aroma of a freshly-baked croissant, ink on newspapers, bird and shoes – for puppies.

Client: colette

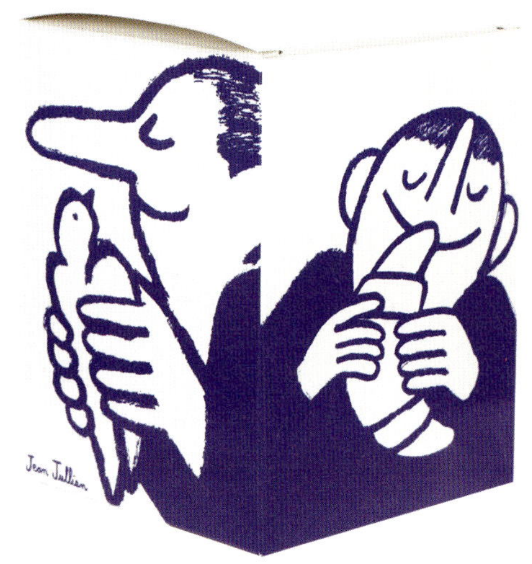

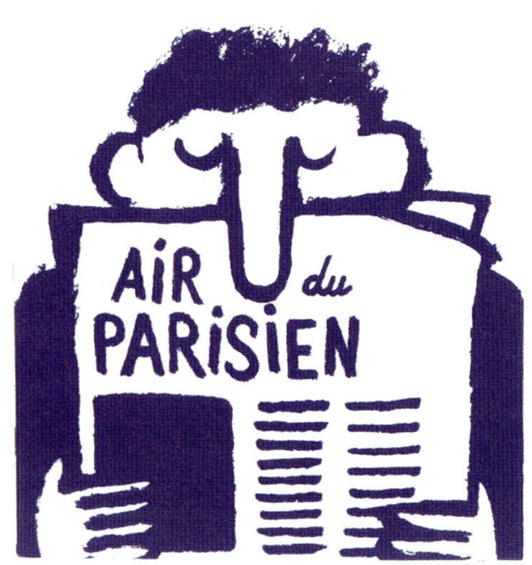

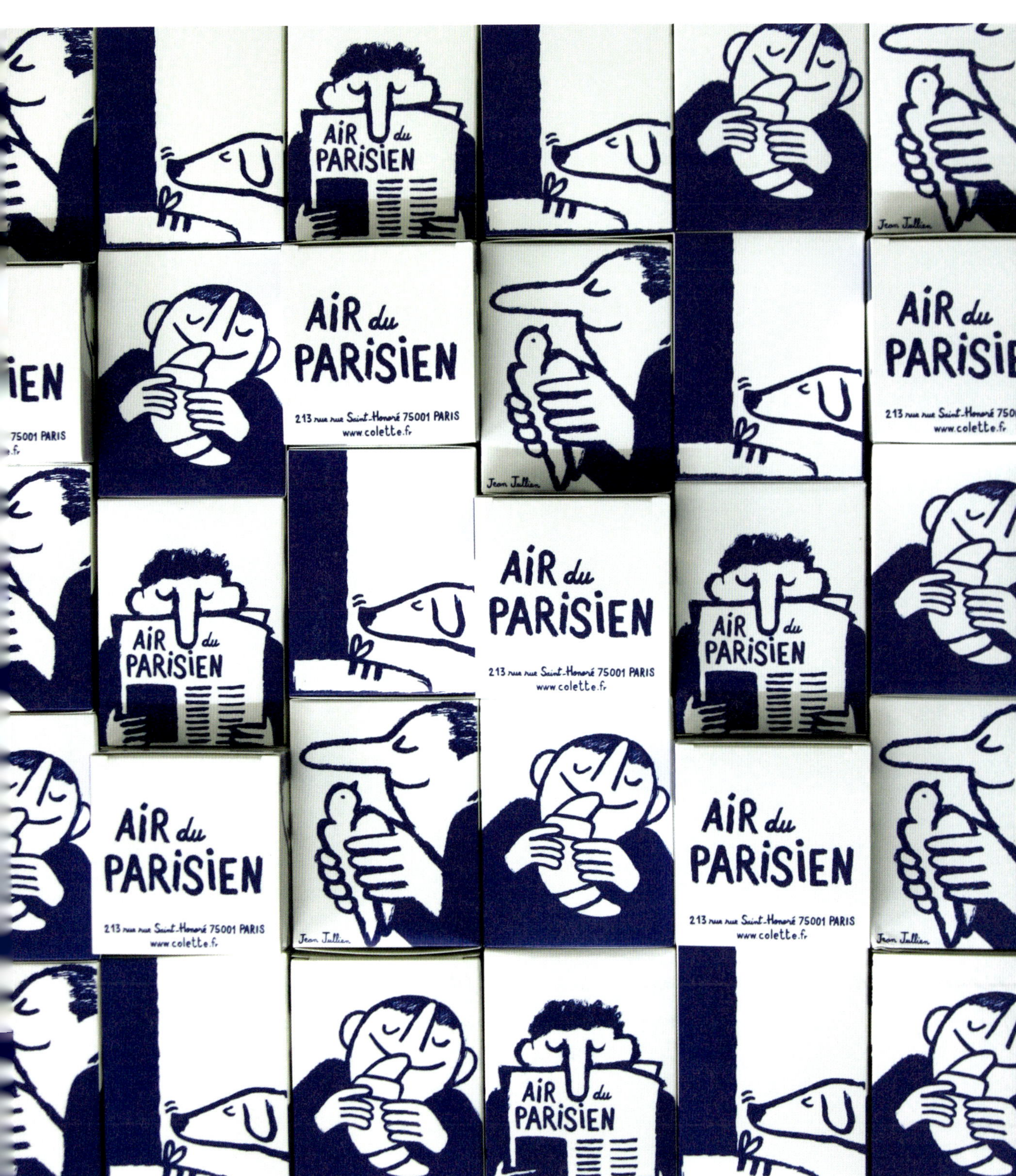
AIR du PARISIEN
213 rue rue Saint-Honoré 75001 PARIS
www.colette.fr
Jean Jullien

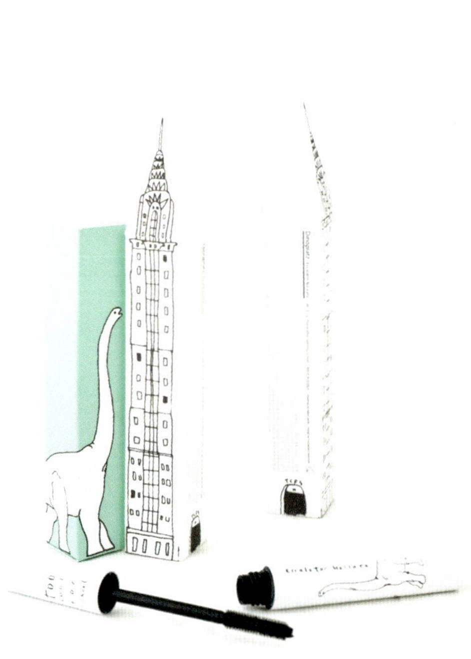

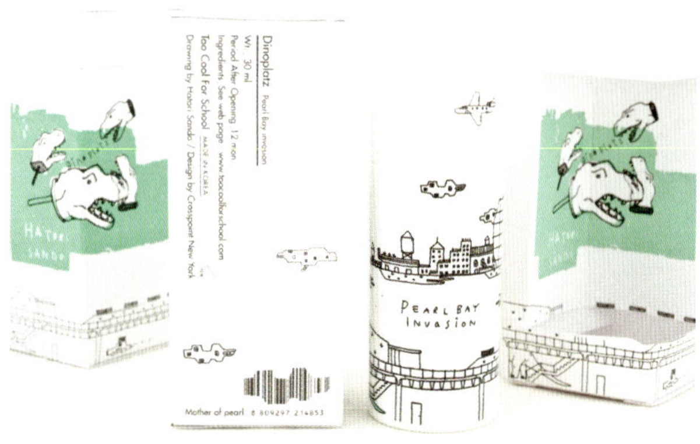

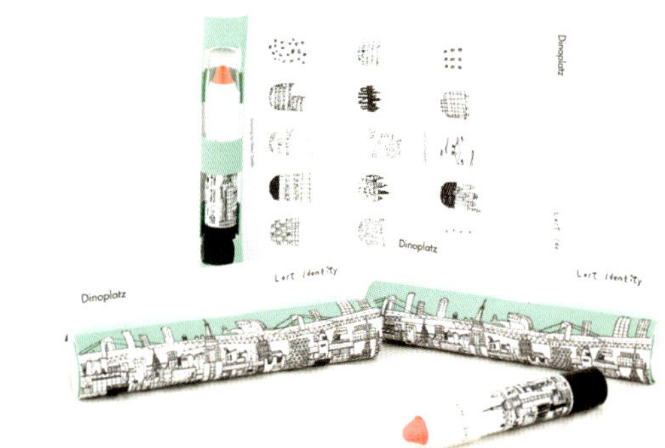

Crosspoint New York, Inc.

Dinoplatz

Hatori Sando's work often demonstrates a creative blend of real to life cityscapes and imagination. Matched with Crosspoint's commitment to minimise waste, minimal paper packaging and Sando's original work made for a byword for cosmopolitan chic for the cosmetic brand's new product line.

Illustration: Hatori Sando
Photo: Jerome Cha
Client: Too Cool for School

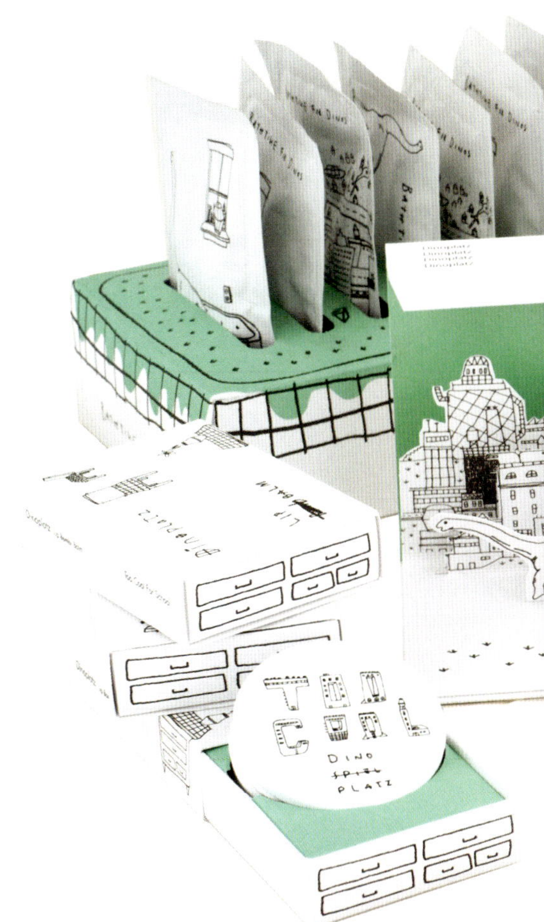

Crosspoint New York, Inc.

Dinoplatz

Hatori Sando's work often demonstrates a creative blend of real to life cityscapes and imagination. Matched with Crosspoint's commitment to minimise waste, minimal paper packaging and Sando's original work made for a byword for cosmopolitan chic for the cosmetic brand's new product line.

Illustration: Hatori Sando

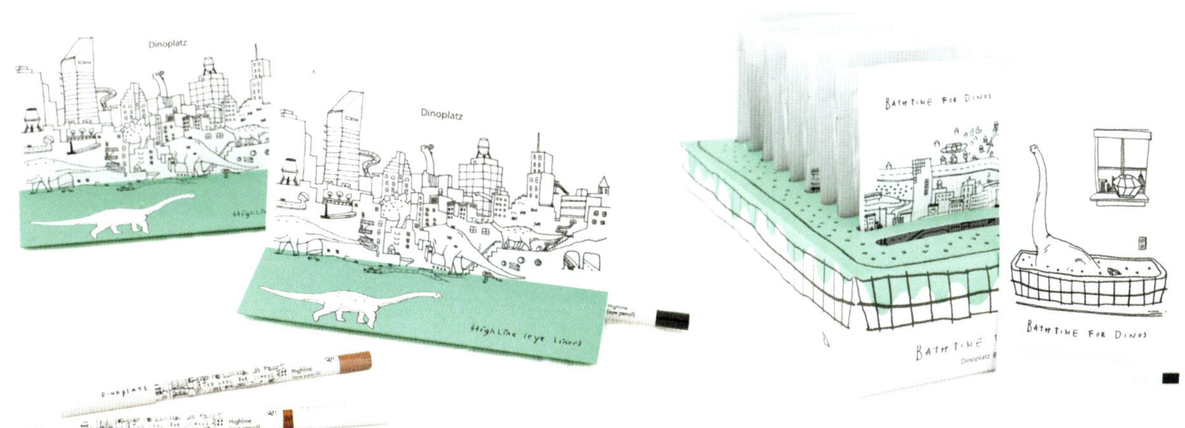
Dinoplatz
Dinoplatz
Highline (eye liner)
BATHTIME FOR DINOS
BATHTIME FOR DINOS

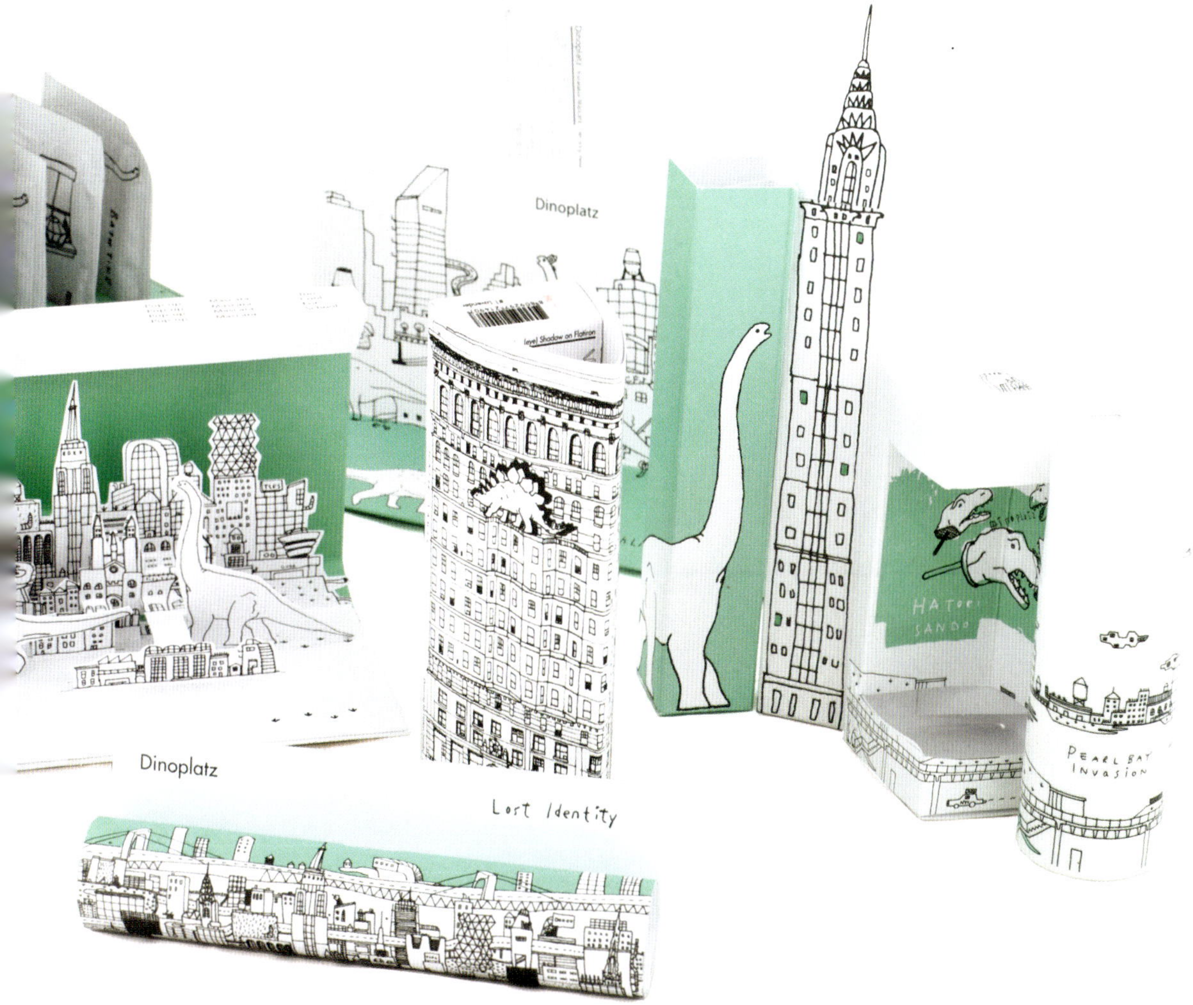

La Patente is a workshop space for day-to-day pleasures like cooking, gardening and crafts. Learning materials hand-drawn with watercolours deliver a clean and direct visual identity that breathes the concepts of 'slow', imperfection of natural things and the 'usual experience' the brand holds dear.

Illustration: Pol Montserrat
Typeface: (Barbedor) Hans Eduard Meier, (Brown) Aurèle Sack
Client: La Patente

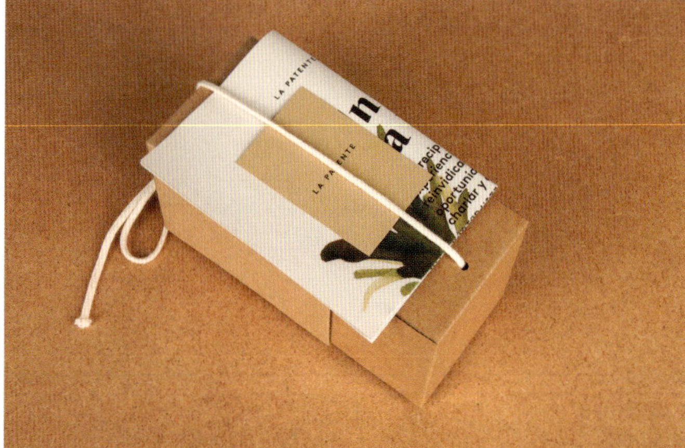

P.A.R

La Patente

La Patente is a workshop space for day-to-day pleasures like cooking, gardening and crafts. Learning materials hand-drawn with watercolours deliver a clean and direct visual identity that breathes the concepts of 'slow', imperfection of natural things and the 'usual experience' the brand holds dear.

Illustration: Pol Montserrat
Typeface: (Barbedor) Hans Eduard Meier, (Brown) Aurèle Sack
Client: La Patente

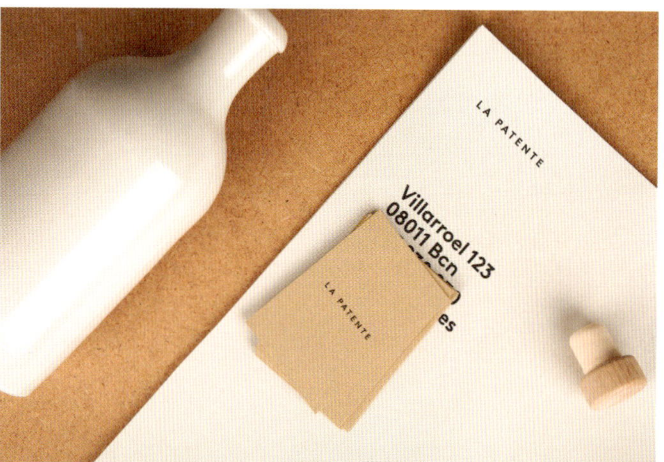

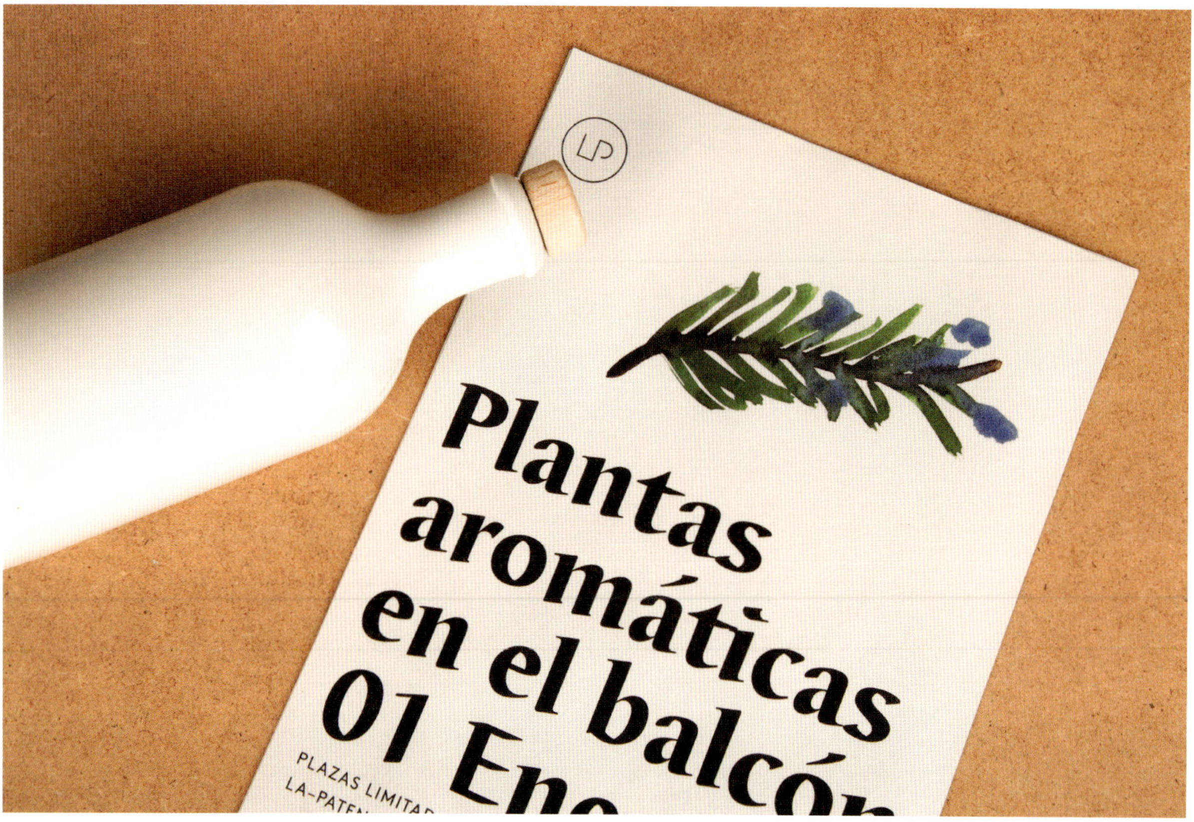

LA PATENTE

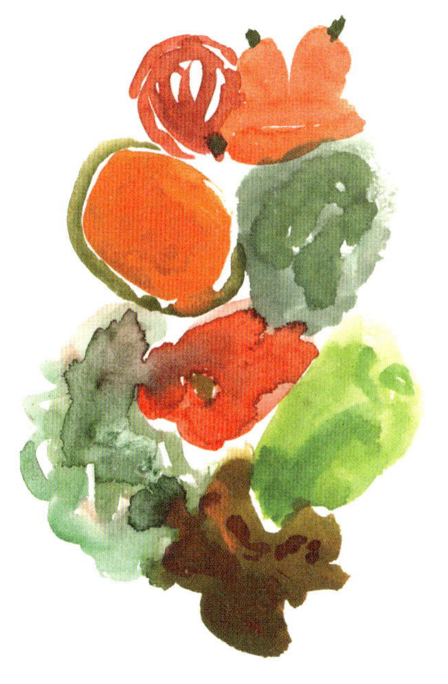

LA-PATENTE.ES

LA PATENTE

Queremos reinterpretar lo cotidiano con un estilo urbano, original y con sentido del humor, que da valor a *lo hecho a mano* o *lo de toda la vida.* Nuestra intención es que cualquiera pueda sentir que está en su cocina o en su salón preparando algo con los amigos.

En La Patente organizamos talleres y cursos monográficos especialmente de cocina y gastronomía, pero también de huerto urbano, handy-craft... y todo lo que tenga que ver con compartir un momento agradable alrededor de una mesa. La Patente ofrece experiencias de ocio cercanas y participativas.

LA-PATENTE.ES

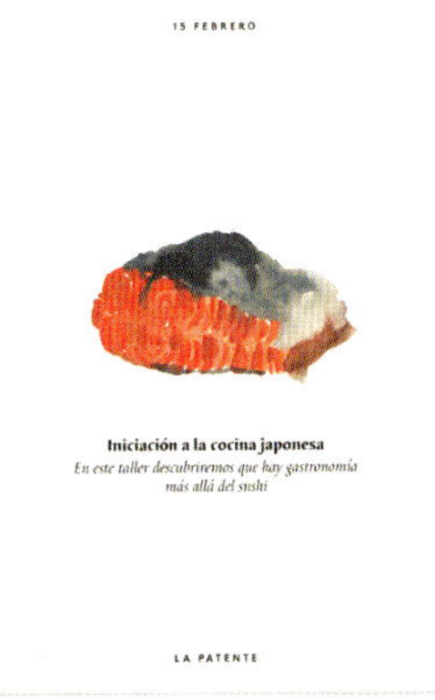

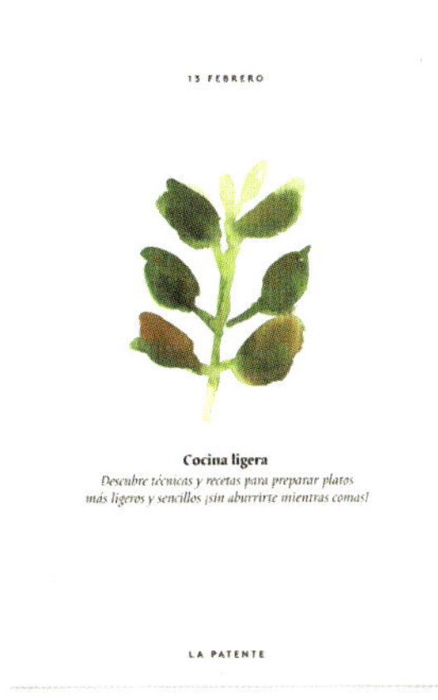

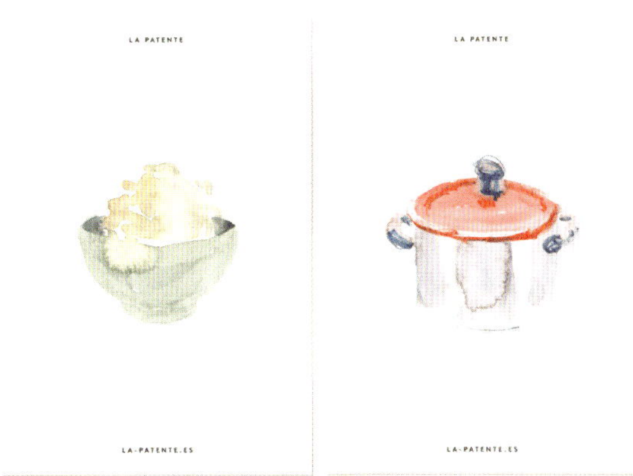

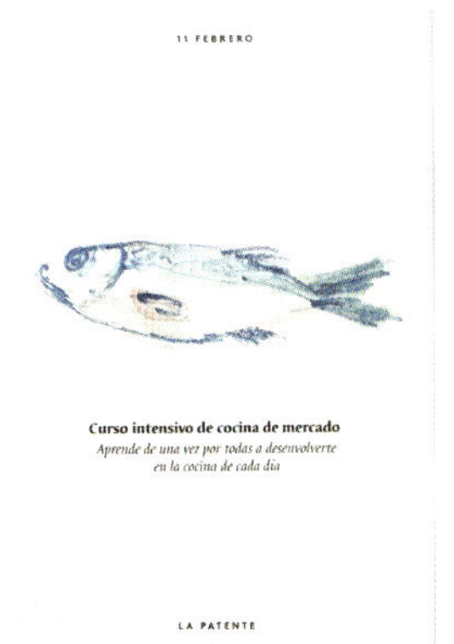

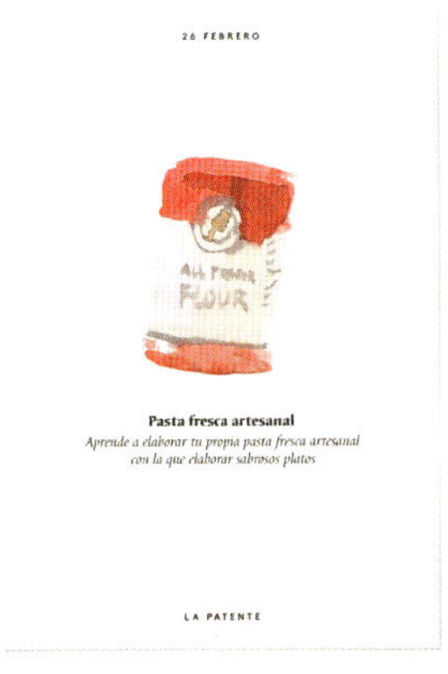

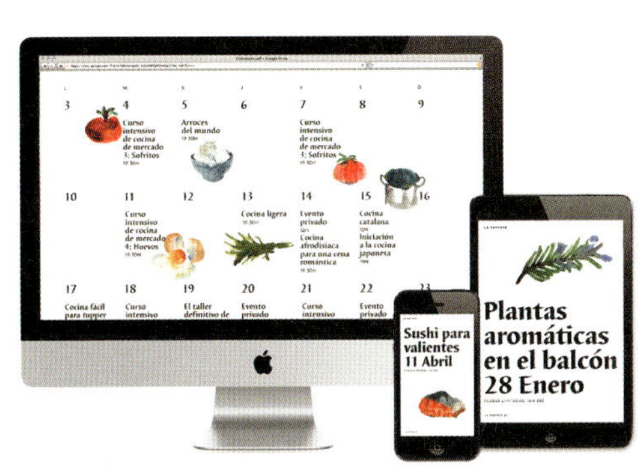

Beautiful Times Spa

Beautiful Times is a high-end women-only spa club. From packaging to deliverables, its visual identity is enchanted with flowers, butterflies and deer in dreamy turquoise that communicates beauty and tenderness that its clients look for at a spa facility.

Client: Beautiful Times Spa

RONCHAM DESIGN OFFICE

Beautiful Times Spa

Beautiful Times is a high-end women-only spa club. From packaging to deliverables, its visual identity is enchanted with flowers, butterflies and deer in dreamy turquoise that communicates beauty and tenderness that its clients look for at a spa facility.

Client: Beautiful Times Spa

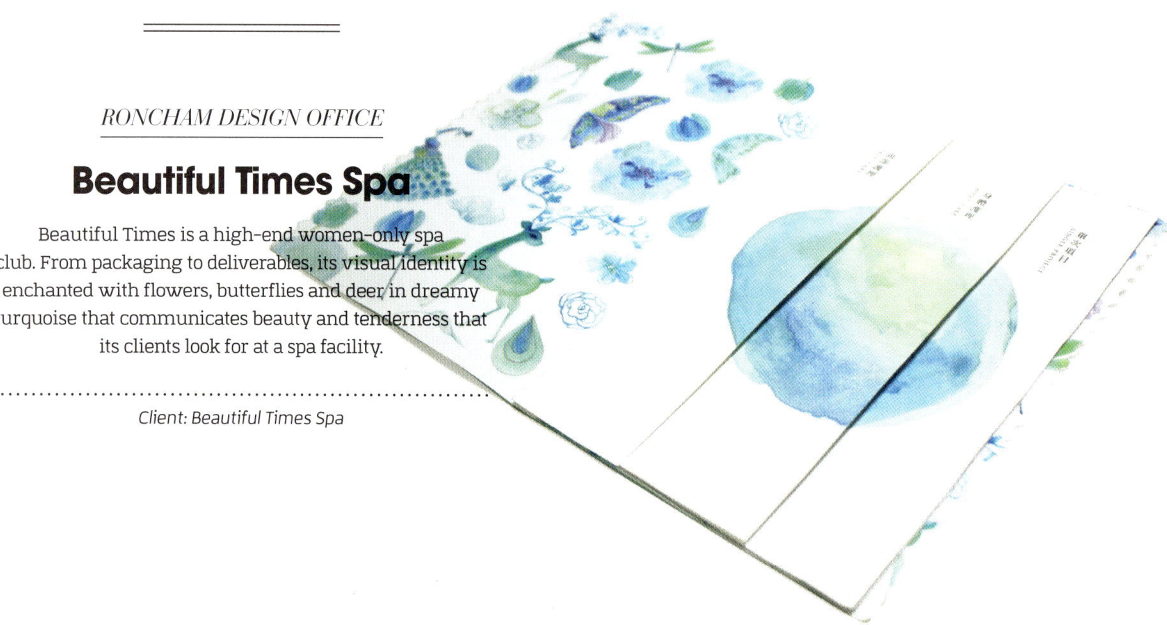

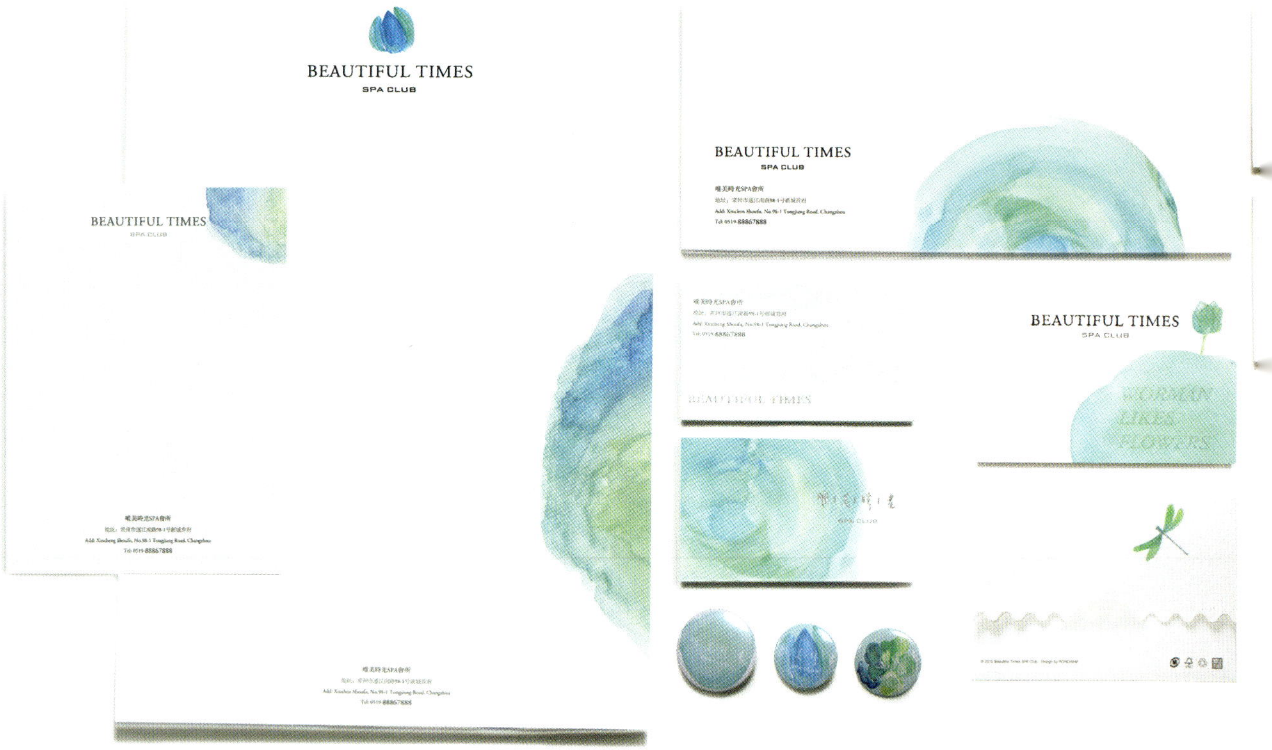

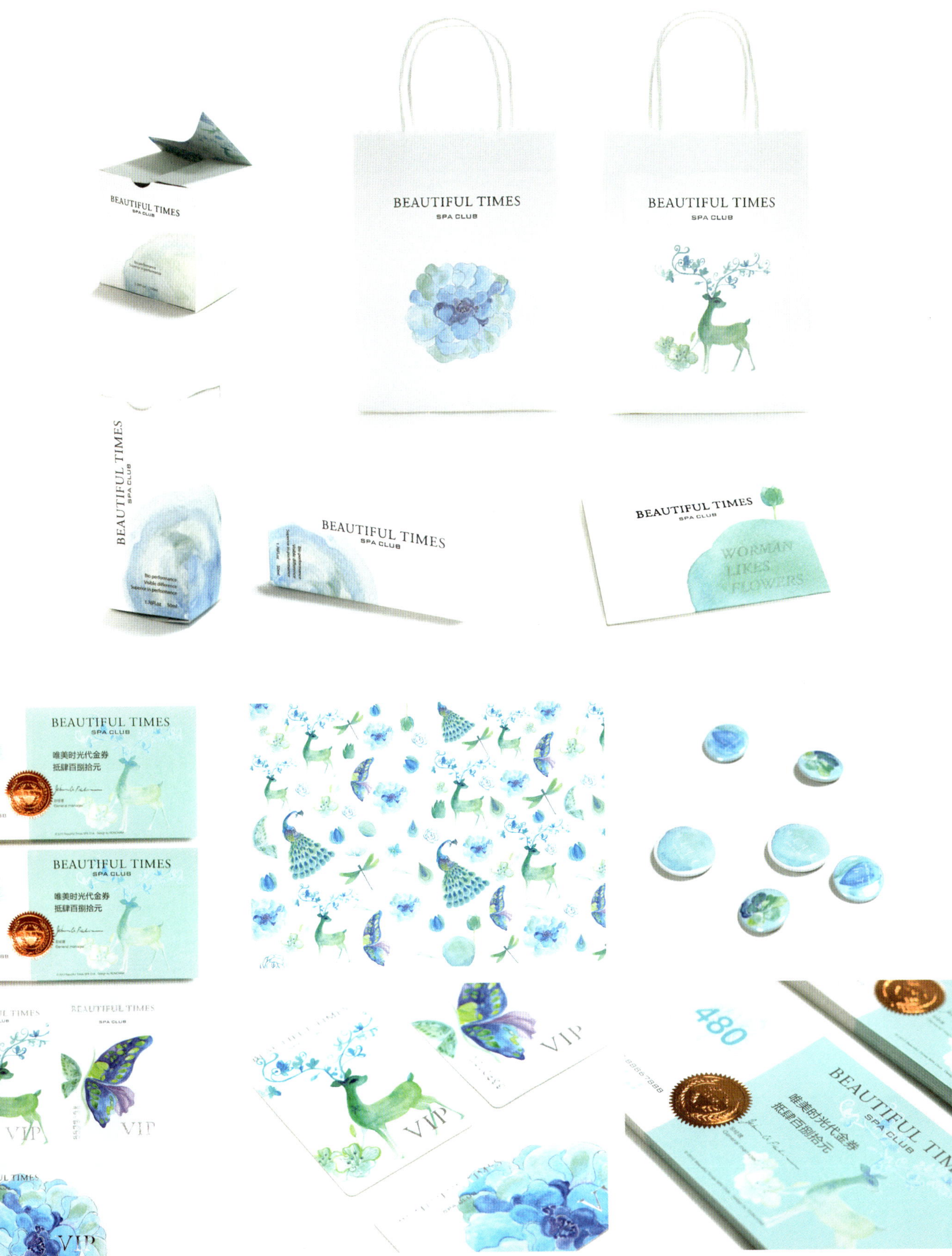
BEAUTIFUL TIMES
SPA CLUB
WORMAN
LIKES
FLOWERS
唯美时光代金券
抵肆百捌拾元
VIP
480

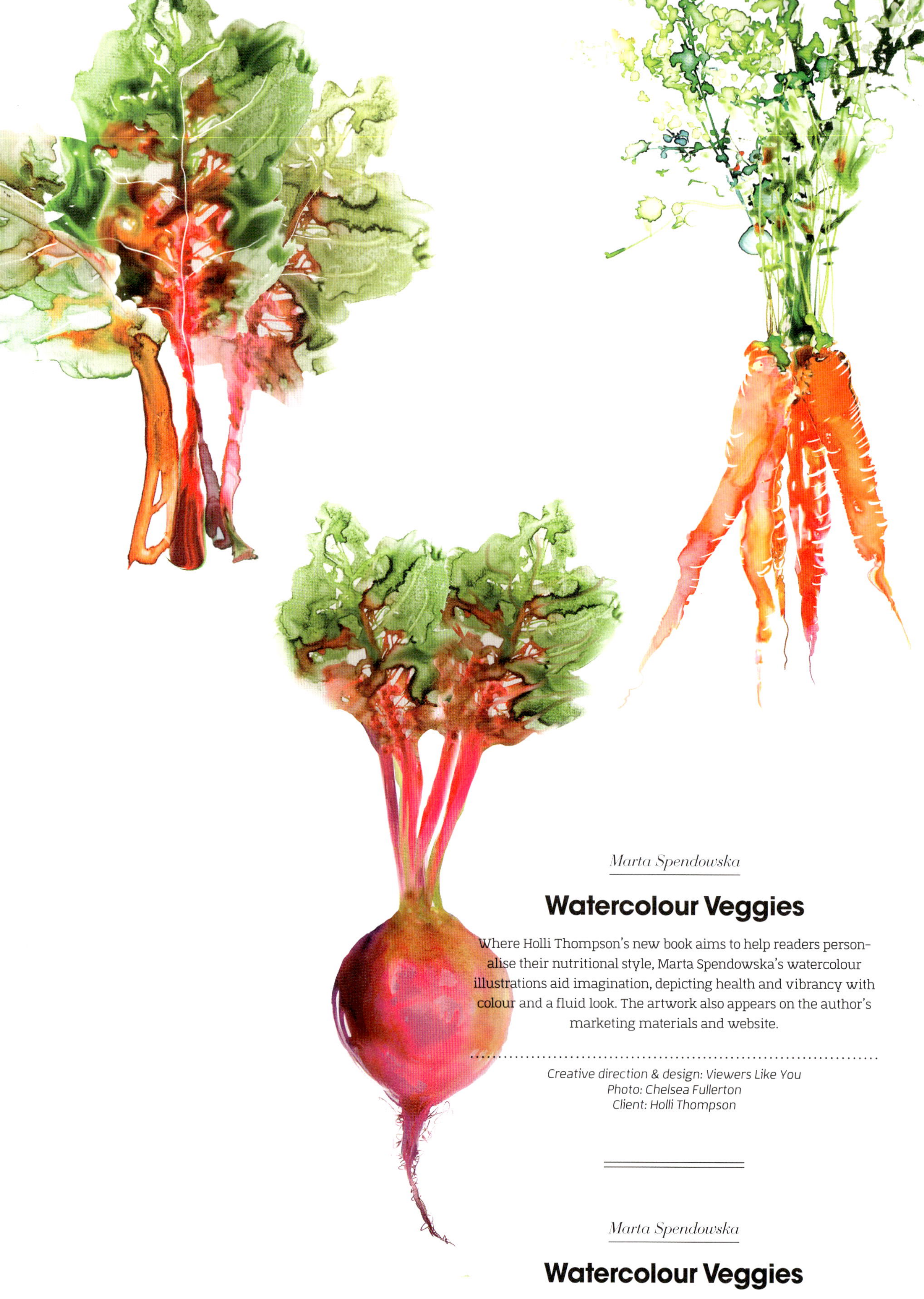

Marta Spendowska

Watercolour Veggies

Where Holli Thompson's new book aims to help readers personalise their nutritional style, Marta Spendowska's watercolour illustrations aid imagination, depicting health and vibrancy with colour and a fluid look. The artwork also appears on the author's marketing materials and website.

Creative direction & design: Viewers Like You
Photo: Chelsea Fullerton
Client: Holli Thompson

Marta Spendowska

Watercolour Veggies

Where Holli Thompson's new book aims to help readers personalise their nutritional style, Marta Spendowska's watercolour illustrations aid imagination, depicting health and vibrancy with

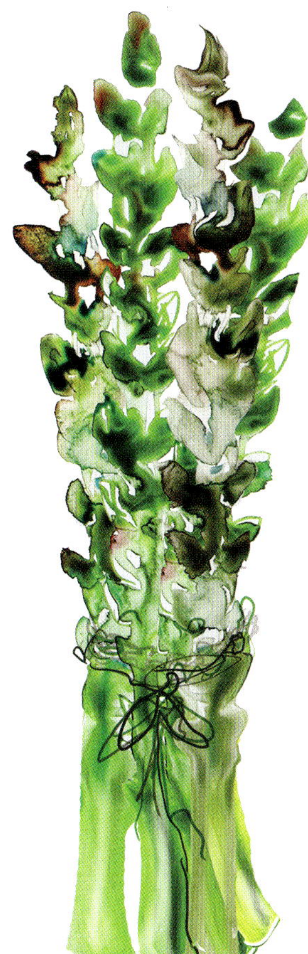

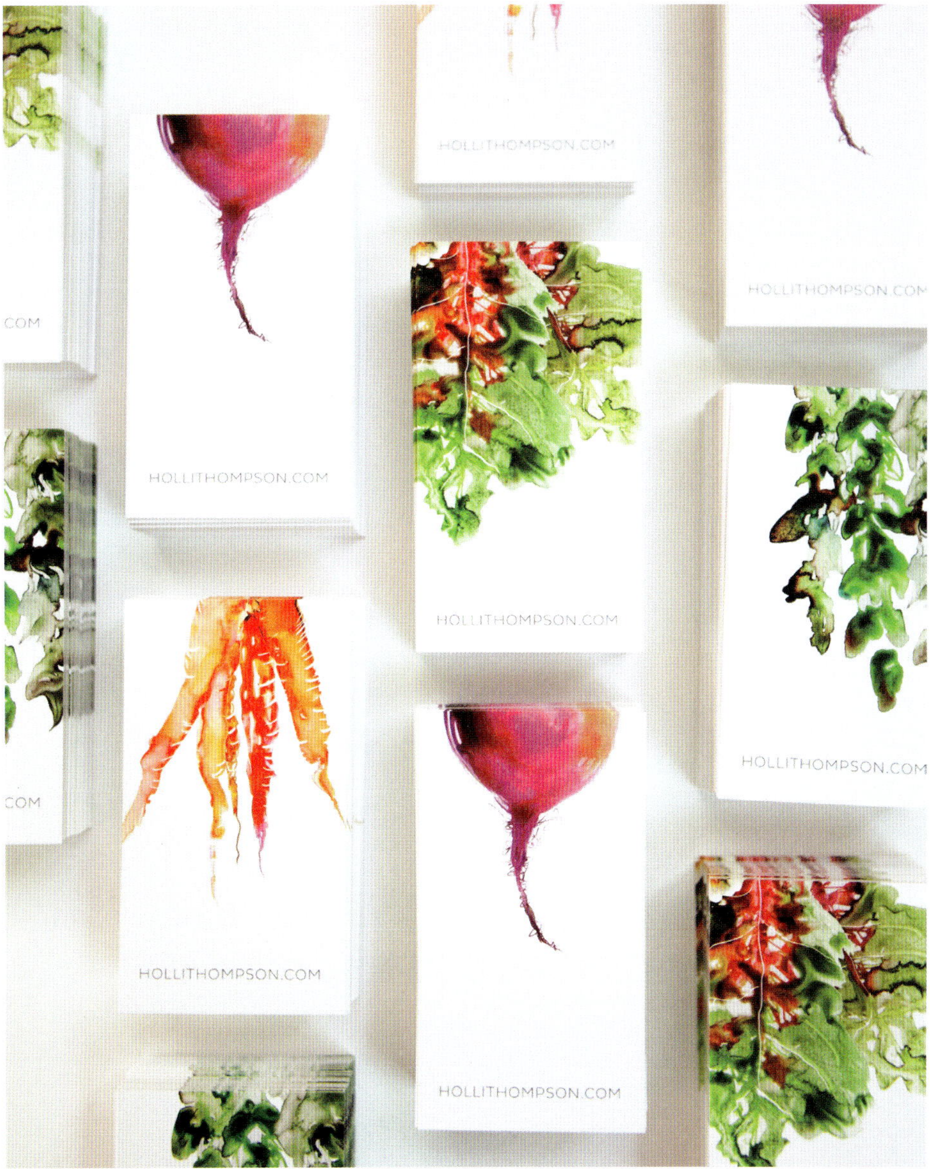

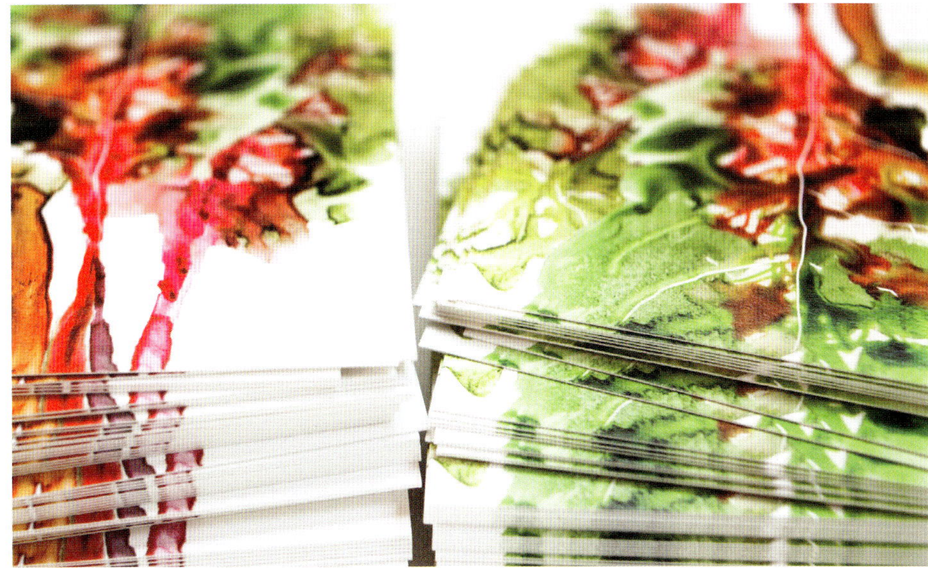

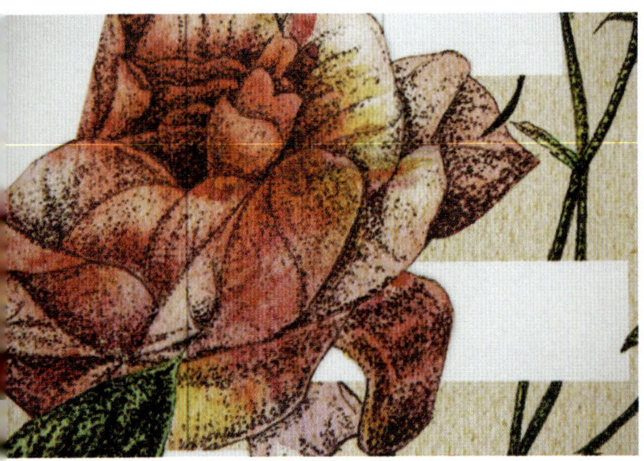

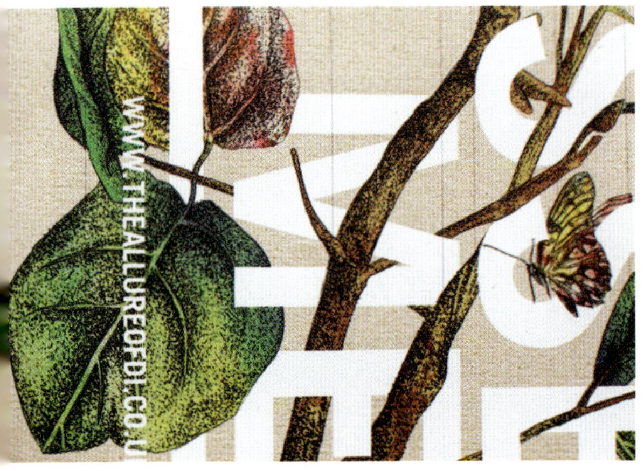

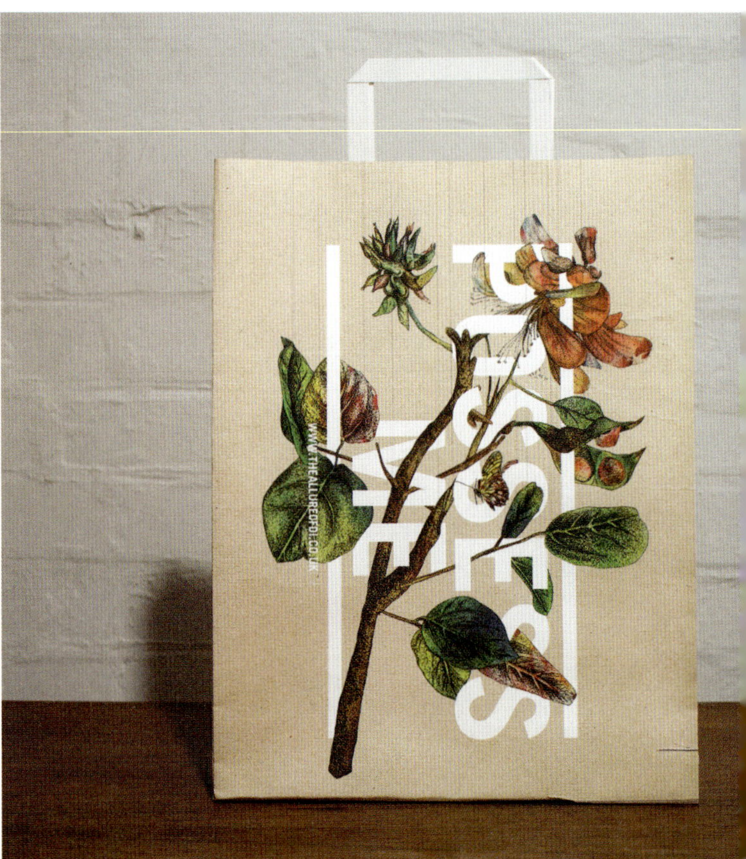

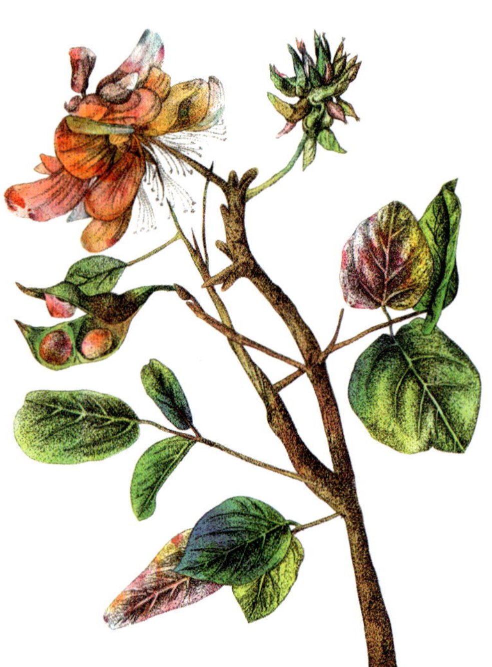

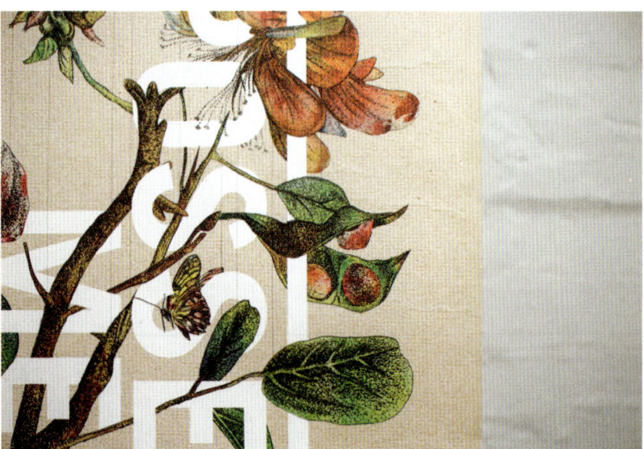

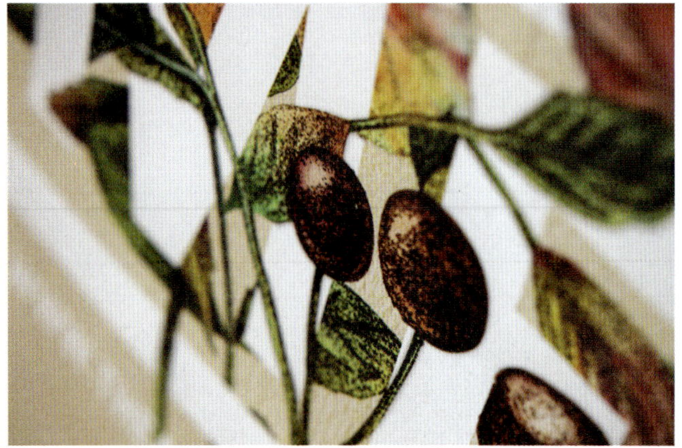

…e, Possess Me

…ion of commercialism, Love Me,
…s seduction and materialism in illustra-
…ndent hand-drawn blossoms and bold
logotype juxta… …e bags and seduce eyes as commercial
graphics do in the commercial world.

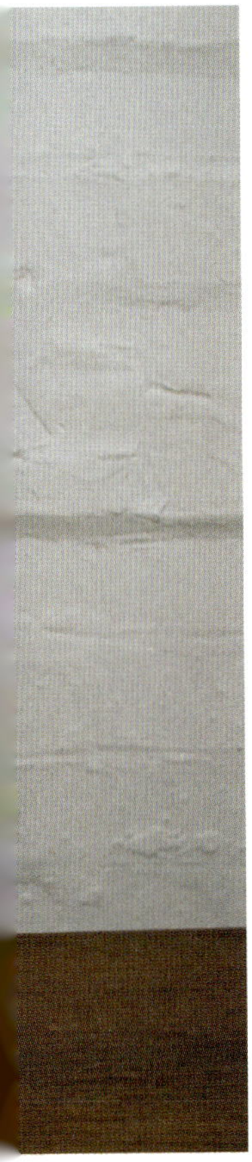

Sidney Lim

Love Me, Possess Me

A graphic rendition of commercialism, Love Me, Possess Me conceptualises seduction and materialism in illustrations and words. Resplendent hand-drawn blossoms and bold logotype juxtapose on the bags and seduce eyes as commercial graphics do in the commercial world.

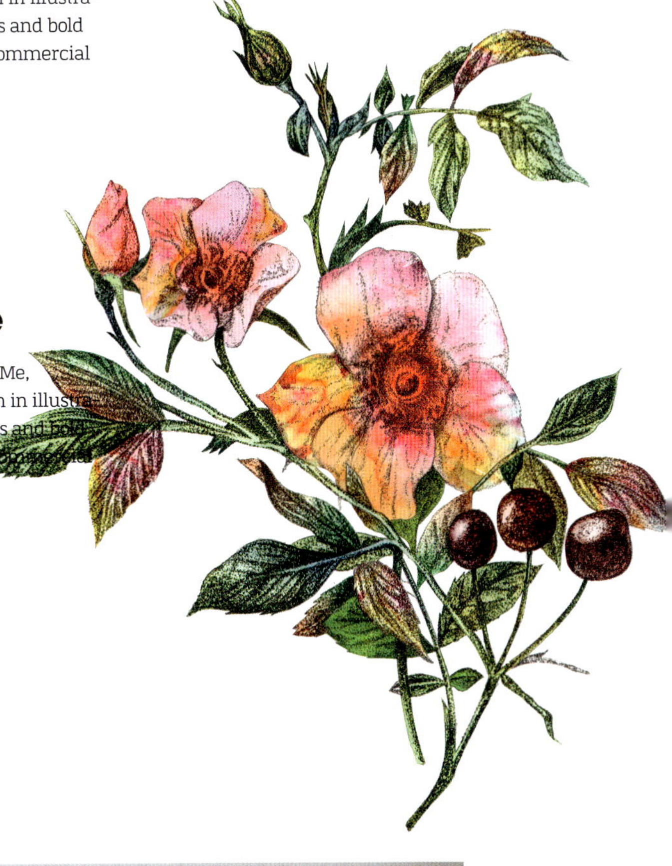

LOVE ME
POSSESS ME

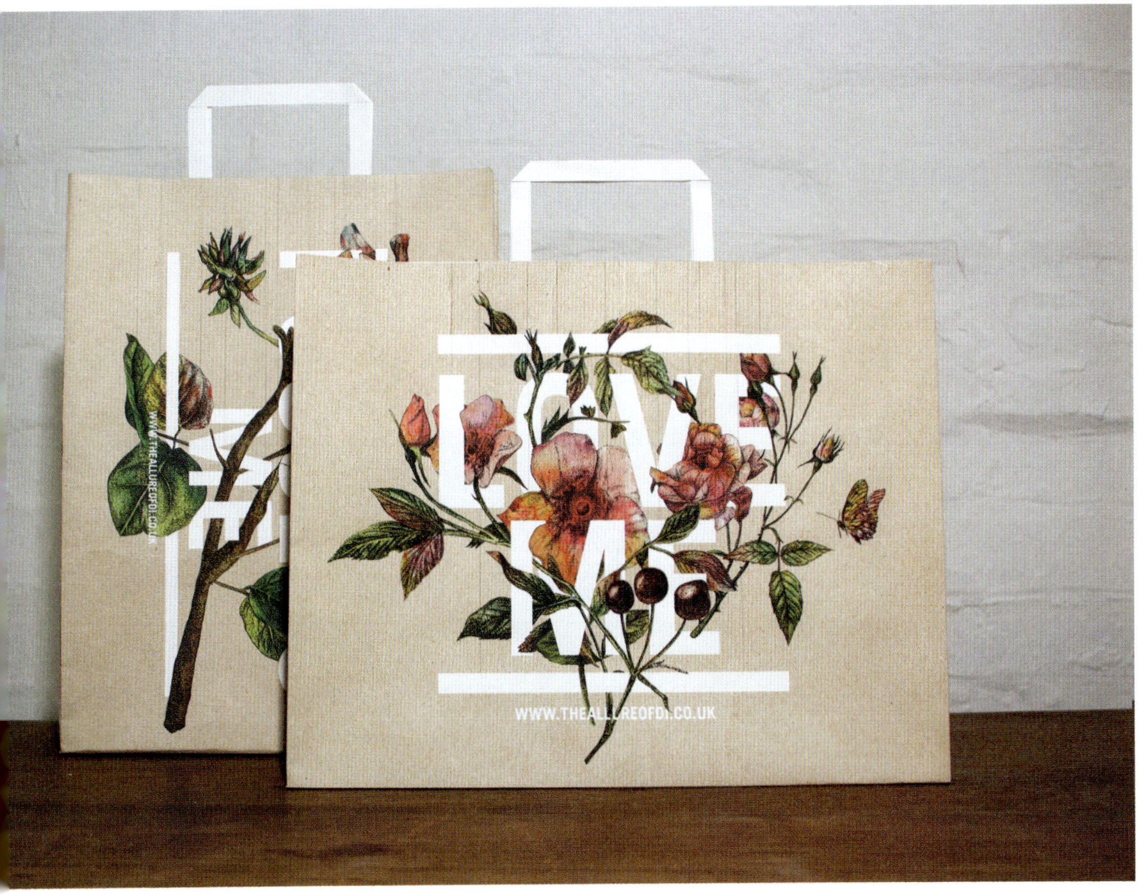

With a notion to explore printing possibilities on unusual objects, TYMOTE collaborated with product designer minna to create a line of quill pens named after the reborn bird. Each pen is individualised by unique graphic print on genuine feather by state-of-the-art technology.

Client: MONOPURI

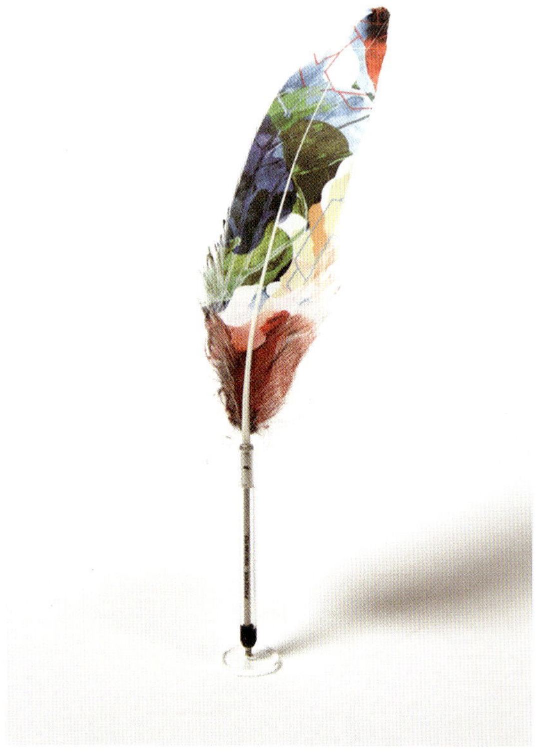

TYMOTE, minna

Phoenix

With a notion to explore printing possibilities on unusual objects, TYMOTE collaborated with product designer minna to create a line of quill pens named after the reborn bird. Each pen is individualised by unique graphic print on genuine feather by state-of-the-art technology.

Client: MONOPURI

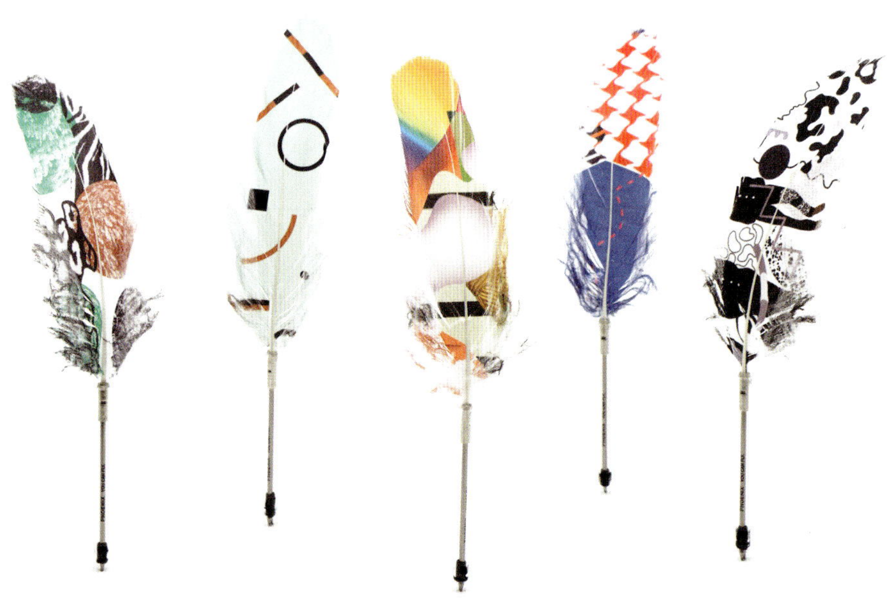

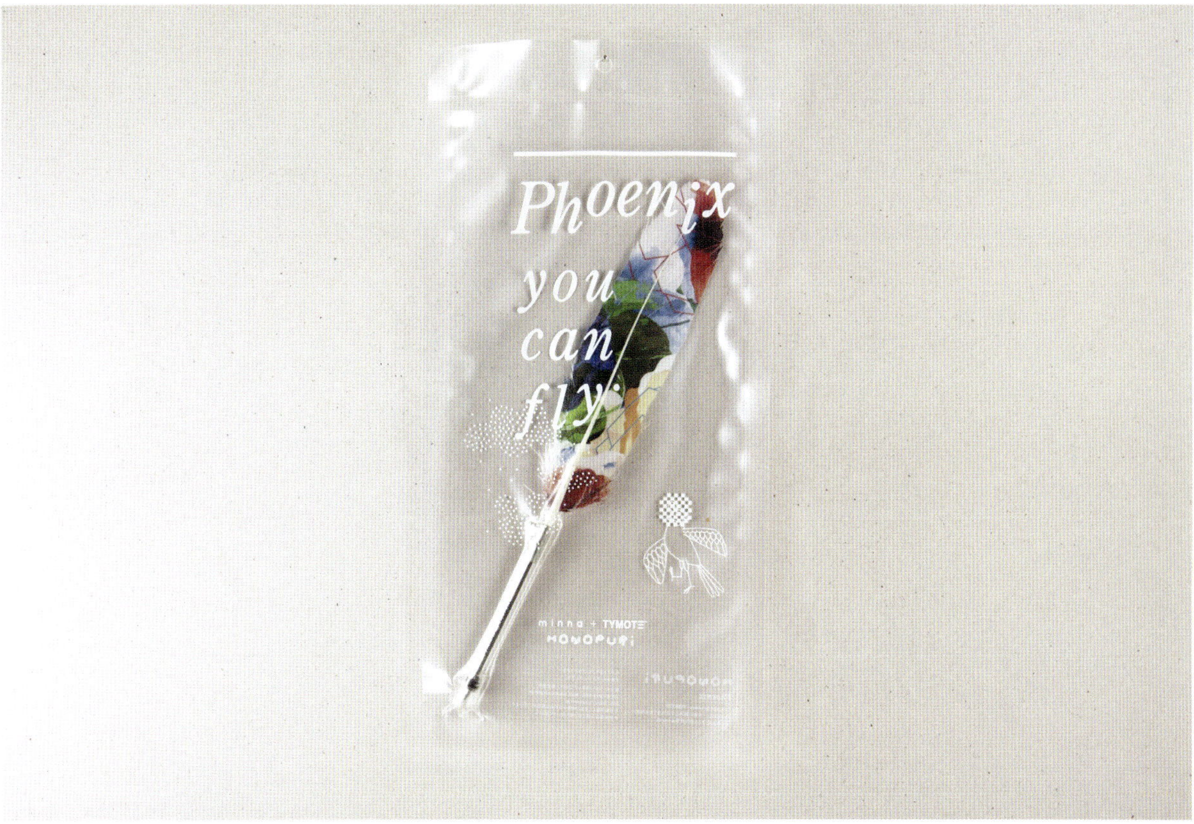
Phoenix
you
can
fly
minna + TYMOTE

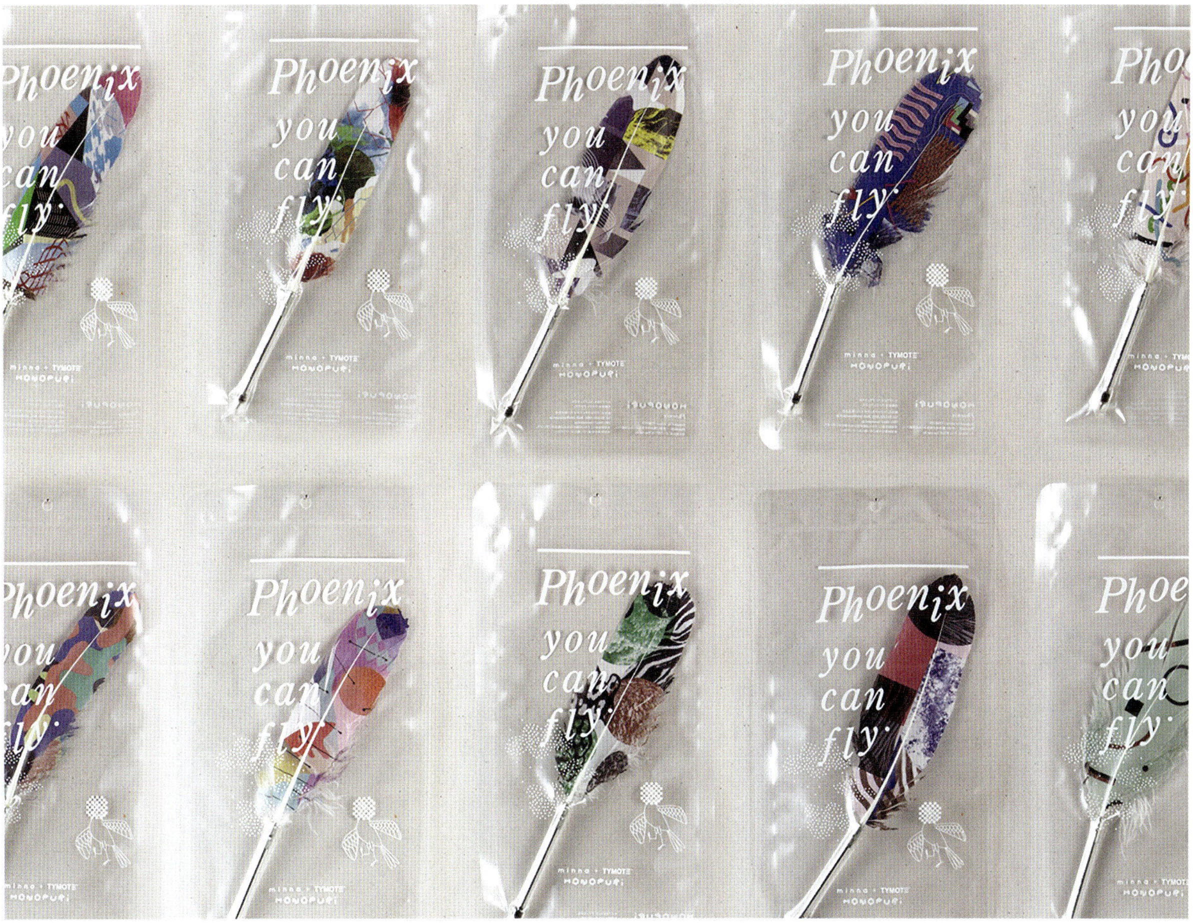
Phoenix
you
can
fly

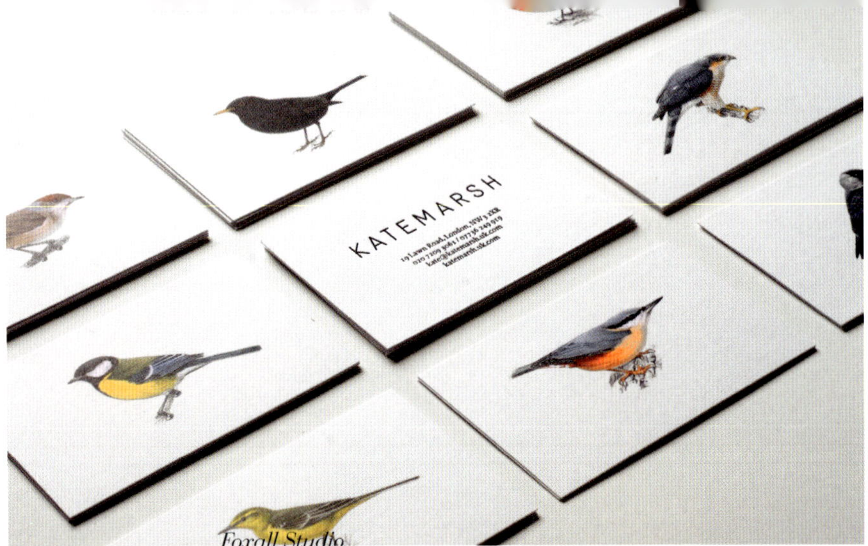

Foxall Studio

Kate Marsh

Kate Marsh is a new recruitment agency in London serving large advertising agencies. Taking on bird drawings by a recognised specialist, the brand identity speaks a creative language as the industry and her potential clients do and boost her image as a professional agent with an agile mind.

Client: Kate Marsh

Foxall Studio

Kate Marsh

Kate Marsh is a new recruitment agency in London serving large advertising agencies. Taking on bird drawings by a recognised specialist, the brand identity speaks a creative language as the industry and her potential clients do and boost her image as a professional agent with an agile mind.

Client: Kate Marsh

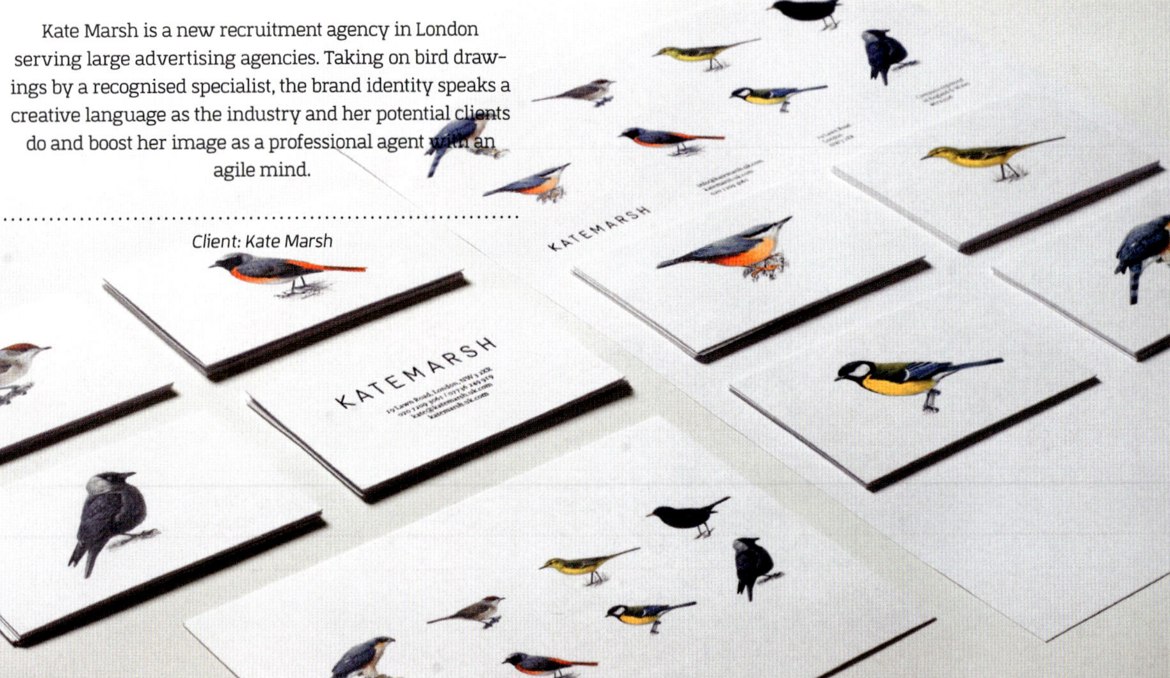

Sweet Greek is a food store in Melbourne's Prahran Market. The blue identity reflected her family origins and spirit, and resulted in an outcome that was honest, raw and filled with character. The project also included Kathy's first cook book celebrating simple food and sumptuous feasts.

Client: Sweet Greek

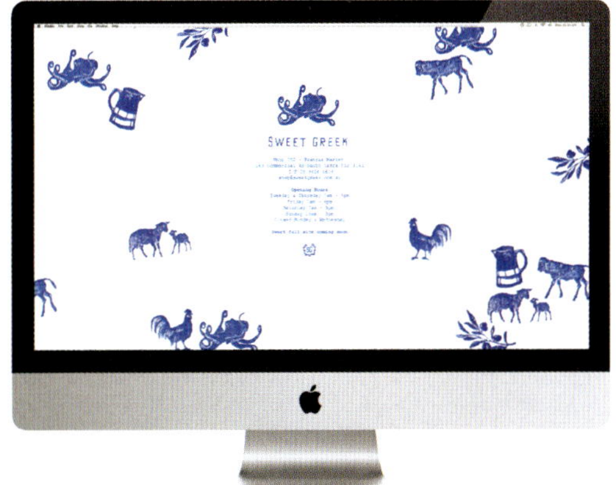

Studio Brave

Sweet Greek

Sweet Greek is a food store in Melbourne's Prahran Market. The blue identity reflected her family origins and spirit, and resulted in an outcome that was honest, raw and filled with character. The project also included Kathy's first cook book celebrating simple food and sumptuous feasts.

Client: Sweet Greek

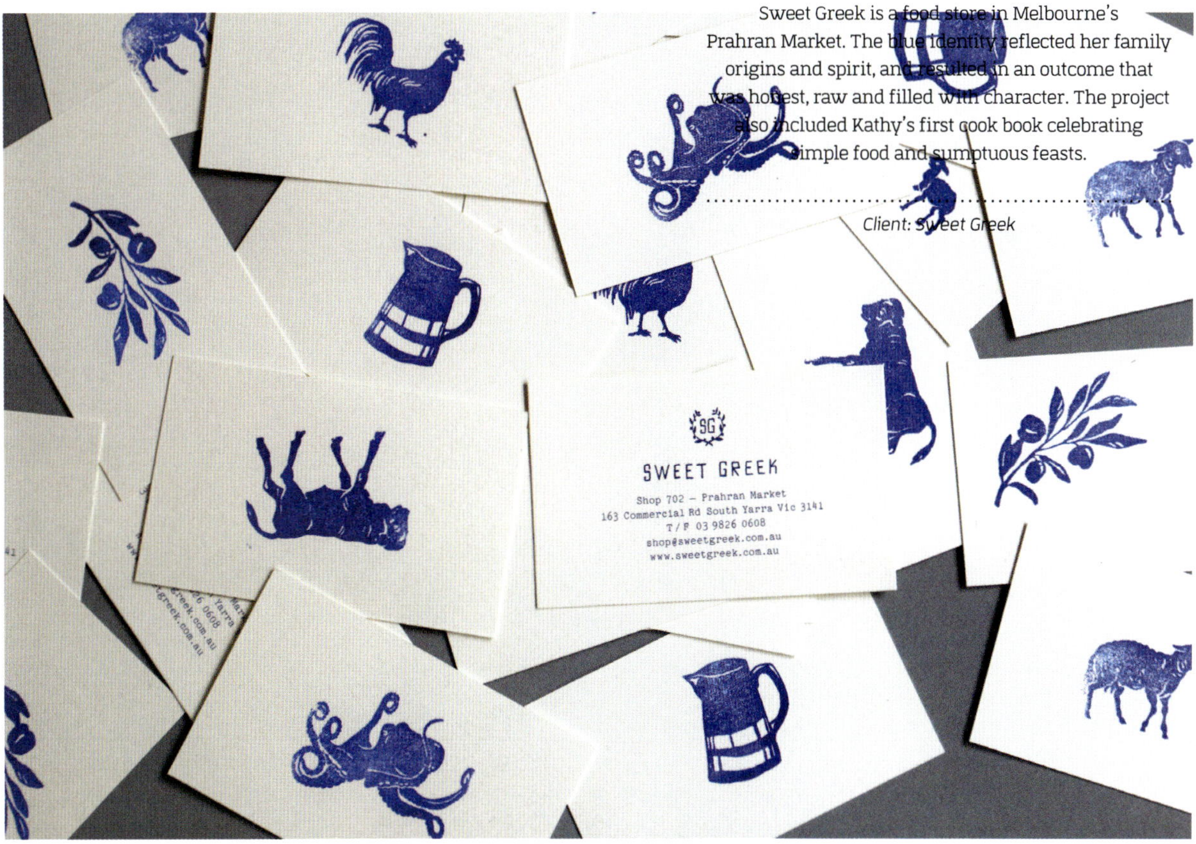

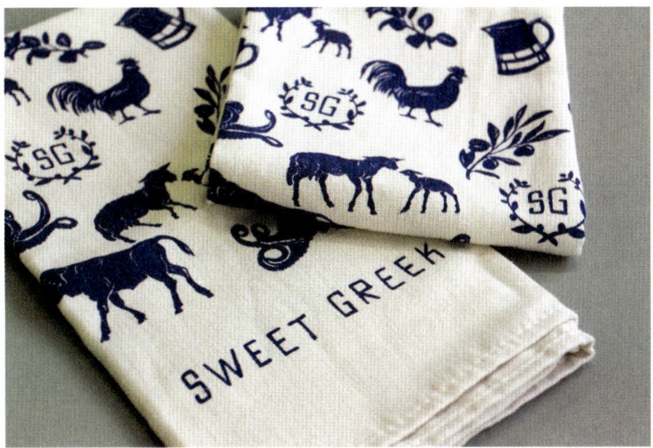

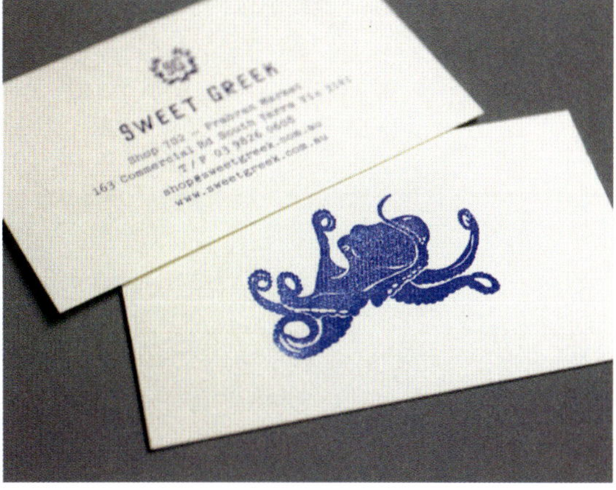

Green Bean Cake

It's Taiwanese culture to show gratitude to the nature through worship and celebration. When bean paste cake meets art, with traditional auspicious animals artistically reworked in Shiu Ruei-jr's style, this collection conveys a happy atmosphere and shares good luck during Chinese New Year.

Illustration: Shiu Ruei-jr
Client: ChaDian Shi Jia Food Co., Ltd

Victor Branding Design Corp.,

ROOOROO Green Bean Cake

It's Taiwanese culture to show gratitude to the nature through worship and celebration. When bean paste cake meets art, with traditional auspicious animals artistically reworked in Shiu Ruei-jr's style, this collection conveys a happy atmosphere and shares good luck during Chinese New Year.

Illustration: Shiu Ruei-jr
Client: ChaDian Shi Jia Food Co., Ltd

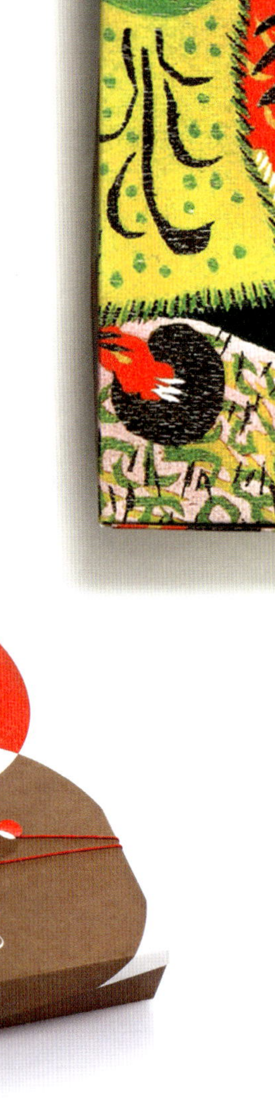

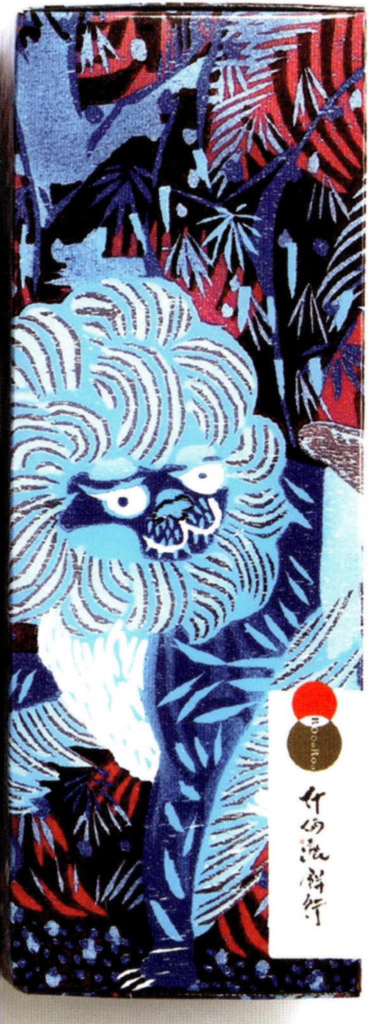

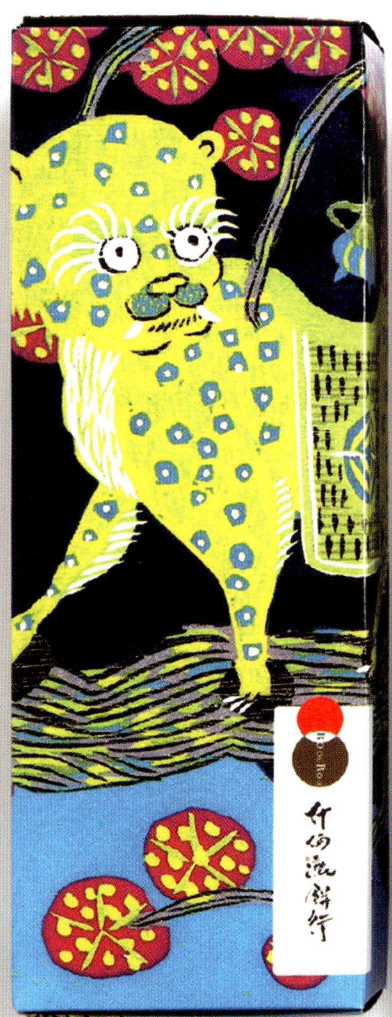

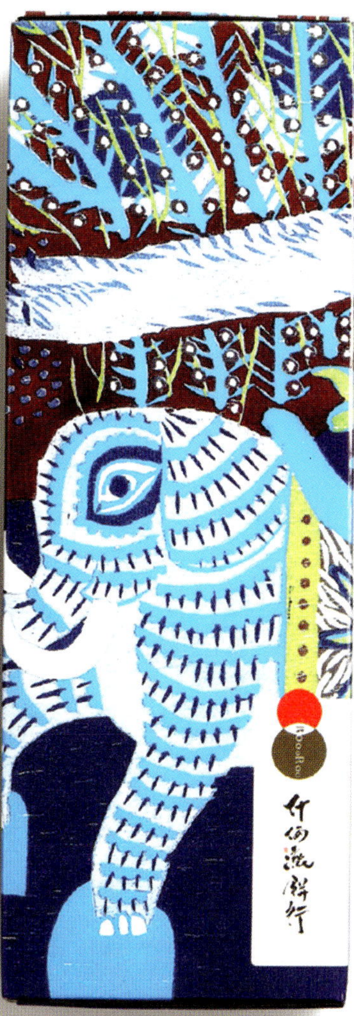

Taking reference from the ancient Greek black-figured vessels, dolphins//communication design created five patterns with different themes for the defining drink of Greece. The tone of the illustration maintains an alternative and lively code of aesthetics.

Client: The Greek Distillation Company (EVA)

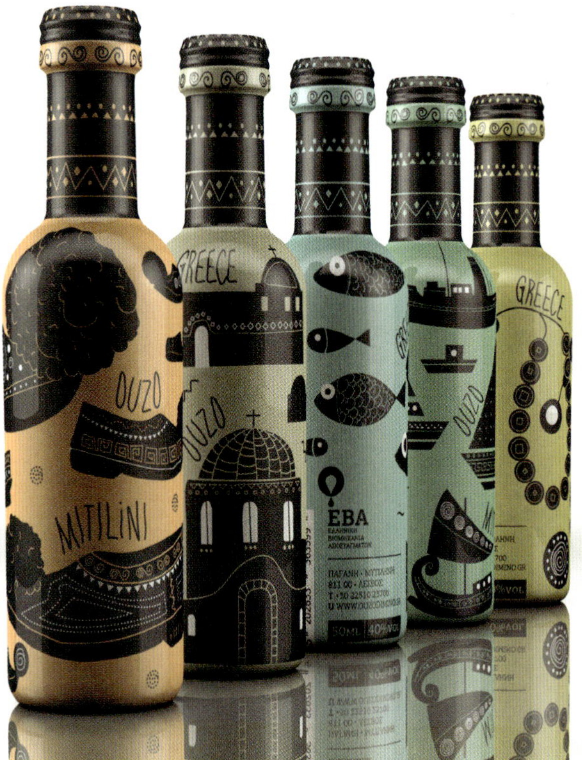

dolphins//communication design

Ouzo Mitilini "Miniatures"

Taking reference from the ancient Greek black-figured vessels, dolphins//communication design created five patterns with different themes for the defining drink of Greece. The tone of the illustration maintains an alternative and lively code of aesthetics.

Client: The Greek Distillation Company (EVA)

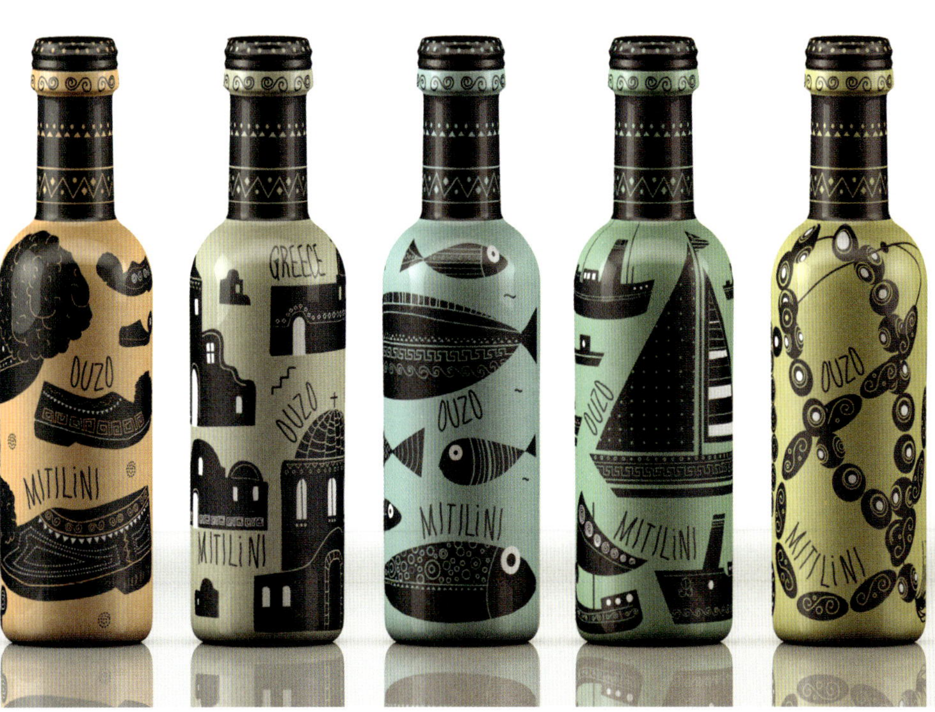

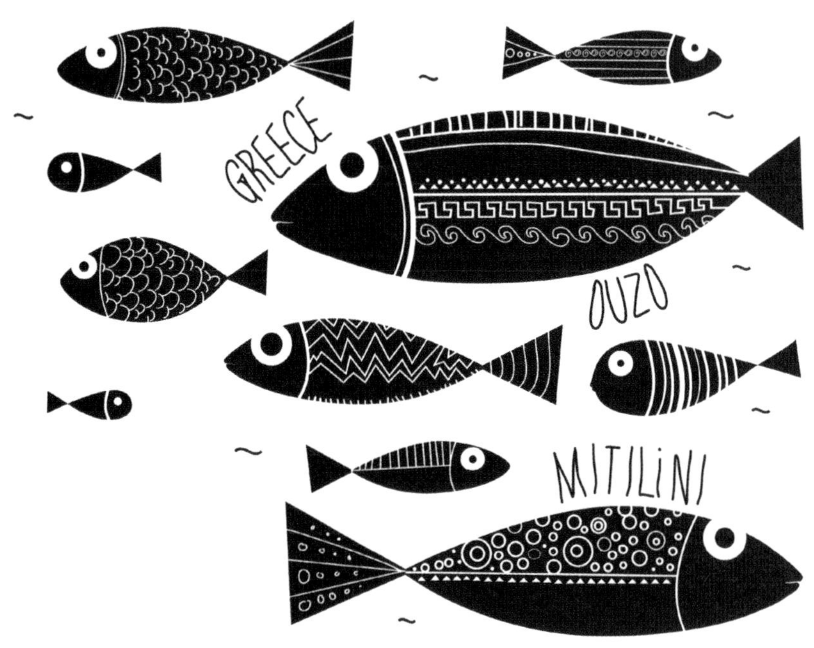
GREECE
OUZO
MITILINI

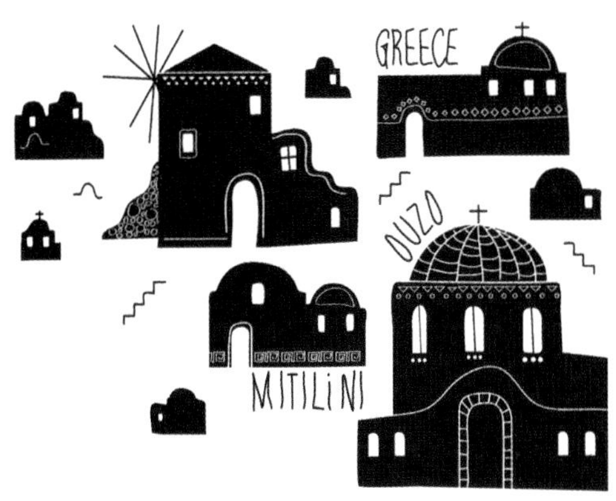
GREECE
OUZO
MITILINI

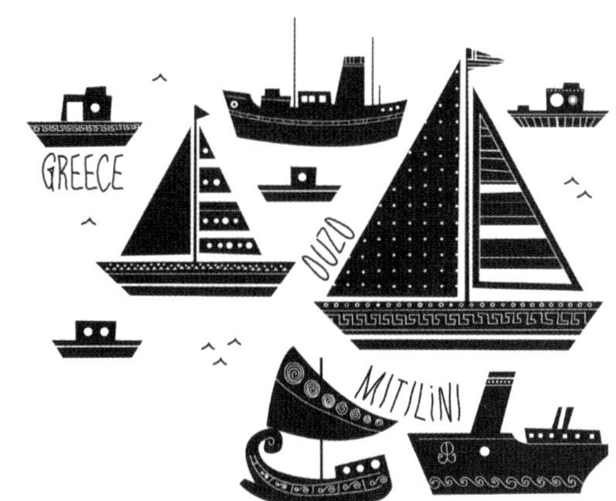
GREECE
OUZO
MITILINI

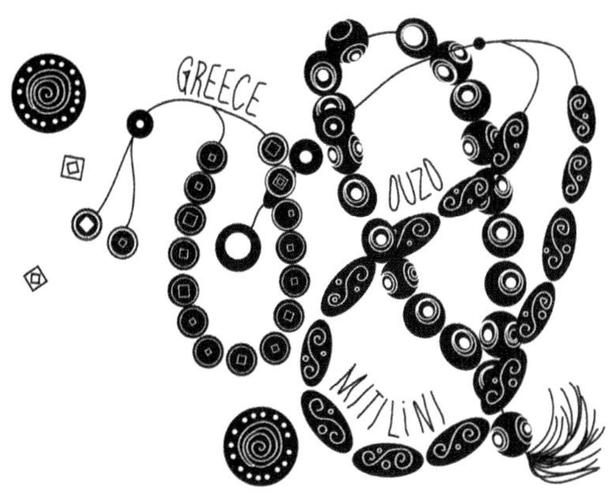
GREECE
OUZO
MITILINI

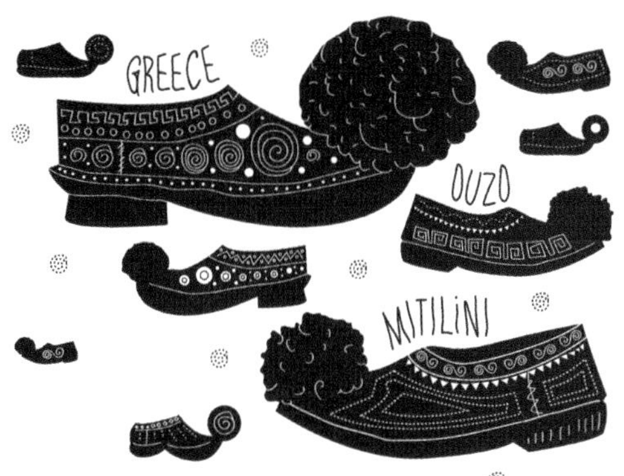
GREECE
OUZO
MITILINI

Once a forgotten architectural masterpiece, No. 1 Regent Street now serves as a world-class restaurant space. Illustration was key in marking the three chapters, with antlers hinting at the restoration, a coffee plant for the rich gastronomic history and a classic ironwork lift to introduce the new architectural space.

Illustration: Emily Robertson
Client: The Crown Estate

dn&co.

No. 1 Regent Street

Once a forgotten architectural masterpiece, No. 1 Regent Street now serves as a world-class restaurant space. Illustration was key in marking the three chapters, with antlers hinting at the restoration, a coffee plant for the rich gastronomic history and a classic ironwork lift to introduce the new architectural space.

Illustration: Emily Robertson
Client: The Crown Estate

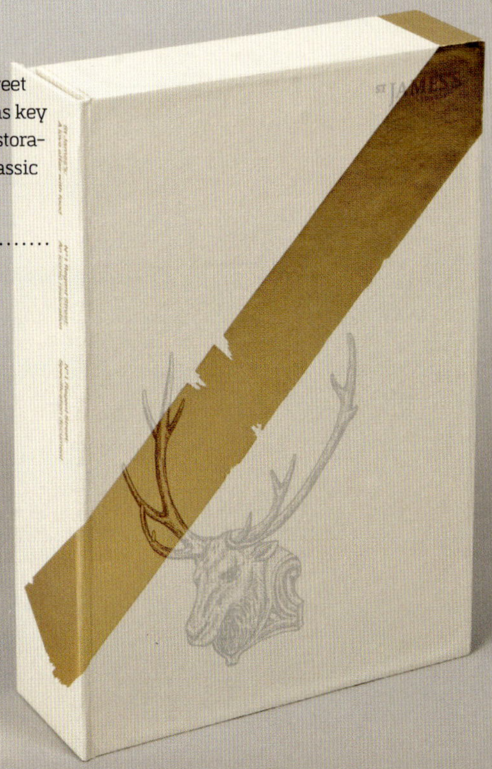

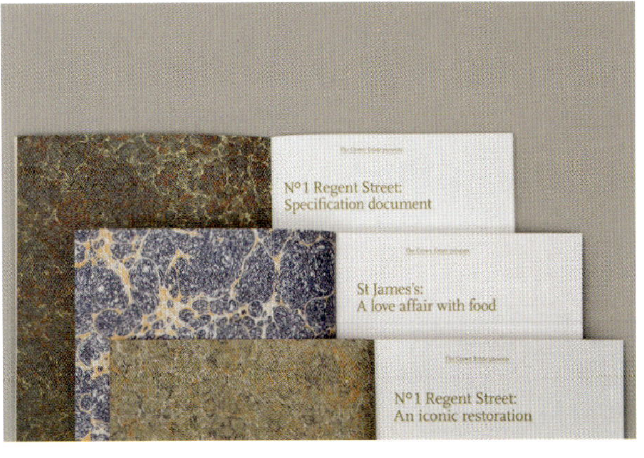

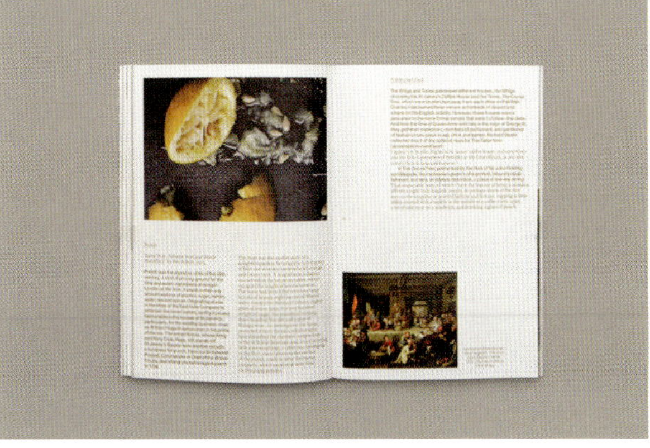

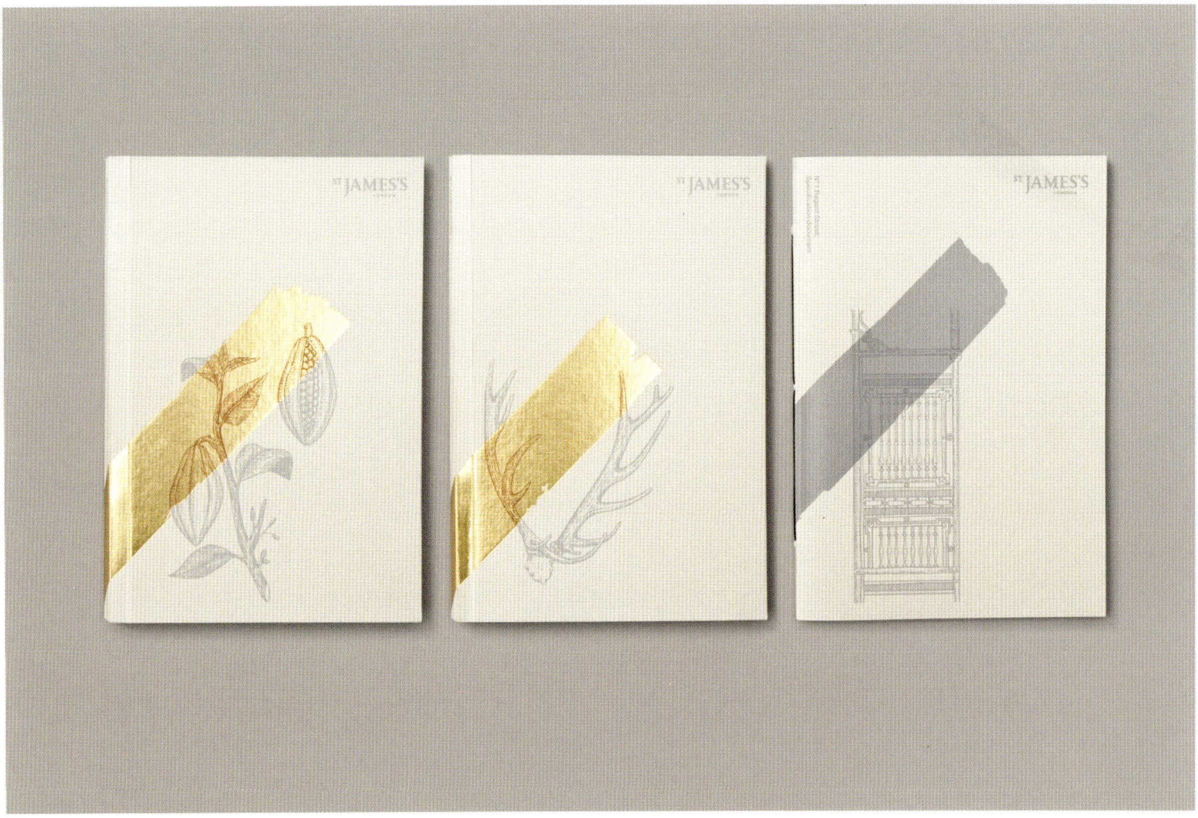

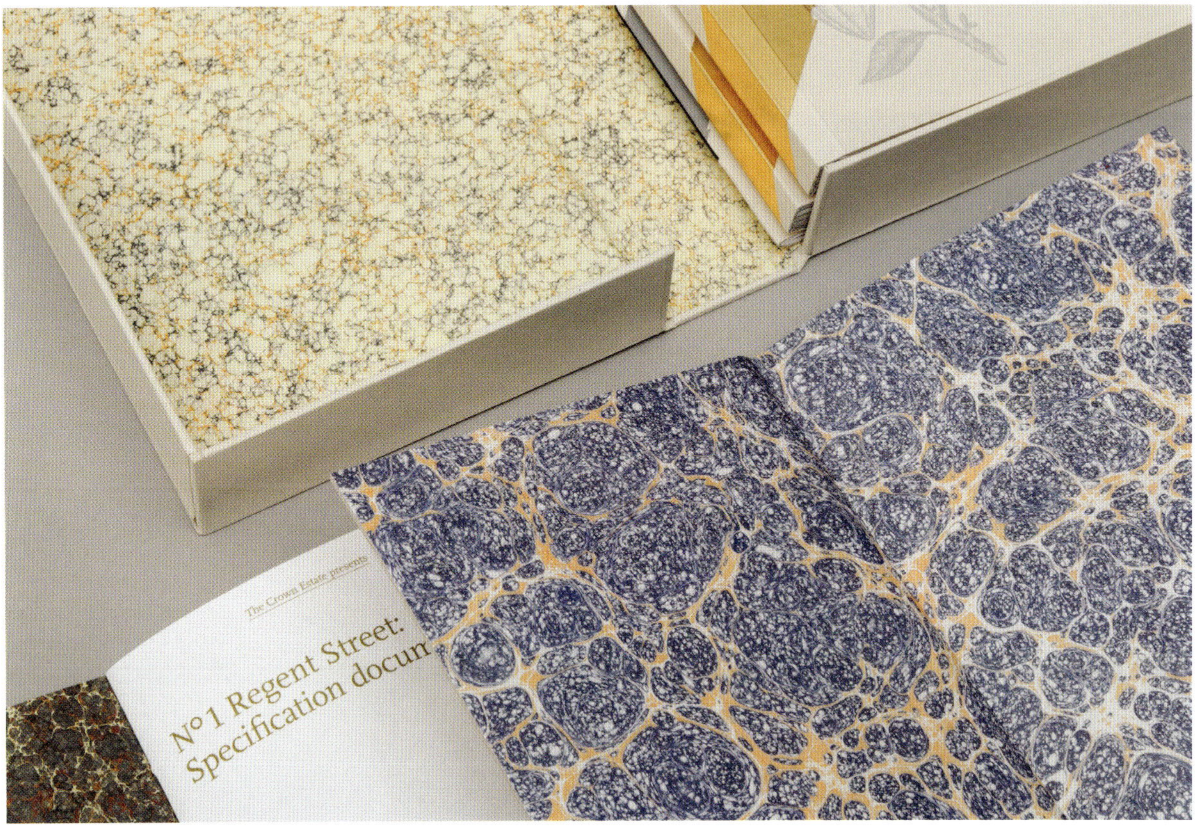

Hushh Stewards Soapery

A soap packaging project featuring five mythical goddesses who claim their own sacred steward to conceal private love lives, fortunes, and tragedies. Each product box features an iconic owls that are historically paired with their deity.

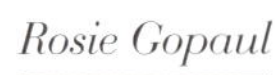

Rosie Gopaul

Hushh Stewards Soapery

A soap packaging project featuring five mythical goddesses who claim their own sacred steward to conceal private love lives, fortunes, and tragedies. Each product box features an iconic owls that are historically paired with their deity.

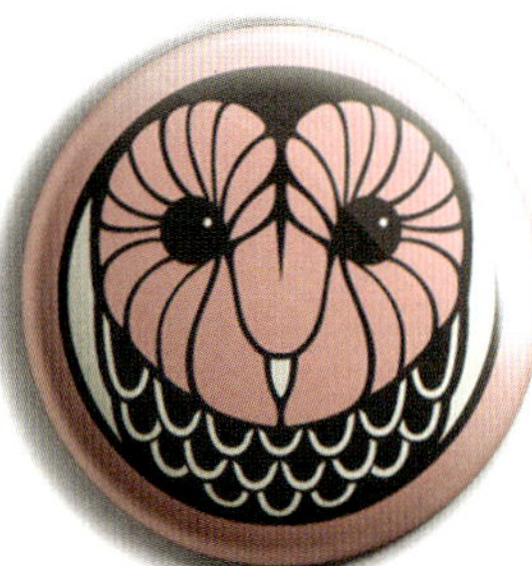

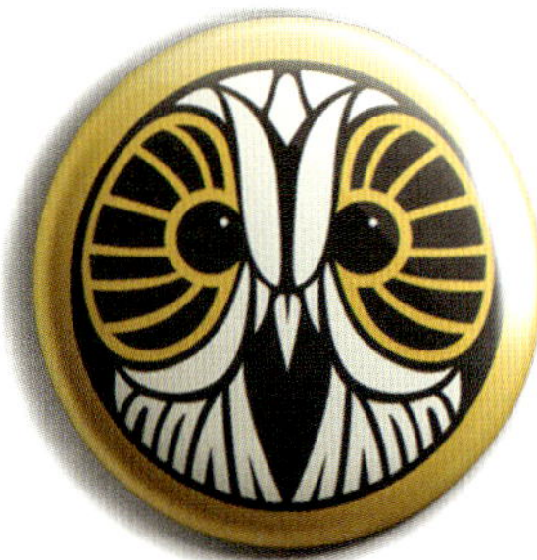

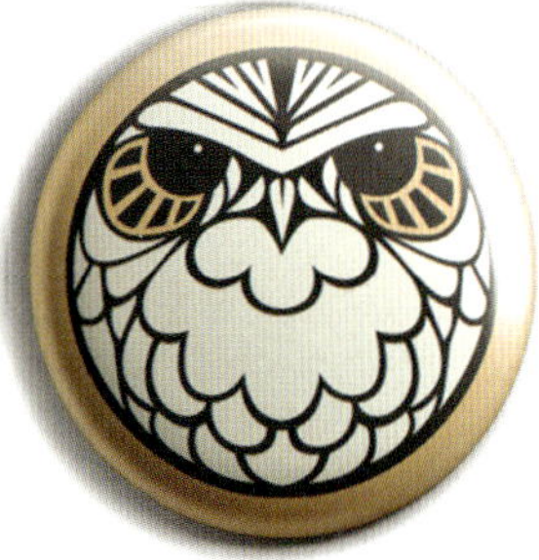

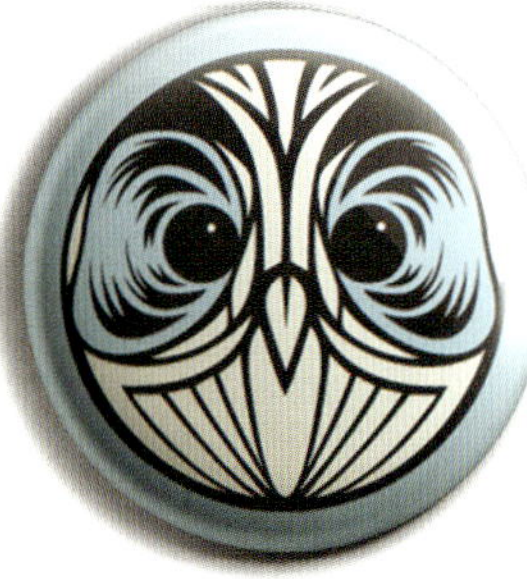

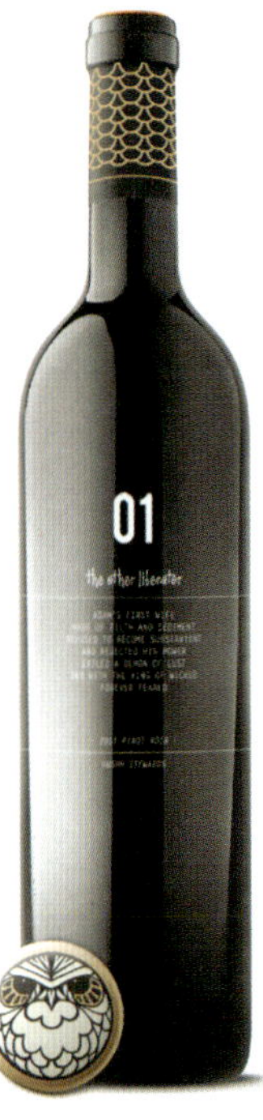

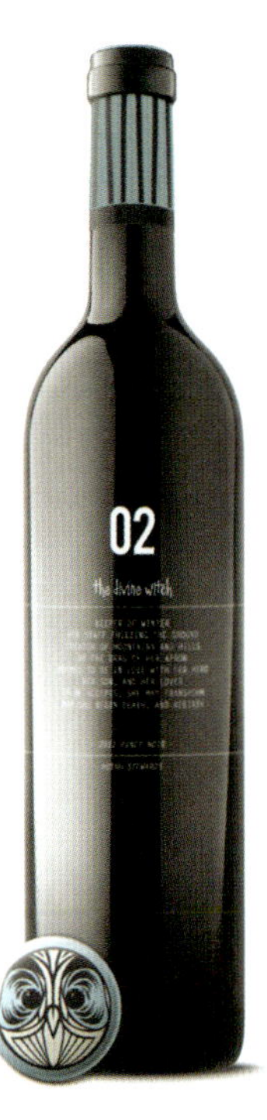

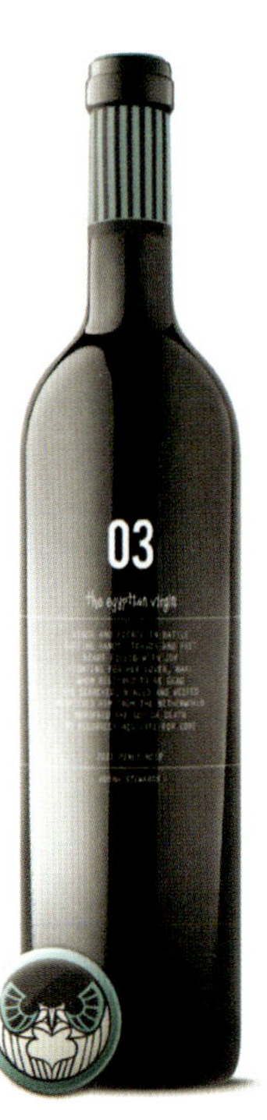

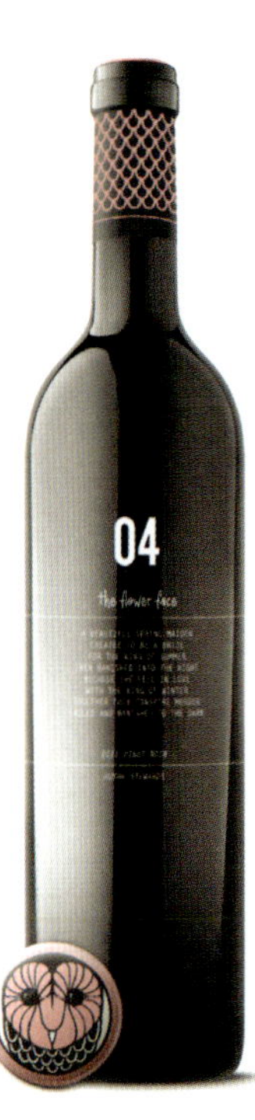

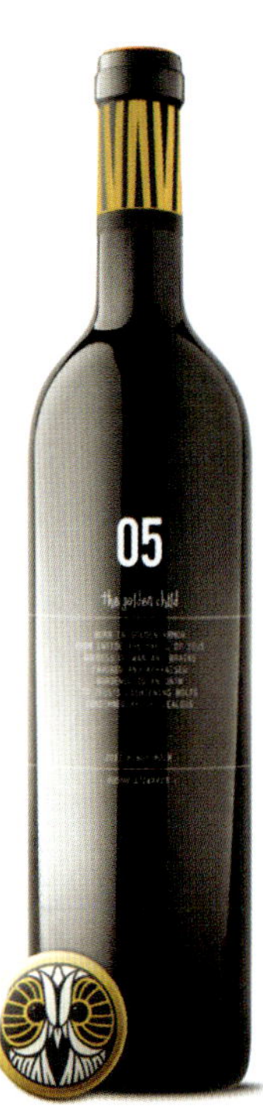

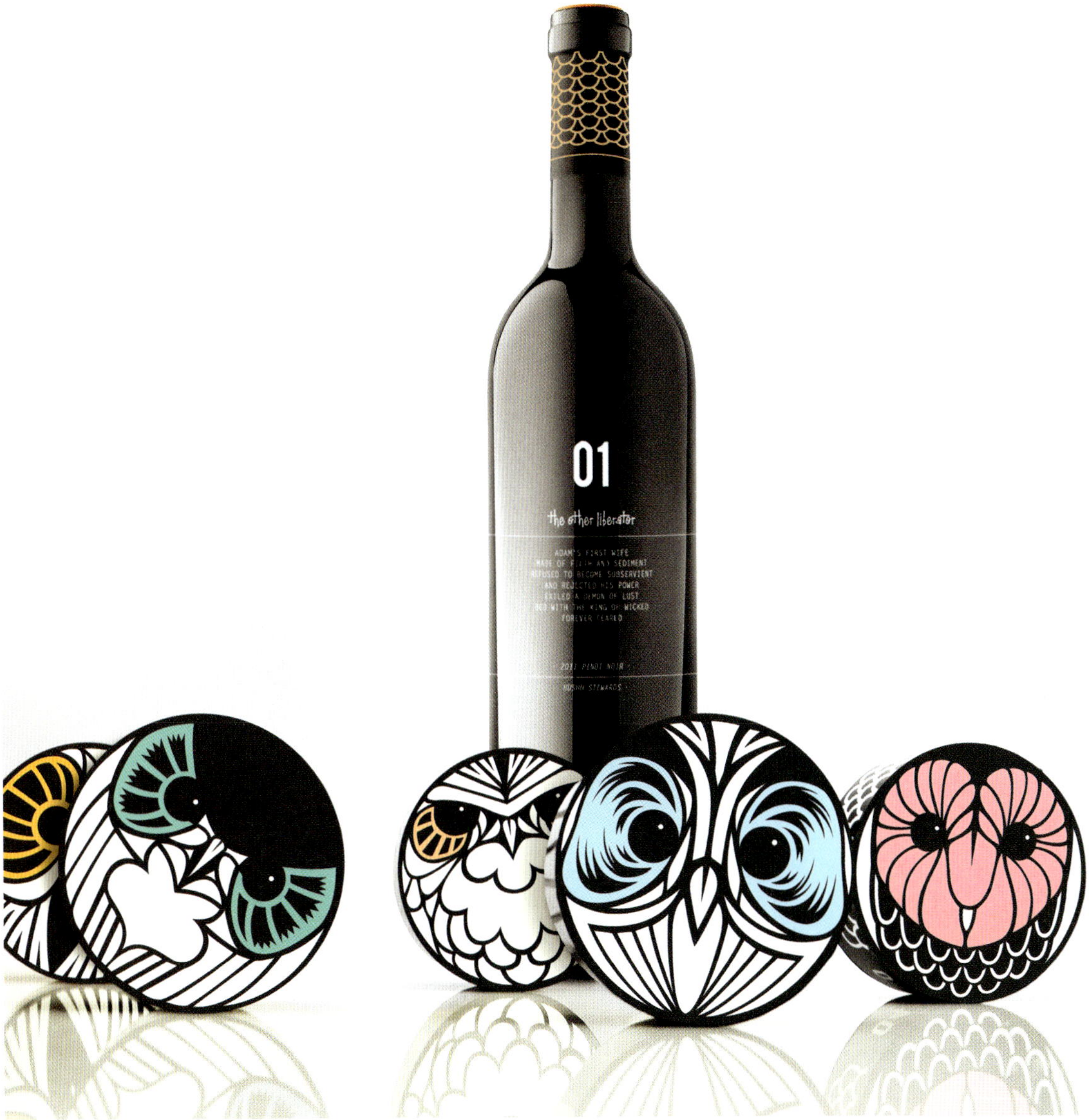

01
the other liberator
ADAM'S FIRST WIFE
REFUSED TO BECOME SUBSERVIENT
AND REJECTED HIS POWER
EXILED A DEMON OF LUST
2011 PINOT NOIR

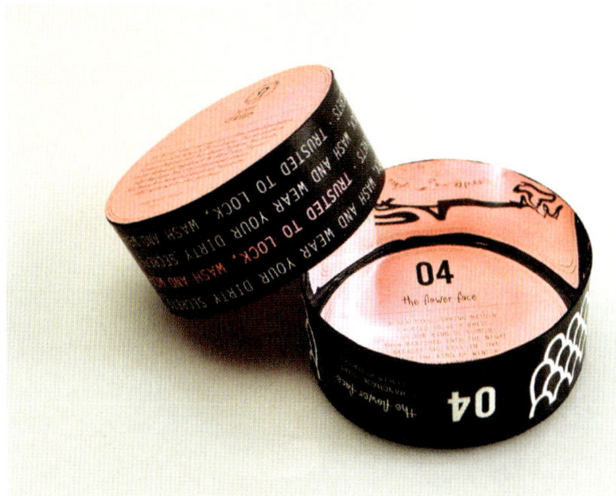
04
the flower face
04

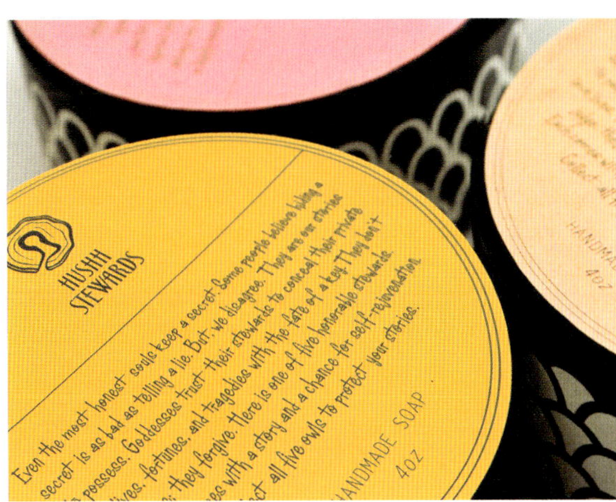
HUSHH STEWARDS
HANDMADE SOAP
4oz

Tattoo Care Range is a specialist product line specially developed for inked skin. A catchy name, hipster-esque typography, classic tattoo designs and striking colours are balanced with clean and cosmetic cred-ibility to attract everyone, from the newly-inked to the hardcore tattoo lovers.

Robot Food

Tattoo Care Range

Tattoo Care Range is a specialist product line specially developed for inked skin. A catchy name, hipster-esque typography, classic tattoo designs and striking colours are balanced with clean and cosmetic cred-ibility to attract everyone, from the newly-inked to the hardcore tattoo lovers.

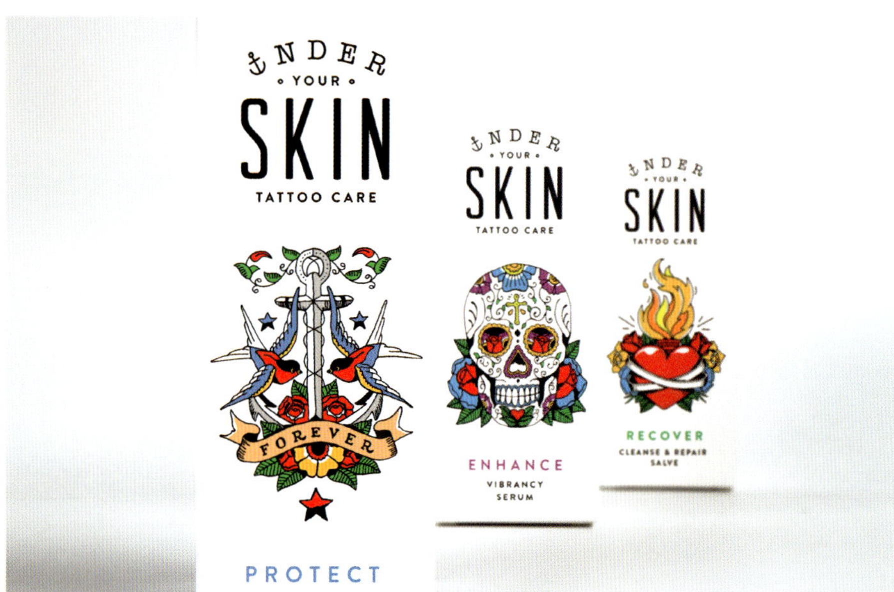

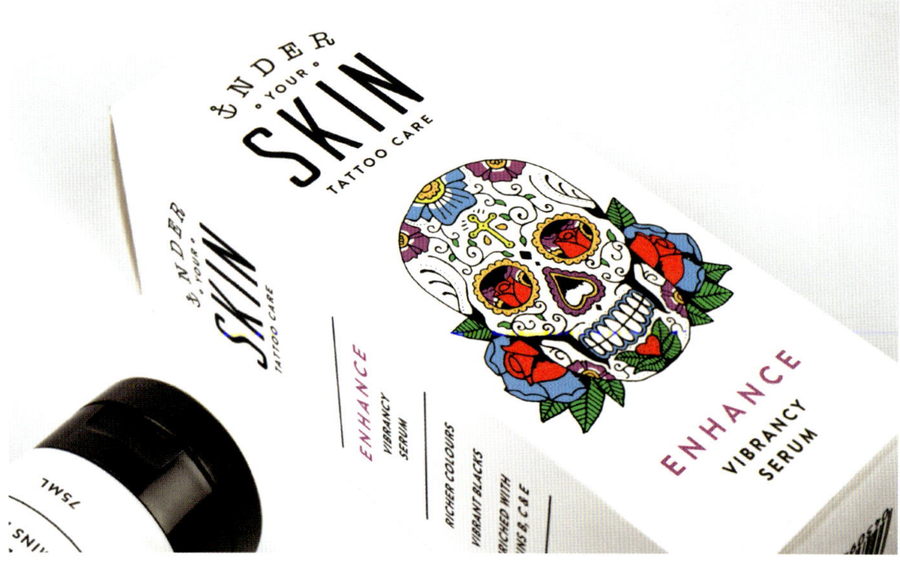

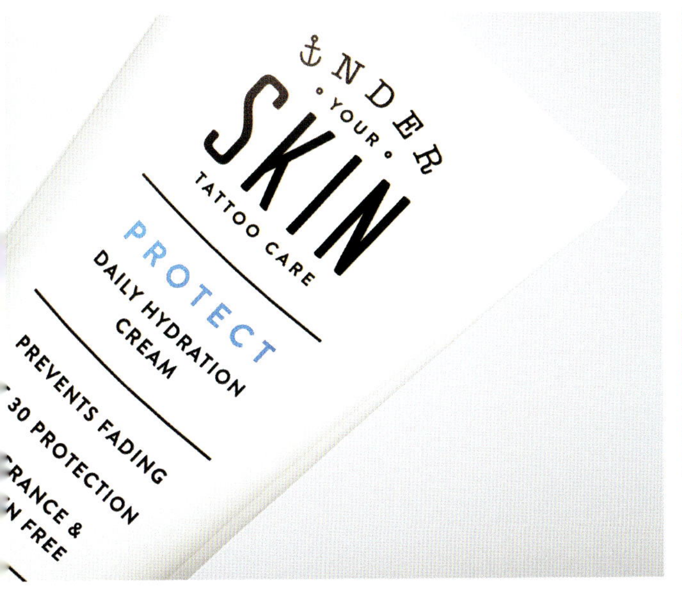
NDER
YOUR
SKIN
TATTOO CARE
PROTECT
DAILY HYDRATION
CREAM
PREVENTS FADING

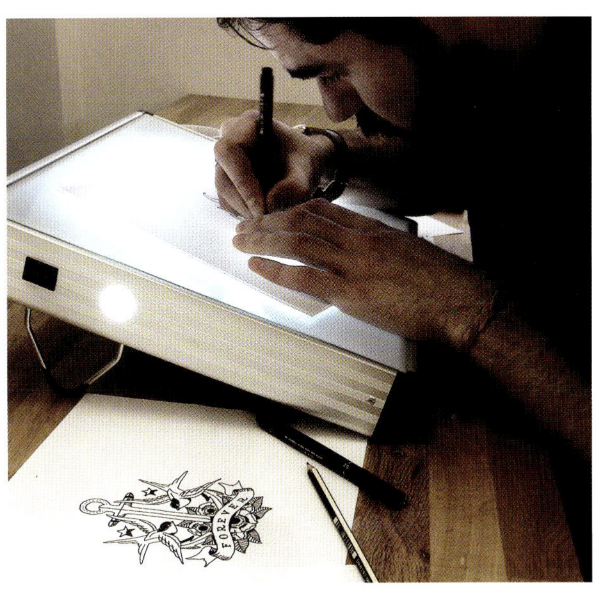
FOREVER

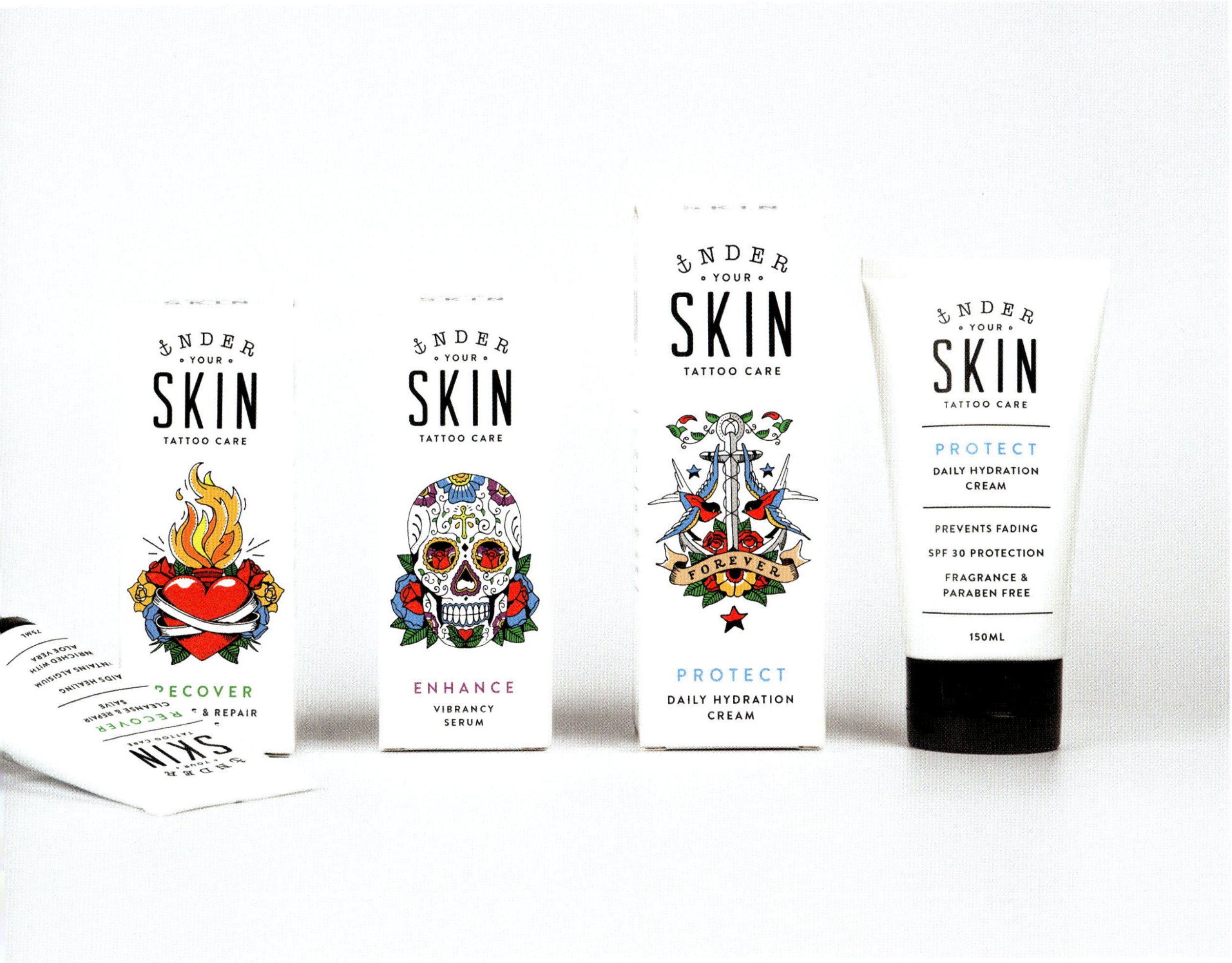

A well-balanced lifestyle is what this mineral water is designed and promoted for. A literal description of its content, a transparent band wrapped in illustrated wild grass enables unobstructed views of the wild-grass-infused mineral water in consumers' hand.

Design: Naonori Yago
Illustration: Toshiaki Watanabe
Client: Patisserie Potager

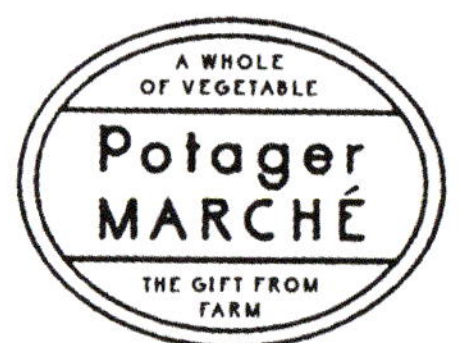

野草の
ふしぎ

WELL-BALANCED WILD GRASS
MINERAL WATER

village®

Potager MARCHÉ

A well-balanced lifestyle is what this mineral water is designed and promoted for. A literal description of its content, a transparent band wrapped in illustrated wild grass enables unobstructed views of the wild-grass-infused mineral water in consumers' hand.

Design: Naonori Yago
Illustration: Toshiaki Watanabe
Client: Patisserie Potager

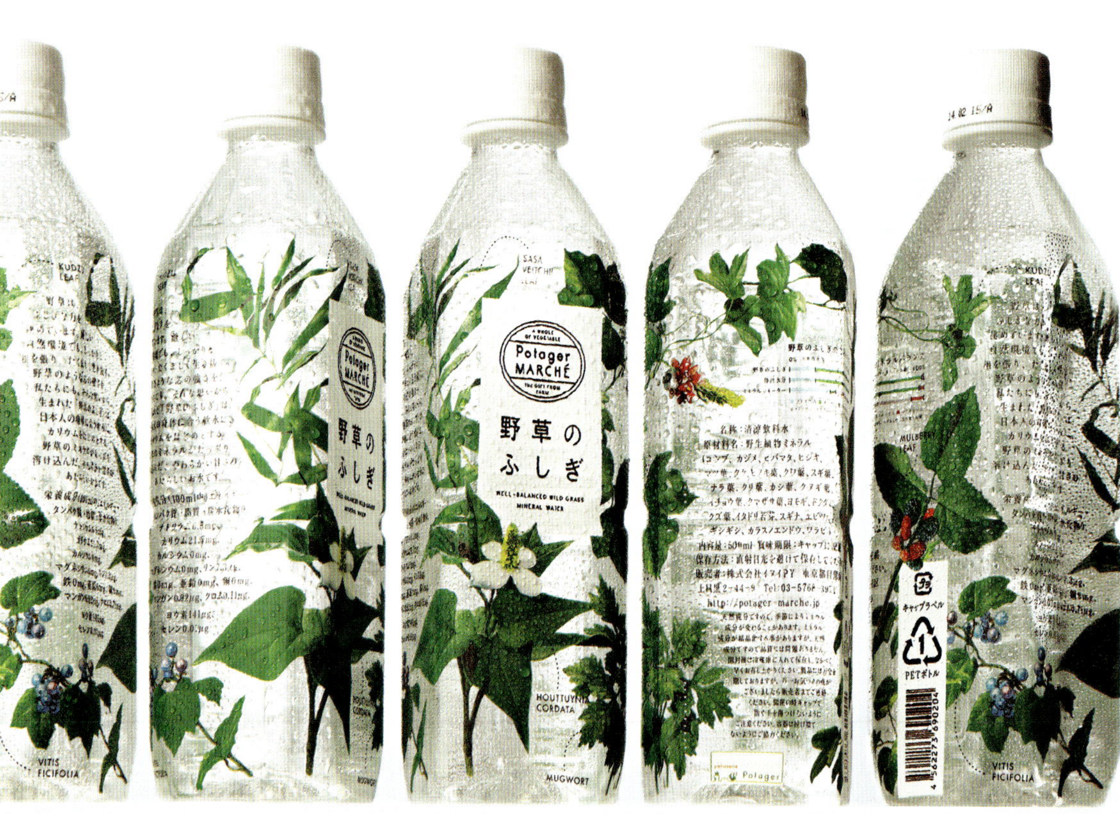

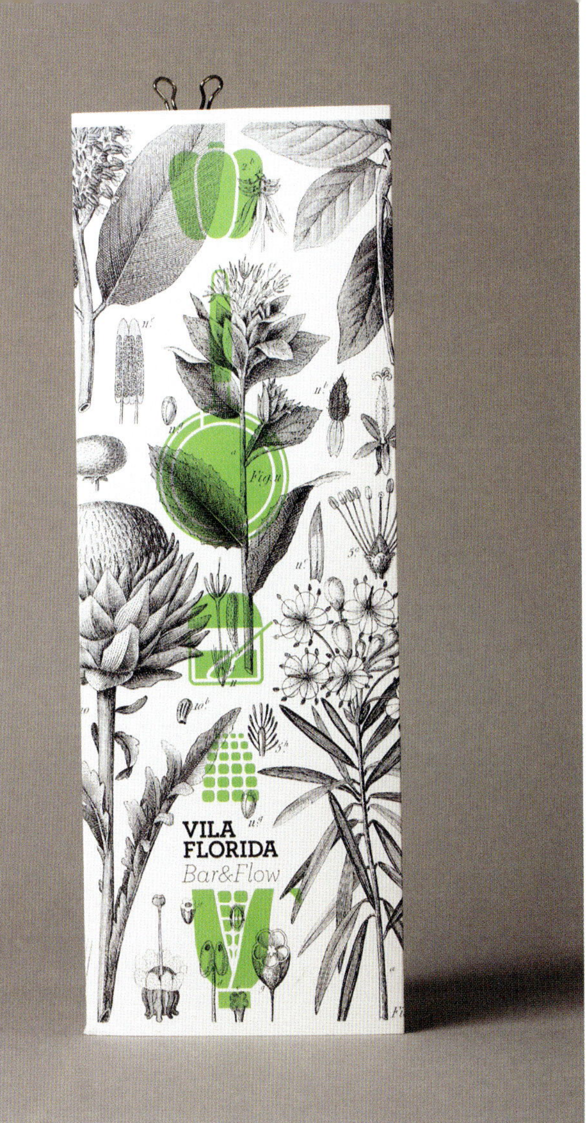

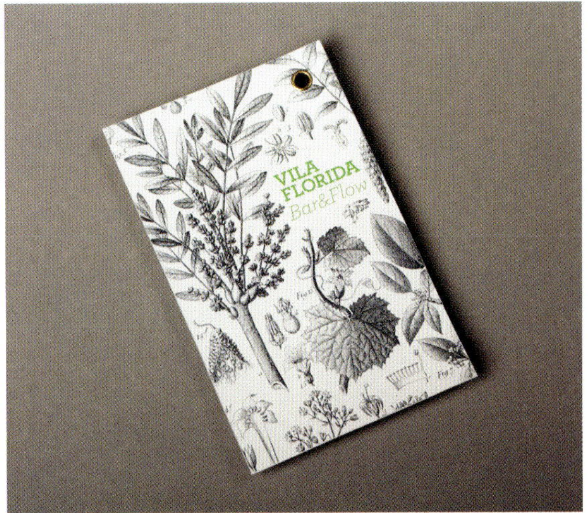

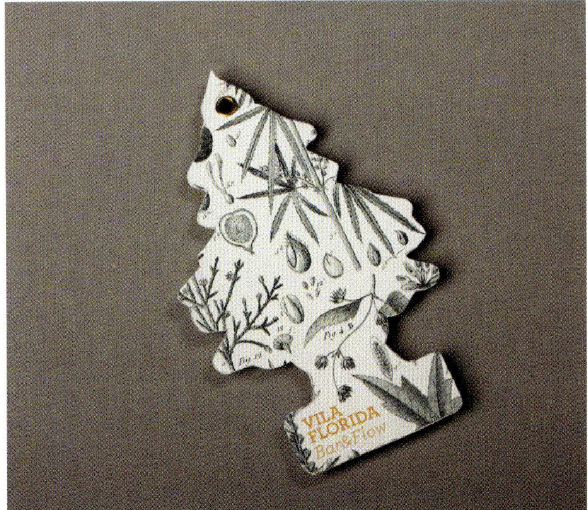

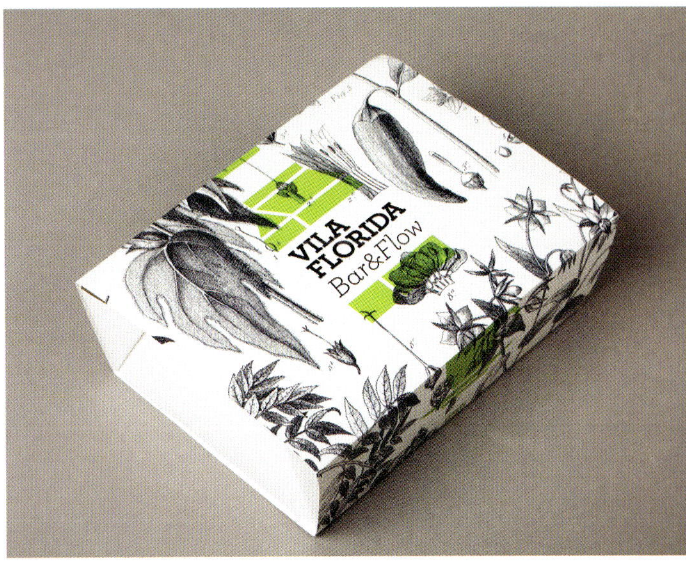

Lo Siento

Vila Florida

Vila Florida is a restaurant and bar set inside a civic centre. Embellished with a garden, the eatery also conceived a visual identity where lush greenery backgrounded its name. A fresh green accents the monochrome details on its packaging and collateral.

Client: Ana&Pitu

Lo Siento

Vila Florida

Vila Florida is a restaurant and bar set inside a civic centre. Embellished with a garden, the eatery also conceived a visual identity where lush greenery backgrounded its name. A fresh green accents the mono-

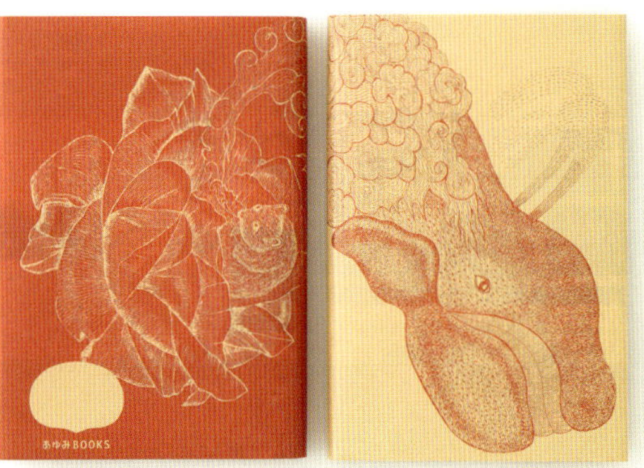

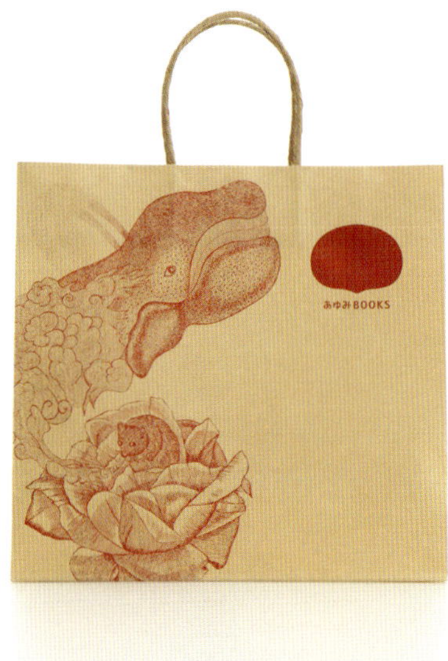

Hara Design Institute

Ayumi Books

It's a custom for Japanese book stores to attach paper covers to every book at check out. Featuring the fantastic animals drawn by Kazumasa Nagai, the shop's signature book covers reveal a strong, artistic individuality next to the book store's logo, where a speech balloon suggests the generation of images and words.

Illustration: Kazumasa Nagai
Client: Ayumi Books

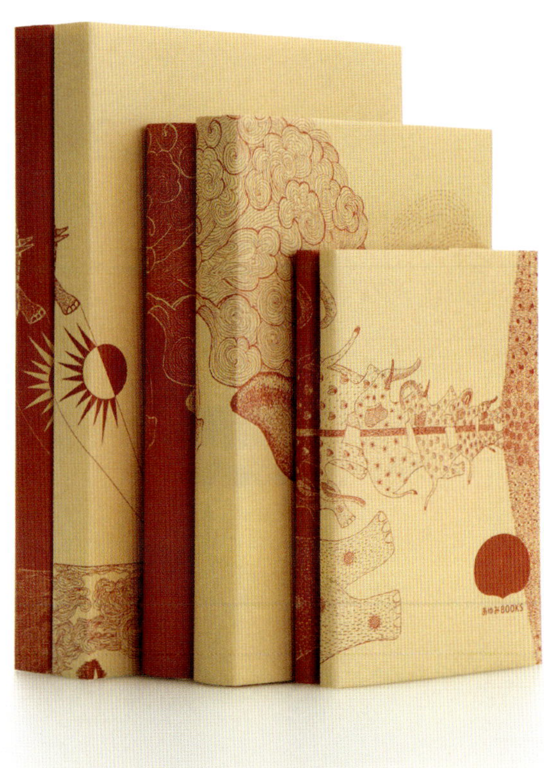

Hara Design Institute

Ayumi Books

It's a custom for Japanese book stores to attach paper covers to every book at check out. Featuring the fantastic animals drawn by Kazumasa Nagai, the shop's signature book covers reveal a strong, artistic individuality next to the book store's logo, where a speech balloon

The Meat Preachers

Zamora Homemade is all about enjoying homemade food, made with fine, natural New Zealand ingredients in traditional South American and European recipes and a modern twist. Graphic elements in the branding system emphasises its belief in staying true to the owners' heritage.

Client: Zamora

Bardo

Zamora
The Meat Preachers

Zamora Homemade is all about enjoying homemade food, made with fine, natural New Zealand ingredients in traditional South American and European recipes and a modern twist. Graphic elements in the branding system emphasises its belief in staying true to the owners' heritage.

Client: Zamora

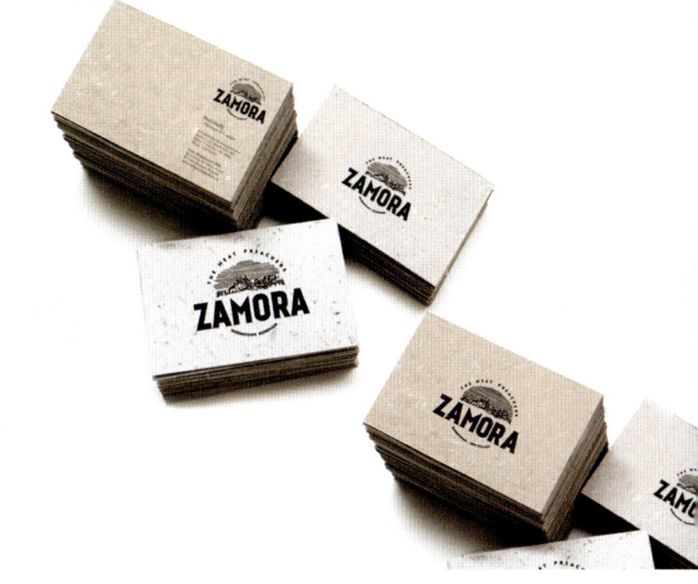

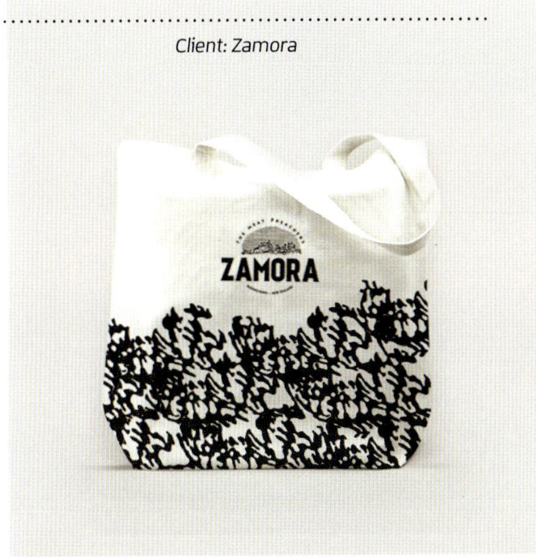

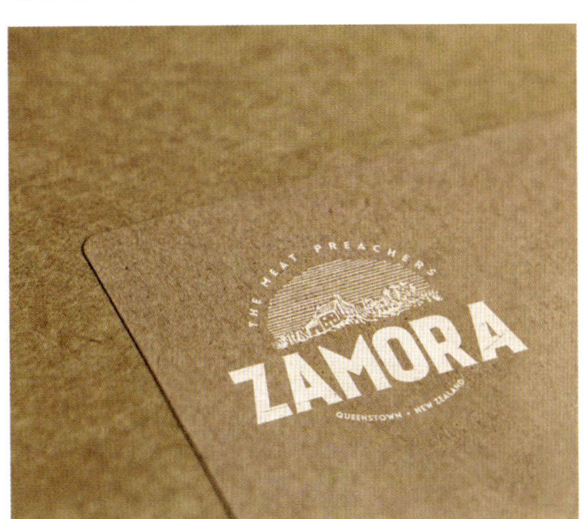

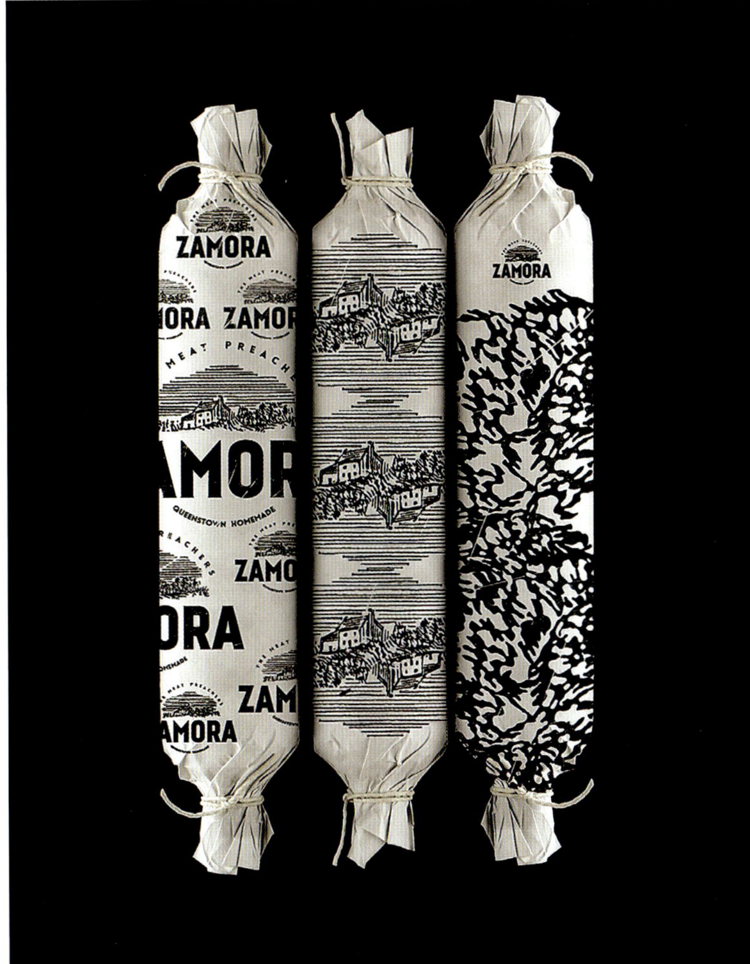

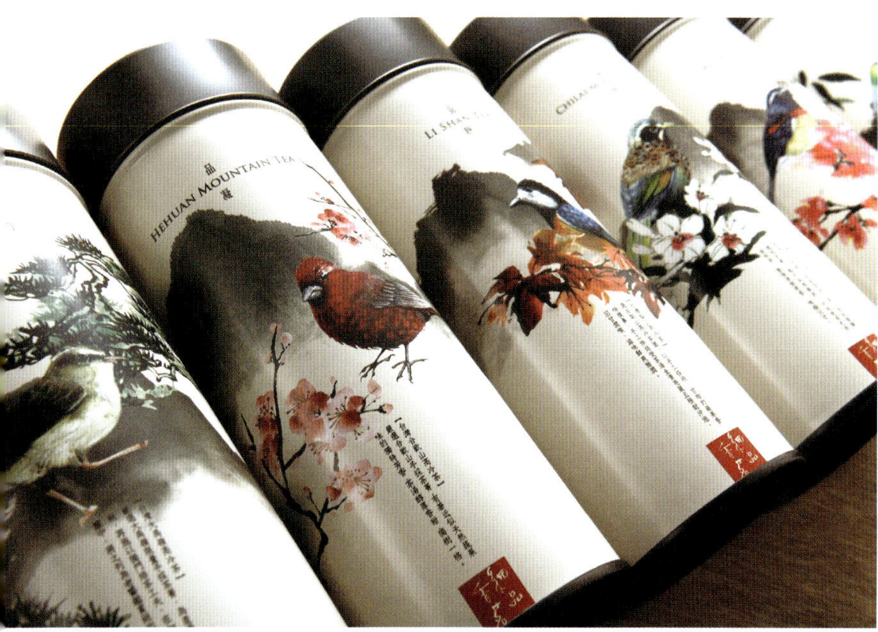
HEHUAN MOUNTAIN TEA

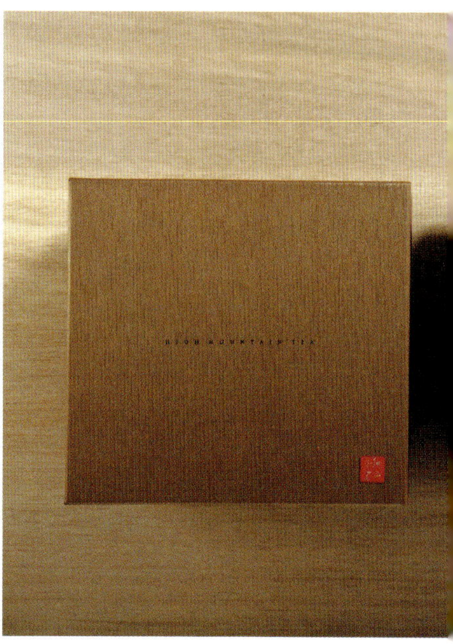

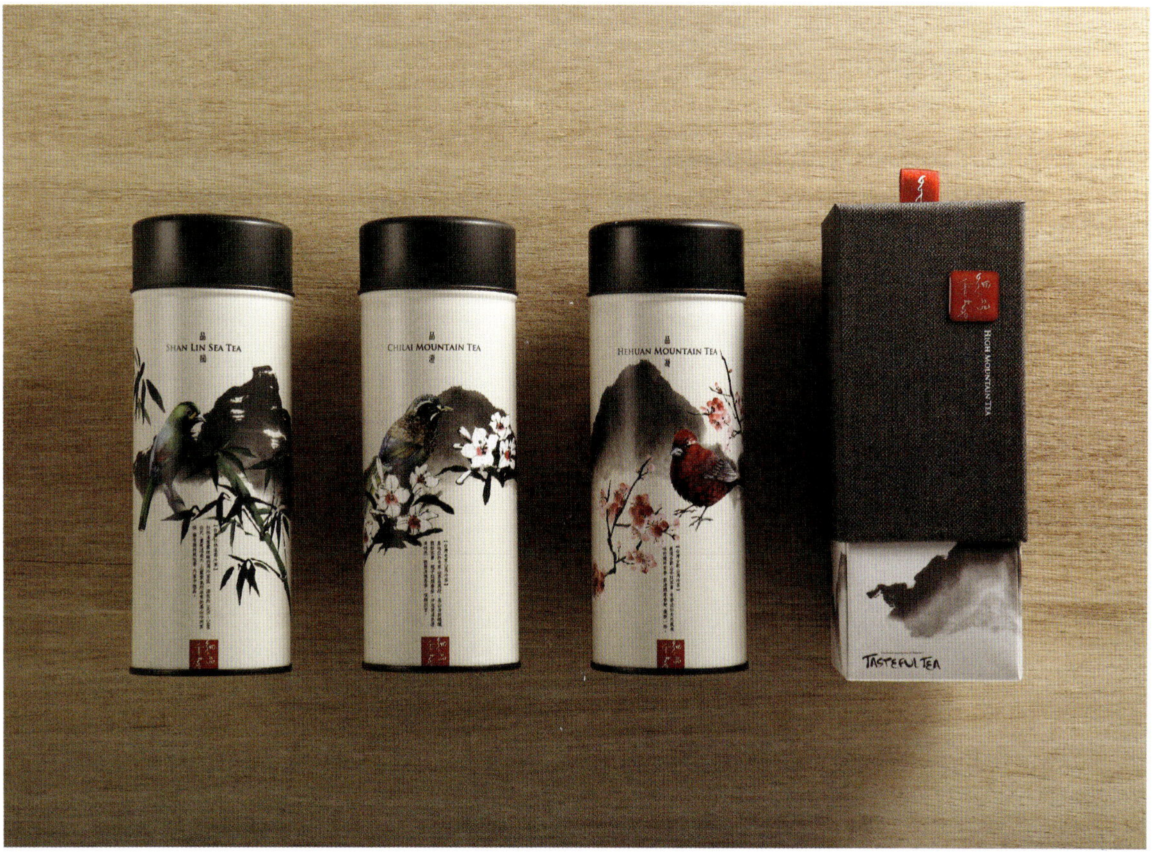

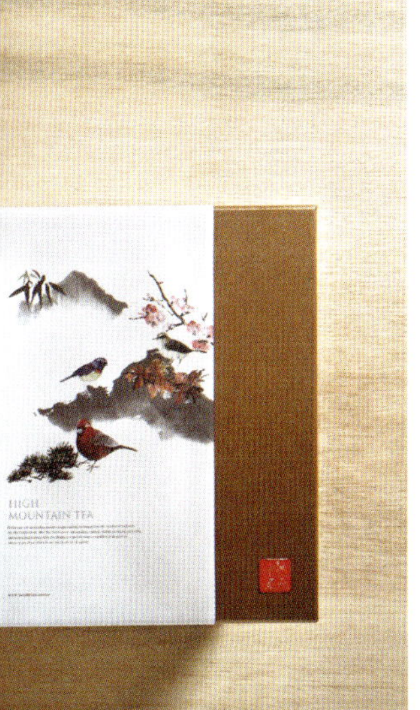

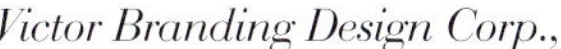

Taiwan High Mountain Tea

Heavenly landscape often suggests where teas are grown and thus its quality. But when traditional Chinese ink painting unites with colour paintings, the result brings the exquisite moments of tea drinking matched with modern lifestyle. Here, plants and bird species specifically represent the tea's origins.

Client: Tasteful Tea

Victor Branding Design Corp.,

Taiwan High Mountain Tea

Heavenly landscape often suggests where teas are grown and thus its quality. But when traditional Chinese ink painting unites with colour paintings, the result brings the exquisite moments of tea drinking matched with modern lifestyle. Here, plants and bird species specifically represent the tea's origins.

Client: Tasteful Tea

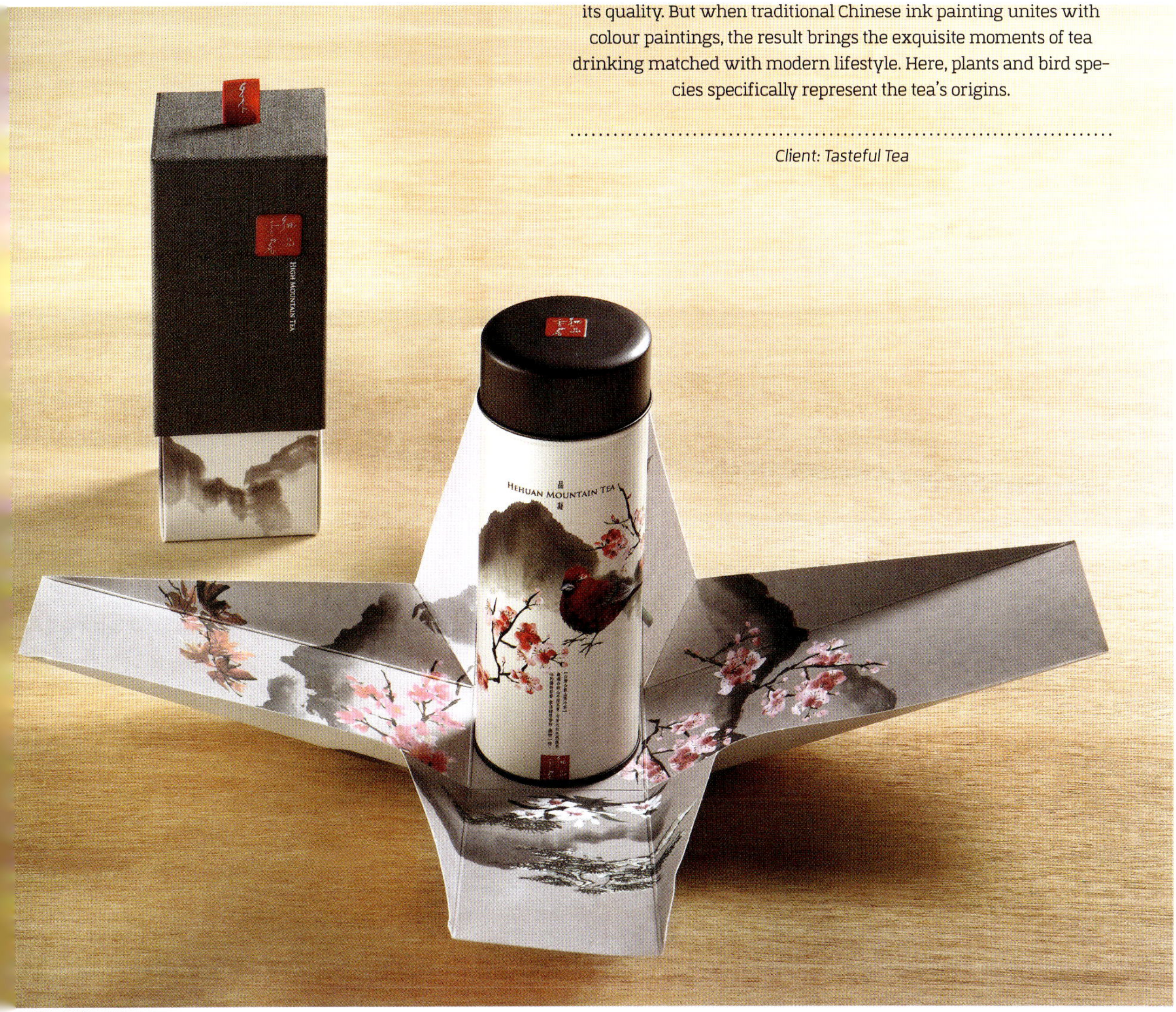

Mingren Mingyan is a tea brand based in China's in Fujian Province. The label presents two teas with distinctive flavours. Named "Mingyin" (chanting of tea) and "Yanyu" (words of rocks), corresponding graphics were used to illustrate the meanings, blended with traditions and culture.

Client: Mingren Mingyan Tea

ONE & ONE DESIGN

Mingren Mingyan

Mingren Mingyan is a tea brand based in China's in Fujian Province. The label presents two teas with distinctive flavours. Named "Mingyin" (chanting of tea) and "Yanyu" (words of rocks), corresponding graphics were used to illustrate the meanings, blended with traditions and culture.

Client: Mingren Mingyan Tea

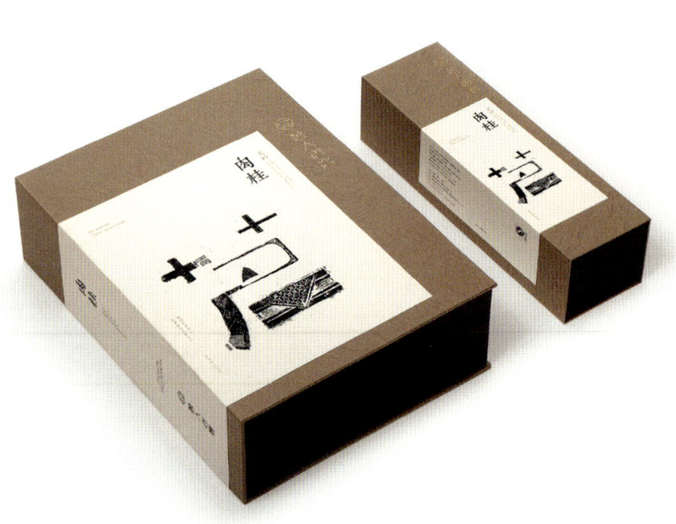

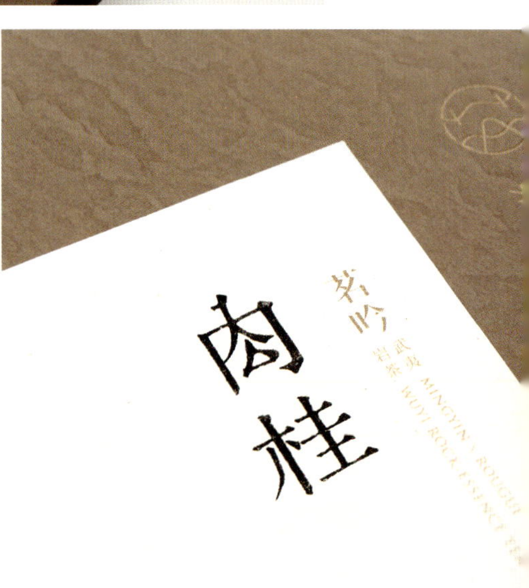

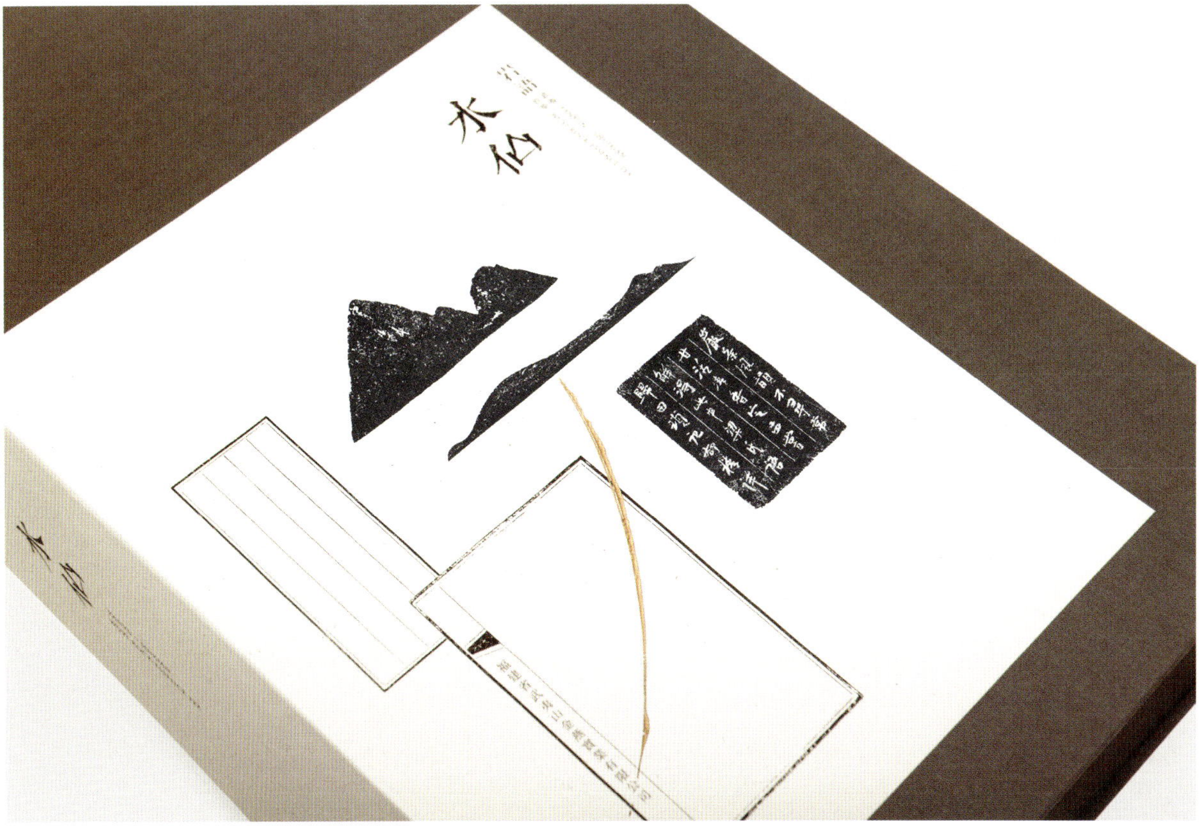

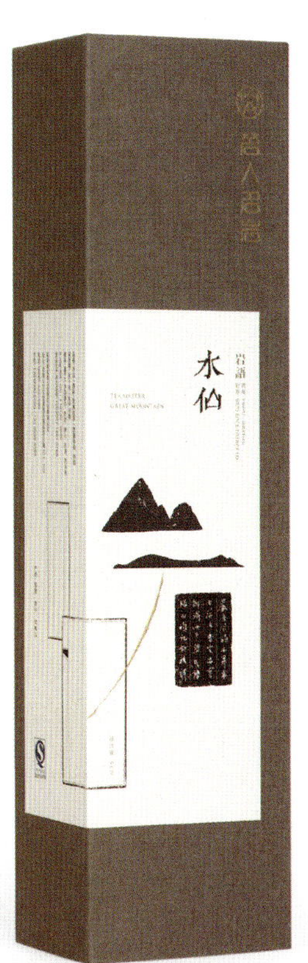

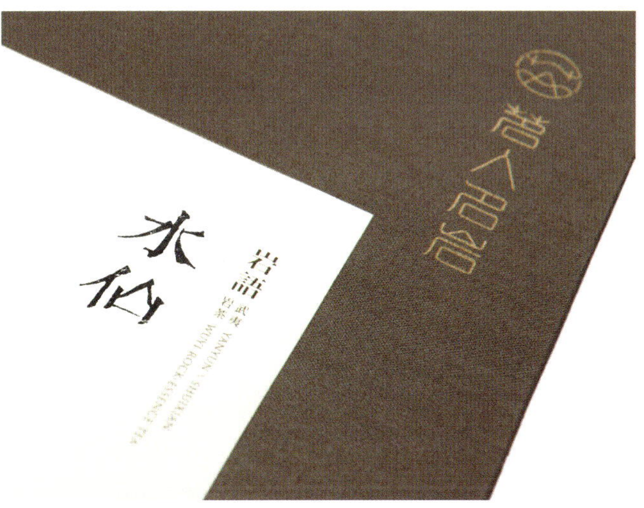

水仙
岩語
武夷
岩茶
YANYUN · SHUIXIAN
WUYI ROCK ESSENCE TEA

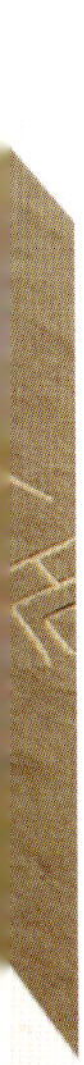

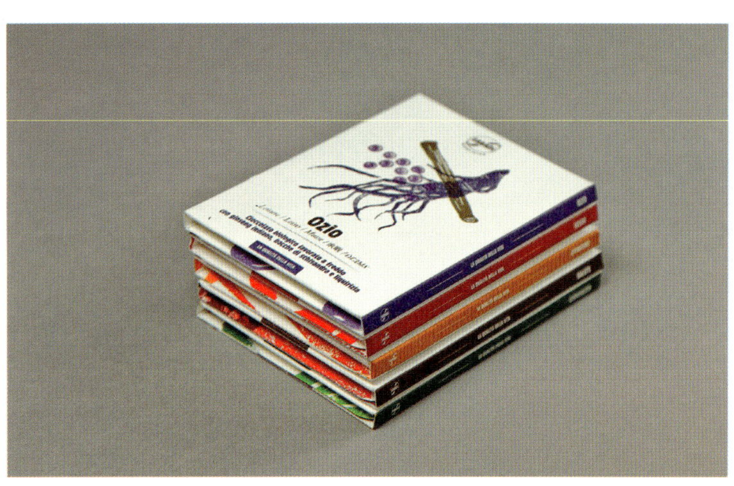

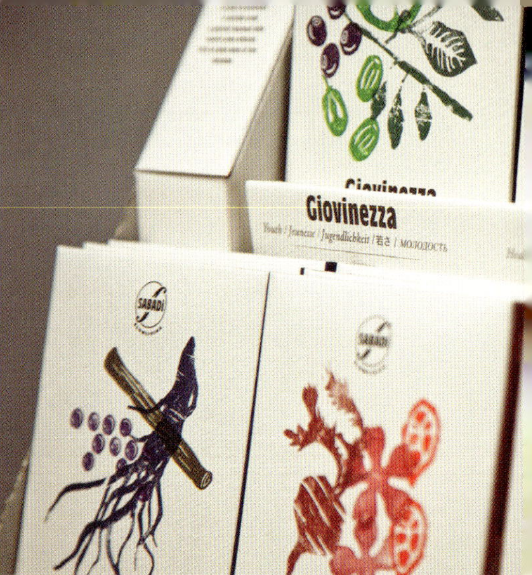

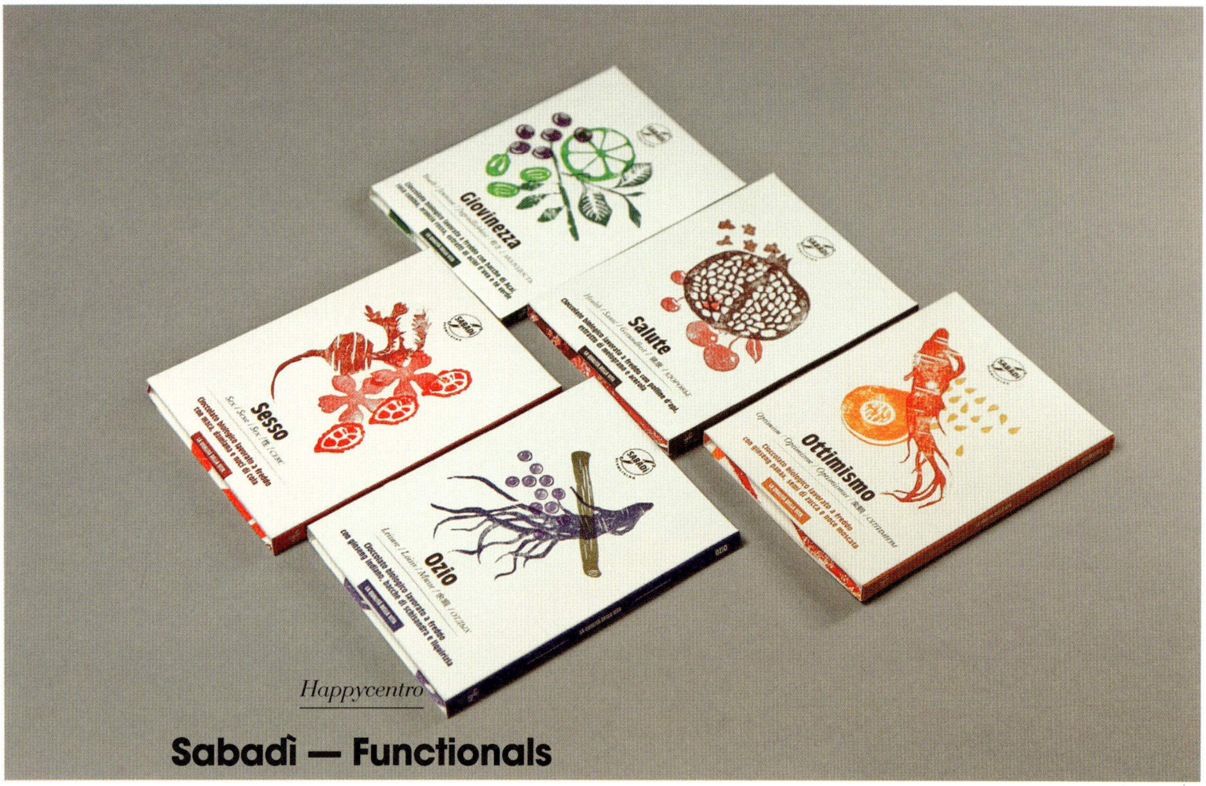

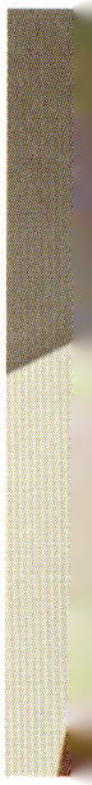

Happycentro

Sabadì — Functionals

Chocolatier Simon Sabaini believes youth, leisure, health, sex and optimism adds up to quality life. These elements can be literally acquired from cold-pressed organic Ecuadorian cocoa. Elemental linocuts hinted at the natural aromatic notes and metaphorically the virtues that affirm the wellness of life.

Design & illustration: Ilaria Roglieri, Roberto Solieri
Linocut: Anna Rodighiero
Client: Sabadì

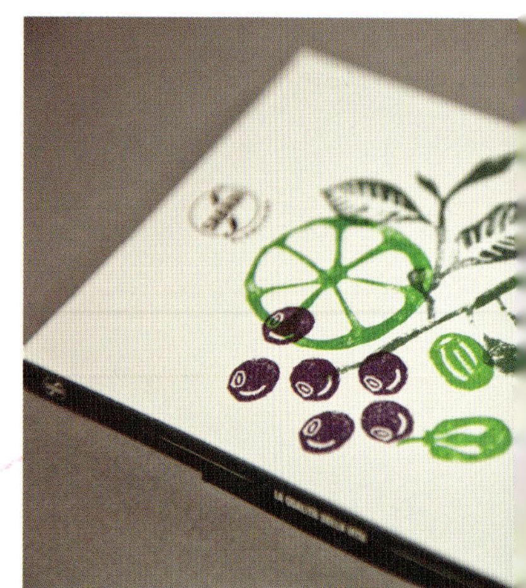

Happycentro

Sabadì — Functionals

Chocolatier Simon Sabaini believes youth, leisure, health, sex and

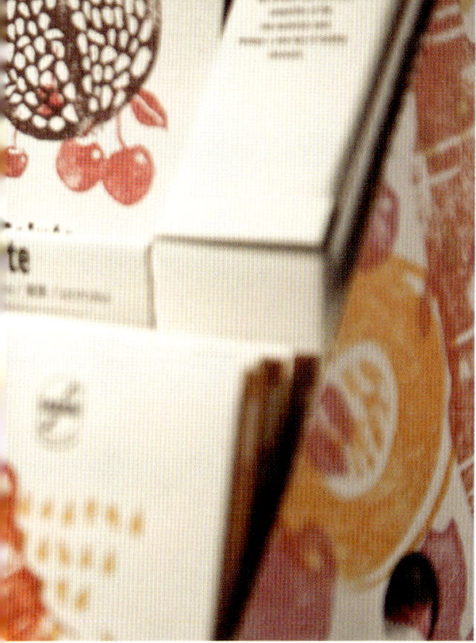

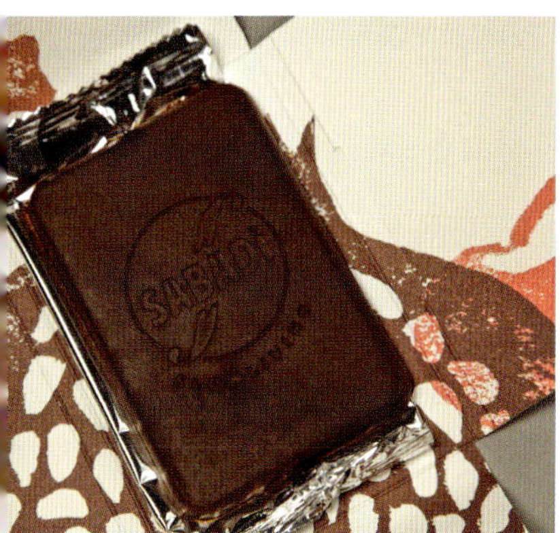

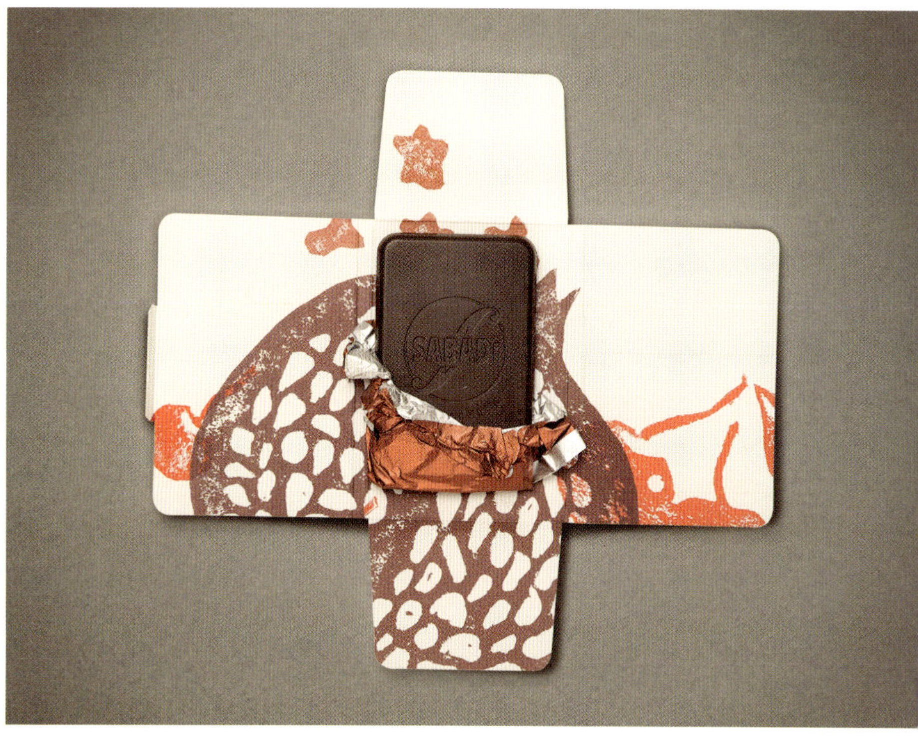

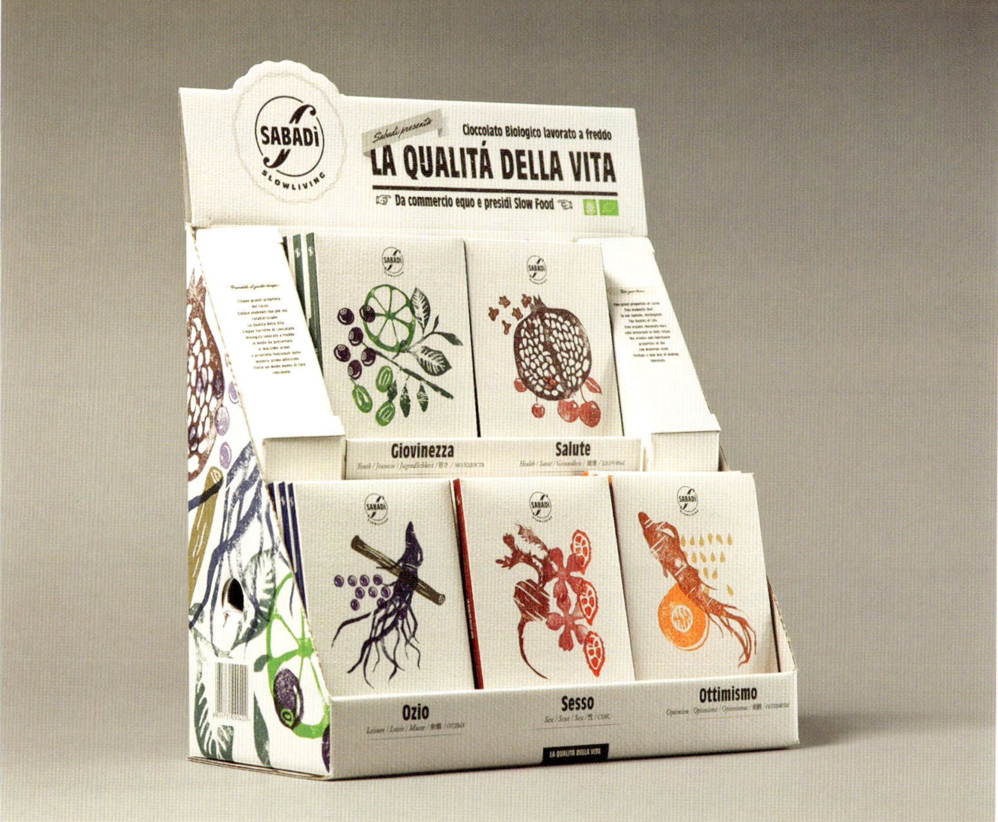
SABADÌ
SLOWLIVING
Cioccolato Biologico lavorato a freddo
LA QUALITÁ DELLA VITA
Da commercio equo e presidi Slow Food
Giovinezza
Salute
Ozio
Sesso
Ottimismo

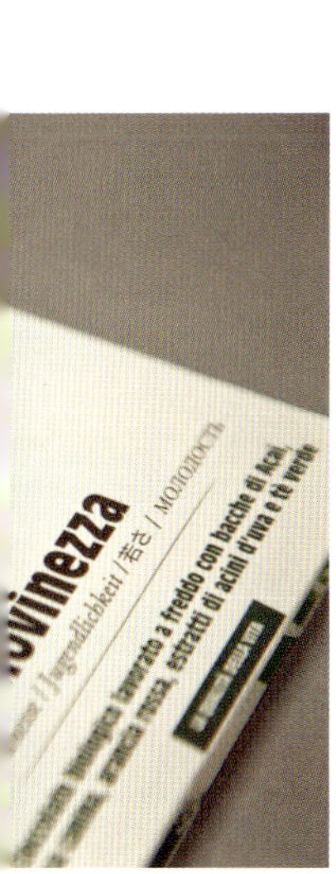

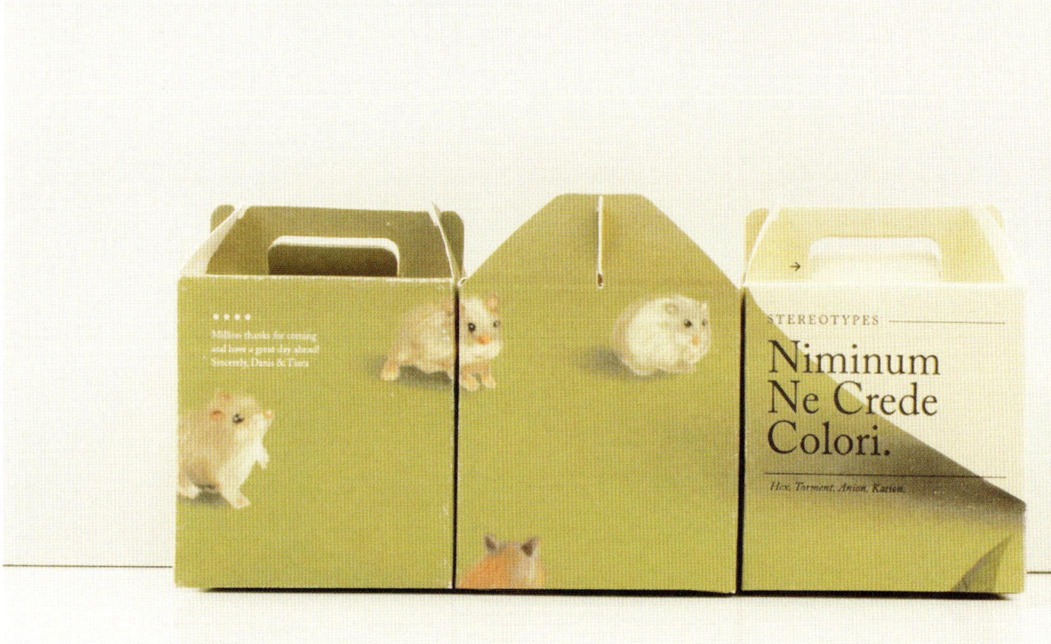

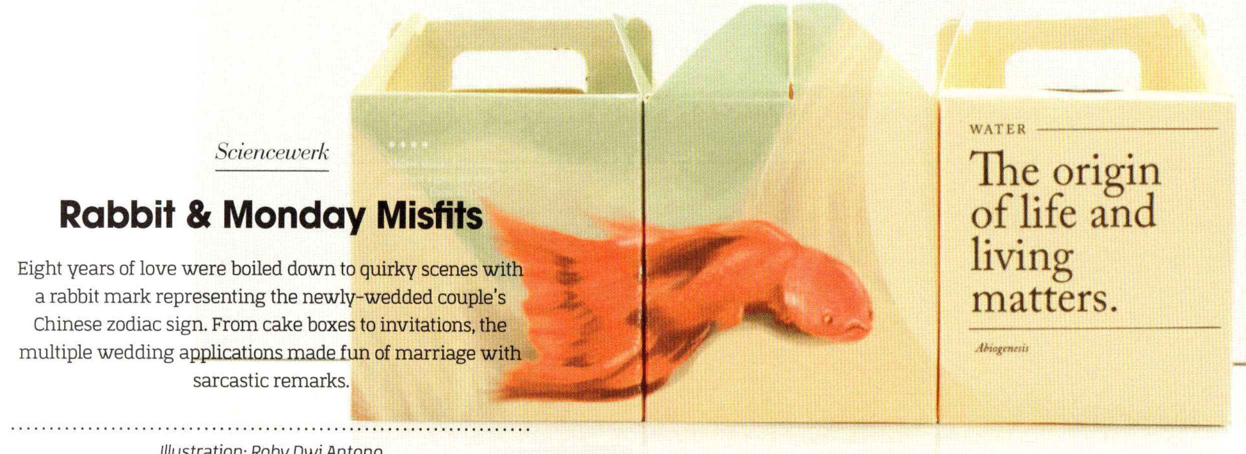

Sciencewerk

Rabbit & Monday Misfits

Eight years of love were boiled down to quirky scenes with a rabbit mark representing the newly-wedded couple's Chinese zodiac sign. From cake boxes to invitations, the multiple wedding applications made fun of marriage with sarcastic remarks.

Illustration: Roby Dwi Antono

Sciencewerk

Rabbit & Monday Misfits

Eight years of love were boiled down to quirky scenes with a rabbit mark representing the newly-wedded couple's Chinese zodiac sign. From cake boxes to invitations, the

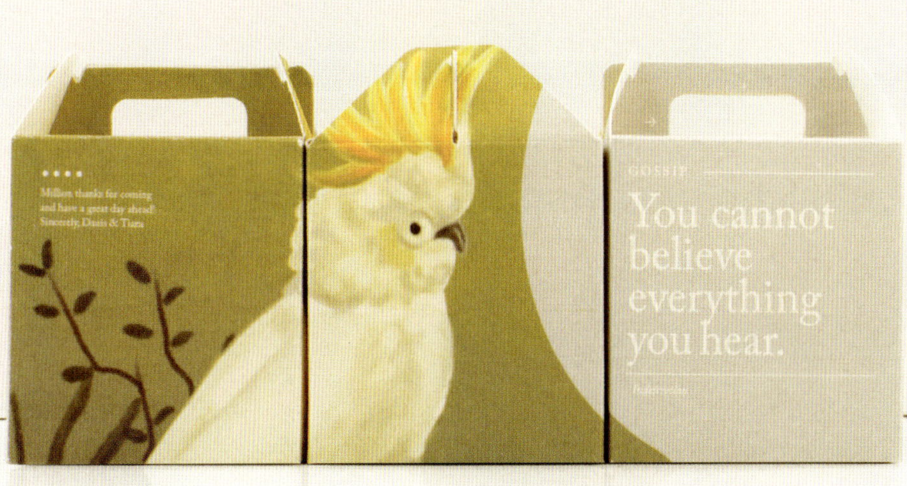
Million thanks for coming
and have a great day ahead!
GOSSIP
You cannot believe everything you hear.

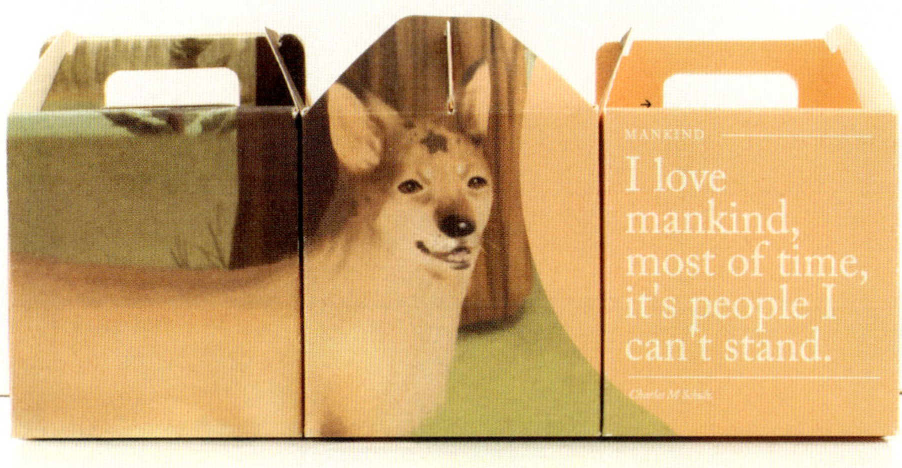
MANKIND
I love mankind, most of time, it's people I can't stand.

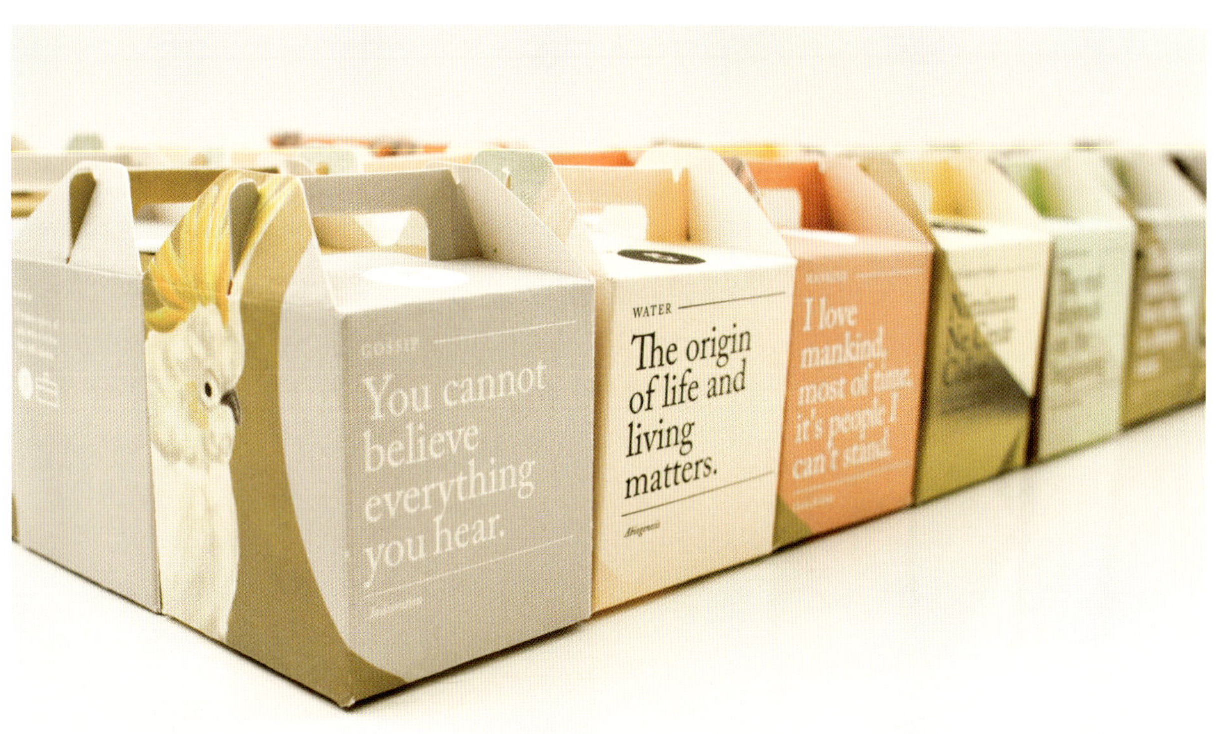
GOSSIP
You cannot believe everything you hear.
WATER
The origin of life and living matters.
I love mankind, most of time, it's people I can't stand.

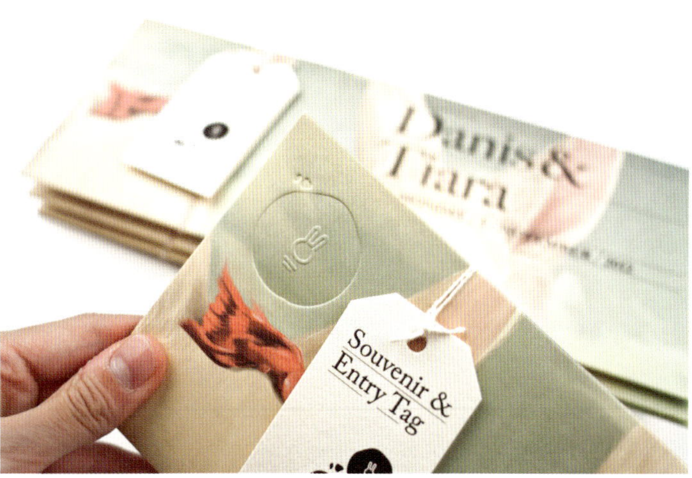
Souvenir & Entry Tag

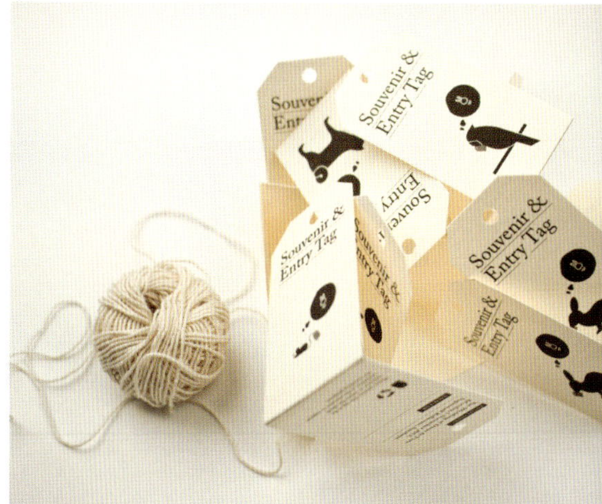
Souvenir & Entry Tag
Souvenir & Entry Tag
Souvenir & Entry Tag

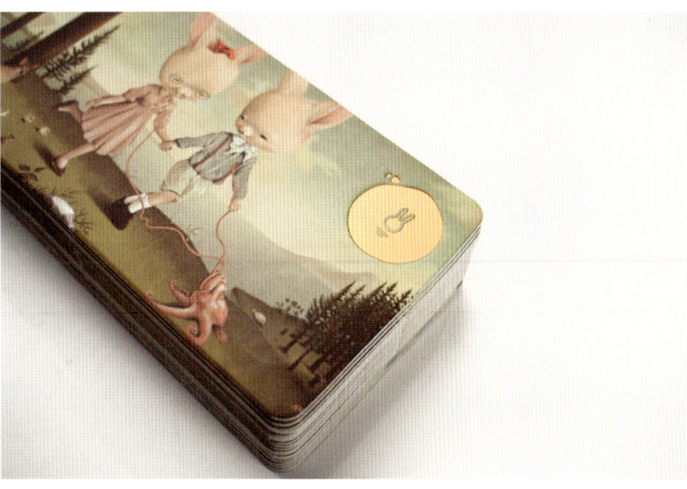

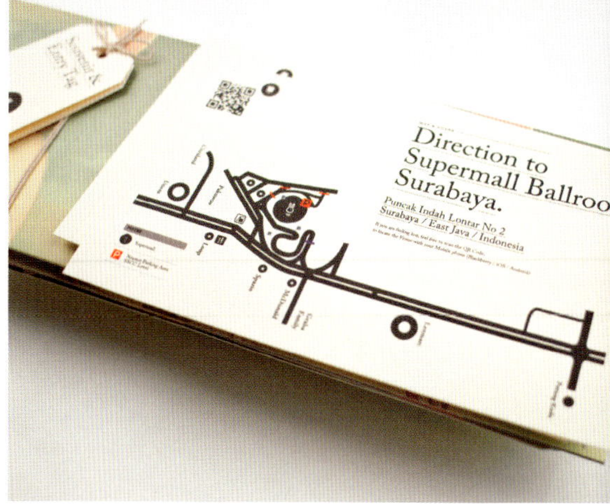
Direction to Supermall Ballroo
Surabaya.
Puncak Indah Lontar No 2
Surabaya / East Java / Indonesia

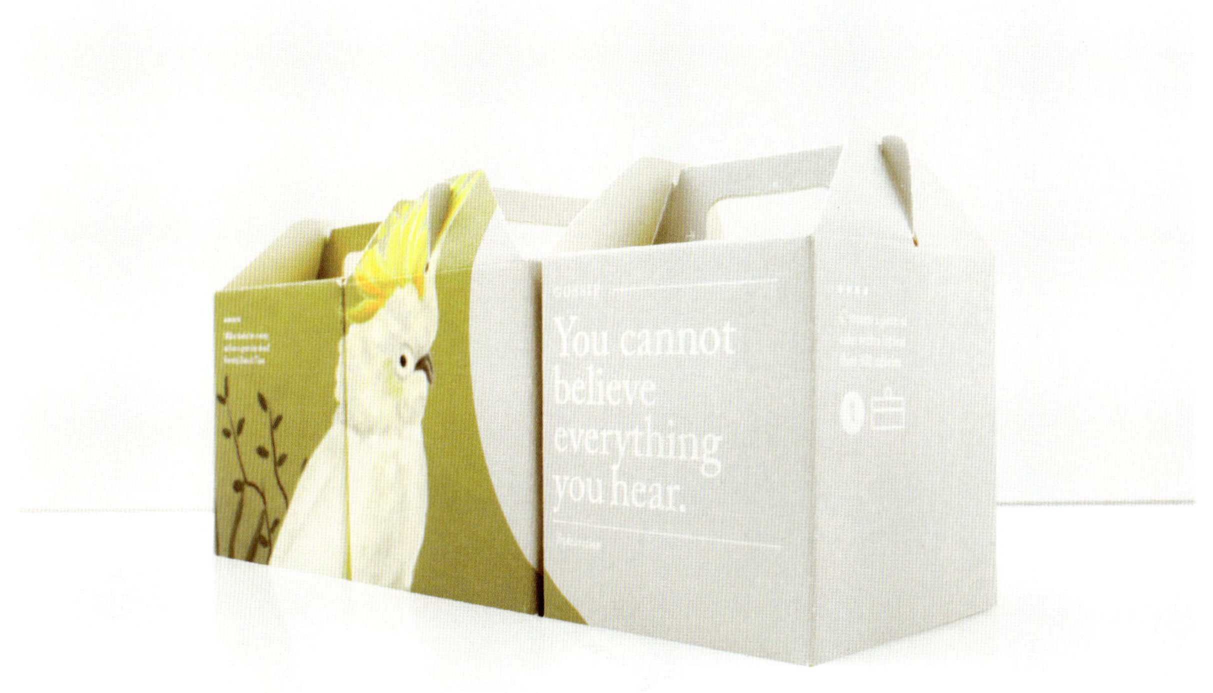
You cannot believe everything you hear.

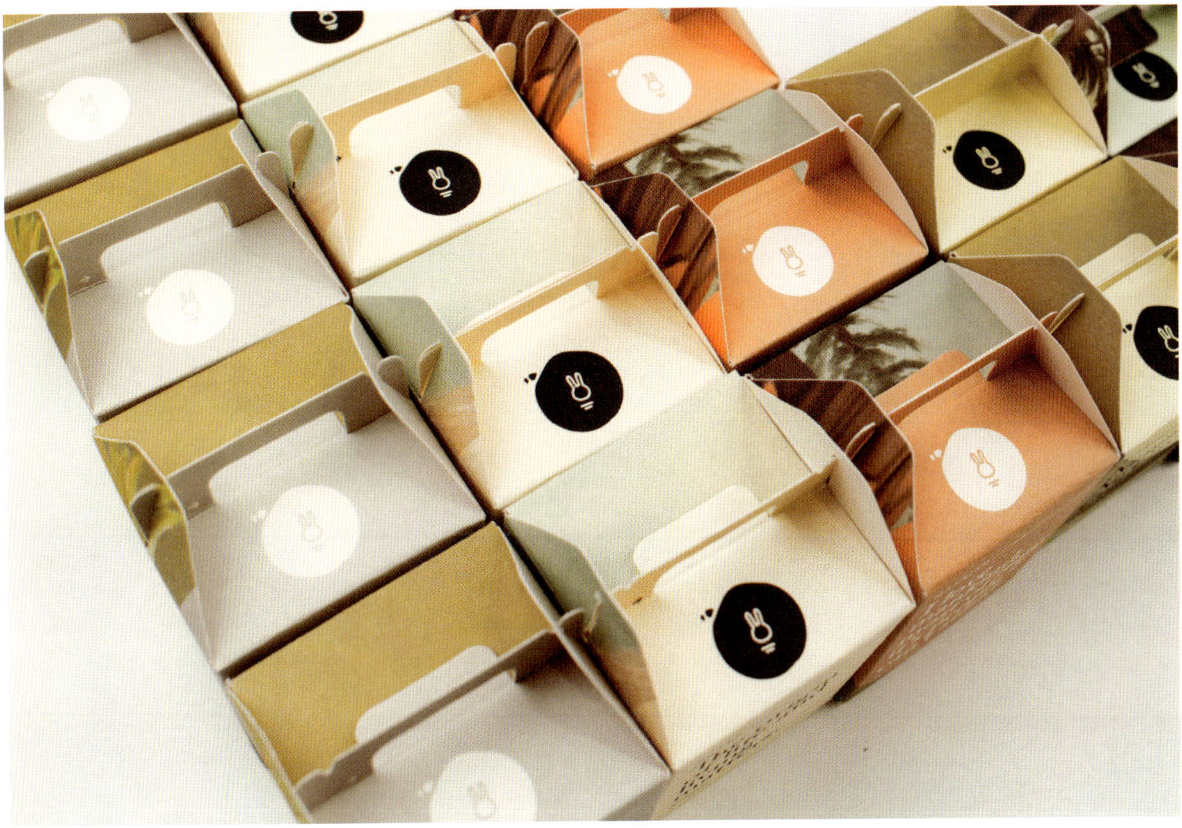

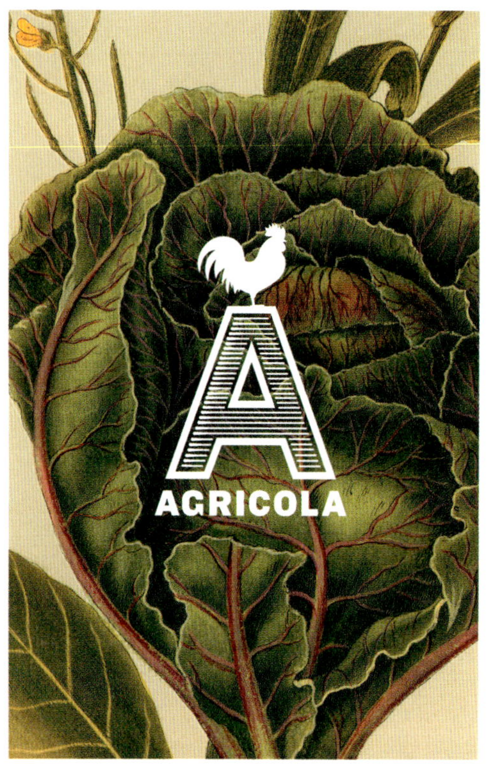

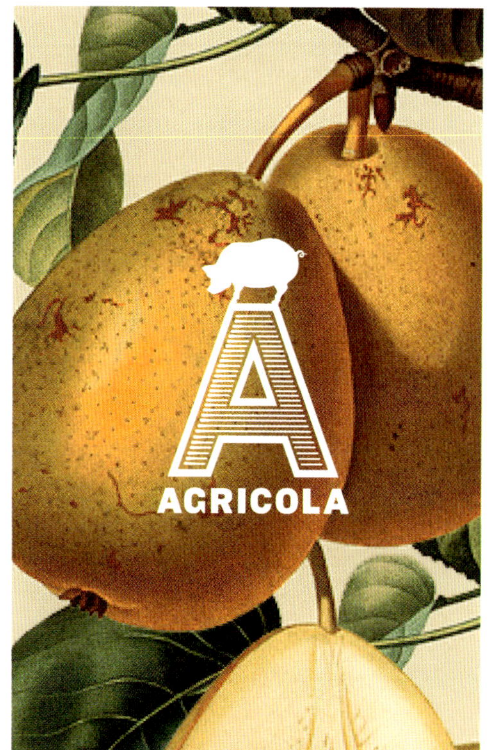

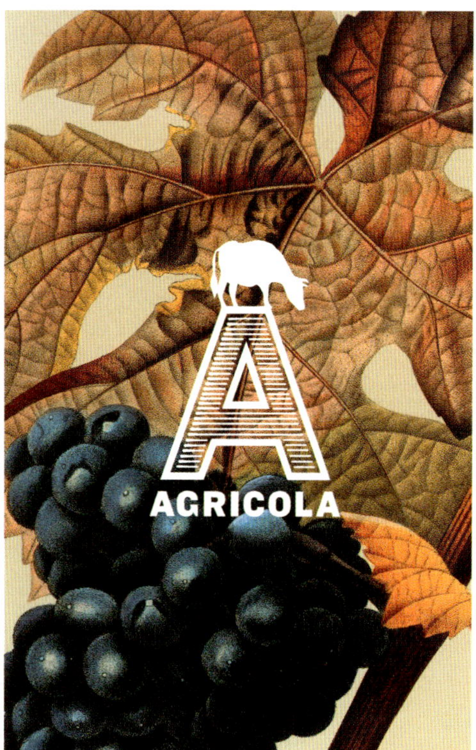

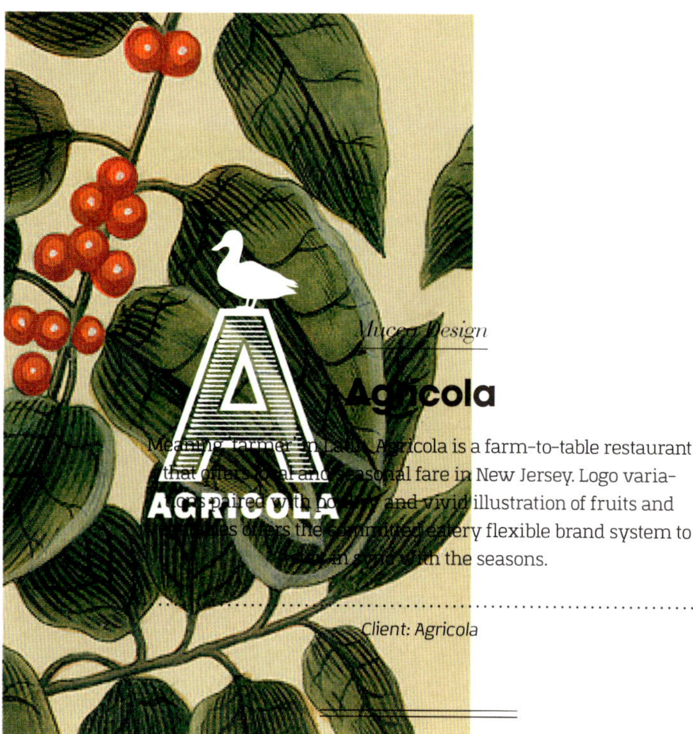

Mucca Design

Agricola

Meaning 'farmer' in Latin, Agricola is a farm-to-table restaurant that offers local and seasonal fare in New Jersey. Logo variations paired with poultry and vivid illustration of fruits and vegetables offers the committed eatery flexible brand system to stay in sync with the seasons.

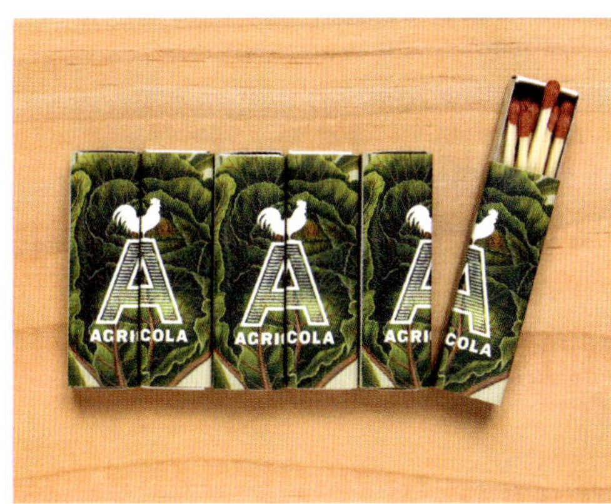
AGRICOLA
AGRICOLA

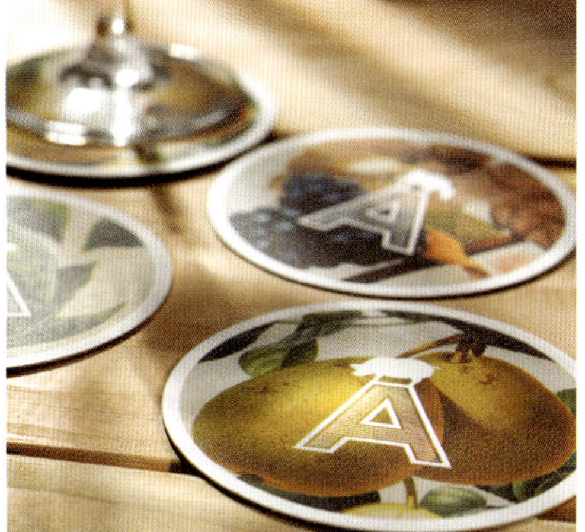

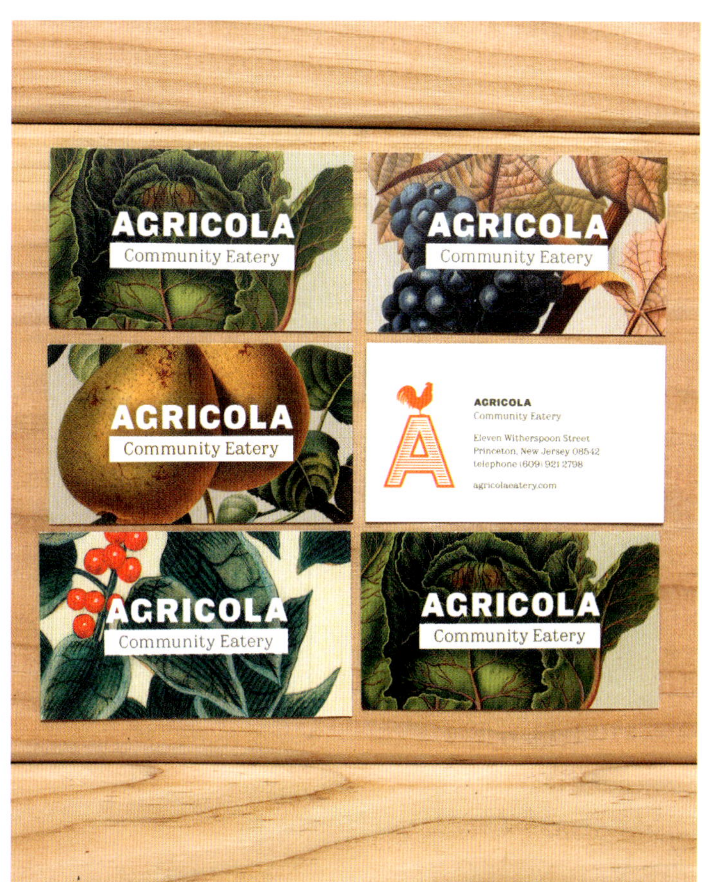
AGRICOLA
Community Eatery
AGRICOLA
Community Eatery
AGRICOLA
Community Eatery
AGRICOLA
Community Eatery
Eleven Witherspoon Street
Princeton, New Jersey 08542
telephone (609) 921 2798
agricolaeatery.com
AGRICOLA
Community Eatery
AGRICOLA
Community Eatery

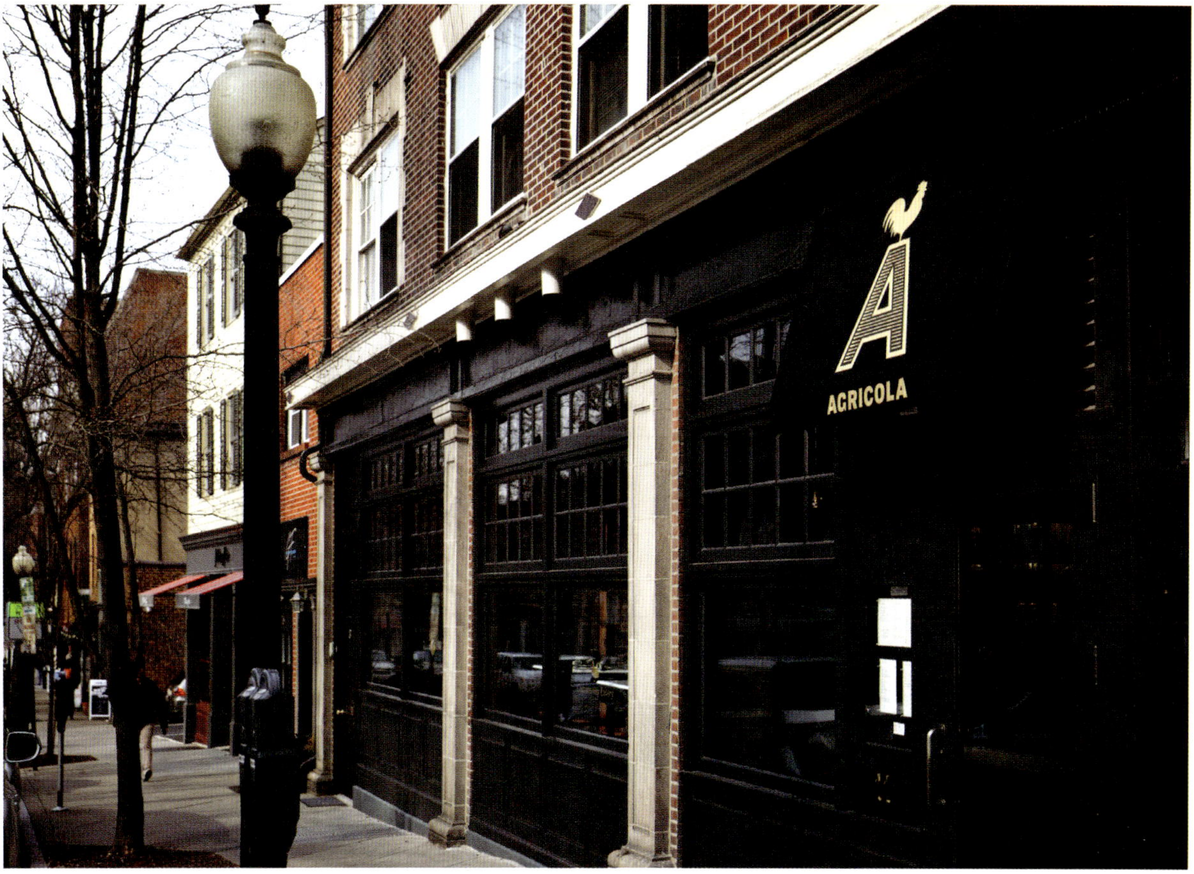

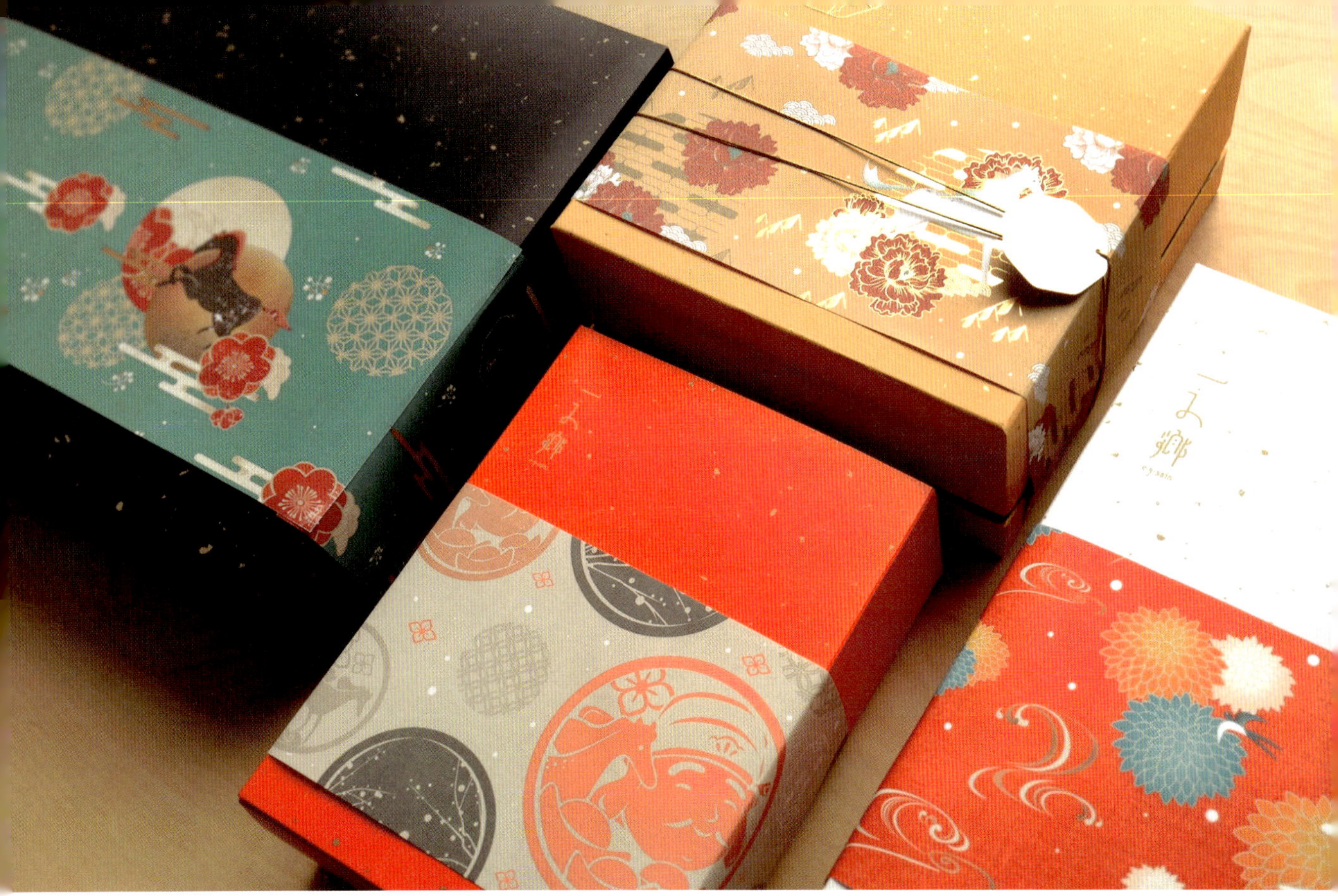

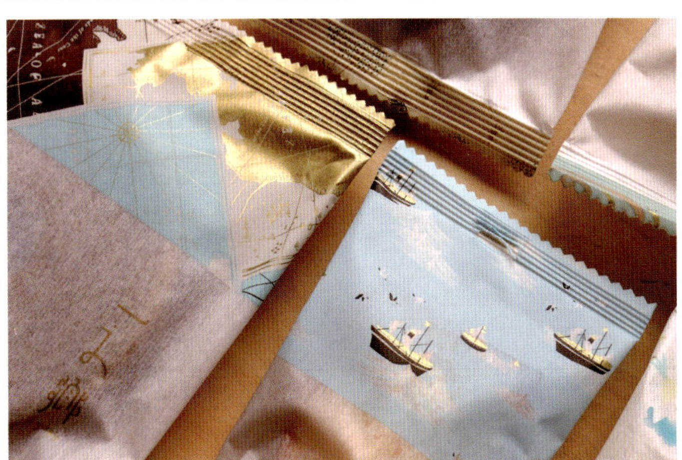

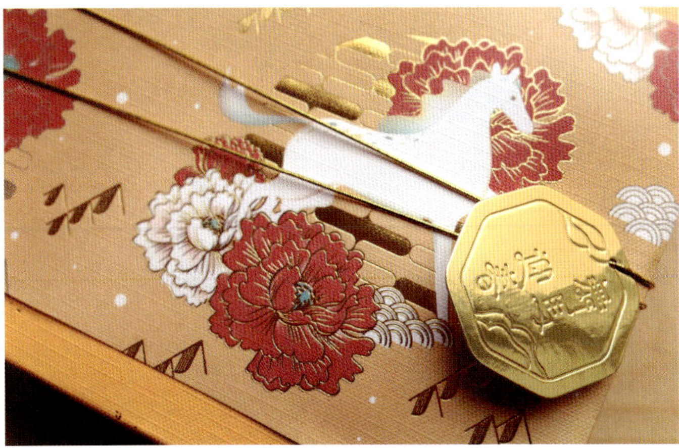

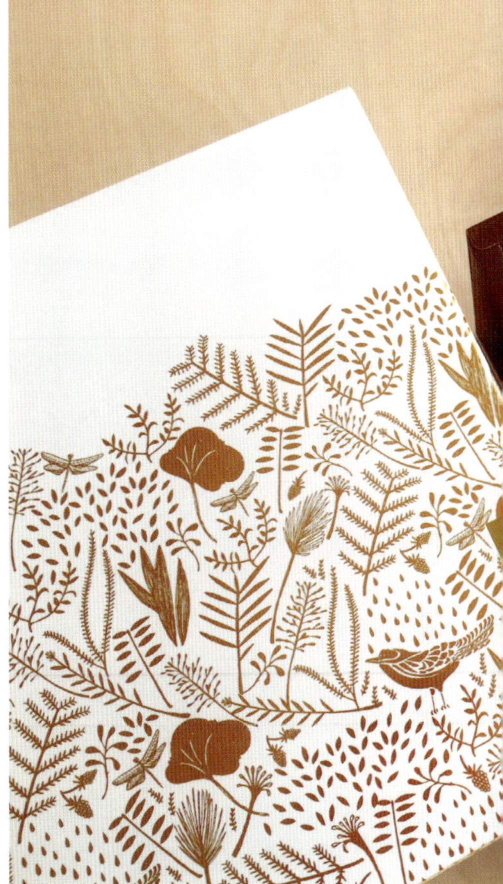

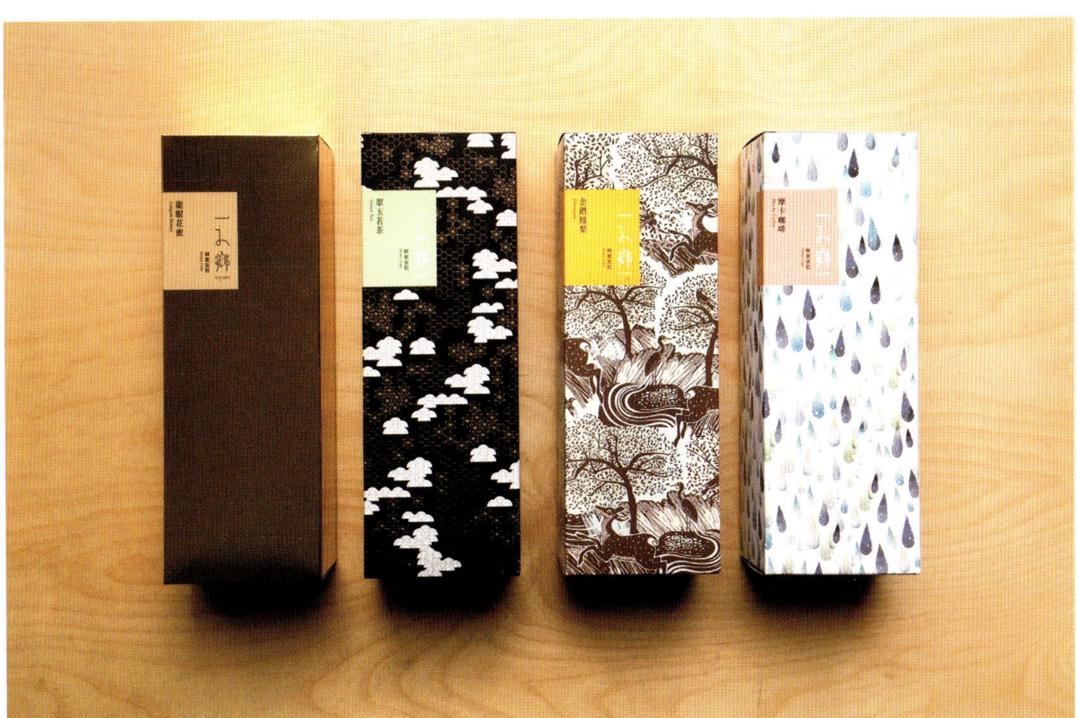

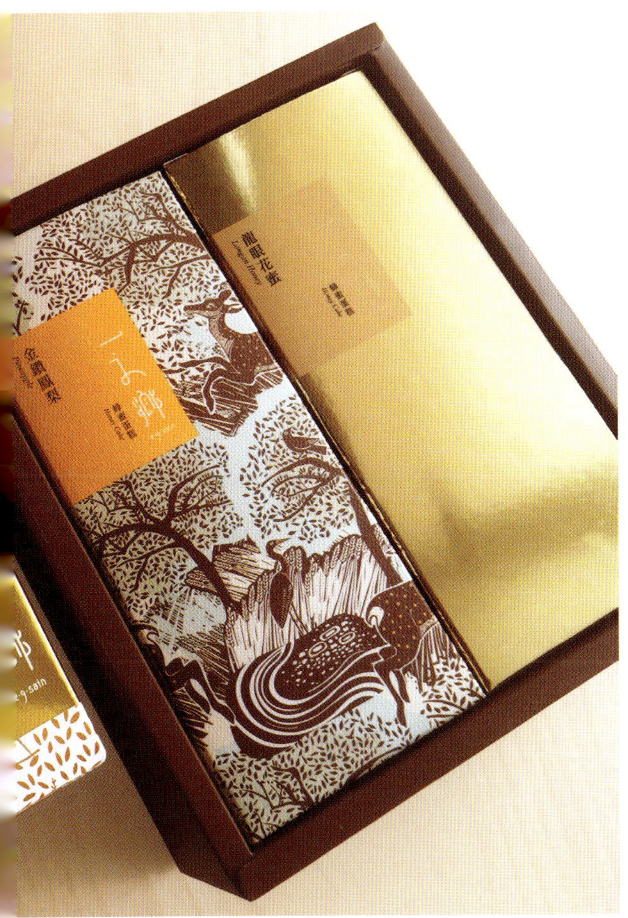

MURA

E-g-sain

Time-honoured Taiwanese cake shop initiates a rebranding that emphasises the transcendence of time and memory. Nostalgic graphical references connecting with brand are refashioned on packaging. The brand's Taipei flagship also underwent an overhaul to include hints of Taiwan back in time.

Client: E-g-sain Co.,Ltd.

MURA

E-g-sain

Time-honoured Taiwanese cake shop initiates a rebranding that emphasises the transcendence of time and memory. Nostalgic graphical references connect-

floresta is a Japanese doughnut chain dedicated to use all-natural ingredients. Elements of forest life were hand-drawn by Ryoji Nakajima to stress the enterprise's commitment across its brand communications. The logo is a pictogram of kanji 'forest'.

Graphic design: asatte design office
Client: floresta

Ryoji Nakajima

floresta

floresta is a Japanese doughnut chain dedicated to use all-natural ingredients. Elements of forest life were hand-drawn by Ryoji Nakajima to stress the enterprise's commitment across its brand communications. The logo is a pictogram of kanji 'forest'.

Graphic design: asatte design office
Client: floresta

floresta
nature
doughnuts
Since 2oo2 Nara

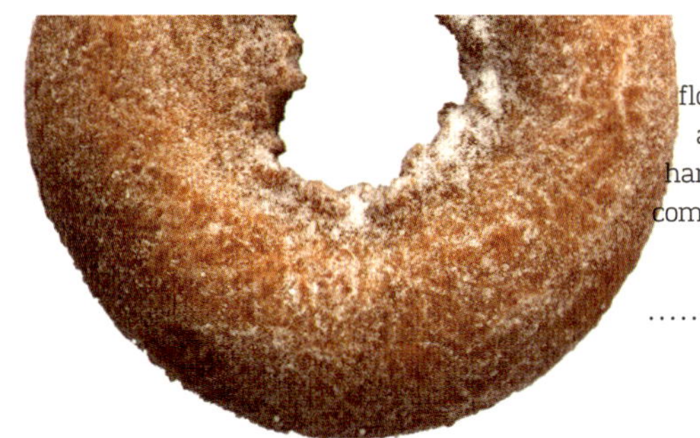

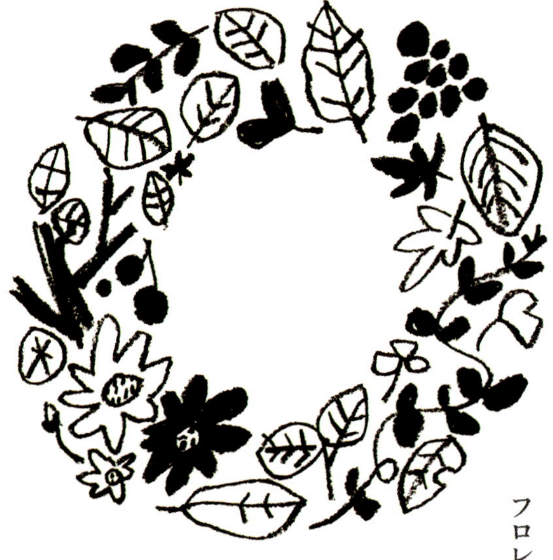

体にやさしく
おいしい
ドーナツのお店
フロレスタ

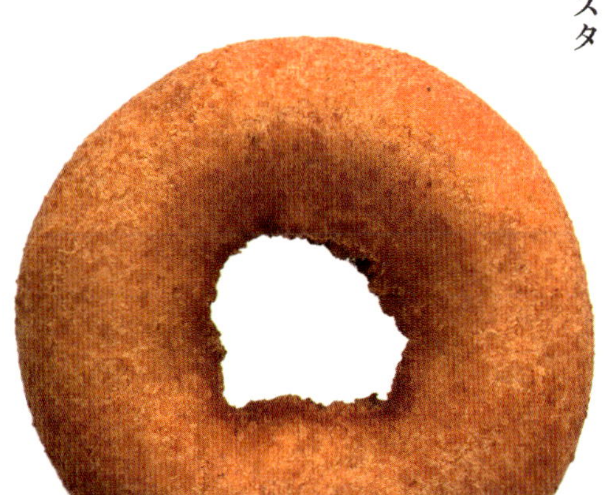

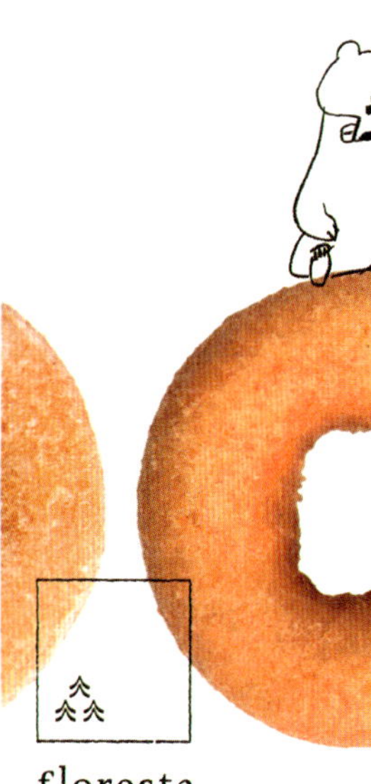

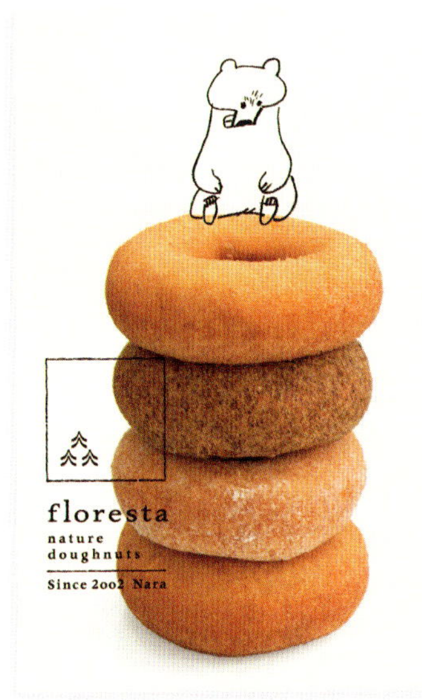
floresta
nature
doughnuts
Since 2002 Nara

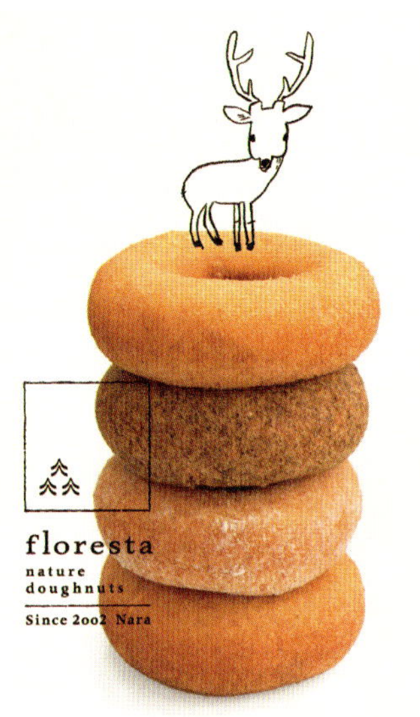
floresta
nature
doughnuts
Since 2002 Nara

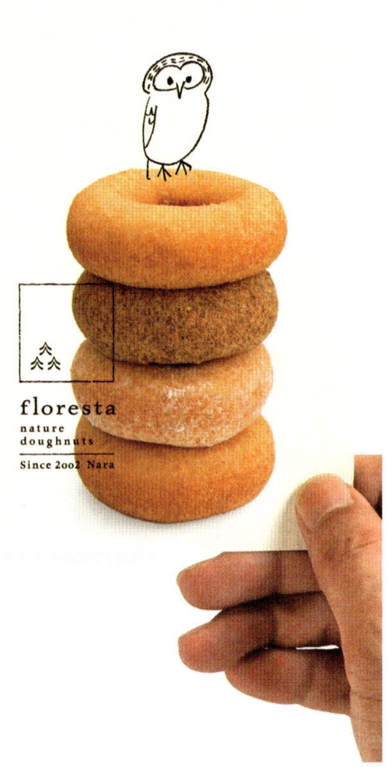
floresta
nature
doughnuts
Since 2002 Nara

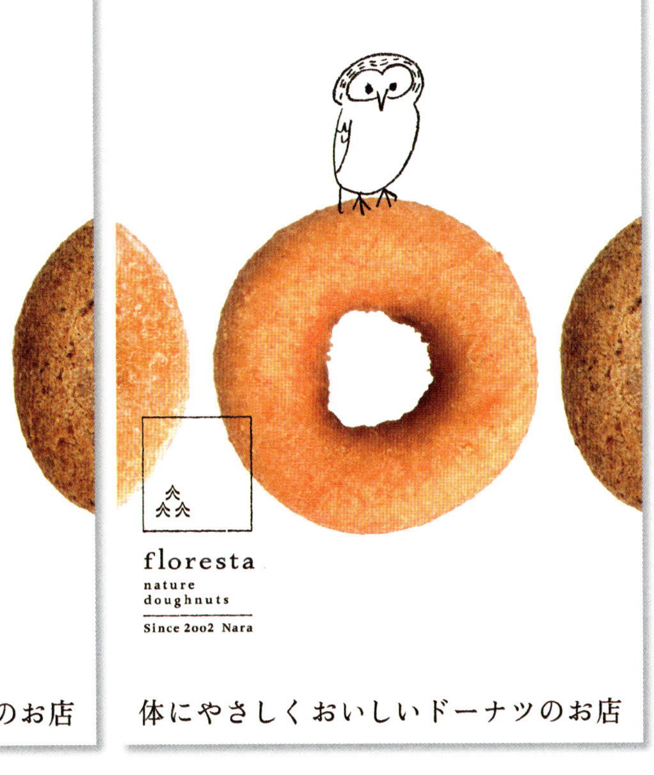
ーナツのお店
floresta
nature
doughnuts
Since 2002 Nara
体にやさしくおいしいドーナツのお店

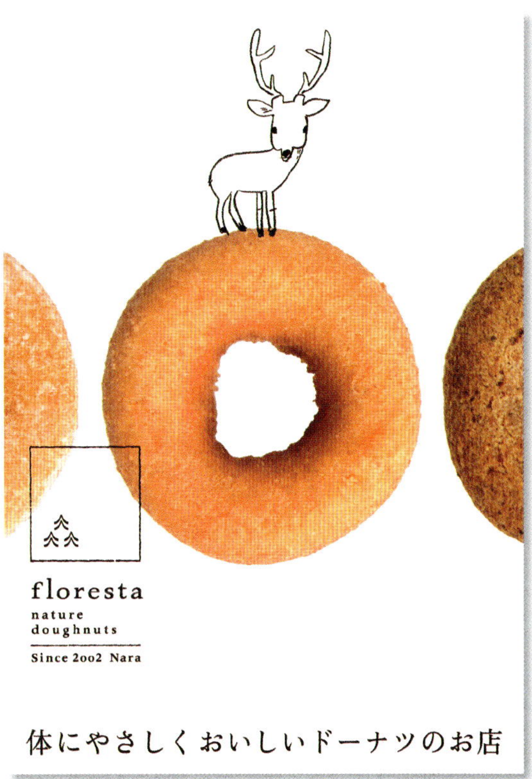
floresta
nature
doughnuts
Since 2002 Nara
体にやさしくおいしいドーナツのお店

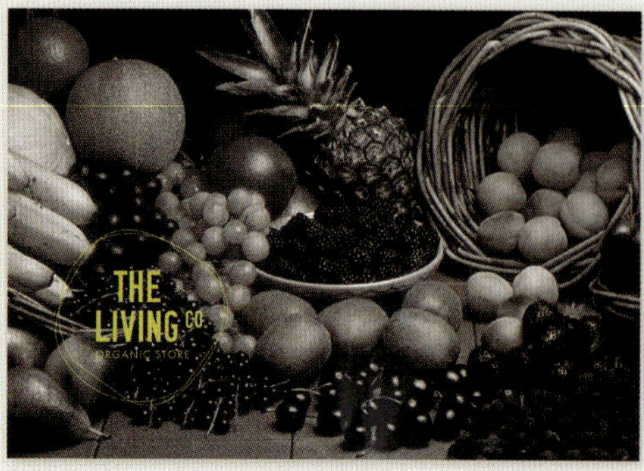

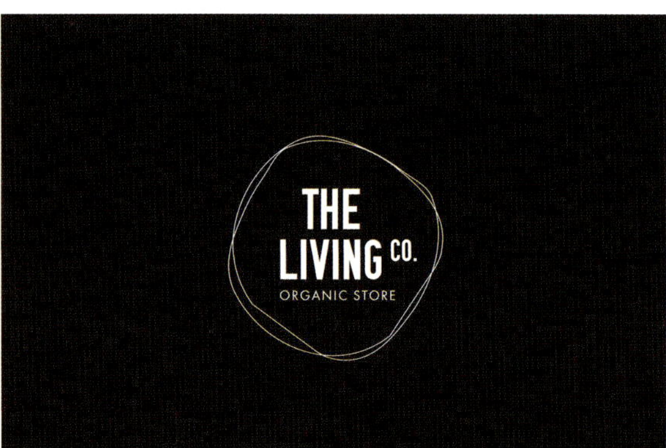

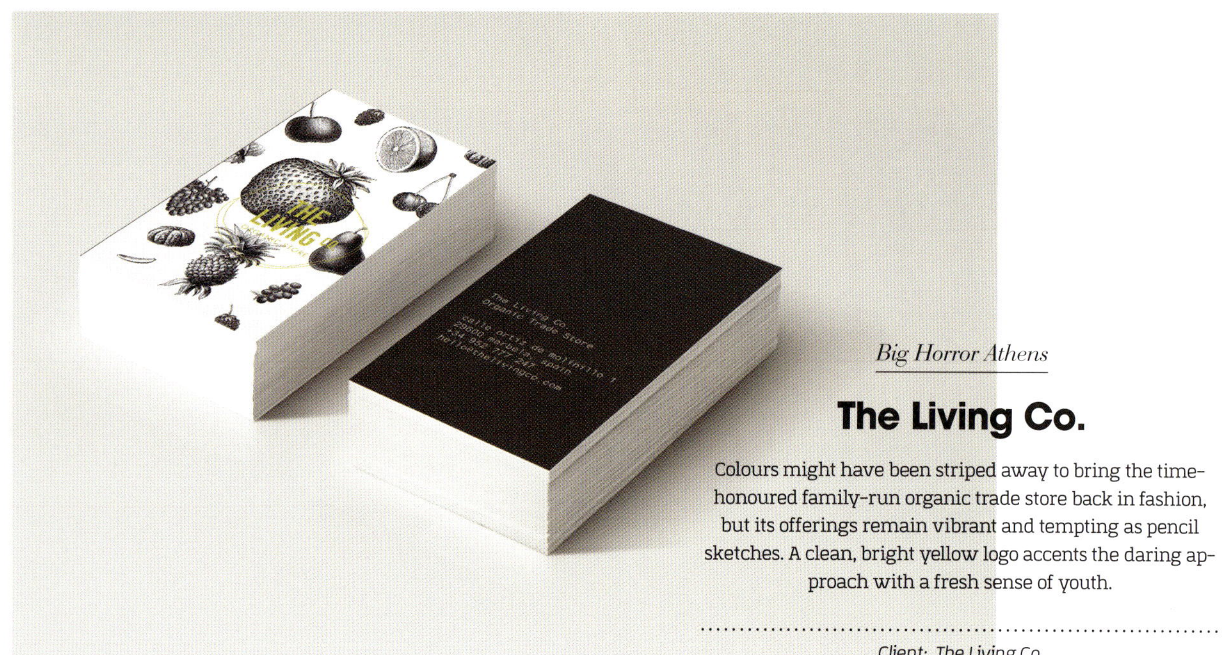

Big Horror Athens

The Living Co.

Colours might have been striped away to bring the time-honoured family-run organic trade store back in fashion, but its offerings remain vibrant and tempting as pencil sketches. A clean, bright yellow logo accents the daring approach with a fresh sense of youth.

Client: The Living Co.

Big Horror Athens

The Living Co.

Colours might have been striped away to bring the time-honoured family-run organic trade store back in fashion, but its offerings remain vibrant and tempting as pencil

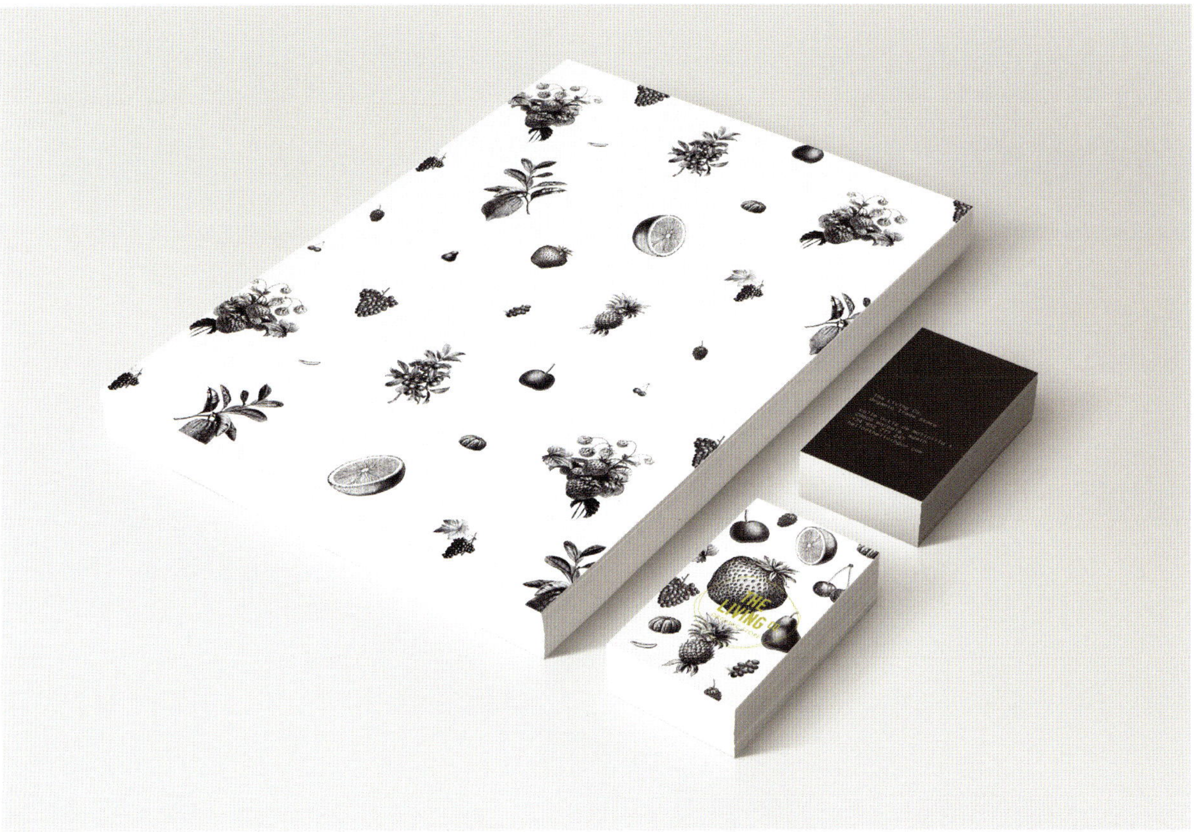

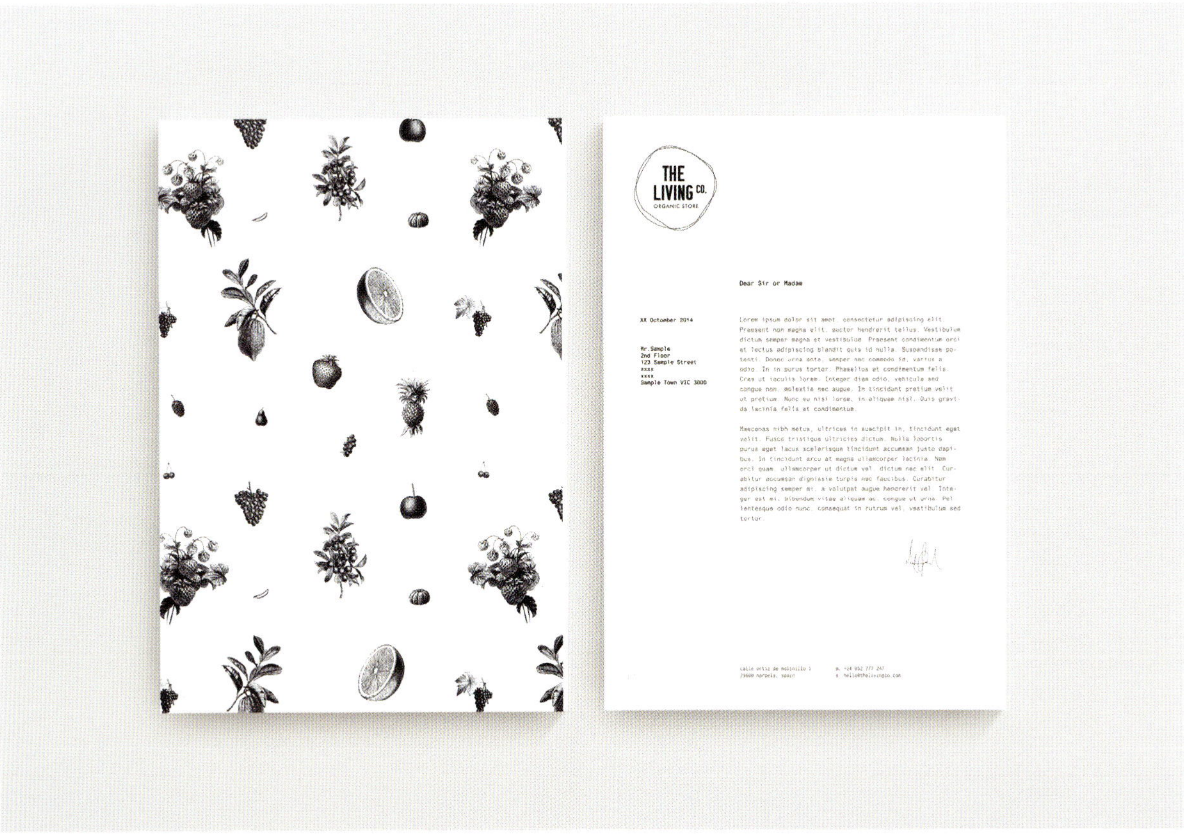

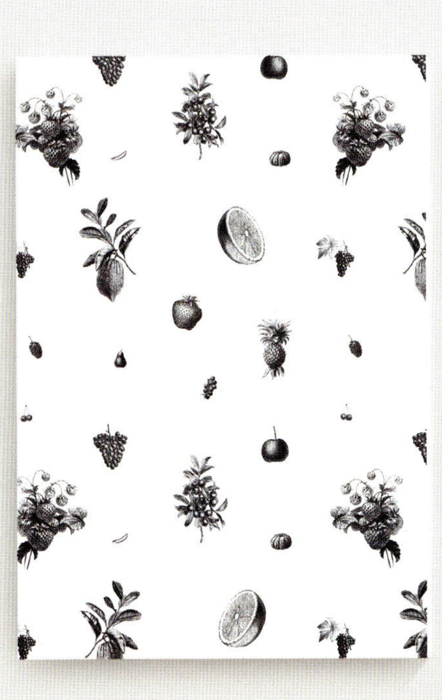

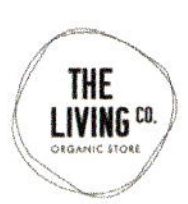
THE
LIVING CO.
ORGANIC STORE

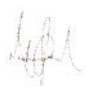

Bruce Leaves

Sleep Projects was asked to create a unique logotype for Bruce Leaves, a salad bar in Sydney. The result is a tongue in cheek approach to the design draws inspiration from their menu items, such as "Big Beef in Little Korea", "Crouching Chicken Hidden Chipotle" and "Sashimi Salmon-ai Warrior".

Client: Bruce Leaves

Sleep Projects

Bruce Leaves

Sleep Projects was asked to create a unique logotype for Bruce Leaves, a salad bar in Sydney. The result is a tongue in cheek approach to the design draws inspiration from their menu items, such as "Big Beef in Little Korea", "Crouching … and "Sashimi Salmon-a…

Client: Bruce Lea…

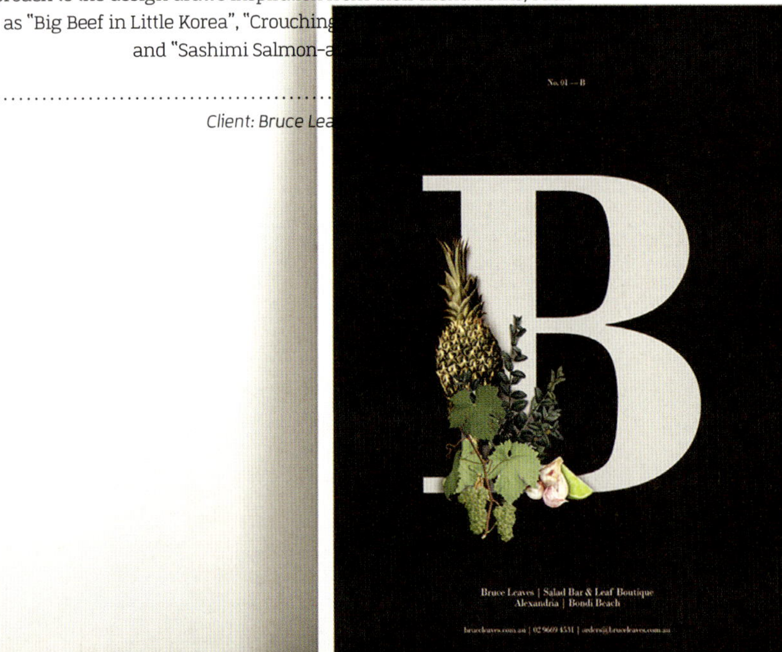

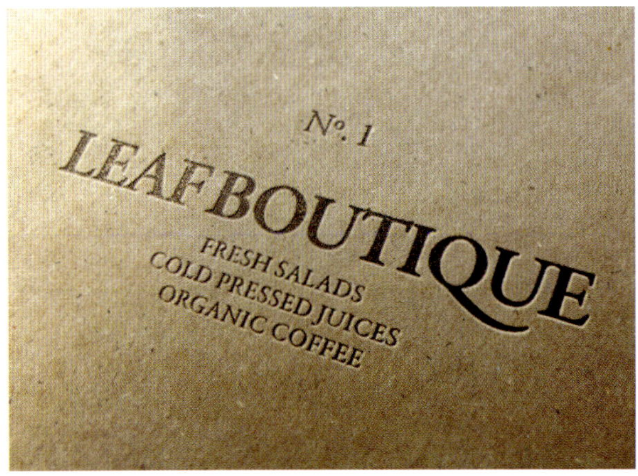

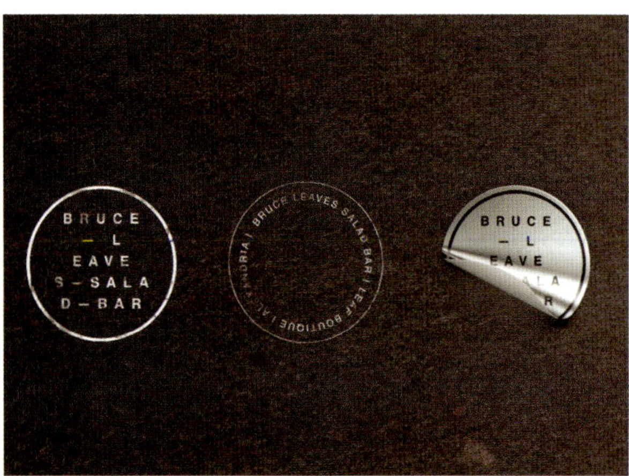

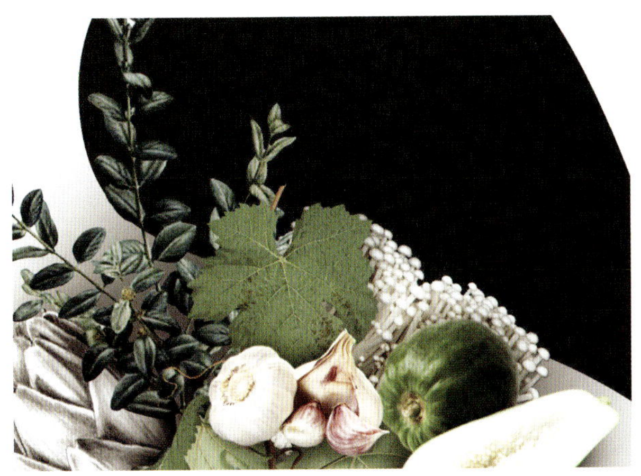

ORGANIC COFFEE | COLD PRESSED JUICES | FRESH SALAD

BRUCE LEAVES

LEAF BOUTIQUE

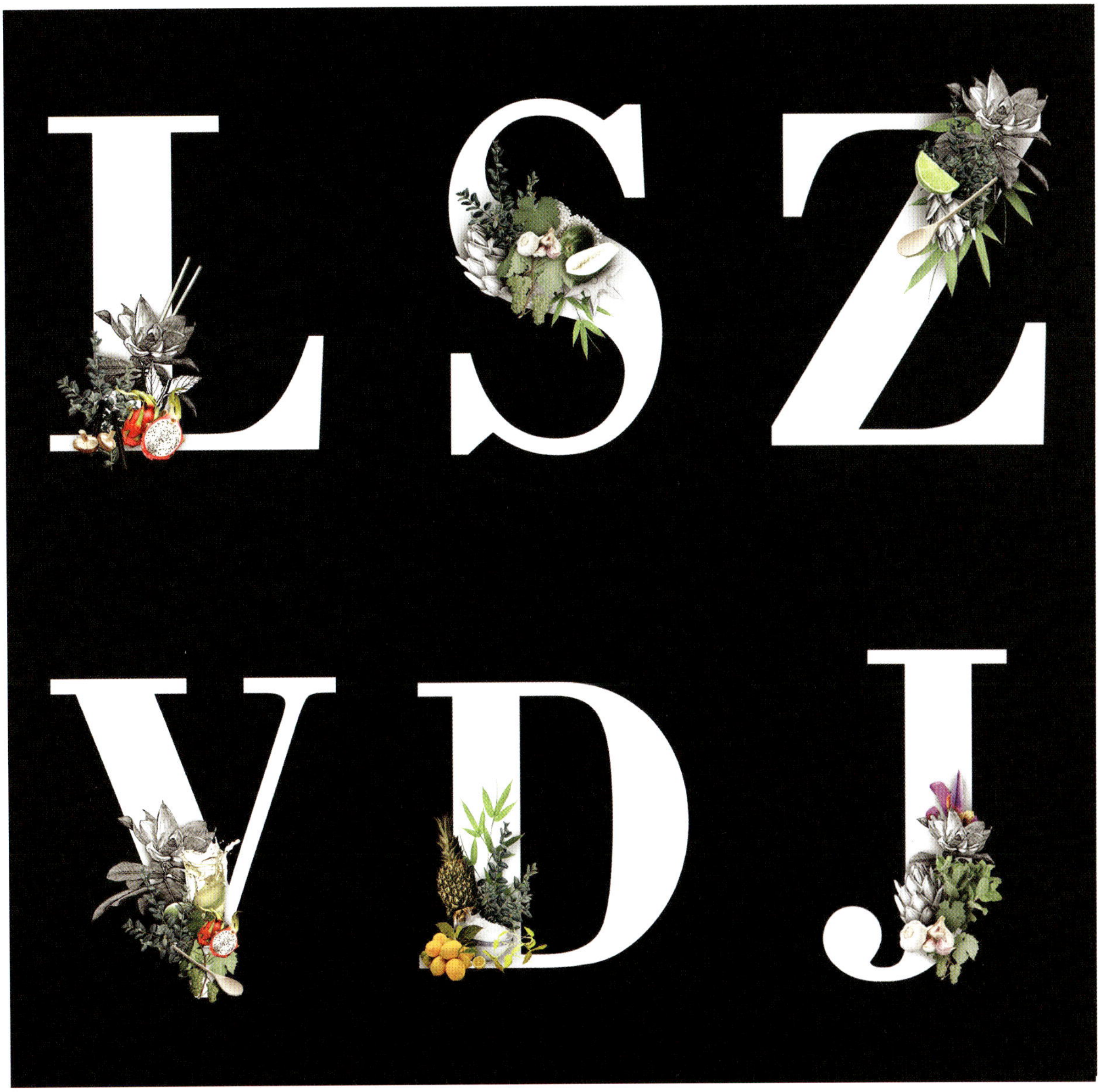

L S Z

V D J

Puree Organics

Puree is an organic medicinal vegetable garden where consumers can access naturally farmed food just around the corner. Lifelike drawings of fresh produce steers their practice away from the typical tokens of health, well-being and organic farms.

Client: Puree Organics

PUREE

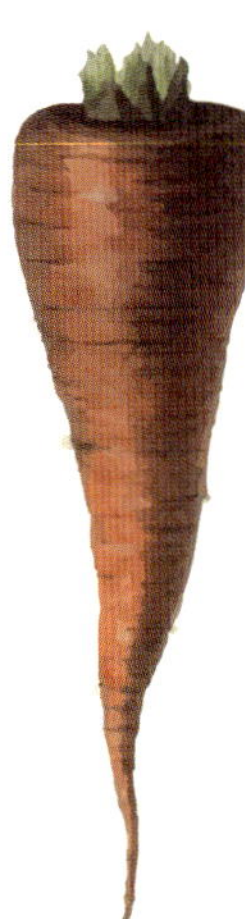

Studioahamed

Puree Organics

Puree is an organic medicinal vegetable garden where consumers can access naturally farmed food just around the corner. Lifelike drawings of fresh produce steers their practice away from the typical tokens of health, well-being and organic farms.

Client: Puree Organics

PUREE

PUREE

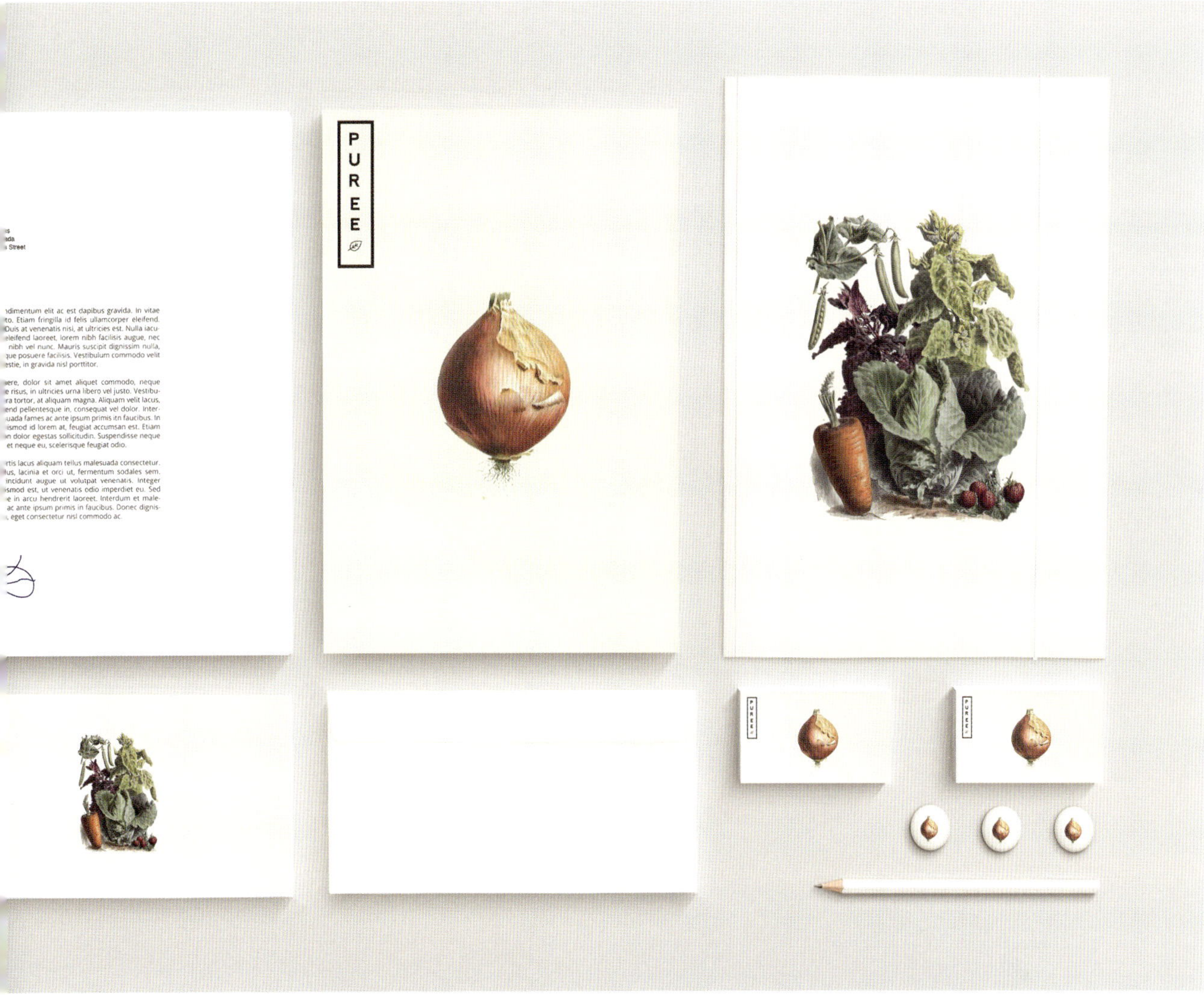

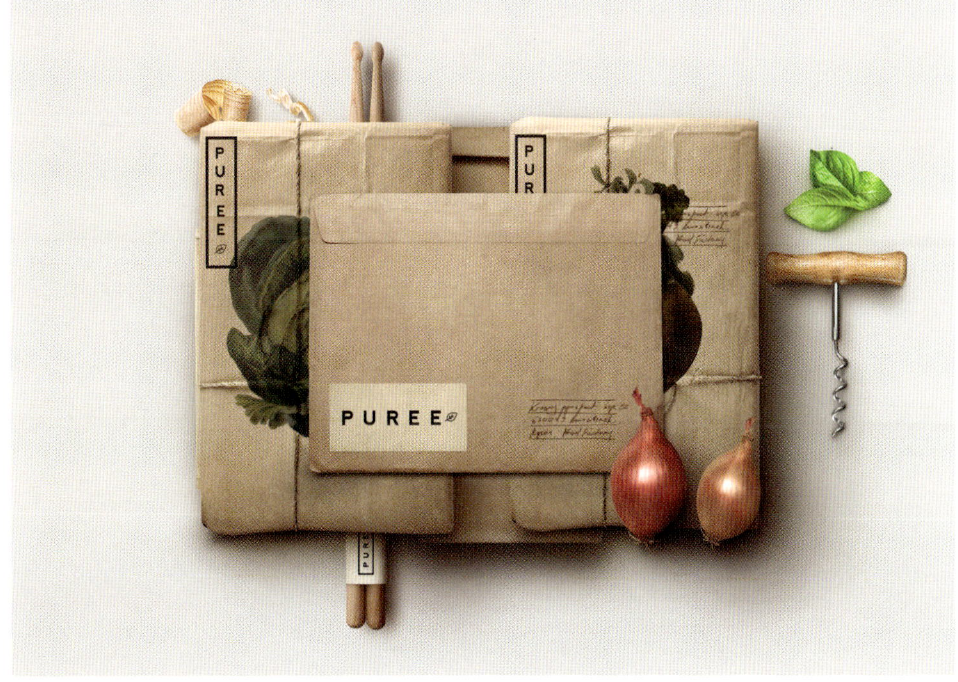
PUREE

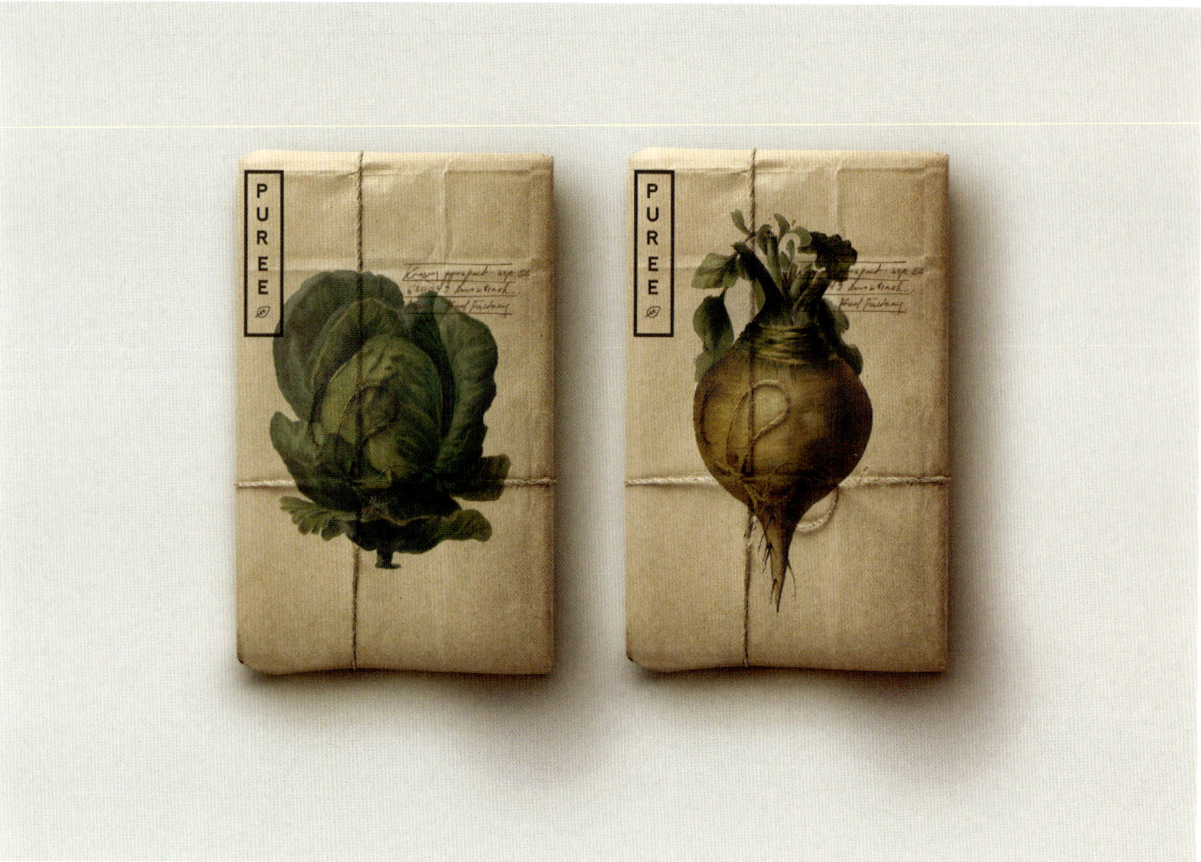
PUREE
PUREE

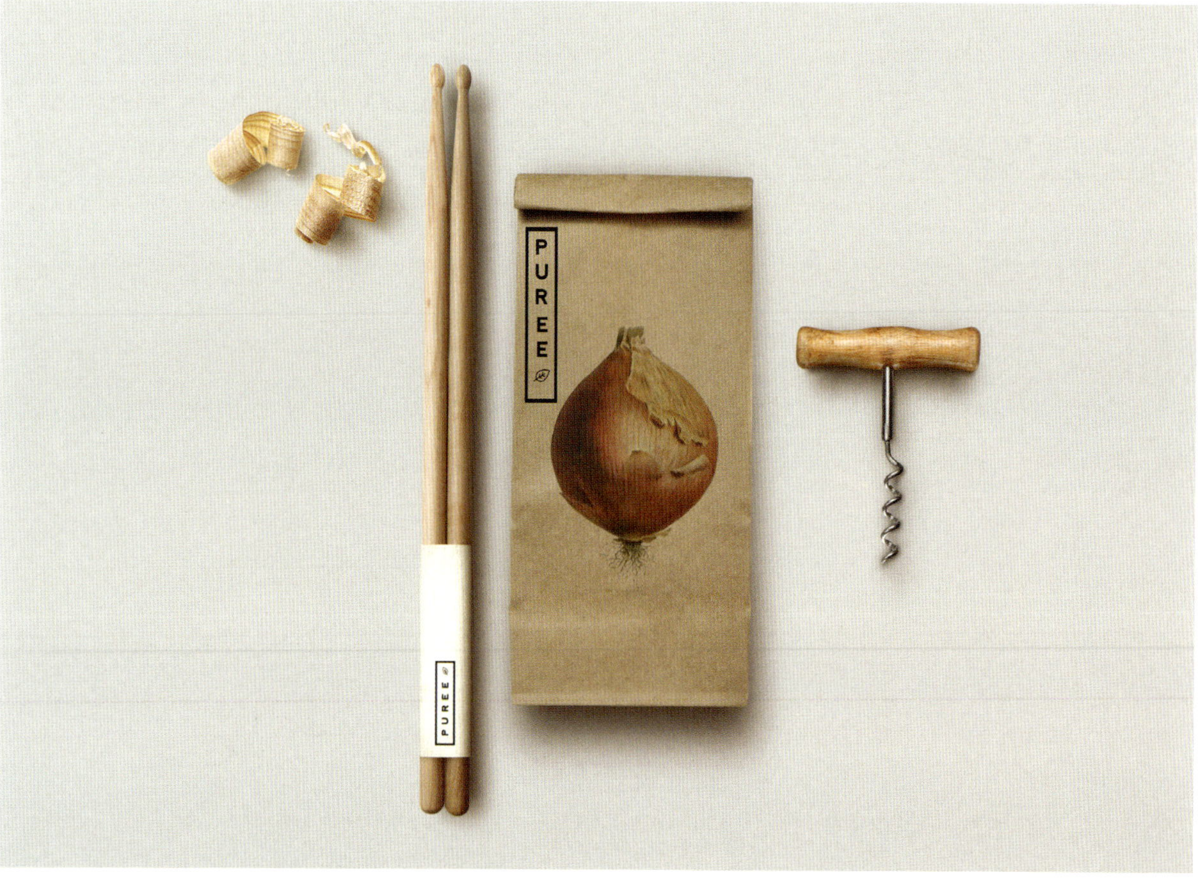
PUREE
PUREE

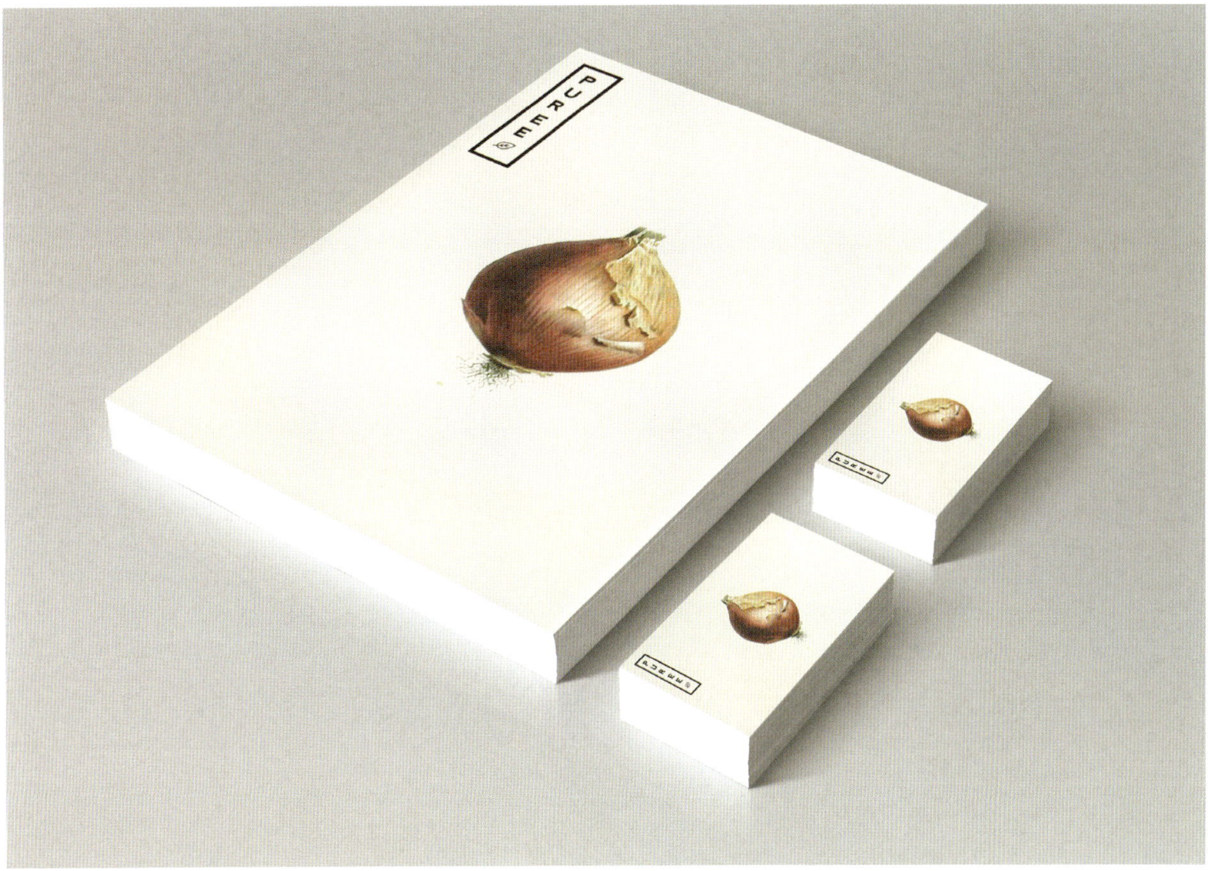

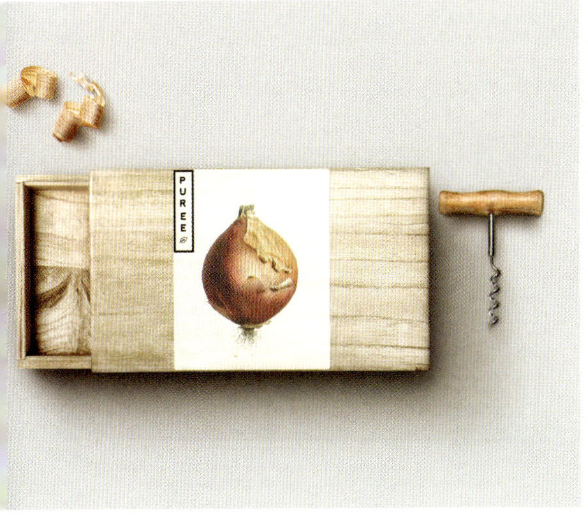
PUREE

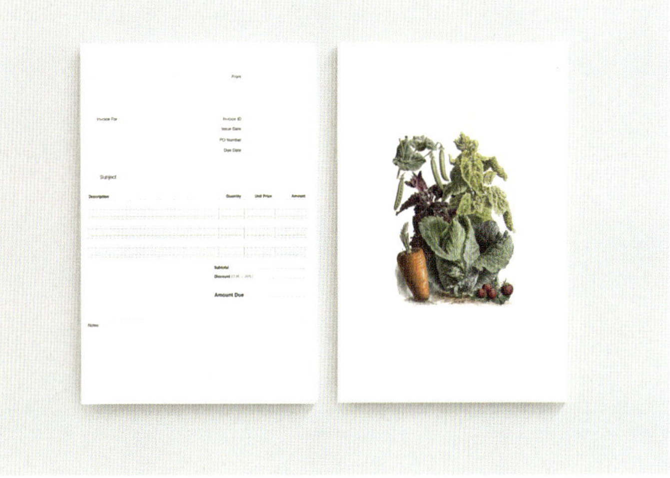
Subject
Description
Quantity
Unit Price
Amount
Subtotal
Amount Due
Notes

Wine Rack is a cosy spot in for casual chats over a nice glasses of wine. Almost like hallucinations, distorted reality made of beasts, food and curiosities takes happy drinkers to look at the world through wine bottles or after a couple of drinks.

Client: Vinniy Shkaf

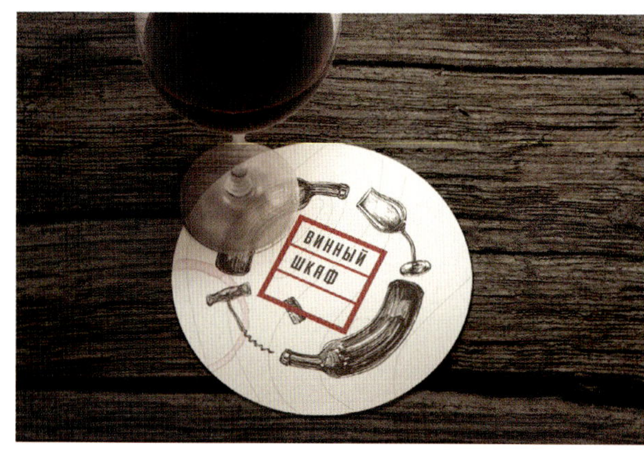

SHISHKI branding agency

Wine Rack

Wine Rack is a cosy spot in for casual chats over a nice glasses of wine. Almost like hallucinations, distorted reality made of beasts, food and curiosities takes happy drinkers to look at the world through wine bottles or after a couple of drinks.

Client: Vinniy Shkaf

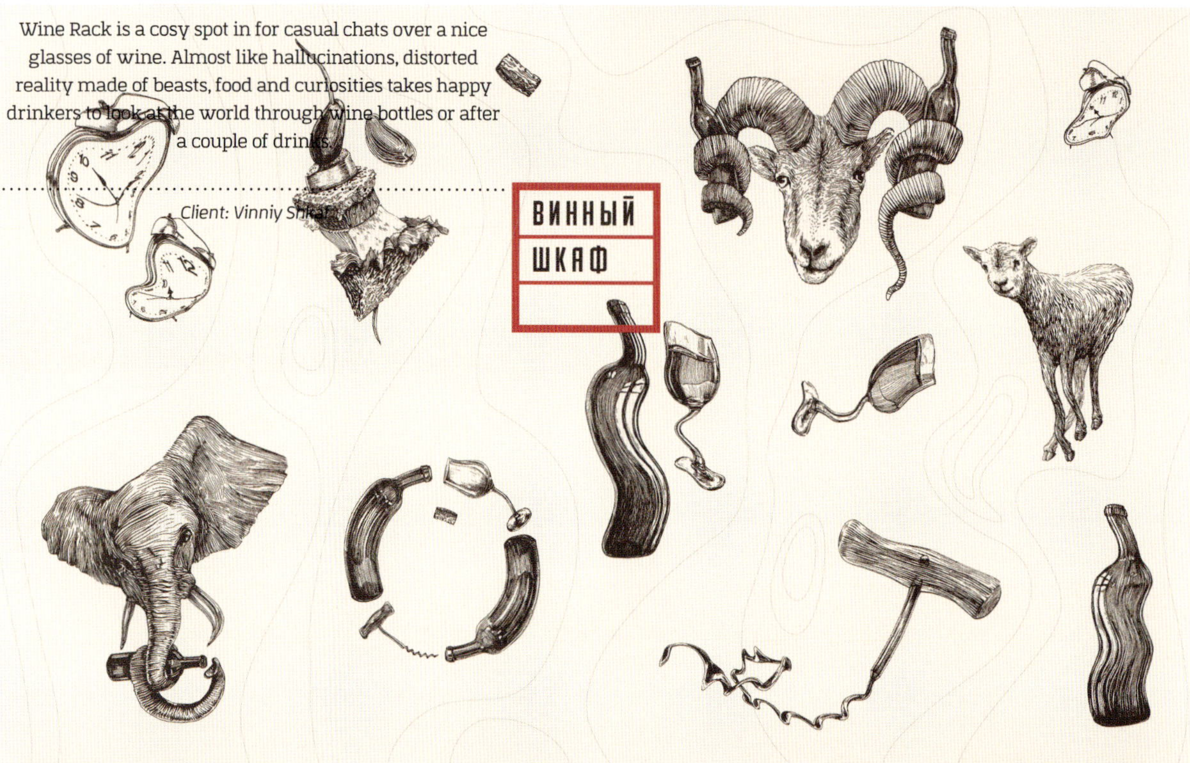

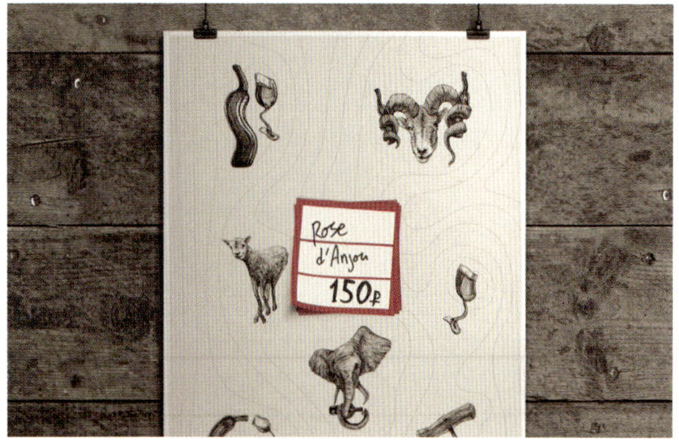

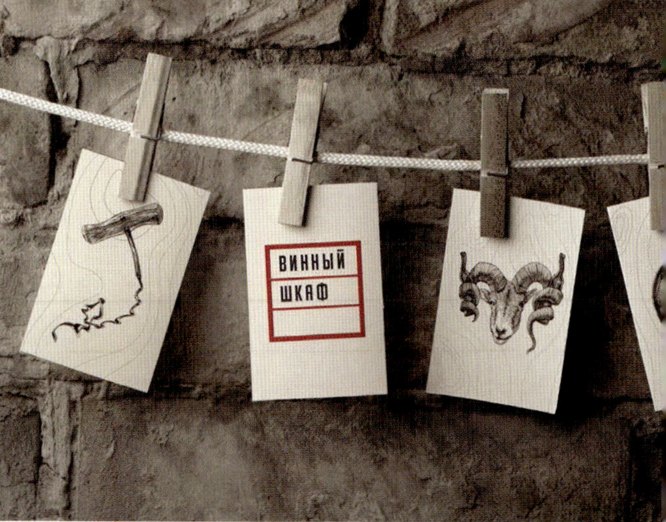

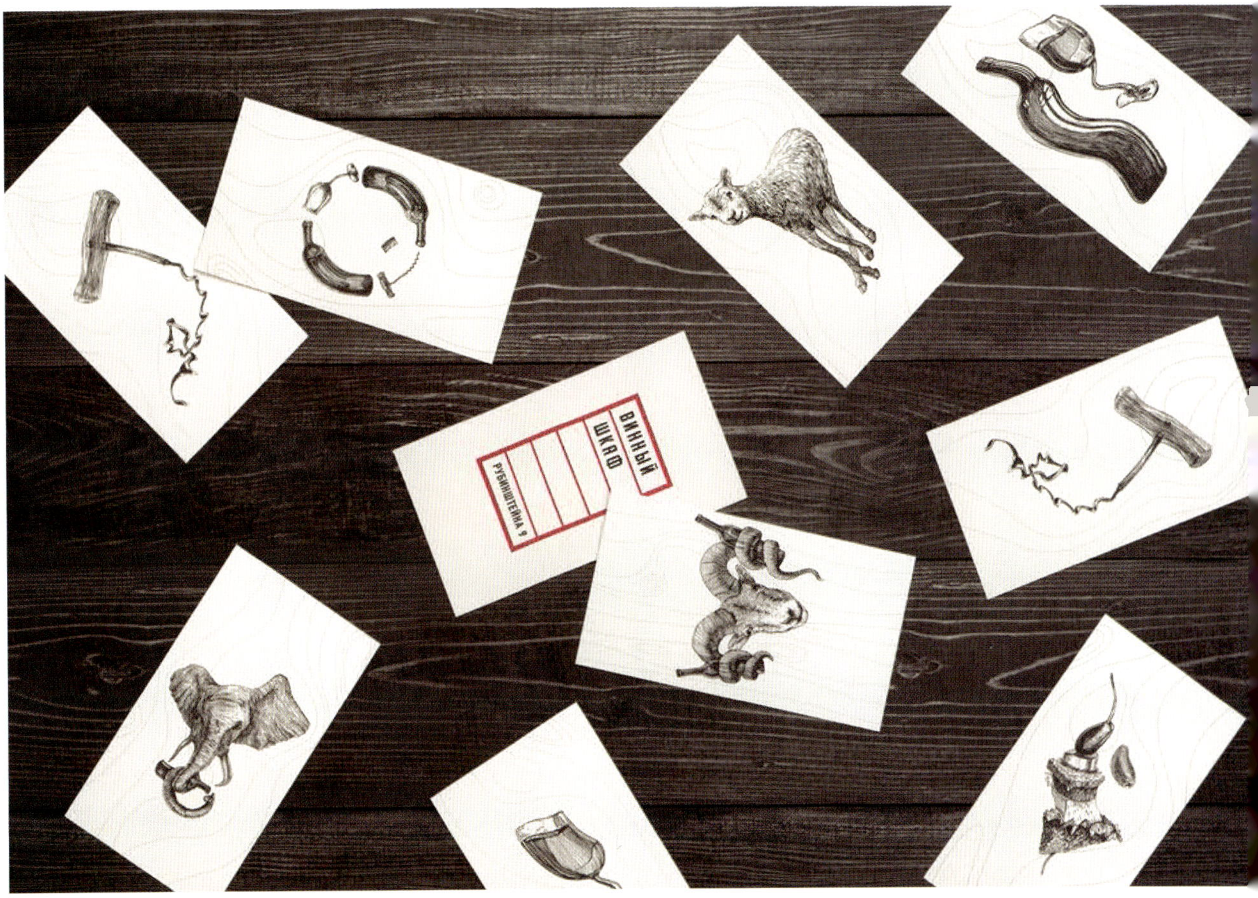

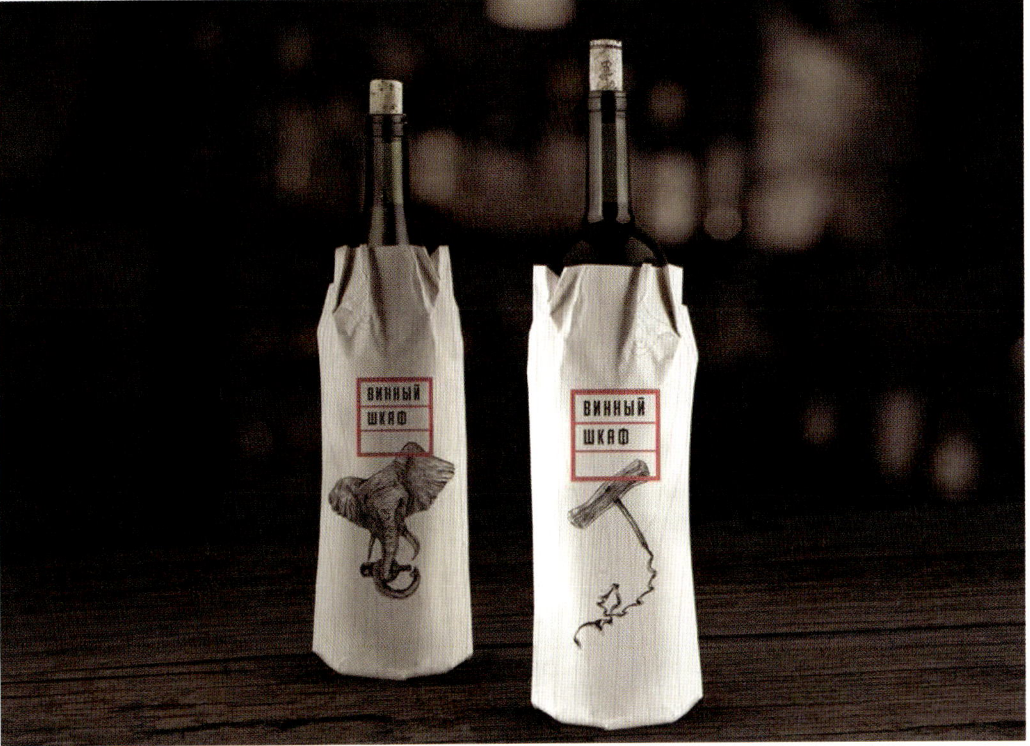
ВИННЫЙ
ШКАФ
ВИННЫЙ
ШКАФ

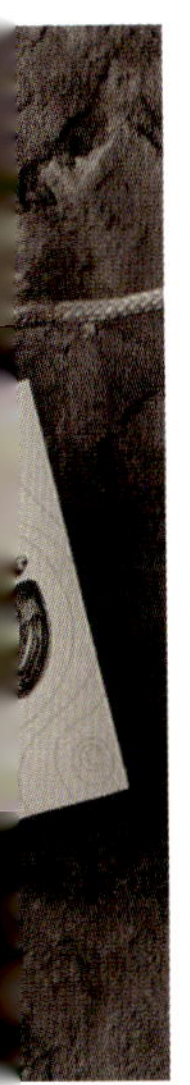

Every weekend Farmers Market dyes the street outside Park Lane by Splendor shopping centre with bountiful colours of locally grown seasonal produce. Simplic… was key to reflect the quality nature of the foo… …ing centre's cheerful spirit in the… …ypeface.

Huang Zhong-xing (Park Lane by Splendor)

Farmers Market

Every weekend Farmers Market dyes the street outside Park Lane by Splendor shopping centre with bountiful colours of locally grown seasonal produce. Simplicity was key to reflect the quality nature of the food and the shopping centre's cheerful spirit in the posters, flyers and typeface.

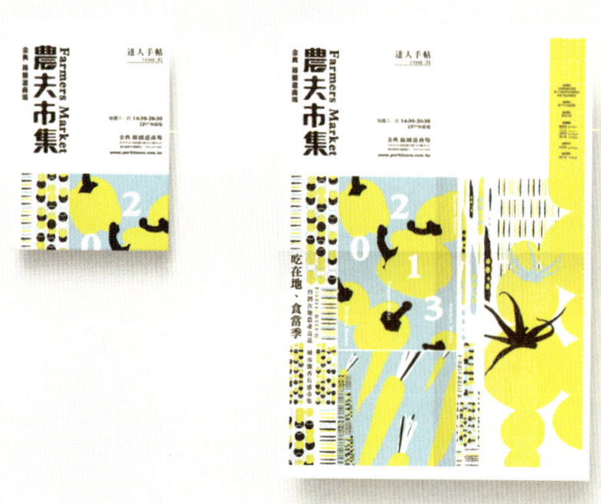

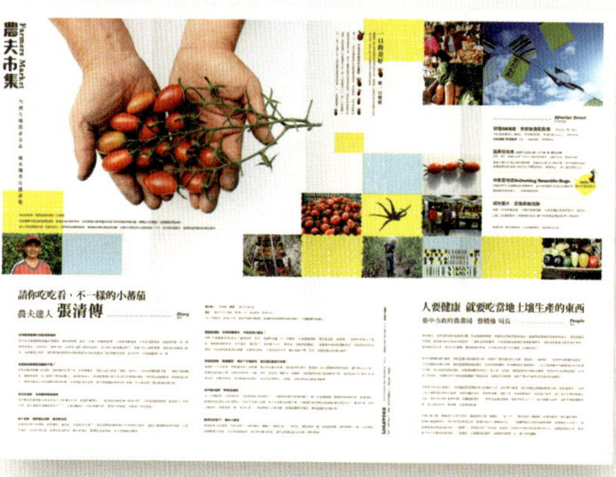

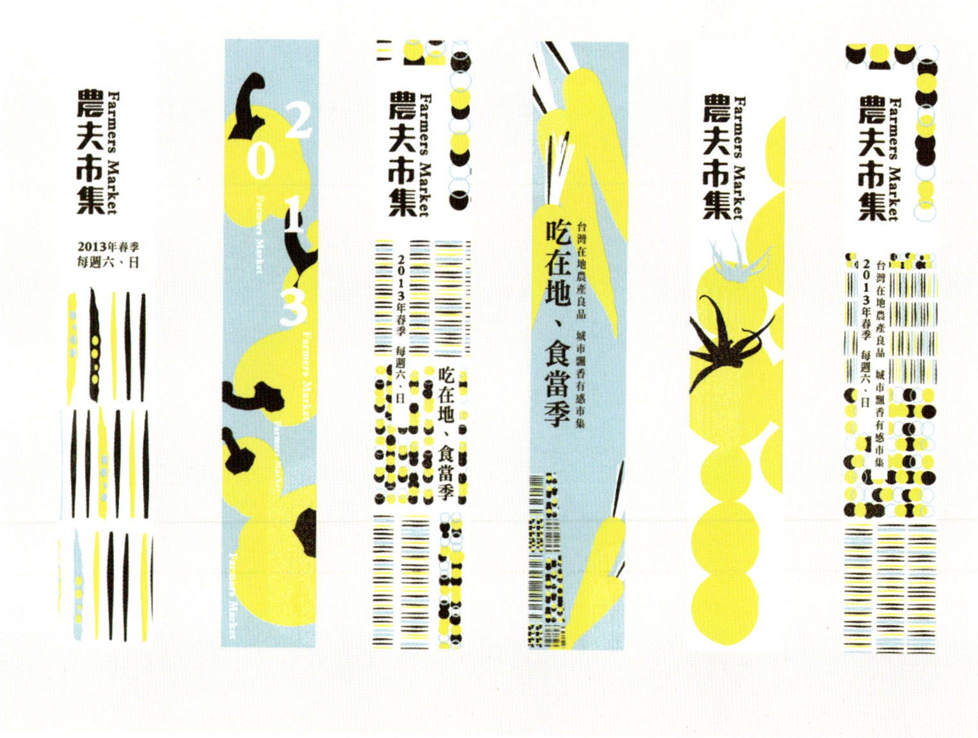

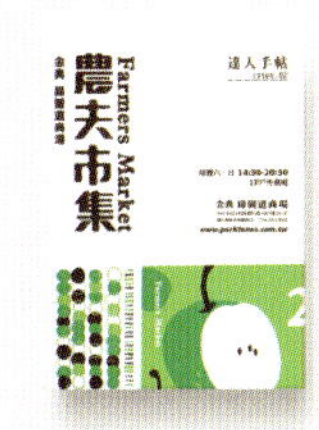
農夫市集
Farmers Market
達人手帖

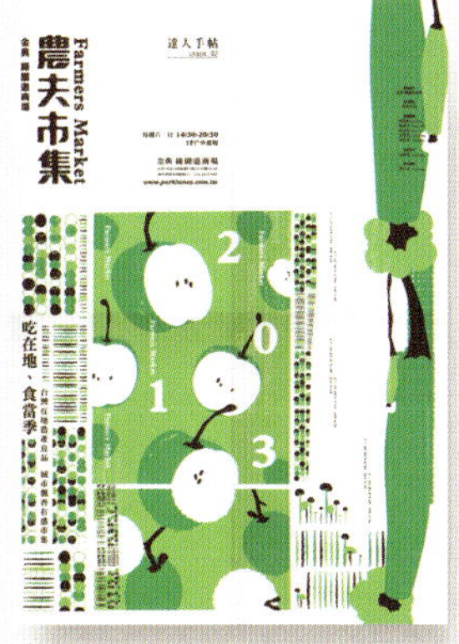
農夫市集
Farmers Market
達人手帖
2
0
1
3
吃在地、食當季

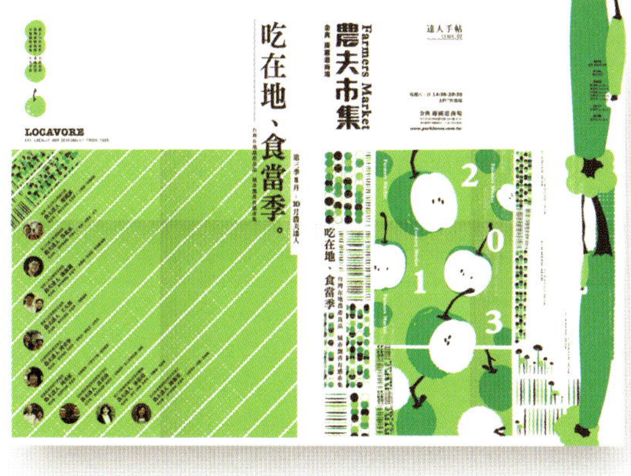
吃在地、食當季。
LOCAVORE
農夫市集
Farmers Market
達人手帖
2
0
1
3
吃在地、食當季

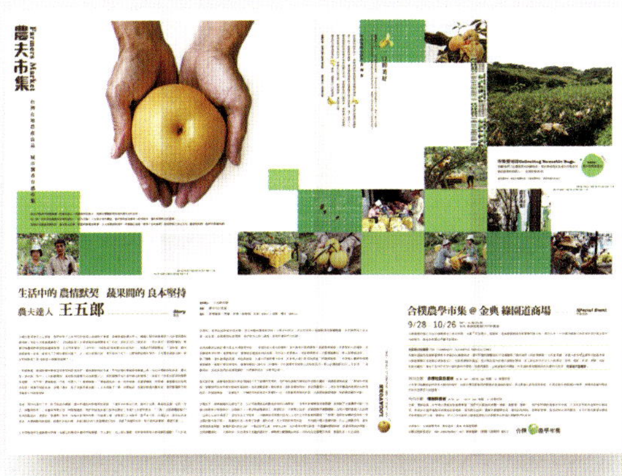
農夫市集
Farmers Market
生活中的 農情默契 蔬果間的 良本堅持
農夫達人 王五郎
合樸農學市集 @ 金典 綠園道商場
9/28 10/26

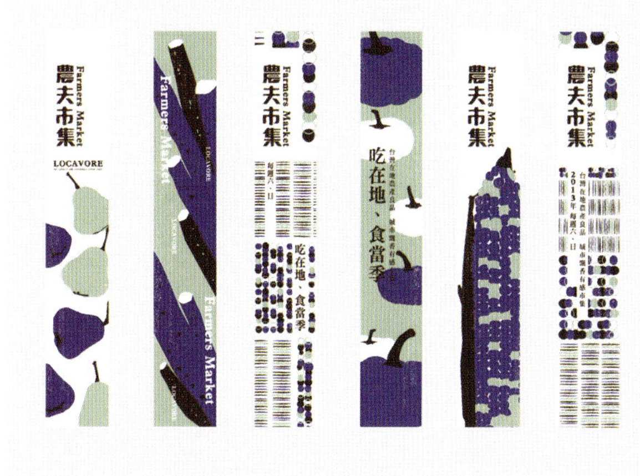
農夫市集
Farmers Market
LOCAVORE
吃在地、食當季

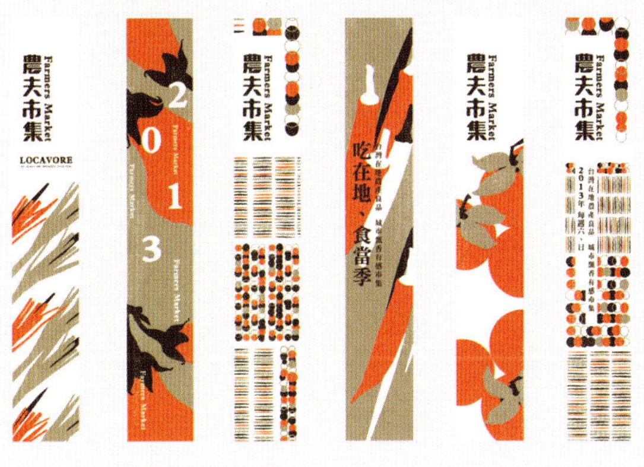
農夫市集
Farmers Market
LOCAVORE
2
0
1
3
吃在地、食當季

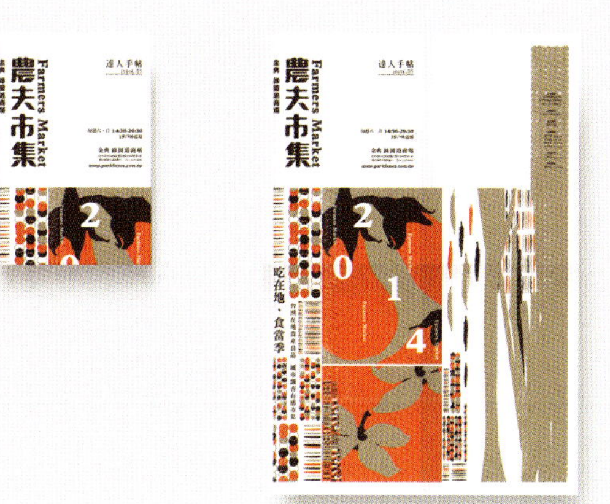
農夫市集
Farmers Market
達人手帖
2
0
1
4
吃在地、食當季

ADC Festival 2014

ADC Festival was moving their base to Miami Beach after 91 years in New York City. Bright colour and blooms suggestive of the new location fuelled the gala's vibe as prints and interactive graphics across the venue and brand applications. The tricolour scheme echoed the event's three days' duration.

Illustration: Christian Villacañas
Photo: Marçal Vaquer
Client: Art Directors Club (ADC)

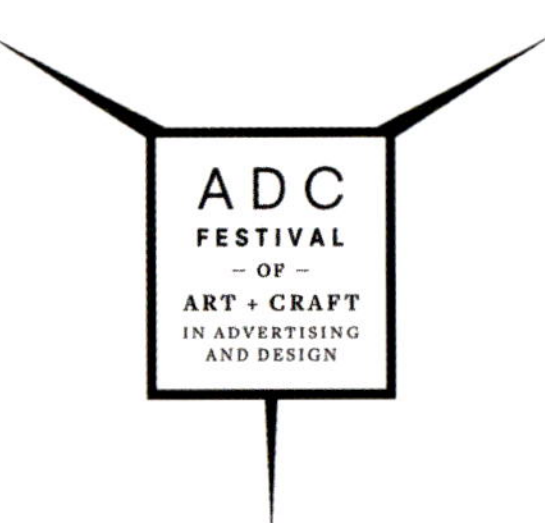

CROWD STUDIO

ADC Festival 2014

ADC Festival was moving their base to Miami Beach after 91 years in New York City. Bright colour and blooms suggestive of the new location fuelled the gala's vibe as prints and interactive graphics across the venue and brand applications. The tricolour scheme echoed the event's three days' duration.

Illustration: Christian Villacañas
Photo: Marçal Vaquer
Client: Art Directors Club (ADC)

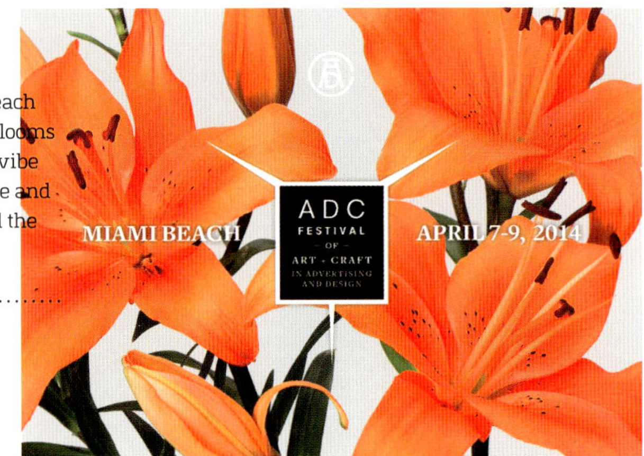

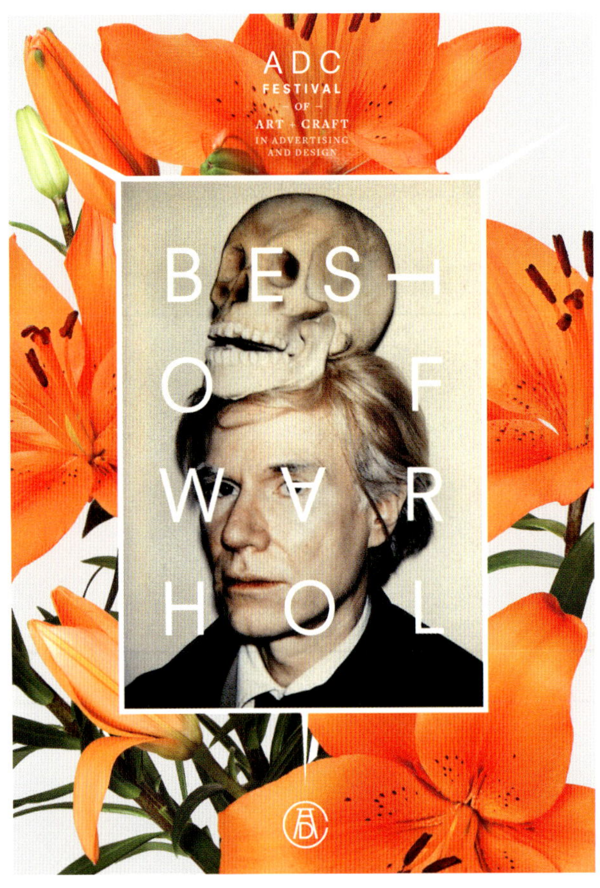

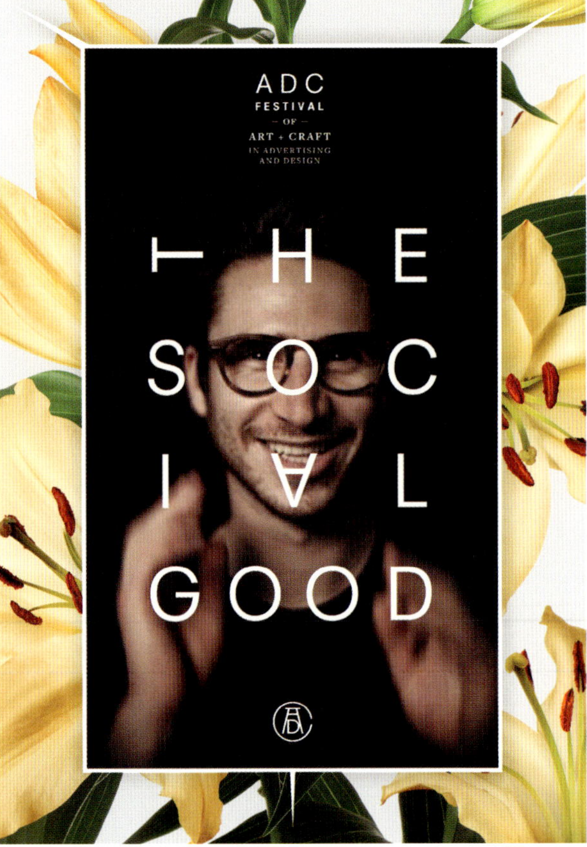

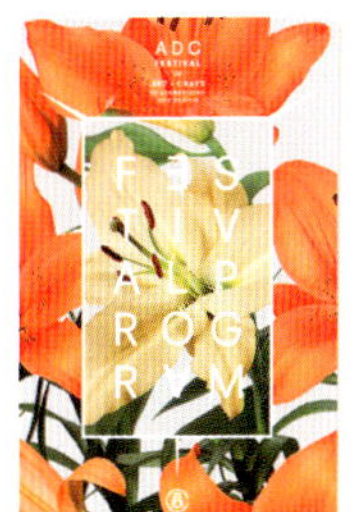

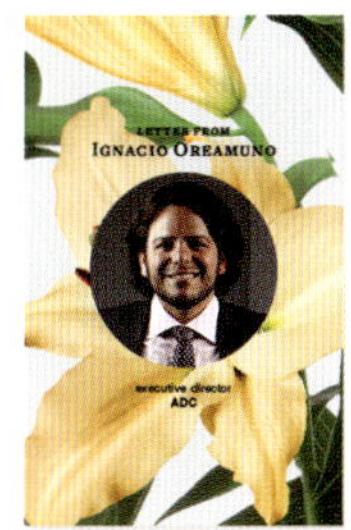
LETTER FROM
IGNACIO OREAMUNO
executive director
ADC

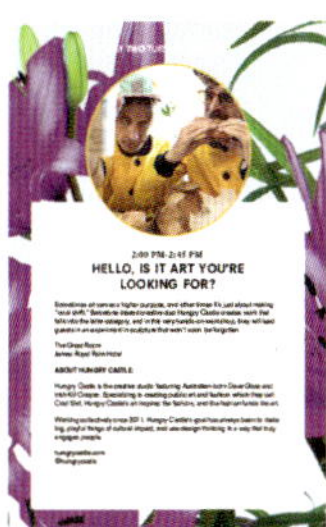
HELLO, IS IT ART YOU'RE LOOKING FOR?

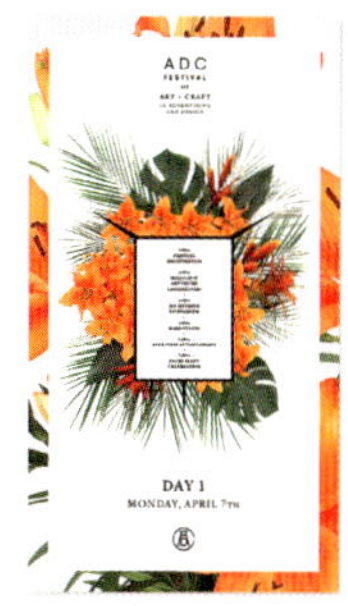
ADC
DAY 1

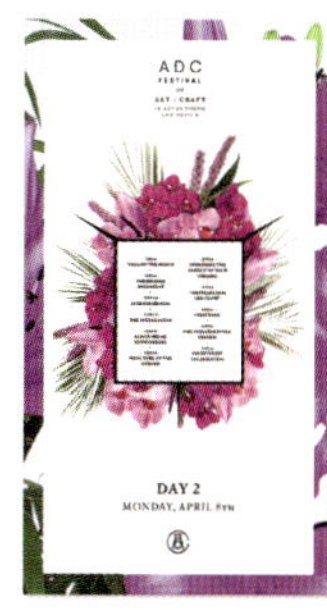
ADC
DAY 2

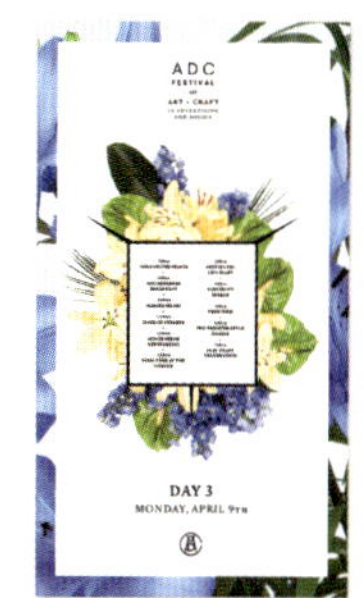
ADC
DAY 3

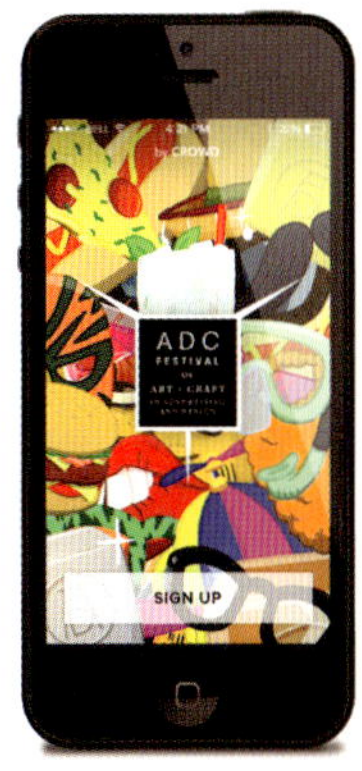
ADC
FESTIVAL
SIGN UP

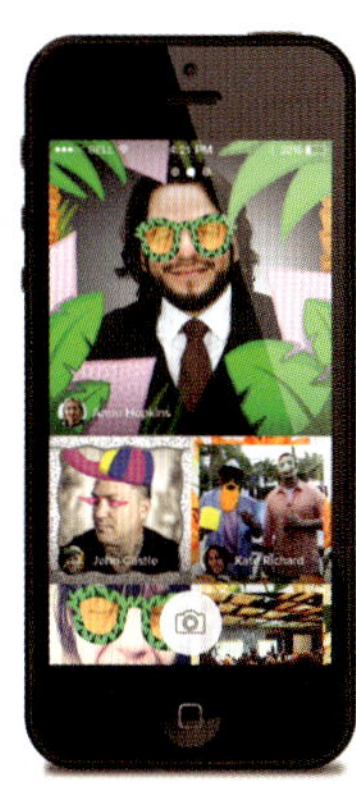

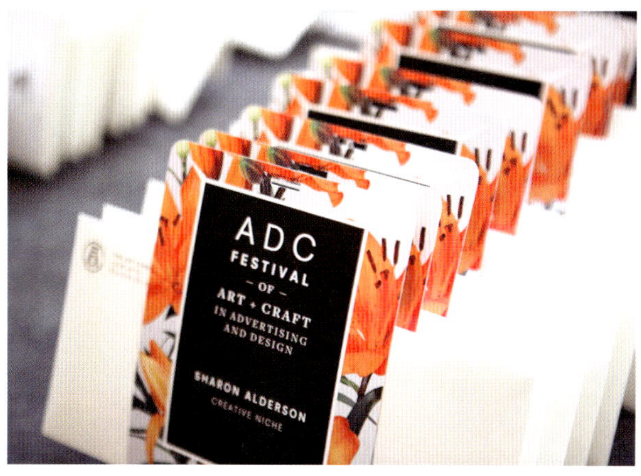
ADC
FESTIVAL
- OF -
ART + CRAFT
IN ADVERTISING
AND DESIGN
SHARON ALDERSON
CREATIVE NICHE

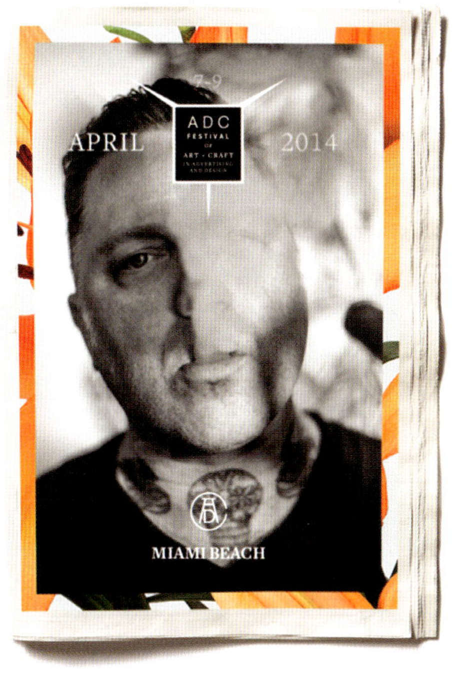
7-9
APRIL
ADC
FESTIVAL
ART + CRAFT
2014
MIAMI BEACH

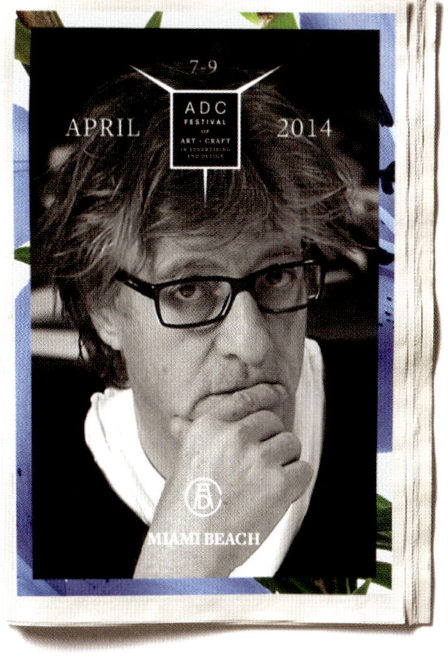
7-9
APRIL
ADC
FESTIVAL
ART + CRAFT
2014
MIAMI BEACH

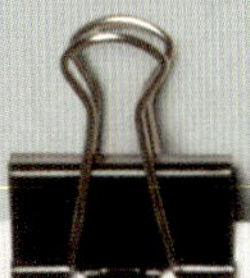

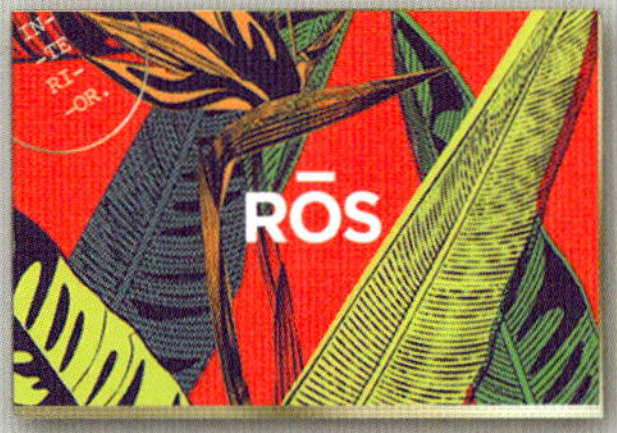
RŌS

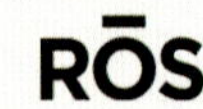
RŌS

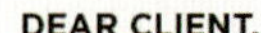
DEAR CLIENT.
Lorem ipsum dolor sit amet, consectetur adipiscing elit. Donec orci purus, luctus
nissim eu, iaculis sed purus. Vivamus faucibus, ipsum nec aliquet viverra, leo
mentum ligula, sit amet sagittis enim ligula quis arcu. Nam egestas tortor id nisi
mattis. In tortor ante, ultricies in suscipit a, tempus non massa. Vivamus et
vel massa nulla. Phasellus nec eros mauris, et scelerisque orci.
Donec malesuada orci vitae nulla accumsan porta a id massa. Quisque accumsan
amet fringilla. Maecenas consequat, magna eget tincidunt semper, odio nibh rutrum
giat ante nisi eu risus. Vestibulum nunc orci, rhoncus a placerat in, ultricies
mattis varius eros, vel fringilla nisi suscipit eget. Quisque scelerisque sagittis
porttitor.
Sed id augue vitae urna euismod commodo aliquet a quam. Pellentesque arcu velit,
malesuada ut, consequat et diam. Nullam erat sem, rhoncus id ullamcorper vitae,
arcu. In ultricies ultricies nulla, ut rutrum nisi iaculis at. Donec eu magna a
faucibus. Fusce aliquet faucibus ultricies. Morbi semper, est id tincidunt
adipiscing lacus, ac bibendum nulla leo eu purus. Quisque nec diam sed risus
ccumsan quis quis nibh. Vestibulum id purus lorem.
(912) 555-1234 / hello@yourwebsite.com
1600 Pennsylvania Ave NW, Washington, DC 20500, United States of America

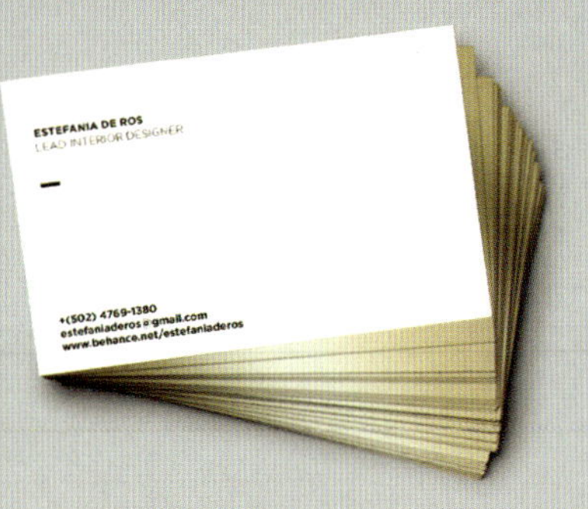
ESTEFANIA DE ROS
LEAD INTERIOR DESIGNER
+(502) 4769-1380
estefaniaderos@gmail.com
www.behance.net/estefaniaderos

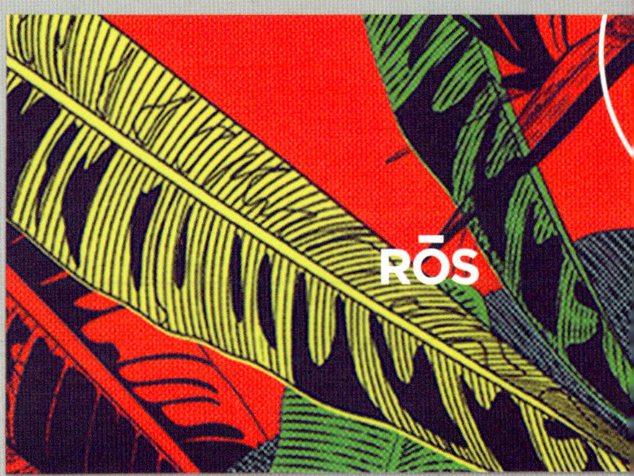
RŌS

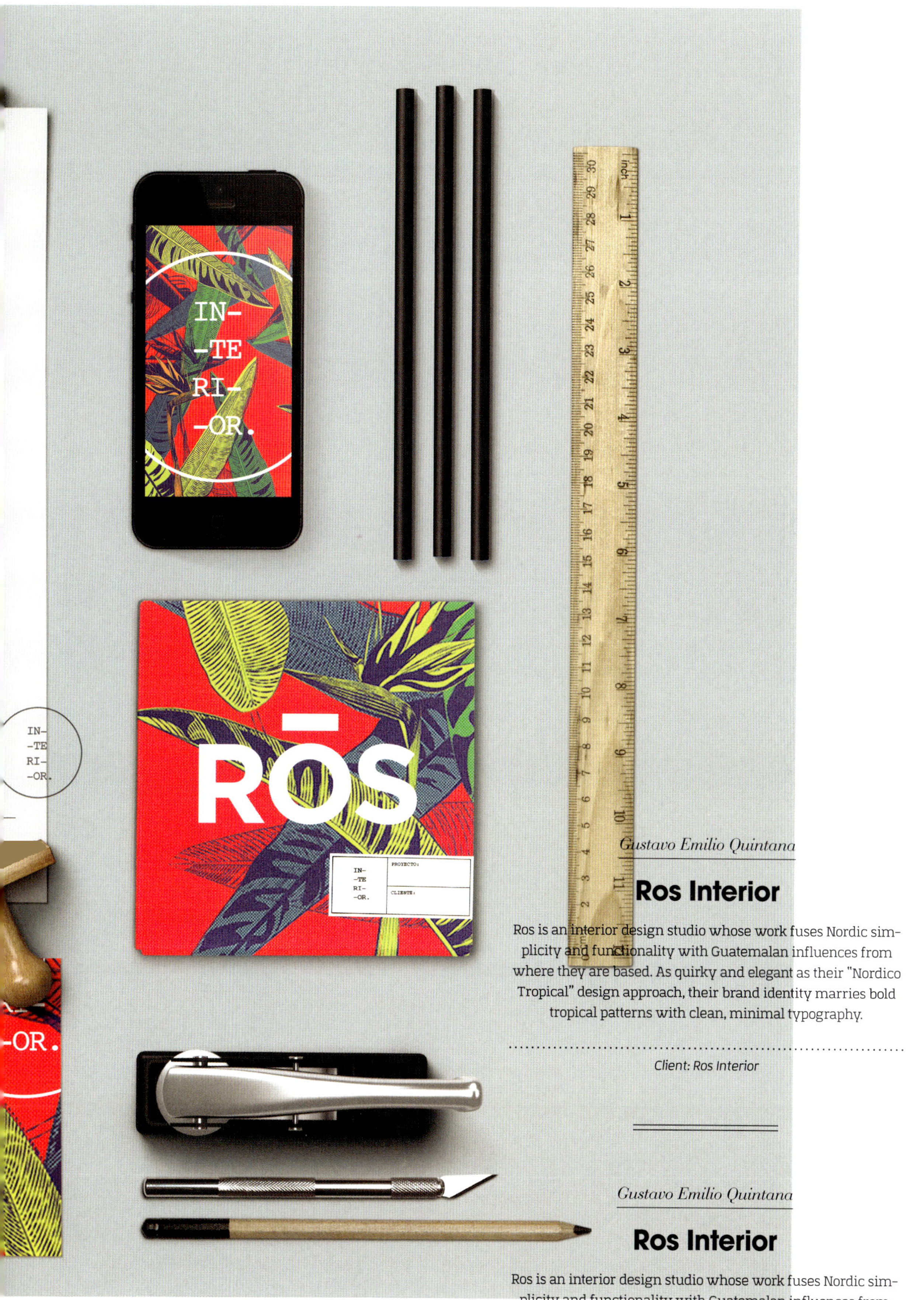

Gustavo Emilio Quintana

Ros Interior

Ros is an interior design studio whose work fuses Nordic simplicity and functionality with Guatemalan influences from where they are based. As quirky and elegant as their "Nordico Tropical" design approach, their brand identity marries bold tropical patterns with clean, minimal typography.

Client: Ros Interior

Gustavo Emilio Quintana

Ros Interior

Ros is an interior design studio whose work fuses Nordic simplicity and functionality with Guatemalan influences from where they are based. As quirky and elegant as their "Nordico Tropical" design approach, their brand identity marries bold

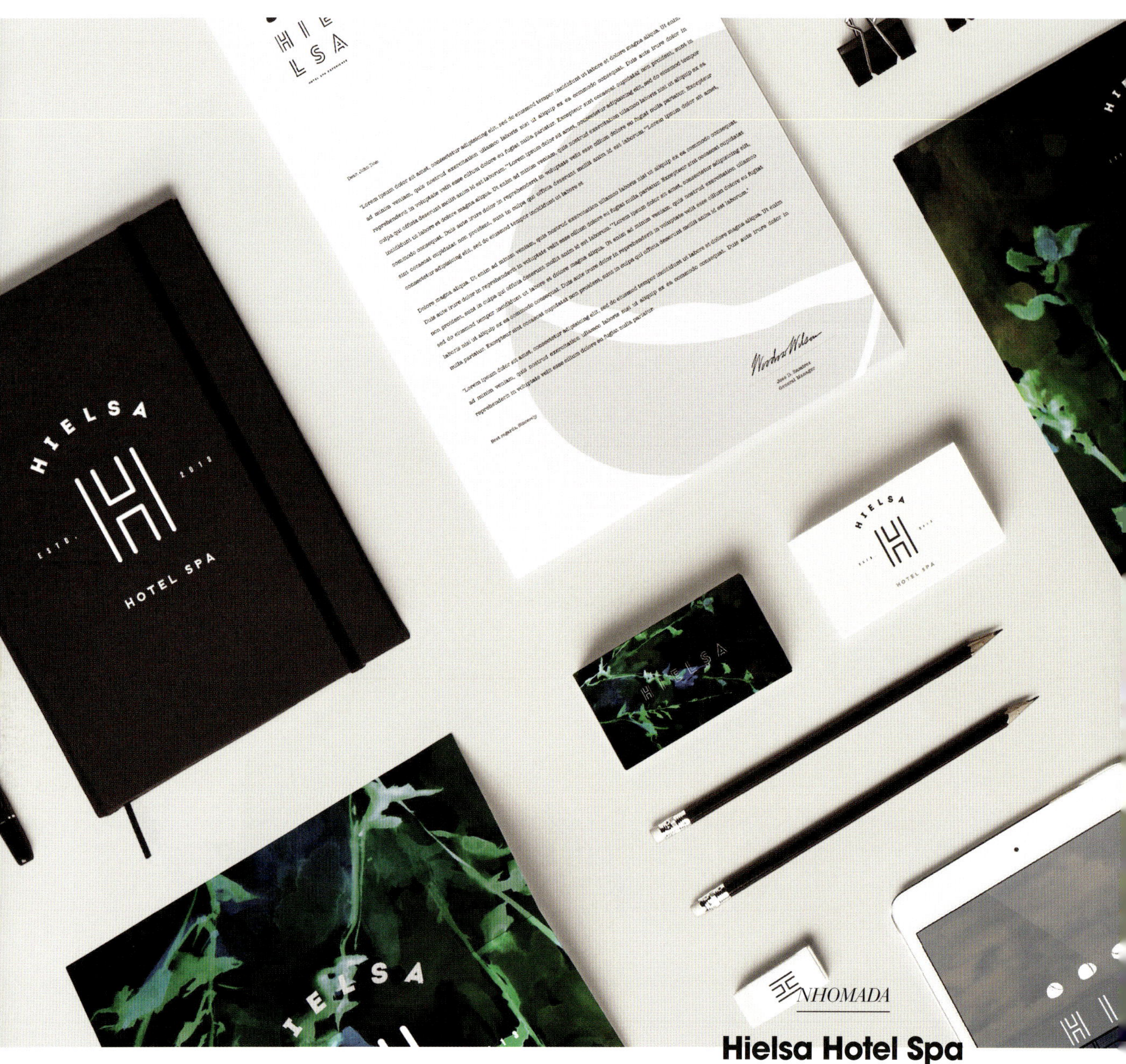

NHOMADA

Hielsa Hotel Spa

Brand design commissioned for a final project at Les Roches, International School of Hotel Management. Newfangled logotype as well as sombrely serene illustrated verso combined to create a modern visual concept focusing on its location in the depths of Iceland.

Client: Ramón Martinez
(Les Roches International School of Hotel Management)

NHOMADA

Hielsa Hotel Spa

Brand design commissioned for a final project at Les Roches, International School of Hotel Manage-

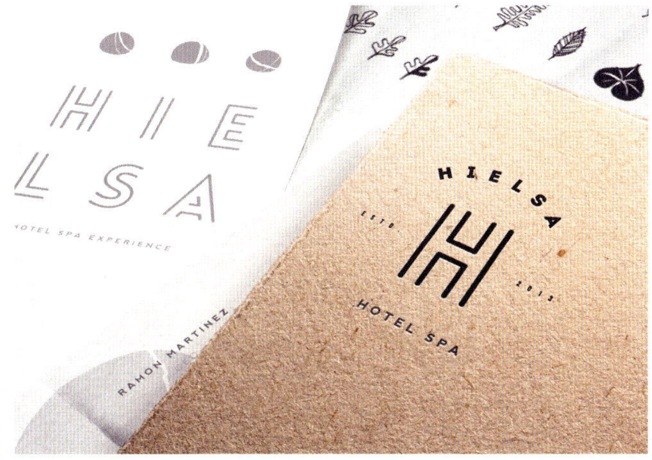
HIE
LSA
HOTEL SPA EXPERIENCE
RAMON MARTINEZ
HIELSA
ESTD.
2013
HOTEL SPA

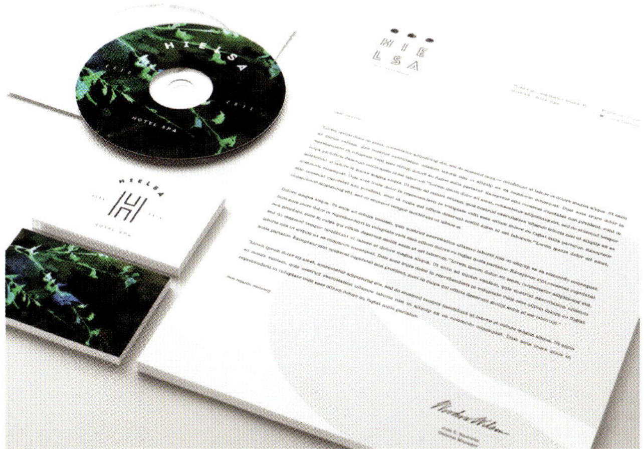
HIELSA
HOTEL SPA

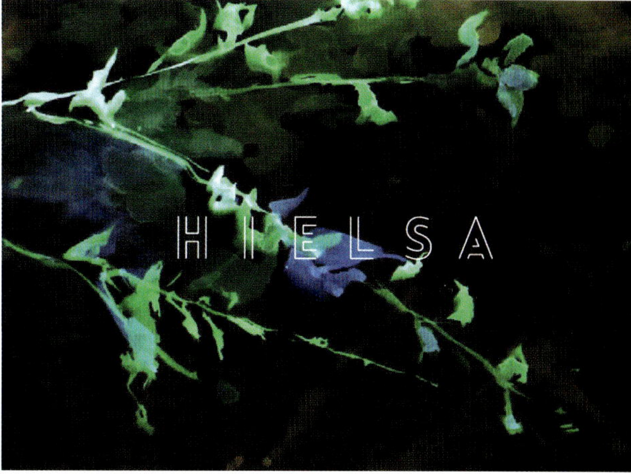
HIELSA

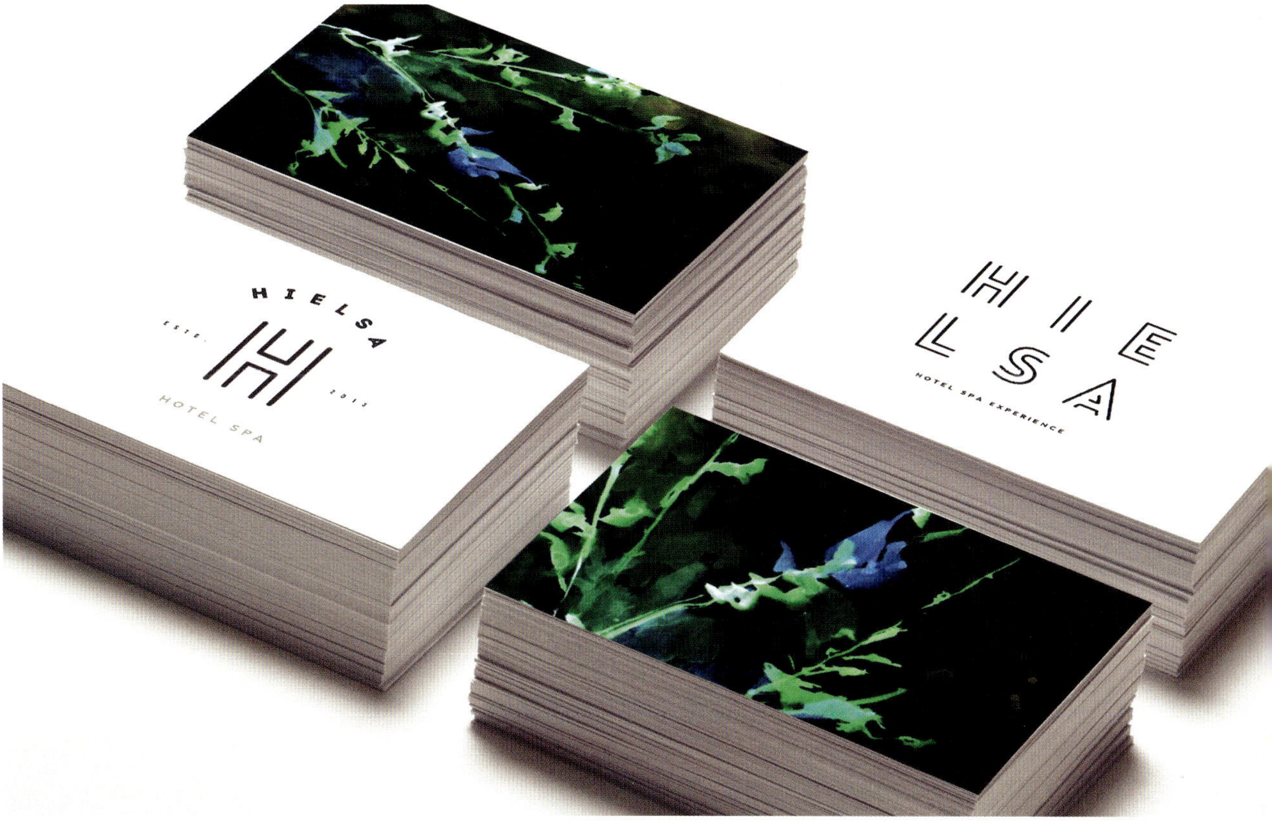

Mushrooms

Mushrooms is a personal project of Sasha Vinogradova where the artist played on surreal colours and funguses of distinctive shapes to produce glyphs and patterns. The dimensional digital artwork was rendered using 3ds Max, ZBrush and Photoshop.

Sasha Vinogradova

Mushrooms

Mushrooms is a personal project of Sasha Vinogradova where the artist played on surreal colours and funguses of distinctive shapes to produce glyphs and patterns. The dimensional digital artwork was rendered using 3ds Max, ZBrush and Photoshop.

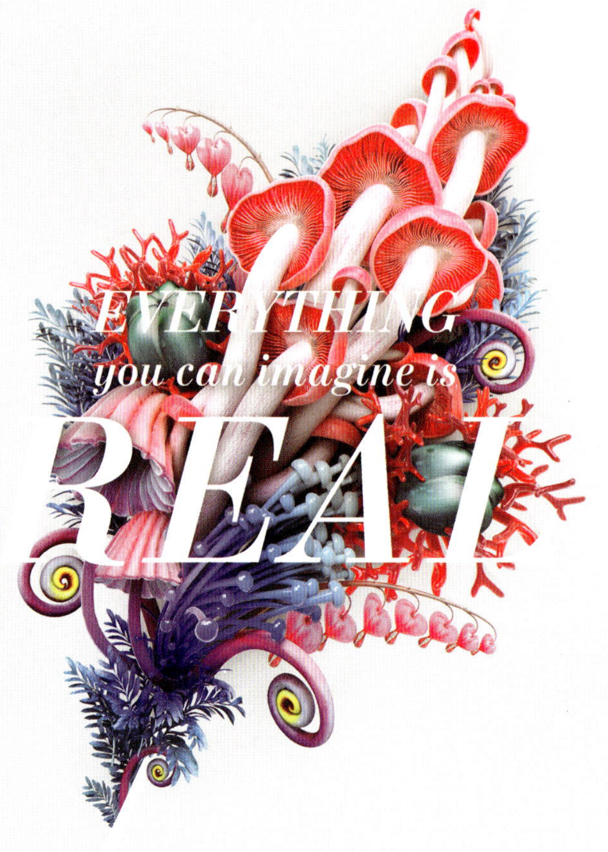

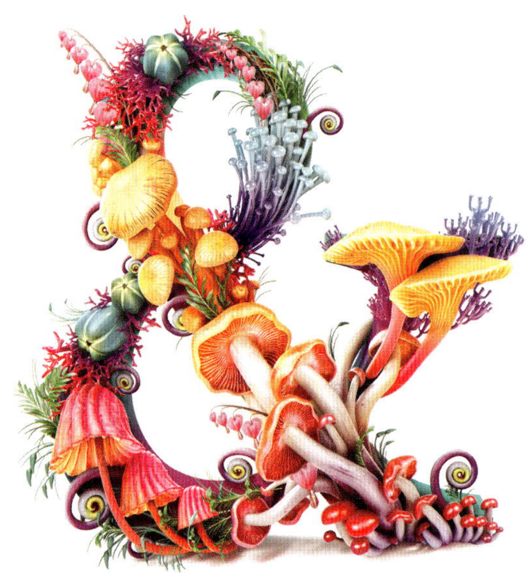

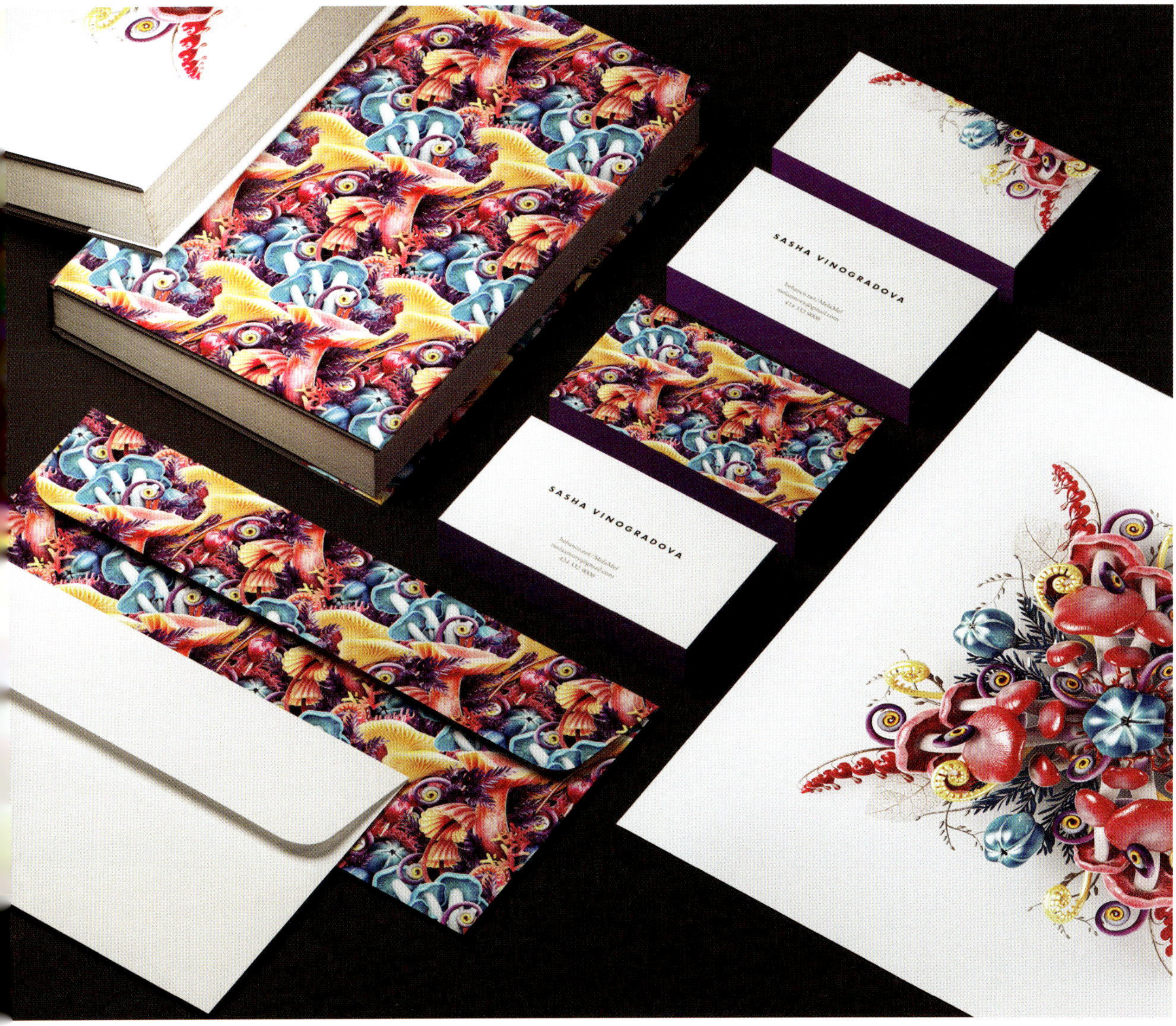

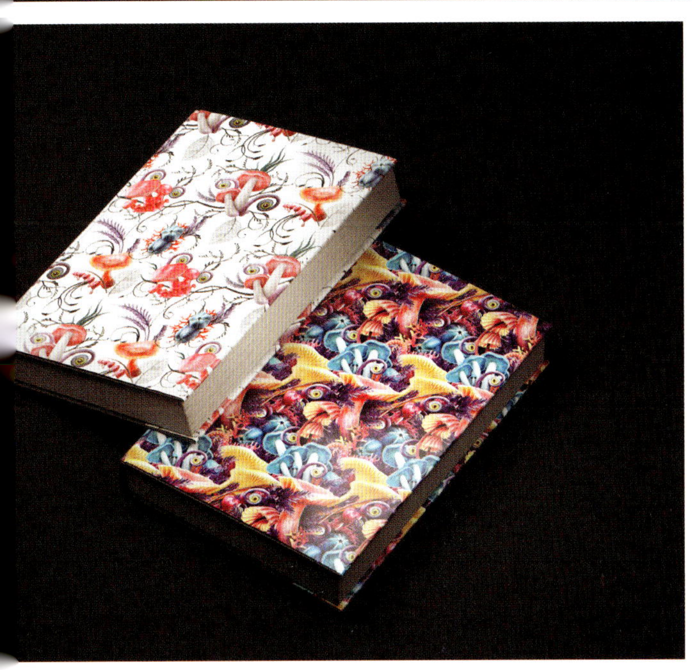

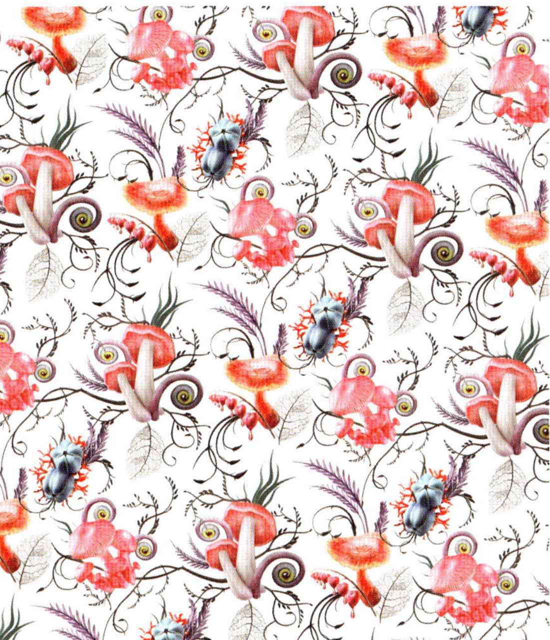

Pure Drops is a passionate team of experts that produces fine wines and olive oil from Greece. While the drop visualises the name, illustrations visualise ingredients and abstract sensations, allowing for a flexible adaptation onto the likes of wrapping paper and press kit.

Client: Pure Drops

Bob Studio

Pure Drops

Pure Drops is a passionate team of experts that produces fine wines and olive oil from Greece. While the drop visualises the name, illustrations visualise ingredients and abstract sensations, allowing for a flexible adaptation onto the likes of wrapping paper and press kit.

Client: Pure Drops

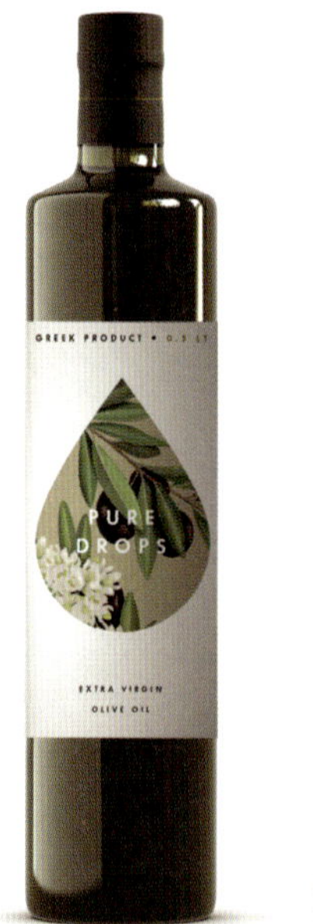

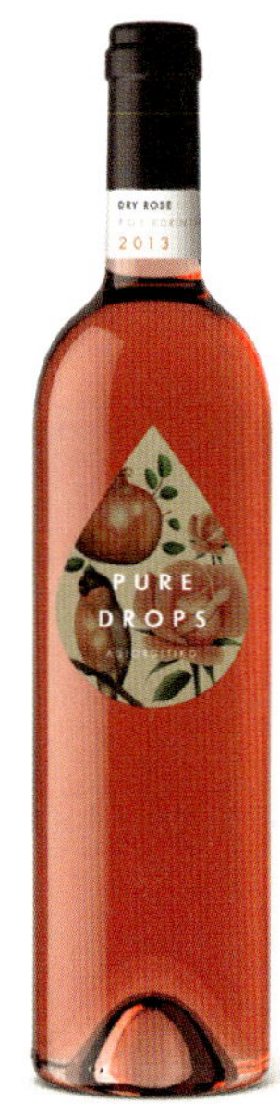

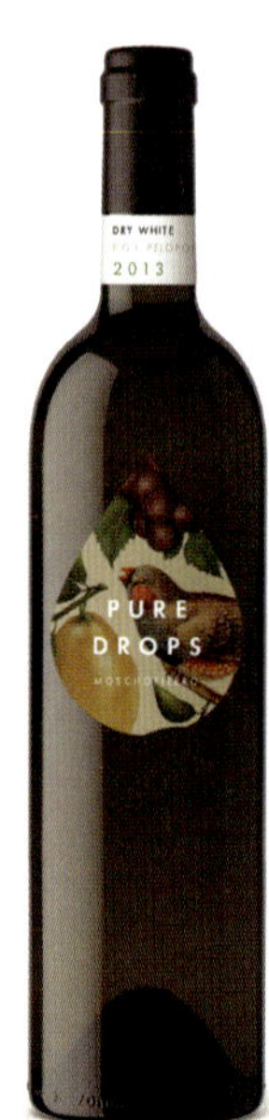

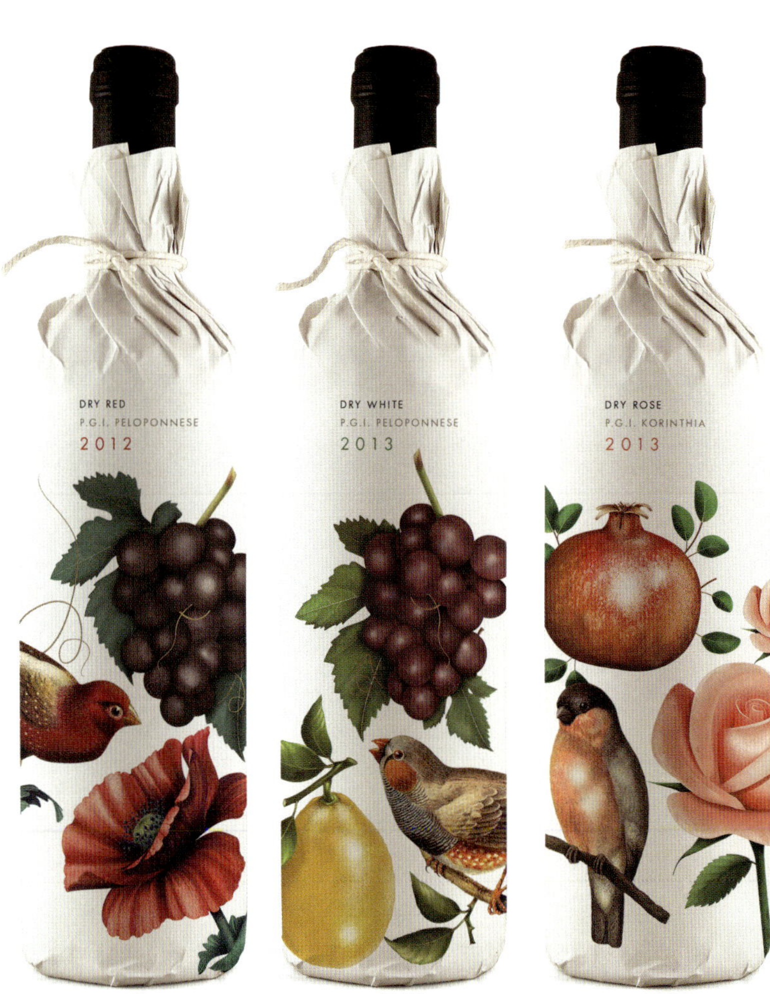

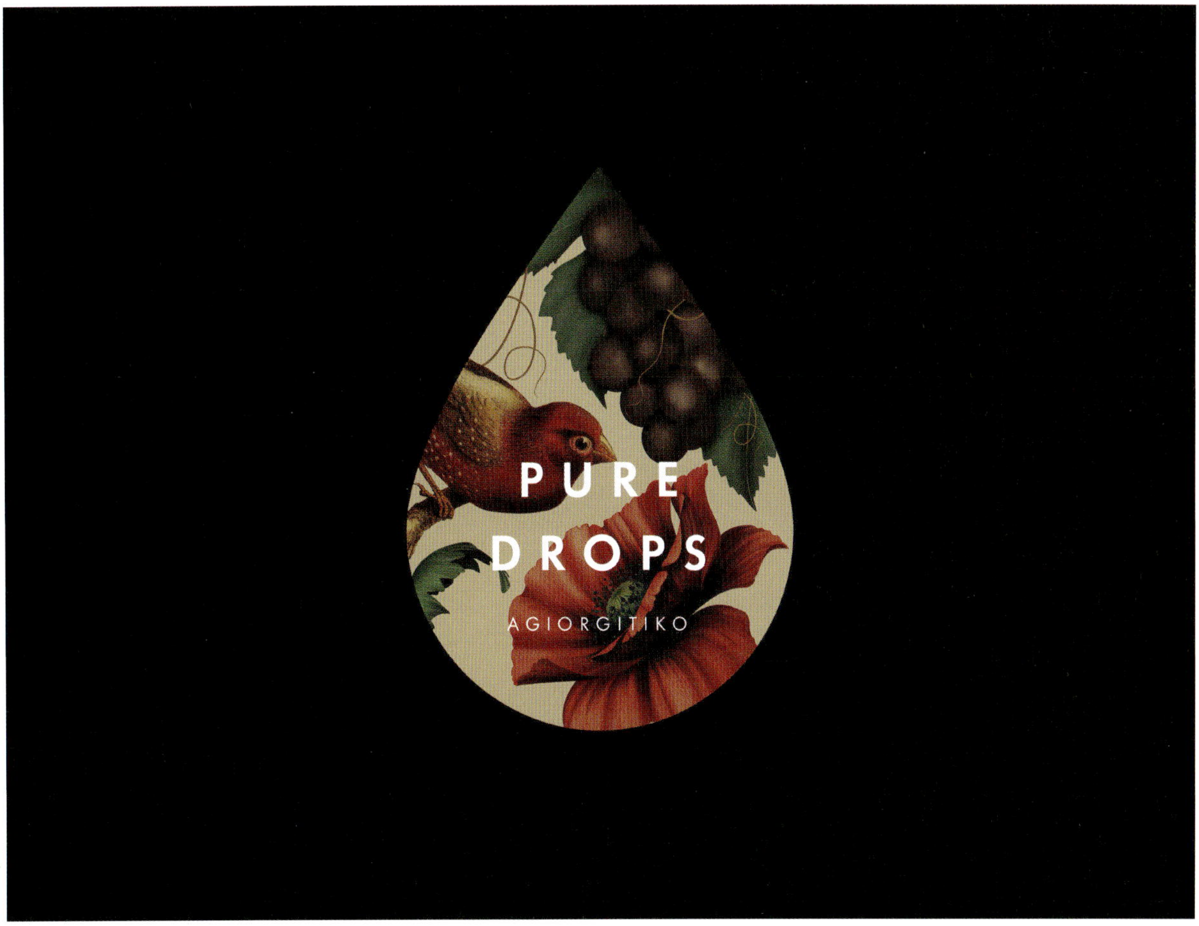

PURE
DROPS
AGIORGITIKO

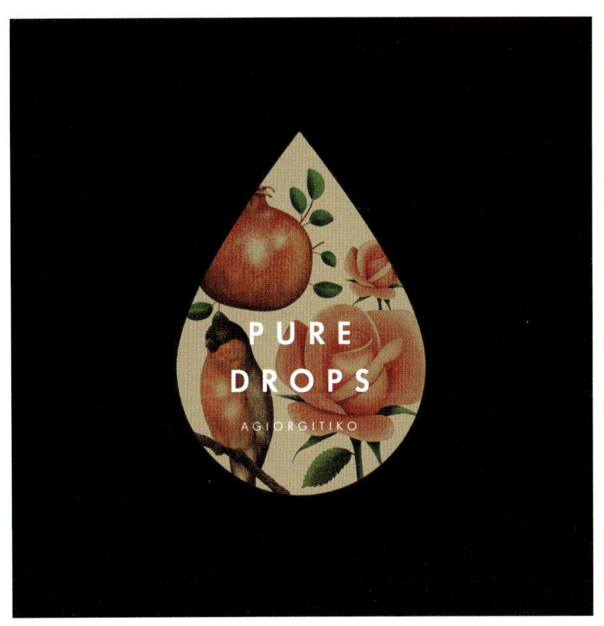
PURE
DROPS
AGIORGITIKO

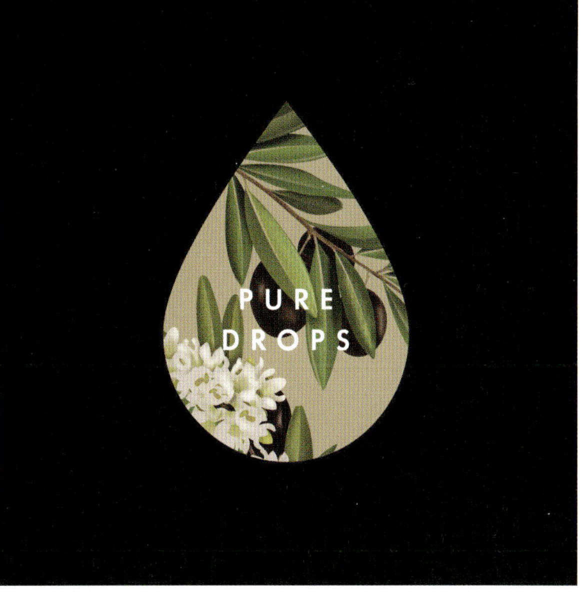
PURE
DROPS

Beto y Carlos

B & C Beer-Wine Steakhouse is a bar and grill started by friends and a food-lover duo. Taking advantage of contrasting colours, Estudio Yeyé yields a whimsical collage in the visual identity about food magic with illustrations and hues likened to vintage posters.

Estudio Yeyé

Beto y Carlos

B & C Beer-Wine Steakhouse is a bar and grill started by friends and a food-lover duo. Taking advantage of contrasting colours, Estudio Yeyé yields a whimsical collage in the visual identity about food magic with illustrations and hues likened to vintage posters.

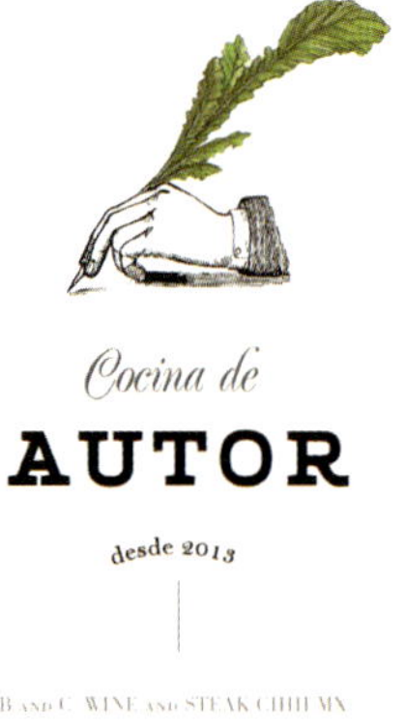

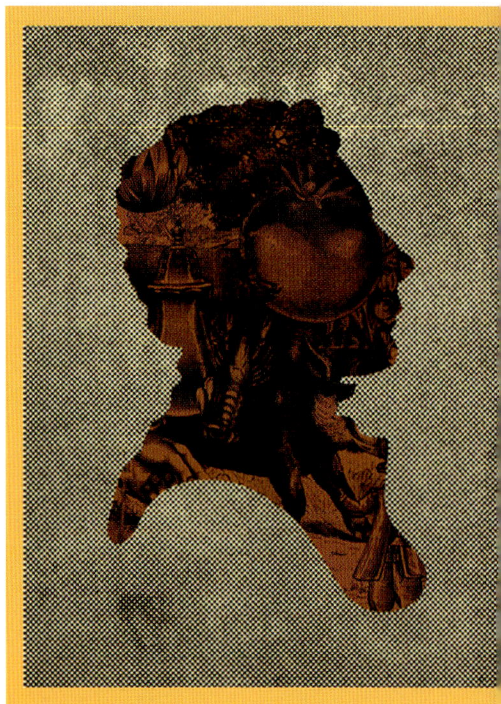

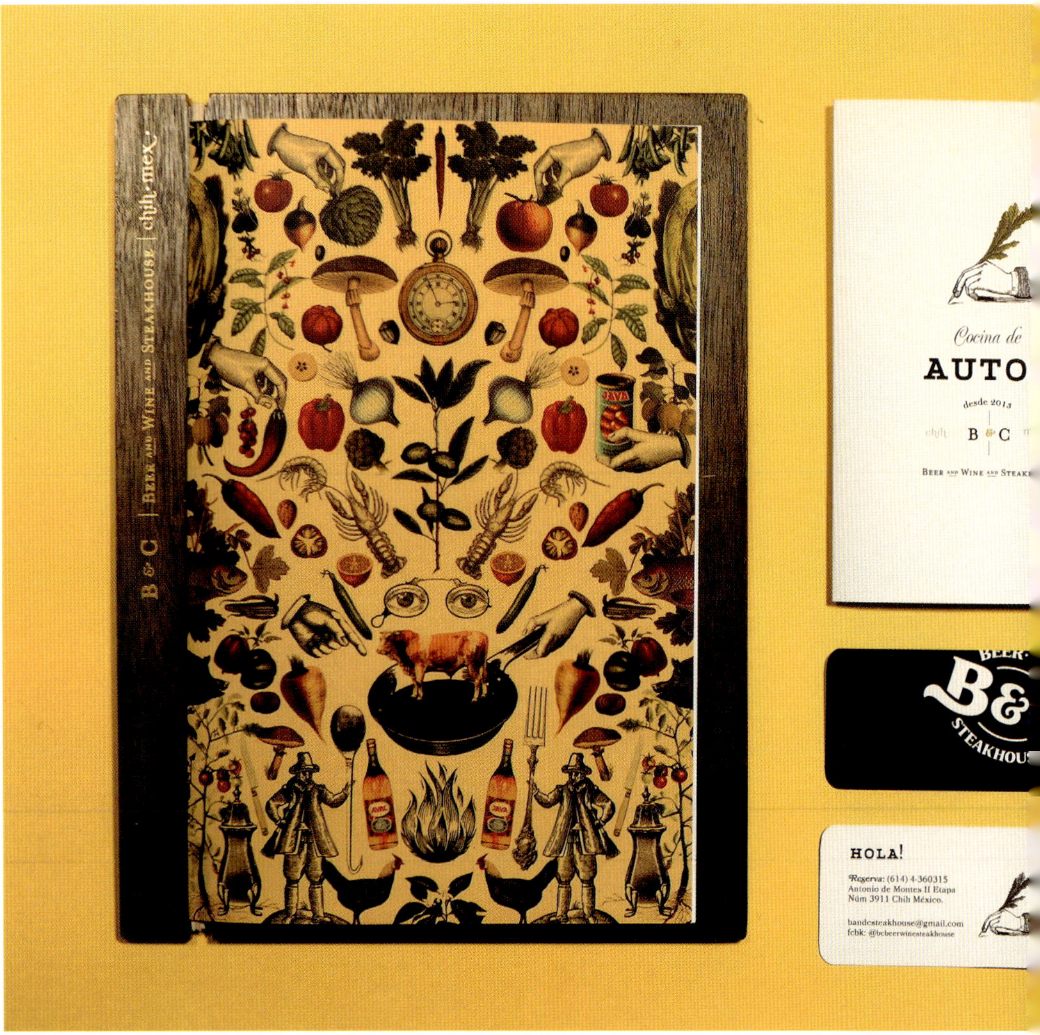

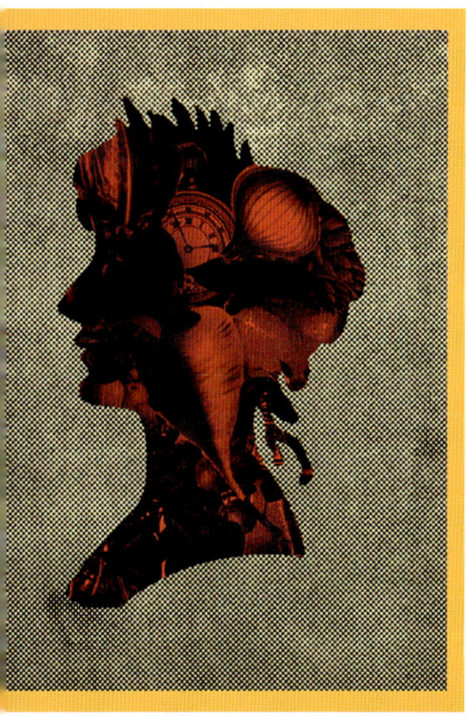

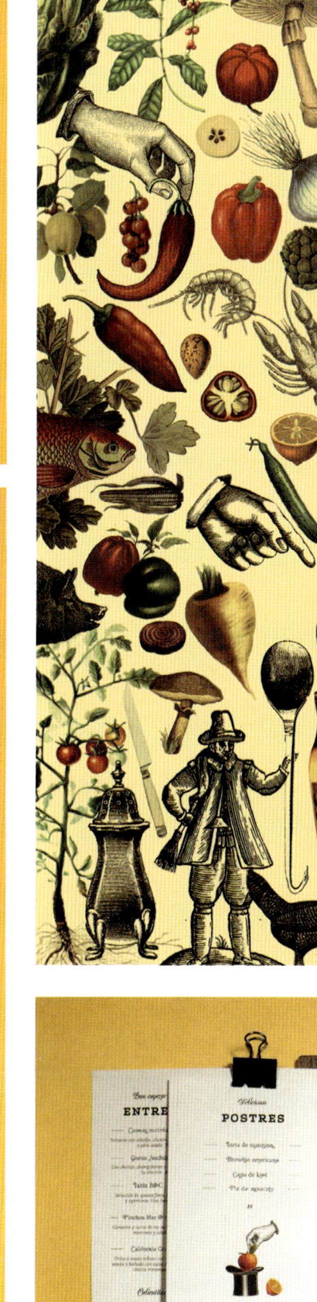

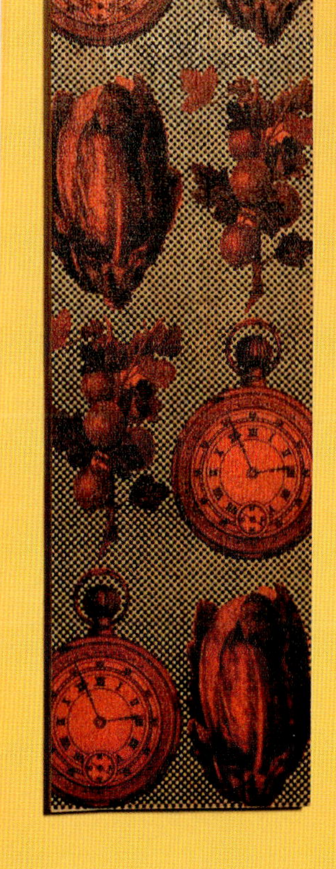

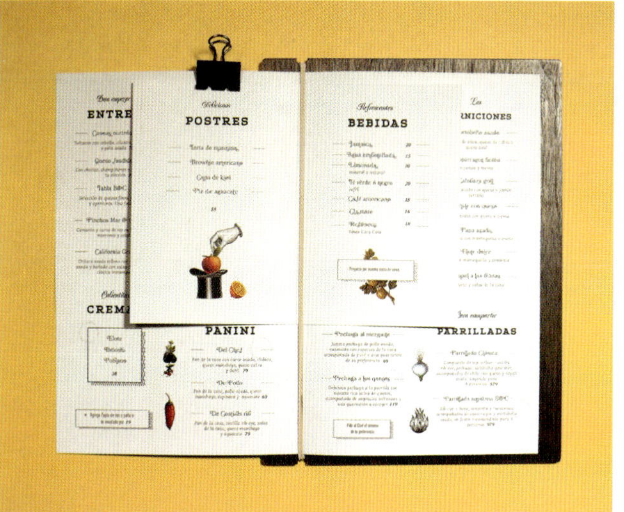
POSTRES
BEBIDAS
PANINI
PARRILLADAS

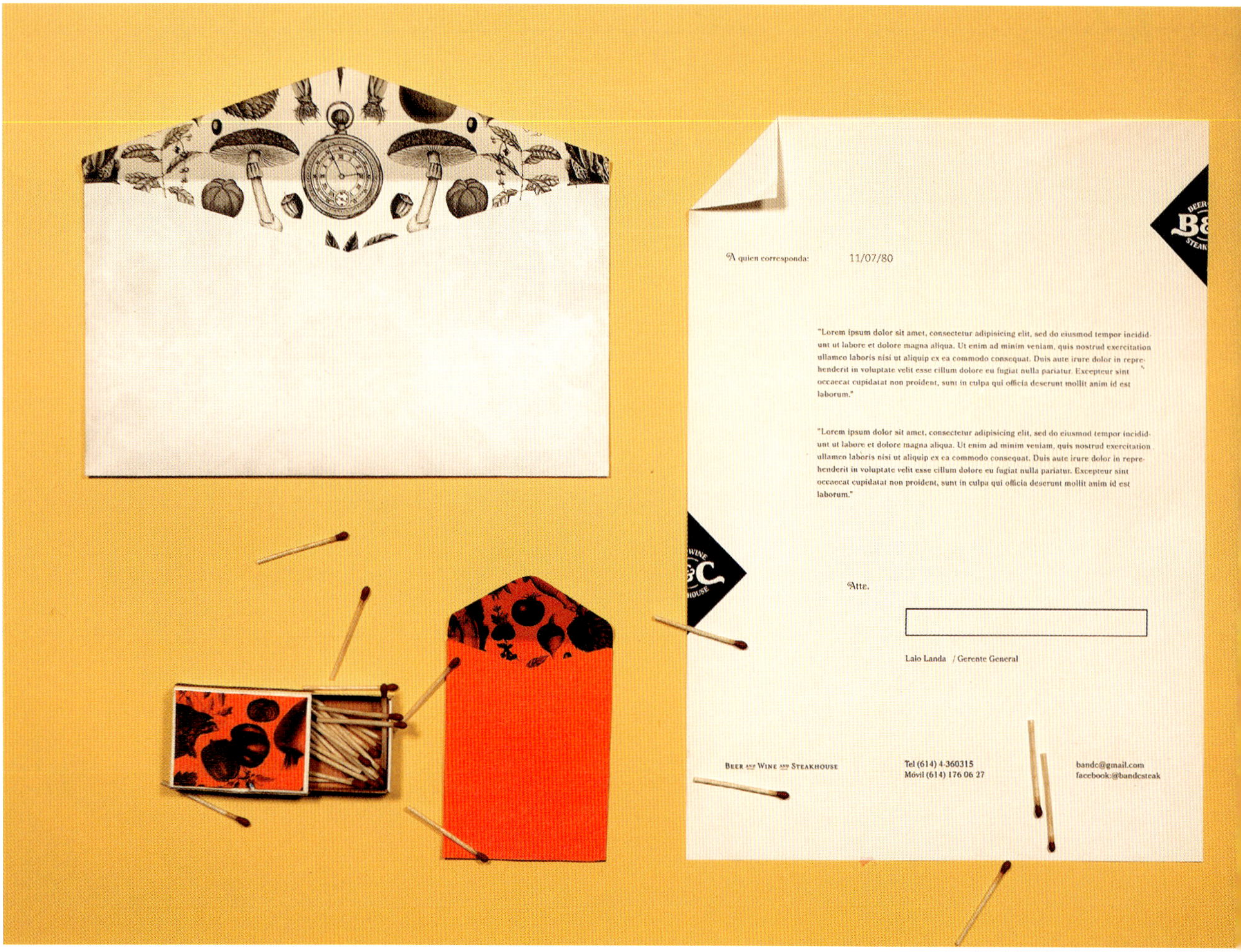

A quien corresponda: 11/07/80

"Lorem ipsum dolor sit amet, consectetur adipisicing elit, sed do eiusmod tempor incididunt ut labore et dolore magna aliqua. Ut enim ad minim veniam, quis nostrud exercitation ullamco laboris nisi ut aliquip ex ea commodo consequat. Duis aute irure dolor in reprehenderit in voluptate velit esse cillum dolore eu fugiat nulla pariatur. Excepteur sint occaecat cupidatat non proident, sunt in culpa qui officia deserunt mollit anim id est laborum."

"Lorem ipsum dolor sit amet, consectetur adipisicing elit, sed do eiusmod tempor incididunt ut labore et dolore magna aliqua. Ut enim ad minim veniam, quis nostrud exercitation ullamco laboris nisi ut aliquip ex ea commodo consequat. Duis aute irure dolor in reprehenderit in voluptate velit esse cillum dolore eu fugiat nulla pariatur. Excepteur sint occaecat cupidatat non proident, sunt in culpa qui officia deserunt mollit anim id est laborum."

Atte.

Lalo Landa / Gerente General

Beer and Wine and Steakhouse

Tel (614) 4-360315
Móvil (614) 176 06 27

bandc@gmail.com
facebook: @bandcsteak

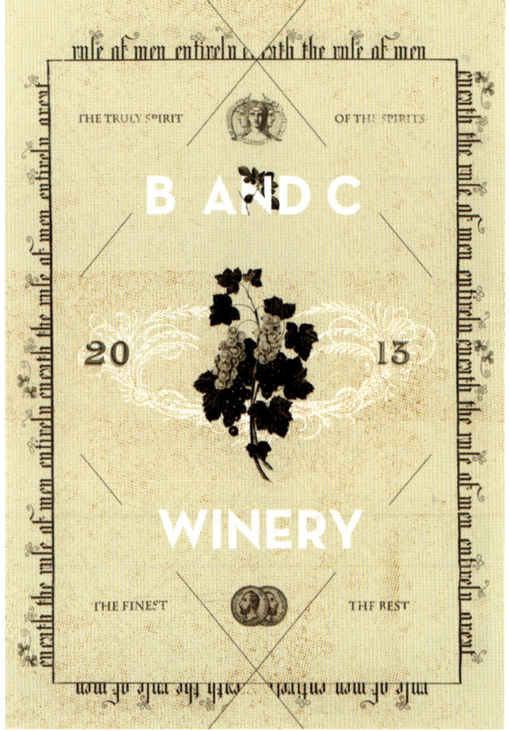

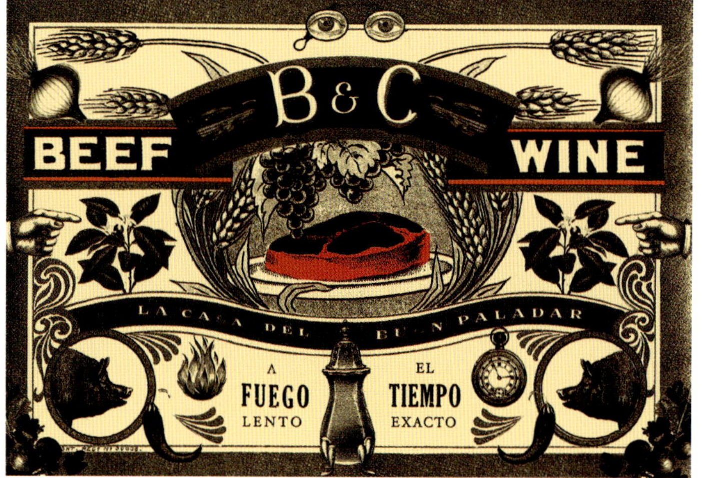

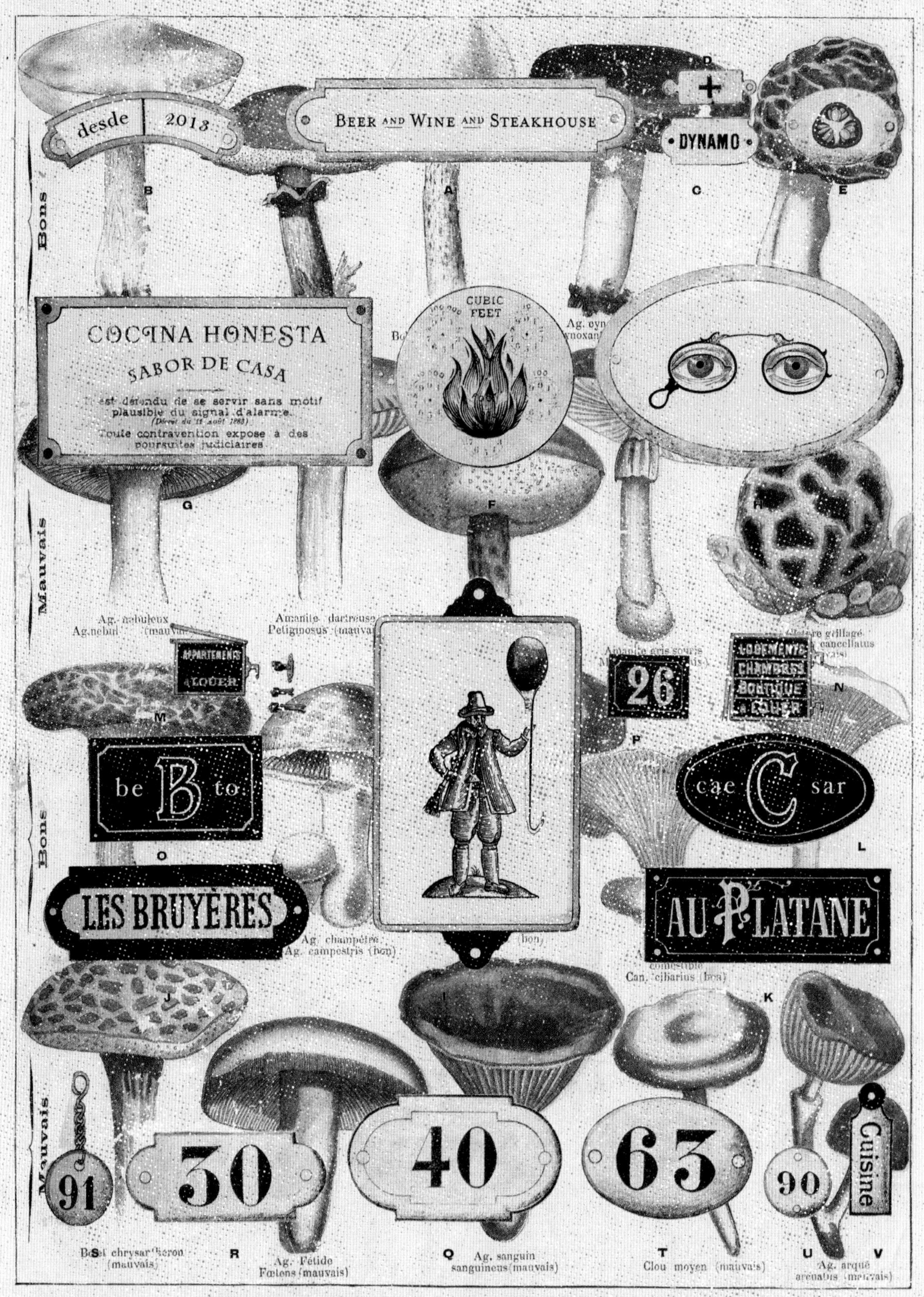
desde 2013
BEER AND WINE AND STEAKHOUSE
DYNAMO
Bons
COCINA HONESTA
SABOR DE CASA
est défendu de se servir sans motif plausible du signal d'alarme.
Toute contravention expose à des poursuites judiciaires.
CUBIC FEET
Mauvais
APPARTEMENTS A LOUER
26
LOGEMENTS CHAMBRES BOUTIQUE A LOUER
be B to.
cae C sar
LES BRUYÈRES
AU PLATANE
91
30
40
63
90
Cuisine
CHAMPIGNONS BONS ET MAUVAIS

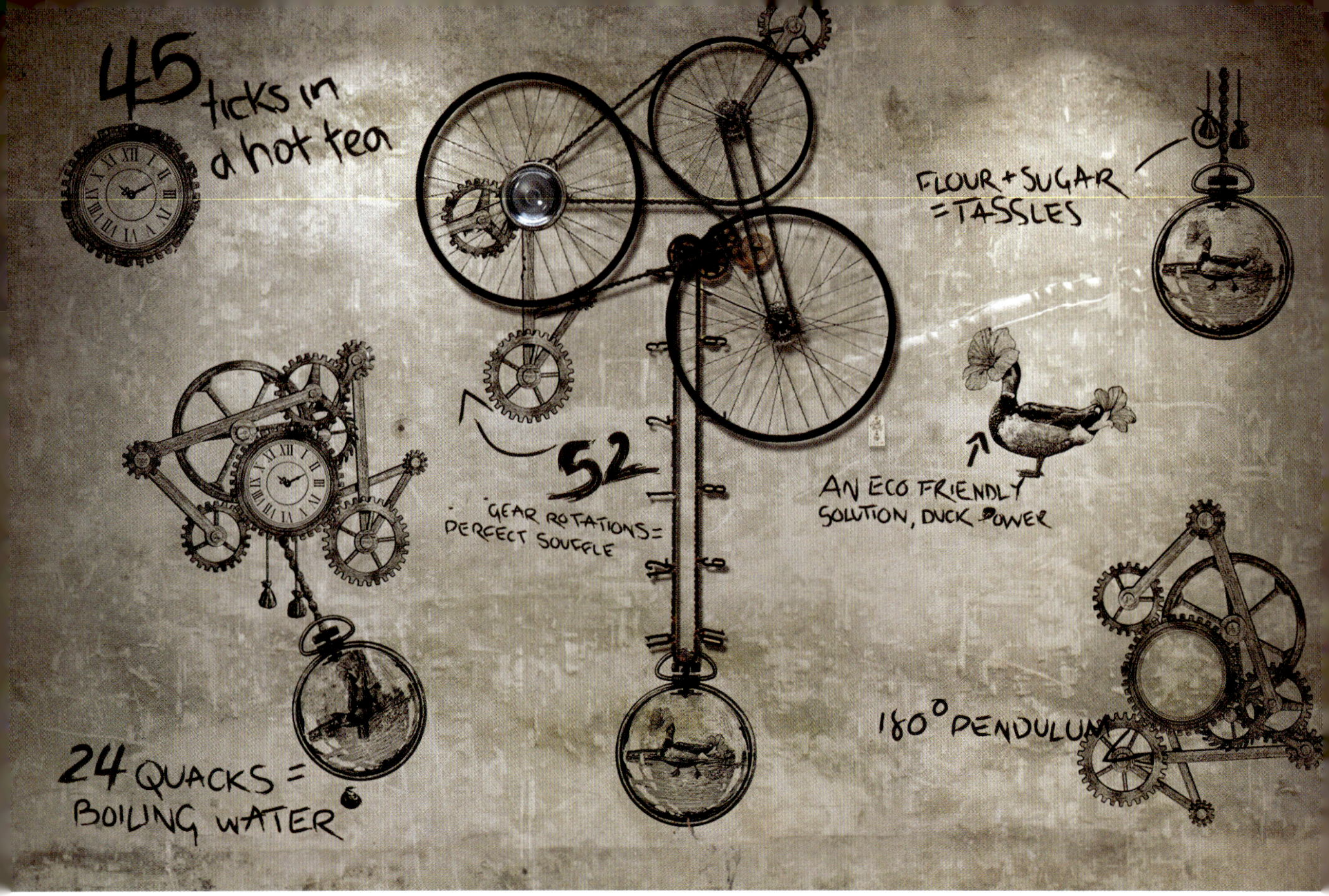

45 ticks in a hot tea

FLOUR + SUGAR = TASSLES

52 GEAR ROTATIONS = PERFECT SOUFFLE

AN ECO FRIENDLY SOLUTION, DUCK POWER

180° PENDULUM

24 QUACKS = BOILING WATER

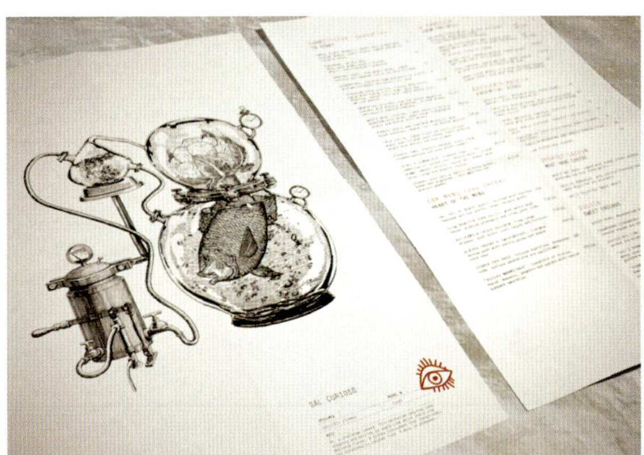

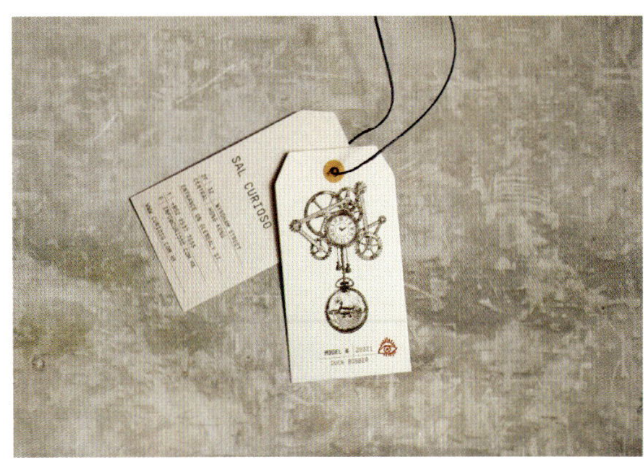

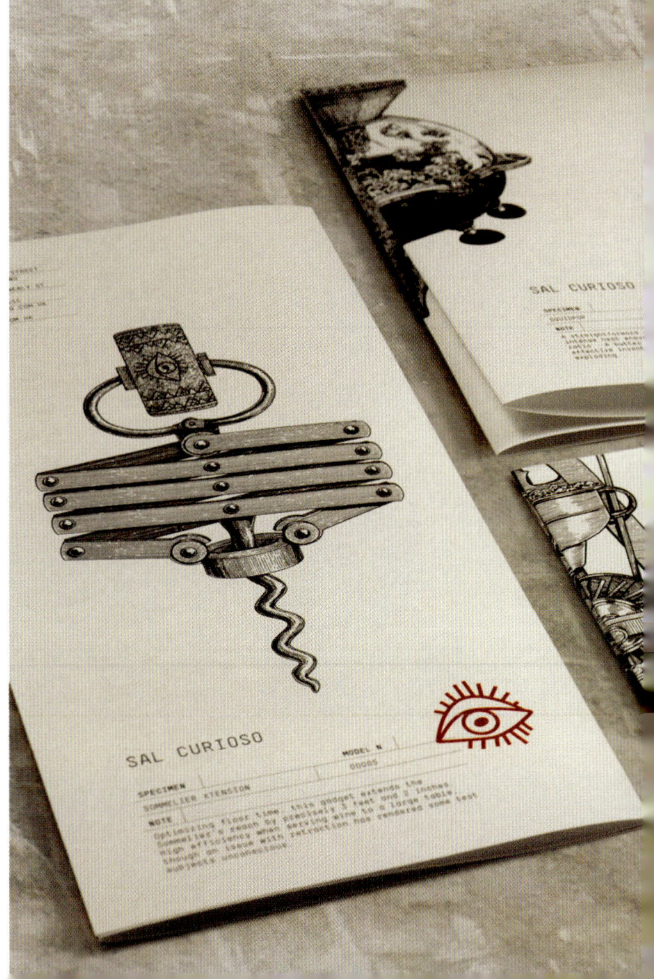

Sal Curioso is a Spanish restaurant committed to offering patrons an innovative taste journey. Substance built on the spirit with bizarre illustrations of culinary experiments. Patent application forms and prototype sketches reflect Sal's quest for perfection.

Client: Elite Grace International Ltd

Substance

Sal Curioso

Sal Curioso is a Spanish restaurant committed to offering patrons an innovative taste journey. Substance built on the spirit with bizarre illustrations of culinary experiments. Patent application forms and prototype sketches reflect Sal's quest for perfection.

Client: Elite Grace International Ltd

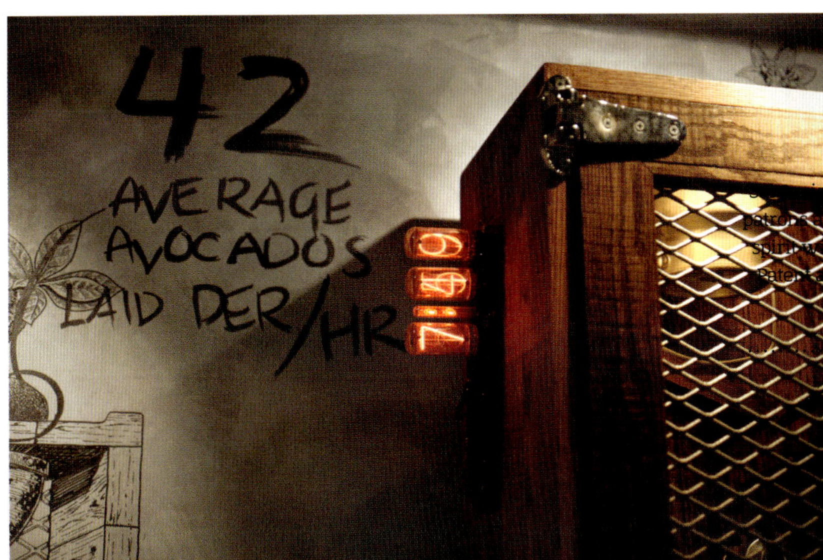

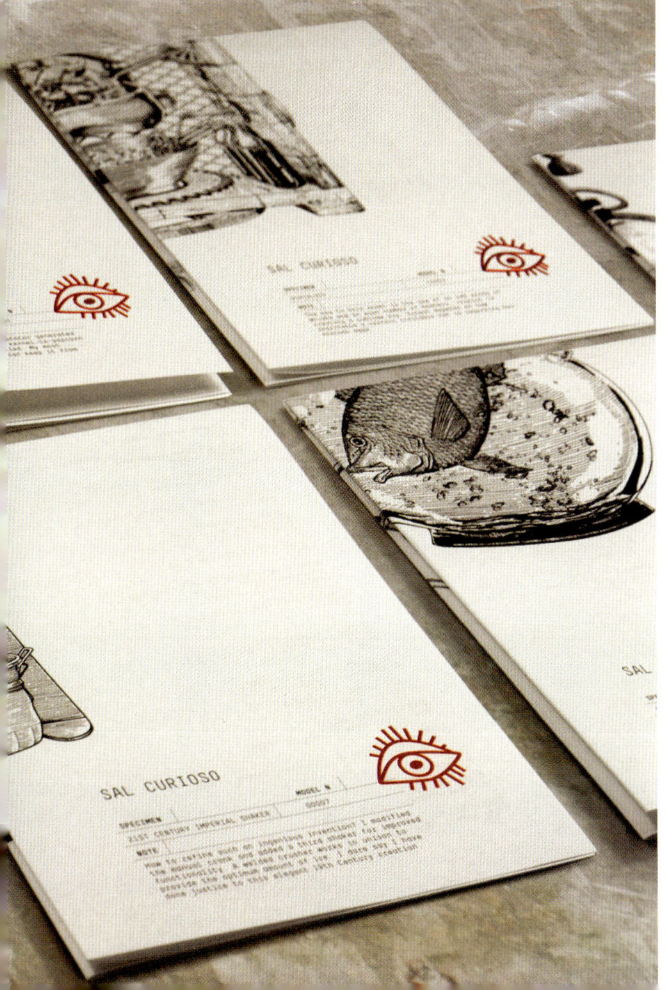

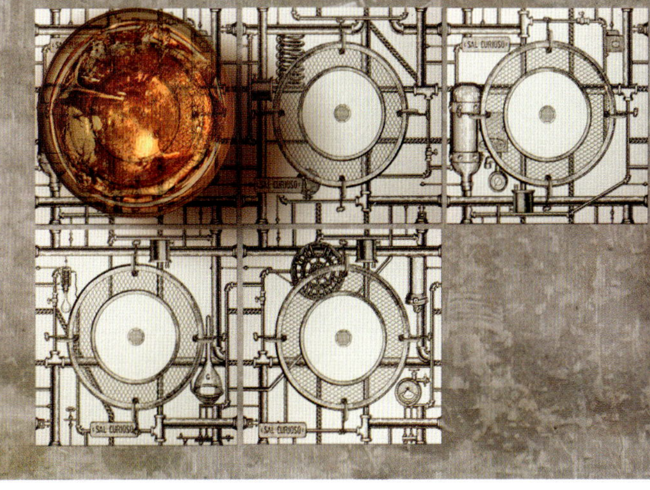

The combination of artisanal production technique and playful approach contributes to the hallmark of Kinga Offert and her label, Offert. Mixed types and the designer's single-eyed alter ego articulate a desire to create thoughtful and tongue-in-cheek products all handmade in-house.

Kinga Offert

Offert

The combination of artisanal production technique and playful approach contributes to the hallmark of Kinga Offert and her label, Offert. Mixed types and the designer's single-eyed alter ego articulate a desire to create thoughtful and tongue-in-cheek products all handmade in-house.

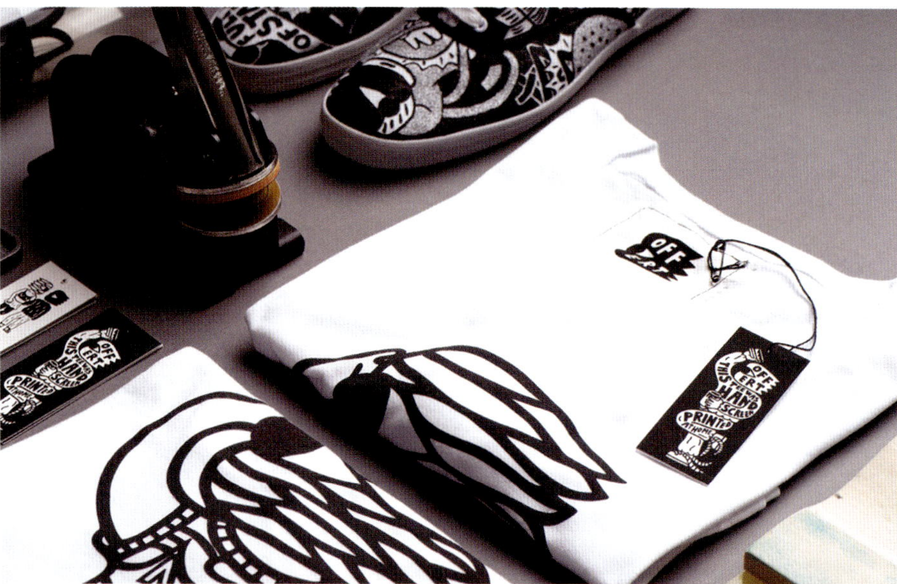

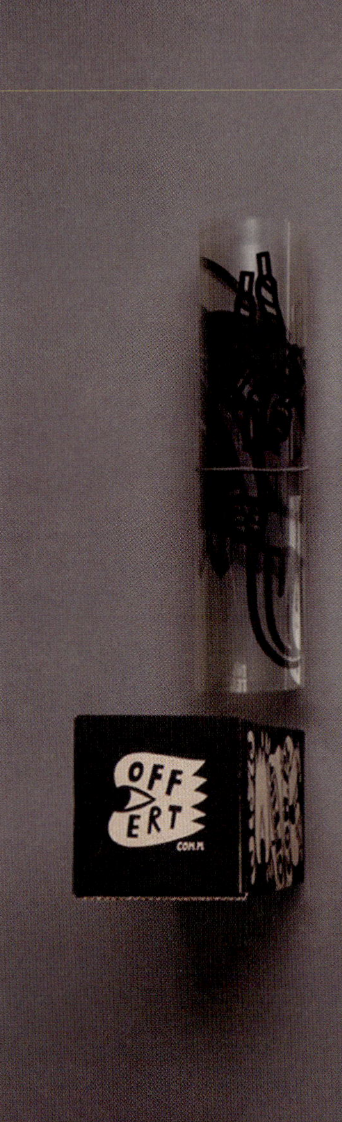

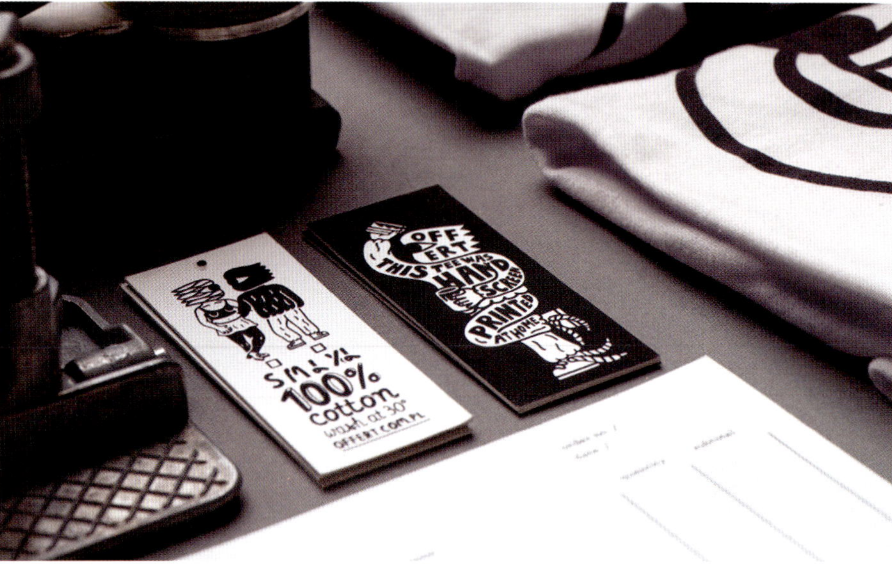

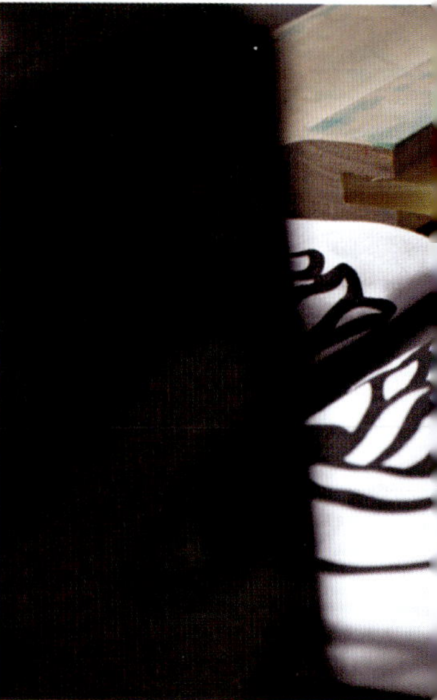

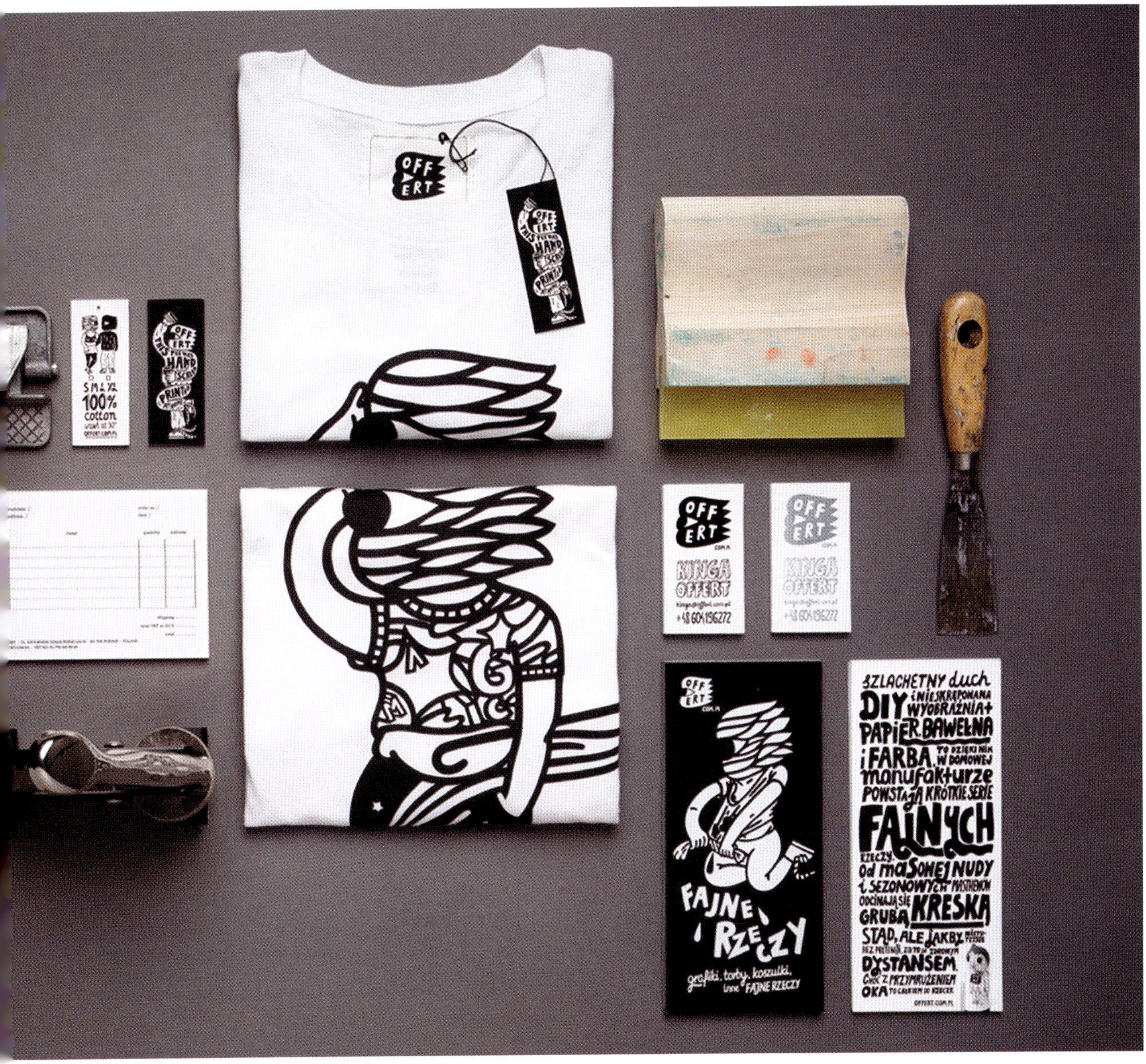

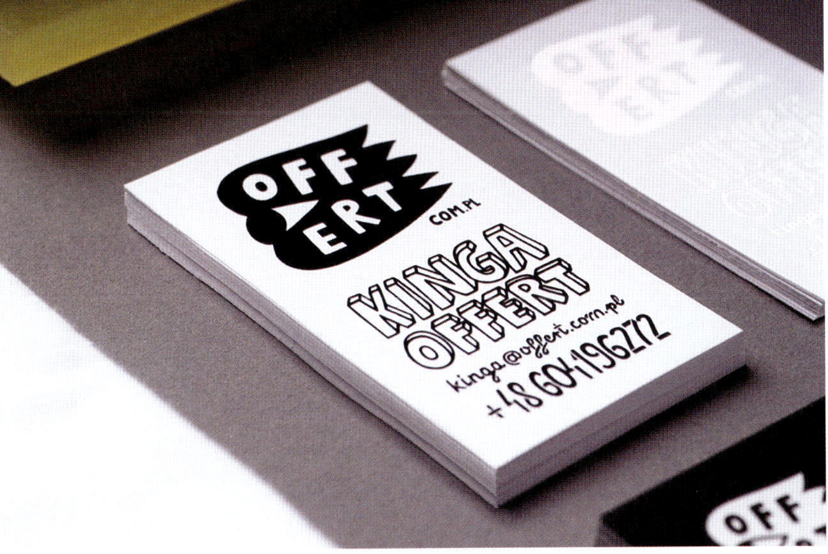
OFF
ERT
COM.PL
KINGA
OFFERT
kinga@offert.com.pl
+48 604196272

In a navy and red-orange palette, the rebranding of a menswear expert tailor has a medley of measuring tools, pins, buttons and markings to celebrate the skilled craftsman's work. The visual chemistry speaks to dandies and young professionals who values quality as much as amusement.

Calvin Tan

Club Man Shop

In a navy and red-orange palette, the rebranding of a menswear expert tailor has a medley of measuring tools, pins, buttons and markings to celebrate the skilled craftsman's work. The visual chemistry speaks to dandies and young professionals who values quality as much as amusement.

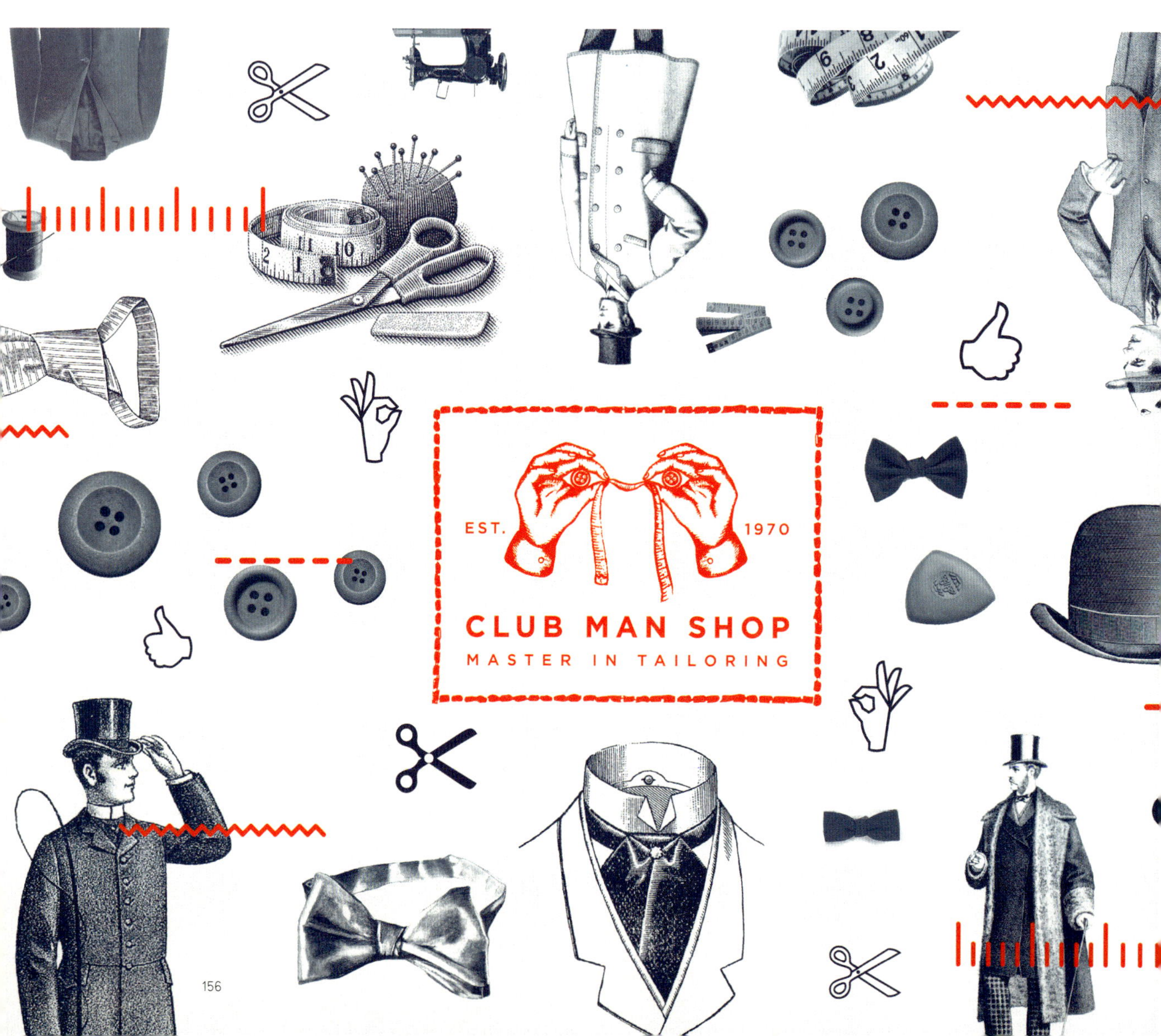

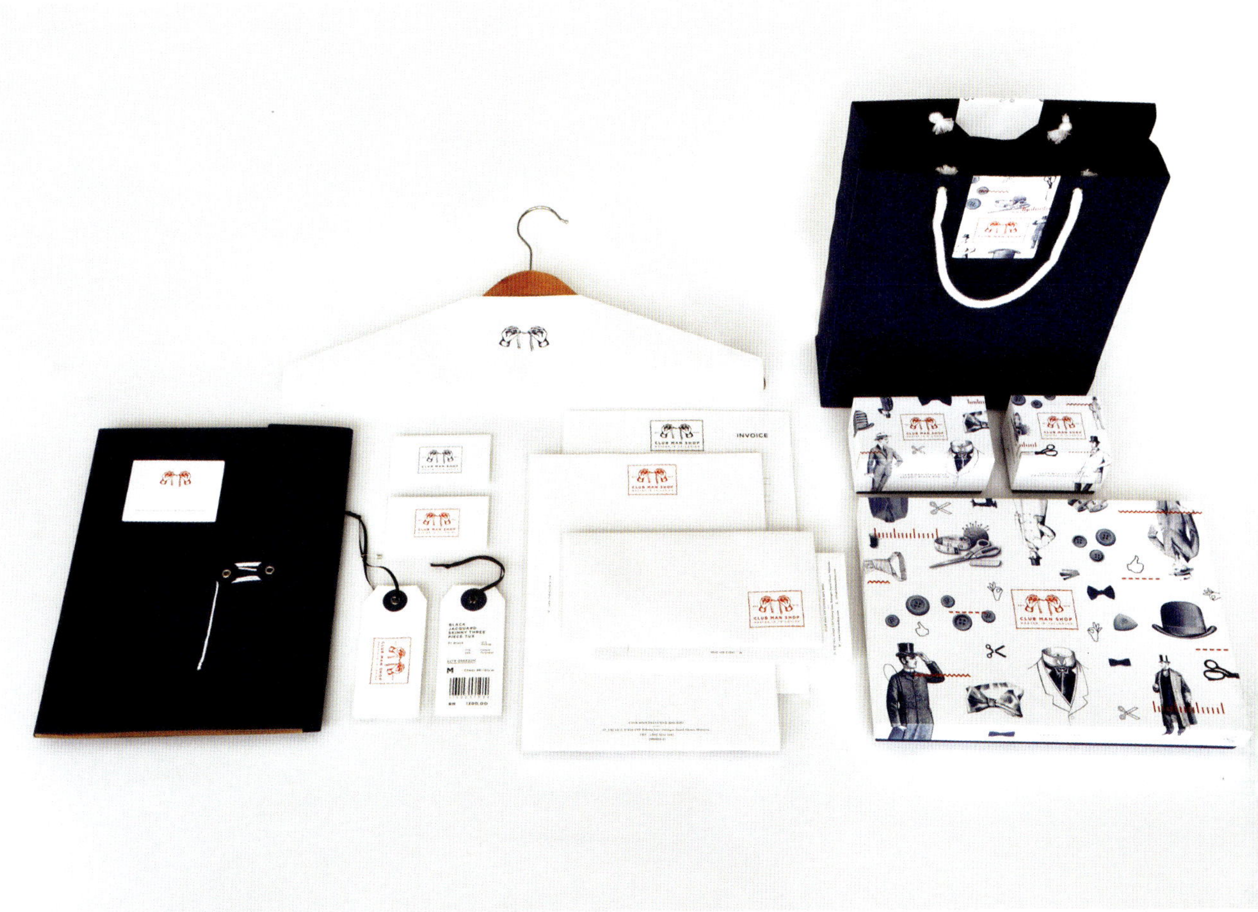

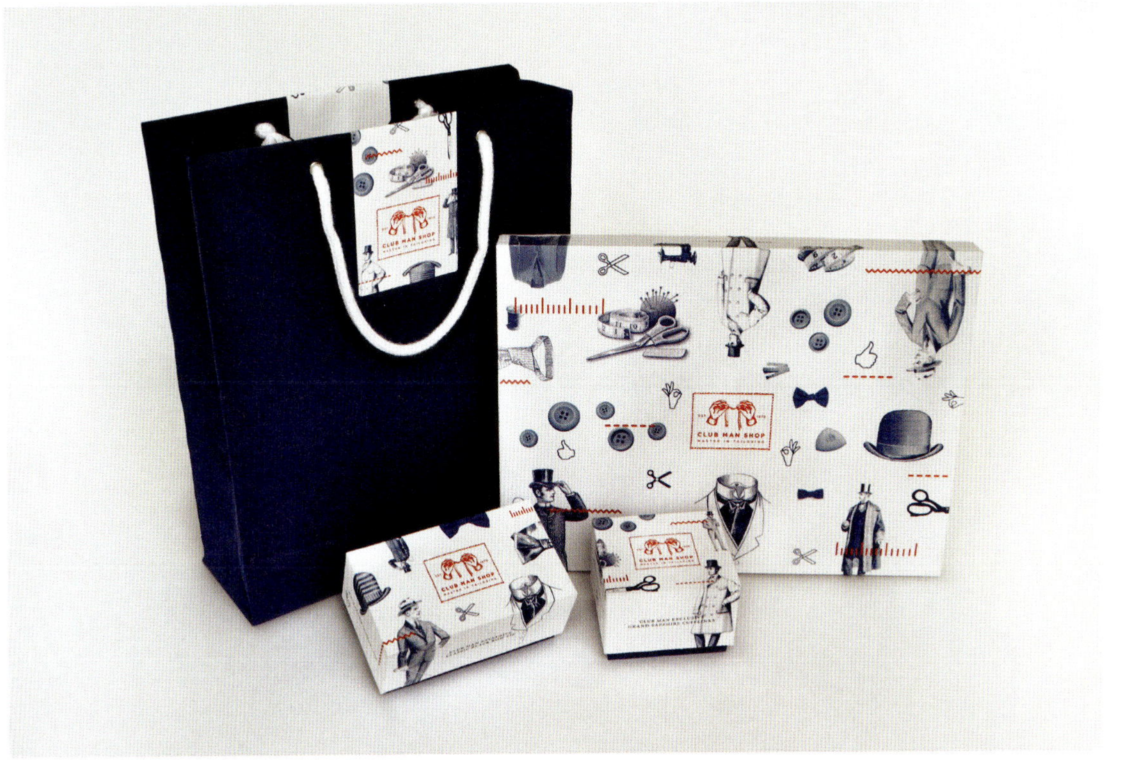
CLUB MAN SHOP

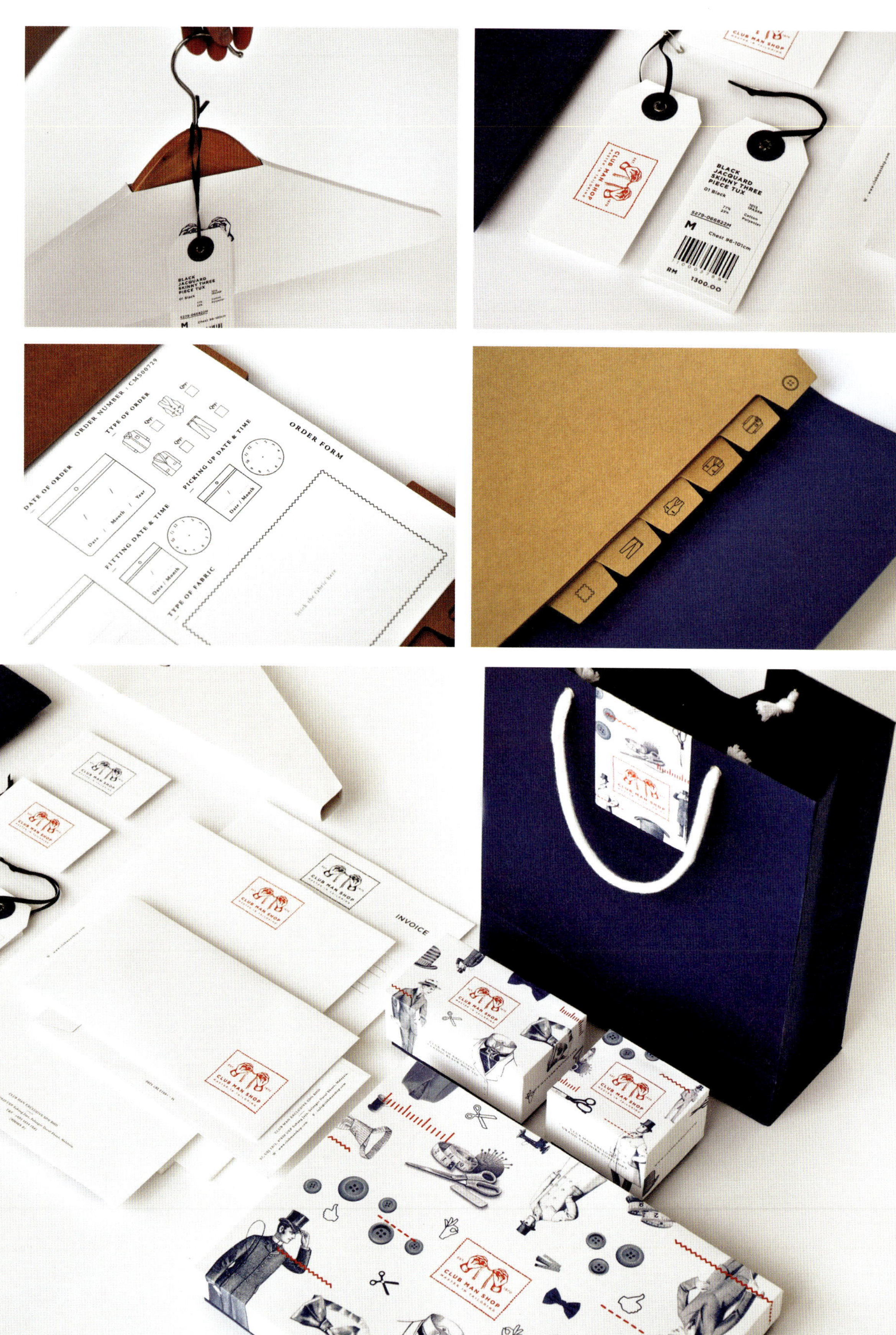

BLACK JACQUARD SKINNY THREE PIECE TUX
01 Black
M
Chest 96-101cm
RM
1300.00
CLUB MAN SHOP
ORDER FORM
TYPE OF ORDER
DATE OF ORDER
Date / Month / Year
PICKING UP DATE & TIME
Date / Month
FITTING DATE & TIME
TYPE OF FABRIC
INVOICE

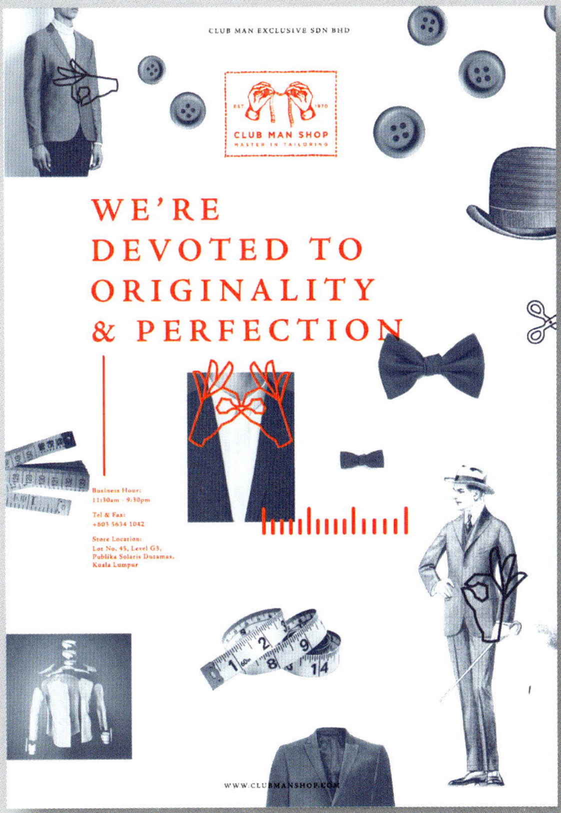

CLUB MAN EXCLUSIVE SDN BHD

EST 1970
CLUB MAN SHOP
MASTER IN TAILORING

WE'RE
DEVOTED TO
ORIGINALITY
& PERFECTION

Business Hour:
11:30am - 9:30pm

Tel & Fax:
+603 5634 1042

Store Location:
Lot No. 45, Level G3,
Publika Solaris Dutamas,
Kuala Lumpur

WWW.CLUBMANSHOP.COM

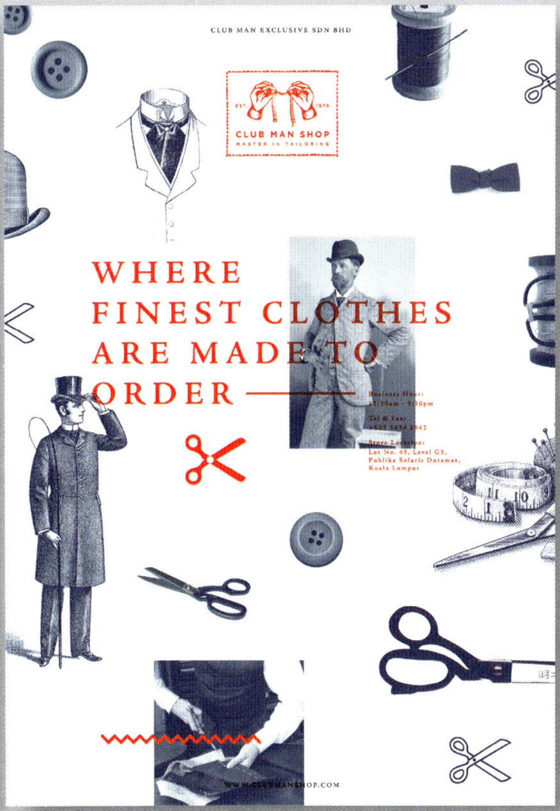

CLUB MAN EXCLUSIVE SDN BHD

EST 1970
CLUB MAN SHOP
MASTER IN TAILORING

WHERE
FINEST CLOTHES
ARE MADE TO
ORDER

Business Hour:
Tel & Fax:
Store Location:
Publika Solaris Dutamas,
Kuala Lumpur

WWW.CLUBMANSHOP.COM

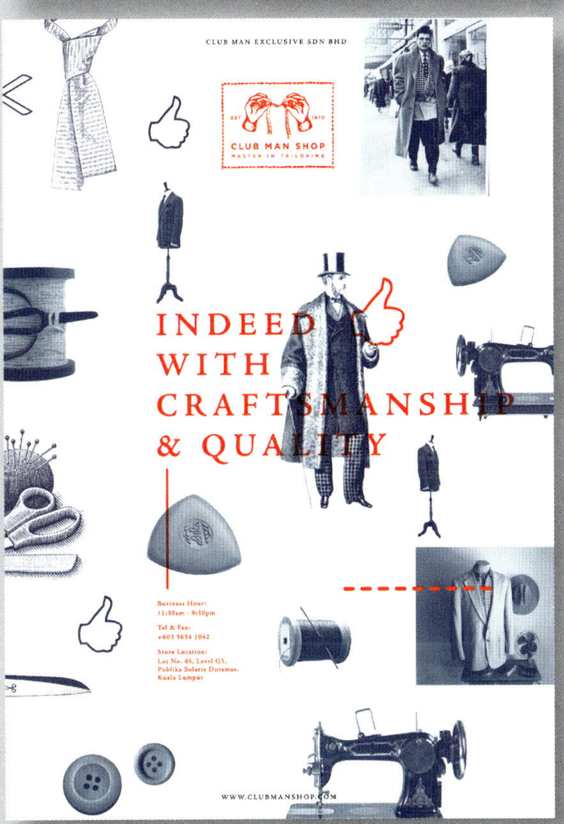

Maravilhas

The red and black, as well as the hearts and checkers, should serve a sufficient hint at the eccentric scenes of Alice in Wonderland, but patterned characters were also composed to ginger up the century-old classic, which All About Dance planned to stage during Christmas. The project covered collateral and souvenir shirts.

Client: All About Dance Academy

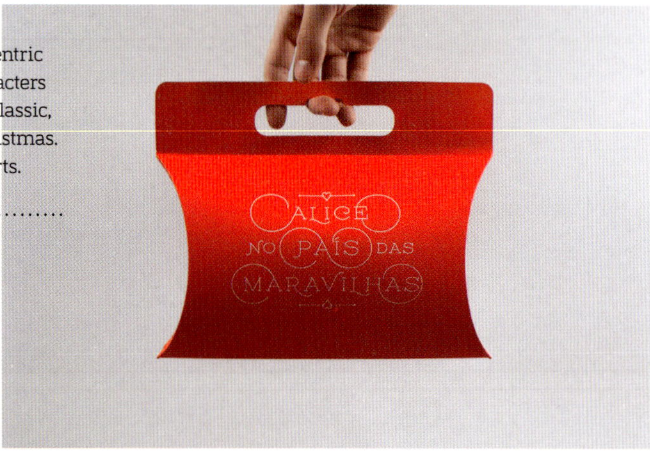

oraviva! designers

Alice no País das Maravilhas

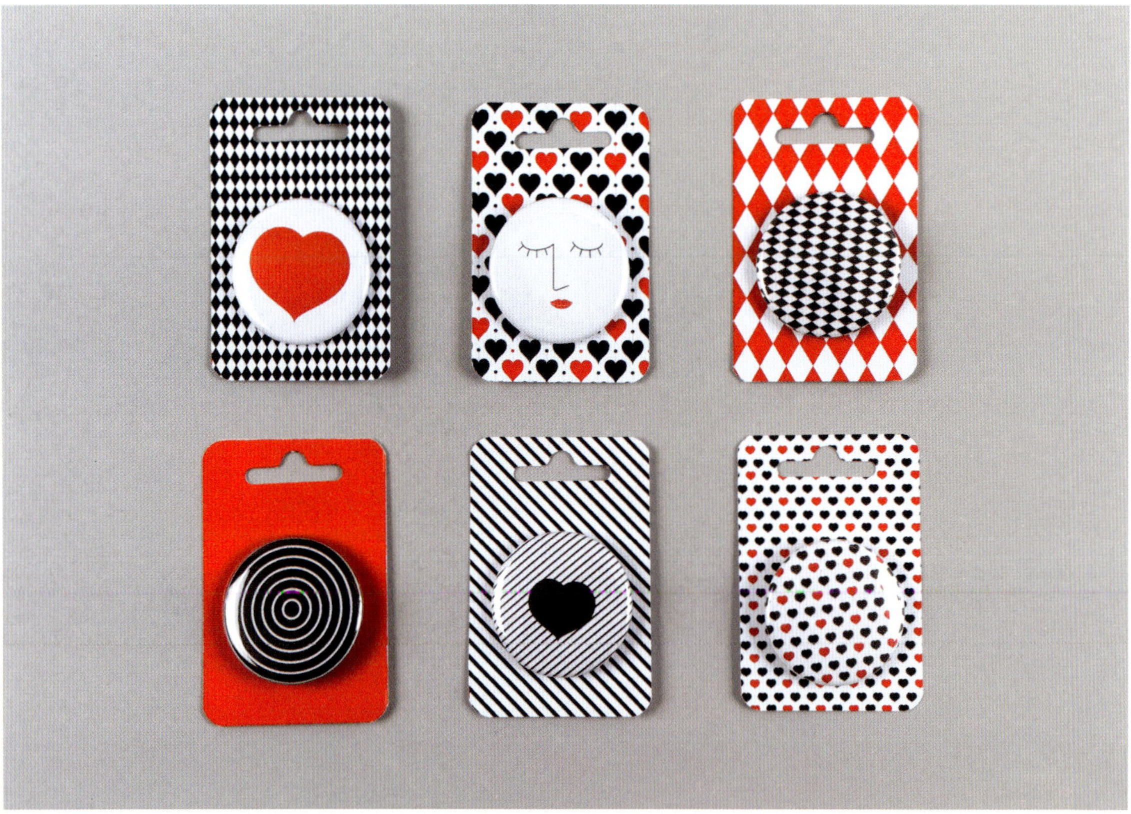

The red and black, as well as the hearts and checkers, should serve a sufficient hint at the eccentric scenes of Alice in Wonderland, but patterned characters were also composed to ginger up the century-old classic, which All About Dance planned to stage during Christmas. The project covered collateral and souvenir shirts.

Client: All About Dance Academy

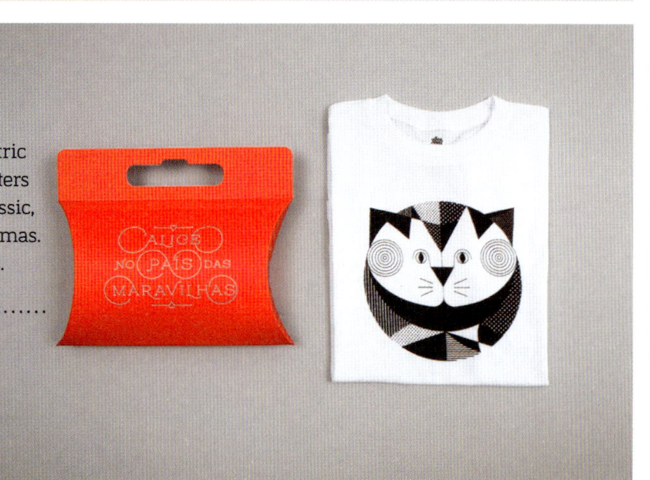

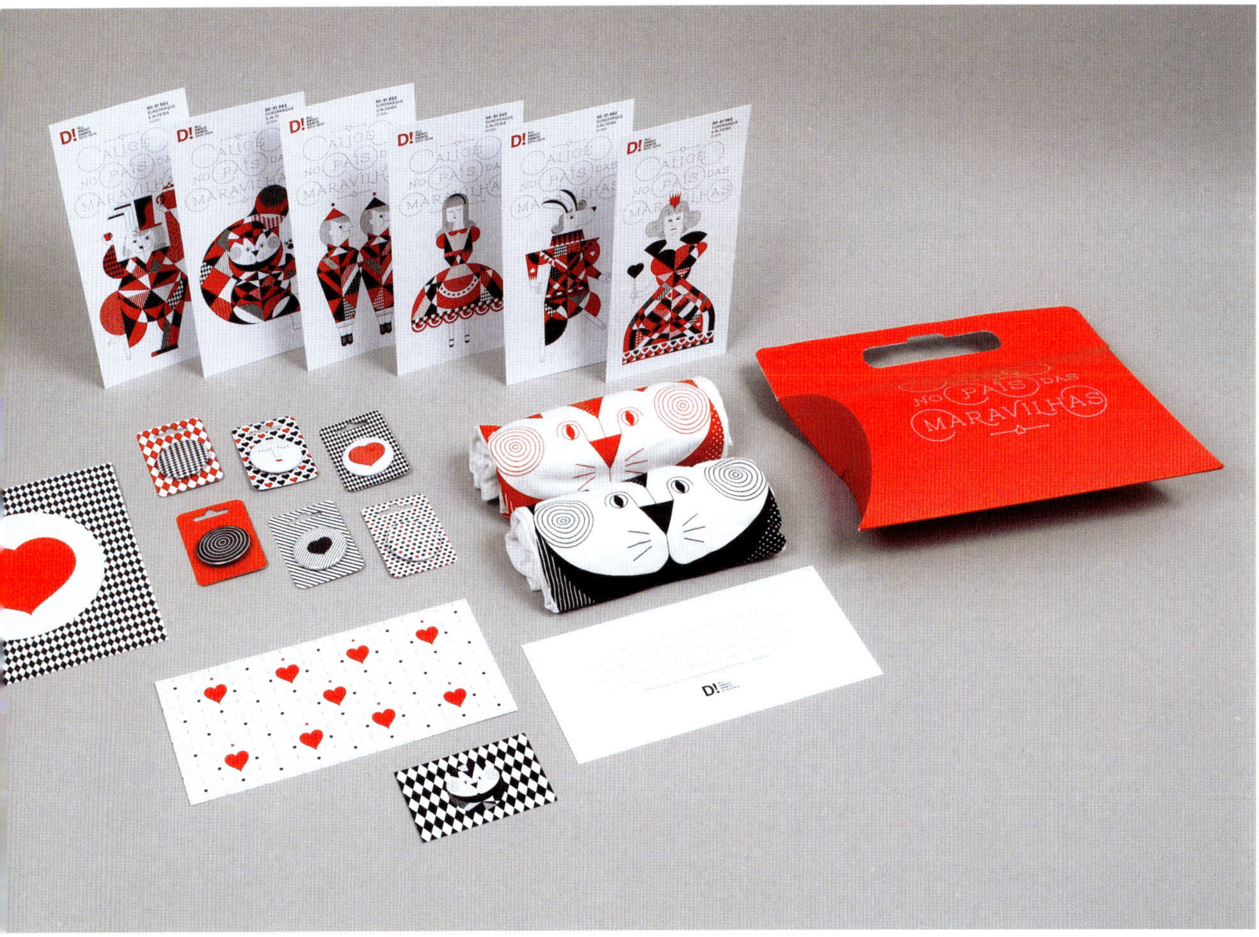

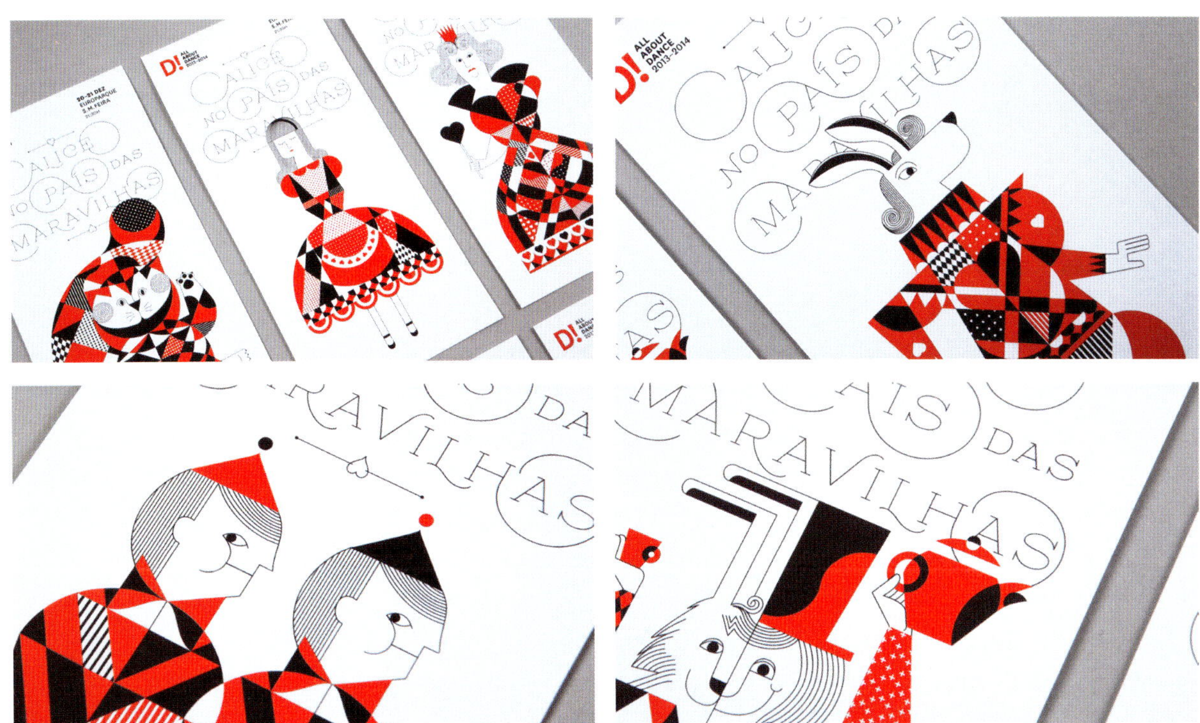
D!
ALL ABOUT DANCE
2013-2014
ALICE
NO PAÍS DAS
MARAVILHAS

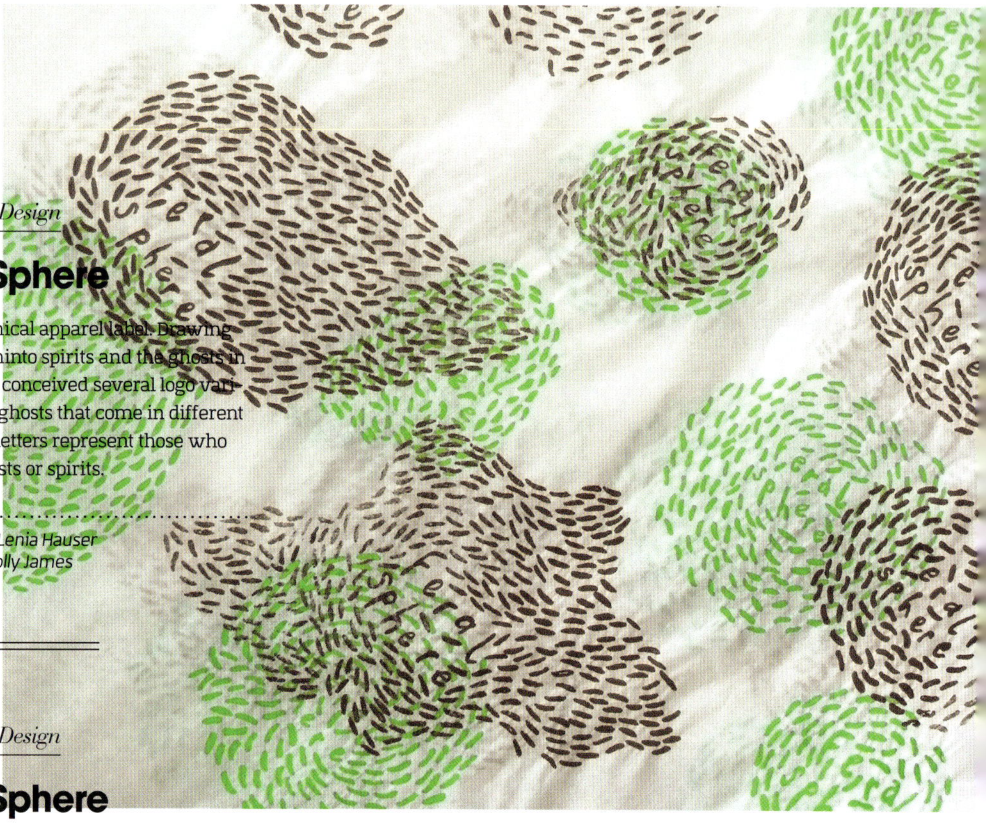

Mind Design

Feral Sphere

Feral Sphere is a British ethical apparel label. Drawing inspiration from Japanese Shinto spirits and the ghosts in the TV series 'Lost', the label conceived several logo variants, as with most spirits or ghosts that come in different shapes and sizes. Flipped letters represent those who can see ghosts or spirits.

Illustration: Lenia Hauser
Client: Holly James

Mind Design

Feral Sphere

Feral Sphere is a British ethical apparel label. Drawing inspiration from Japanese Shinto spirits and the ghosts in the TV series 'Lost', the label conceived several logo variants, as with most spirits or ghosts that come in different shapes and sizes. Flipped letters represent those who can see ghosts or spirits.

Illustration: Lenia Hauser
Client: Holly James

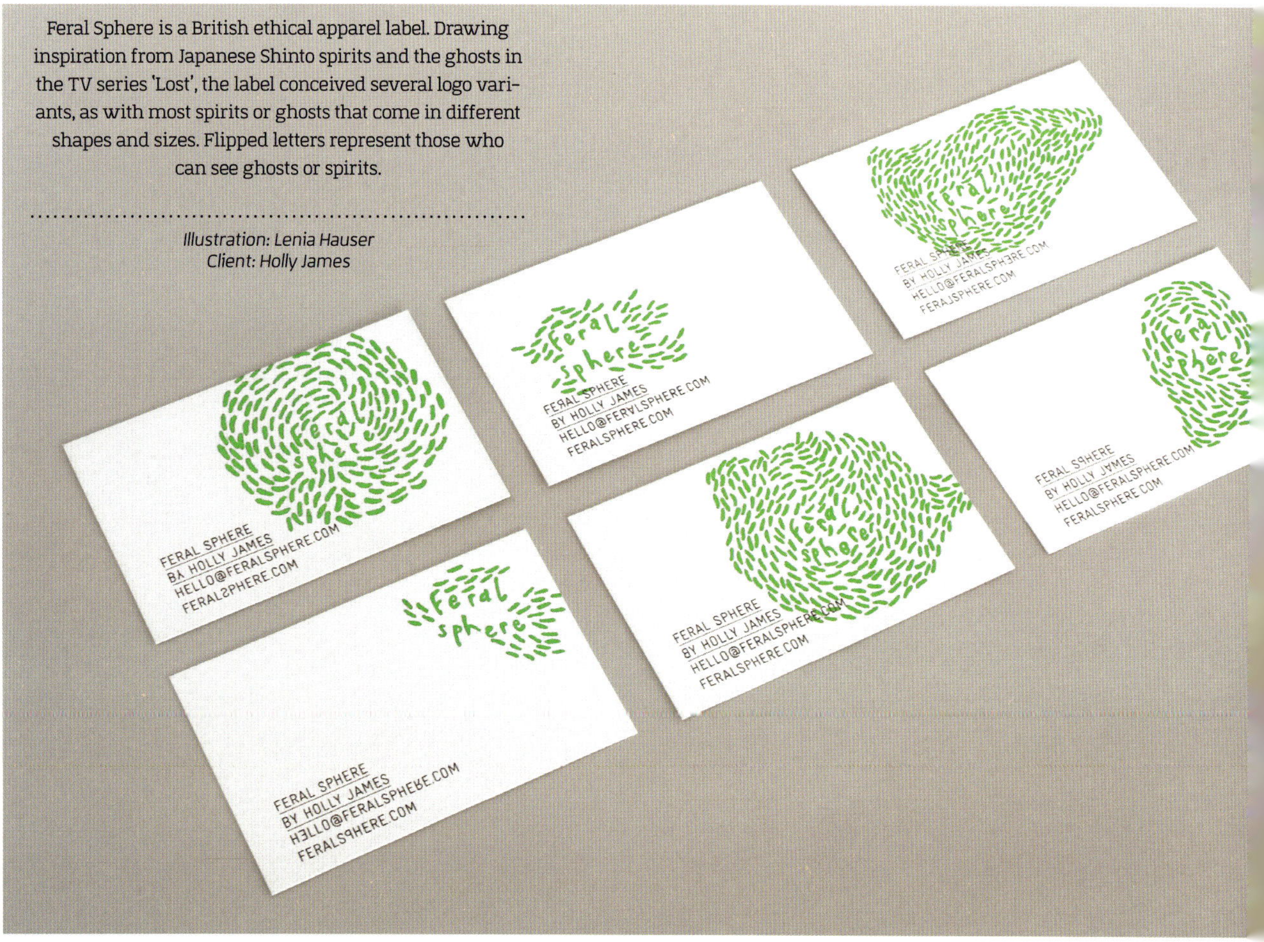

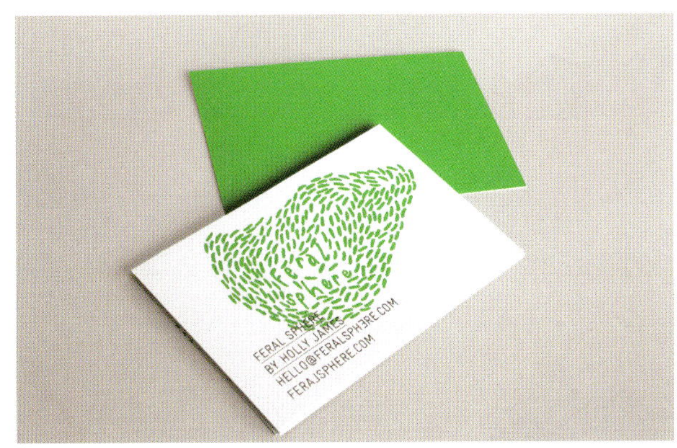
feral sphere
FERAL SPHERE
BY HOLLY JAMES
HELLO@FERALSPH3RE.COM
FERAJSPHERE.COM

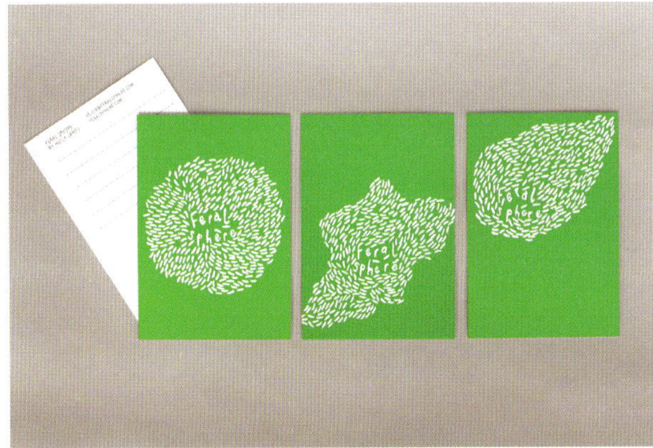
feral sphere

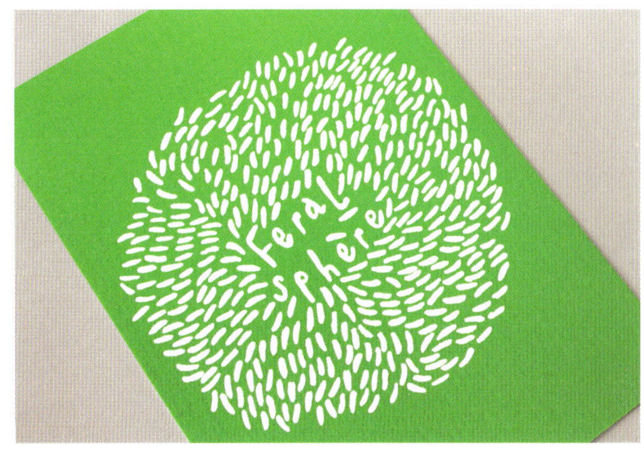
feral sphere

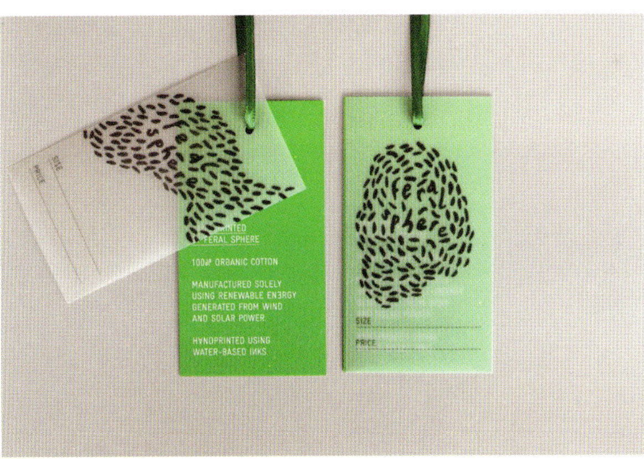
feral sphere
FERAL SPHERE
100% ORGANIC COTTON
MANUFACTURED SOLELY USING RENEWABLE EN3RGY GENERATED FROM WIND AND SOLAR POWER.
HANDPRINTED USING WATER-BASED INKS.
SIZE
PRICE

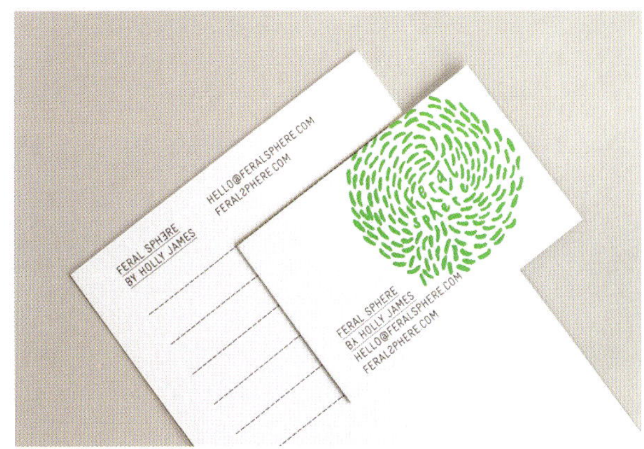
FERAL SPH3RE
BY HOLLY JAMES
HELLO@FERALSPHERE.COM
FERAL2PHERE.COM
feral sphere
FERAL SPHERE
BA HOLLY JAMES
HELLO@FERALSPHERE.COM
FERAL2PHERE.COM

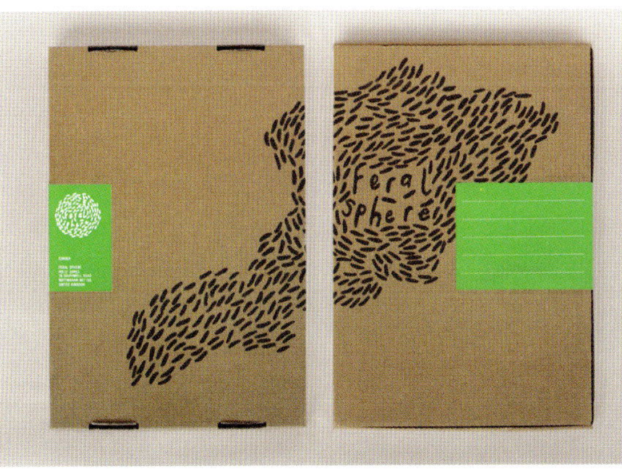
feral sphère

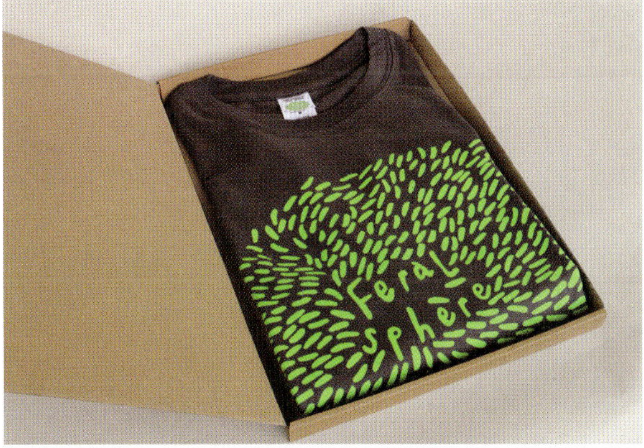
feral sphere

The Secret Garde

The Secret Garden is a traditional bed and breakfast in Cape Cod hidden away in a lush green garden. The little guest house refreshed its brand identity with artwork imagining a native fauna outside the window and boosting a quaint and cosy atmosphere with flair.

Client: The Secret Garden Inn

Booth

The Secret Garden

The Secret Garden is a traditional bed and breakfast in Cape Cod hidden away in a lush green garden. The little guest house refreshed its brand identity with artwork imagining a native fauna outside the window and boosting a quaint and cosy atmosphere with flair.

Client: The Secret Garden Inn

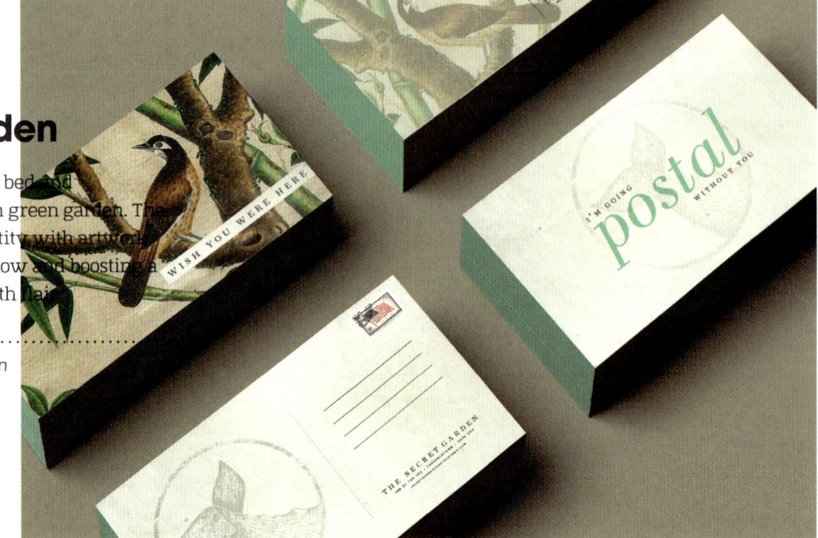

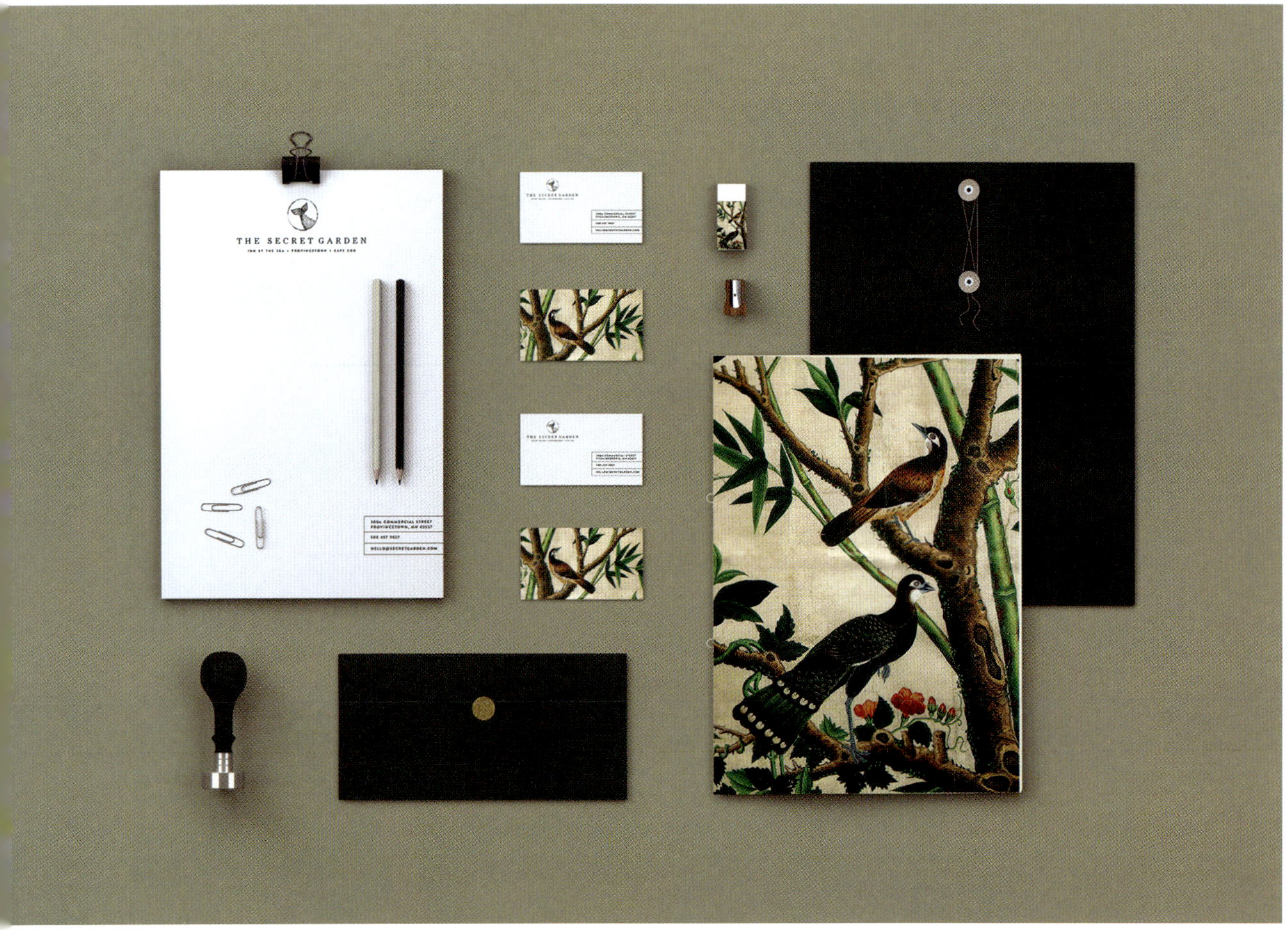

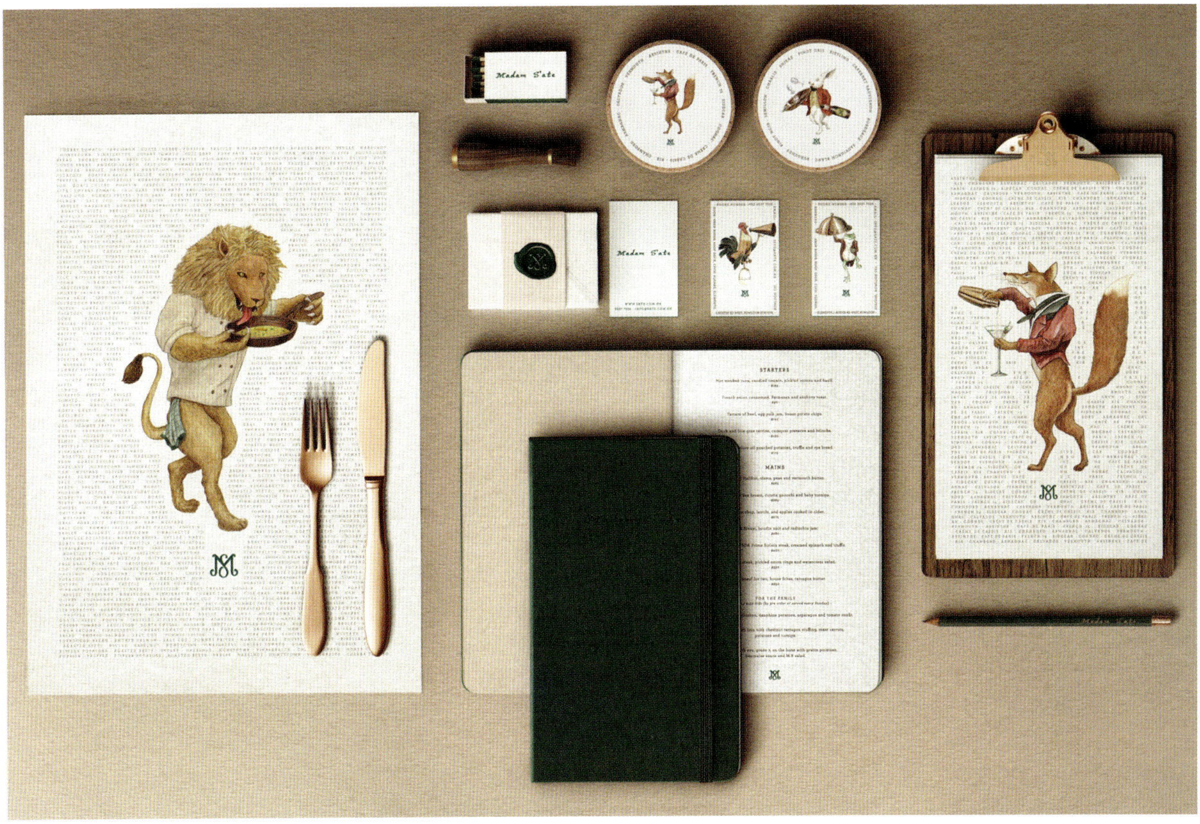

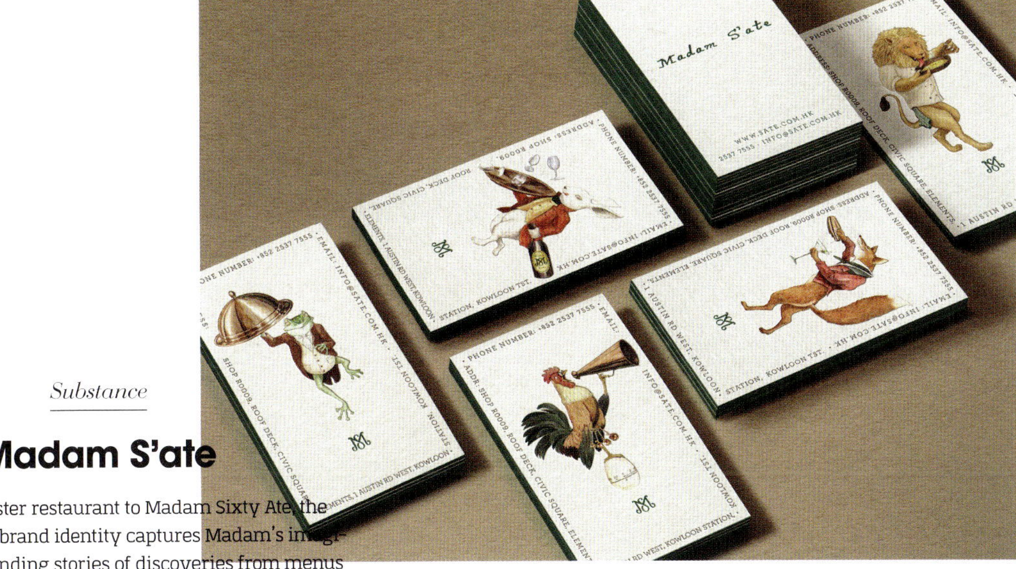

Substance

Madam S'ate

A bohemian sister restaurant to Madam Sixty Ate, the French kitchen's brand identity captures Madam's imagination and astounding stories of discoveries from menus through to its corporate stationery. Each of the quirky characters will identify with a piece of personal memory that is fun and farce.

Substance

Madam S'ate

A bohemian sister restaurant to Madam Sixty Ate, the French kitchen's brand identity captures Madam's imagination and astounding stories of discoveries from menus

CITIx60 City Guides

CITIx60 guides explore what living in creative capitals is like through original thinkers' eyes. Driven by artistic collaborations, the publisher asks an artist from each city to portray their hometown as a wrapper and souvenir for the readers. Each city's specialties are also highlighted with lively hand drawings in place of photographs.

---

viction workshop ltd

CITIx60 City Guides

CITIx60 guides explore what living in creative capitals is like through original thinkers' eyes. Driven by artistic collaborations, the publisher asks an artist from each city to portray their hometown as a wrapper and souvenir for the readers. Each city's specialties are also highlighted with lively hand drawings in place of photographs.

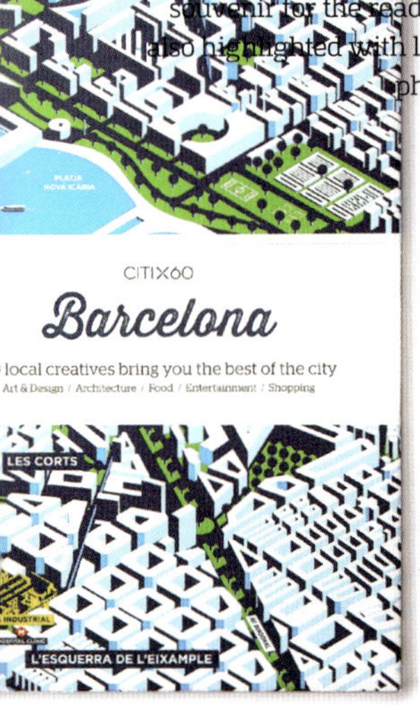

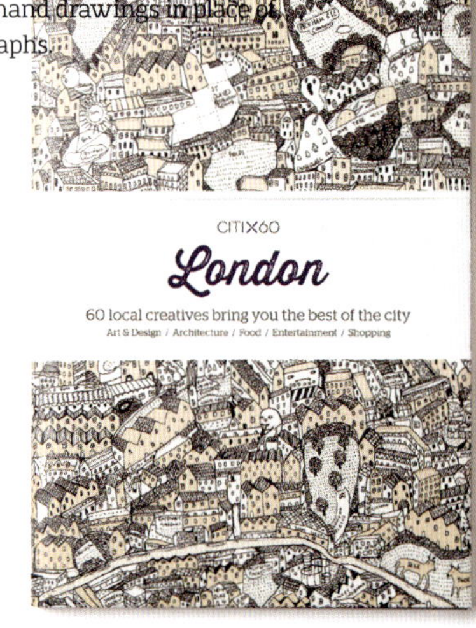

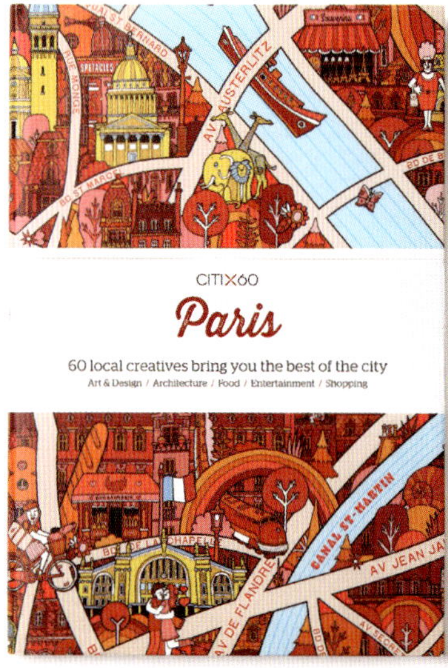

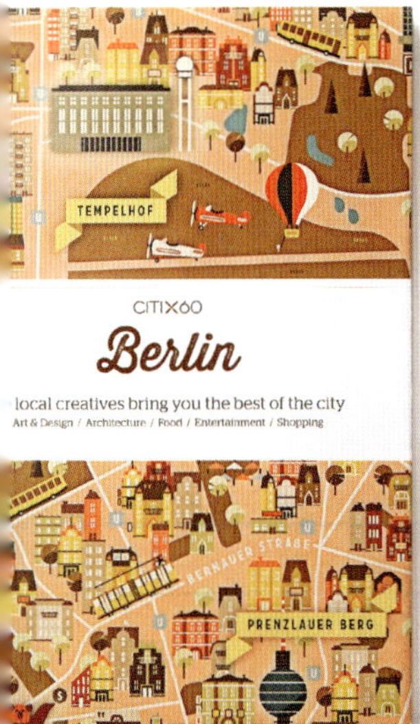

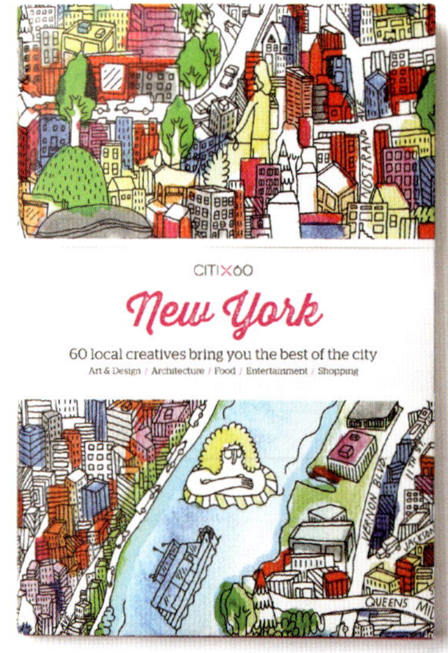

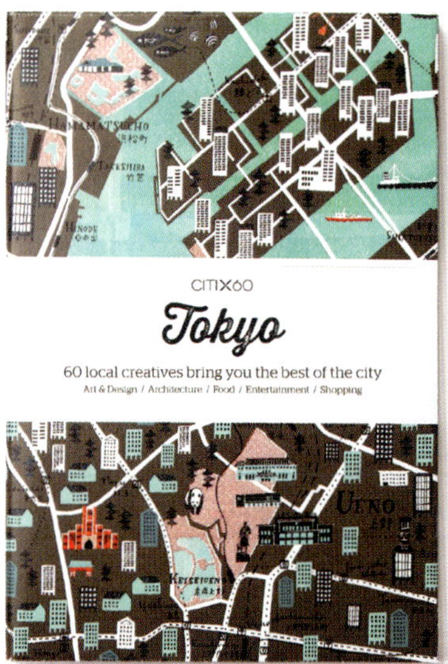

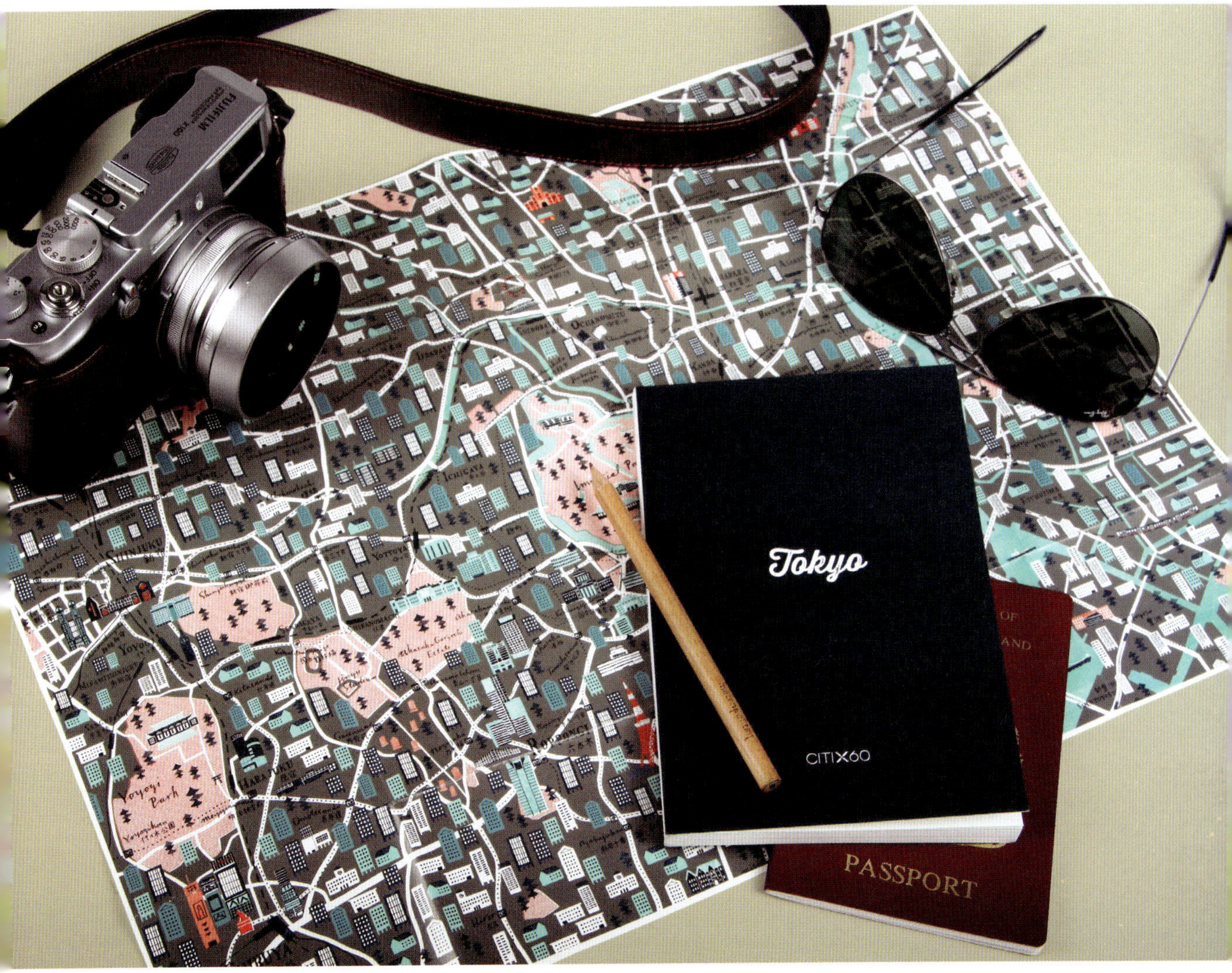

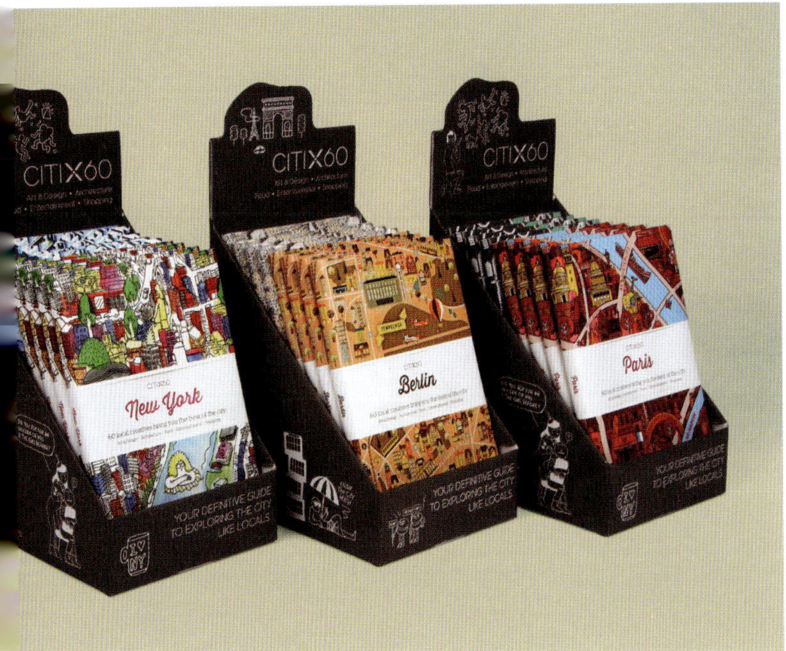
CITIX60
New York
CITIX60
Berlin
CITIX60
Paris
YOUR DEFINITIVE GUIDE TO EXPLORING THE CITY LIKE LOCALS
YOUR DEFINITIVE GUIDE TO EXPLORING THE CITY LIKE LOCALS
YOUR DEFINITIVE GUIDE TO EXPLORING THE CITY LIKE LOCALS

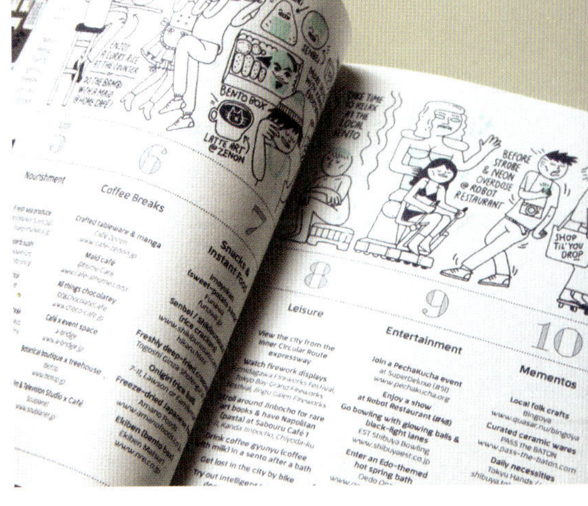
Coffee Breaks
Leisure
Entertainment
Mementos
BEFORE STROBE & NEON OVERDOSE @ ROBOT RESTAURANT

Today is the Day is a mini project of Studio AH–HA specialising in design graphics for parties, special events and weddings. The team let imagination go wild in this project identity with nature-inspired patterns alluding to their artisanal approach that appeals to the young and sophisticated.

Illustration: Mariana Sameiro

Studio AH–HA

Today is the Day

Today is the Day is a mini project of Studio AH–HA specialising in design graphics for parties, special events and weddings. The team let imagination go wild in this project identity with nature-inspired patterns alluding to their artisanal approach that appeals to the young and sophisticated.

Illustration: Mariana Sameiro

TO INVITE

TO LAUGH

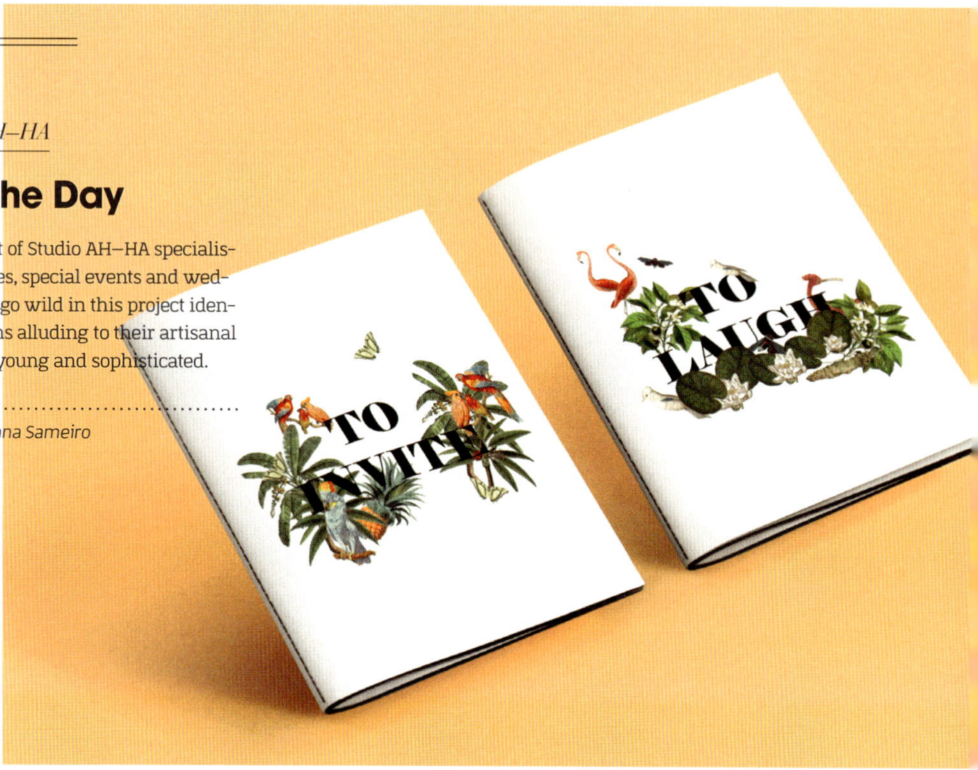

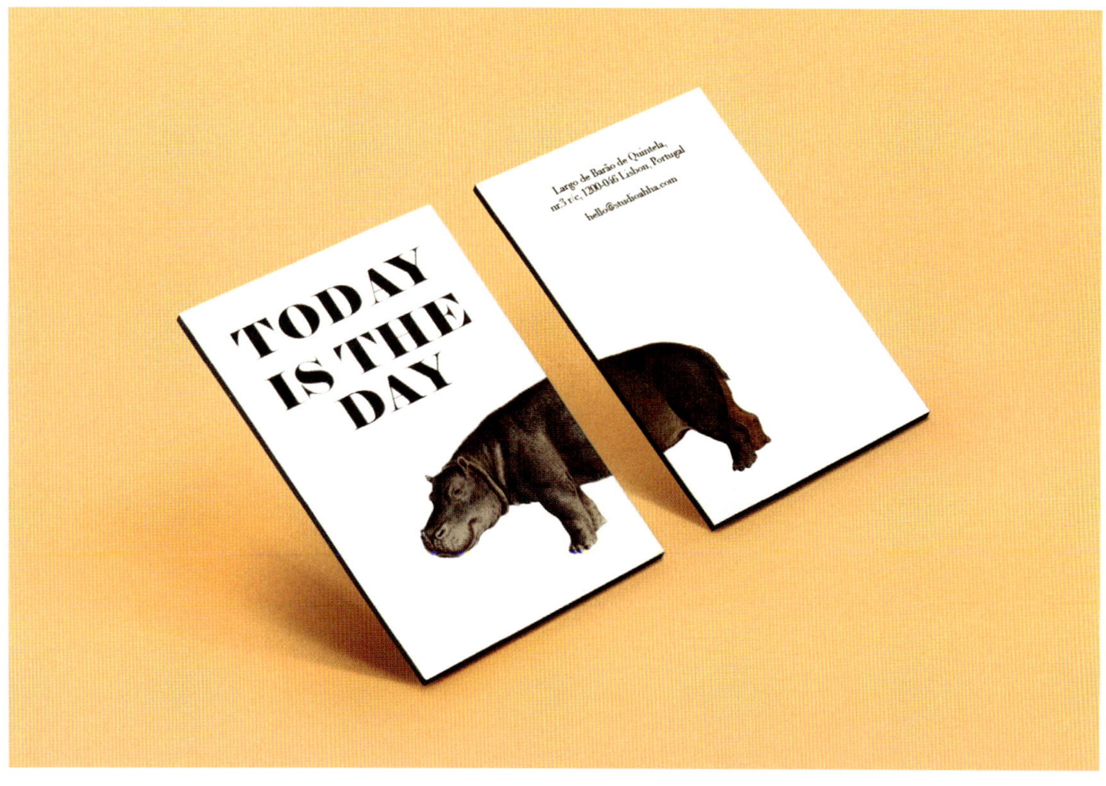

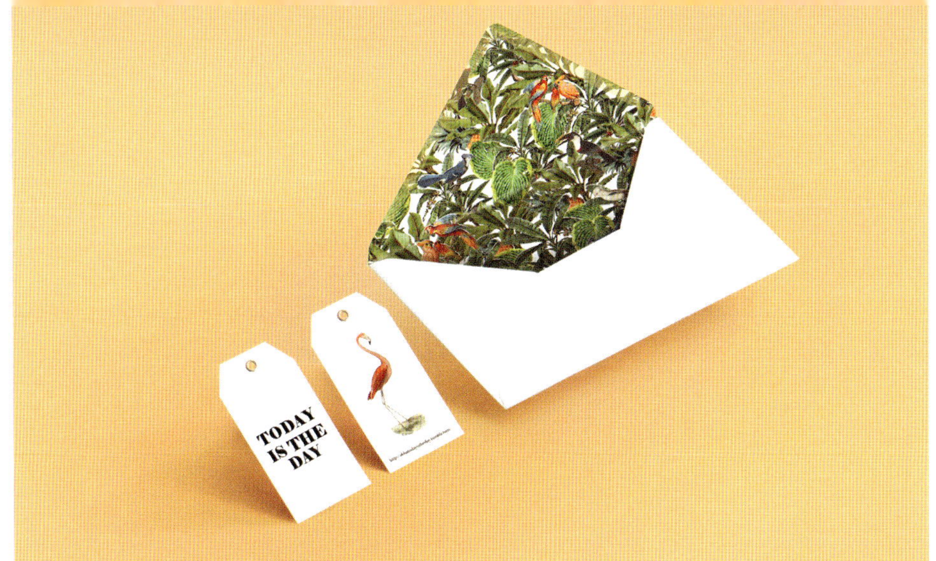
TODAY
IS THE
DAY

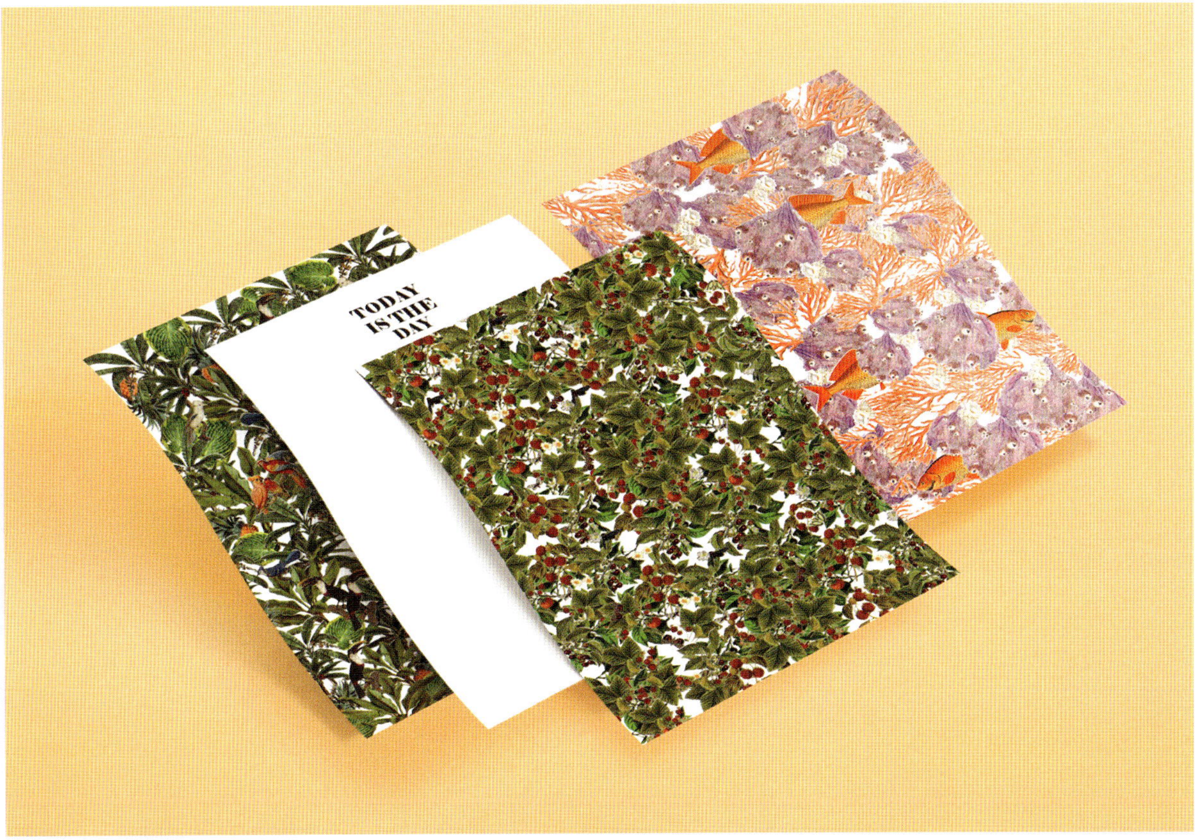

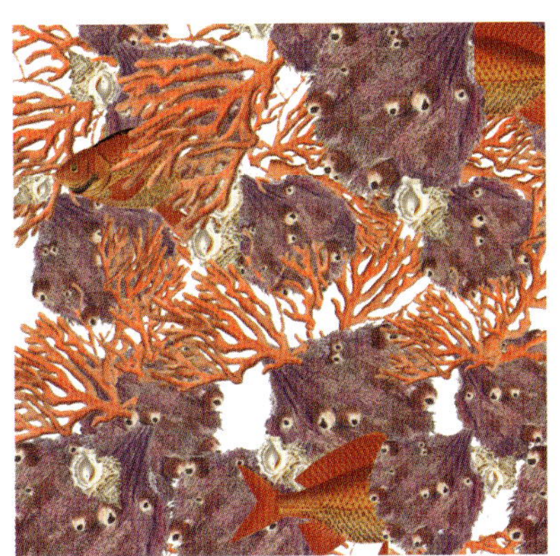

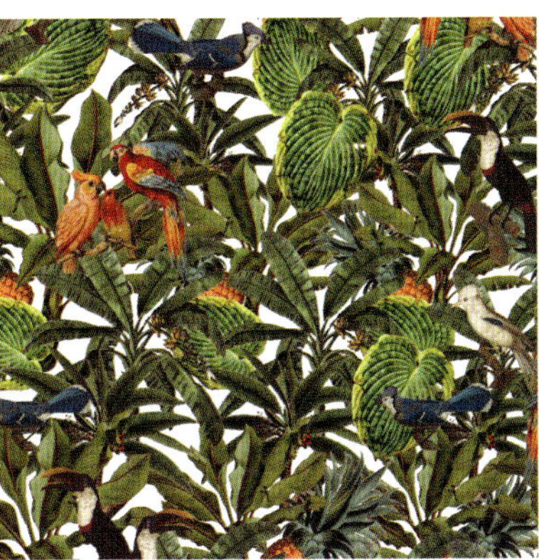

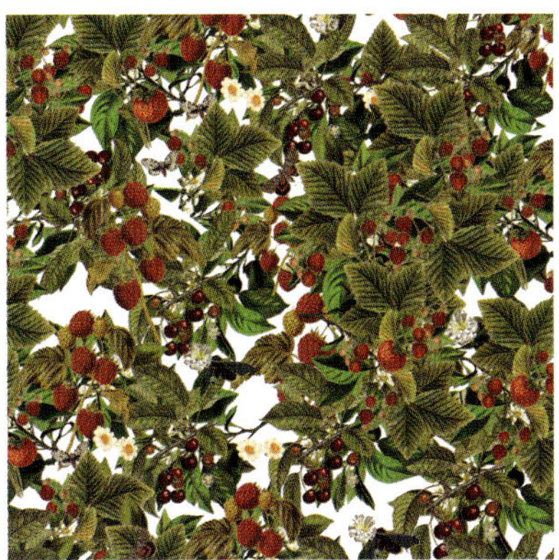

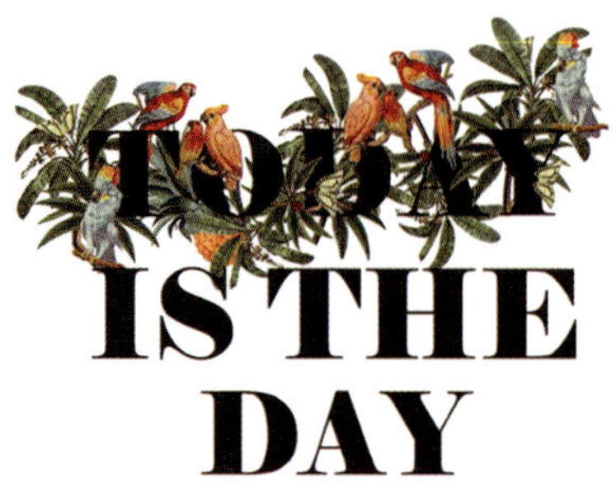
TODAY
IS THE
DAY

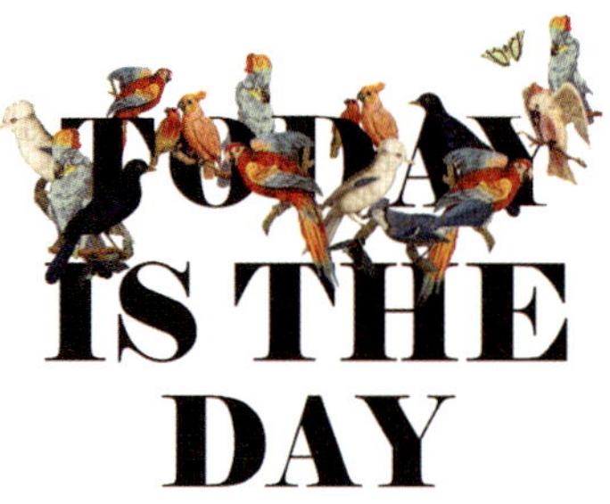
TODAY
IS THE
DAY

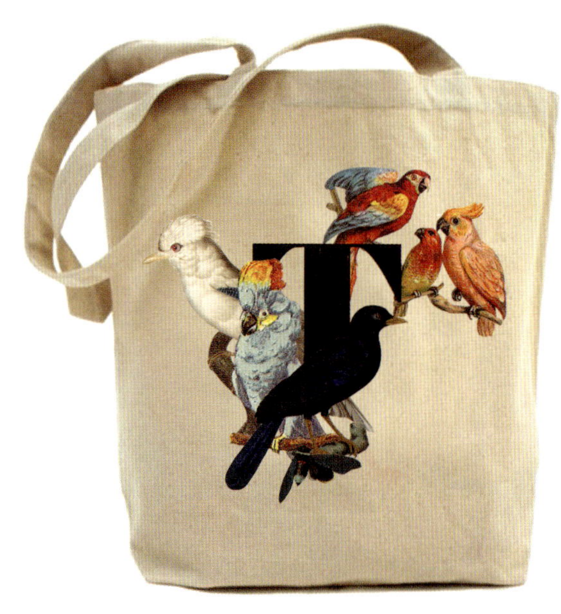
T

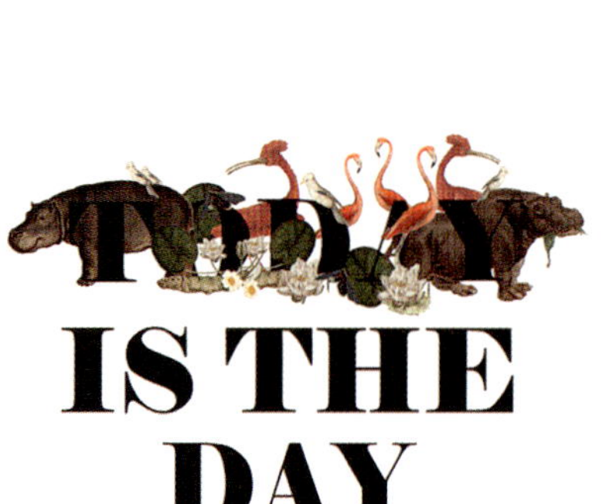
TODAY
IS THE
DAY

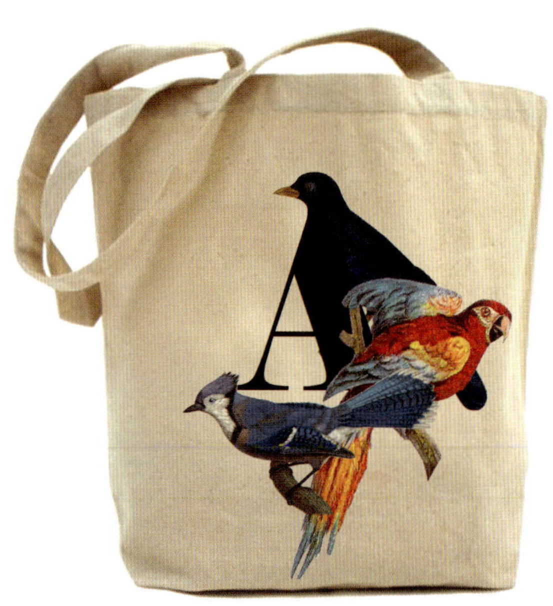
A

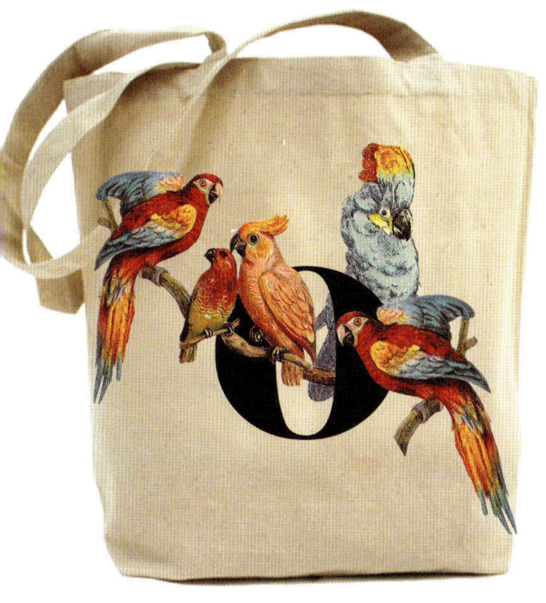
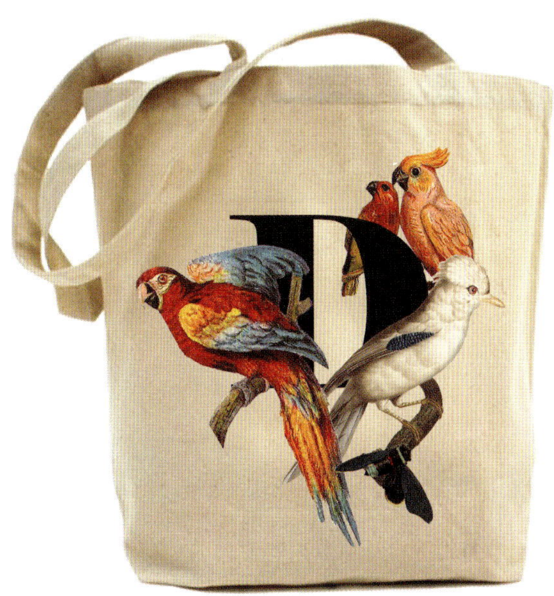
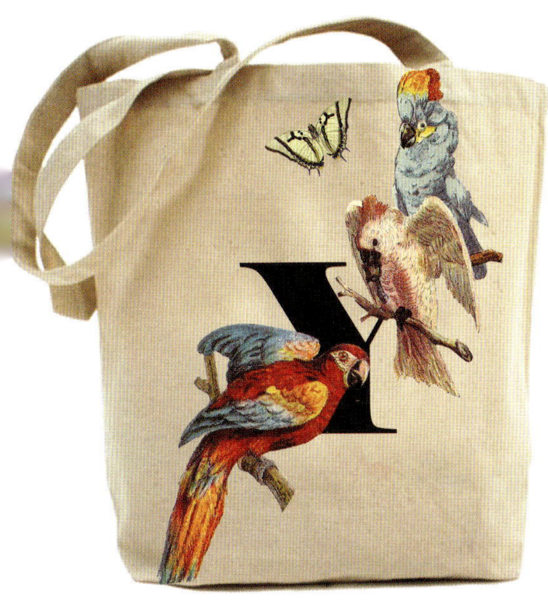
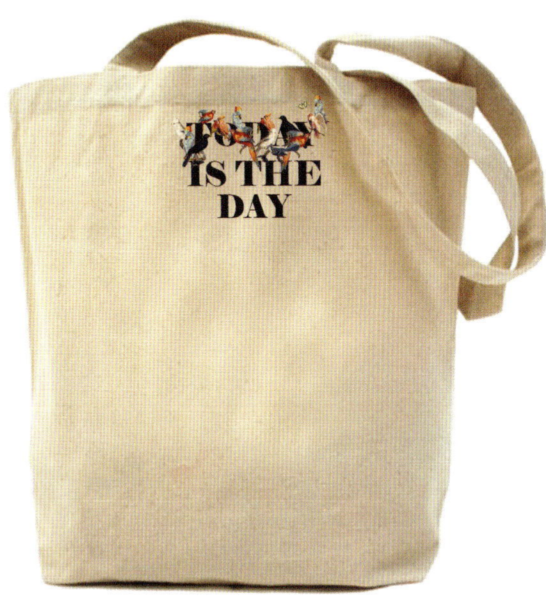
TODAY
IS THE
DAY

Dutch newspaper Het Parool was giving out recipes and columns from its gourmet section as Christmas gifts for its potential subscribers. Detailed illustrations inserted kitchen adventures in between the ingredients and drew focus to the basics. The Illustrated bookmarks were also part of the gift.

Illustration: Wieneke Claxton
Client: Het Parool

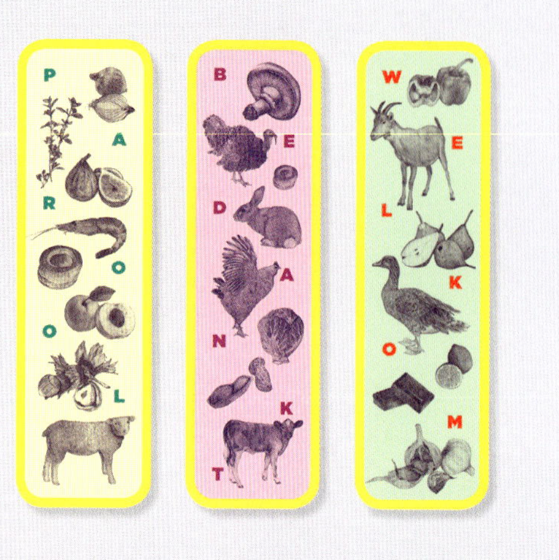

Mara Vissers

Smulpapen Kerstmenu's

Dutch newspaper Het Parool was giving out recipes and columns from its gourmet section as Christmas gifts for its potential subscribers. Detailed illustrations inserted kitchen adventures in between the ingredients and drew focus to the basics. The Illustrated bookmarks were also part of the gift.

Illustration: Wieneke Claxton
Client: Het Parool

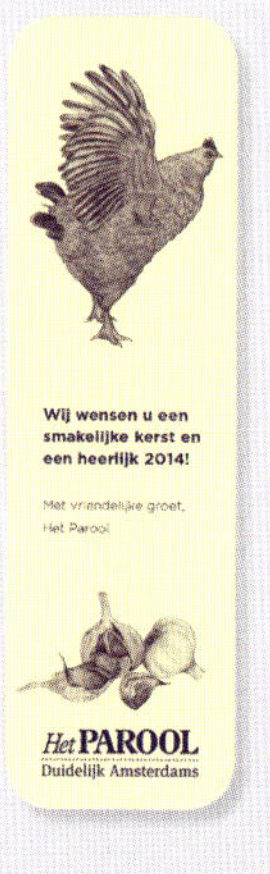

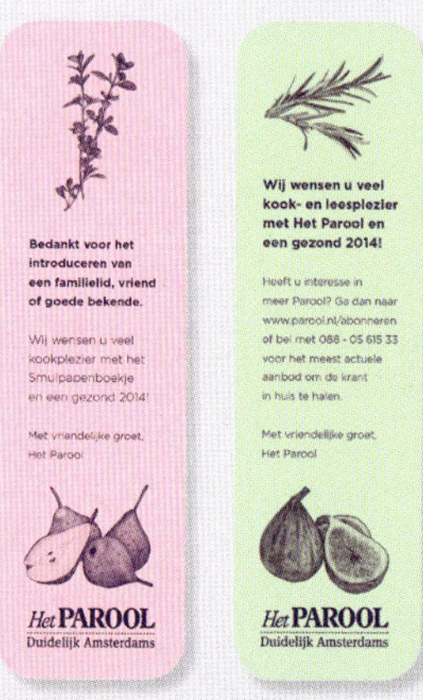

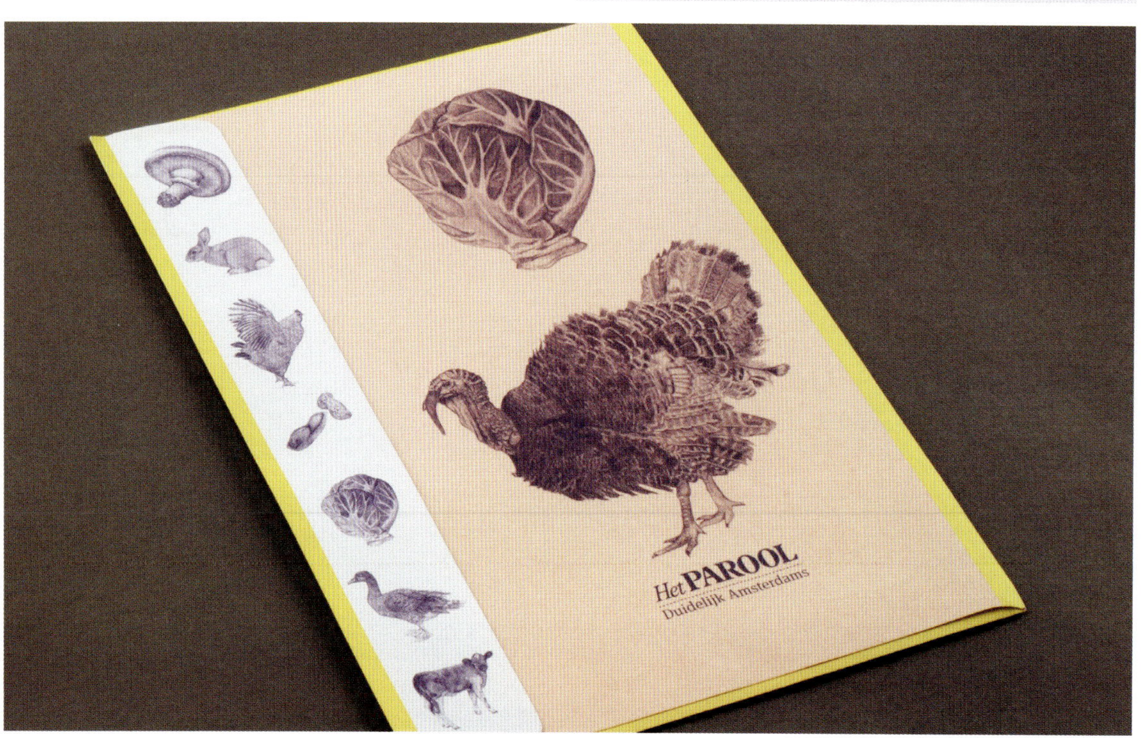

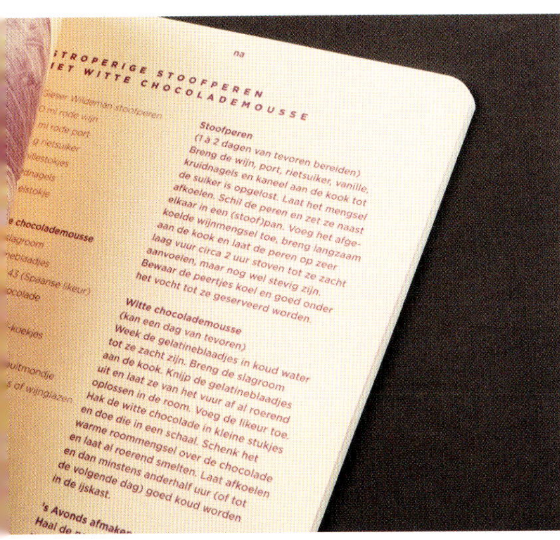
Stoofperen
Witte chocolademousse

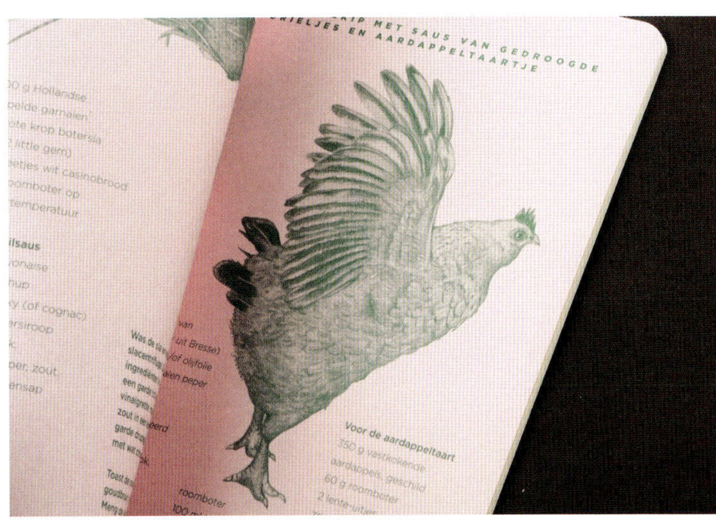
Voor de aardappeltaart

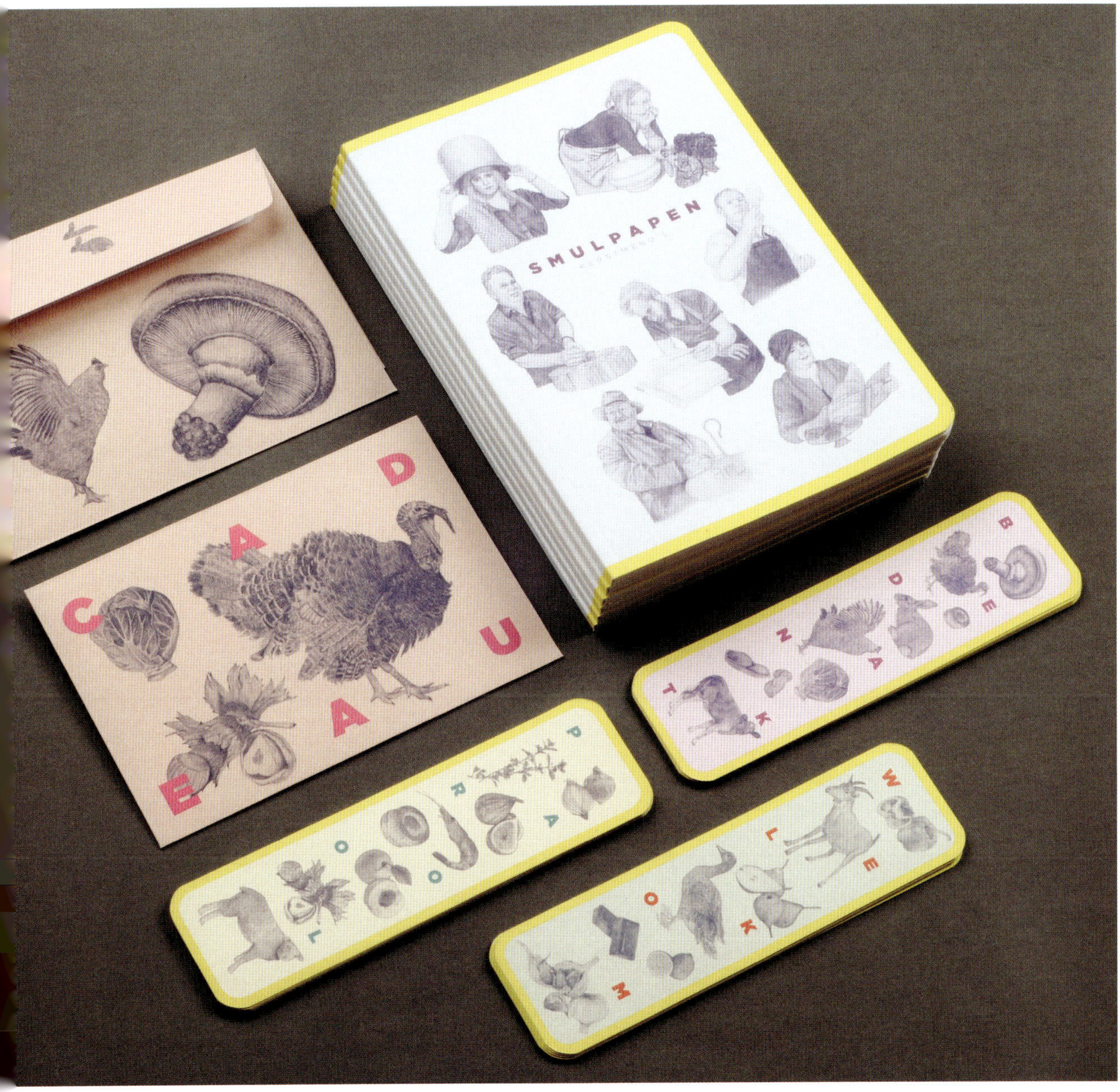

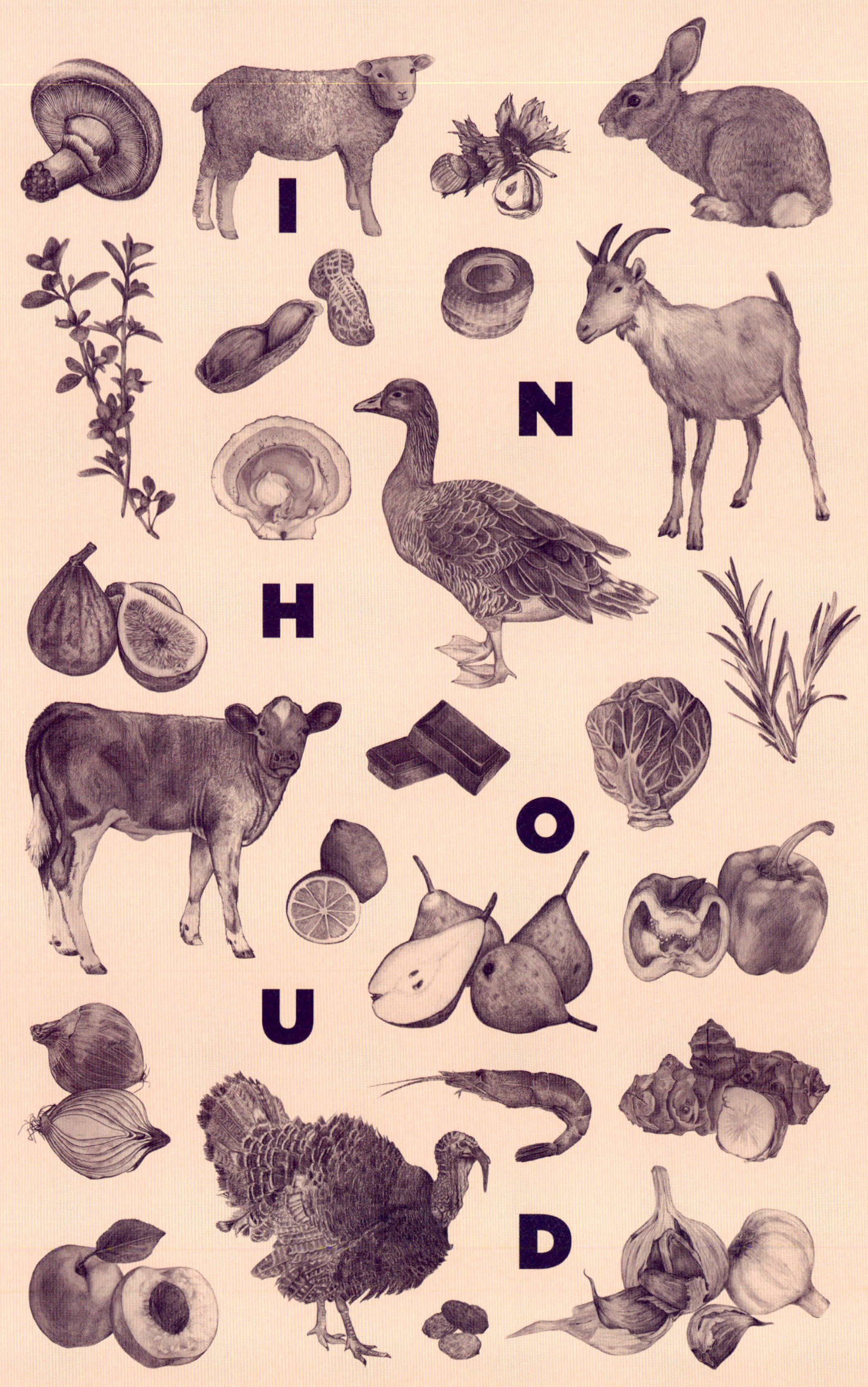
I
N
H
O
U
D

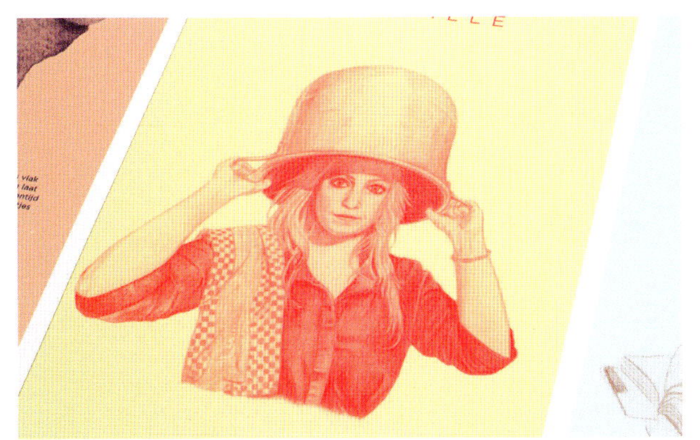

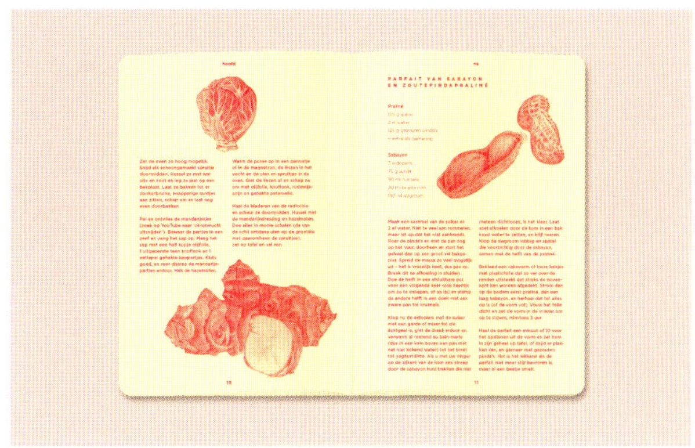

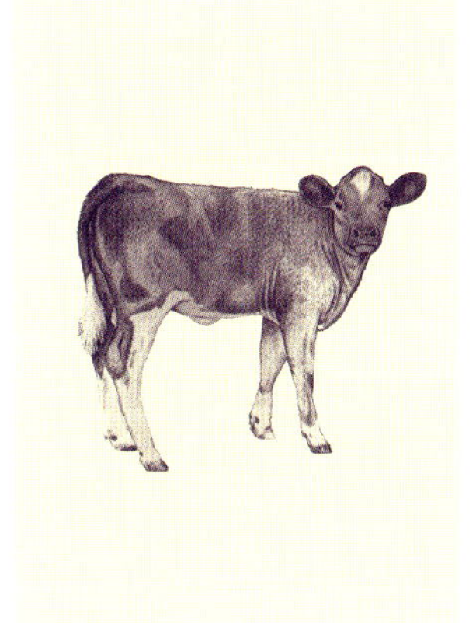

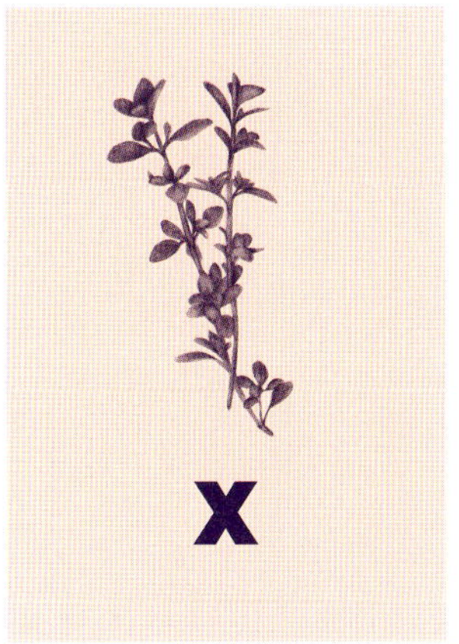
X

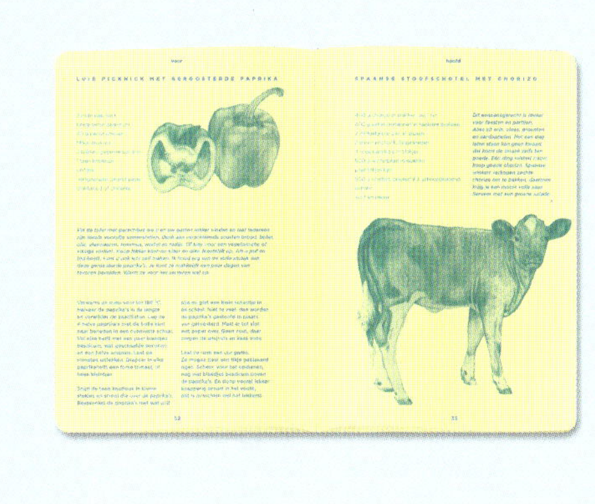

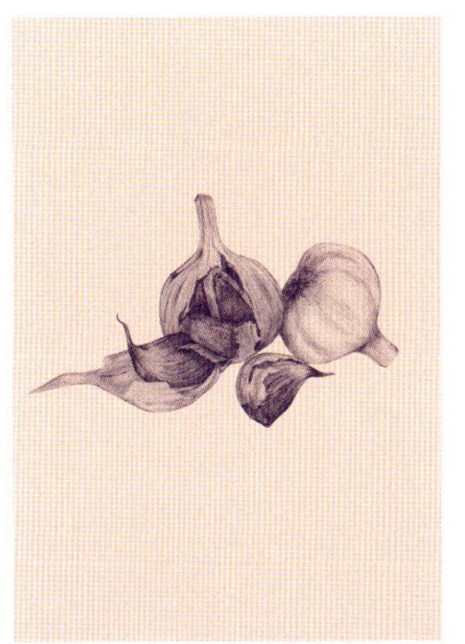

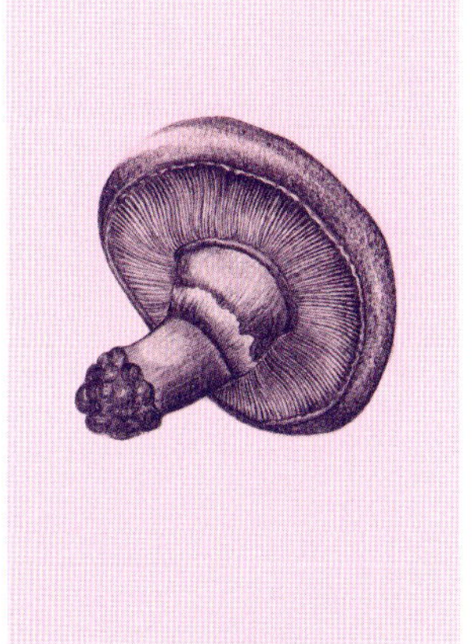

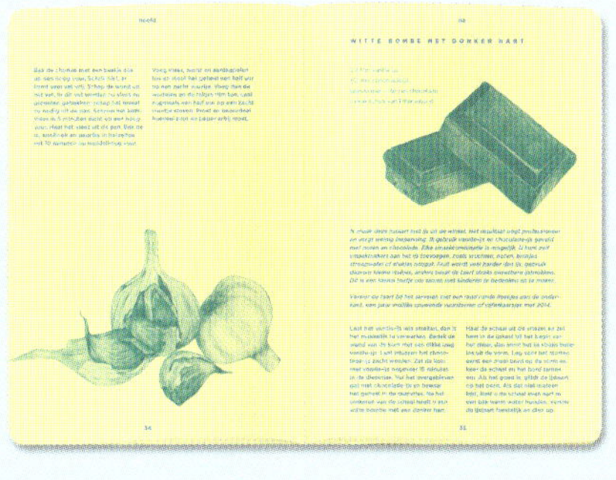

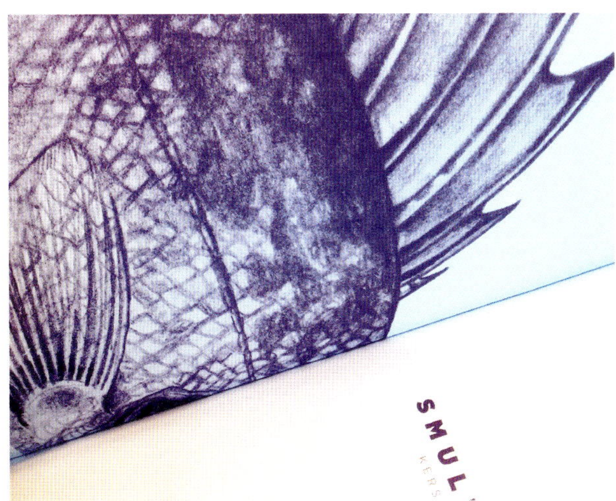

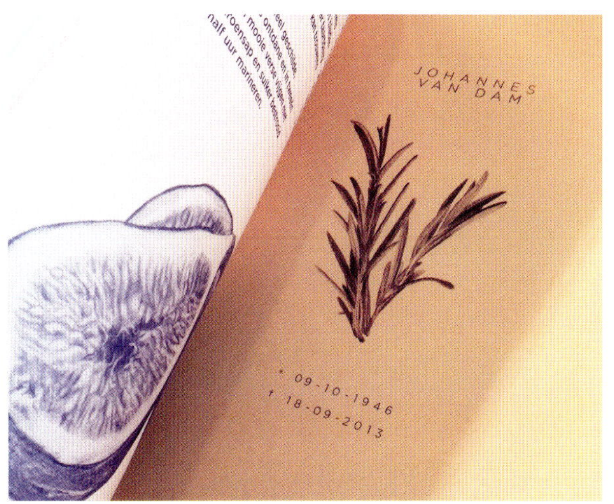
JOHANNES
VAN DAM
* 09-10-1946
† 18-09-2013

El Cariñito is a Mexican restaurant located in downtown Querétaro. Drawing graphic and typographic inspiration from Mexican icons like Guadalupe Posada, Frida Kahlo and golden age movie titles, its visual identity evokes a laid-back marketplace atmosphere to complement the dining experience.

Client: El Cariñito, Cocina con Sentimiento

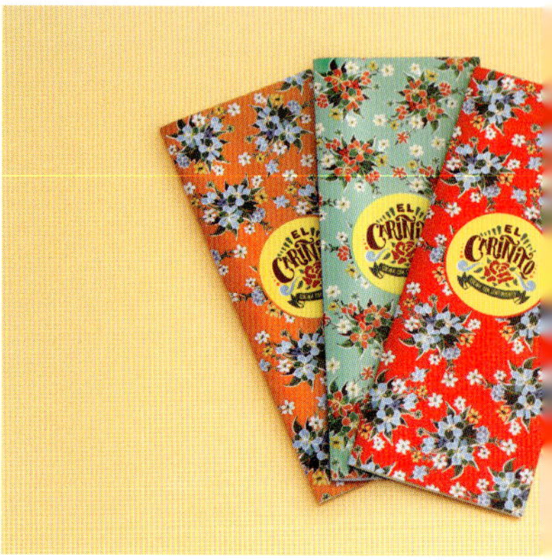

Abraham Lule & Kuro Strada

El Cariñito

El Cariñito is a Mexican restaurant located in downtown Querétaro. Drawing graphic and typographic inspiration from Mexican icons like Guadalupe Posada, Frida Kahlo and golden age movie titles, its visual identity evokes a laid-back marketplace atmosphere to complement the dining experience.

Client: El Cariñito, Cocina con Sentimiento

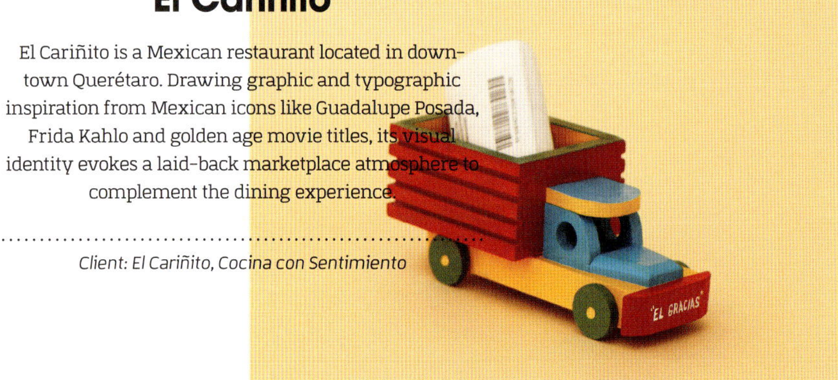

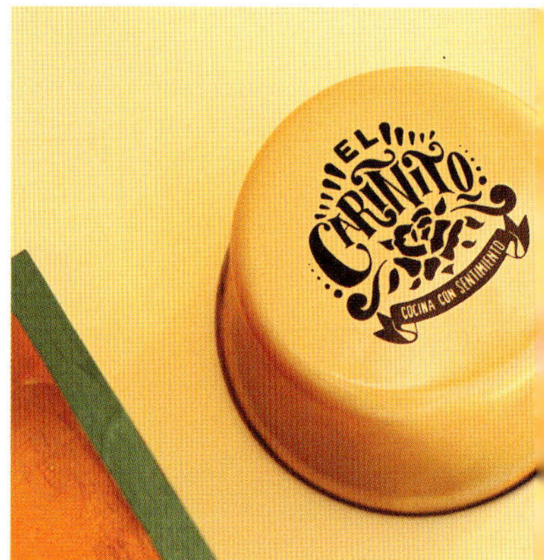

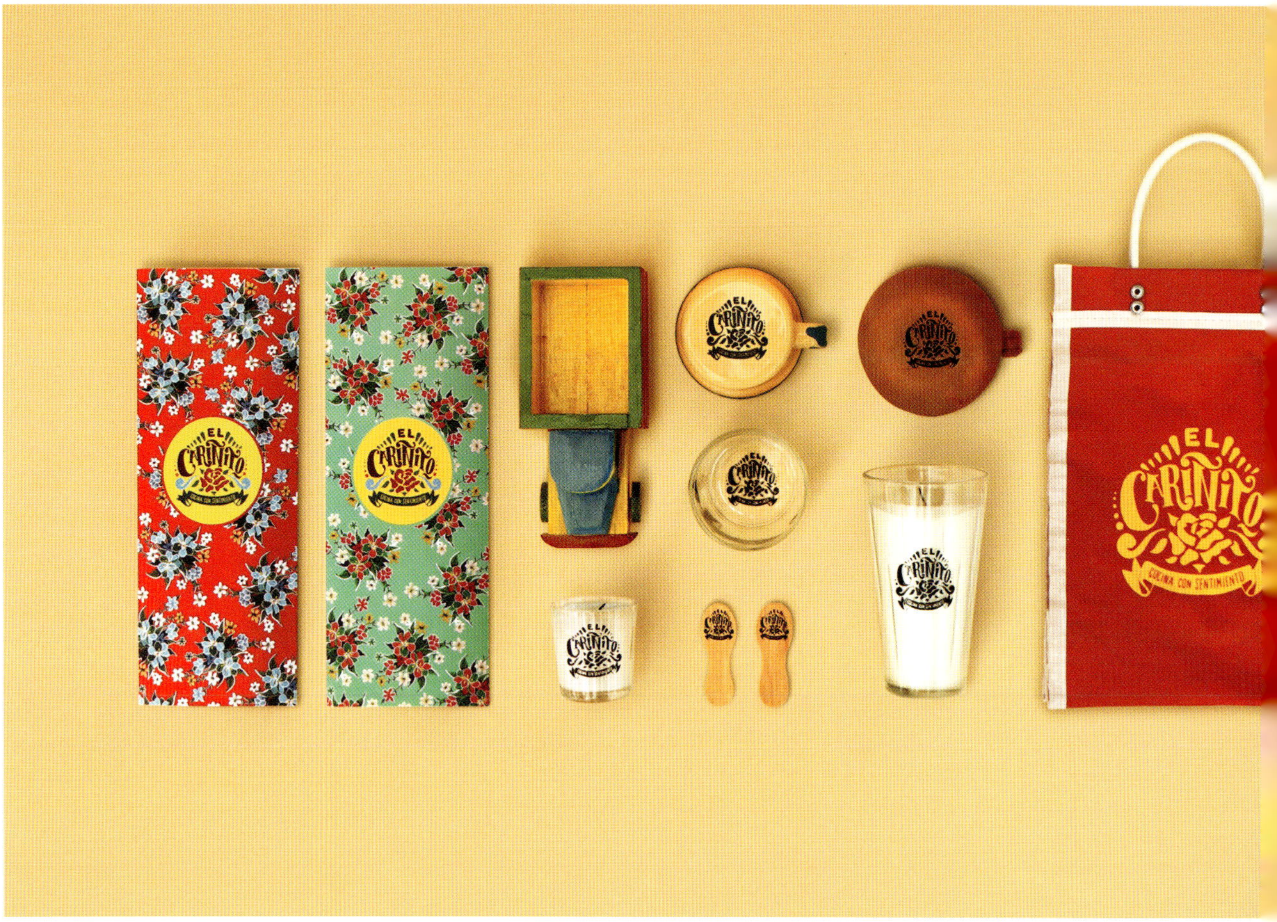

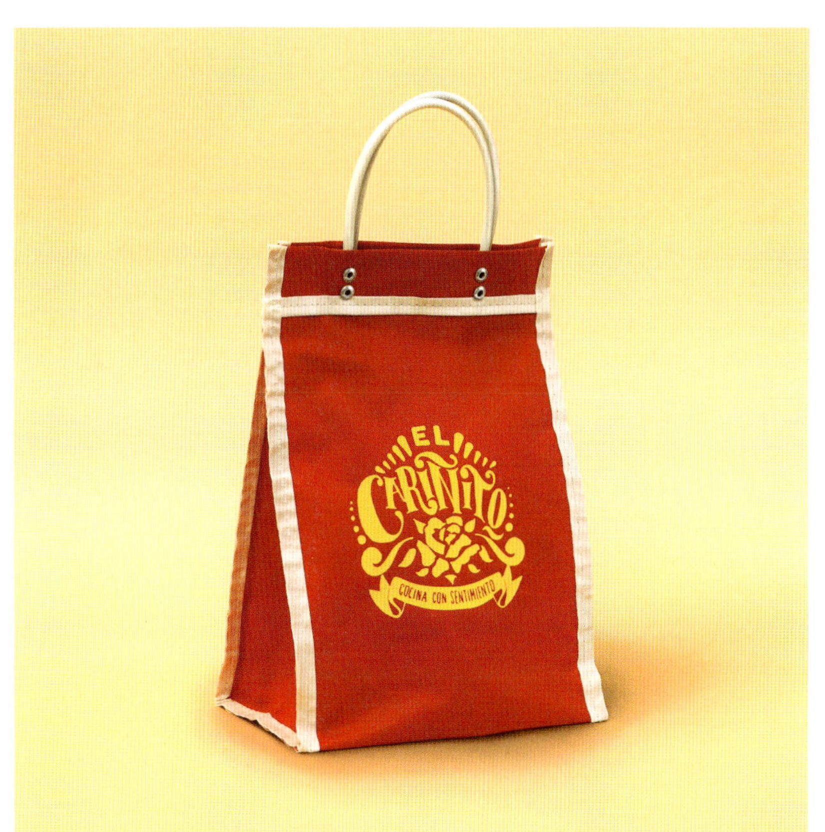
EL
CARIÑITO
COCINA CON SENTIMIENTO

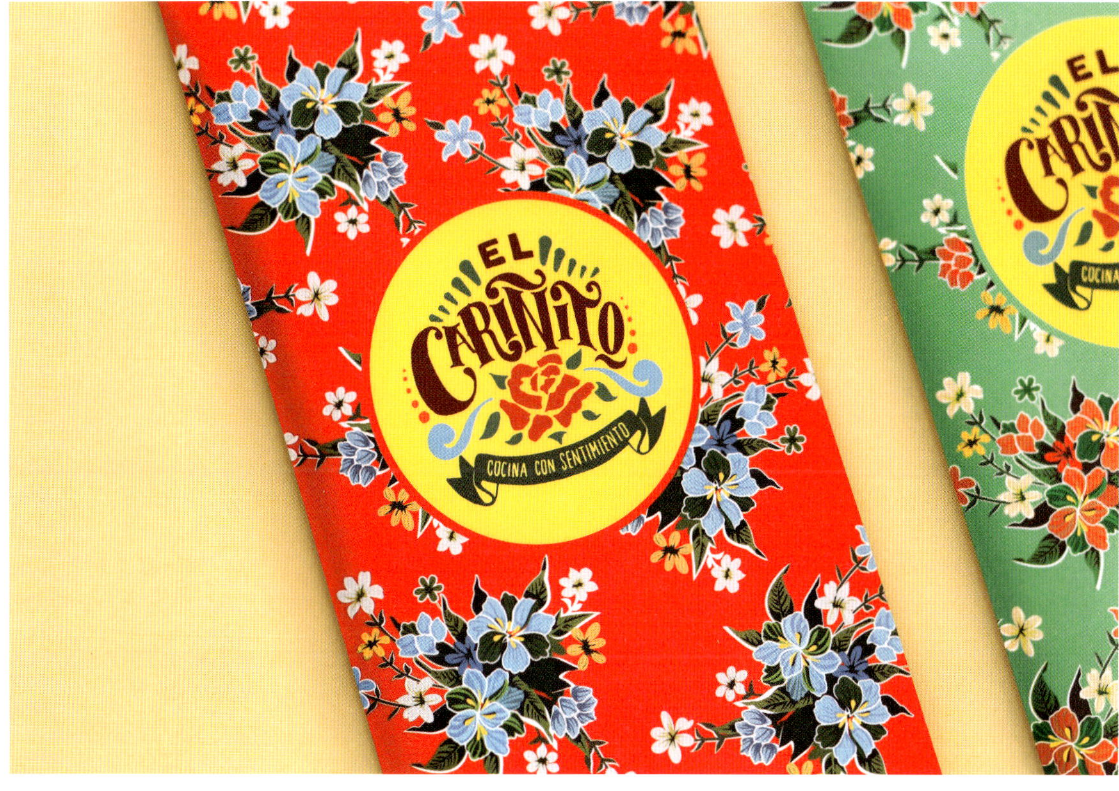
EL
CARIÑITO
COCINA CON SENTIMIENTO

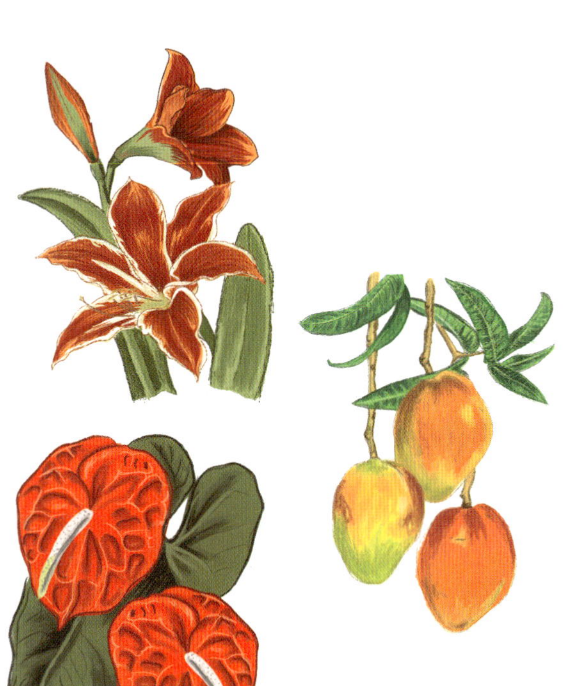

Welcome Veranito

Invitation and visual identity for Spanish media consultancy Pulsa's summer party. Summer cool and heat clashed on the collaterals as soft ice-cream meets tropical flora and fauna. A typographic logo and vintage tone asked guests to expect something different from the bash.

Client: Pulsa Media Consulting

Andrea Ferrandis (Kinton)

Welcome Veranito

Invitation and visual identity for Spanish media consultancy Pulsa's summer party. Summer cool and heat clashed on the collaterals as soft ice-cream meets tropical flora and fauna. A typographic logo and vintage tone asked guests to expect something different from the bash.

Client: Pulsa Media Consulting

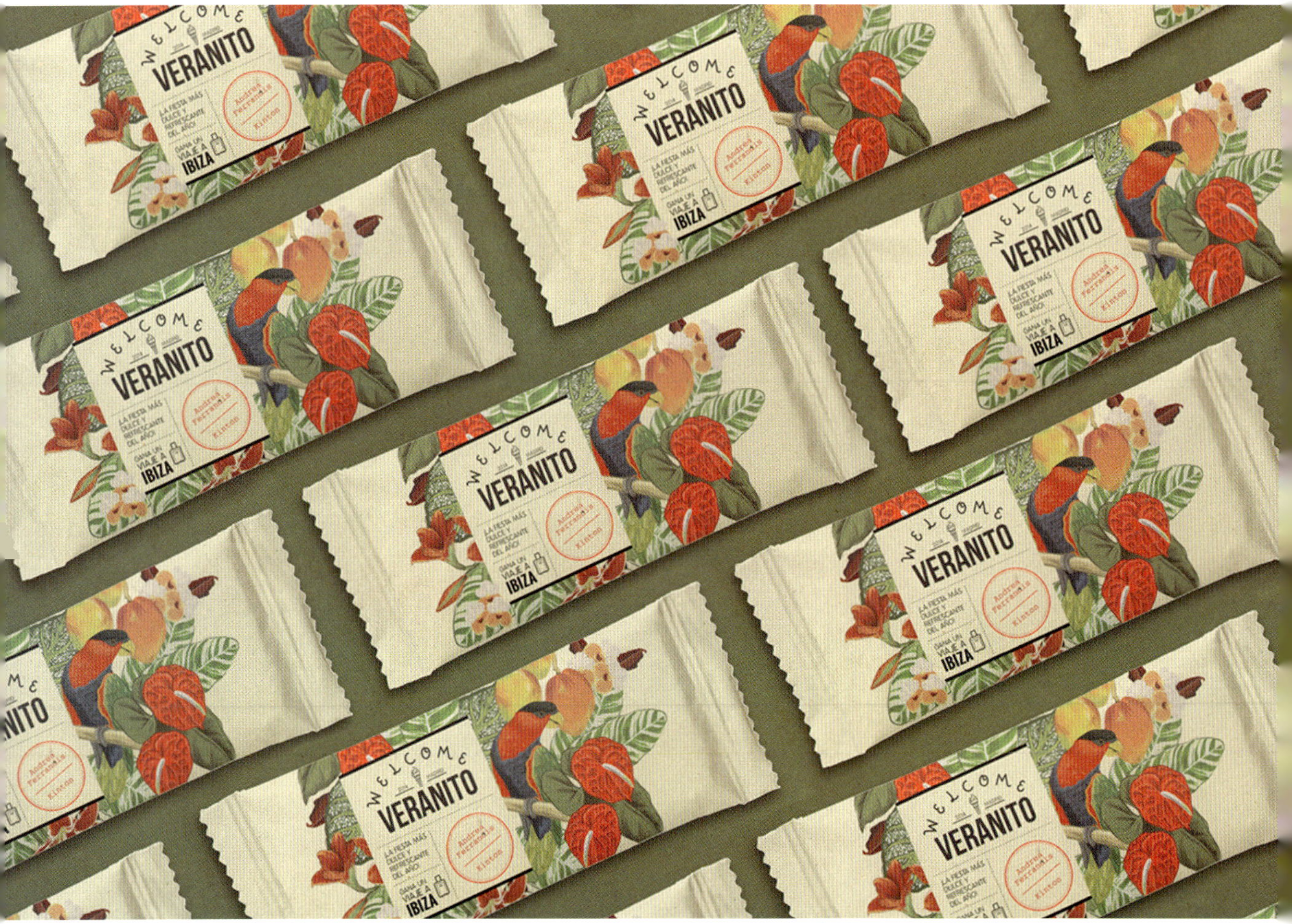

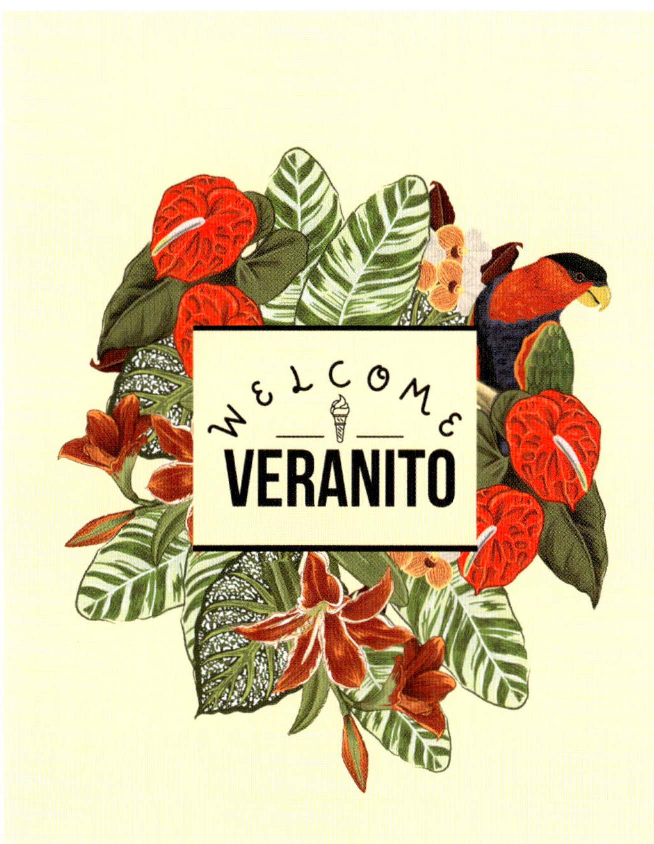
WELCOME
VERANITO

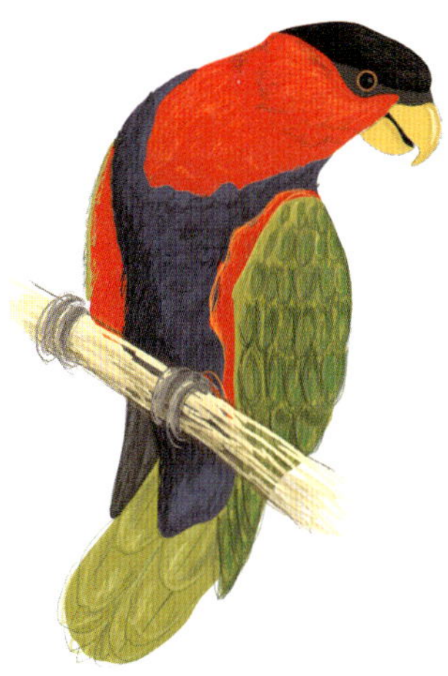

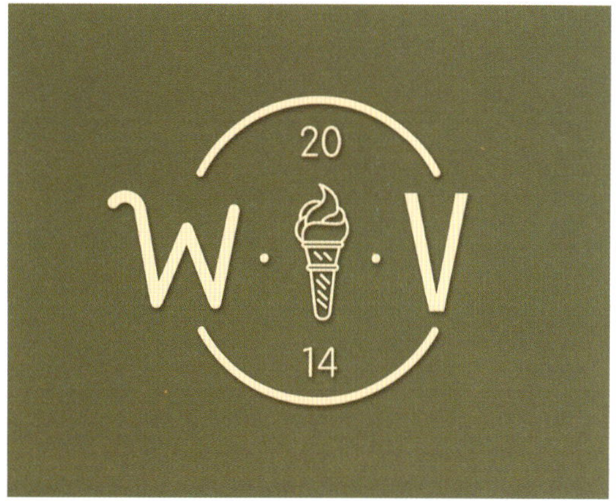
20
W · V
14

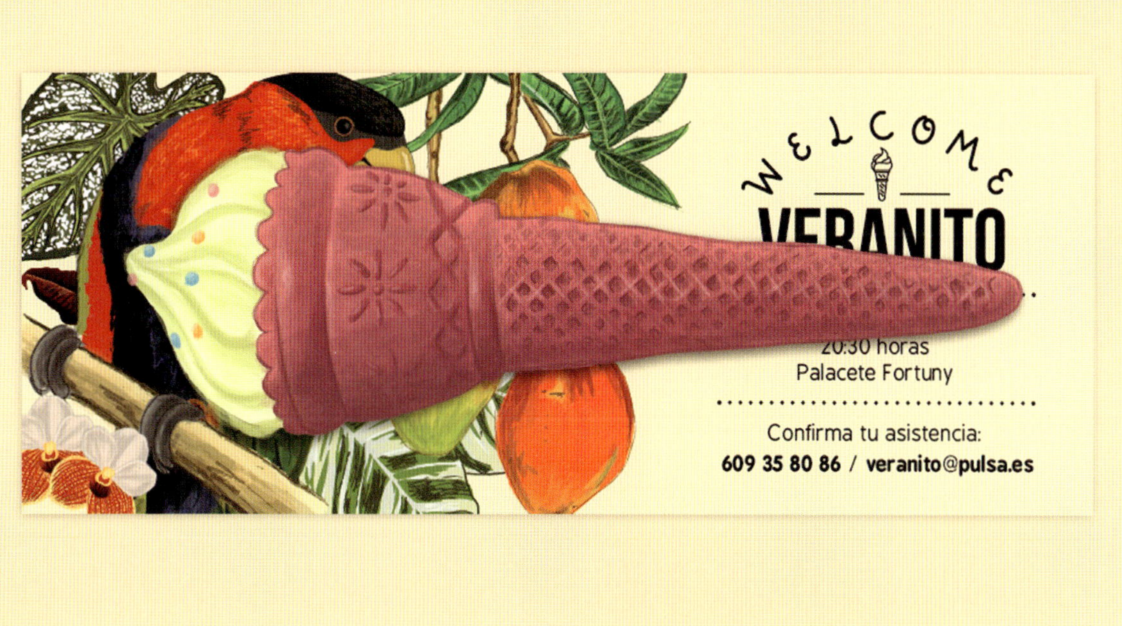
WELCOME
20:30 horas
Palacete Fortuny
Confirma tu asistencia:
609 35 80 86 / veranito@pulsa.es

FLEUR

Femininity, purity and romance dominate Judit Besze's idea of a dream flower store. Botanical flower prints tossed around modern and classical types give a balanced personality with spare elegance on wrapping papers, posters, bags and sign book covers.

Judit Besze

FLEUR

Femininity, purity and romance dominate Judit Besze's idea of a dream flower store. Botanical flower prints tossed around modern and classical types give a balanced personality with spare elegance on wrapping papers, posters, bags and sign book covers.

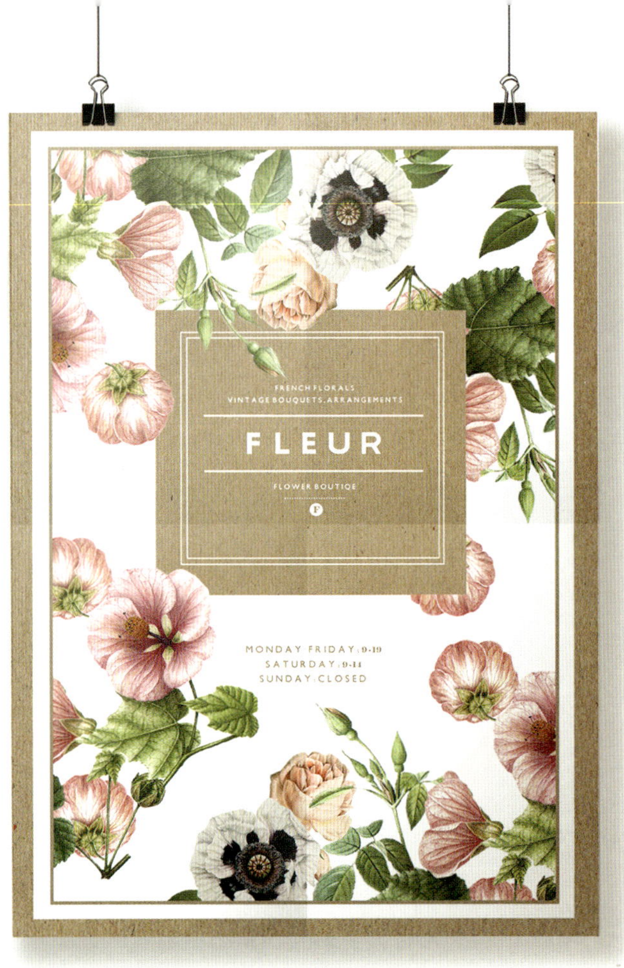

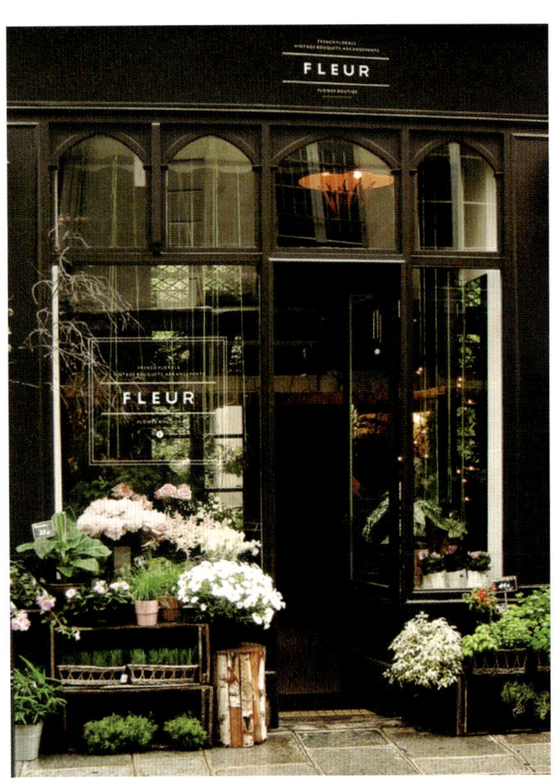

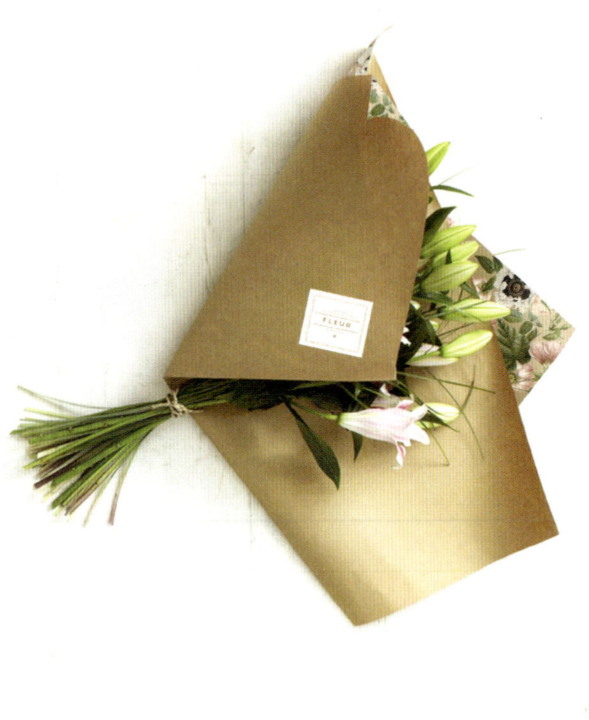

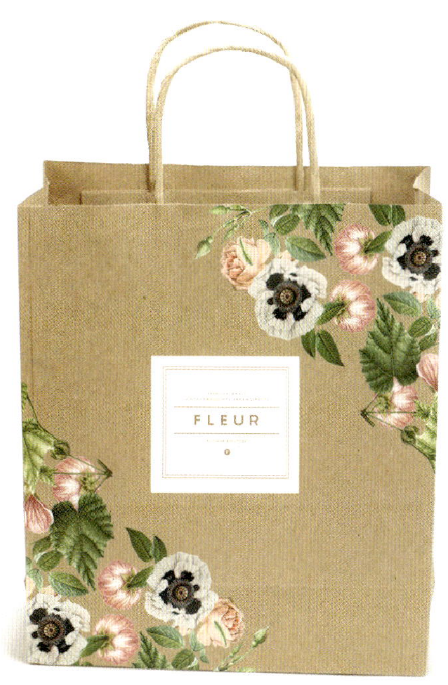
FLEUR

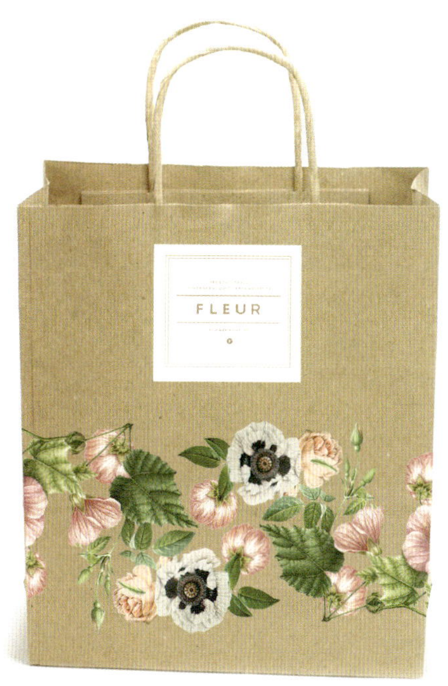
FLEUR

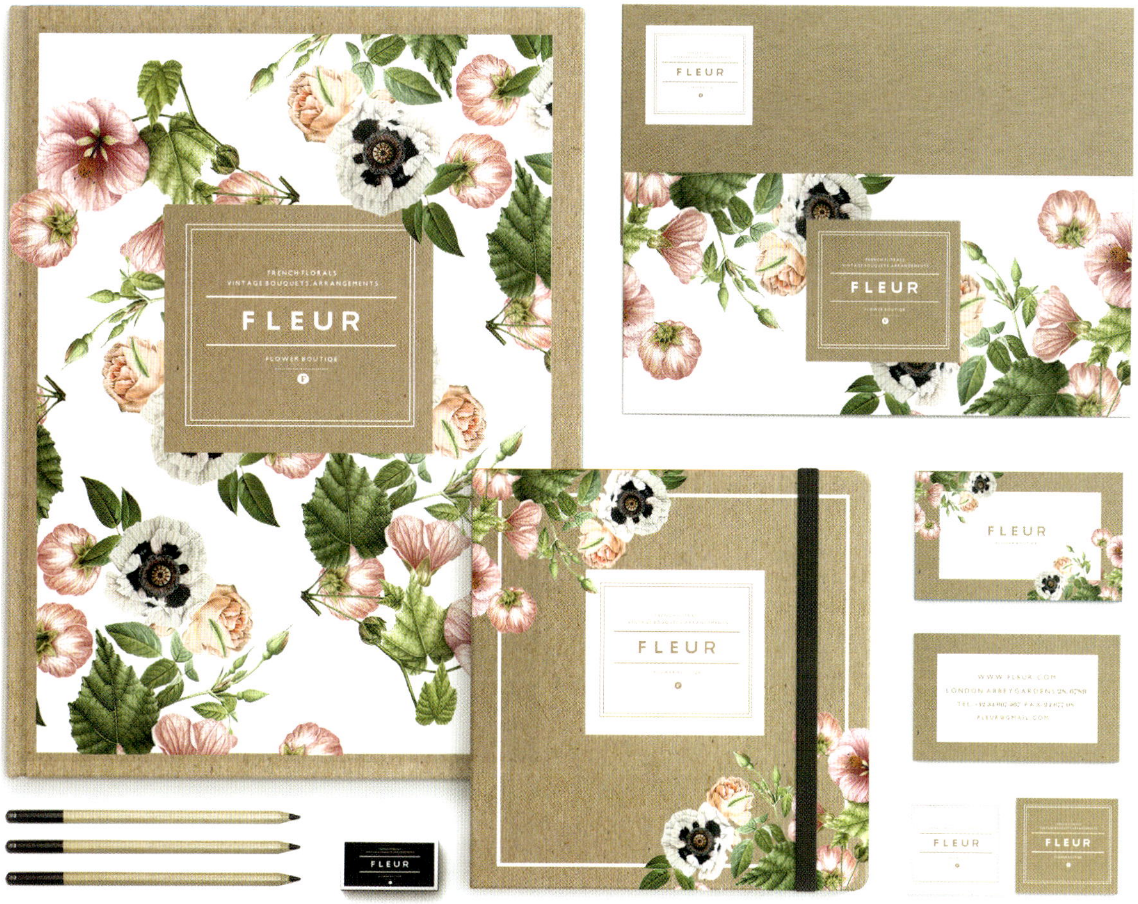

FRENCH FLORALS
VINTAGE BOUQUETS ARRANGEMENTS
FLEUR
FLOWER BOUTIQUE

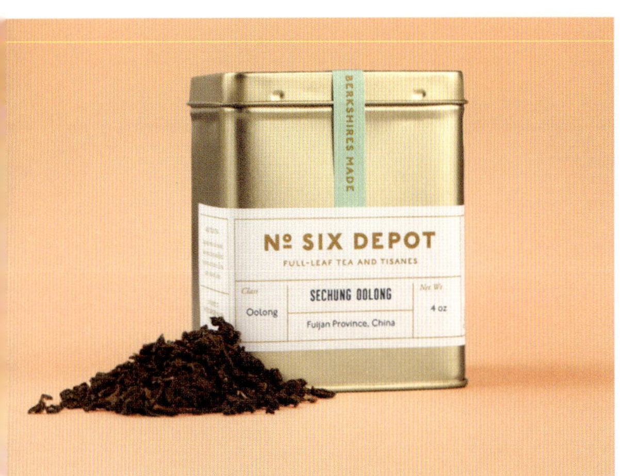
BERKSHIRES MADE
Nº SIX DEPOT
FULL-LEAF TEA AND TISANES
SECHUNG OOLONG
Oolong
4 oz
Fujian Province, China

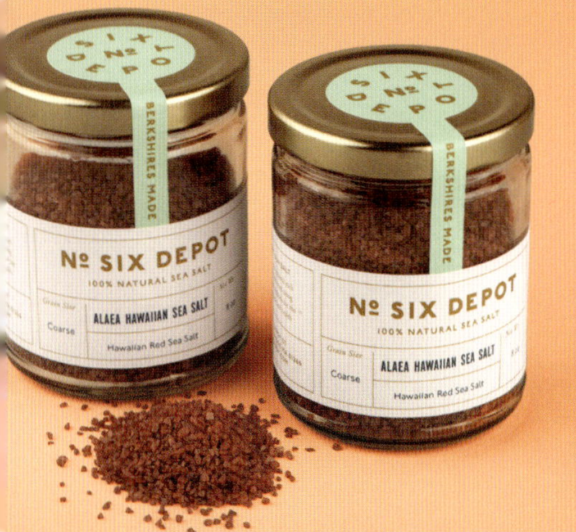
SIX Nº DEPOT
BERKSHIRES MADE
Nº SIX DEPOT
100% NATURAL SEA SALT
Coarse
ALAEA HAWAIIAN SEA SALT
Hawaiian Red Sea Salt

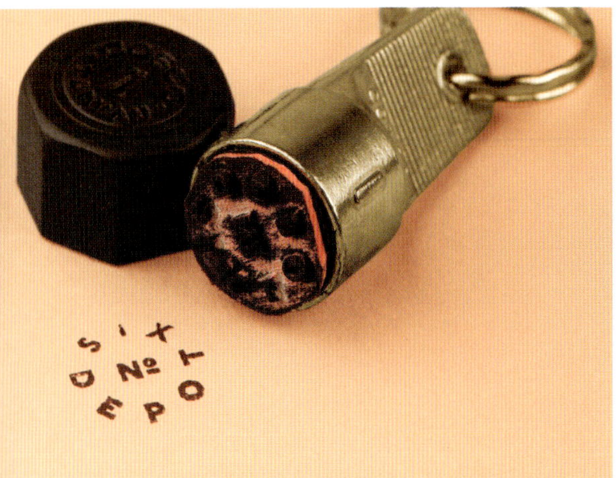
SIX Nº DEPOT

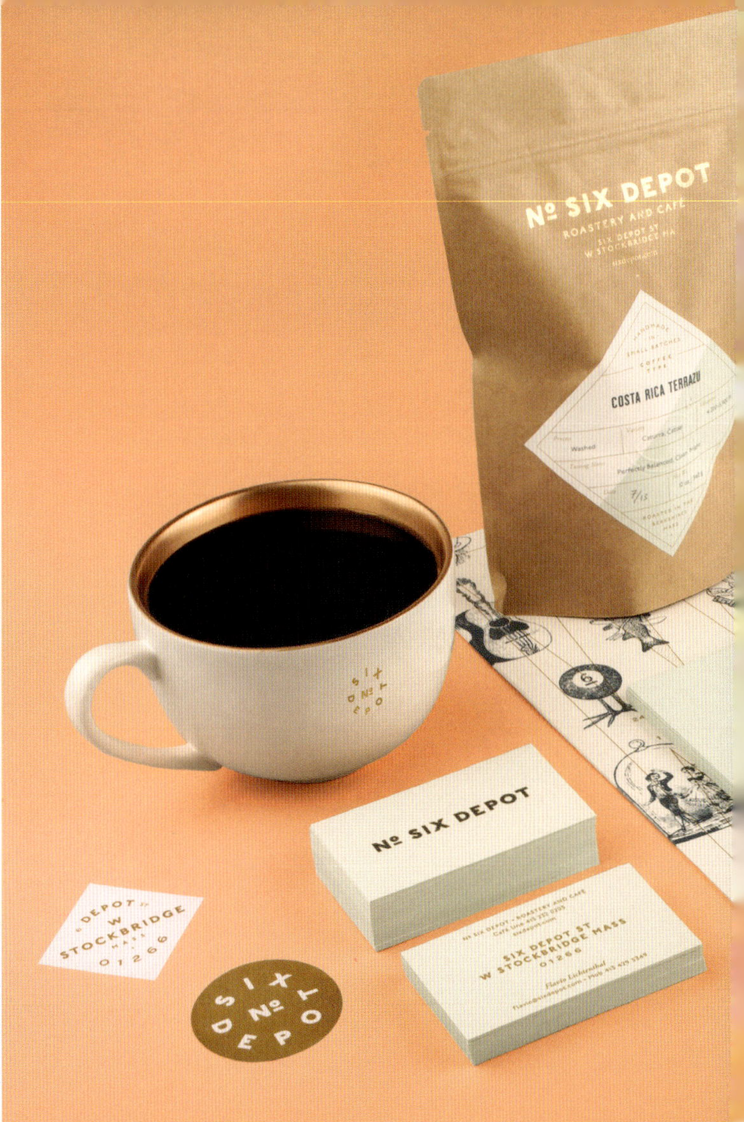
Nº SIX DEPOT
ROASTERY AND CAFE
COSTA RICA TERRAZU
Nº SIX DEPOT
DEPOT W STOCKBRIDGE MASS 01266
SIX Nº DEPOT
SIX DEPOT ST
W STOCKBRIDGE MASS
01266

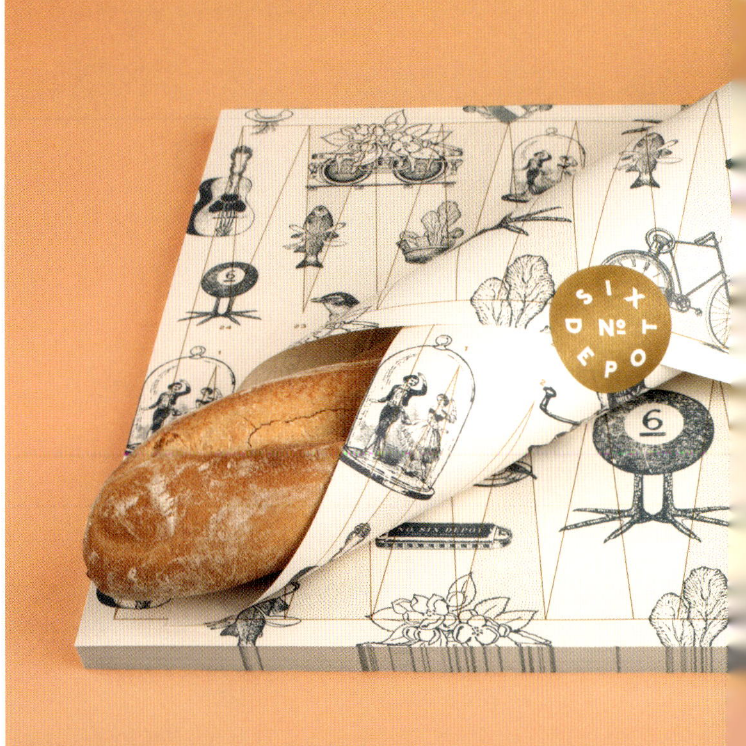
SIX Nº DEPOT
6

ix Depot

Nº Six Depot is a family-owned coffee roaster and café nested in beautiful Berkshires. A visual link to its location in a historic train station, the identity juxtaposes a mix of modern and rural elements inspired by their backyard railroad. The idea was to keep it simple and make it true.

Photo: Jennifer May
Client: Nº Six Depot

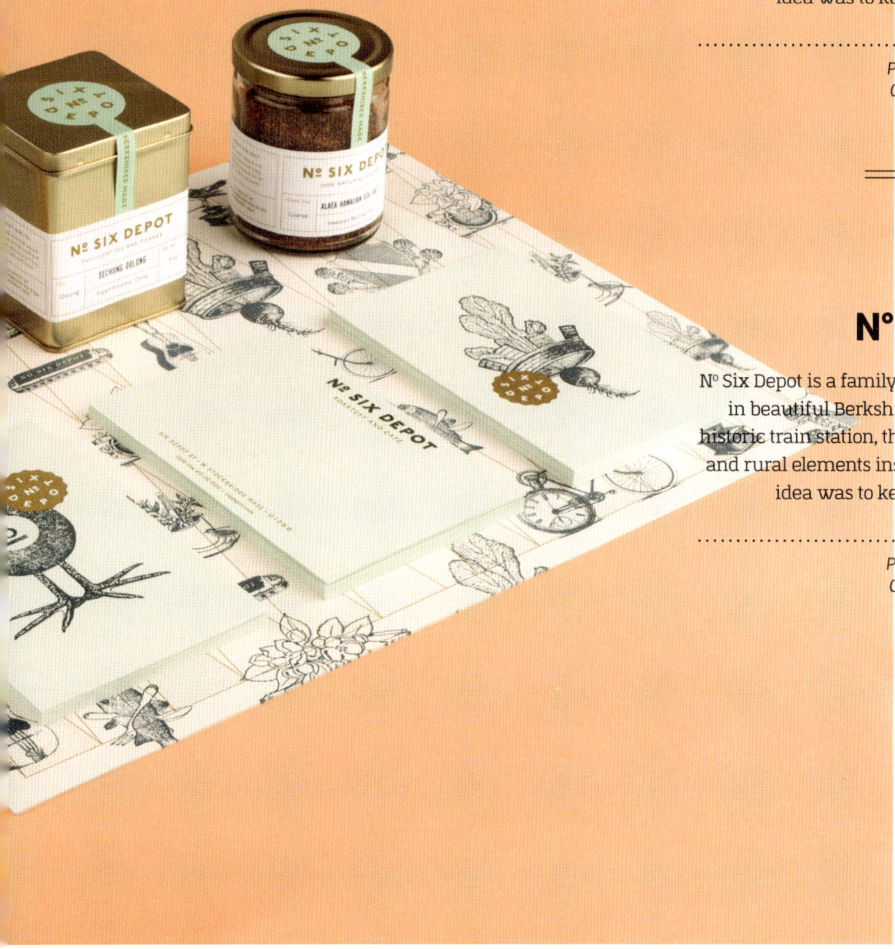

Perky Bros llc

Nº Six Depot

Nº Six Depot is a family-owned coffee roaster and café nested in beautiful Berkshires. A visual link to its location in a historic train station, the identity juxtaposes a mix of modern and rural elements inspired by their backyard railroad. The idea was to keep it simple and make it true.

Photo: Jennifer May
Client: Nº Six Depot

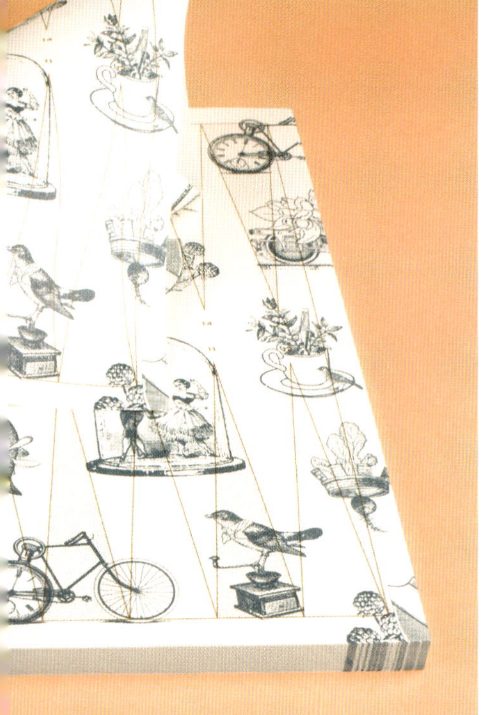

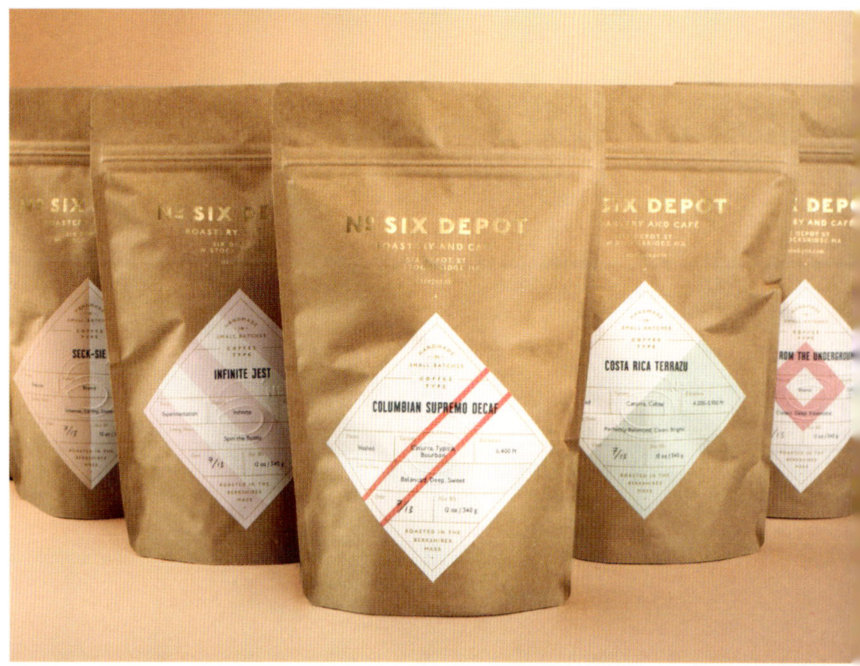

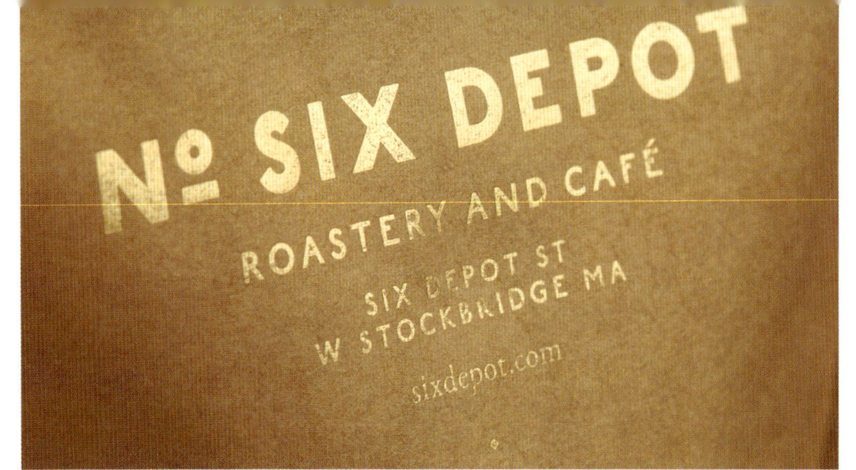
Nº SIX DEPOT
ROASTERY AND CAFÉ
SIX DEPOT ST
W STOCKBRIDGE MA
sixdepot.com

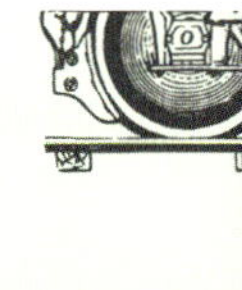

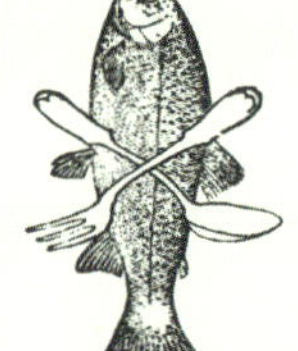

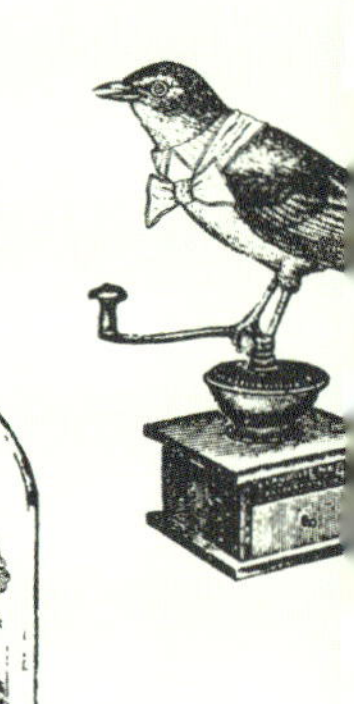

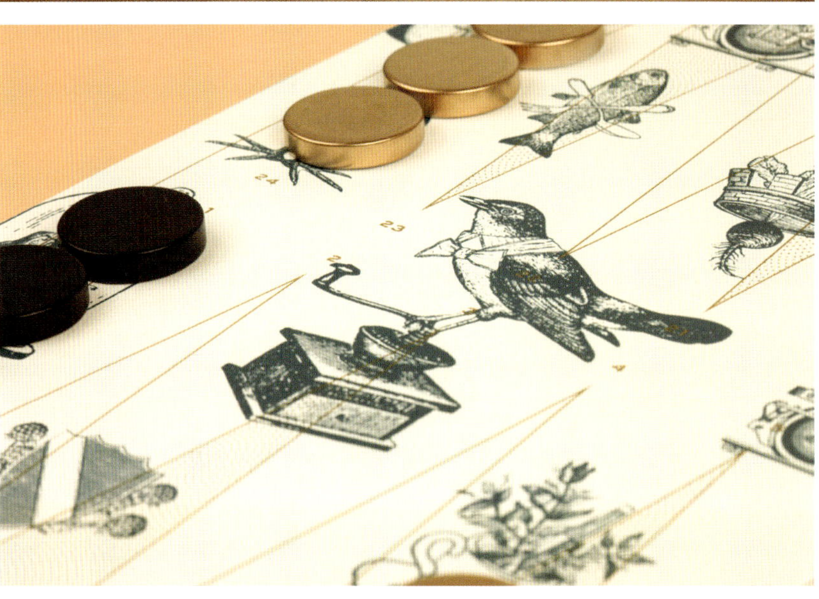

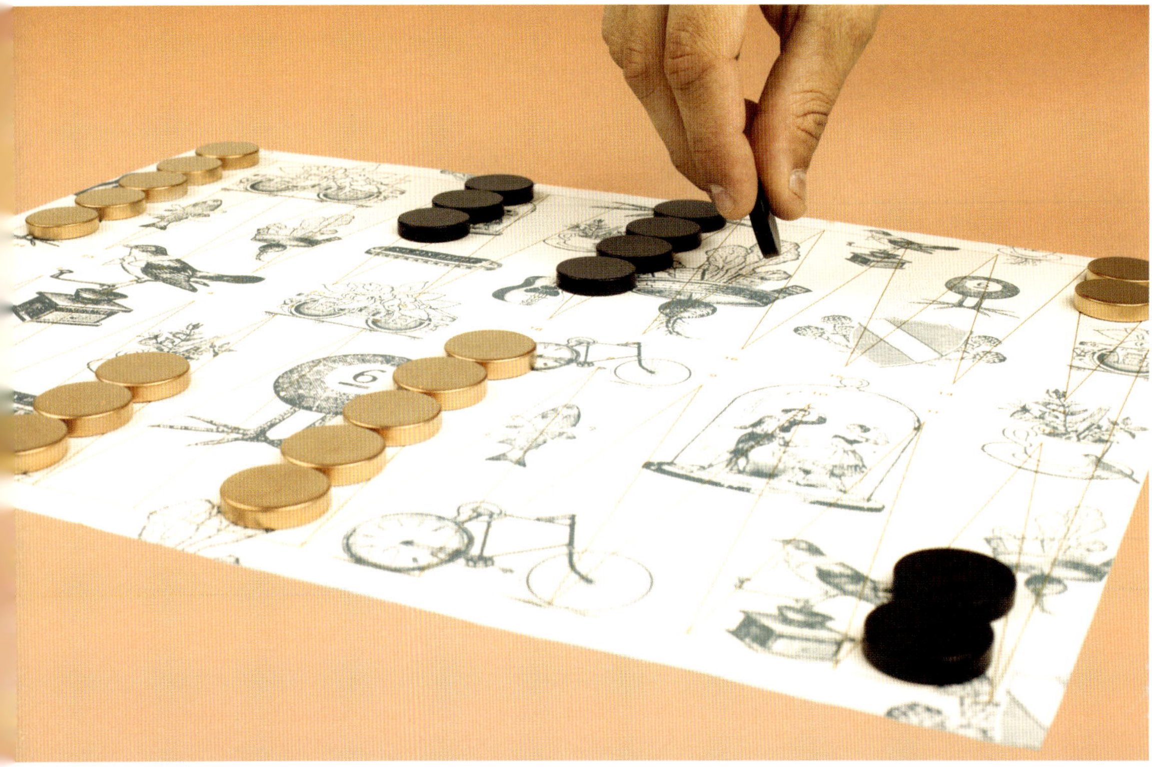

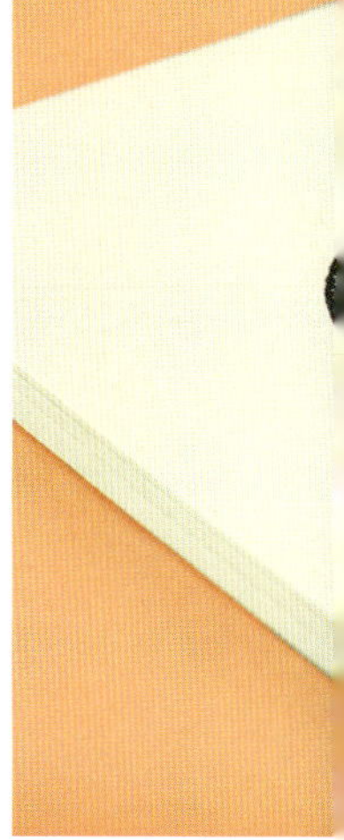

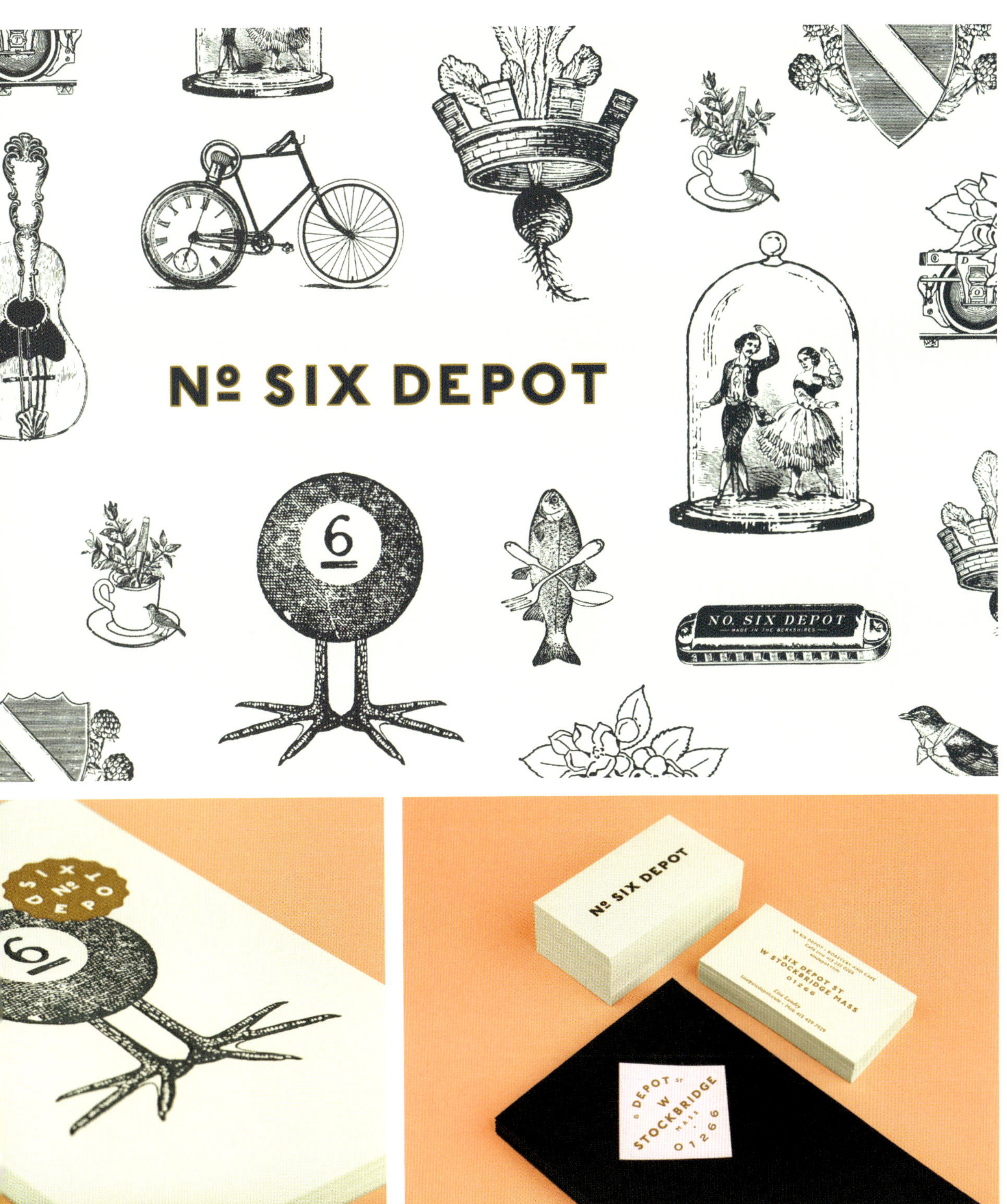

Nº SIX DEPOT
6
NO. SIX DEPOT
MADE IN THE BERKSHIRES
SIX Nº DEPOT
Nº SIX DEPOT
SIX DEPOT ST
W STOCKBRIDGE MASS
01266
DEPOT ST
W
STOCKBRIDGE
MASS
01266

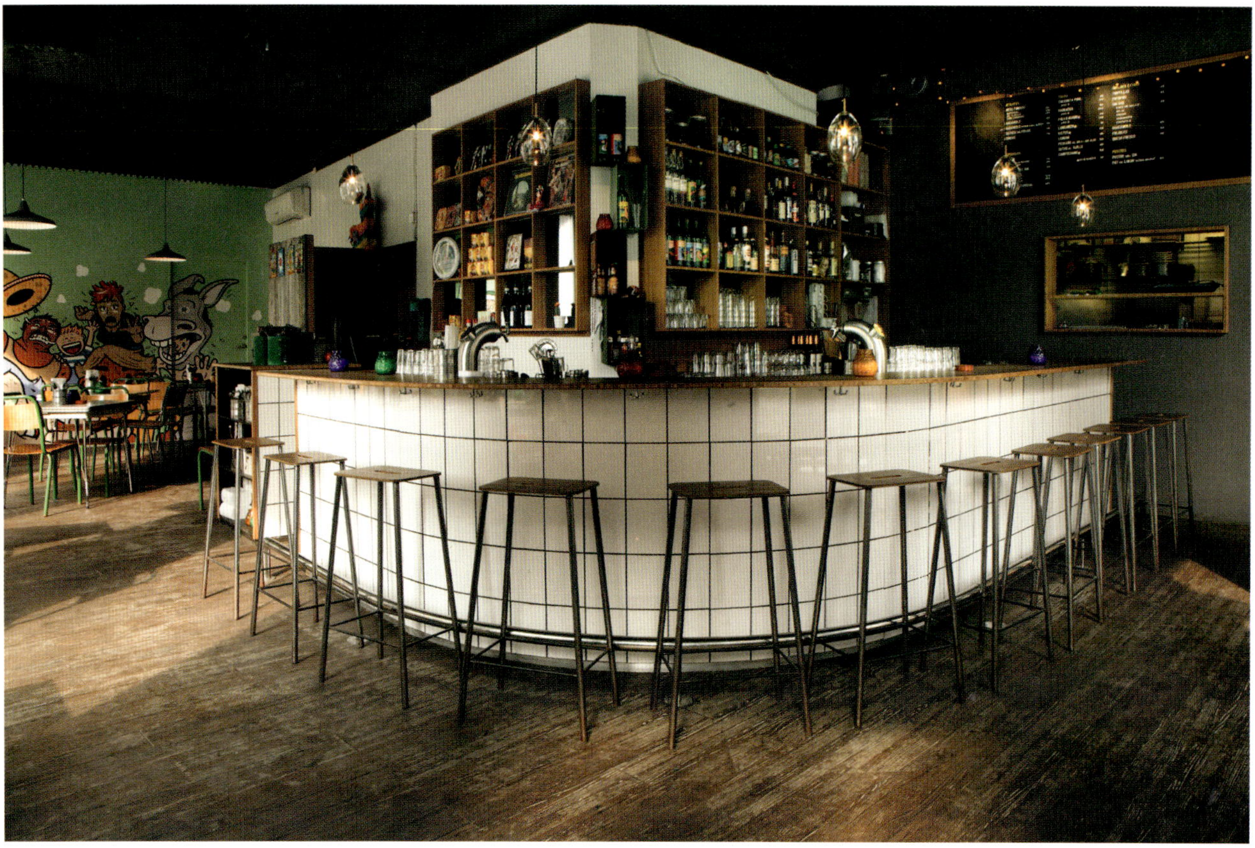

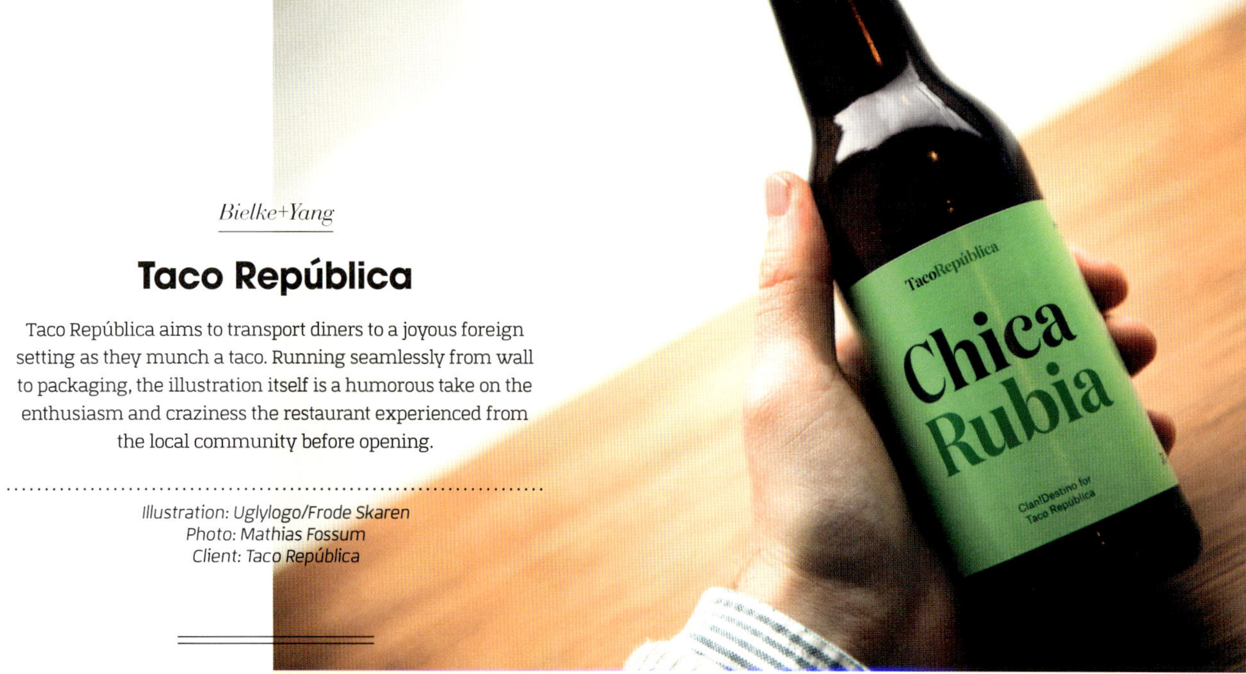

Bielke+Yang

Taco República

Taco República aims to transport diners to a joyous foreign setting as they munch a taco. Running seamlessly from wall to packaging, the illustration itself is a humorous take on the enthusiasm and craziness the restaurant experienced from the local community before opening.

Illustration: Uglylogo/Frode Skaren
Photo: Mathias Fossum
Client: Taco República

Bielke+Yang

Taco República

Taco República aims to transport diners to a joyous foreign setting as they munch a taco. Running seamlessly from wall to packaging, the illustration itself is a humorous take on the enthusiasm and craziness the restaurant experienced from the local community before opening.

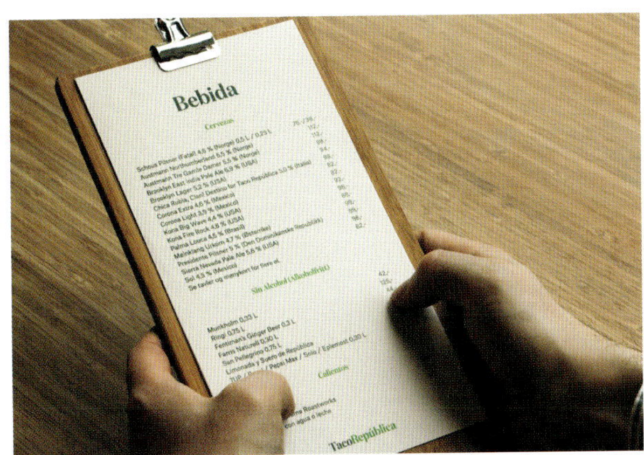
Bebida
Cervezas
TacoRepública

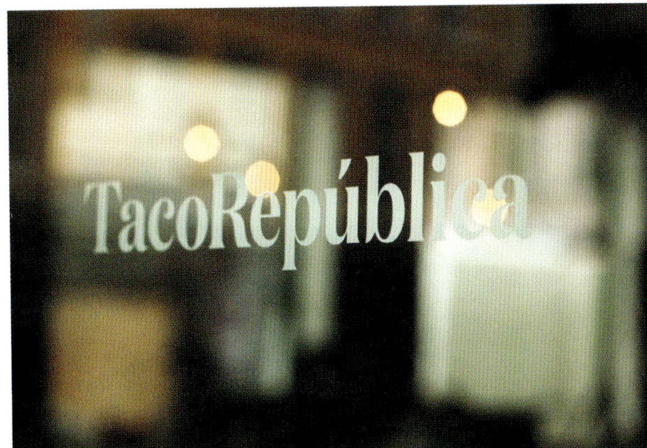
TacoRepública

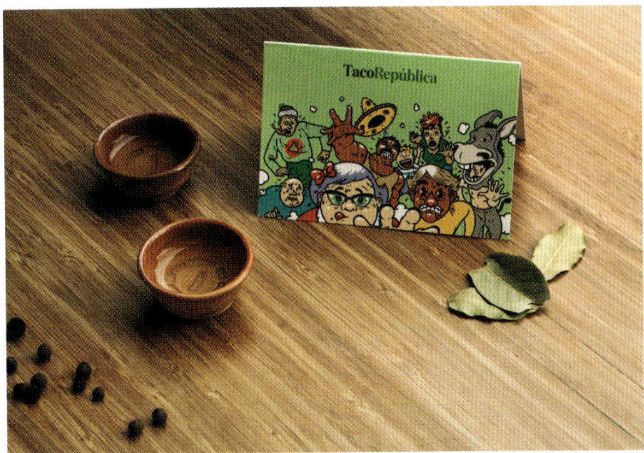
TacoRepública

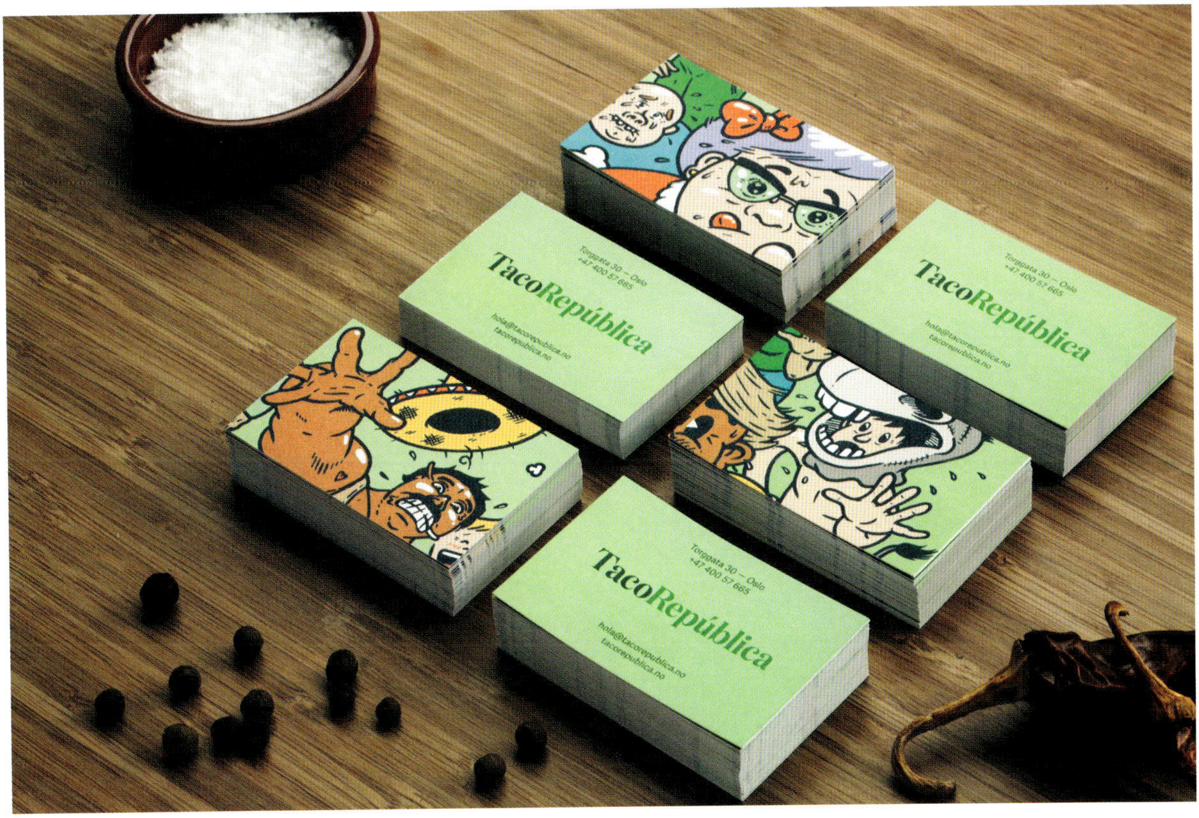

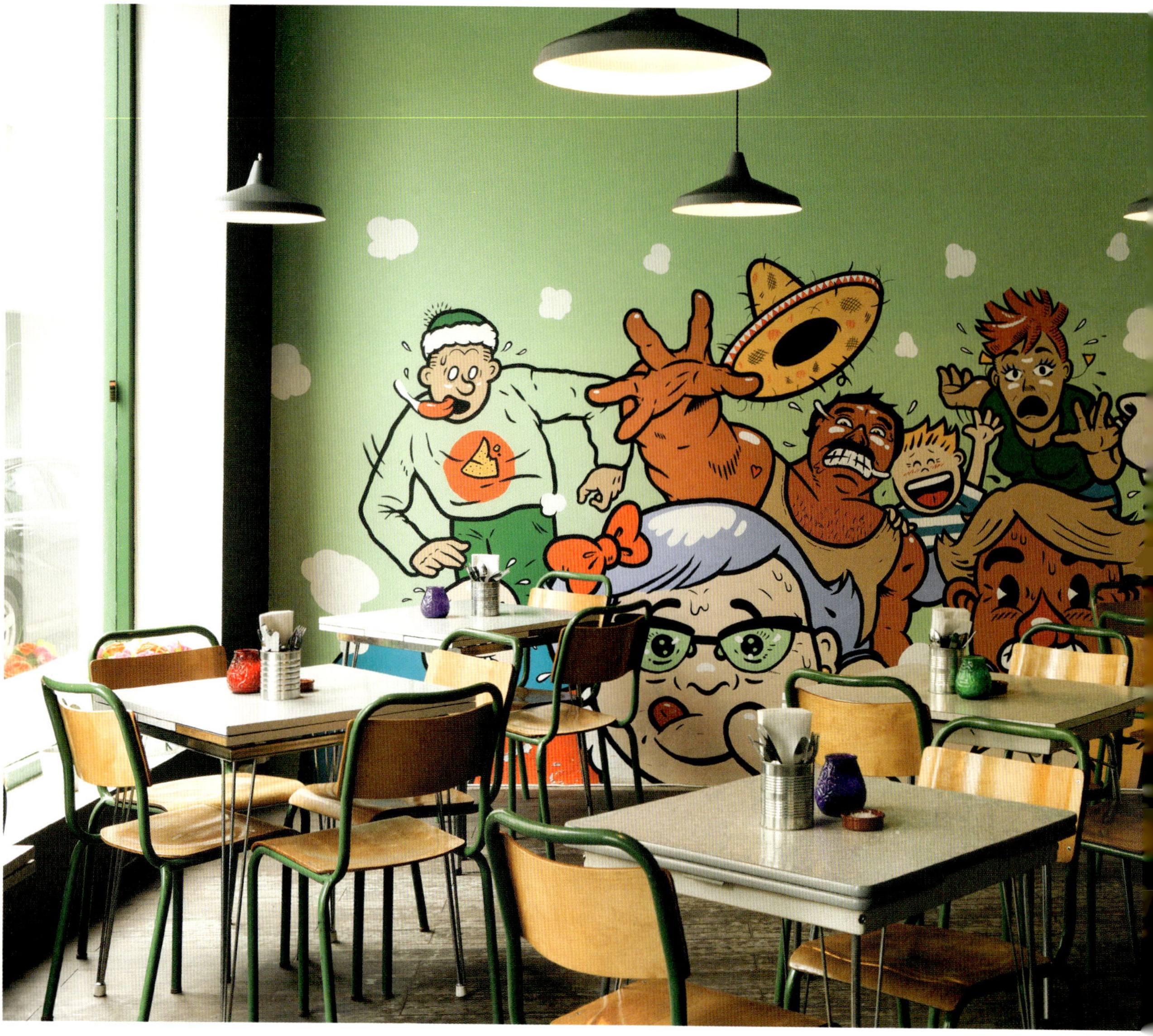

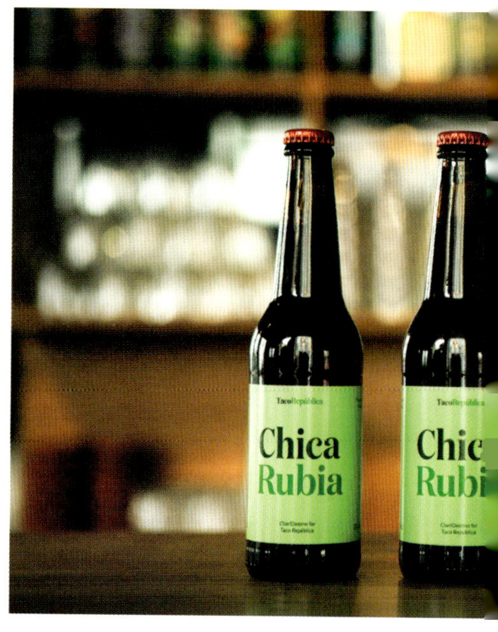
Chica
Rubia

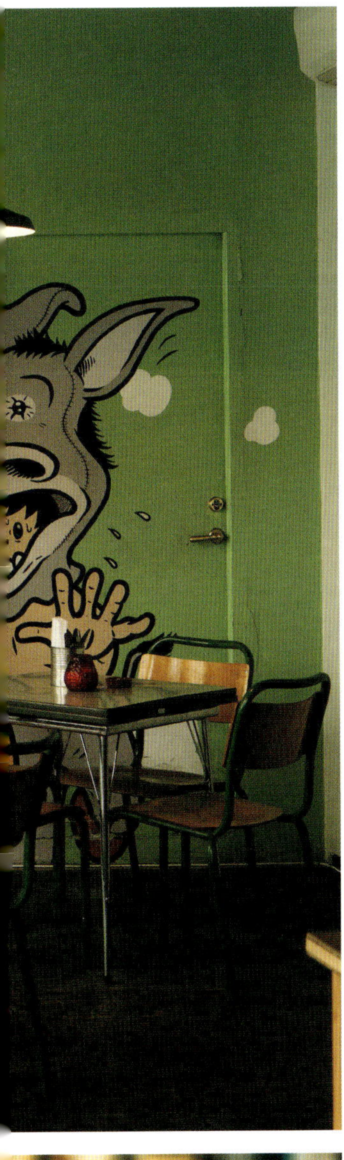

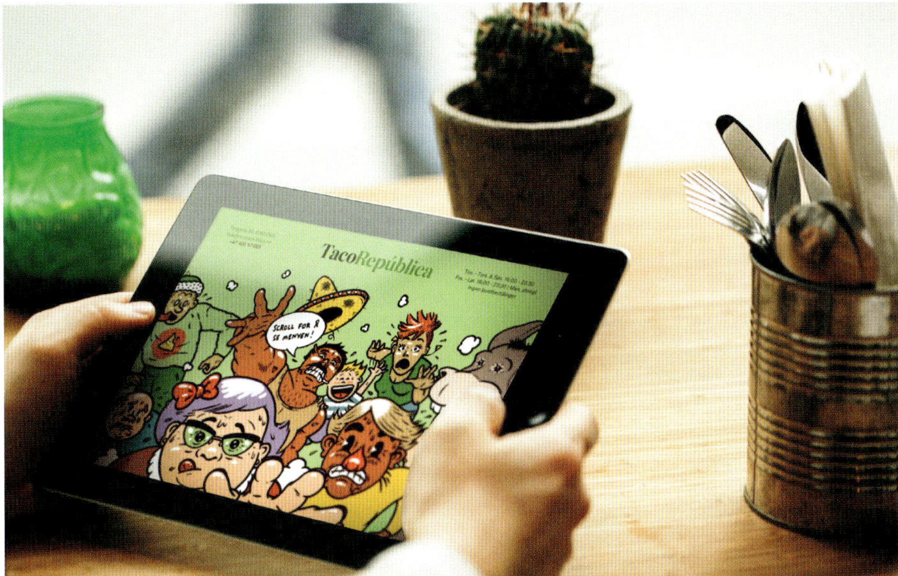

TacoRepública
SCROLL FOR Å SE MENYEN!

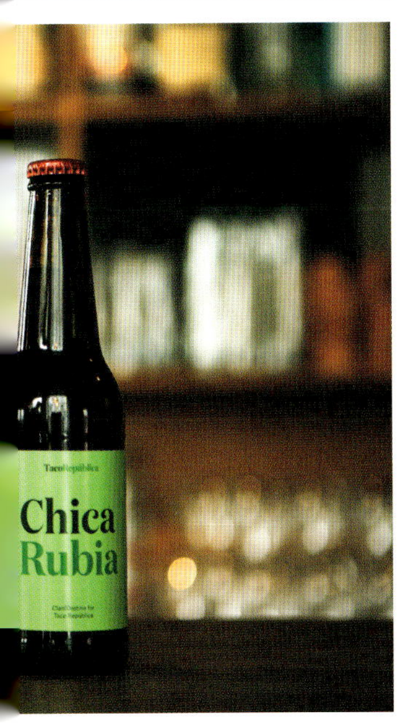

TacoRepública
Chica Rubia

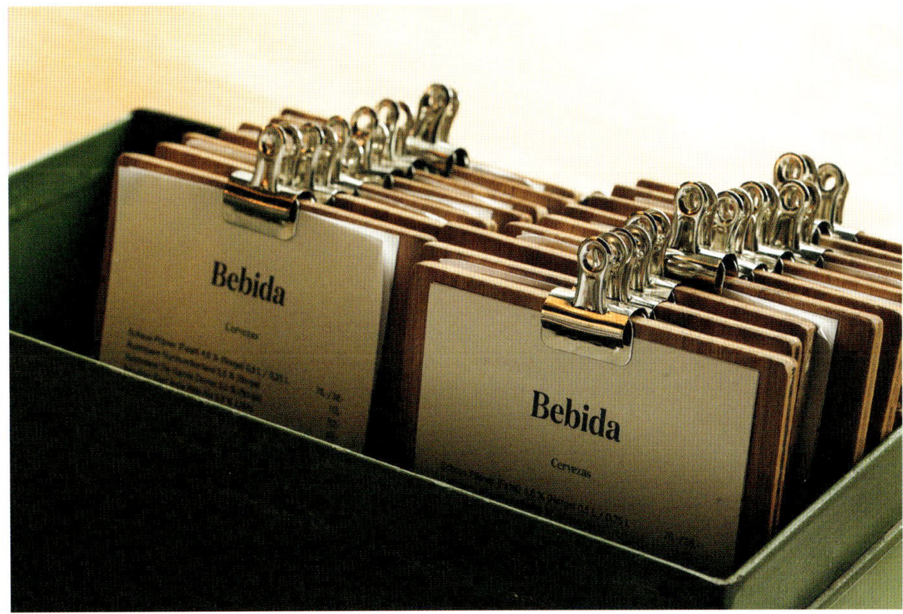

Bebida
Cervezas
Bebida
Cervezas

VE KIDS

The Elbe Housing Association (BVE) founded its own cooperative for children to engage them in the design of living spaces. A vibrant parallel world is built up in the brand system where imaginative residents tell stories of what it means to build and live alongside one another in the city.

Client: BVE Bauverein der Elbgemeinden eG

EIGA Design

BVE KIDS

The Elbe Housing Association (BVE) founded its own cooperative for children to engage them in the design of living spaces. A vibrant parallel world is built up in the brand system where imaginative residents tell stories of what it means to build and live alongside one another in the city.

Client: BVE Bauverein der Elbgemeinden eG

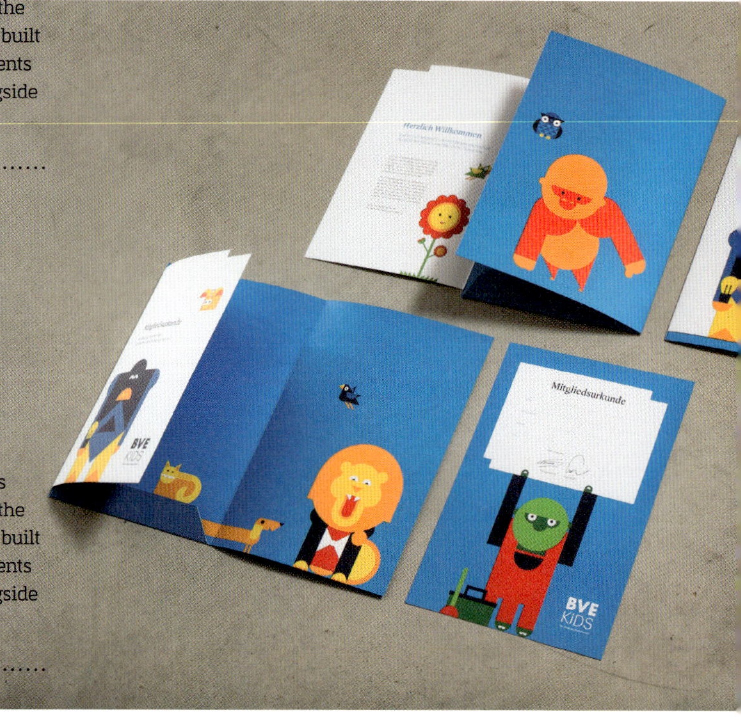

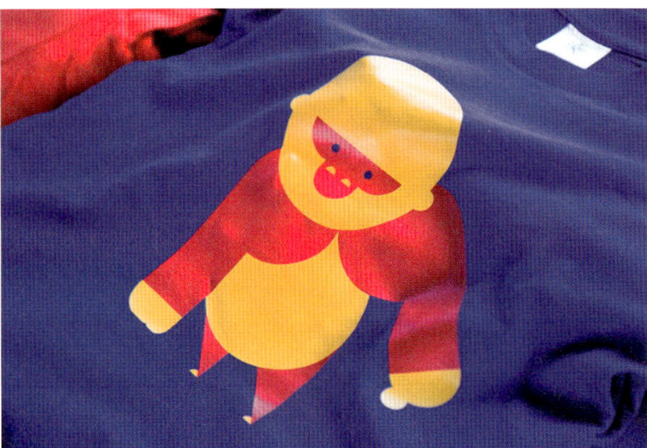

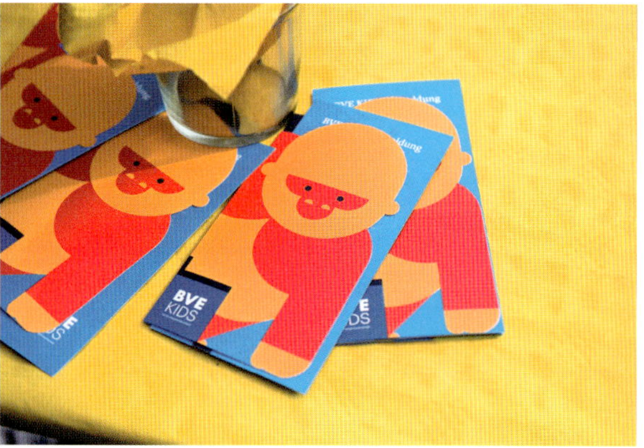

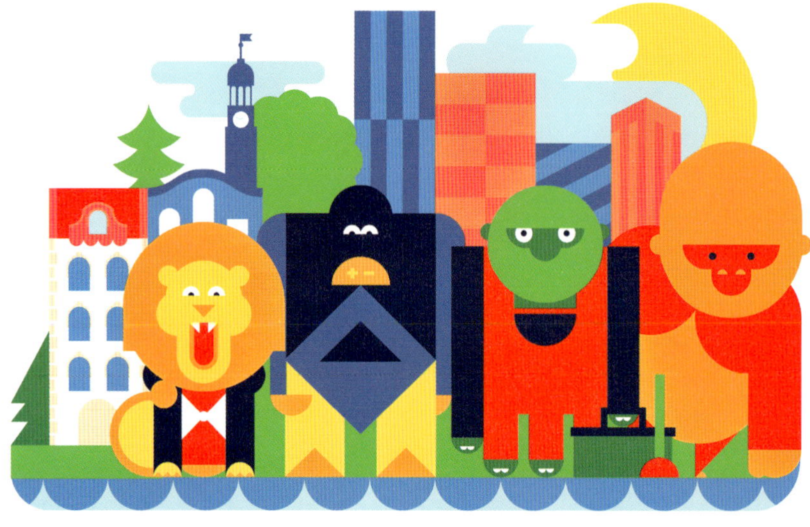

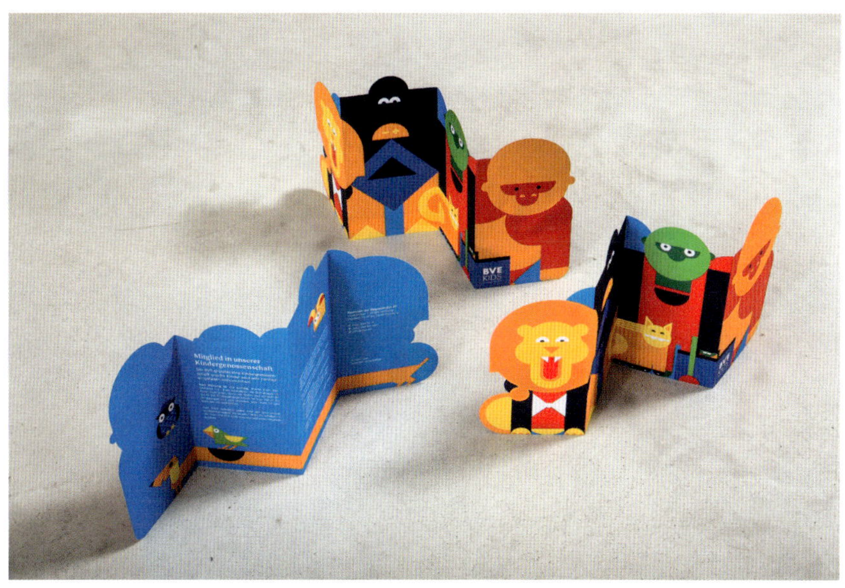

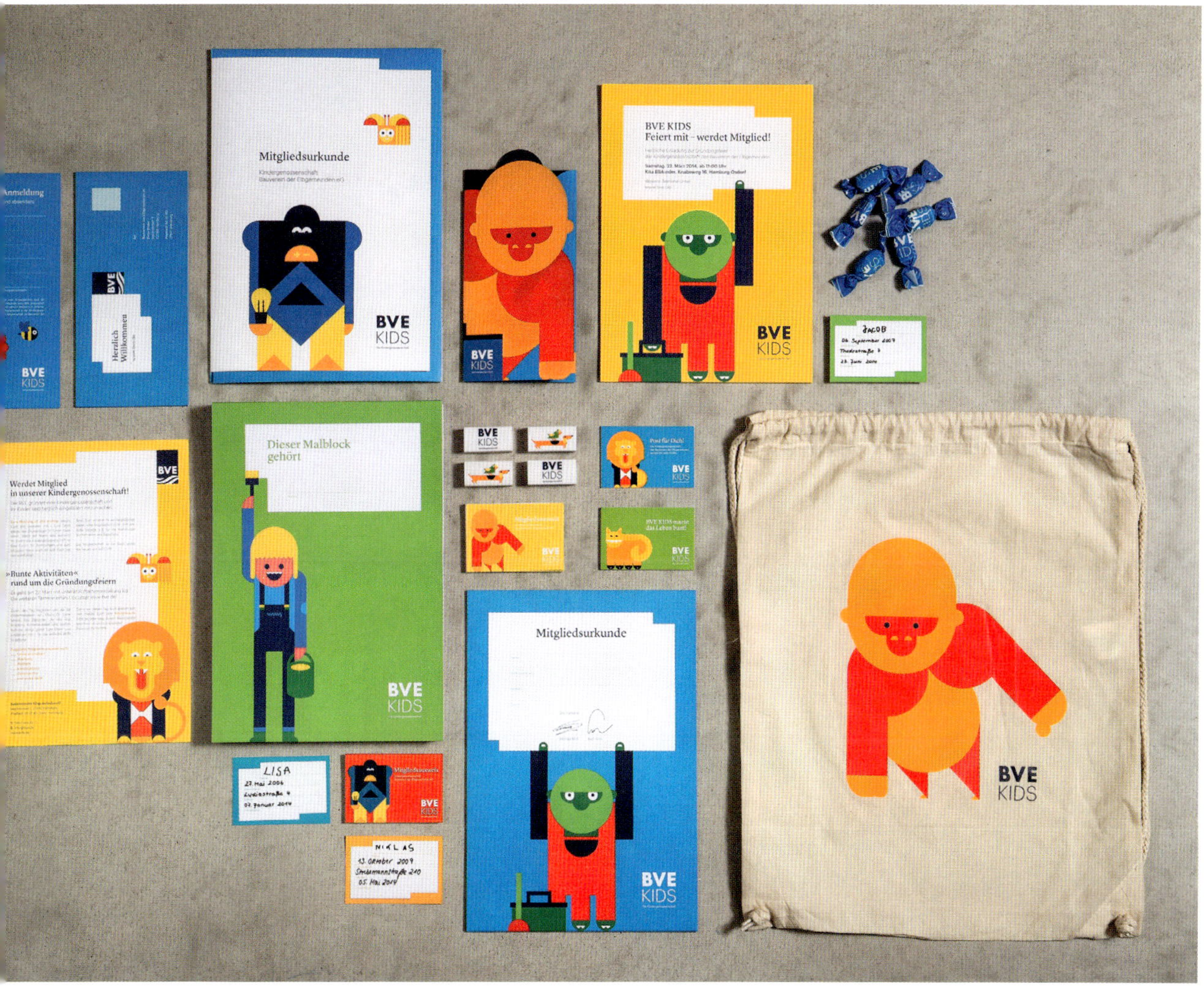

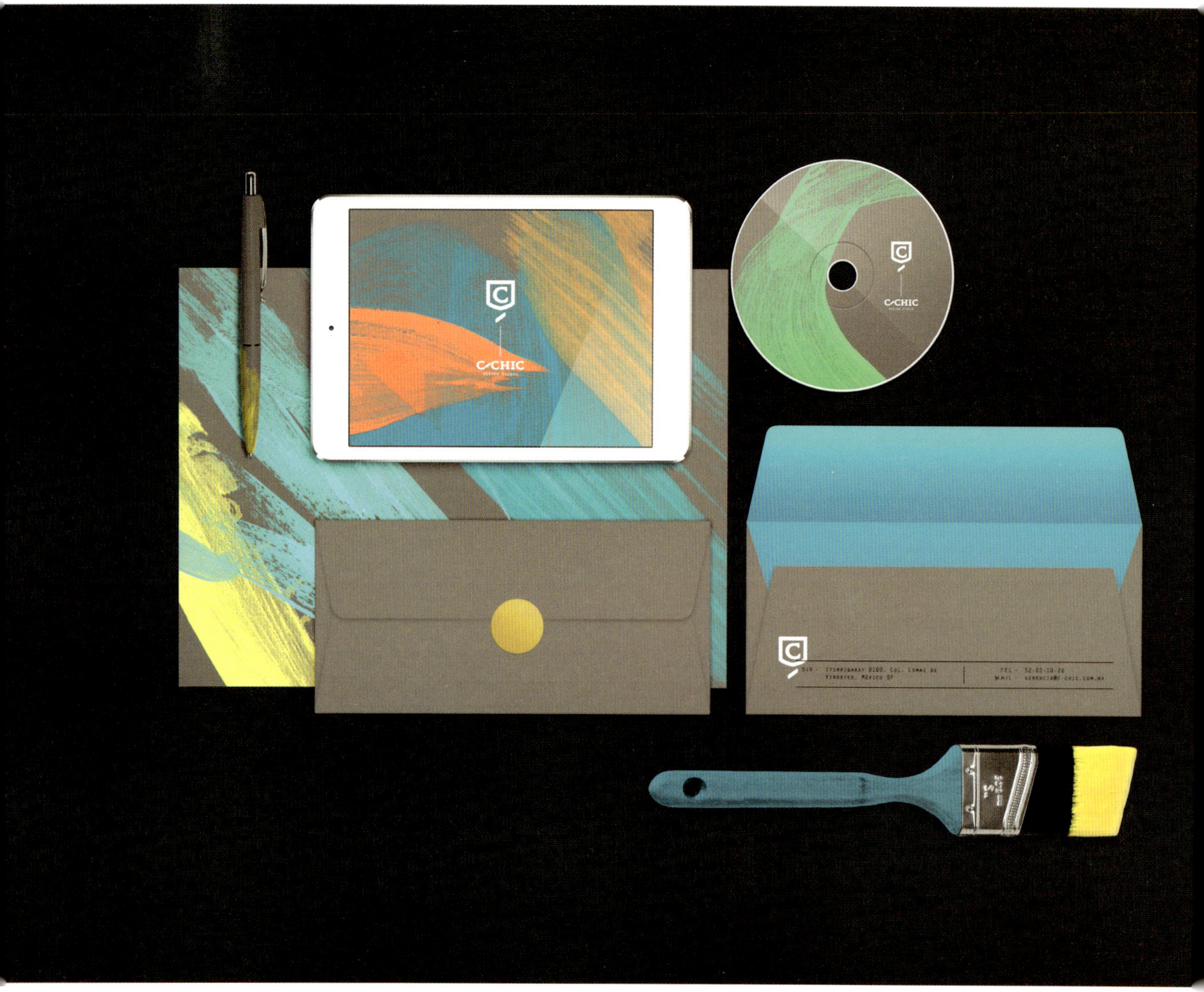

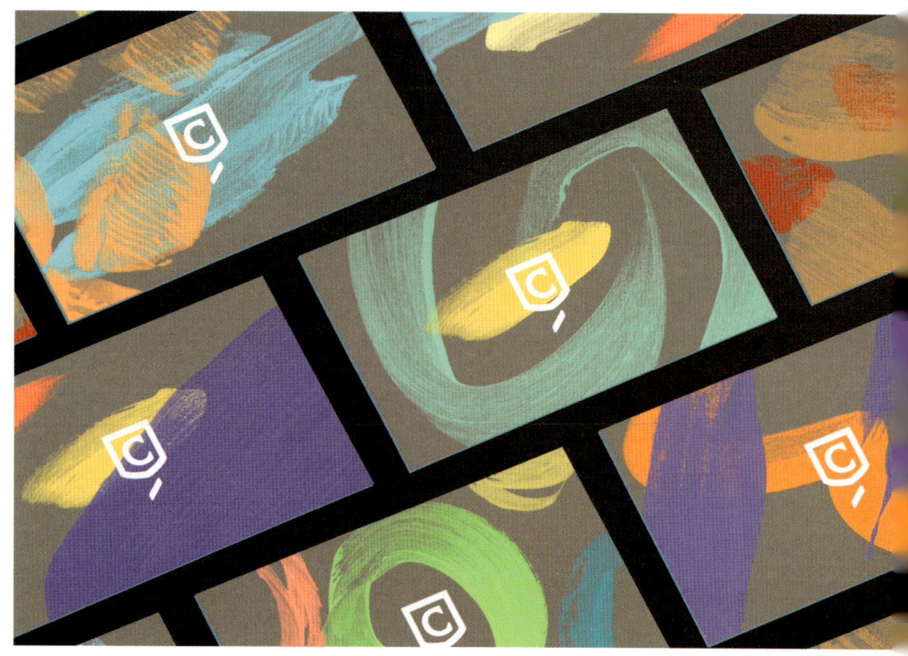

C Chic Design Studio

A complete makeover for the brand was aimed at reflecting its personality and the years of experience the interior design house has spent in the field. Abstract imagery conceived with flowing brushstrokes and vibrant colours fostered a contemporary look yet allow rooms for free interpretation.

Client: C Chic Design Studio

Enrique Larios

C Chic Design Studio

A complete makeover for the brand was aimed at reflecting its personality and the years of experience the interior design house has spent in the field. Abstract imagery conceived with flowing brushstrokes and vibrant colours fostered a contemporary look yet allow rooms for free interpretation.

Client: C Chic Design Studio

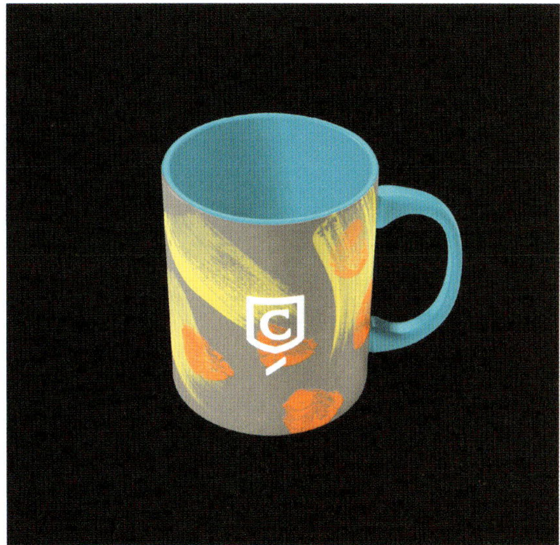

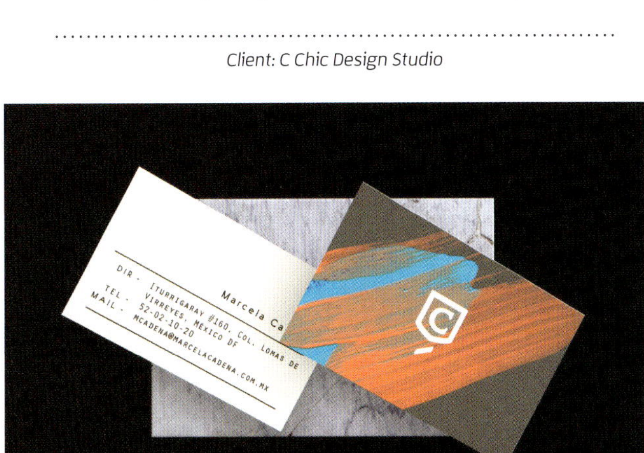

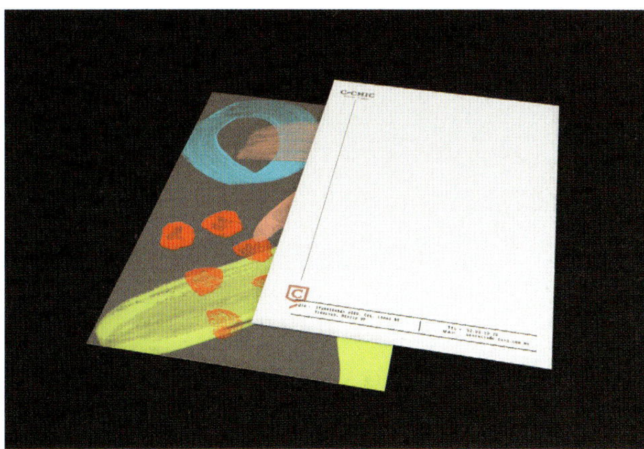

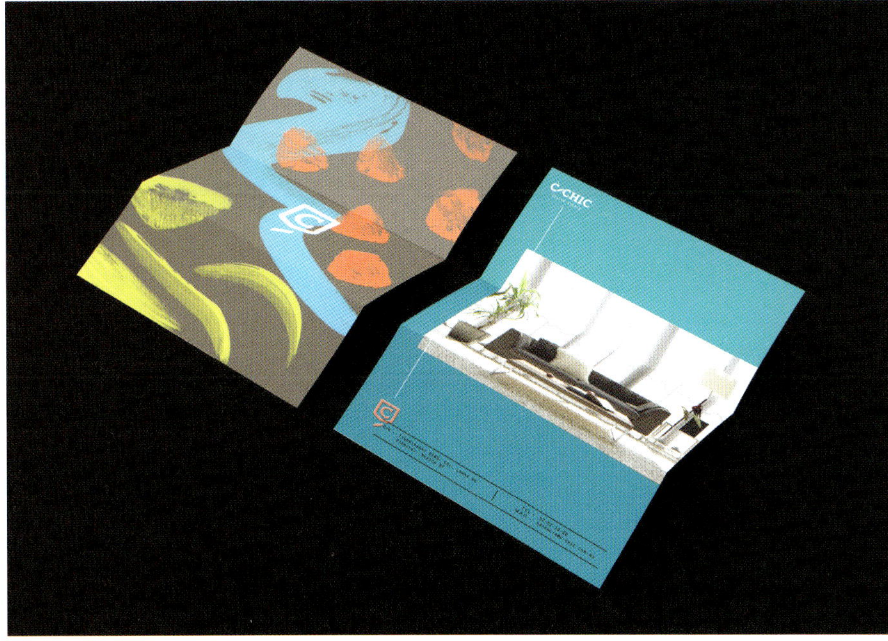

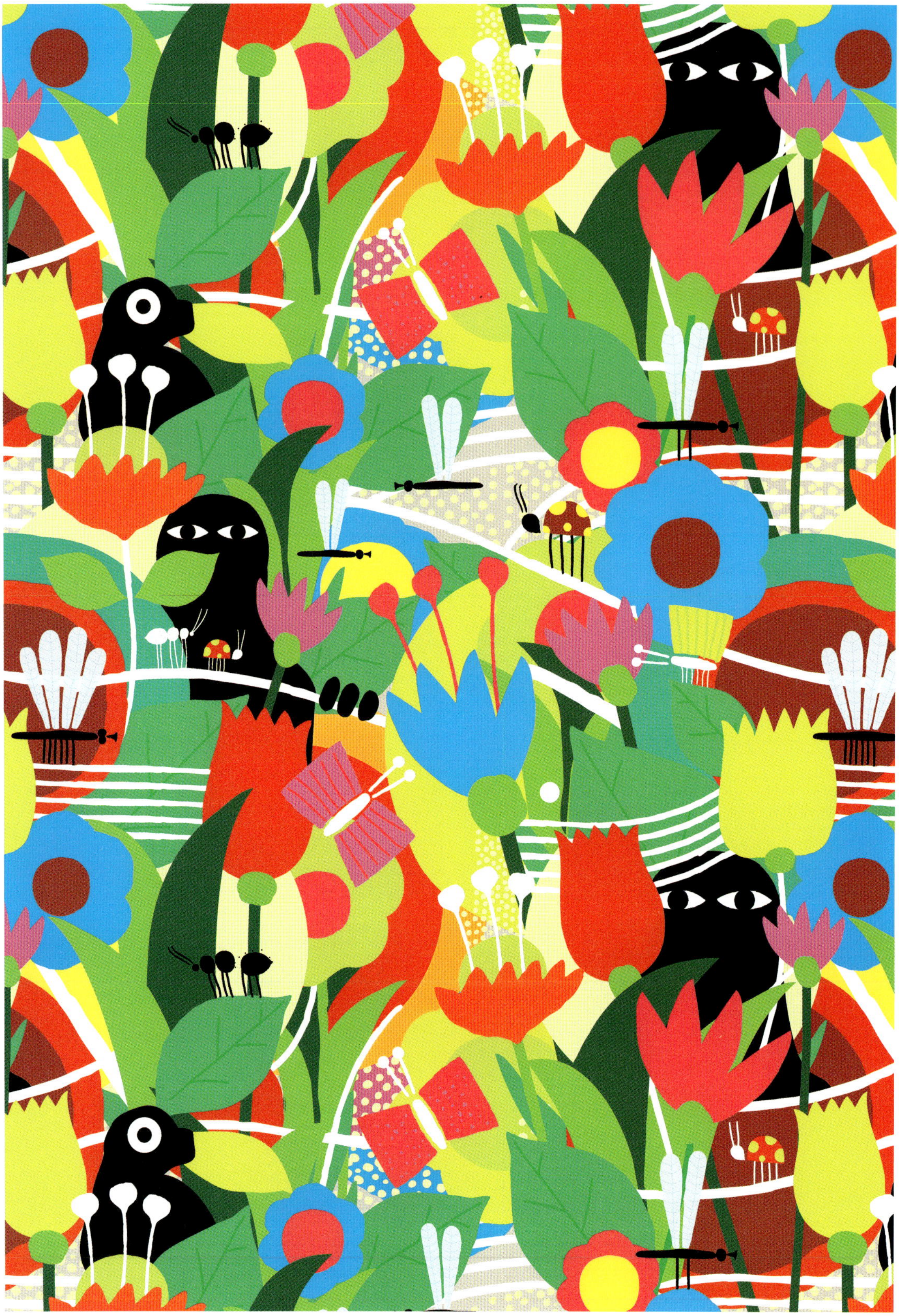

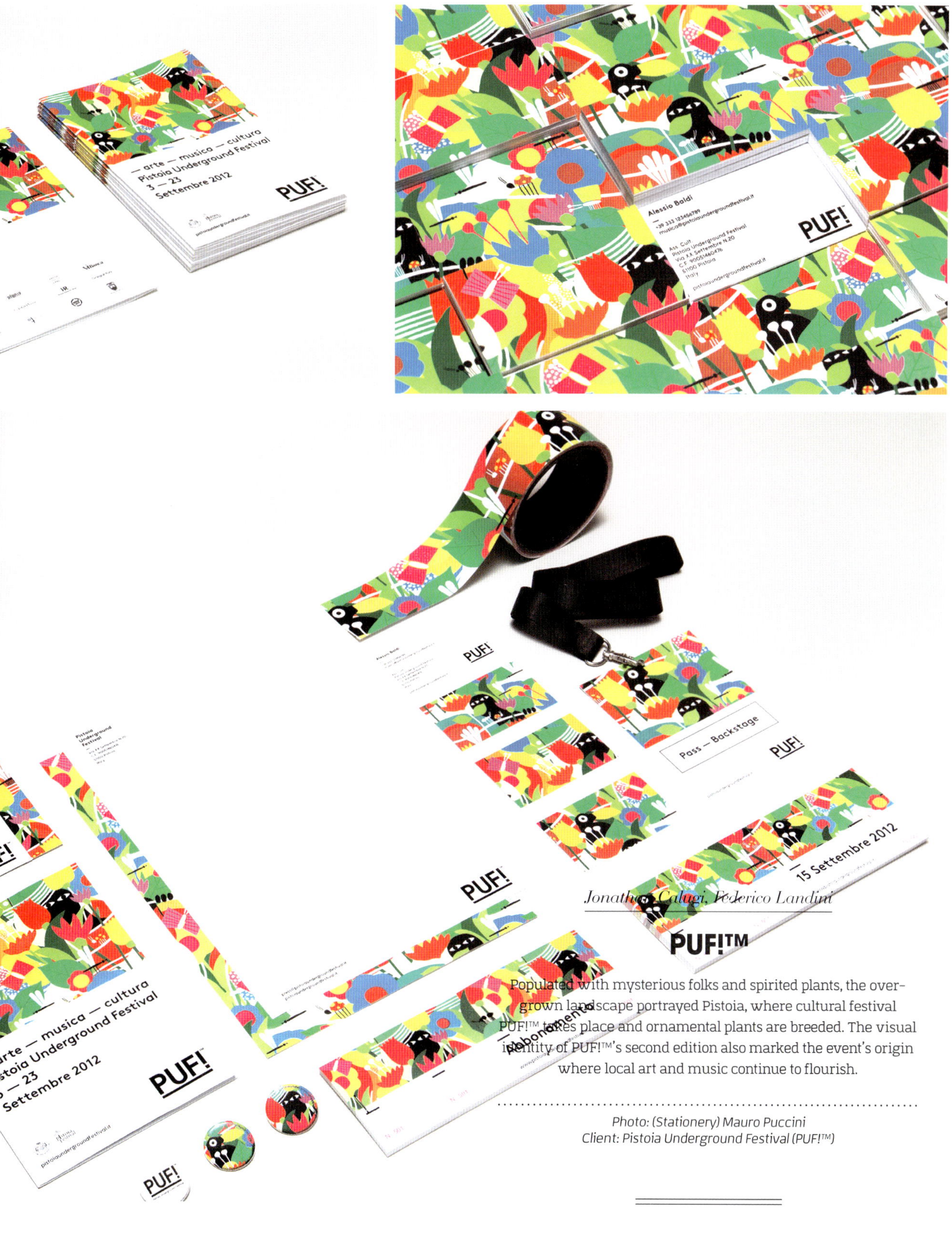

Jonathan Calugi, Federico Landini

PUF!™

Populated with mysterious folks and spirited plants, the overgrown landscape portrayed Pistoia, where cultural festival PUF!™ takes place and ornamental plants are breeded. The visual identity of PUF!™'s second edition also marked the event's origin where local art and music continue to flourish.

Photo: (Stationery) Mauro Puccini
Client: Pistoia Underground Festival (PUF!™)

Jonathan Calugi, Federico Landini

PUF!™

Populated with mysterious folks and spirited plants, the overgrown landscape portrayed Pistoia, where cultural festival

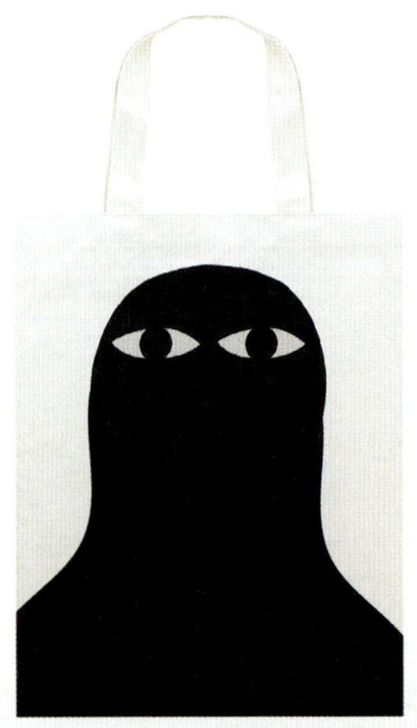

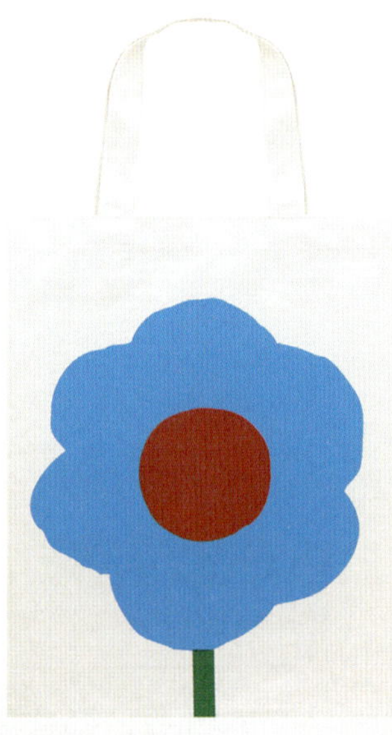

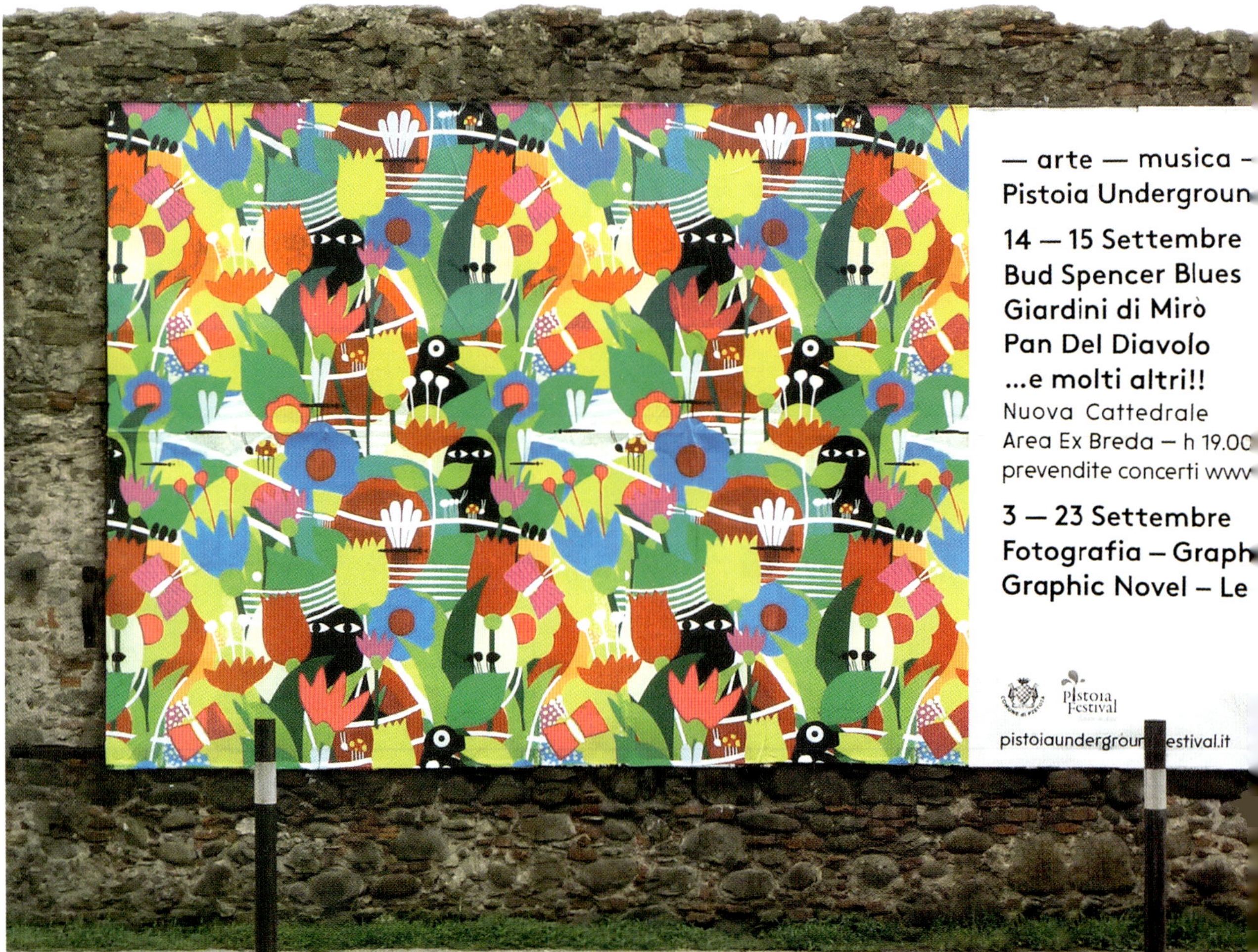

— arte — musica
Pistoia Undergroun
14 — 15 Settembre
Bud Spencer Blues
Giardini di Mirò
Pan Del Diavolo
...e molti altri!!
Nuova Cattedrale
Area Ex Breda — h 19.00
prevendite concerti www
3 — 23 Settembre
Fotografia – Graph
Graphic Novel – Le
Pistoia Festival
pistoiaundergroun estival.it

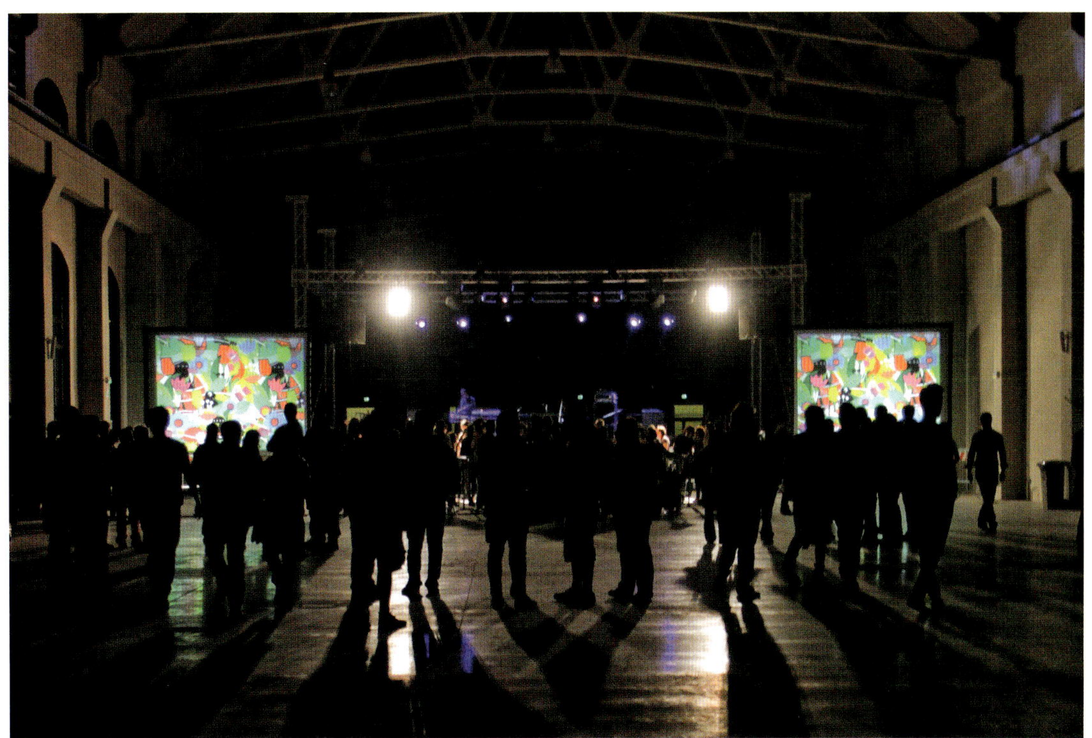

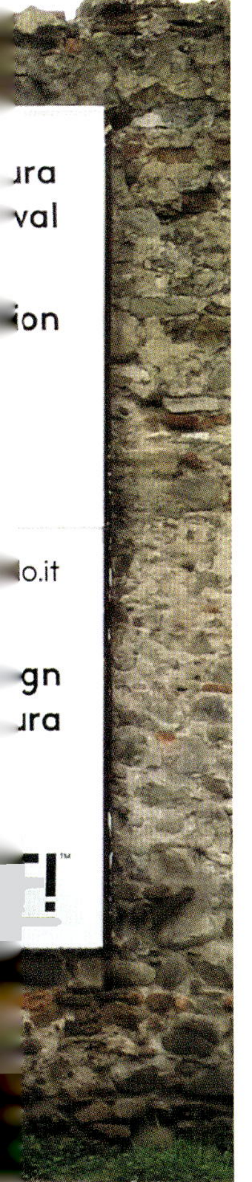

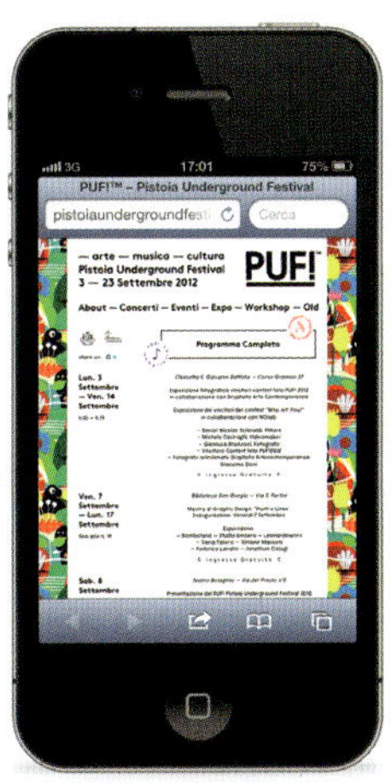
17:01
PUF!™ – Pistoia Underground Festival
— arte — musica — cultura
Pistoia Underground Festival
3 — 23 Settembre 2012
PUF!
About — Concerti — Eventi — Expo — Workshop — Old
Programma Completo

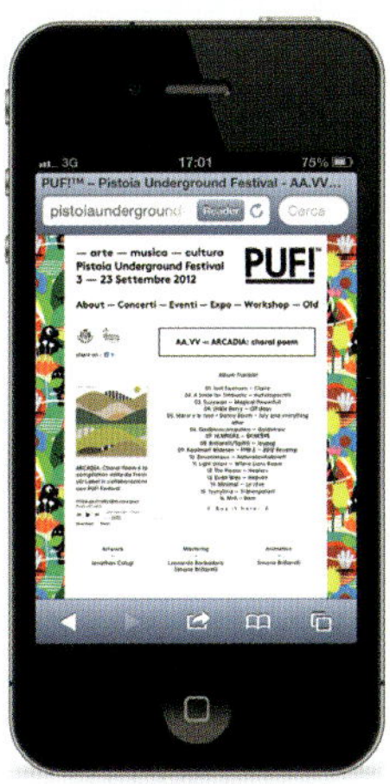
17:01
PUF!™ – Pistoia Underground Festival - AA.VV...
— arte — musica — cultura
Pistoia Underground Festival
3 — 23 Settembre 2012
PUF!
About — Concerti — Eventi — Expo — Workshop — Old
AA.VV — ARCADIA: choral poem

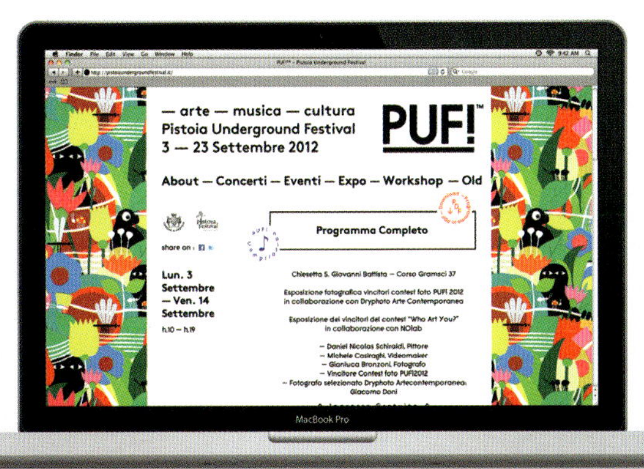
— arte — musica — cultura
Pistoia Underground Festival
3 — 23 Settembre 2012
PUF!™
About — Concerti — Eventi — Expo — Workshop — Old
Programma Completo
share on :
Lun. 3 Settembre — Ven. 14 Settembre
h.10 — h.19
Chiesetta S. Giovanni Battista — Corso Gramsci 37
Esposizione fotografica vincitori contest foto PUF! 2012
in collaborazione con Dryphoto Arte Contemporanea
Esposizione dei vincitori del contest "Who Art You?"
in collaborazione con NOlab
— Daniel Nicolas Schiraldi, Pittore
— Michele Casiraghi, Videomaker
— Gianluca Bronzoni, Fotografo
— Vincitore Contest foto PUF!2012
— Fotografo selezionato Dryphoto Artecontemporanea:
Giacomo Doni
MacBook Pro

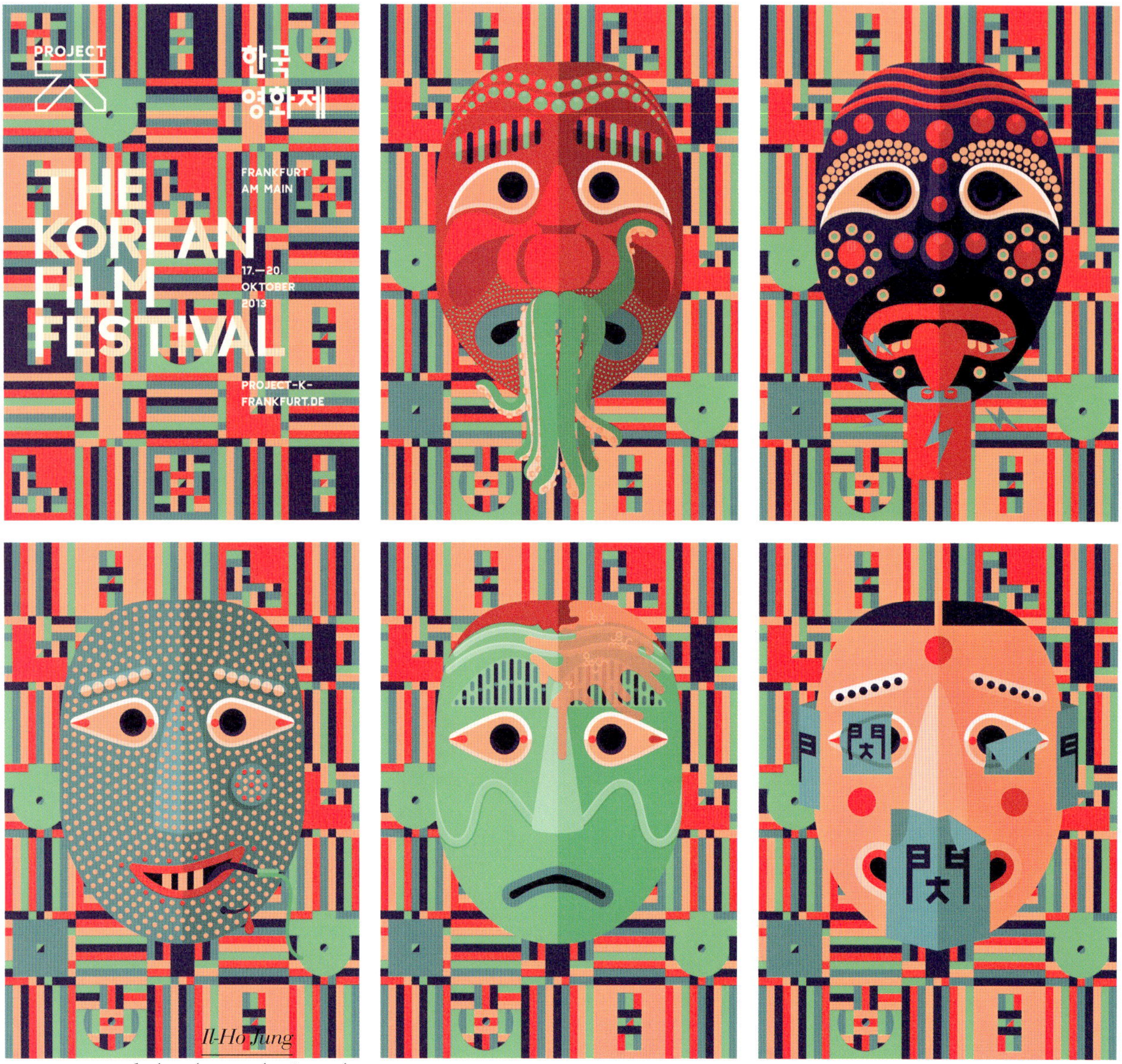

PROJECT
한국 영화제
THE KOREAN FILM FESTIVAL
FRANKFURT AM MAIN
17.–20. OKTOBER 2013
PROJECT-K-FRANKFURT.DE

Il-Ho Jung

design, interactive & motion

Project K

Comprised of classic Korean stripes and type, a dancheong-inspired decorative pattern started off the second Korean Film Festival in Frankfurt on the theme of '4 Days in Seoul'. Traditional Korean masks re-enacted memorable scenes from famous Korean movies, bringing 'film' back in the spotlight.

Client: Project K e.V.

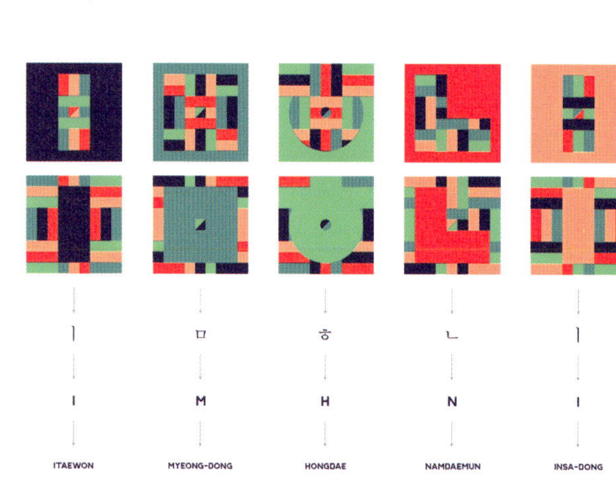

Il-Ho Jung

design, interactive & motion

Project K

Comprised of classic Korean stripes and type, a

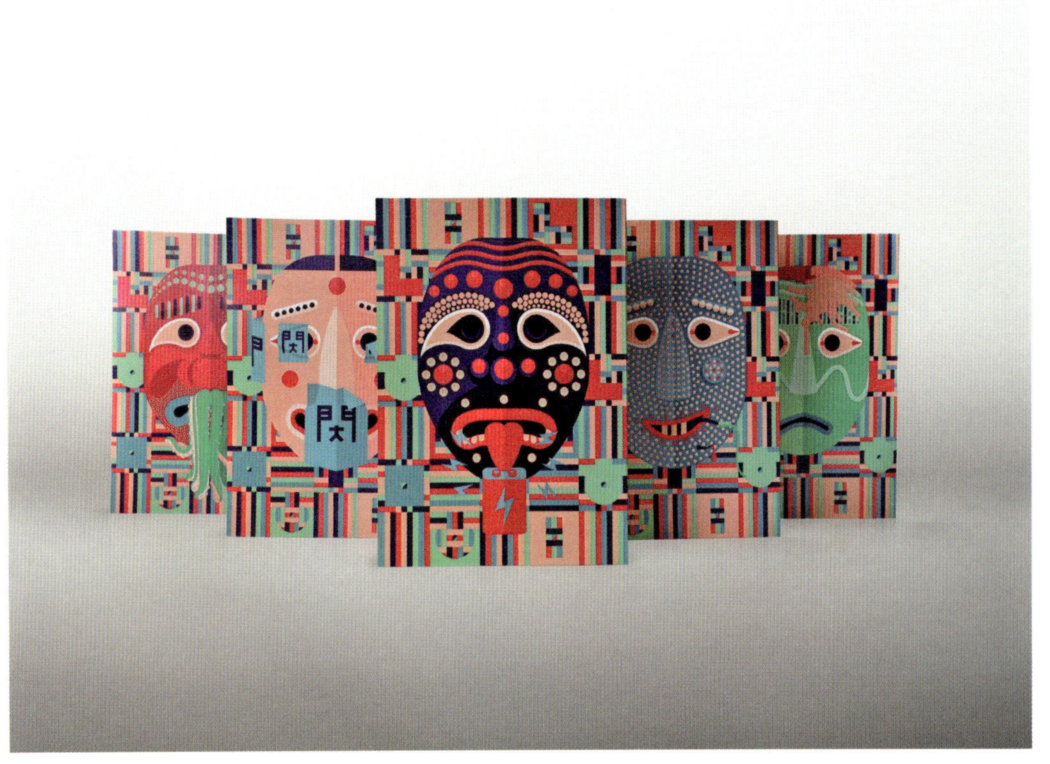

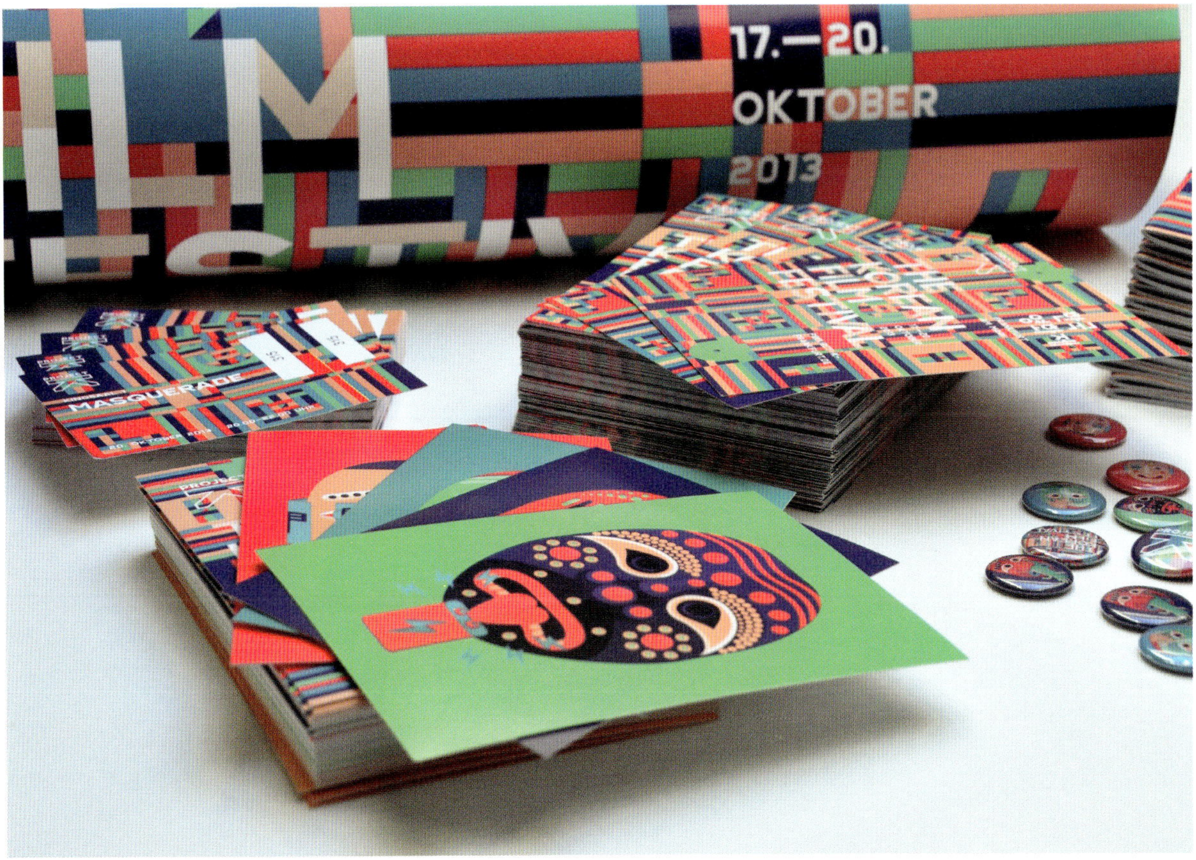

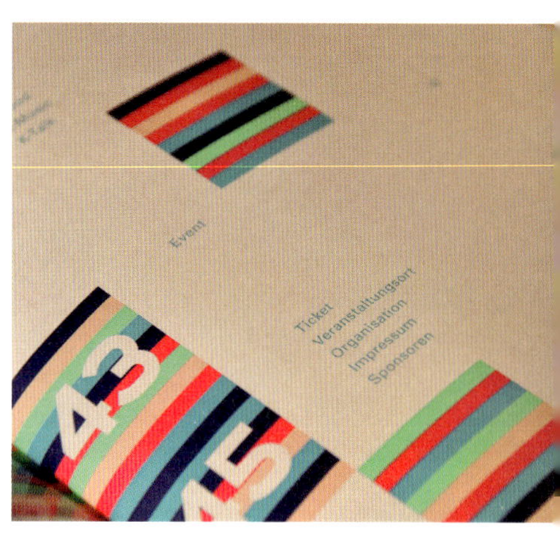

Event
Ticket
Veranstaltungsort
Organisation
Impressum
Sponsoren
43
45

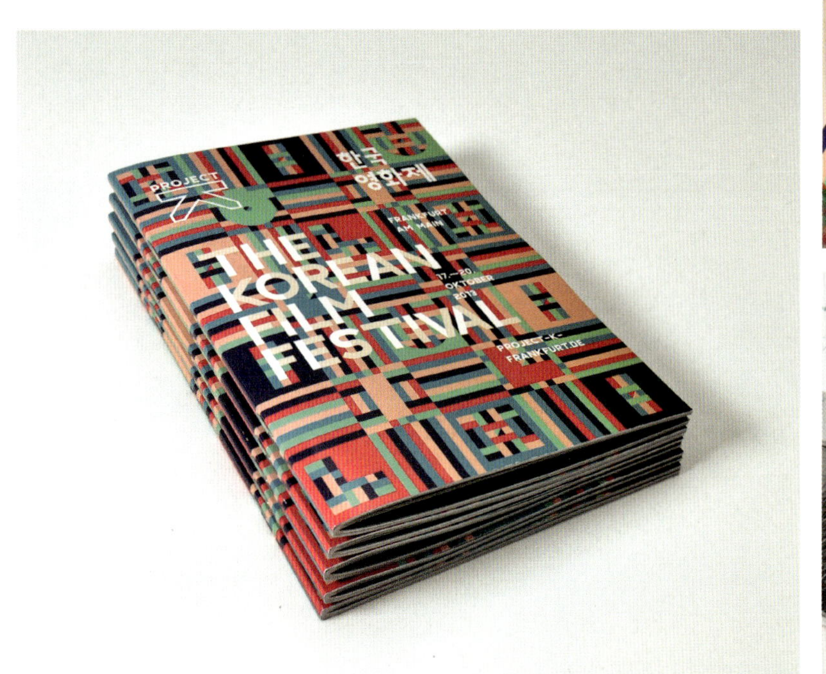

PROJECT
한국영화제
FRANKFURT AM MAIN
THE KOREAN FILM FESTIVAL
17.—20. OKTOBER 2013
PROJECT-K-FRANKFURT.DE

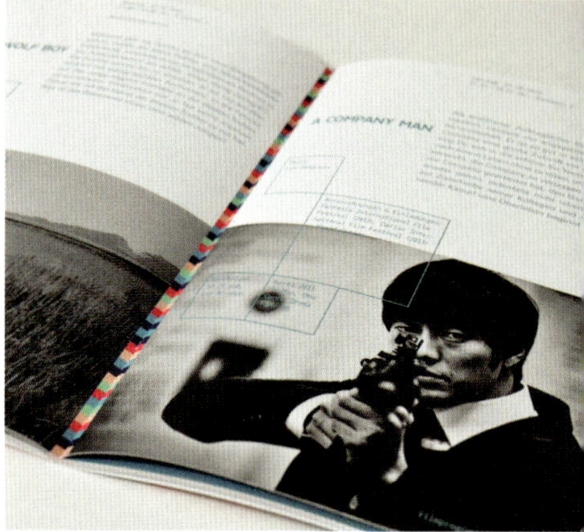

A COMPANY MAN

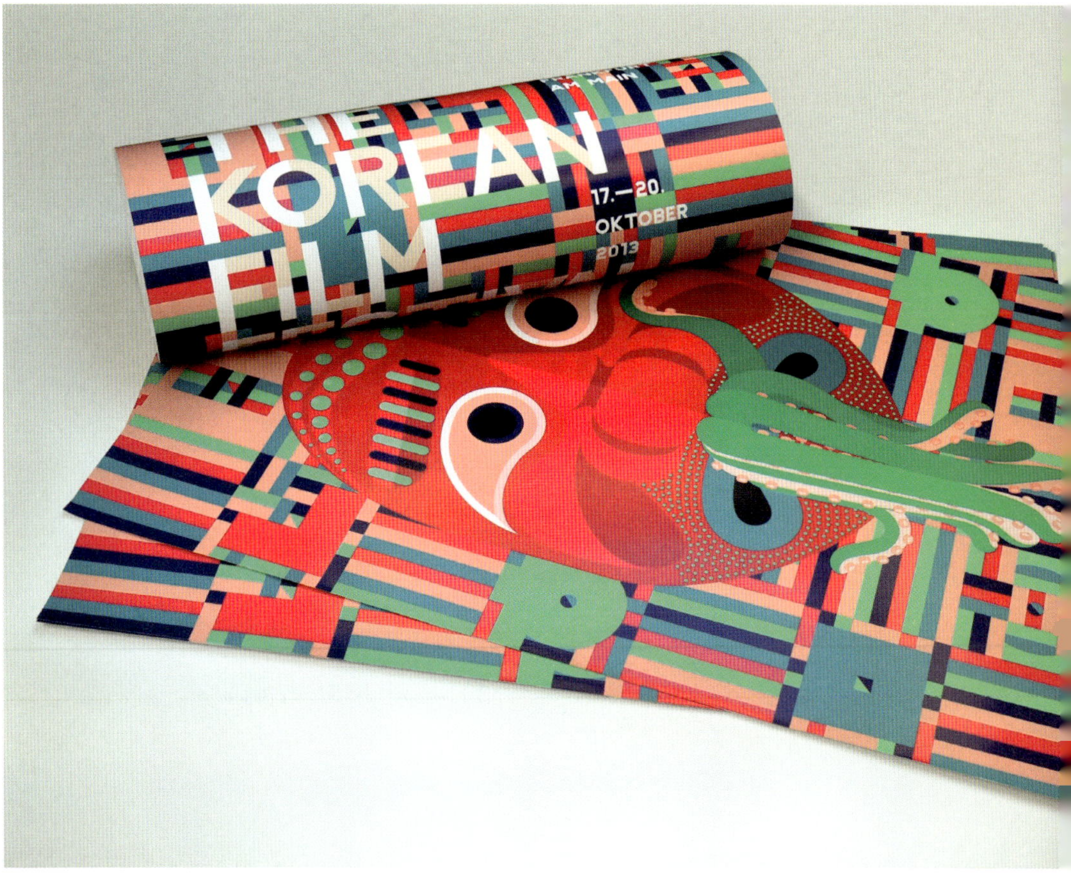

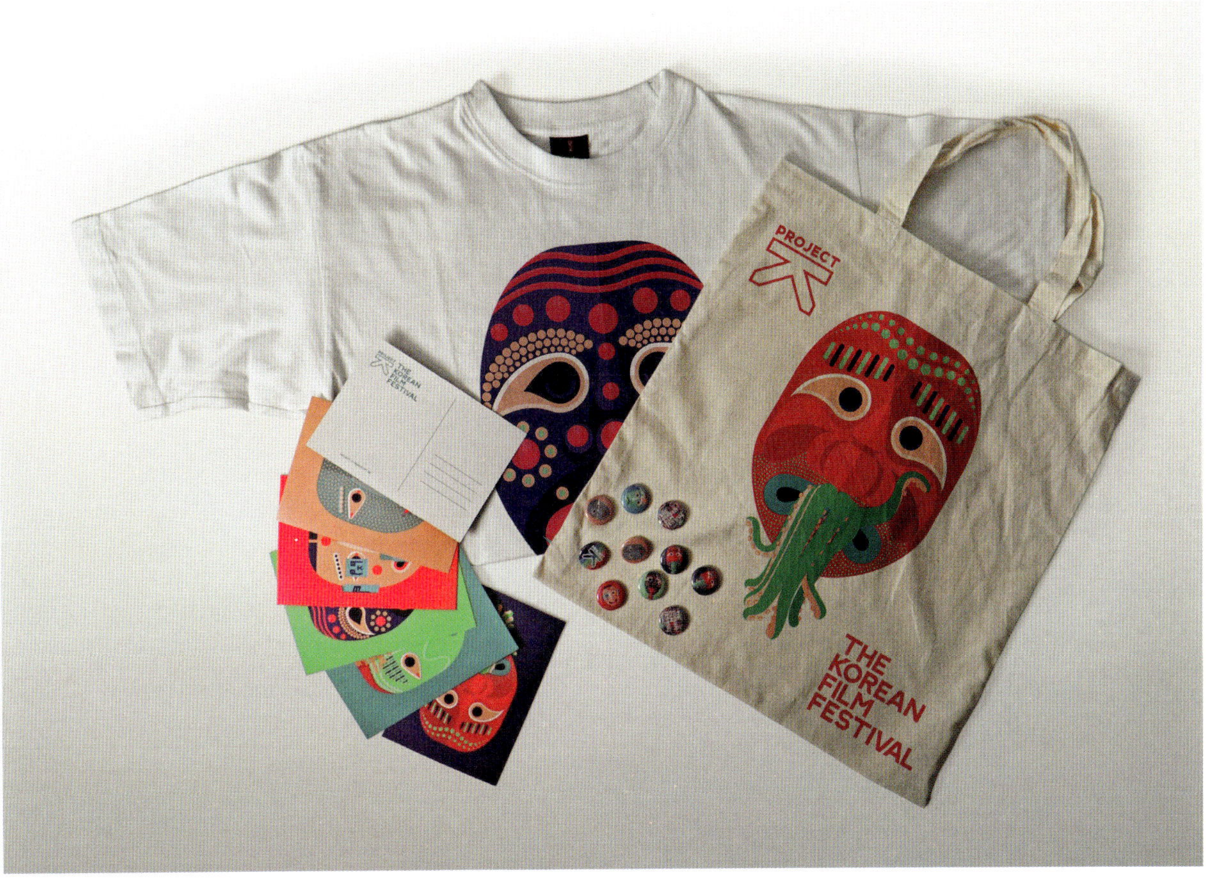

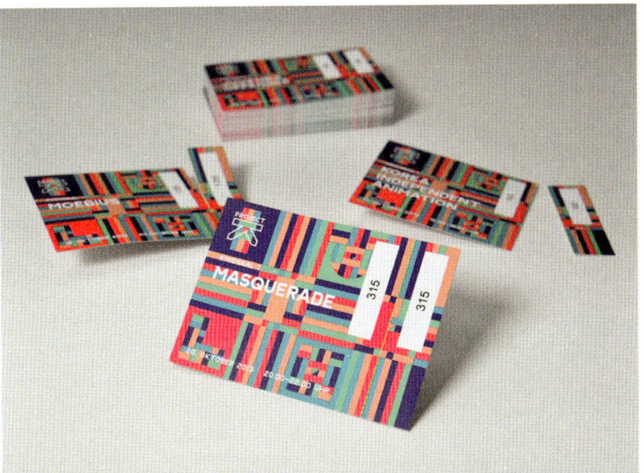
MOEBIUS
MASQUERADE
315
315

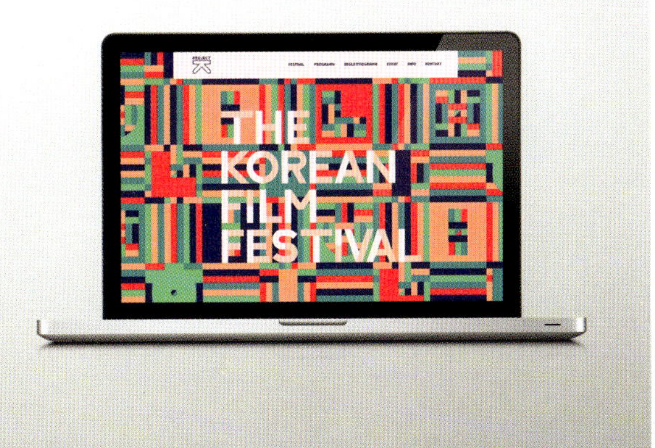
THE
KOREAN
FILM
FESTIVAL

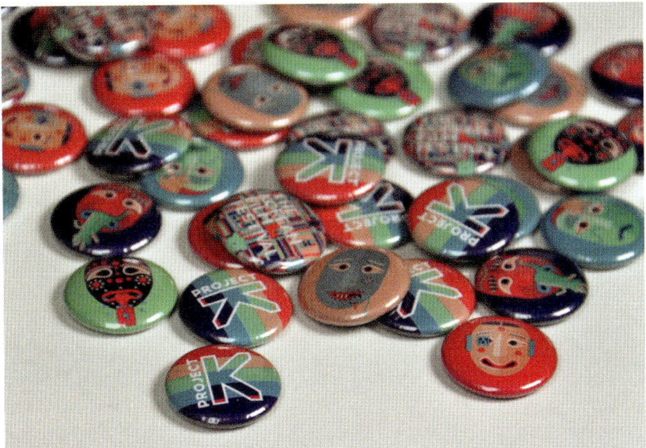
PROJECT
K

Inspired by vibrant colours, national symbols as well as inclusive multiculture, the deluxe hotel brand from Malaysia boosts an artistic journey with hints of Nanyang culture and art. The bold colours and varied patterns translate passion to every touchpoint of the brand system.

Client: The Happy 8

1983 ASIA, SUSU & YAO

The Happy 8

Inspired by vibrant colours, national symbols as well as inclusive multiculture, the deluxe hotel brand from Malaysia boosts an artistic journey with hints of Nanyang culture and art. The bold colours and varied patterns translate passion to every touchpoint of the brand system.

Client: The Happy 8

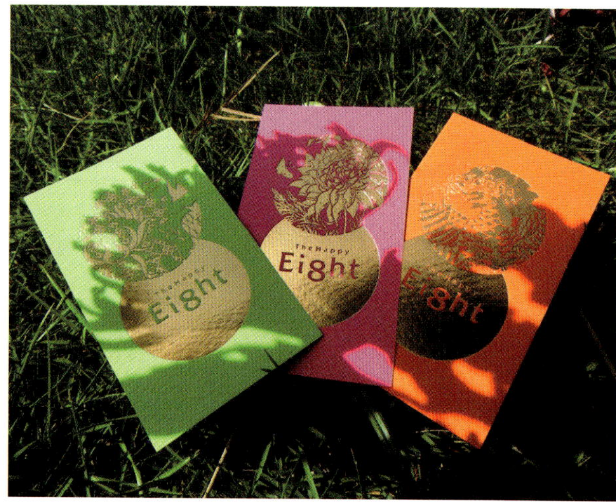

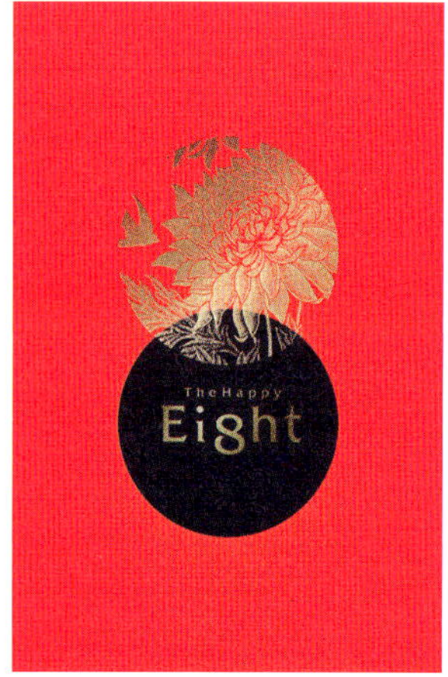

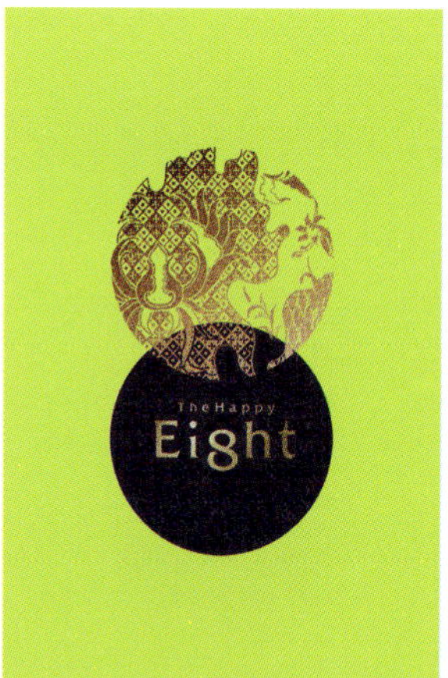

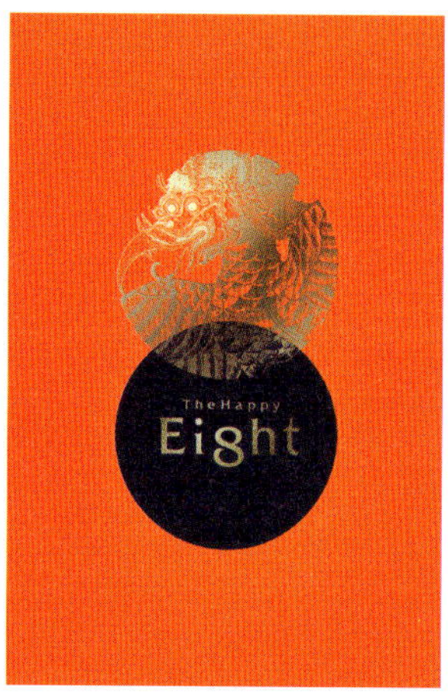

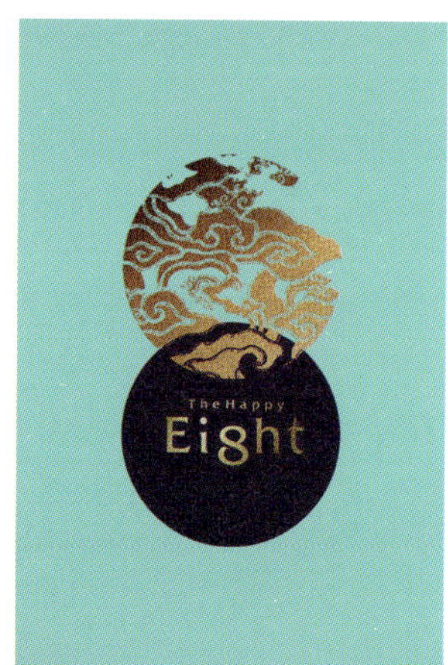

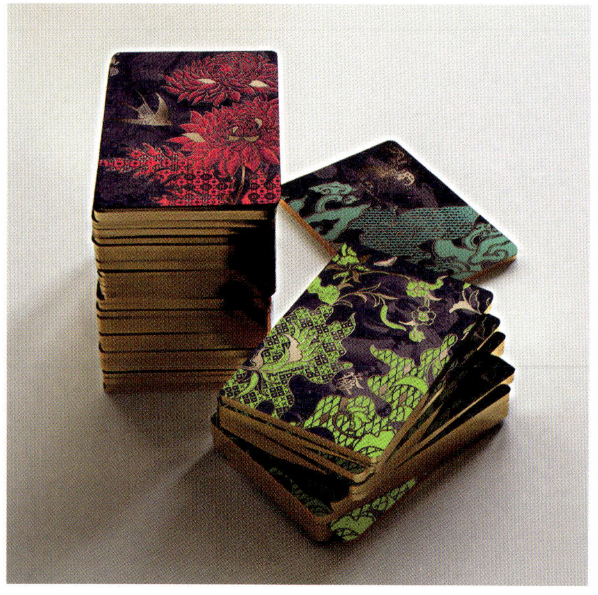

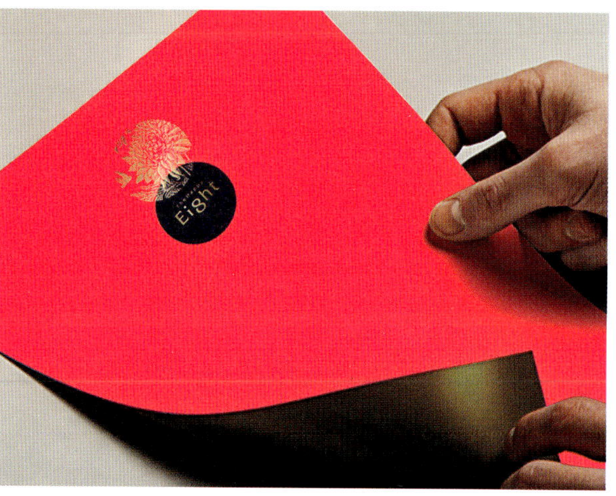

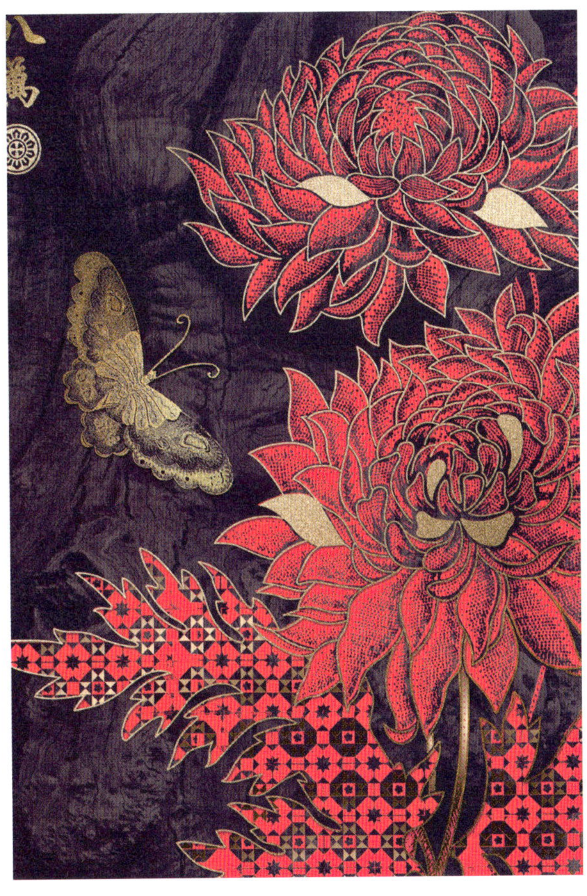

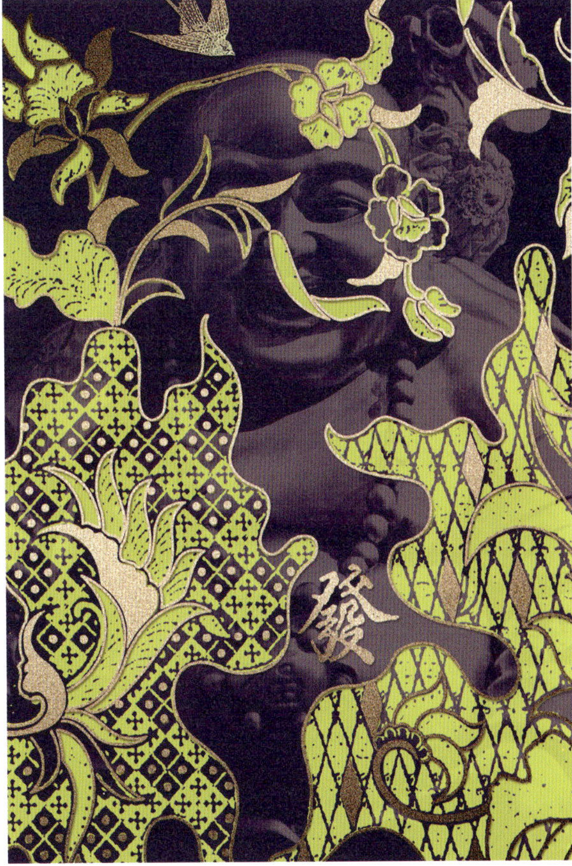
發

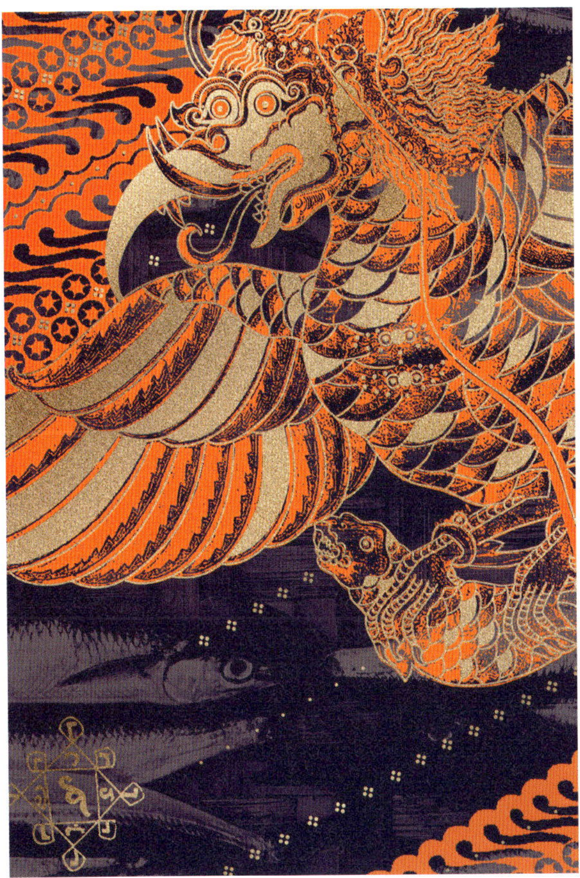

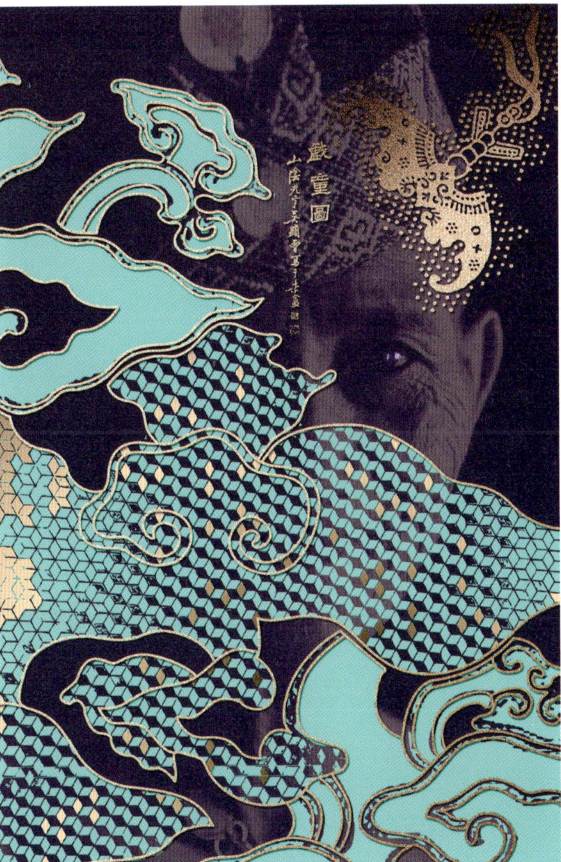

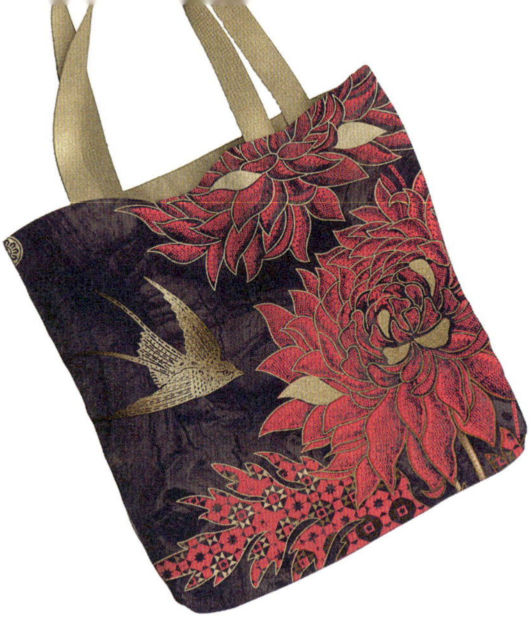

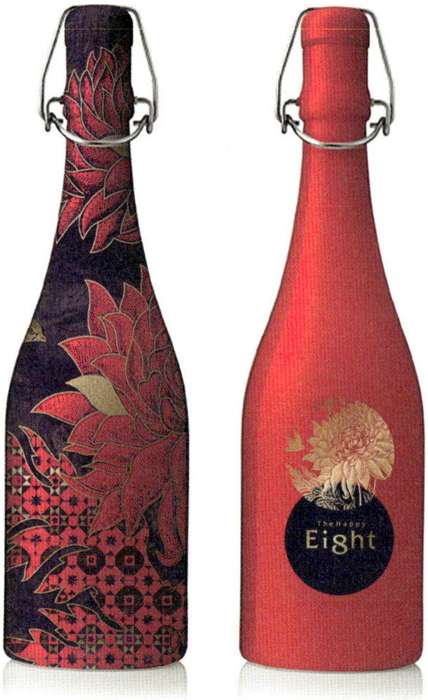

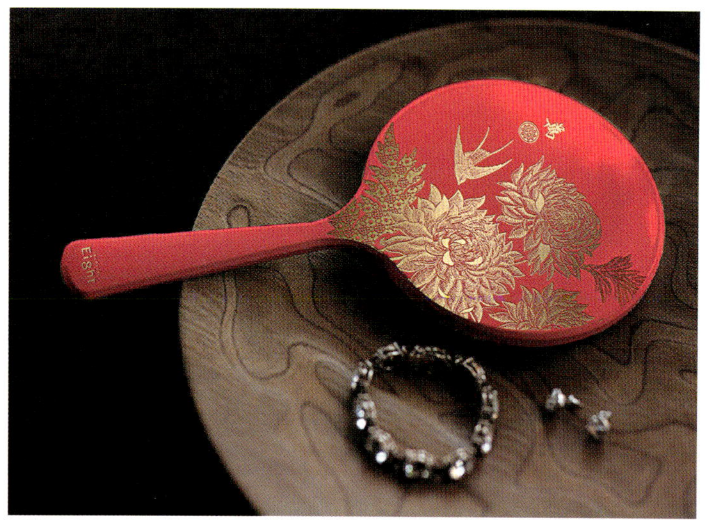

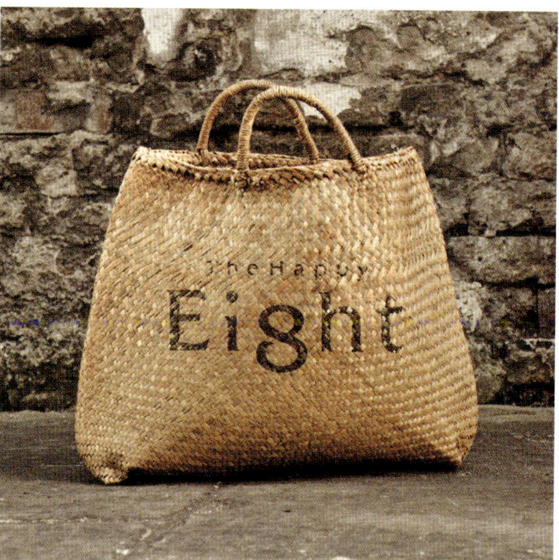
The Happy
Eight

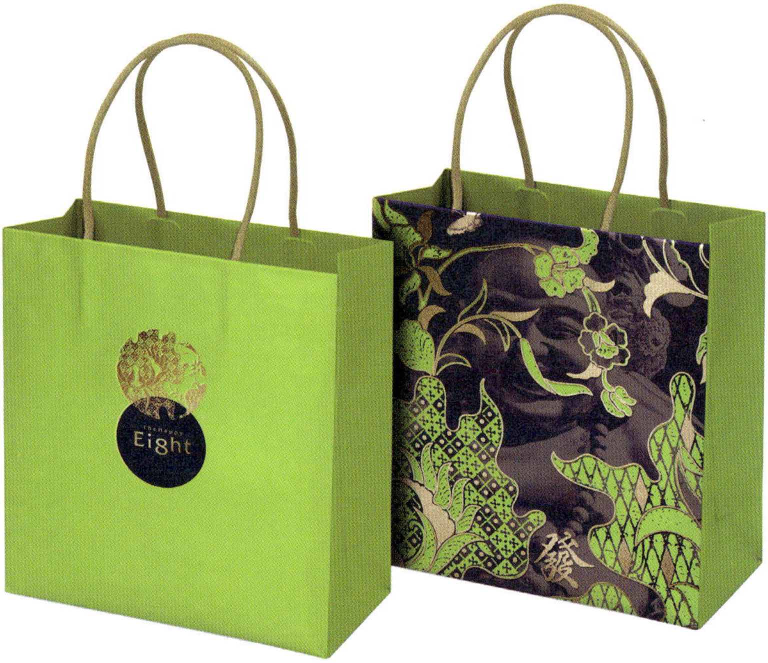

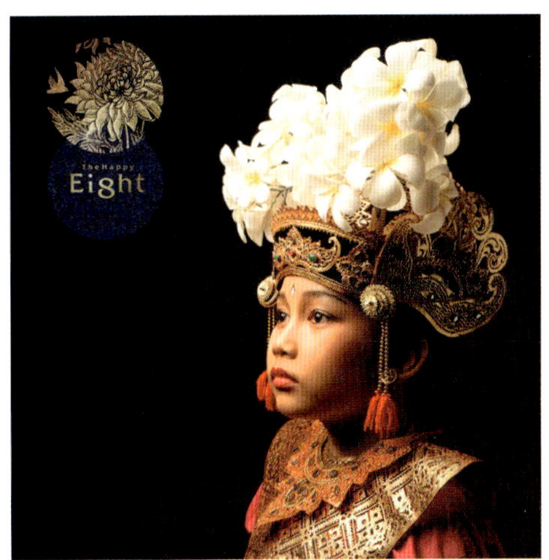
The Happy
Eight
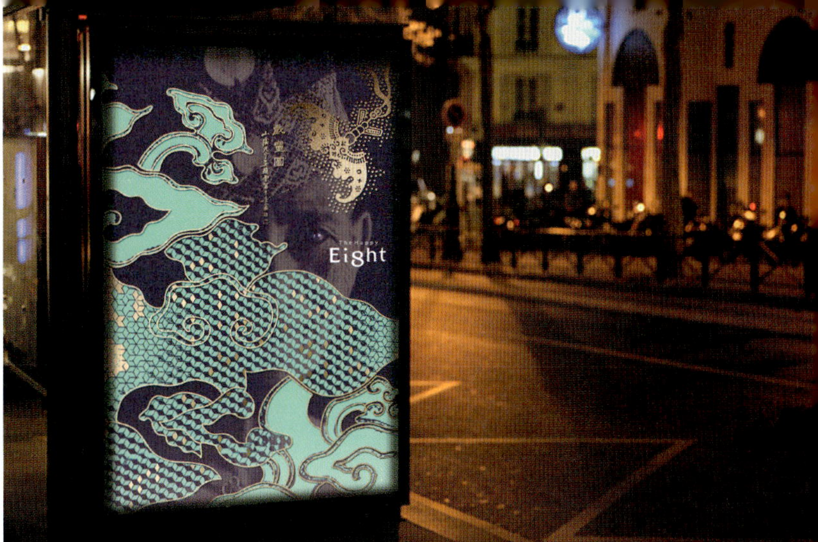
The Happy
Eight
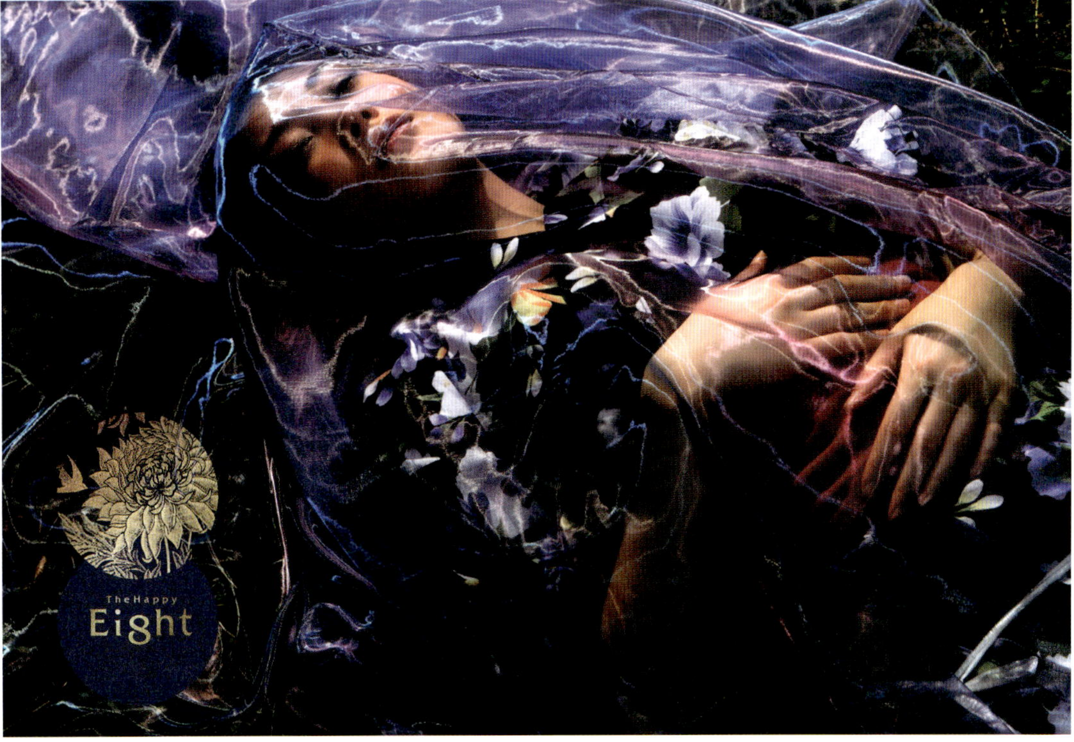
The Happy
Eight
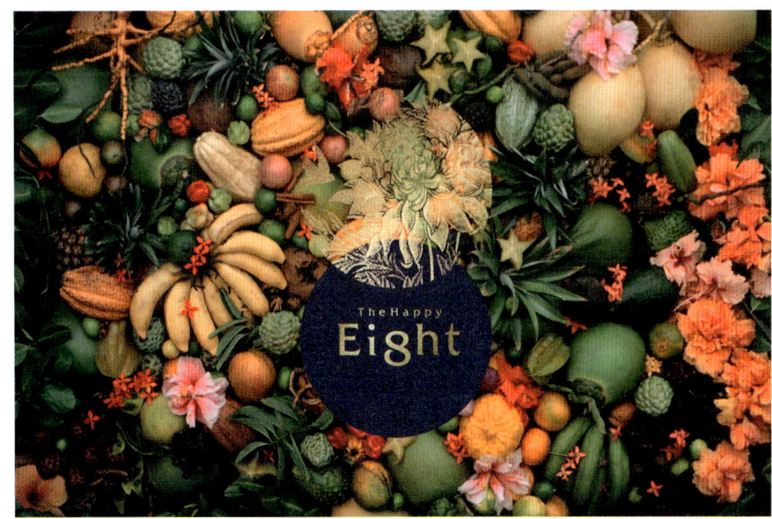
The Happy
Eight

Located at the heart of Mexico's La Condesa, Xinampa is a restaurant where Chef Ricardo Ocejo elevates Asian-Mexican street food. Its identity blooms in four woodcut style floral illustrations exuding a sense of exquisiteness unique to its offerings across its environment.

Illustration: Emilio Canton, Diego Leyva
Client: Xinampa

NHOMADA

Xinampa

Located at the heart of Mexico's La Condesa, Xinampa is a restaurant where Chef Ricardo Ocejo elevates Asian-Mexican street food. Its identity blooms in four woodcut style floral illustrations exuding a sense of exquisiteness unique to its offerings across its environment.

Illustration: Emilio Canton, Diego Leyva
Client: Xinampa

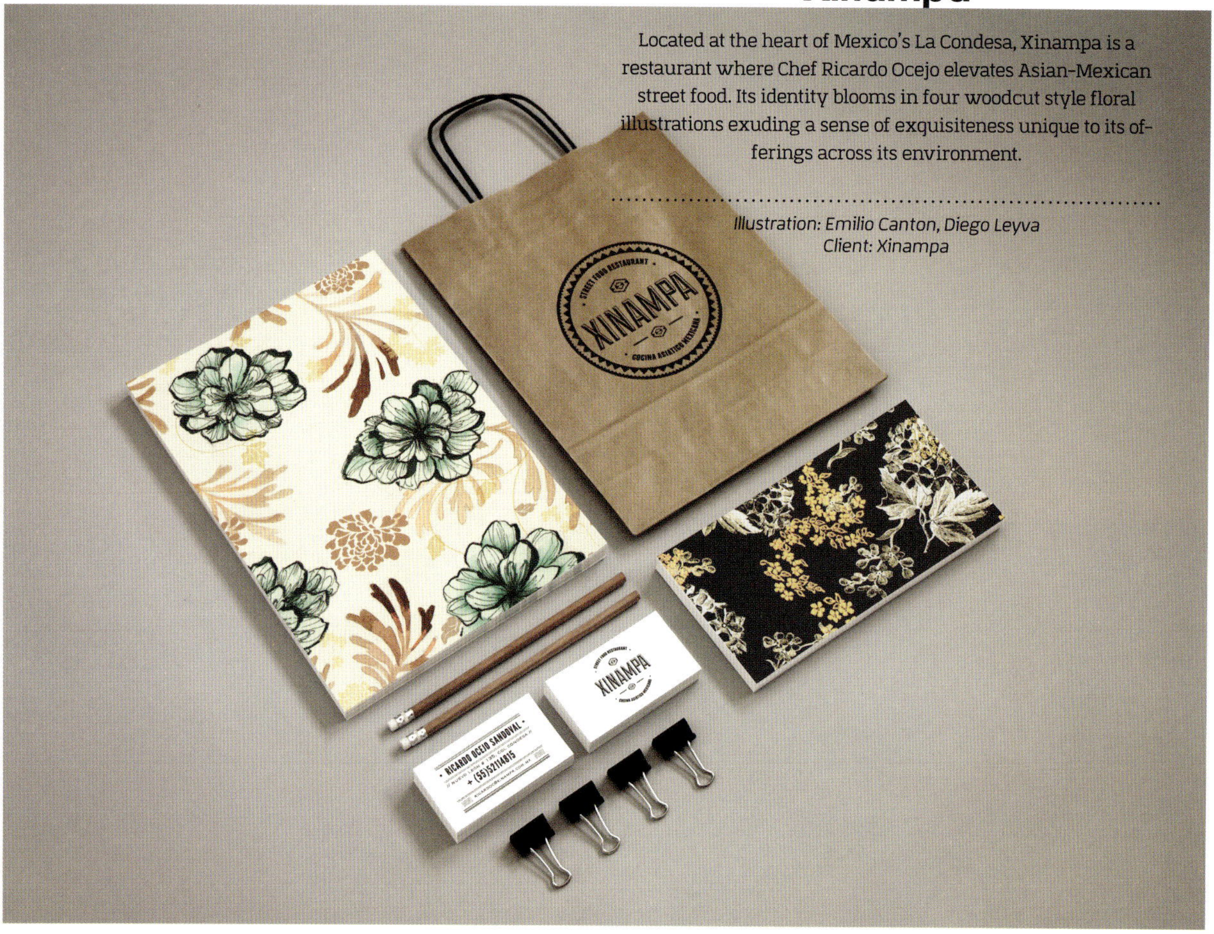

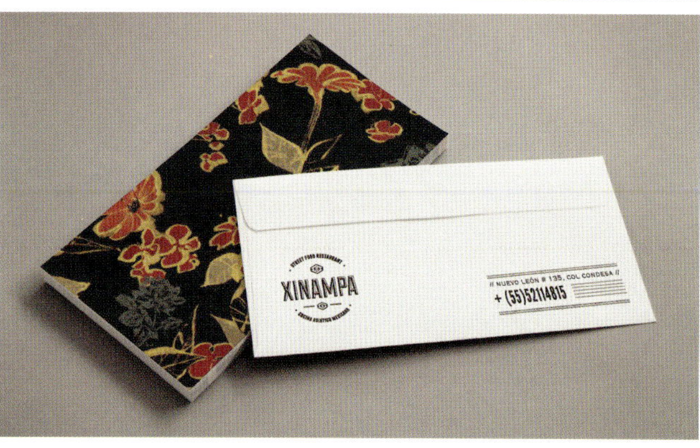

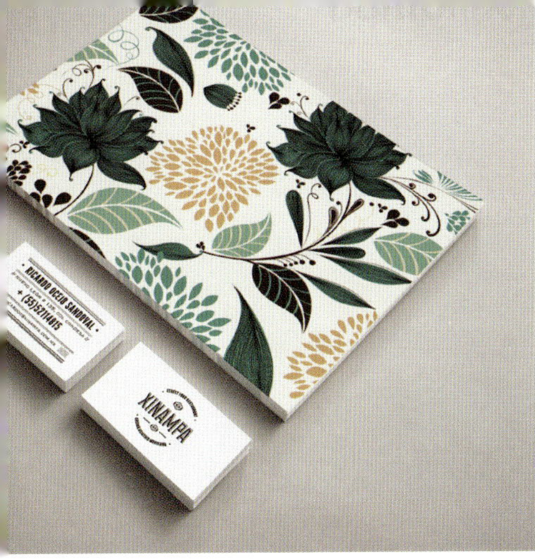
RICARDO OCEJO SANDOVAL
(55)52114815
XINAMPA

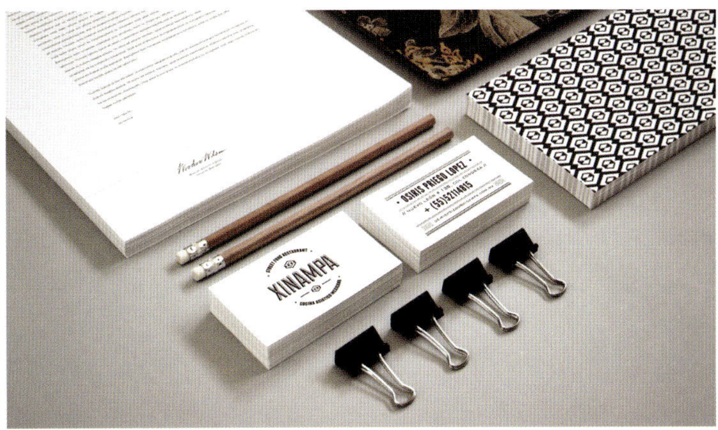
OSIRIS PRIEGO LOPEZ
(55)52114815
STREET FOOD RESTAURANT
XINAMPA

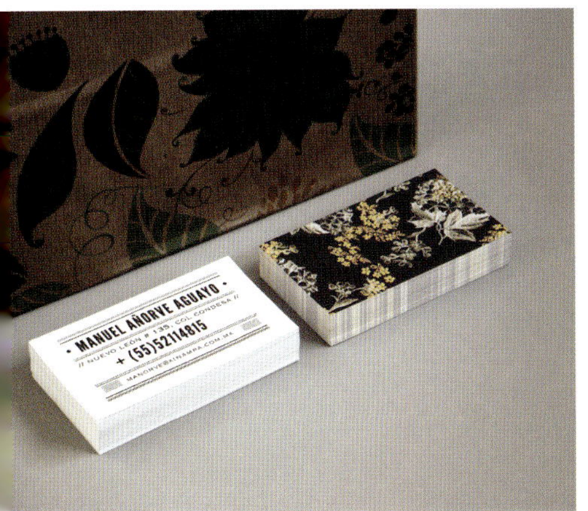
MANUEL AÑORVE AGUAYO
// NUEVO LEÓN # 135, COL. CONDESA //
+ (55)52114815

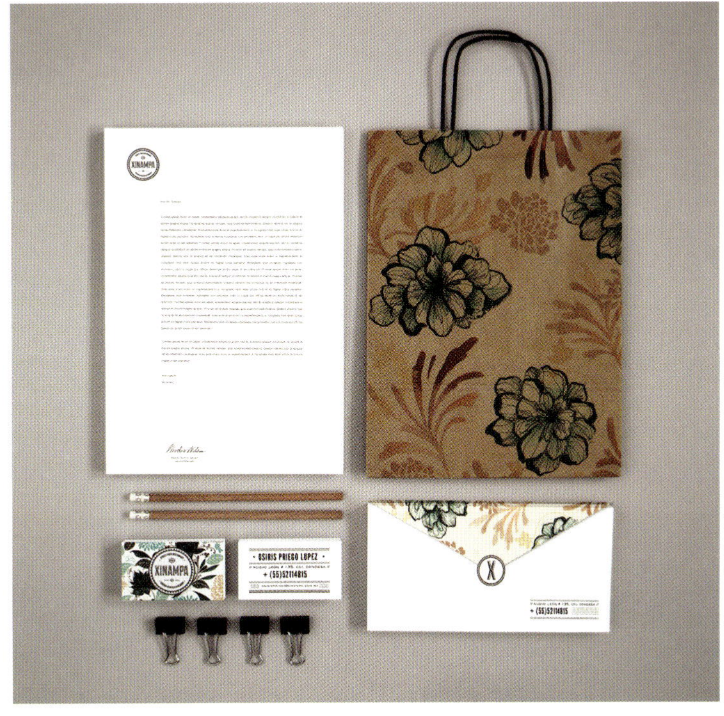
XINAMPA
OSIRIS PRIEGO LOPEZ
+ (55)52114815

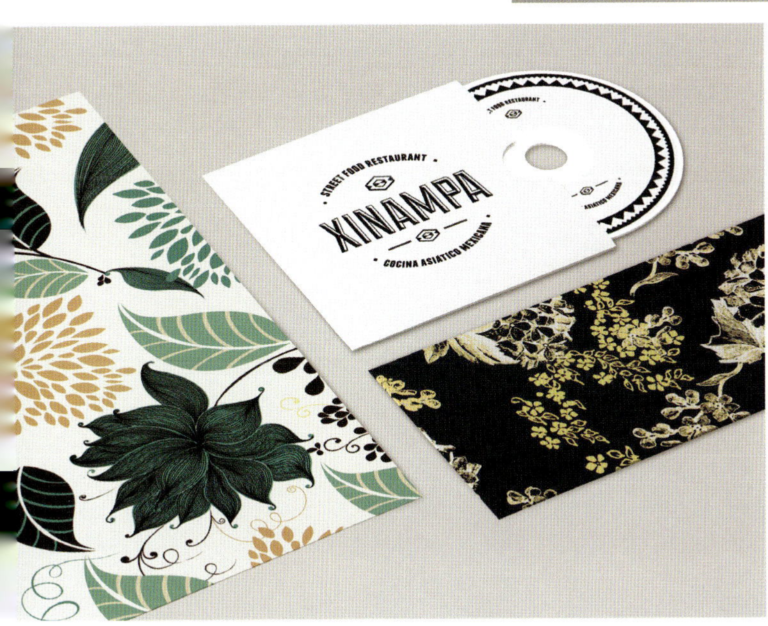
STREET FOOD RESTAURANT
XINAMPA
COCINA ASIATICO MEXICANA

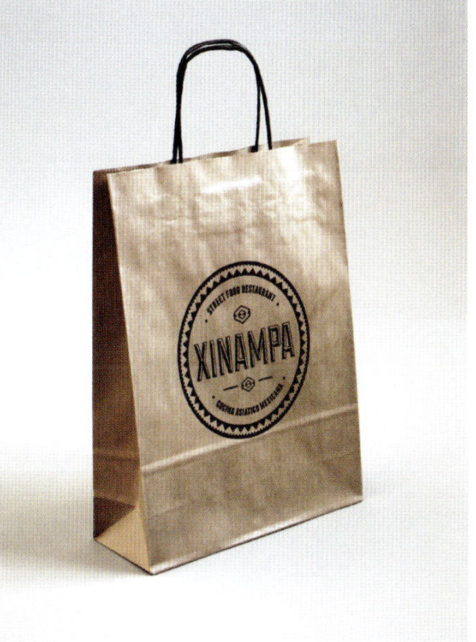
STREET FOOD RESTAURANT
XINAMPA
COCINA ASIATICO MEXICANA

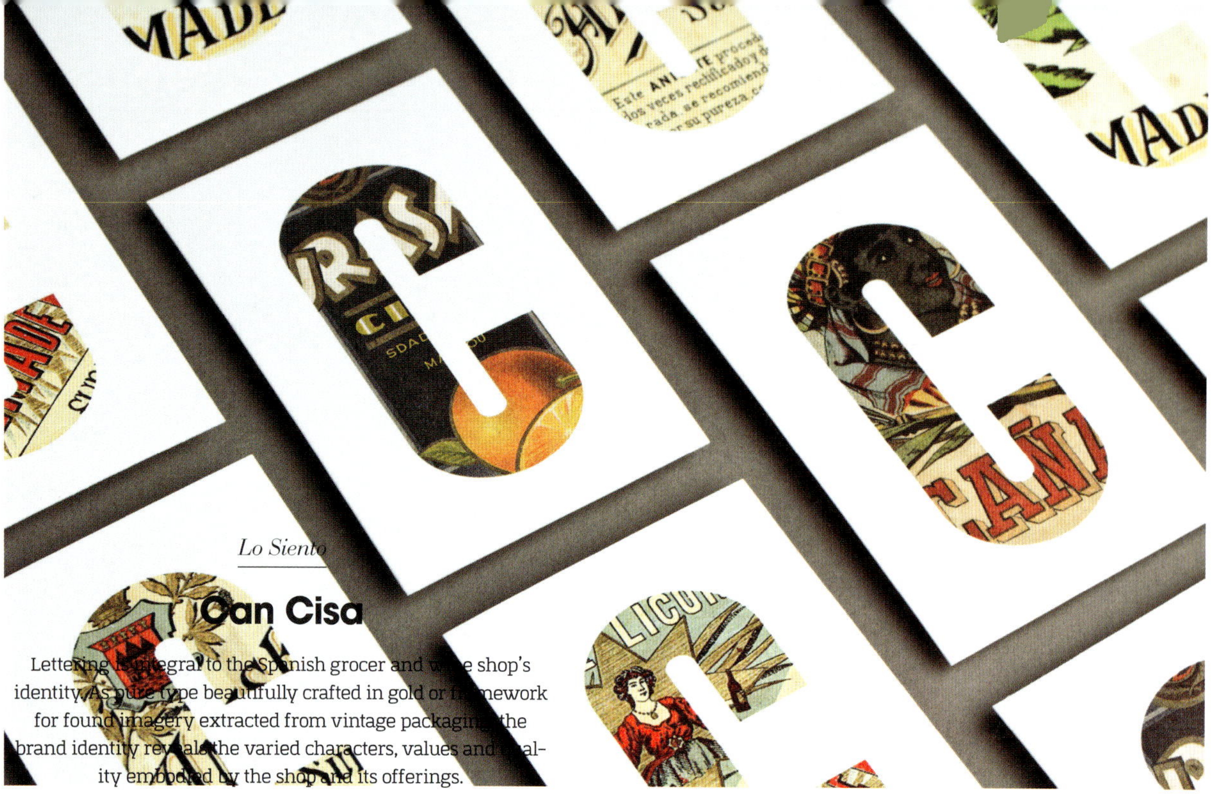

Lo Siento

Can Cisa

Lettering is integral to the Spanish grocer and wine shop's identity. As pure type beautifully crafted in gold or framework for found imagery extracted from vintage packaging, the brand identity reveals the varied characters, values and quality embodied by the shop and its offerings.

Client: Joan Valencia, Colombo Brothers

Lo Siento

Can Cisa

Lettering is integral to the Spanish grocer and wine shop's identity. As pure type beautifully crafted in gold or framework for found imagery extracted from vintage packaging, the brand identity reveals the varied characters, values and quality embodied by the shop and its offerings.

Client: Joan Valencia, Colombo Brothers

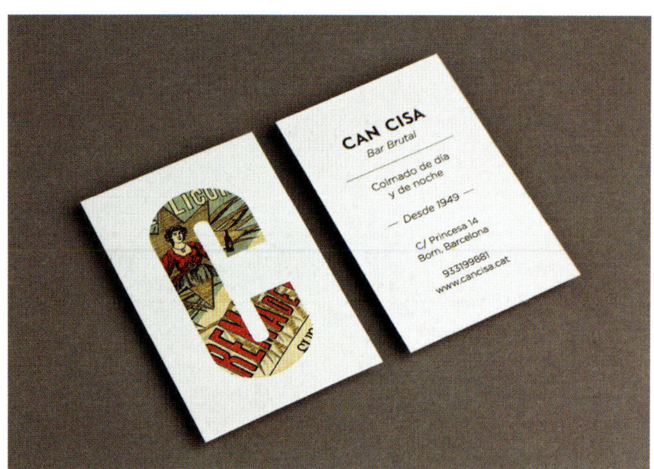

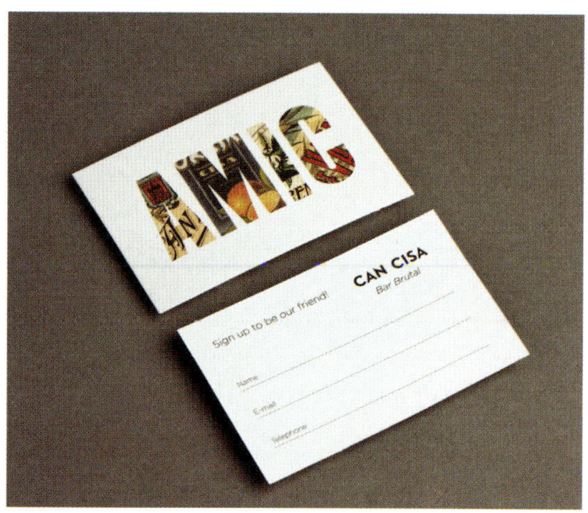

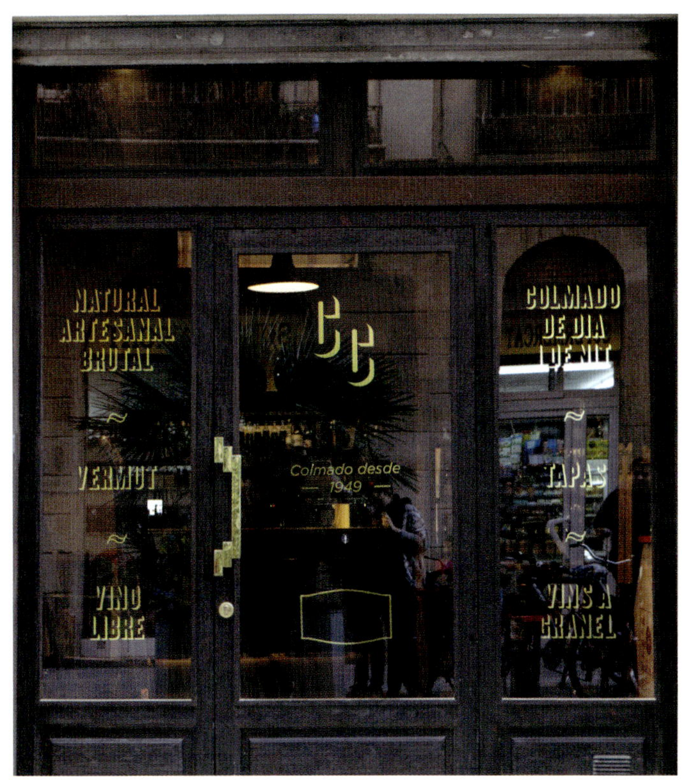
NATURAL
ARTESANAL
BRUTAL
VERMUT
VINO
LIBRE
Colmado desde
1949
COLMADO
DE DIA
I DE NIT
TAPAS
VINS A
GRANEL

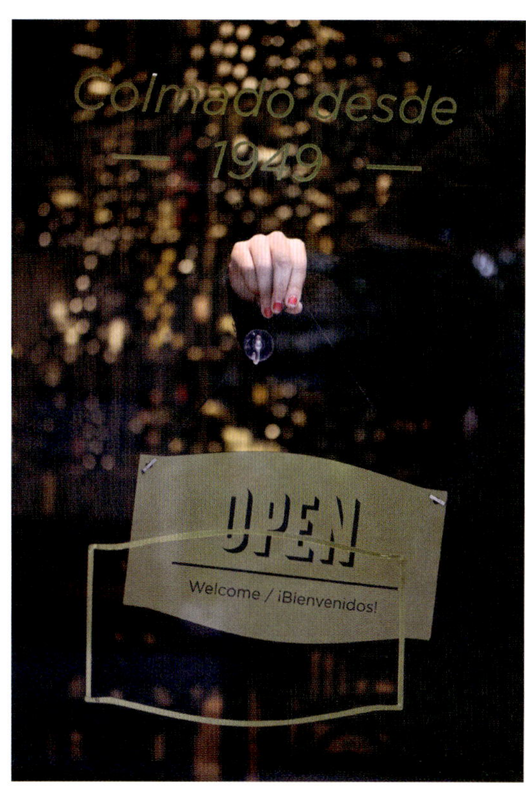
Colmado desde
1949
OPEN
Welcome / ¡Bienvenidos!

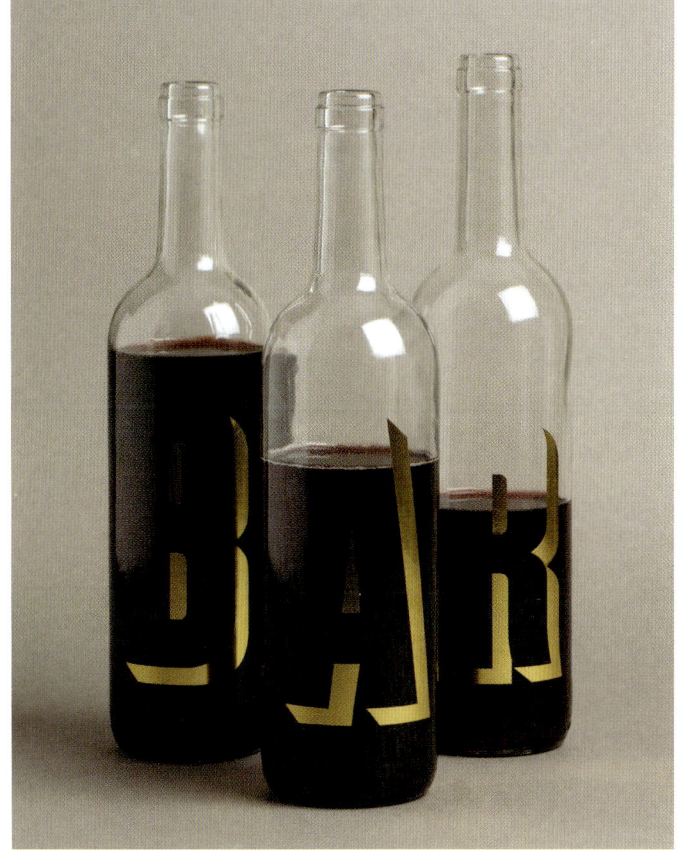

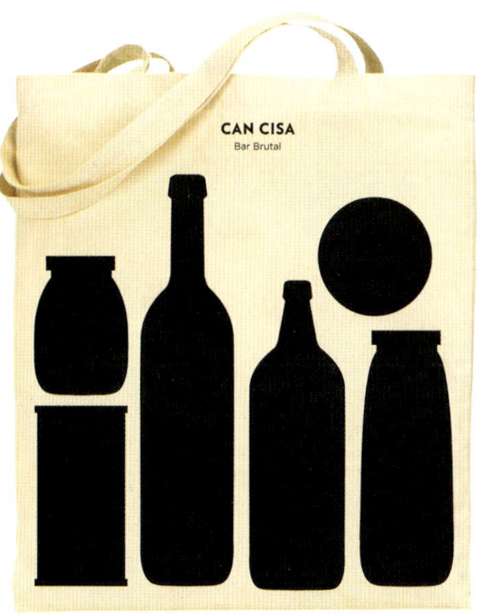
CAN CISA
Bar Brutal

10 A DAY

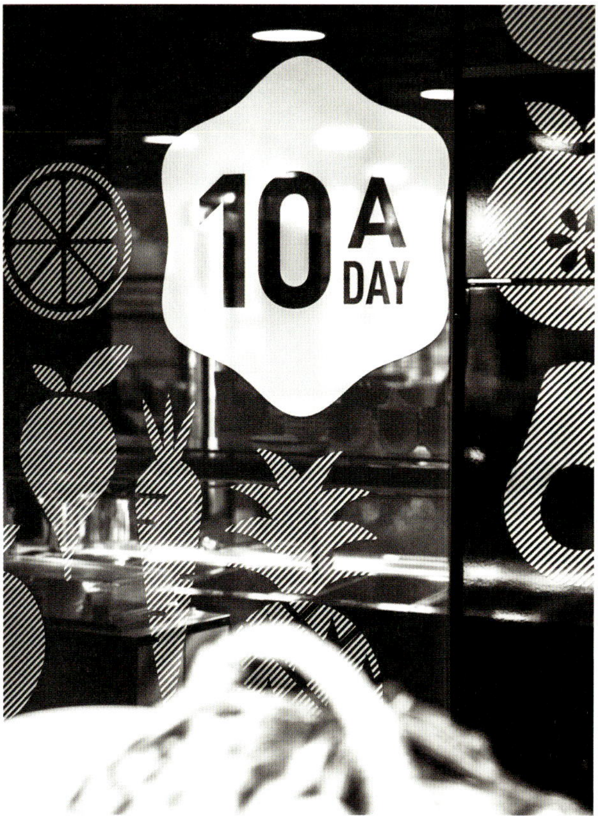

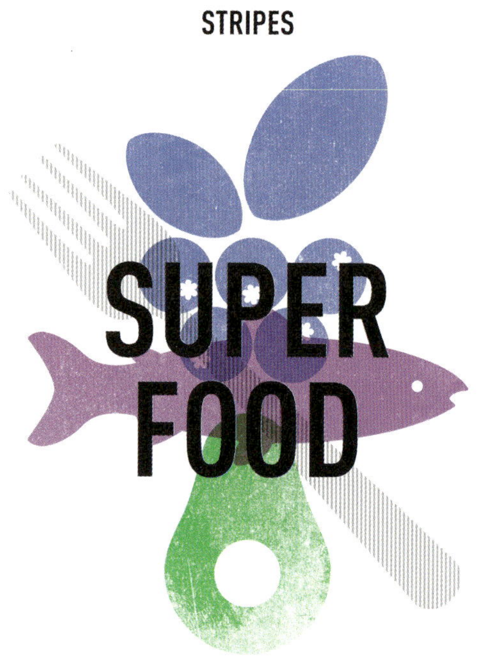
STRIPES
SUPER FOOD
FOOD THAT BOOSTS YOUR HEALTH

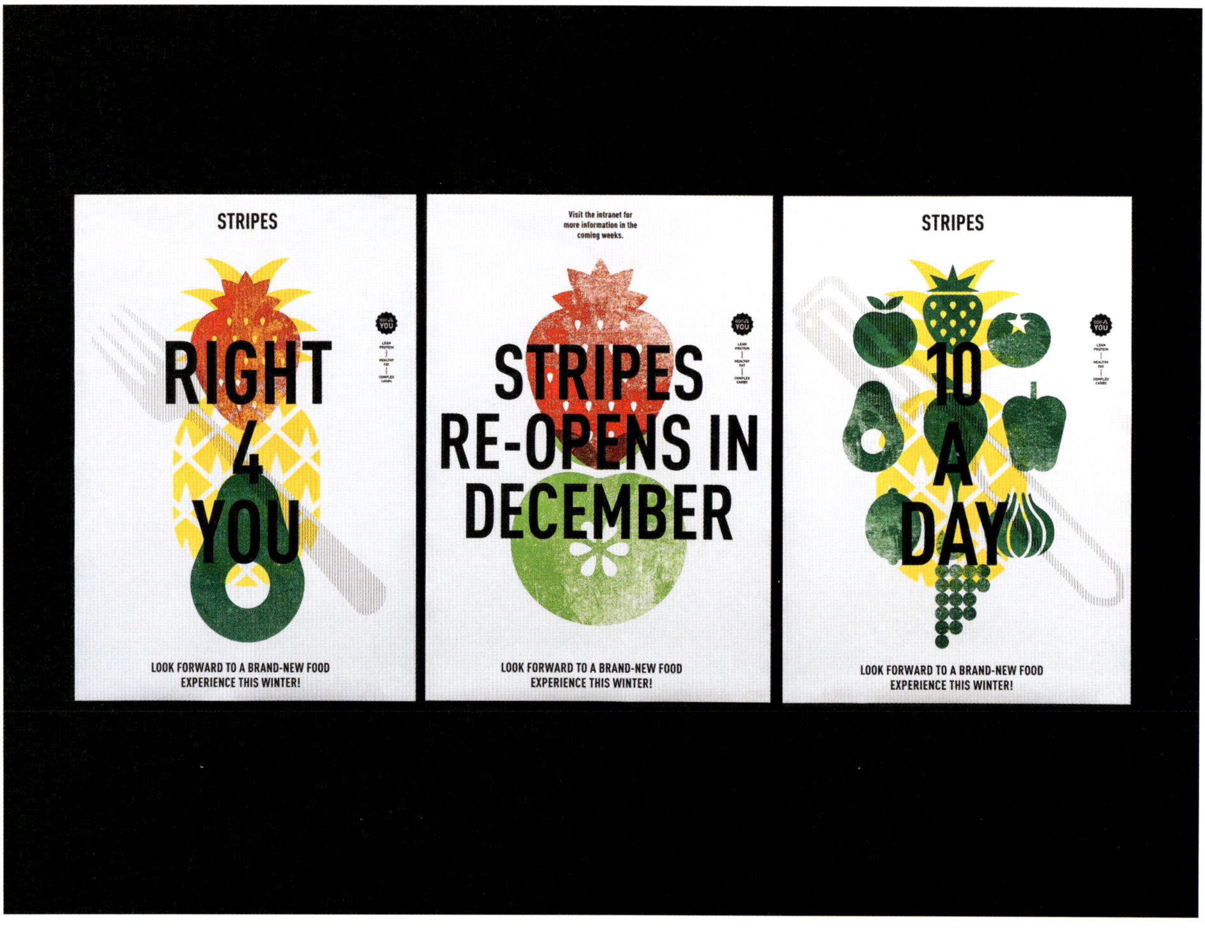

STRIPES
RIGHT 4 YOU
LOOK FORWARD TO A BRAND-NEW FOOD EXPERIENCE THIS WINTER!
Visit the intranet for more information in the coming weeks.
STRIPES RE-OPENS IN DECEMBER
LOOK FORWARD TO A BRAND-NEW FOOD EXPERIENCE THIS WINTER!
STRIPES
10 A DAY
LOOK FORWARD TO A BRAND-NEW FOOD EXPERIENCE THIS WINTER!

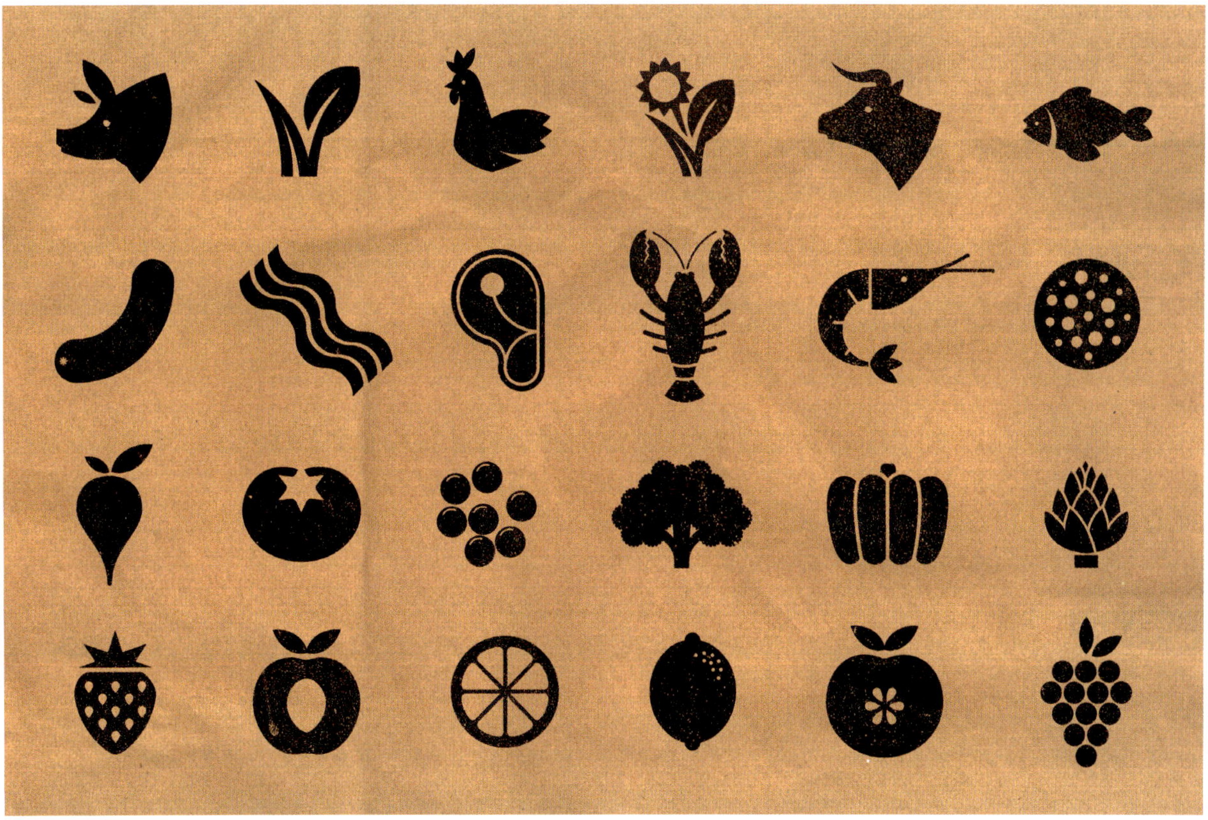

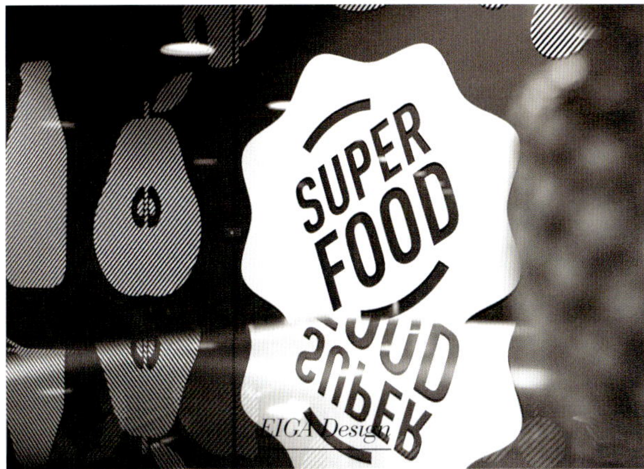

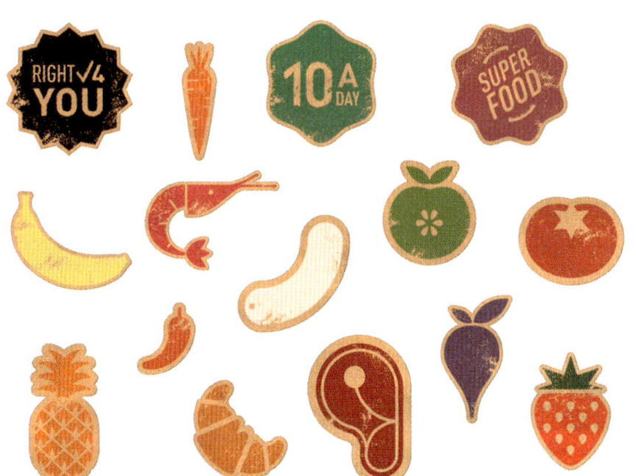

EIGA Design

STRIPES

Visual identity of adidas Group cafeteria STRIPES is united by a fluid set of pictograms that can be used to identify the different ingredients and nutritional content of the daily lunch menus. The taste also ensures fast orientation and easy recognition especially during midday rush hours.

Client: adidas AG

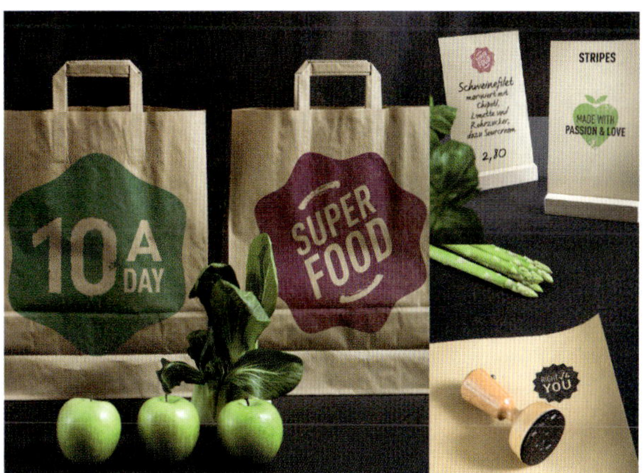

EIGA Design

STRIPES

Visual identity of adidas Group cafeteria STRIPES
is united by a fluid set of pictograms that can be used to identi-

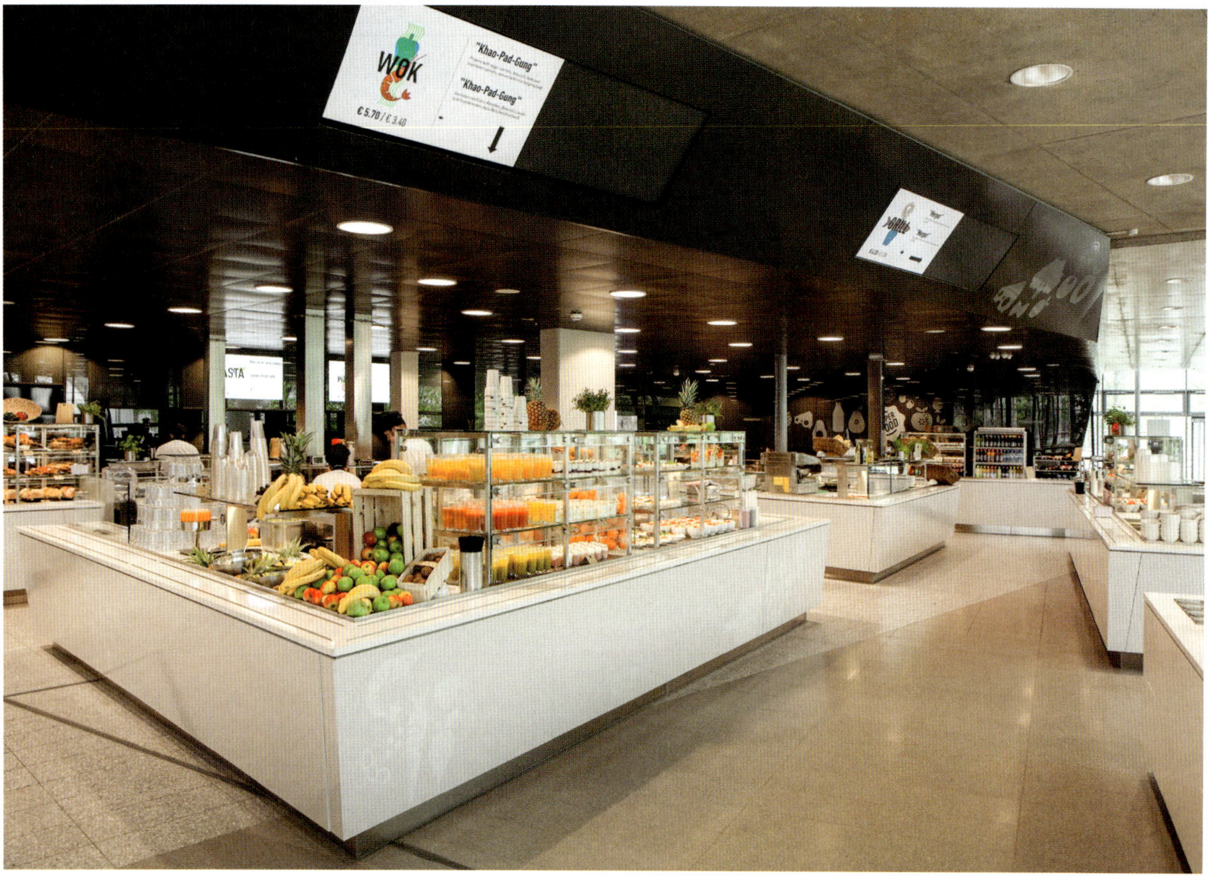

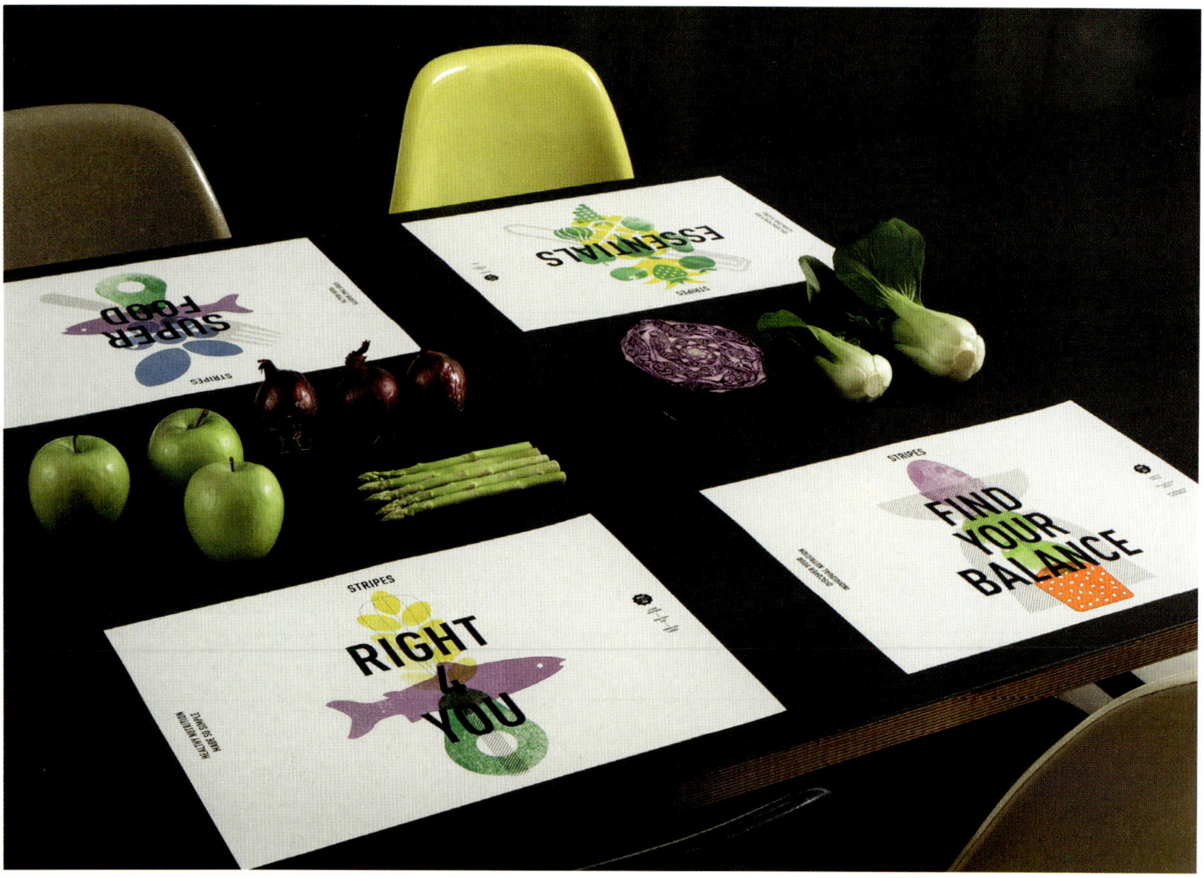

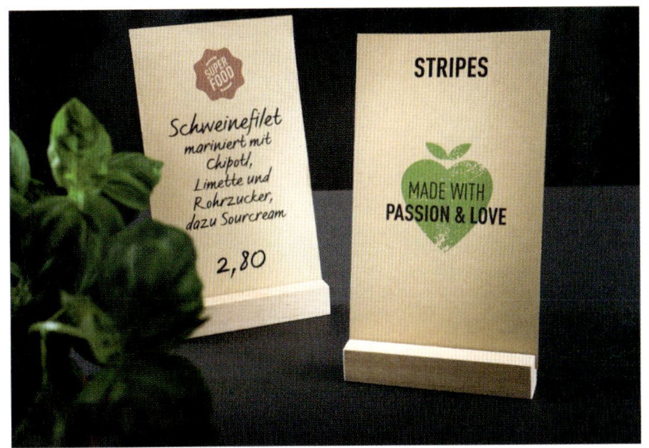
SUPER FOOD
Schweinefilet mariniert mit Chipotl, Limette und Rohrzucker, dazu Sourcream
2,80
STRIPES
MADE WITH PASSION & LOVE

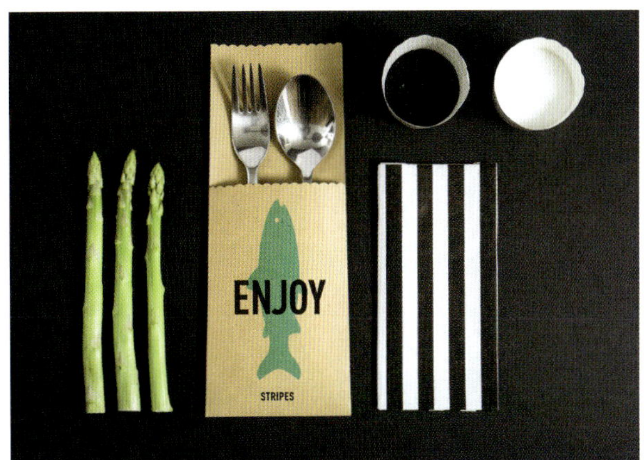
ENJOY
STRIPES

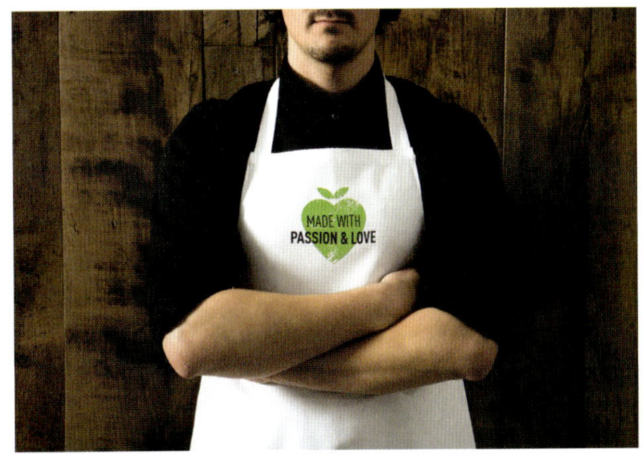
MADE WITH PASSION & LOVE

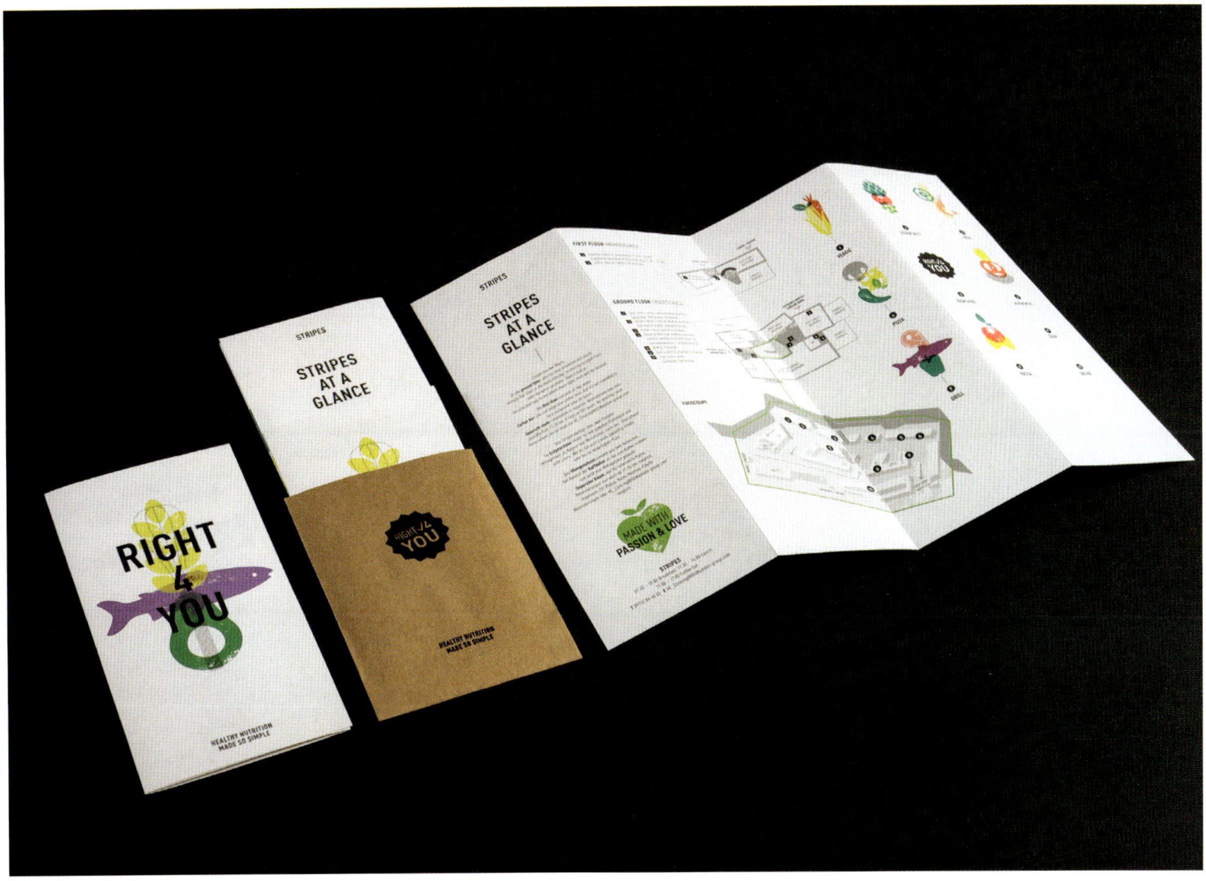

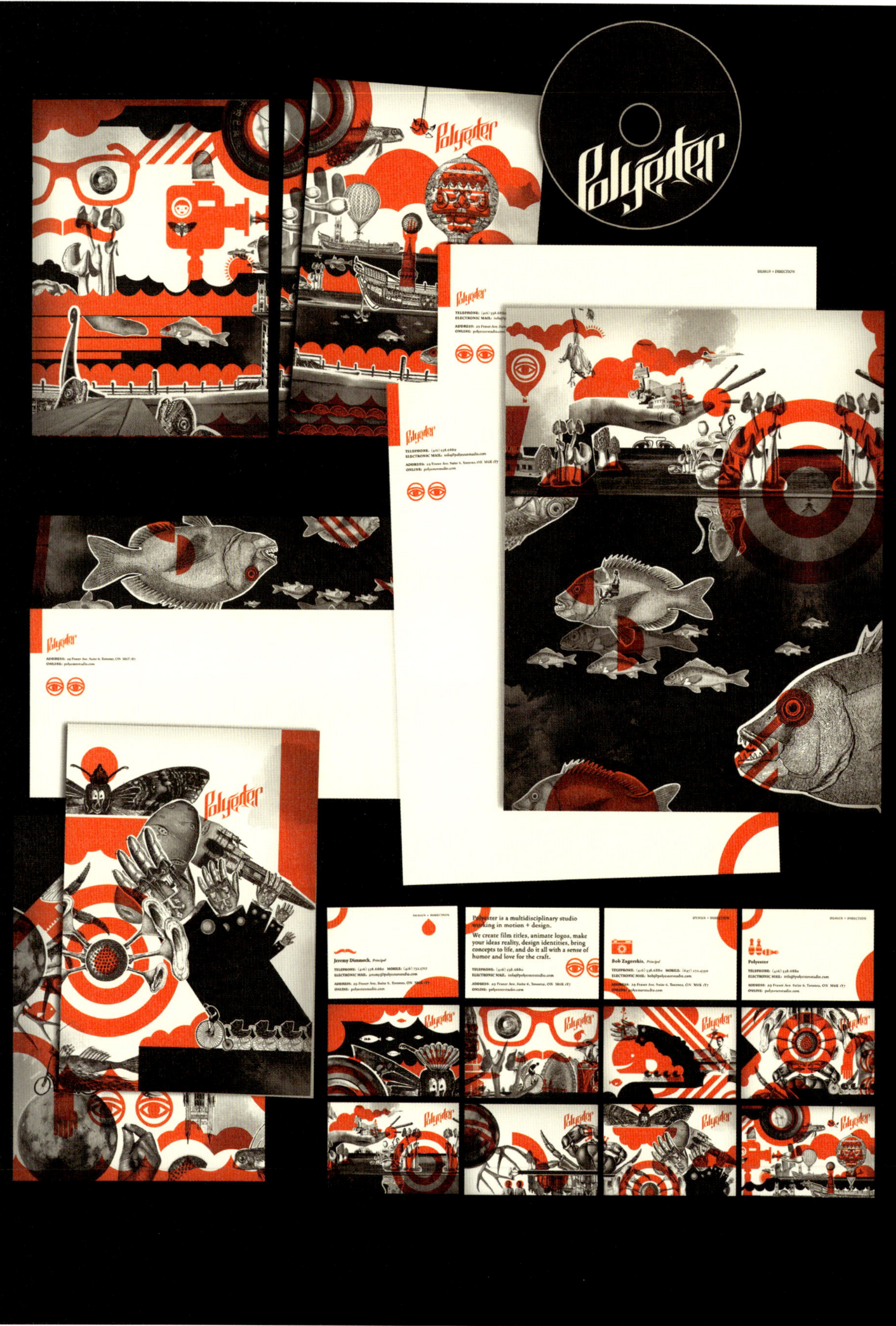
Polyester
Polyester is a multidisciplinary studio working in motion + design.
We create film titles, animate logos, make your ideas reality, design identities, bring concepts to life, and do it all with a sense of humor and love for the craft.
Jeremy Dinmock, Principal
Bob Zagorskis, Principal
DESIGN + DIRECTION

Polyester Studio

Polyester's own brand identity embraces both their digital art and motion picture work. Graphics in red and black were overlaid by found imagery on its stationery meld the two realms to evoke flexibility and possibilities over its identity suite, including stationery and letters.

Printing: CJ Graphics
Letterpress: Lunar Caustic

Polyester Studio

Polyester Studio

Polyester's own brand identity embraces both their digital art and motion picture work. Graphics in red and black were overlaid by found imagery on its stationery meld the two realms to evoke flexibility and possibilities over its identity suite, including stationery and letters.

Printing: CJ Graphics
Letterpress: Lunar Caustic

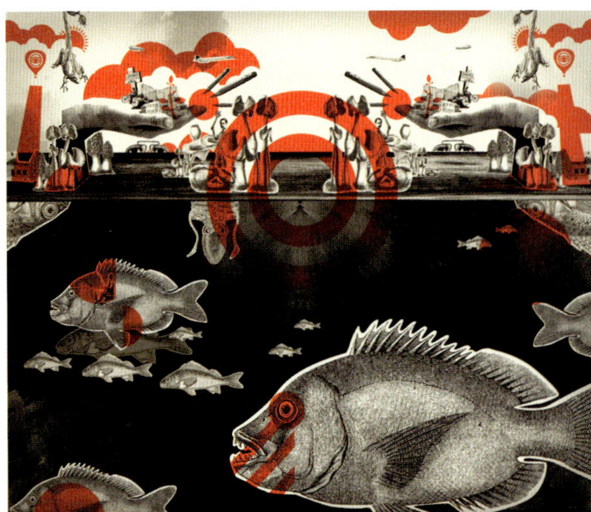

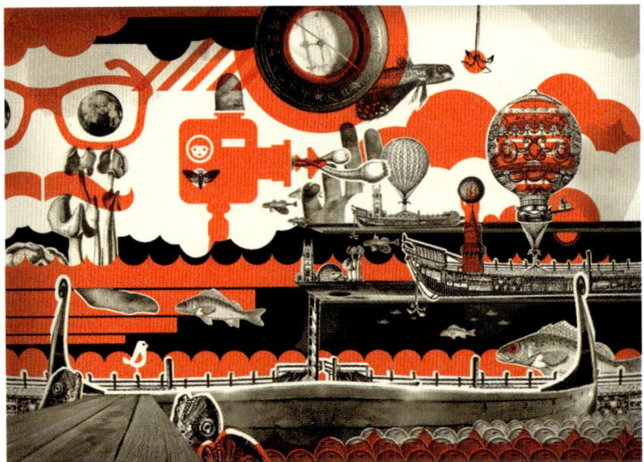

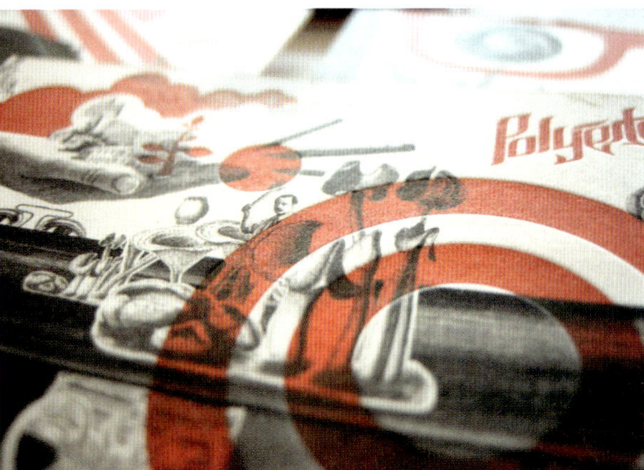

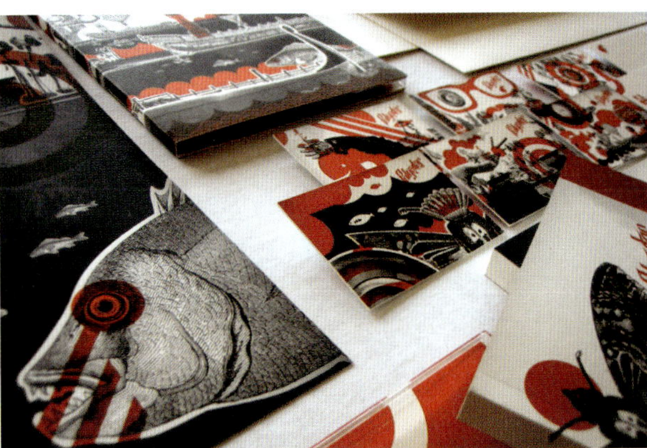

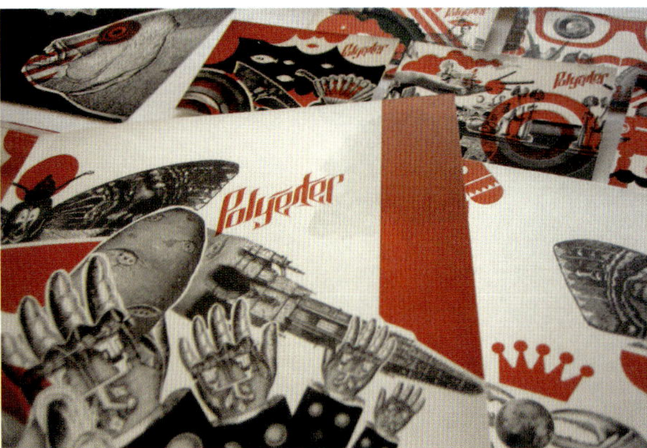

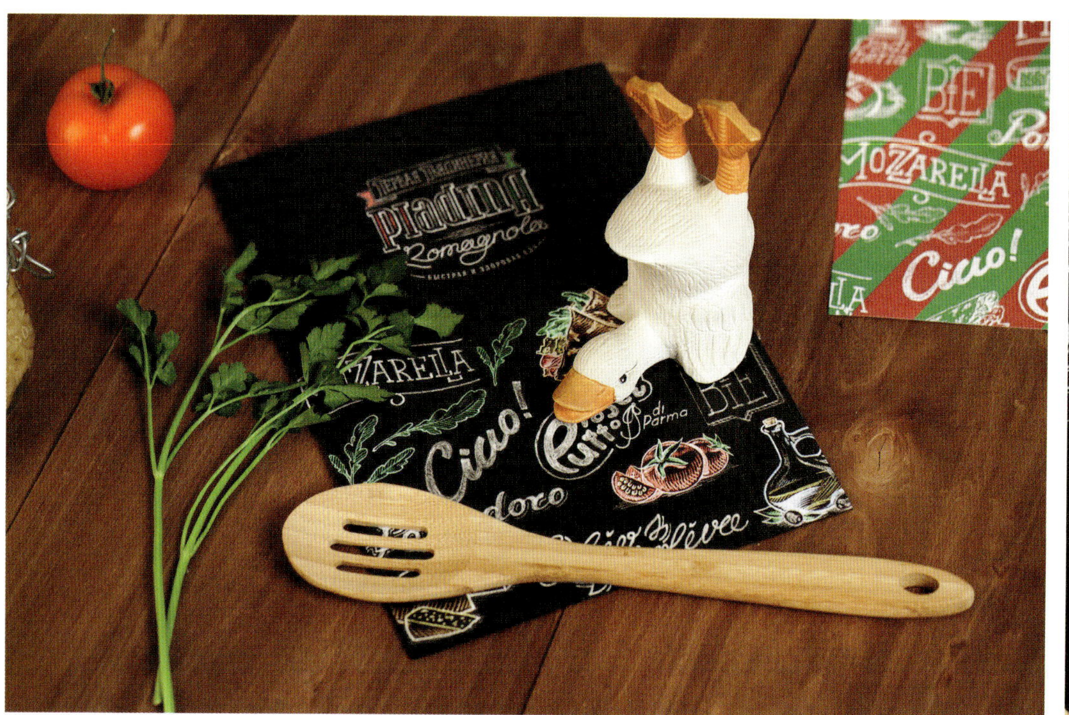

MOZARELLA
Ciao!
di Parma

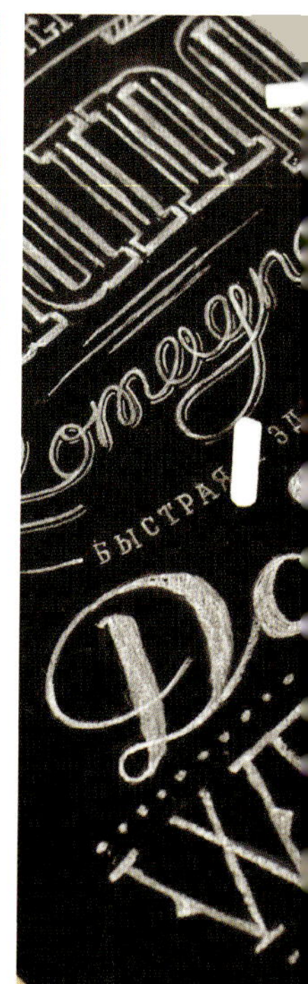

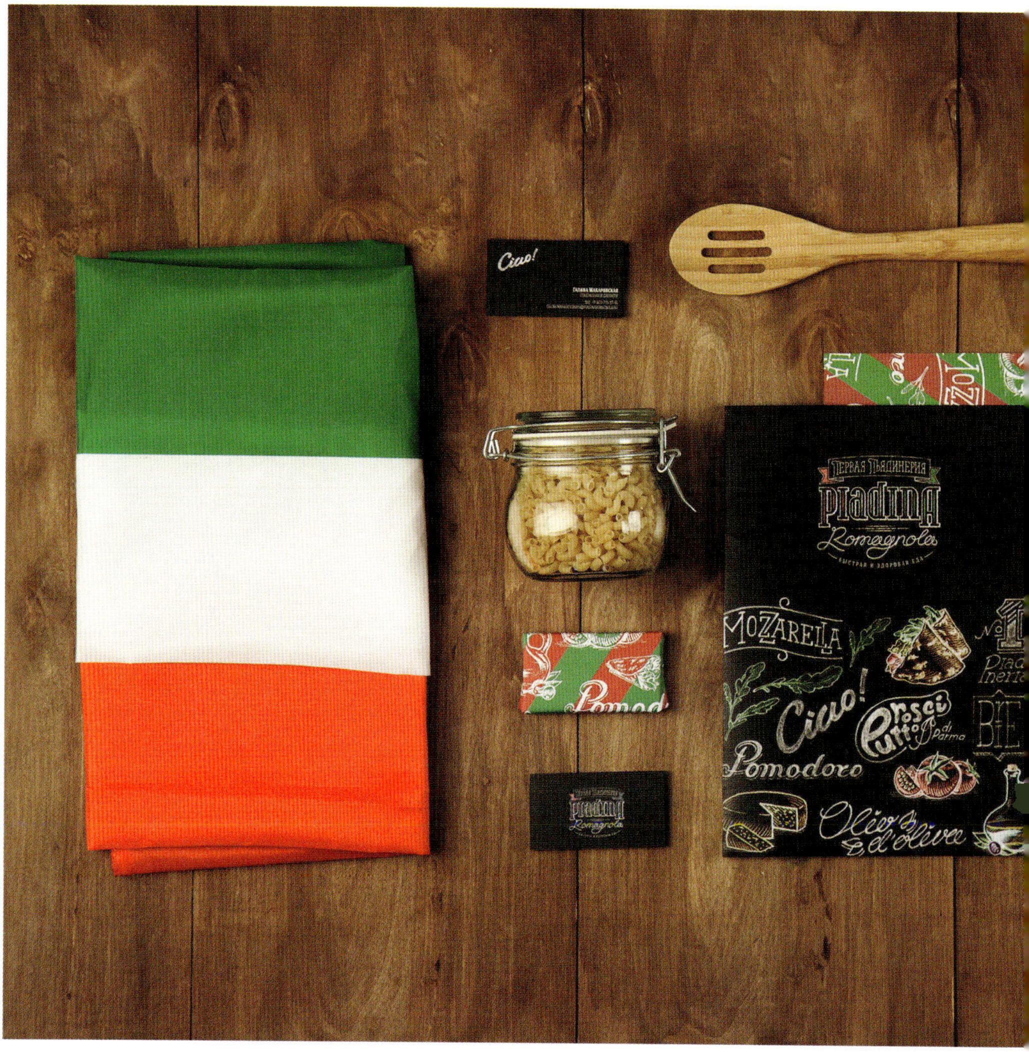

Piadina Ro agnola

Symbolic of the taste and quality highly sought-after in Italy's fast food culture, Piadina Romagnola brings delicious Italian cooking into Russian living. Classic chalkboard typography of Italian eateries form the basis of the graphic identity, with colours taken from the country's flag.

Client: Piadina Romagnola

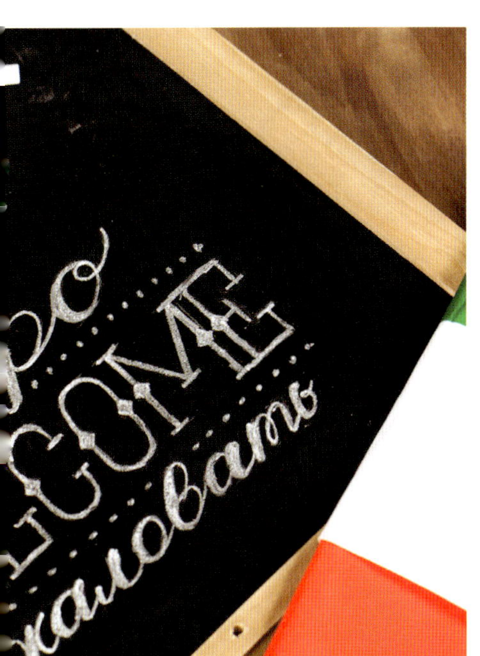

Eskimo Design Studio

Piadina Romagnola

Symbolic of the taste and quality highly sought-after in Italy's fast food culture, Piadina Romagnola brings delicious Italian cooking into Russian living. Classic chalkboard typography of Italian eateries form the basis of the graphic identity, with colours taken from the country's flag.

Client: Piadina Romagnola

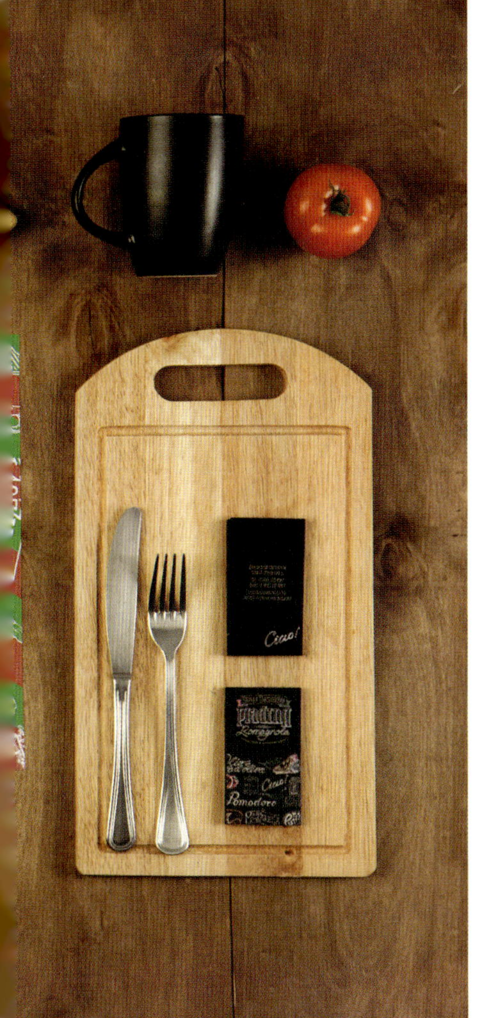

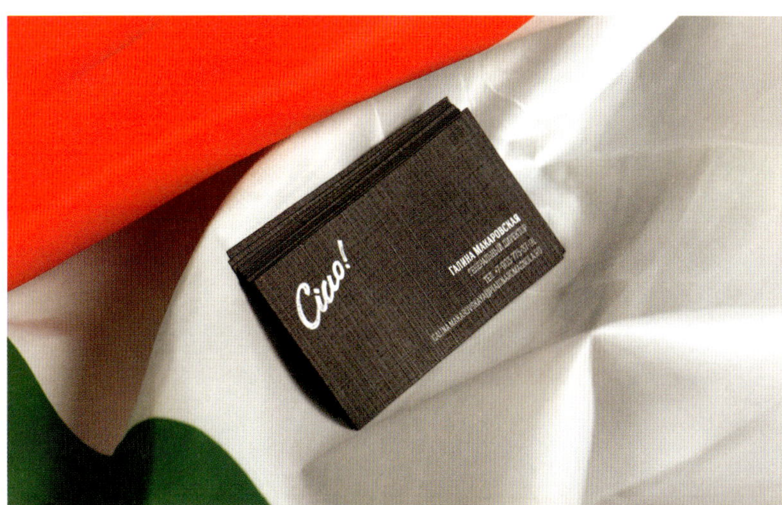

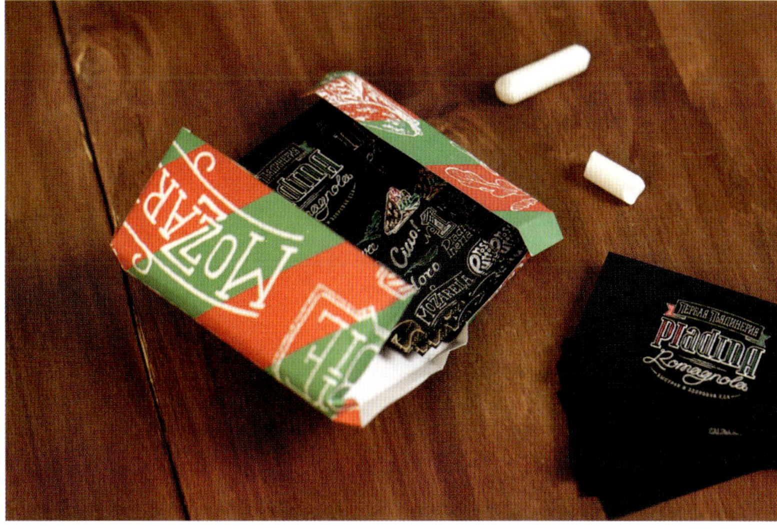

Botanica Real Food

Textured paper, cardboard, crafted food illustrations and a mixed typeface reflect the simple, authentic and real food experience of Botanica. Botanica stresses a whole foods approach to take away, and this pared-down brand and packaging resonant with the shop's core belief.

Client: Botanica Real Food

Oh Babushka

Botanica Real Food

Textured paper, cardboard, crafted food illustrations and a mixed typeface reflect the simple, authentic and real food experience of Botanica. Botanica stresses a whole foods approach to take away, and this pared-down brand and packaging resonant with the shop's core belief.

Client: Botanica Real Food

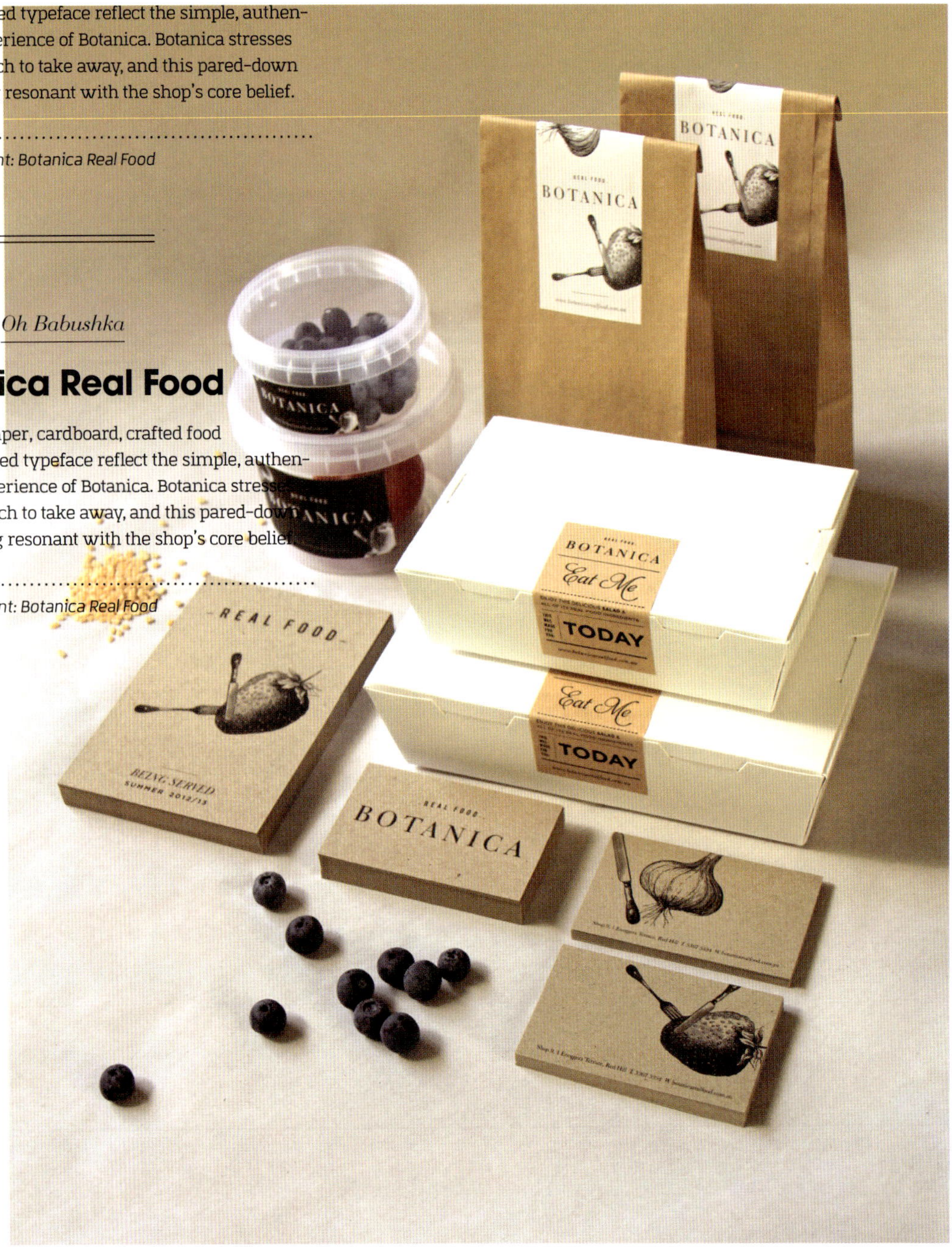

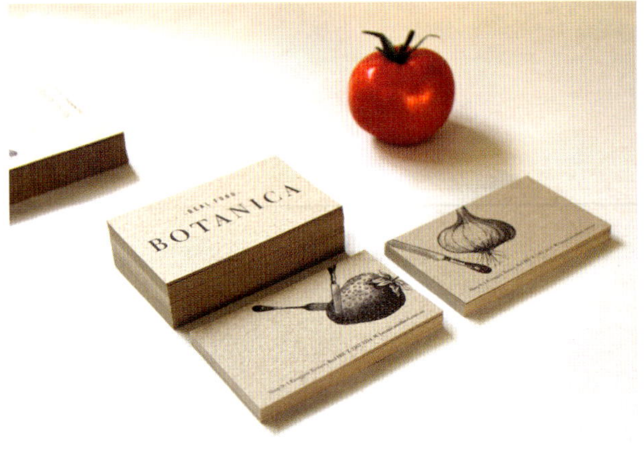

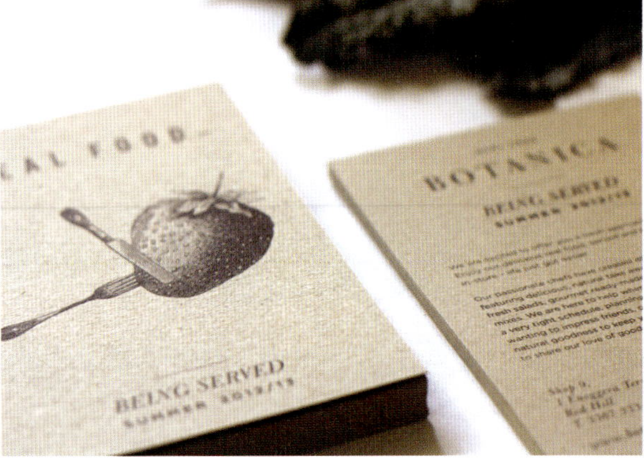

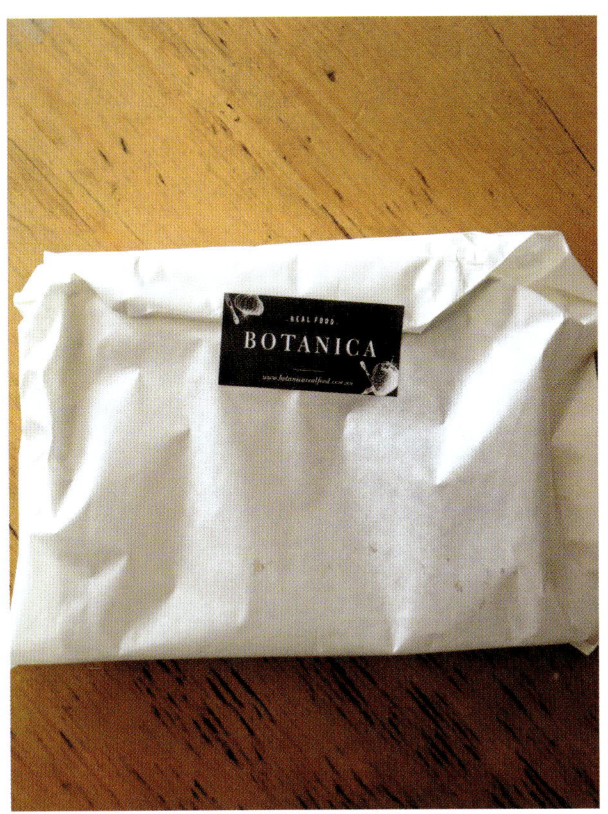
REAL FOOD
BOTANICA

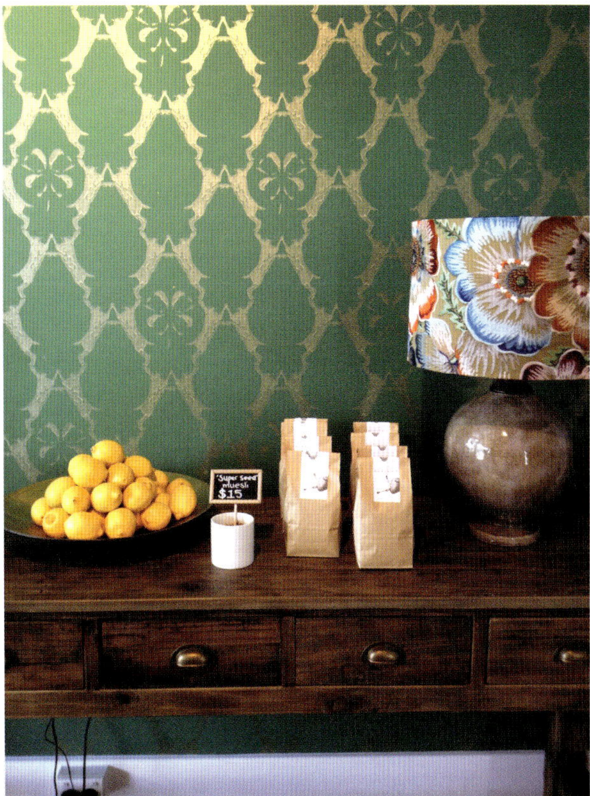
Super Seed Muesli
$15

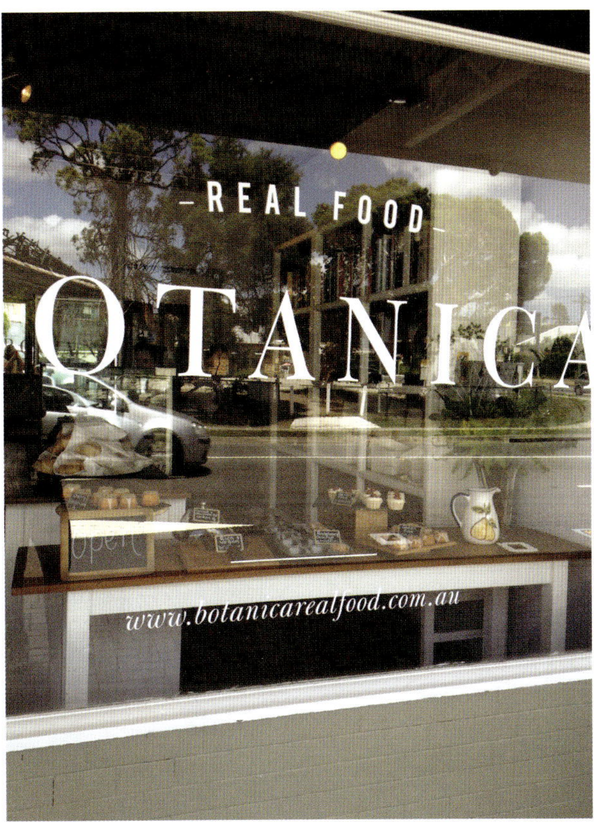
REAL FOOD
OTANICA
www.botanicarealfood.com.au

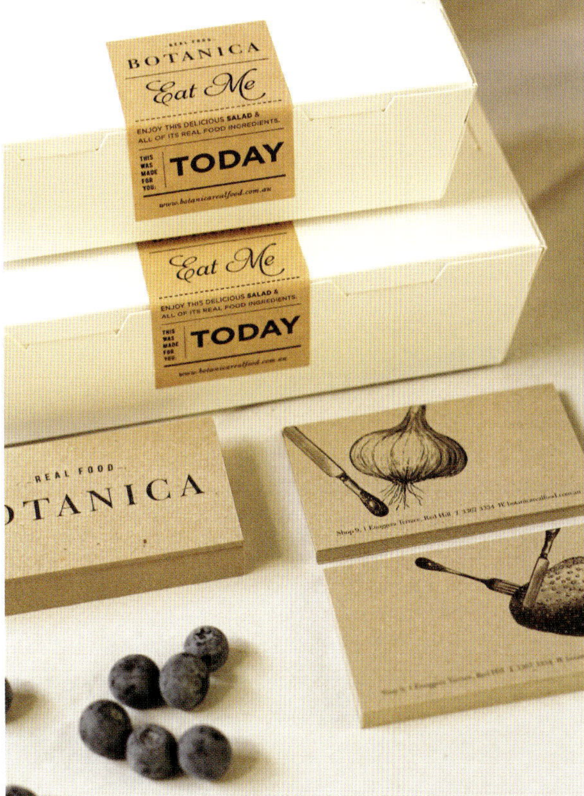
BOTANICA
Eat Me
ENJOY THIS DELICIOUS SALAD & ALL OF ITS REAL FOOD INGREDIENTS.
THIS WAS MADE FOR YOU:
TODAY
www.botanicarealfood.com.au
Eat Me
ENJOY THIS DELICIOUS SALAD & ALL OF ITS REAL FOOD INGREDIENTS.
THIS WAS MADE FOR YOU:
TODAY
REAL FOOD
OTANICA

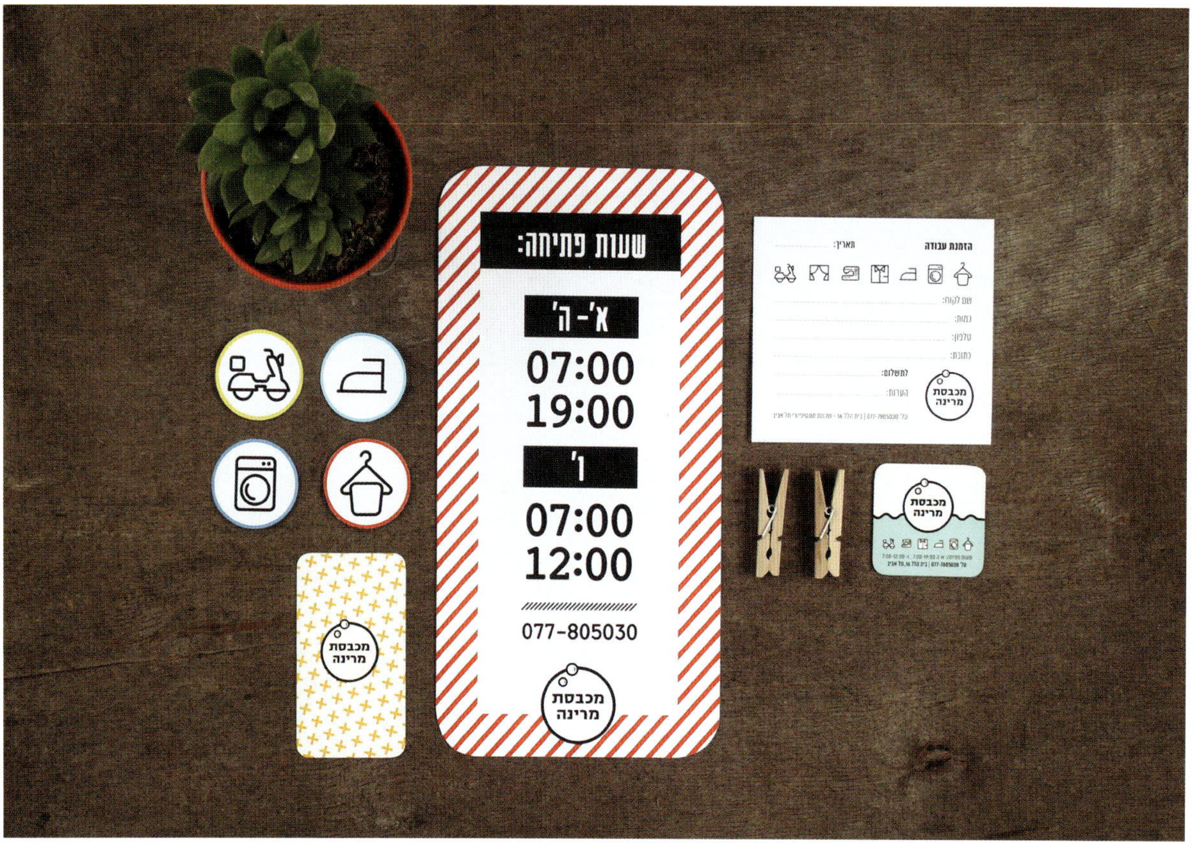
שעות פתיחה:
א׳-ה׳
07:00
19:00
ו׳
07:00
12:00
077-805030
מכבסת
מרינה
הזמנת עבודה
תאריך:
מכבסת
מרינה
מכבסת
מרינה
מכבסת
מרינה

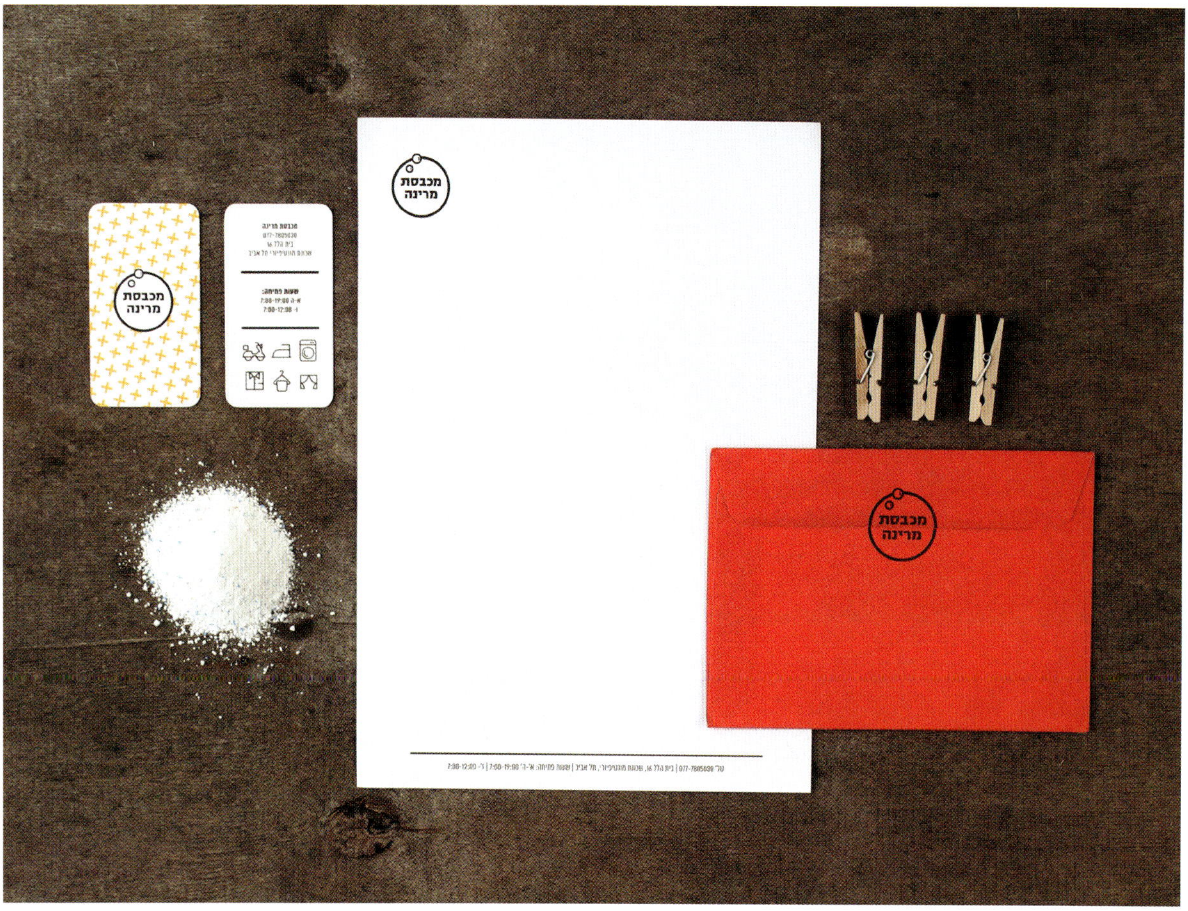
מכבסת
מרינה
מכבסת
מרינה
שעות פתיחה:
מכבסת
מרינה

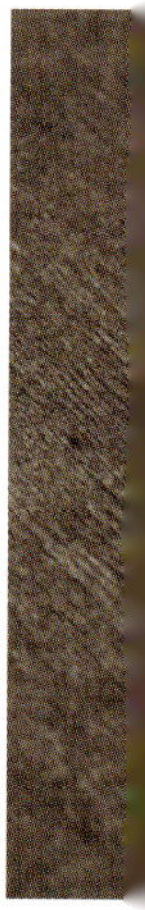

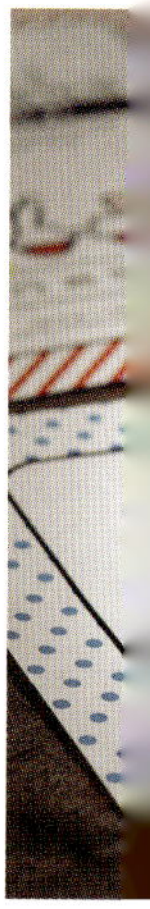

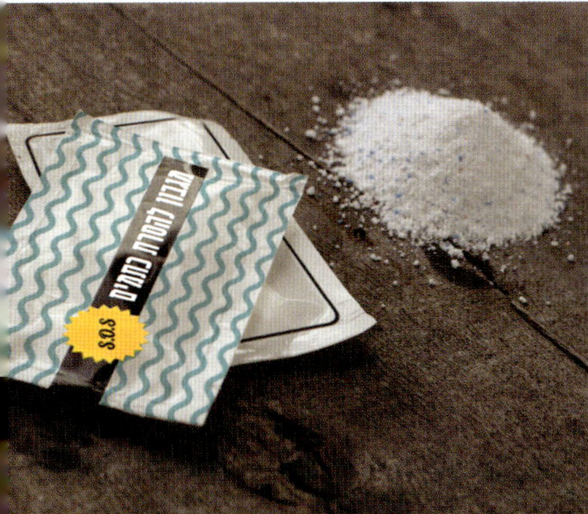

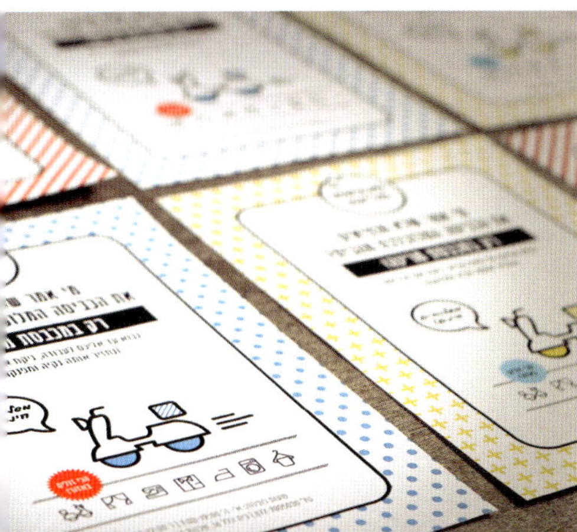

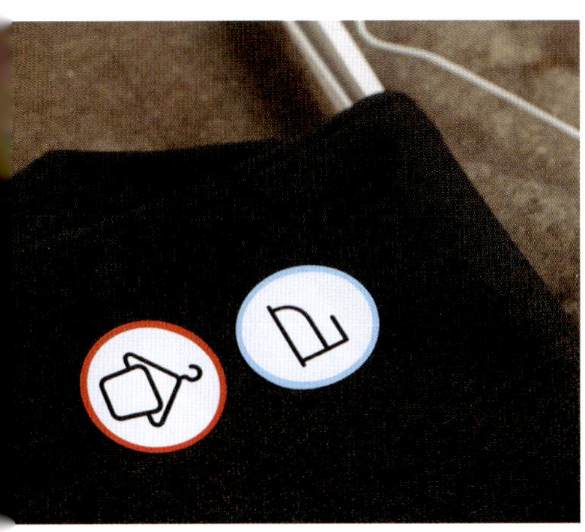

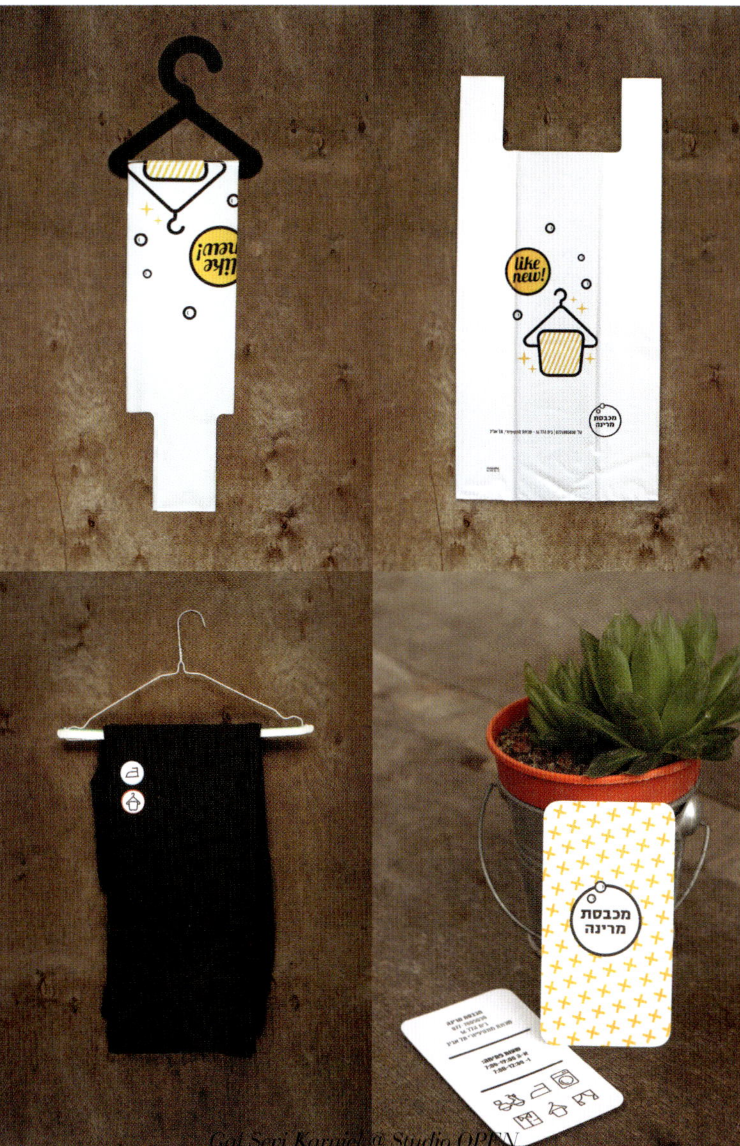

Gal Sevi Karniel @ Studio OPEN.

Total Brand Experience

Marina's Laundry Service

Marina's laundry service is a small business located in a young and dynamic neighbourhood in Central Tel Aviv. A clean, icon-based visual and operating system was devised alongside colour patterns to turn laundry into an efficient and delightful task.

Client: Marina's Laundry Service

Gal Sevi Karniel @ Studio OPEN.

Total Brand Experience

Marina's Laundry Service

Marina's laundry service is a small business located in a young and dynamic neighbourhood in Central Tel Aviv. A clean, icon-based visual

Koultoura Coffee

Steering itself away from coffee chains that fill Jakarta's streets, Koultoura in the school district seeks to bring a fresh stand-alone coffee shop and hipster hangout with masterfully brewed coffee to match. Animal portraits and mural ask customers to forget about the real world as they recharge.

Client: Koultoura Coffee

FullFill Artplication

Koultoura Coffee

Steering itself away from coffee chains that fill Jakarta's streets, Koultoura in the school district seeks to bring a fresh stand-alone coffee shop and hipster hangout with masterfully brewed coffee to match. Animal portraits and mural ask customers to

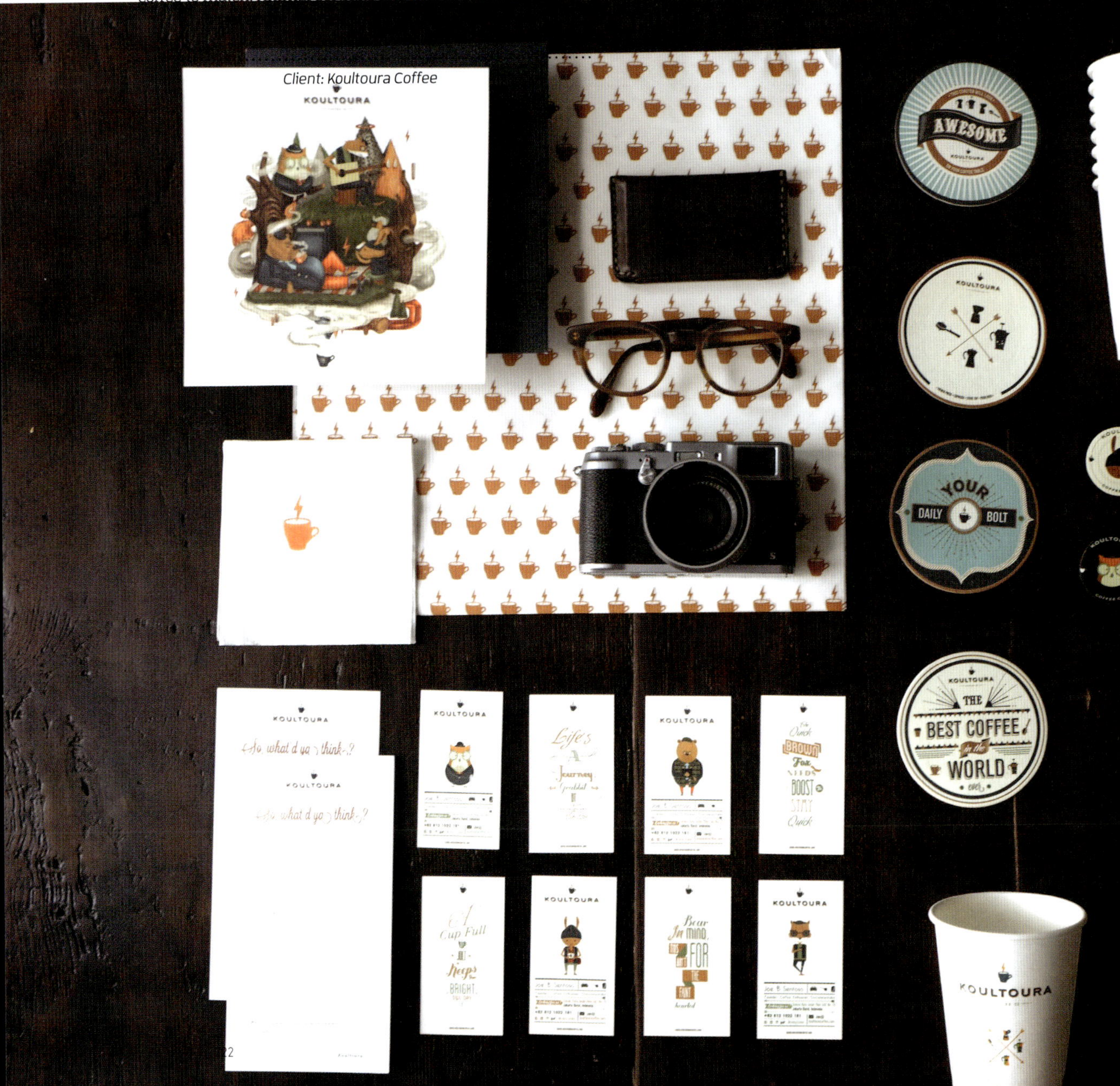

Client: Koultoura Coffee

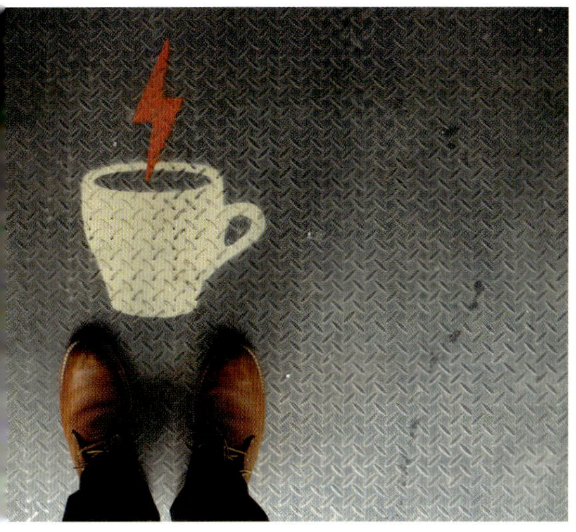

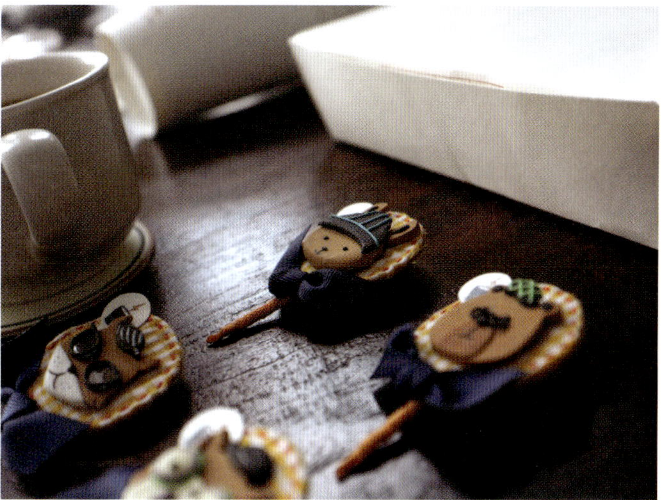

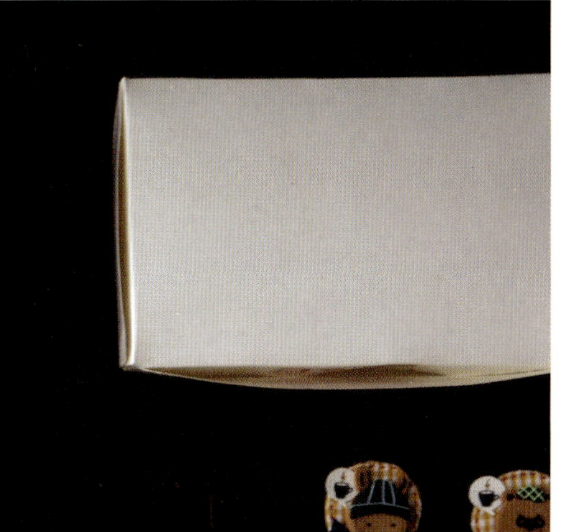

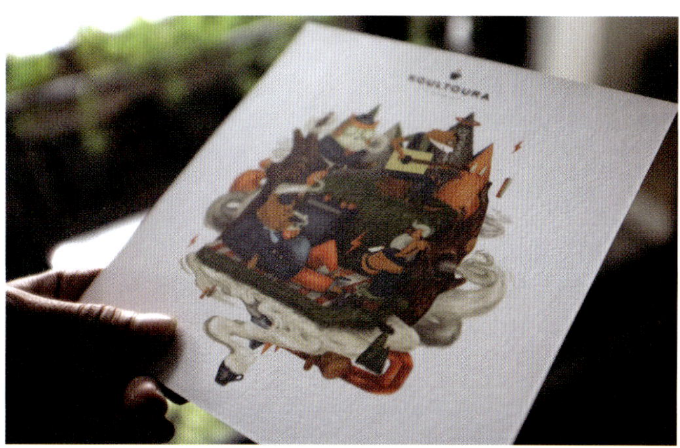
KOULTOURA

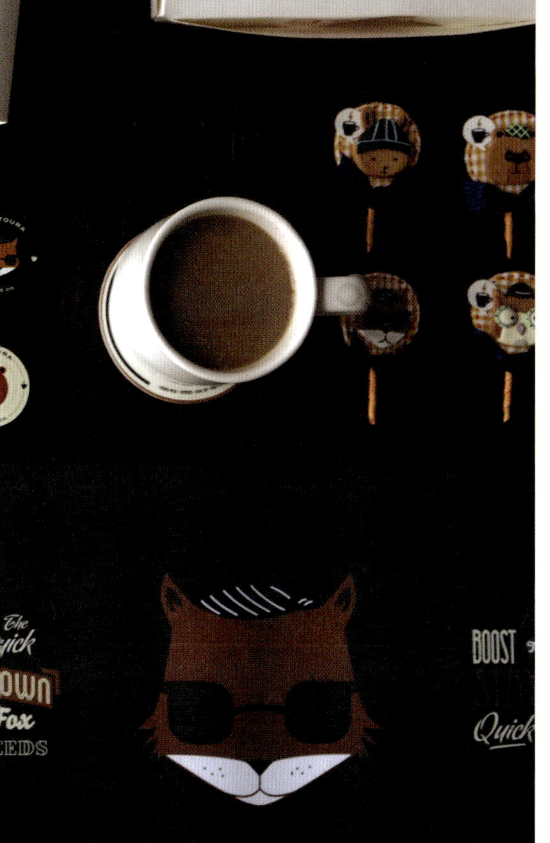
BOOST
Quick
KOULTOURA

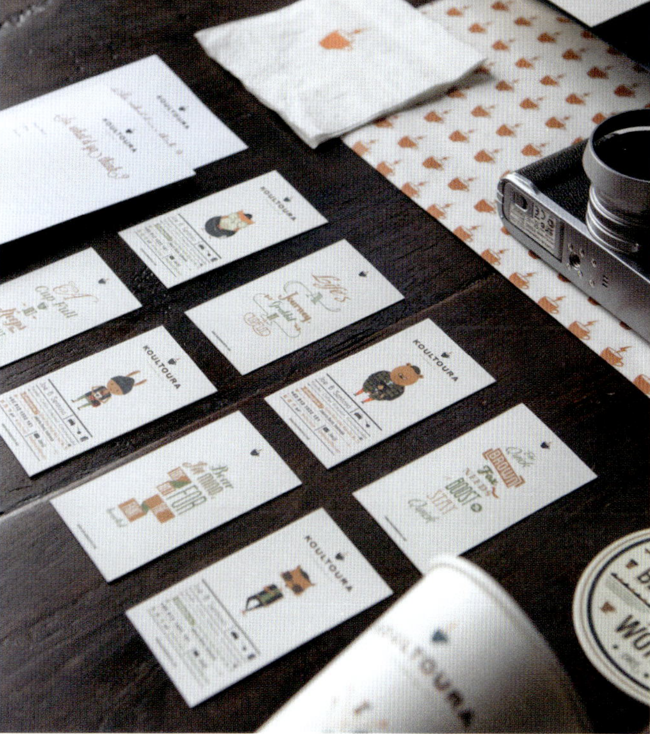
KOULTOURA

Molo10

Branding design for seafood restaurant Molo10 is born out of a desire to transform the sea into a fantastic place full of wonderful characters. Submerged in a palette symbolic of the marine world, Octopus King and Gentleman Seahorse among others accompany patrons to discover delicious treats.

Illustration: Andrea Indini
Photo: Marie Sjoberg
Client: Molo10

Rossoamaranto

Molo10

Branding design for seafood restaurant Molo10 is born out of a desire to transform the sea into a fantastic place full of wonderful characters. Submerged in a palette symbolic of the marine world, Octopus King and Gentleman Seahorse among others accompany patrons to discover delicious treats.

Illustration: Andrea Indini
Photo: Marie Sjoberg
Client: Molo10

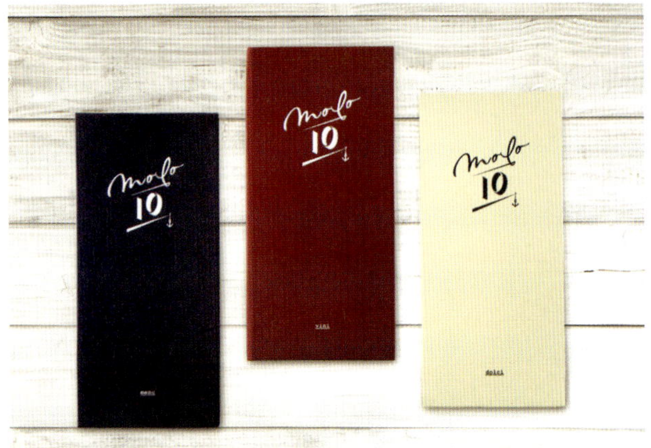

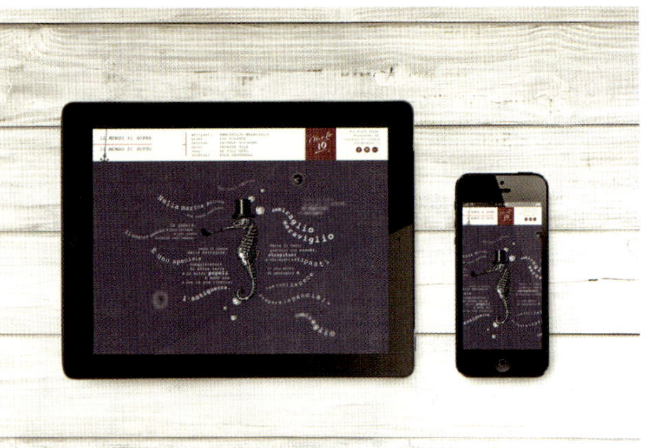

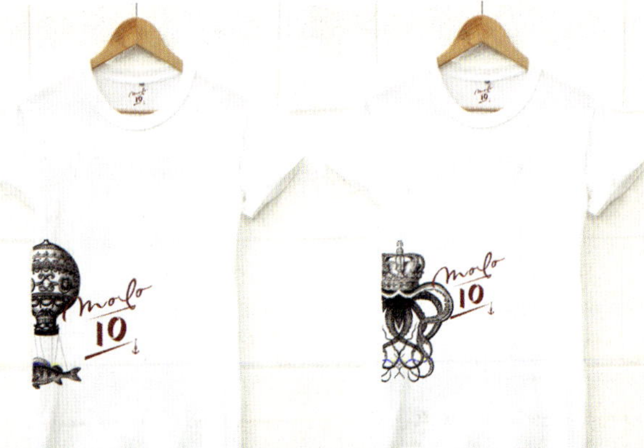

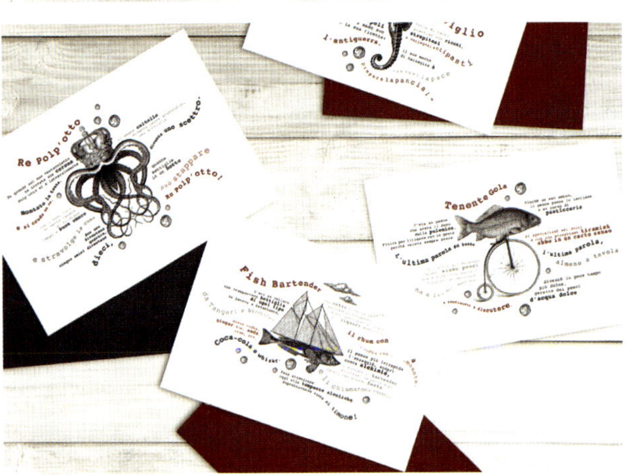

molo 10

Via Prati della Farnesina, 10/14
00135 Roma
tel. 06 3336166
cell. 3351695516

www.molo10.it

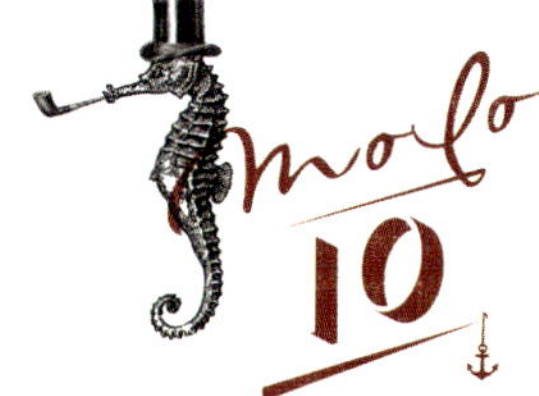

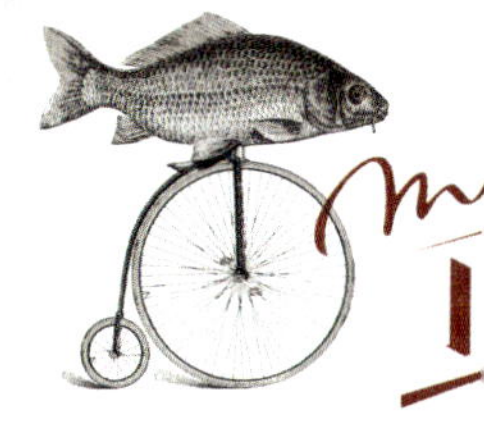

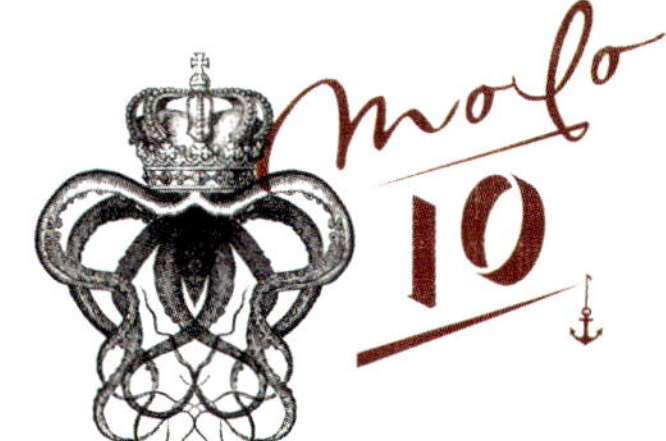

molo 10

Via Prati della Farnesina, 10/14
00135 Roma
tel. 06 3336166
cell. 3351695516

www.molo10.it

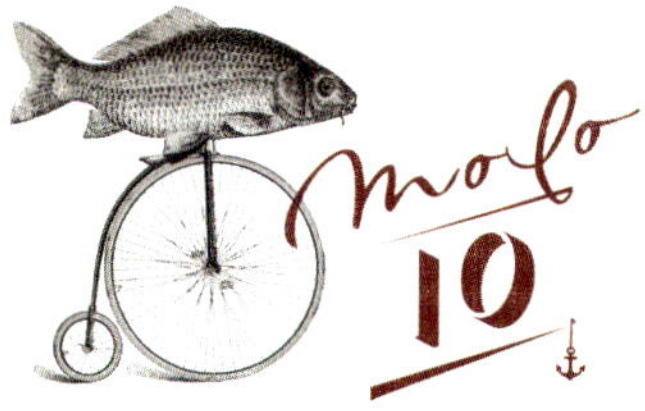

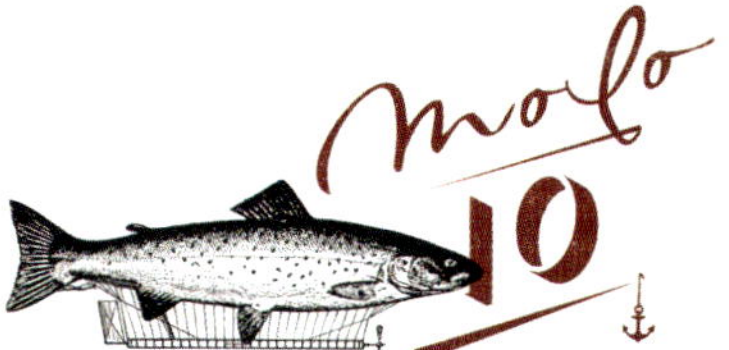

molo 10

Via Prati della F
00135 Roma
tel. 06 3336166
cell. 3351695516

www.molo10.it

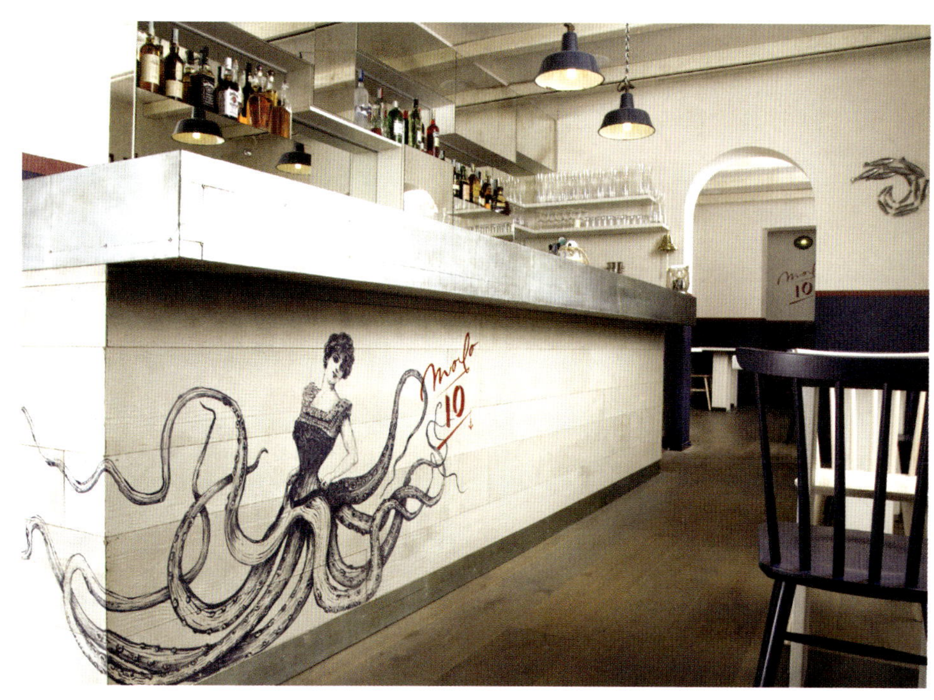

Té de Querer

Té de Querer is a tearoom dedicated to serving rich tisanes and infusions that remind customers of their grandma's love. Its branding system takes a vintage approach with the logo, palette, motifs and portraits construing to an aura that revives the beauty of grandmas' good old days.

Estudio Yeyé

Té de Querer

Té de Querer is a tearoom dedicated to serving rich tisanes and infusions that remind customers of their grandma's love. Its branding system takes a vintage approach with the logo, palette, motifs and portraits construing to an aura that revives the beauty of grandmas' good old days.

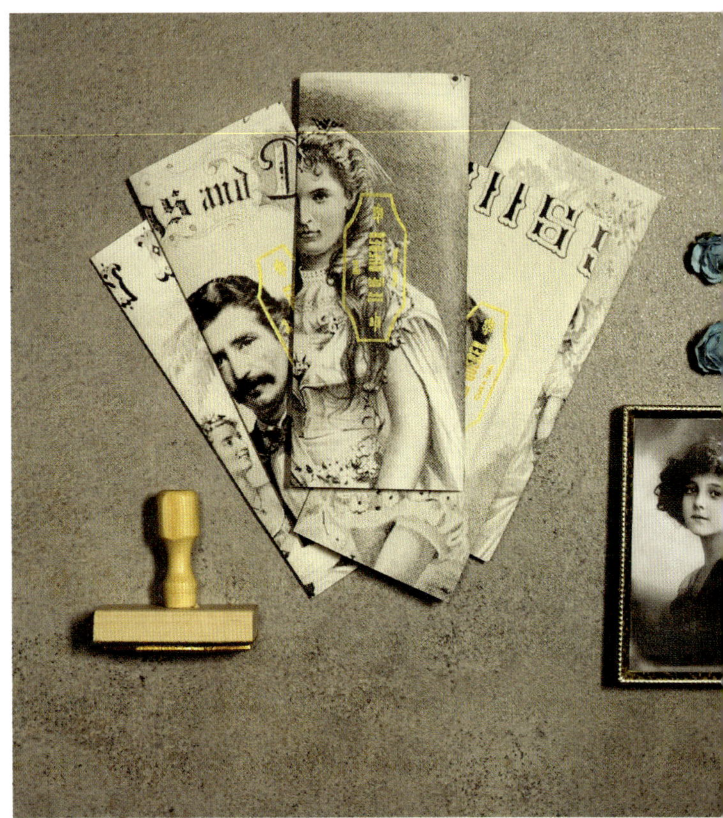

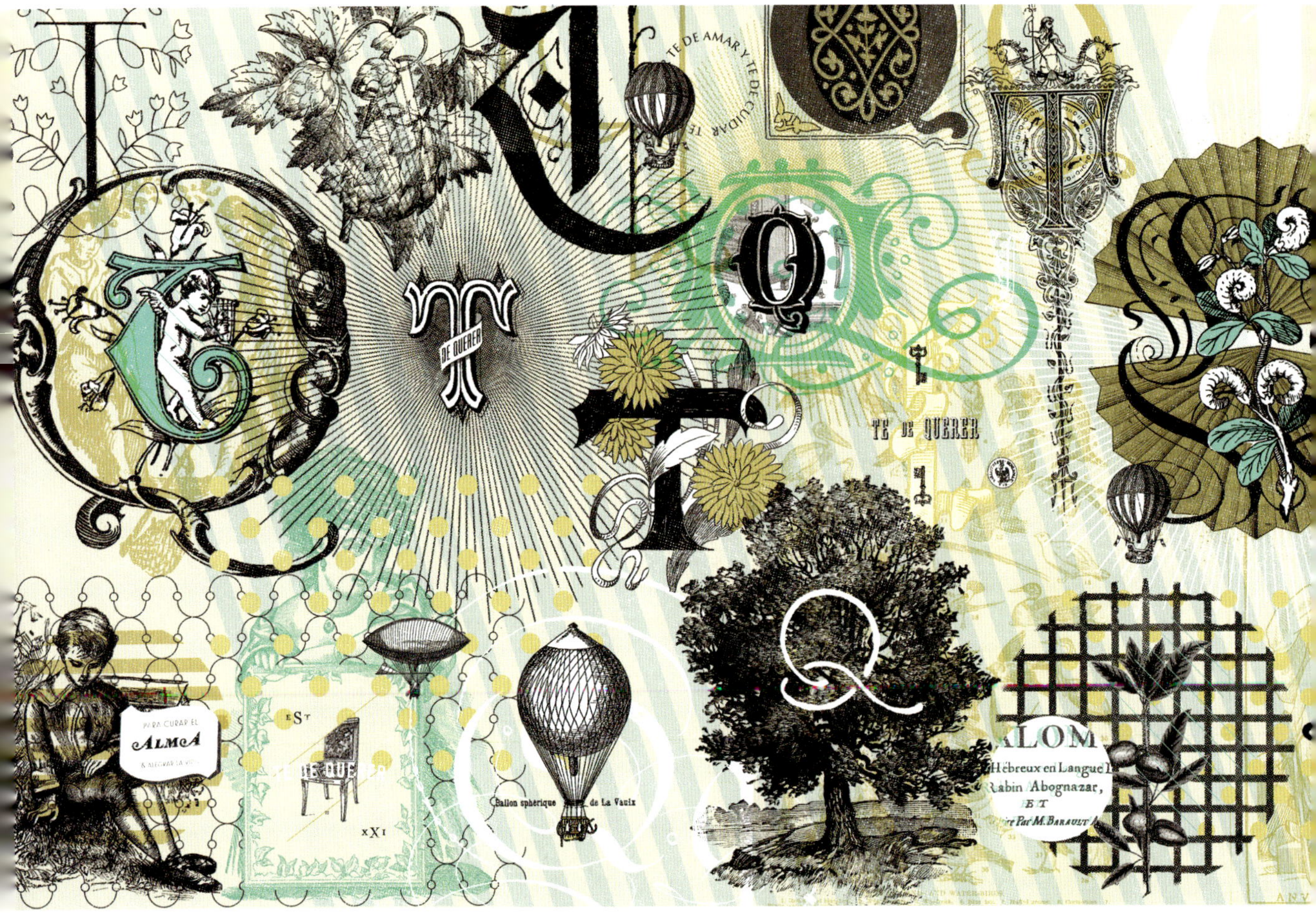

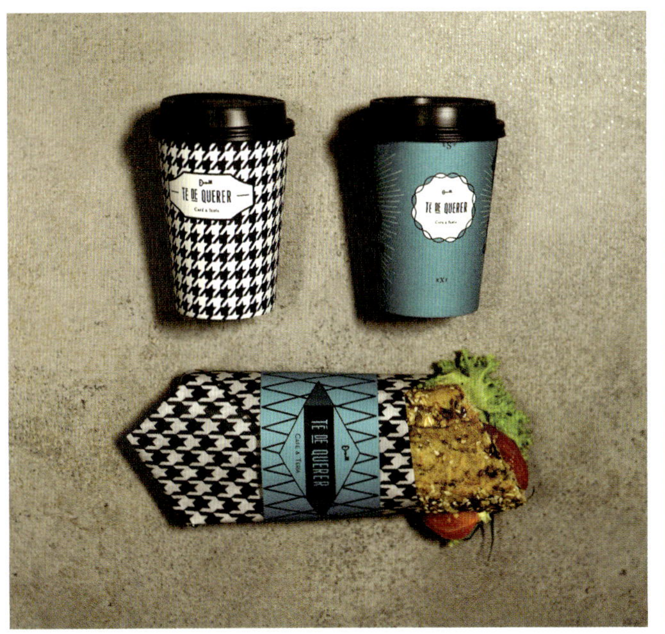
TÉ DE QUERER
TÉ DE QUERER
TÉ DE QUERER
CAFÉ & TERÍA

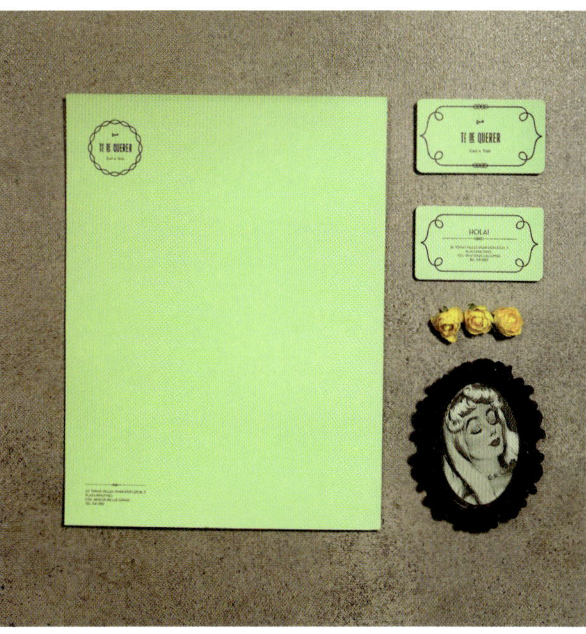
TÉ DE QUERER
HOLA!

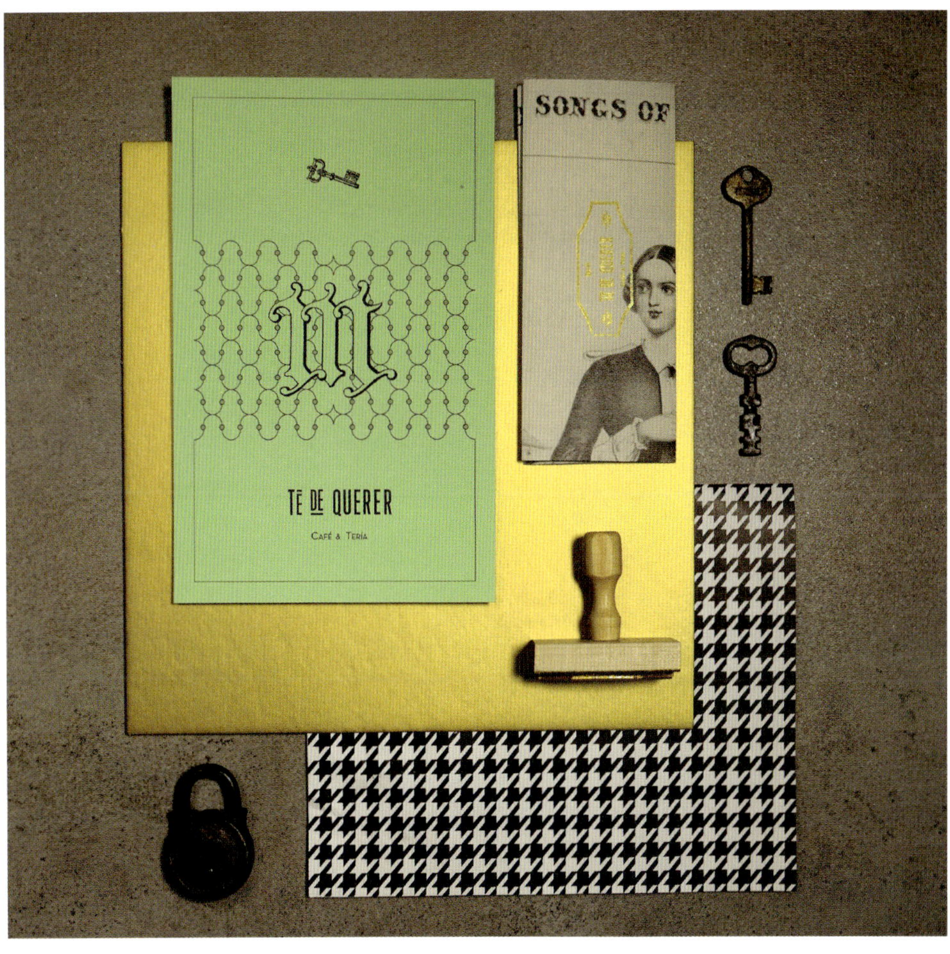
SONGS OF
TÉ DE QUERER
CAFÉ & TERÍA

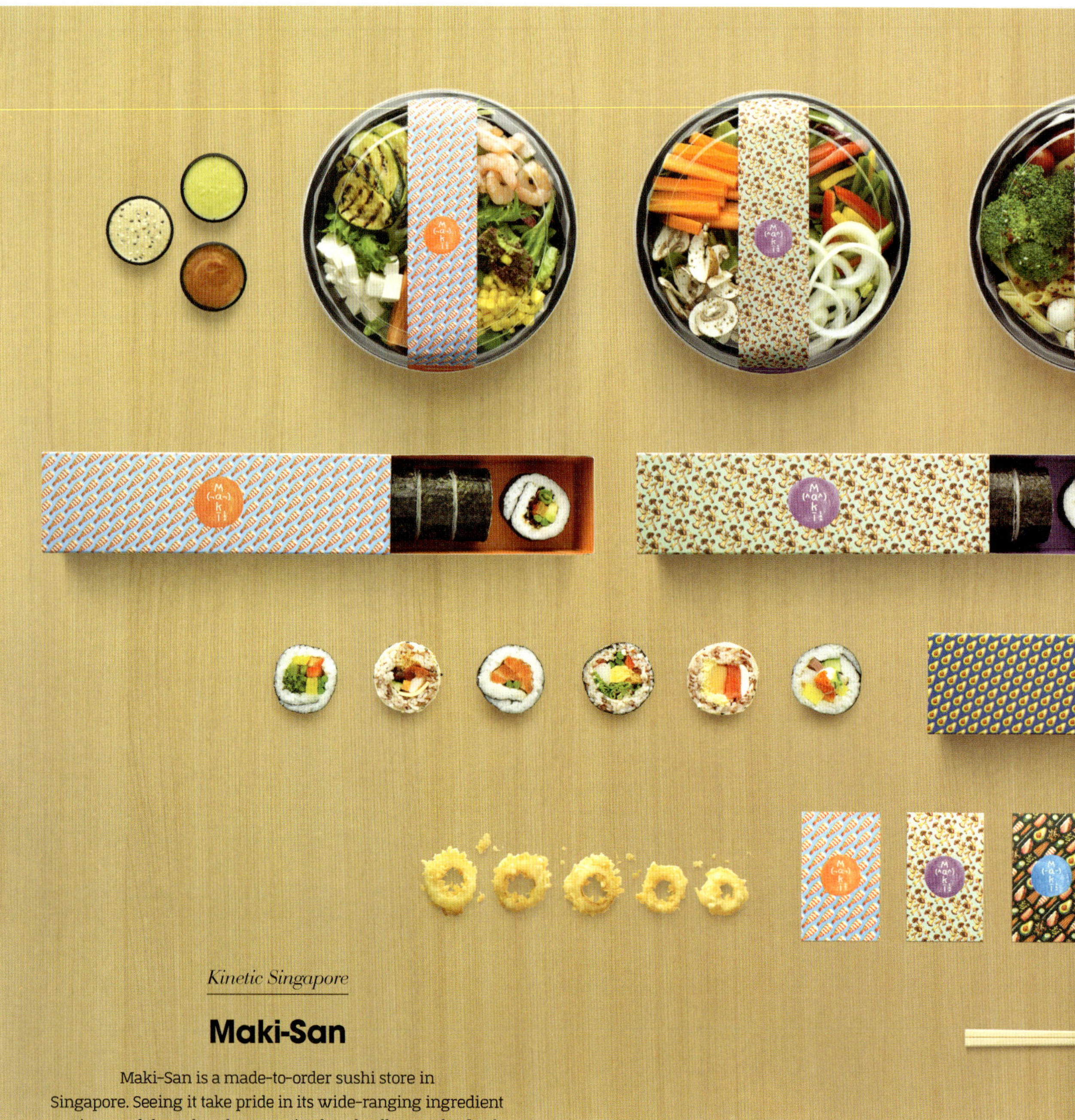

Kinetic Singapore

Maki-San

Maki-San is a made-to-order sushi store in Singapore. Seeing it take pride in its wide-ranging ingredient options and thus abundant creative hand-rolls, popular food and combinations were hand-drawn to deck the store's interior and communications. Selected usual culprits are personified into villains straight out of Japanese manga.

Client: Maki-San

Kinetic Singapore

Maki-San

Maki-San is a made-to-order sushi store in Singapore. Seeing it take pride in its wide-ranging ingredient options and thus abundant creative hand-rolls, popular food

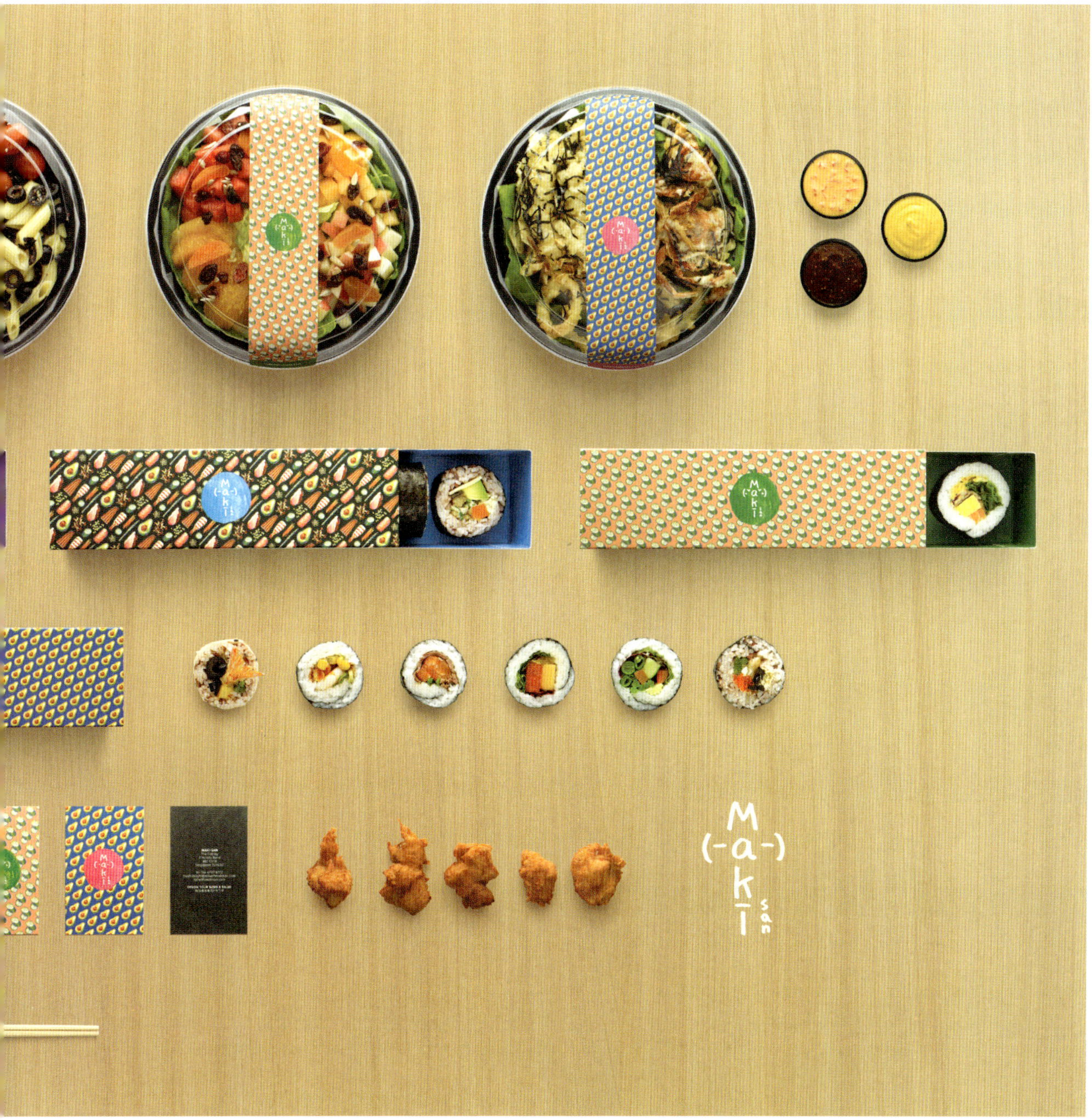

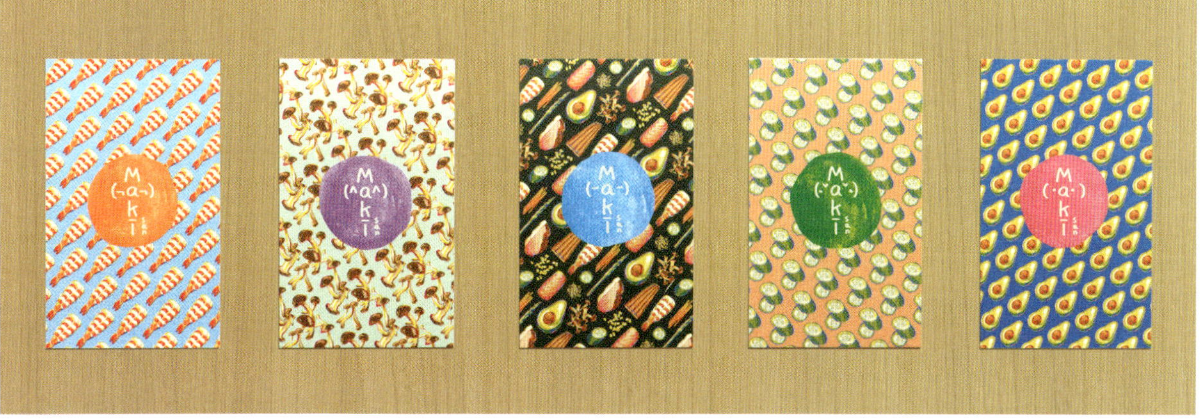

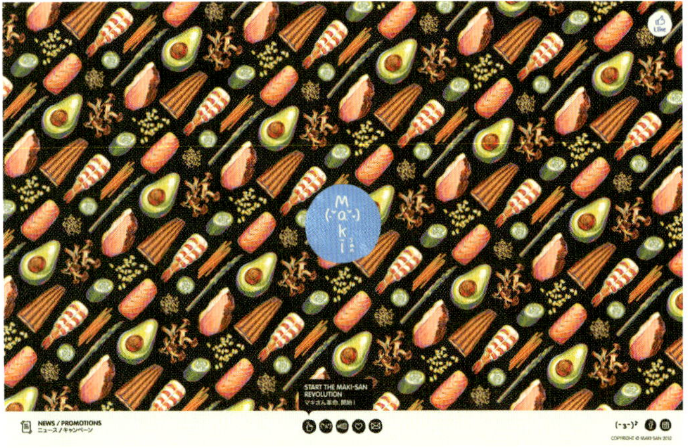
START THE MAKI-SAN REVOLUTION
NEWS / PROMOTIONS
ニュース / キャンペーン
COPYRIGHT © MAKI-SAN 2012

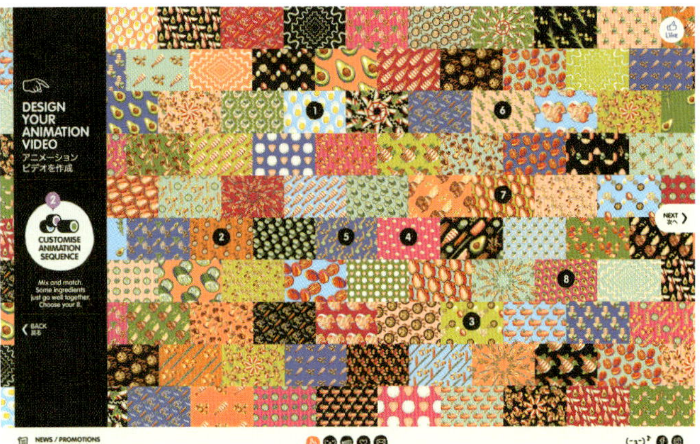
DESIGN YOUR ANIMATION VIDEO
アニメーション
ビデオを作成
CUSTOMISE ANIMATION SEQUENCE
Mix and match. Some ingredients just go well together. Choose your 8.
BACK
戻る
NEXT
NEWS / PROMOTIONS
ニュース / キャンペーン
COPYRIGHT © MAKI-SAN 2012

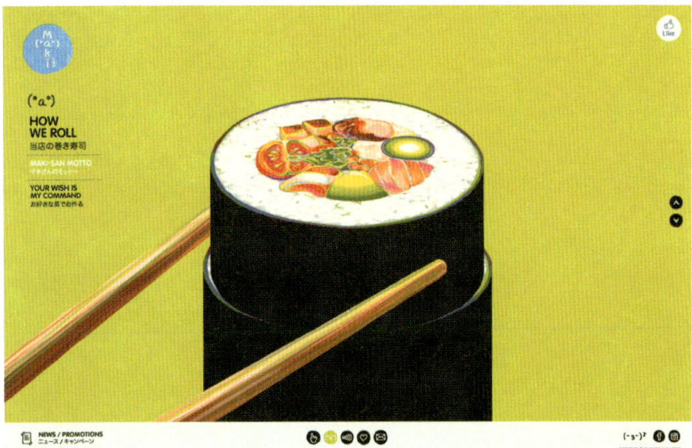
HOW WE ROLL
当店の巻き寿司
MAKI-SAN MOTTO
YOUR WISH IS MY COMMAND
お好きな具でお作る
NEWS / PROMOTIONS
ニュース / キャンペーン
COPYRIGHT © MAKI-SAN 2012

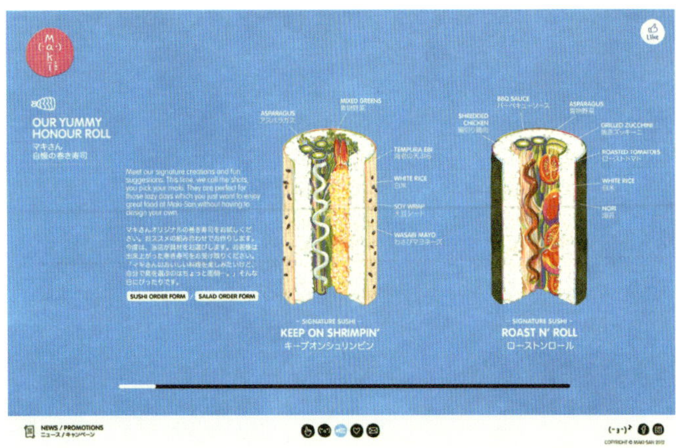
OUR YUMMY HONOUR ROLL
マキさん
自慢の巻き寿司
Meet our signature creations and fun suggestions. This time, we call the shots, you pick your maki. They are perfect for those lazy days which you just want to enjoy great food at Maki-San without having to design your own.
SUSHI ORDER FORM
SALAD ORDER FORM
ASPARAGUS
MIXED GREENS
TEMPURA EBI
WHITE RICE
SOY WRAP
WASABI MAYO
- SIGNATURE SUSHI -
KEEP ON SHRIMPIN'
キープオンシュリンピン
BBQ SAUCE
SHREDDED CHICKEN
ASPARAGUS
GRILLED ZUCCHINI
ROASTED TOMATOES
WHITE RICE
NORI
- SIGNATURE SUSHI -
ROAST N' ROLL
ローストンロール
NEWS / PROMOTIONS
ニュース / キャンペーン
COPYRIGHT © MAKI-SAN 2012

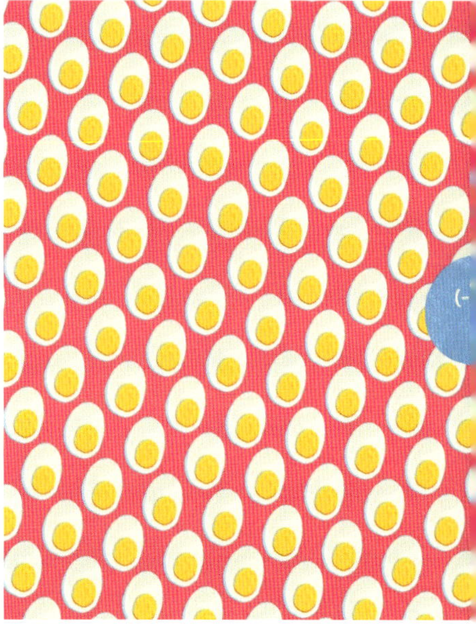

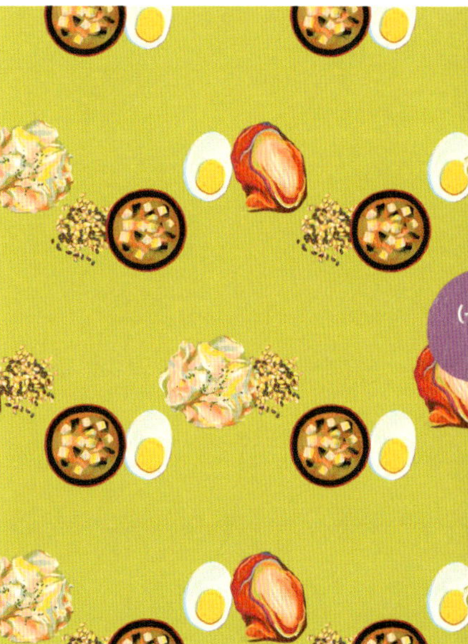

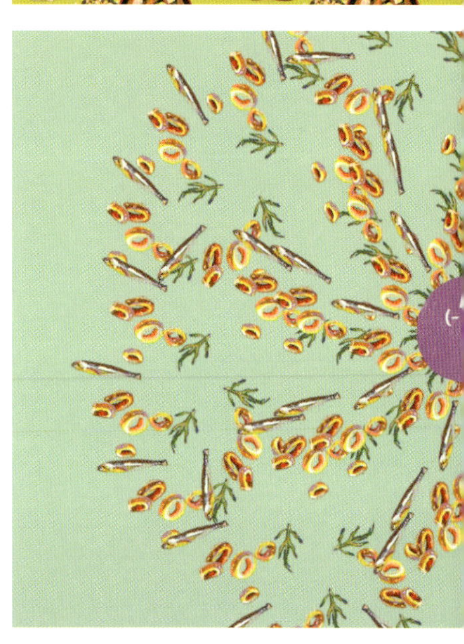

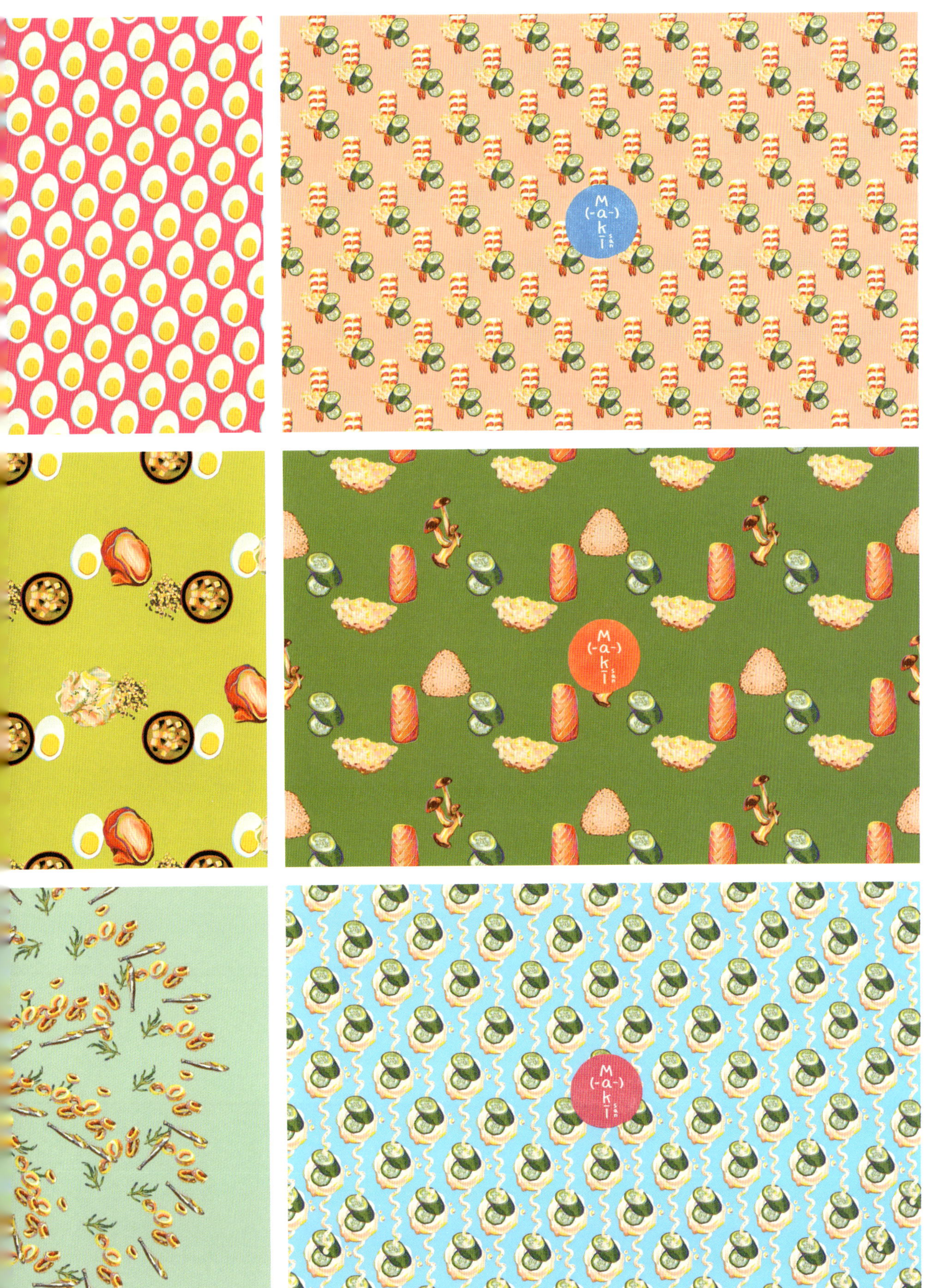
M
(-a-)
k
i
san

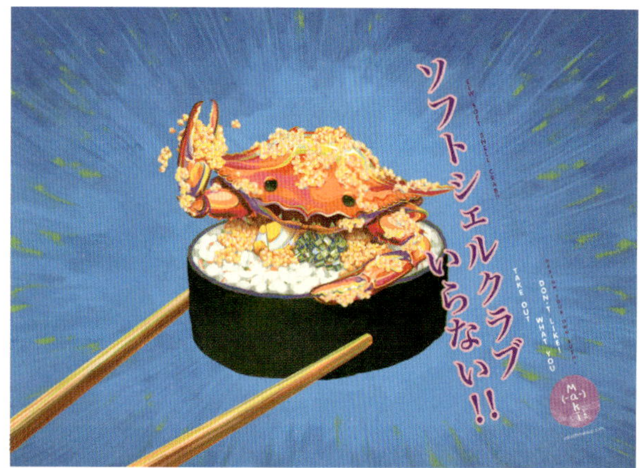
ソフトシェルクラブいらない!!
DON'T LIKE? TAKE OUT WHAT YOU
Ma(-_-)ki

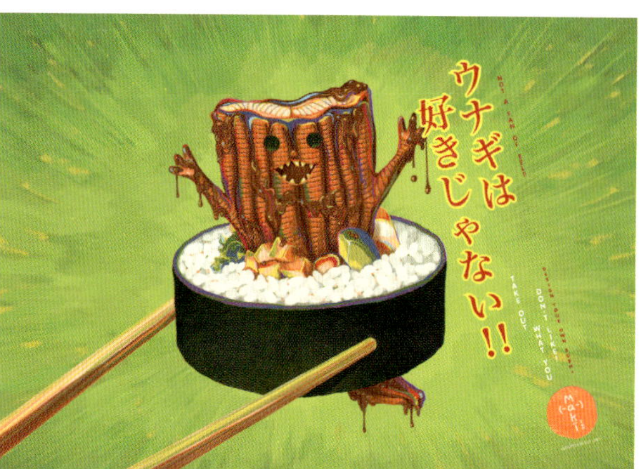
ウナギは好きじゃない!!
DON'T LIKE? TAKE OUT WHAT YOU
Ma(-_-)ki

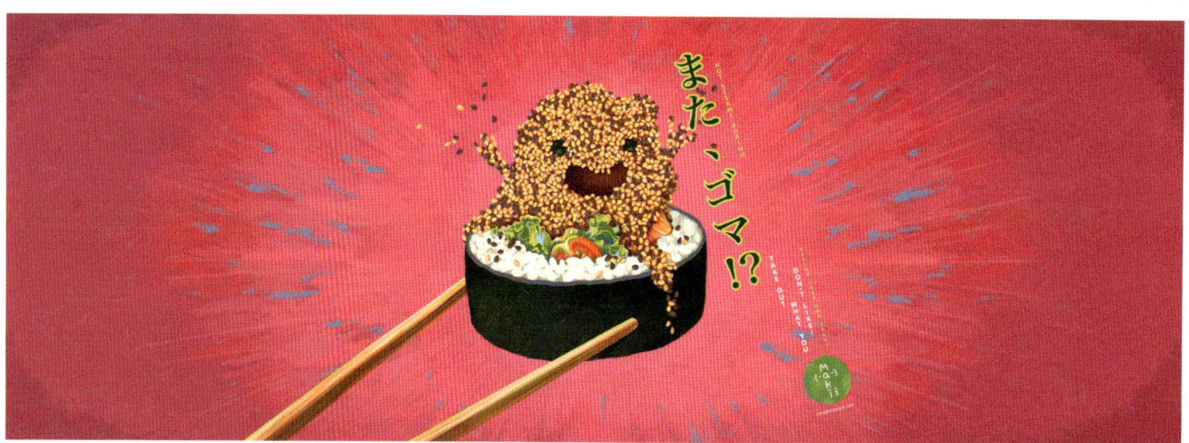
また、ゴマ!?
DON'T LIKE? TAKE OUT WHAT YOU
Ma(-_-)ki

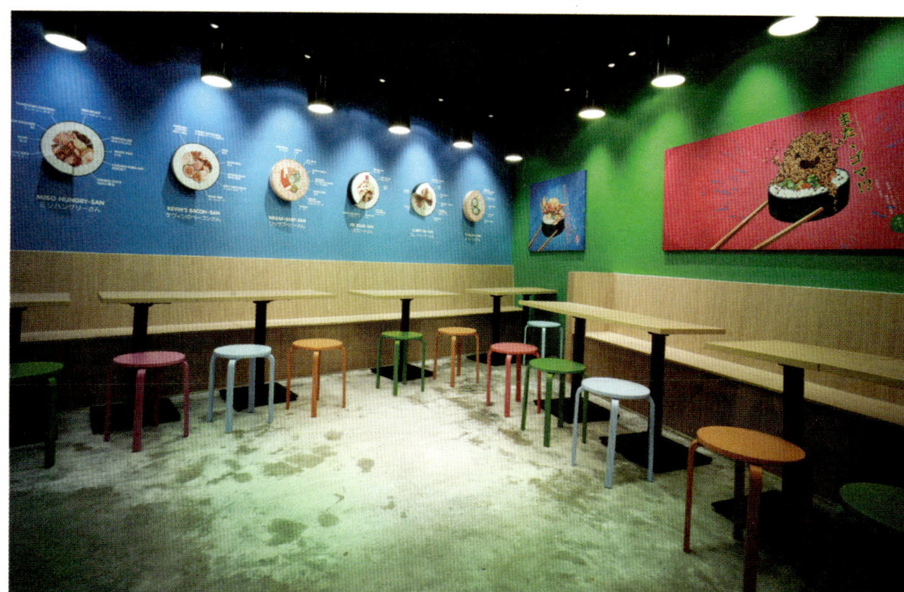
MISO HUNGRY-SAN
ミソハングリーさん
KEVIN'S BACON-SAN
また、ゴマ!?

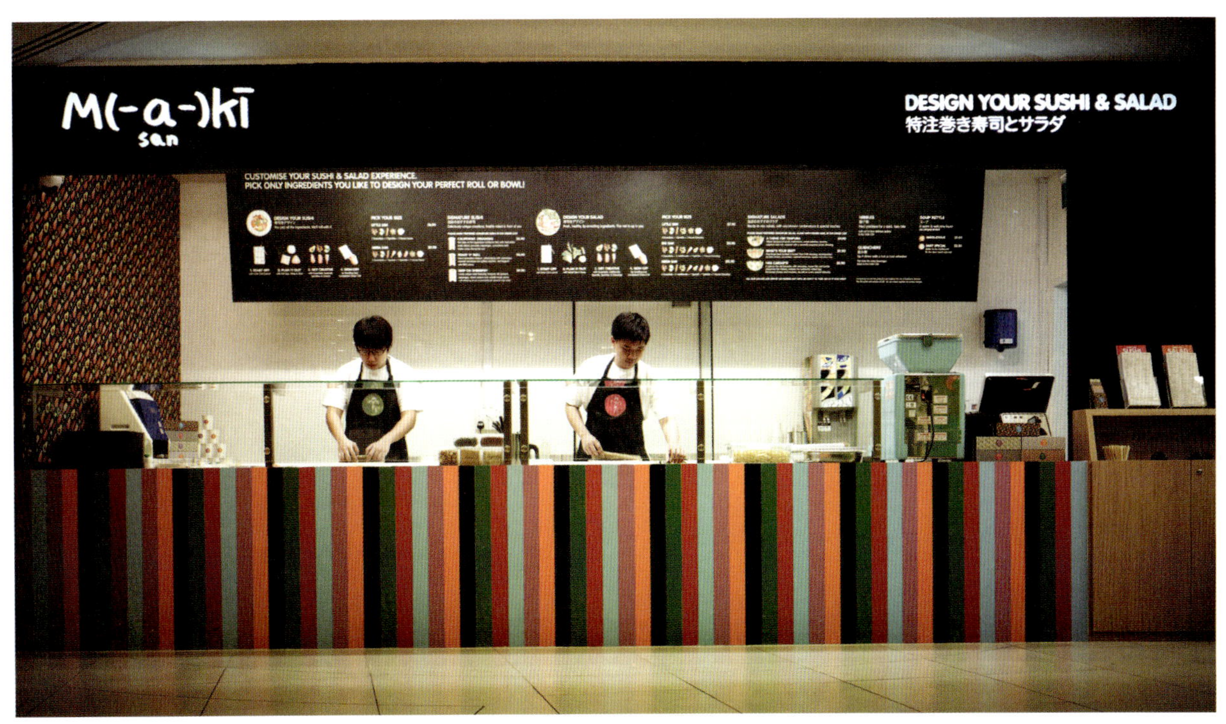
M(-a-)kī
san
DESIGN YOUR SUSHI & SALAD
特注巻き寿司とサラダ
CUSTOMISE YOUR SUSHI & SALAD EXPERIENCE.
PICK ONLY INGREDIENTS YOU LIKE TO DESIGN YOUR PERFECT ROLL OR BOWL!

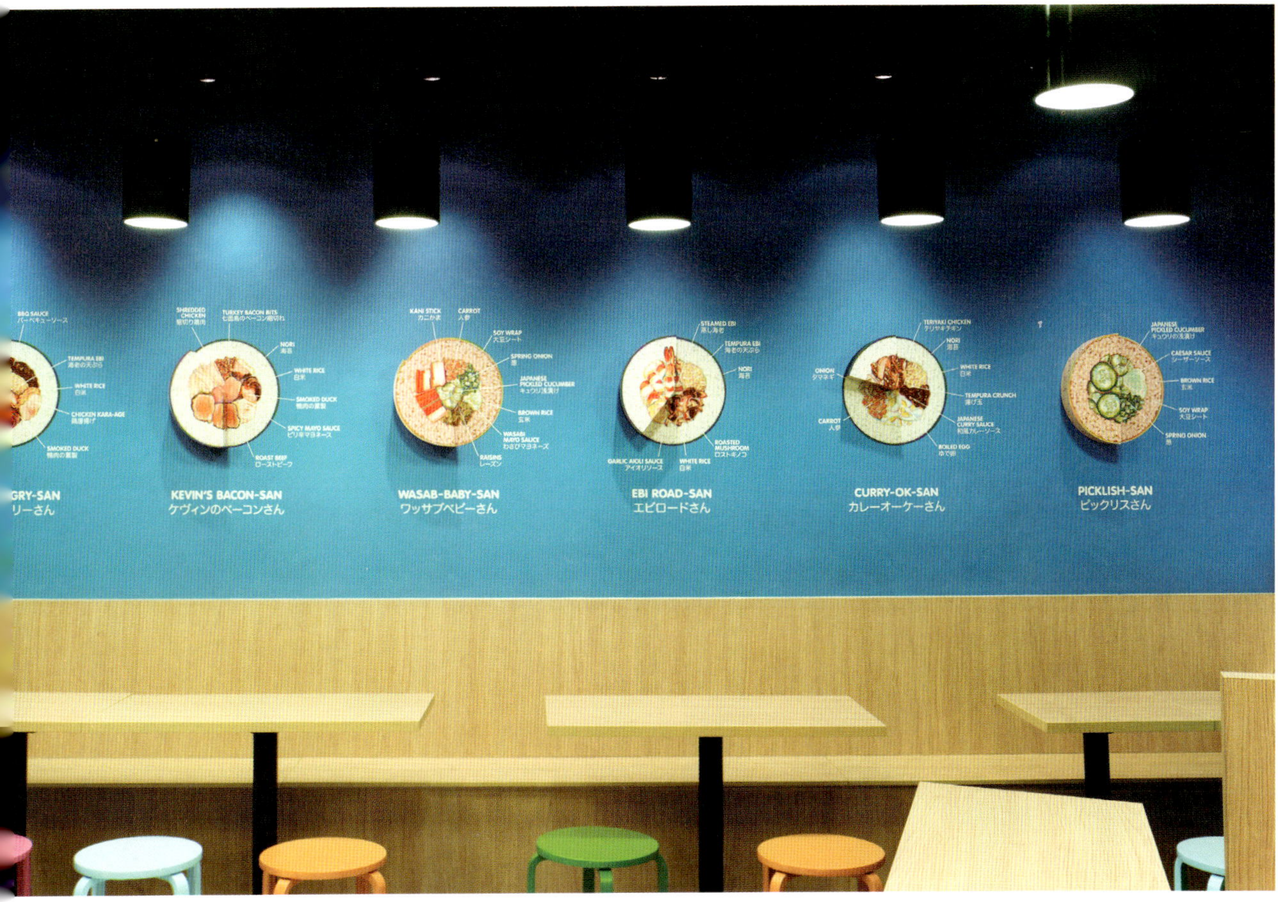

Launched by Shinsegae Department Store in 2012, SSG Food Market is one of South Korea's premier indoor food markets. To celebrate its first anniversary, a refreshing and scrumptious-looking visual identity is conceived to stir the festive air from brand communications to in-store promotion.

Art Direction: Hyojung Ryu
Design: Hyojung Ryu, Jooyeon Oh
Client: SSG Food Market

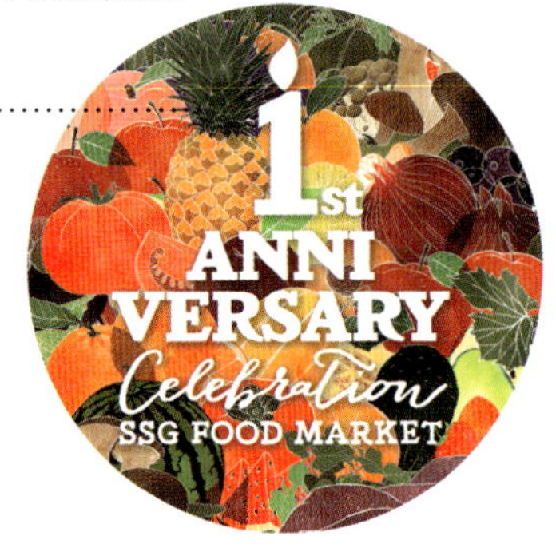

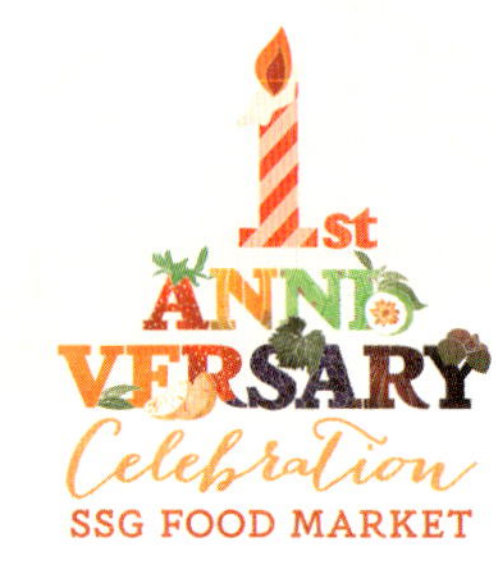

Shinsegae Graphic Design

SSG Food Market

Launched by Shinsegae Department Store in 2012, SSG Food Market is one of South Korea's premier indoor food markets. To celebrate its first anniversary, a refreshing and scrumptious-looking visual identity is conceived to stir the festive air from brand communications to in-store promotion.

Art Direction: Hyojung Ryu
Design: Hyojung Ryu, Jooyeon Oh
Client: SSG Food Market

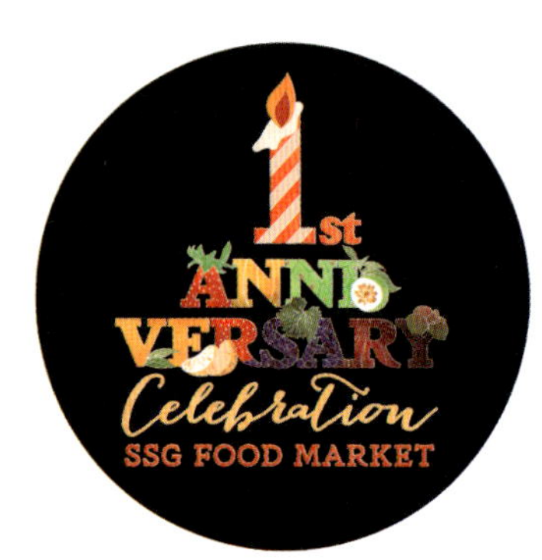

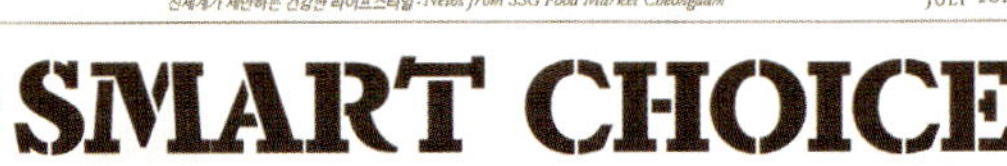

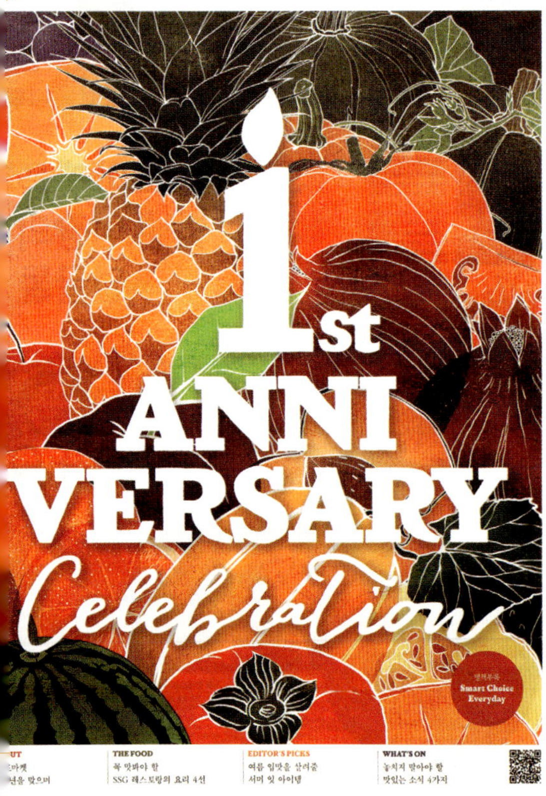

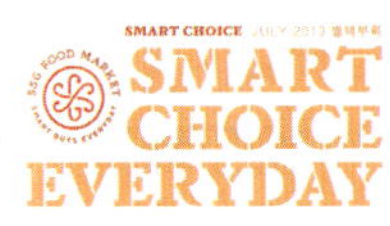

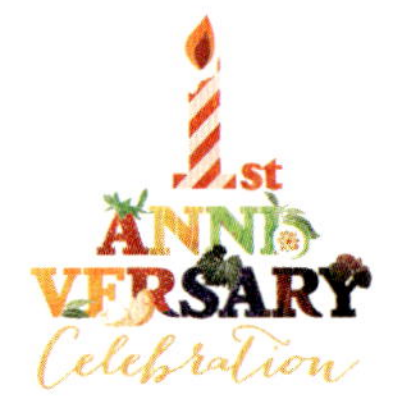

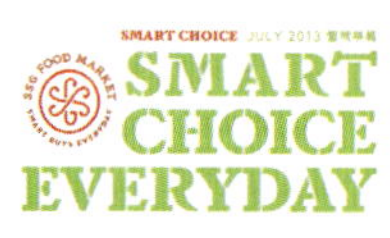

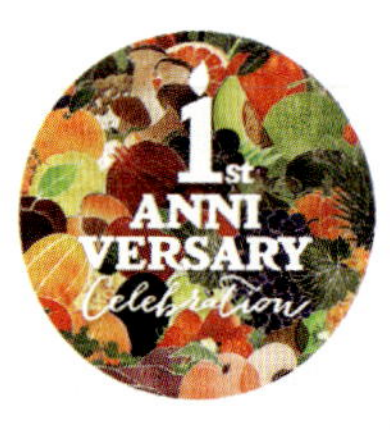

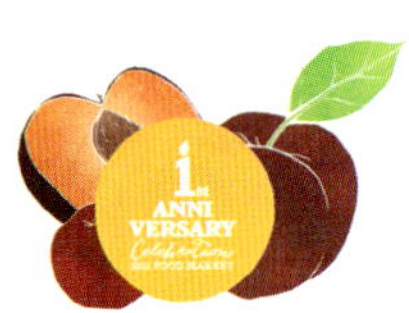

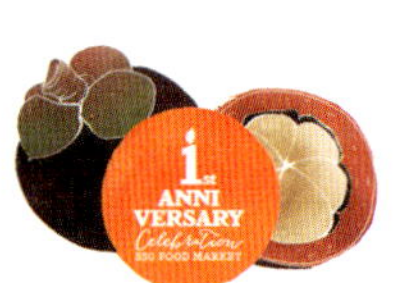

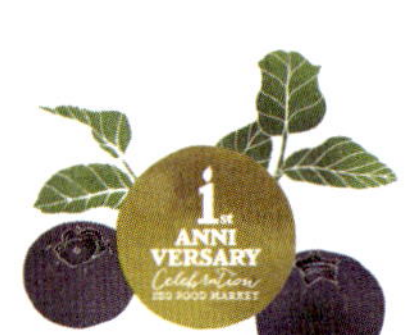

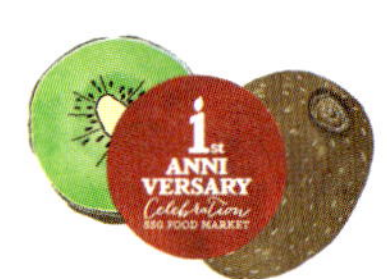

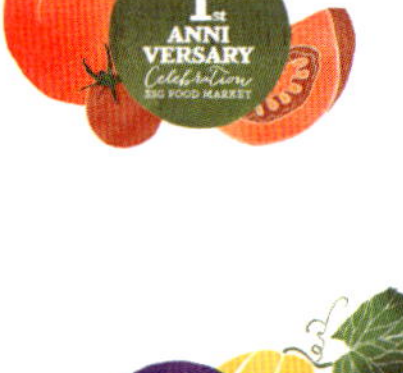

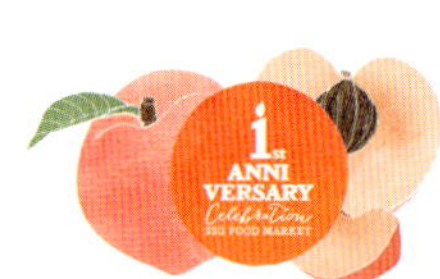

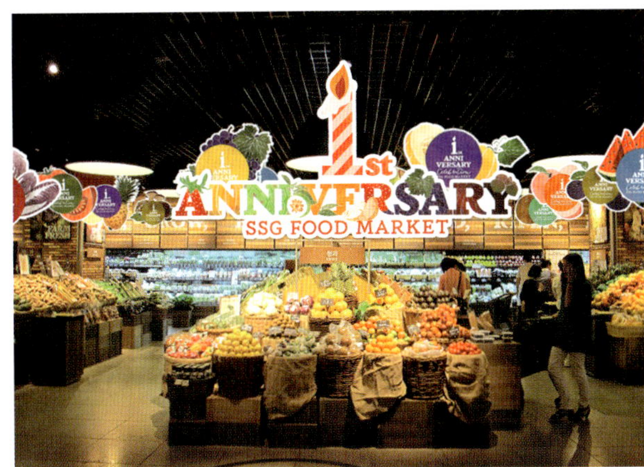
1st
ANNIVERSARY
SSG FOOD MARKET

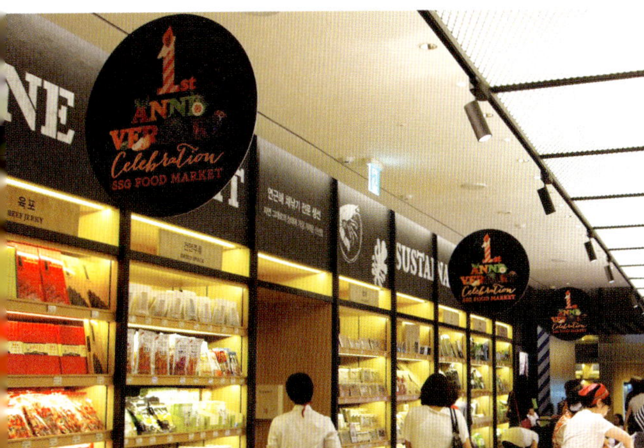
1st
ANNI
VERSARY
Celebration
SSG FOOD MARKET

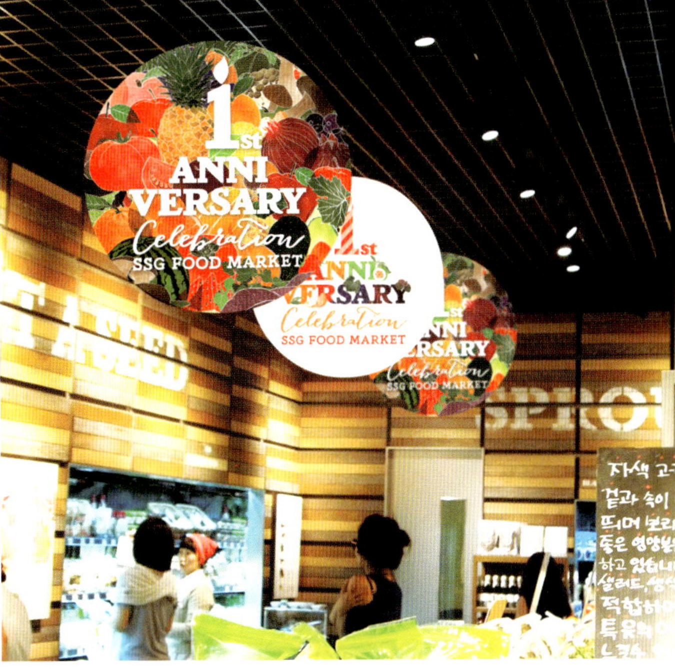
1st
ANNI
VERSARY
Celebration
SSG FOOD MARKET

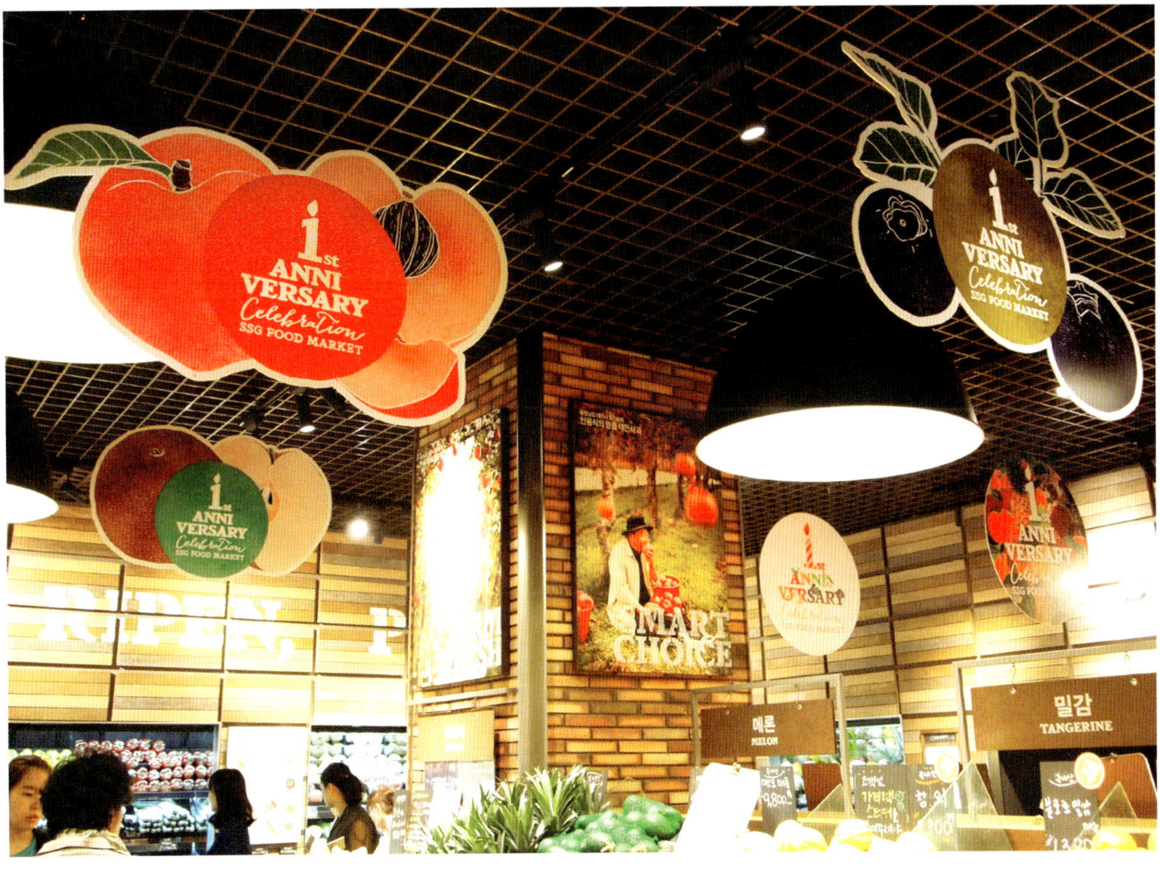

El Aguafuerte is a restaurant and bar located in Hotel San Juan, a historical site in the city of Chihuahua. Estudio Yeyé dips into original graphical resource to convey the weight of the venue, together with the rural Mexican drunk story told through curiosities put on display.

Special credits: Labor Studio, Gerardo Vargas, Francisco Leon

Estudio Yeyé

El Aguafuerte

El Aguafuerte is a restaurant and bar located in Hotel San Juan, a historical site in the city of Chihuahua. Estudio Yeyé dips into original graphical resource to convey the weight of the venue, together with the rural Mexican drunk story told through curiosities put on display.

Special credits: Labor Studio, Gerardo Vargas, Francisco Leon

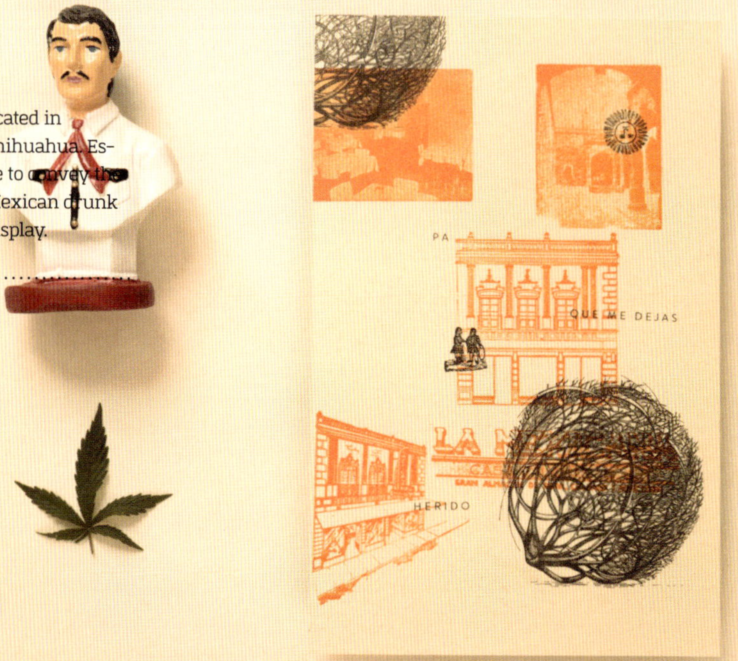

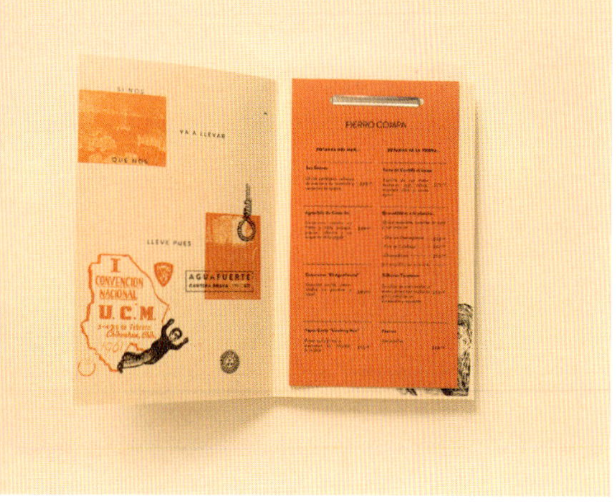

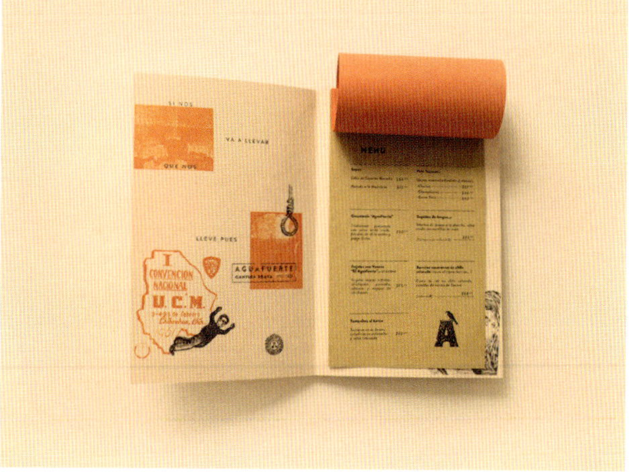

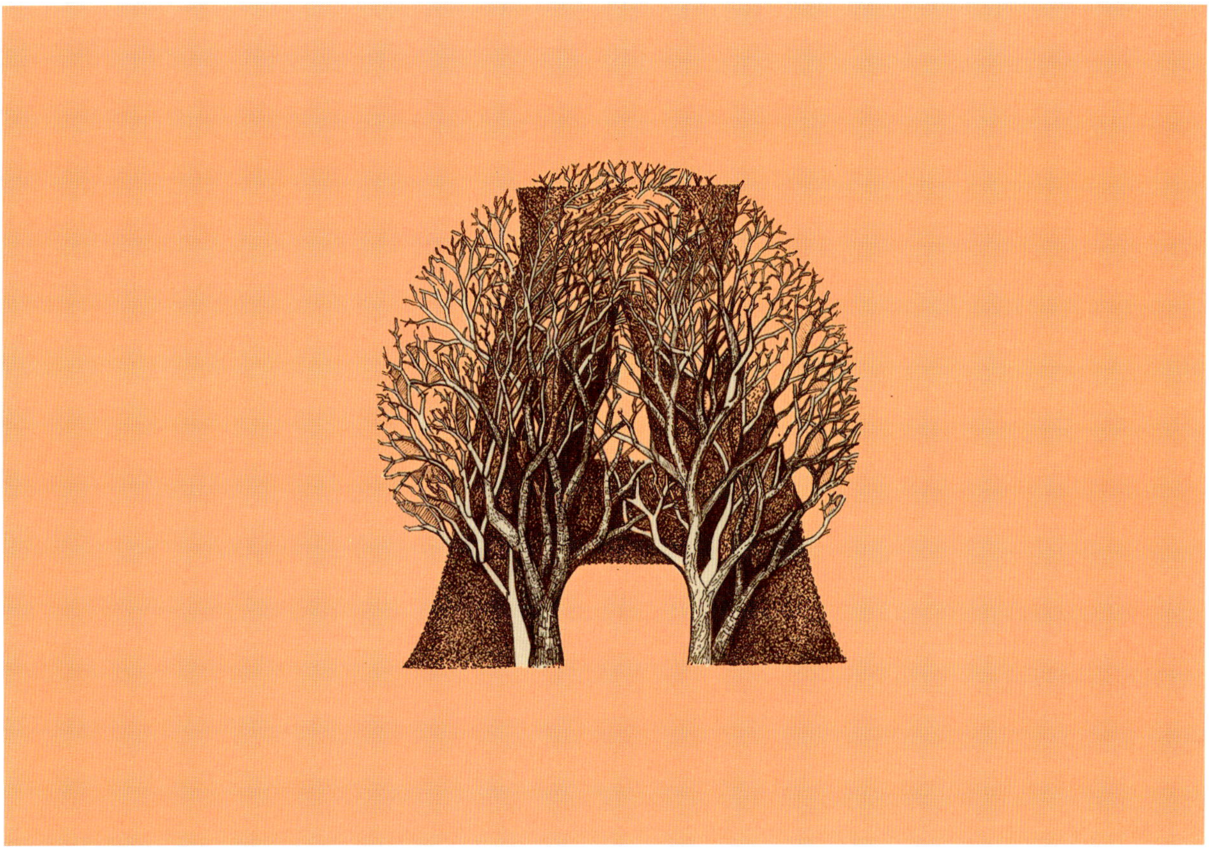

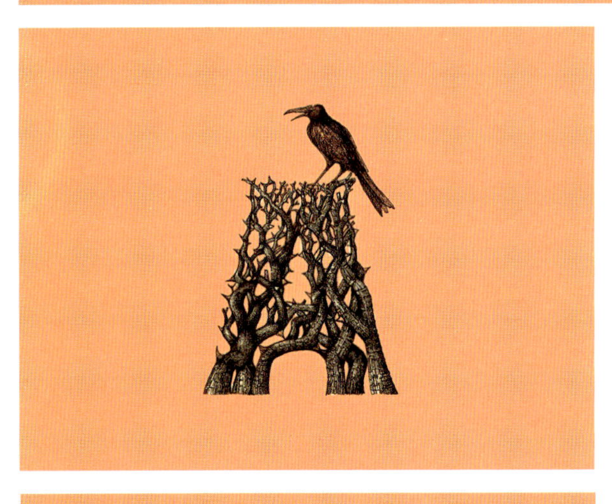

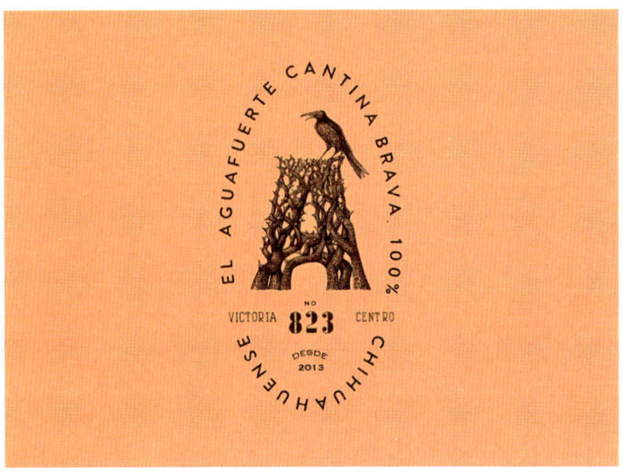
EL AGUAFUERTE CANTINA BRAVA. 100% CHIHUAHUENSE
VICTORIA
NO
823
CENTRO
DESDE
2013

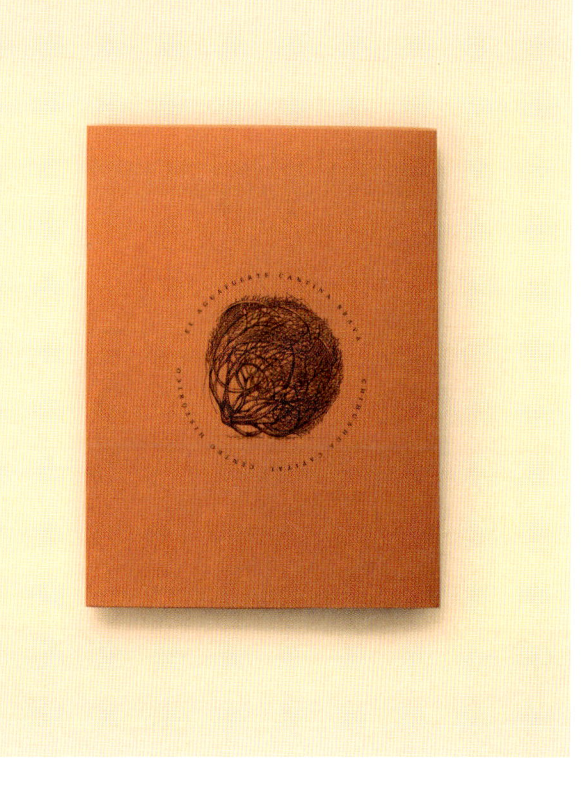

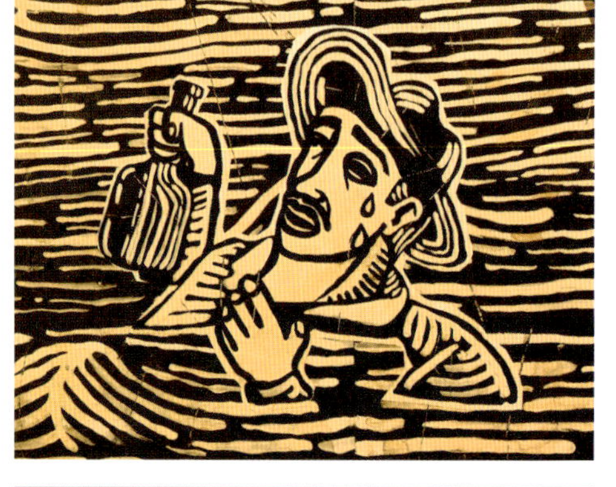

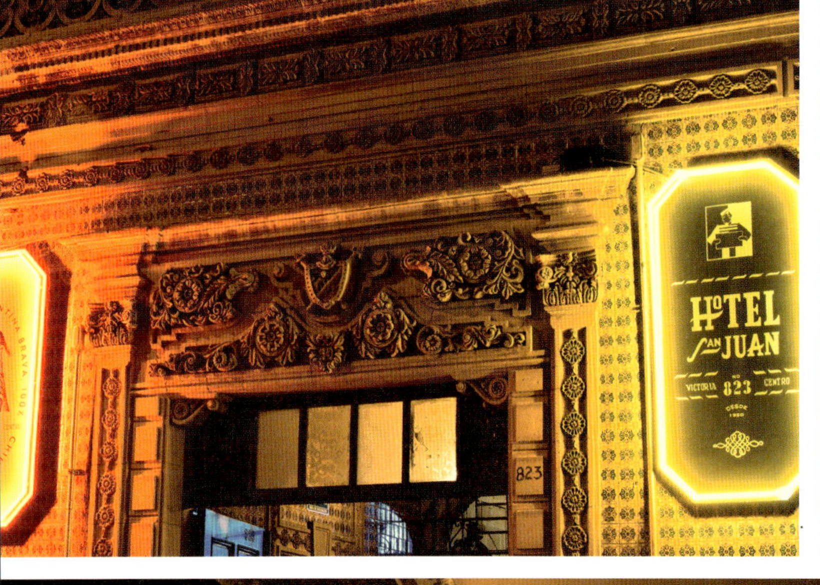
HOTEL
SAN JUAN
VICTORIA
823
CENTRO
823

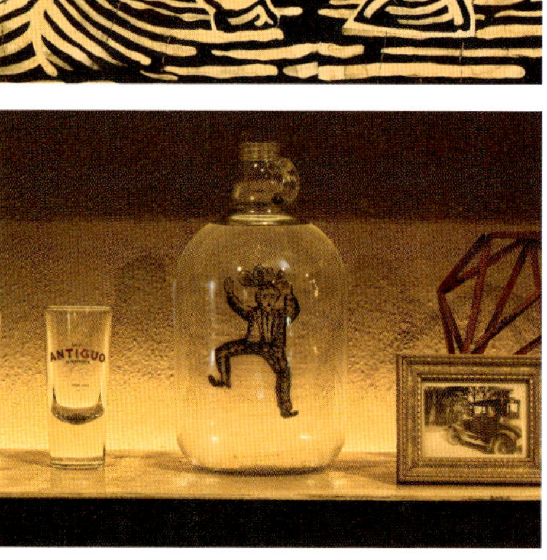
ANTIGUO

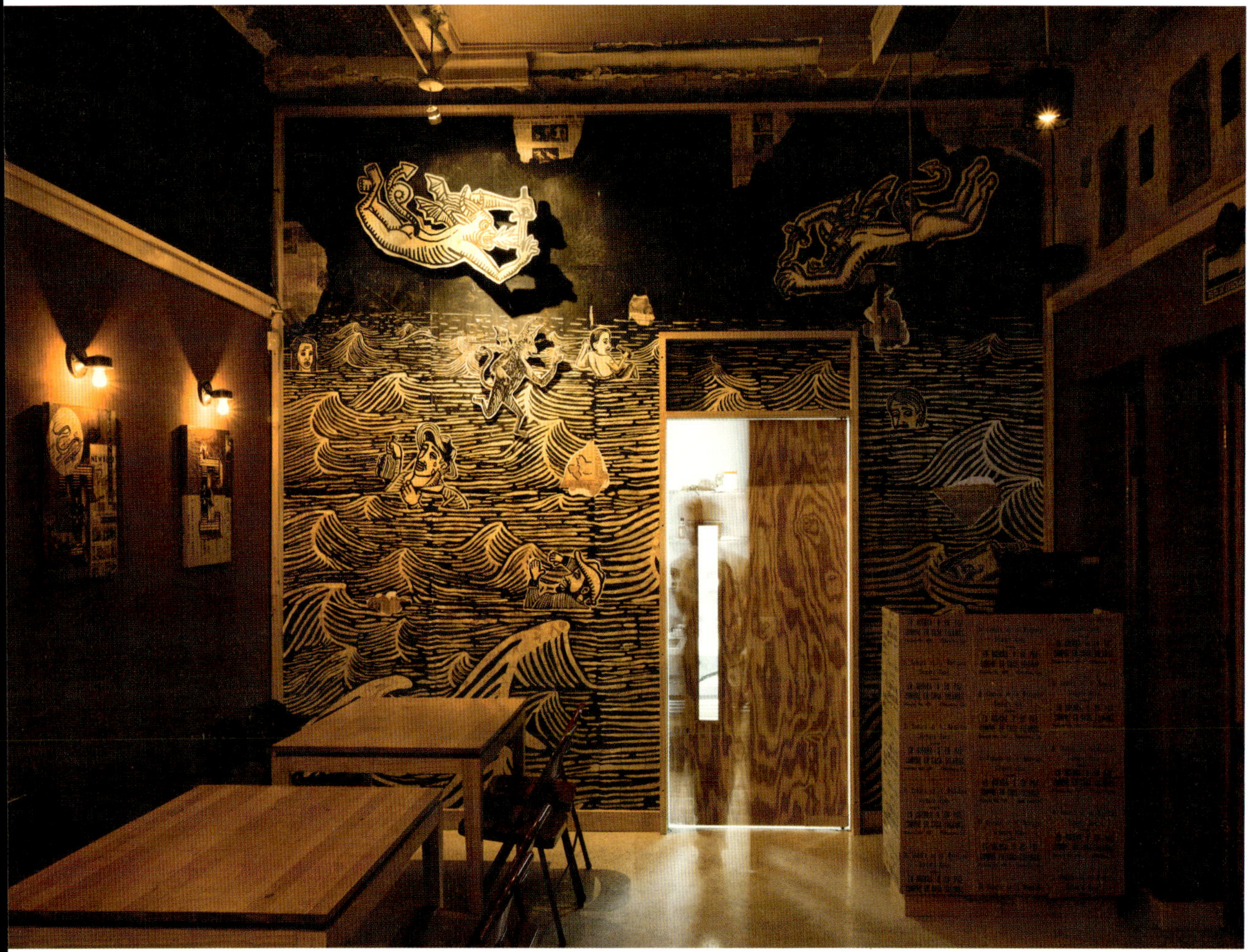

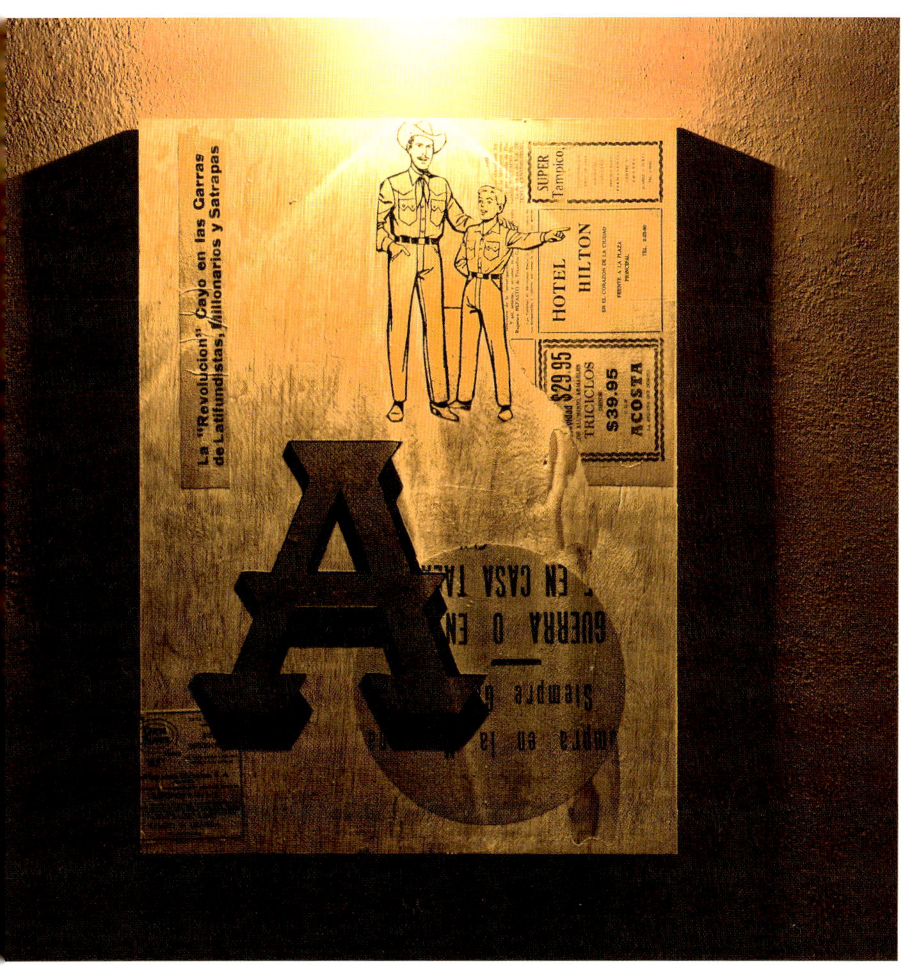
La "Revolución" Cayo en las Garras
de Latifundistas, Millonarios y Satrapas
HOTEL
HILTON
TRICICLOS
$39.95
ACOSTA

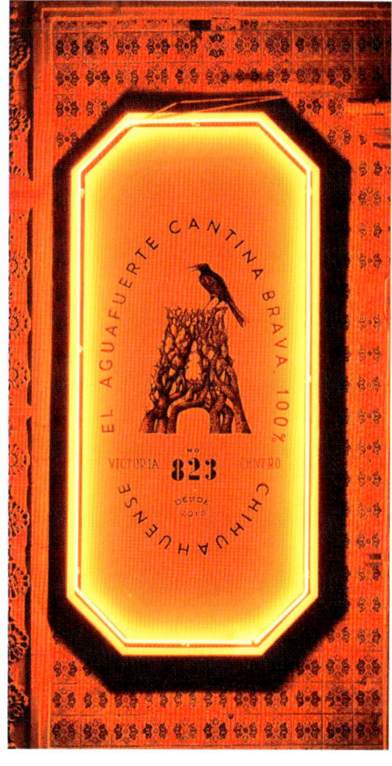
EL AGUAFUERTE CANTINA BRAVA 100% CHIHUAHUENSE
823

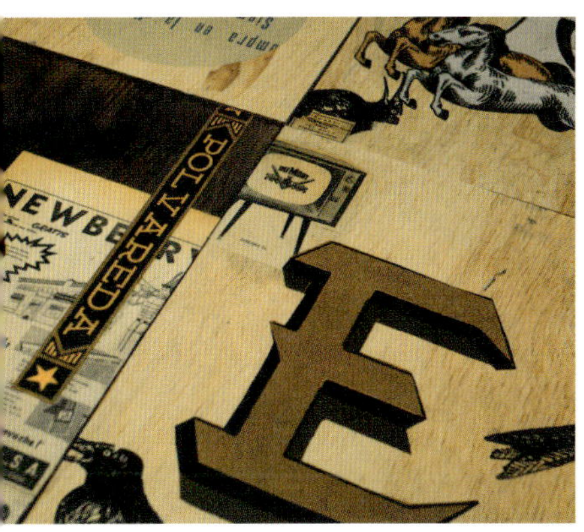
POLVAREDA

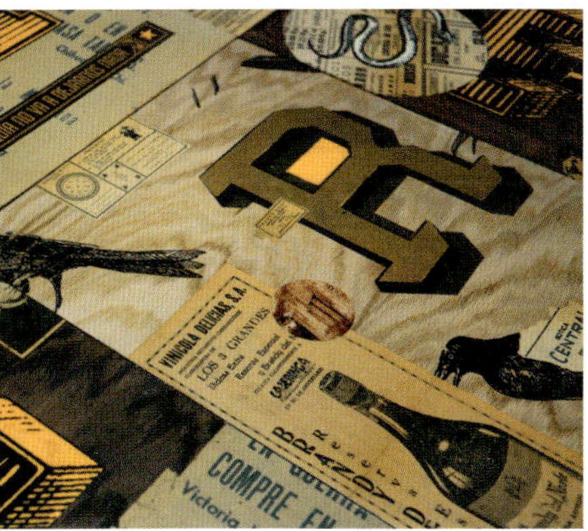

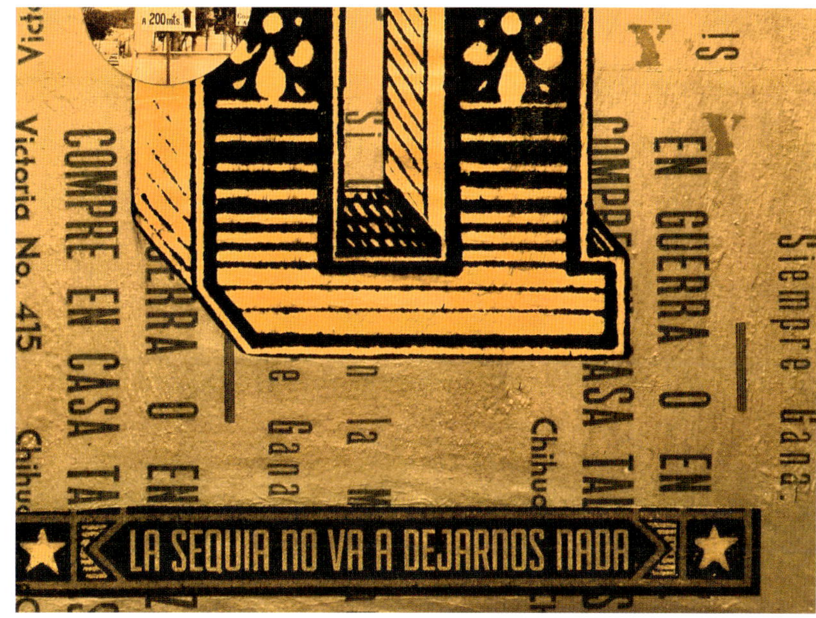
Victoria No. 415
COMPRE EN CASA
EN GUERRA O EN
Siempre Gana
LA SEQUIA NO VA A DEJARNOS NADA

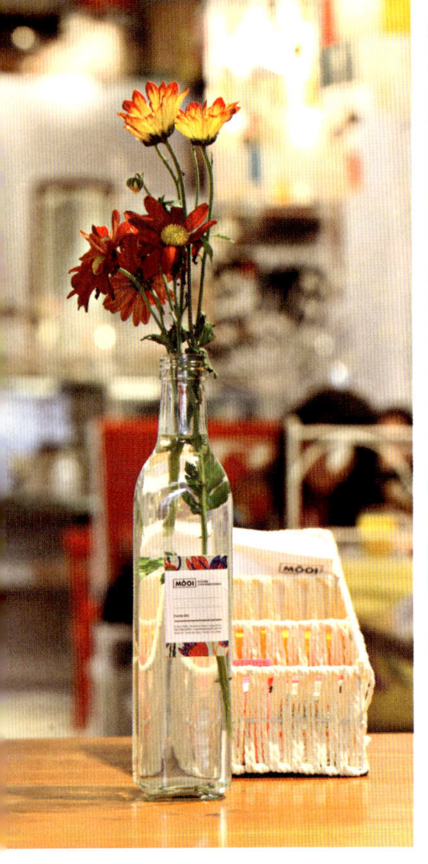

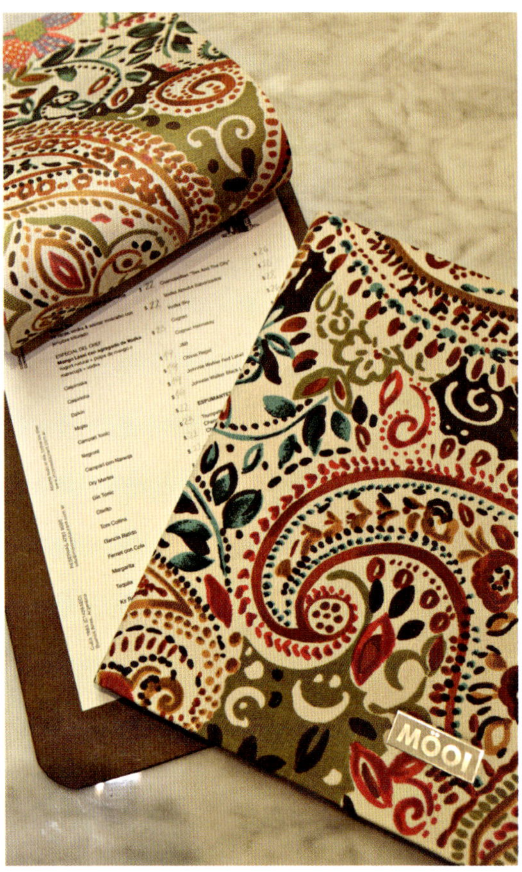

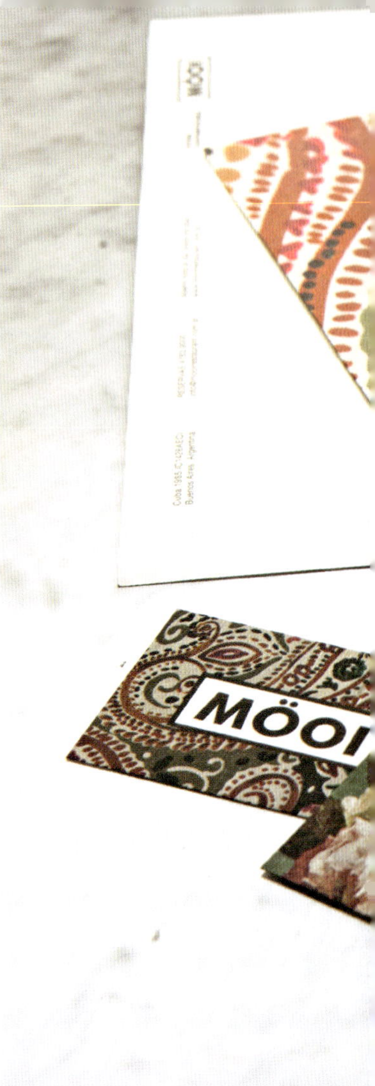

SeventhDesign™

Möoi

Möoi is set to introduce contemporaneous food to Buenos Aires. This wave has been merged in this project with themes fusing shapes, cultural influences, colours and textures. From visual identity to interior fixtures, the strong brand image matches its menu and locale in Belgrano town.

Photo: Mauro Roll
Client: Grupo Multifood
Special credits: María José Rojas

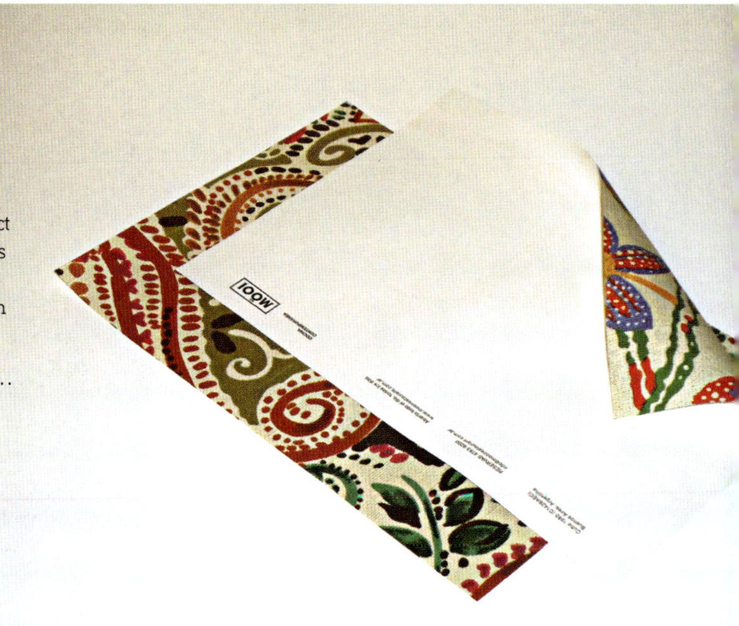

SeventhDesign™

Möoi

Möoi is set to introduce contemporaneous food to Buenos Aires. This wave has been merged in this project with themes fusing shapes, cultural influences, colours

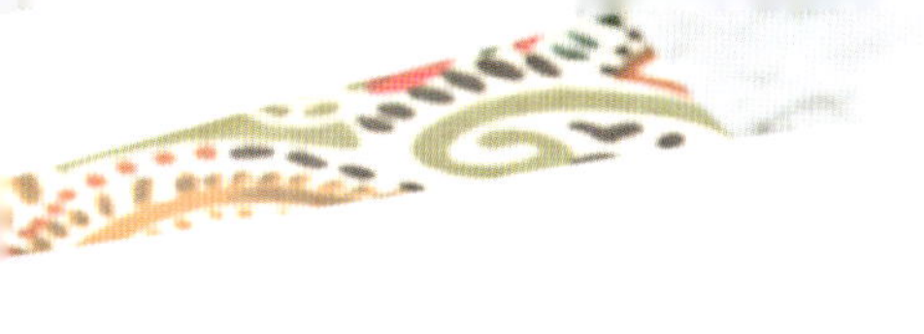

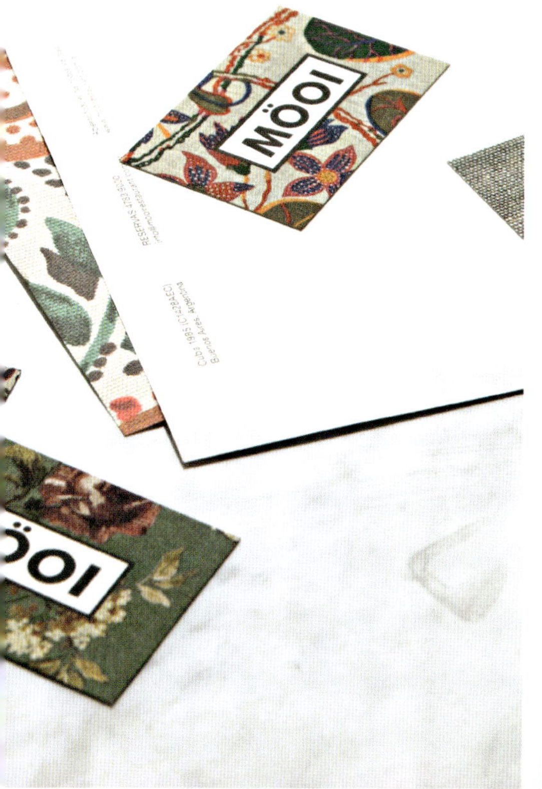
MÖOI
MÖOI

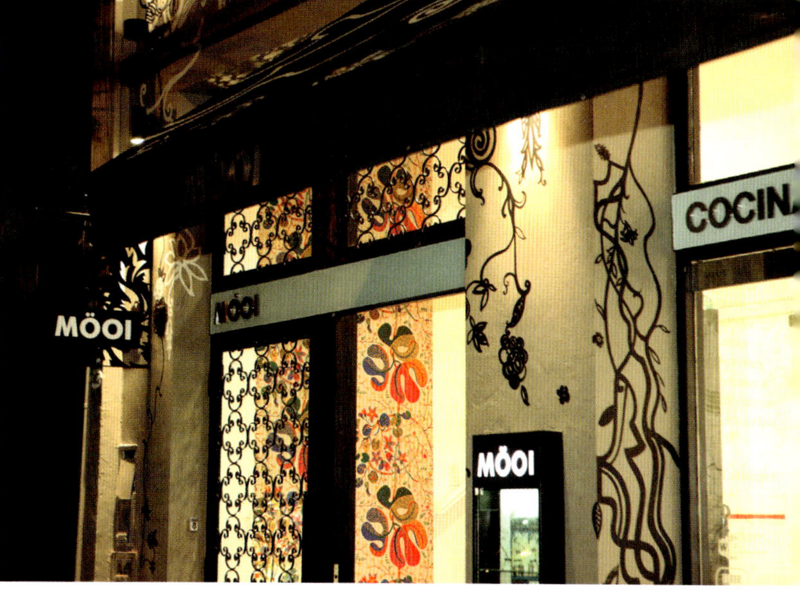
MÖOI
MÖOI
MÖOI
COCIN

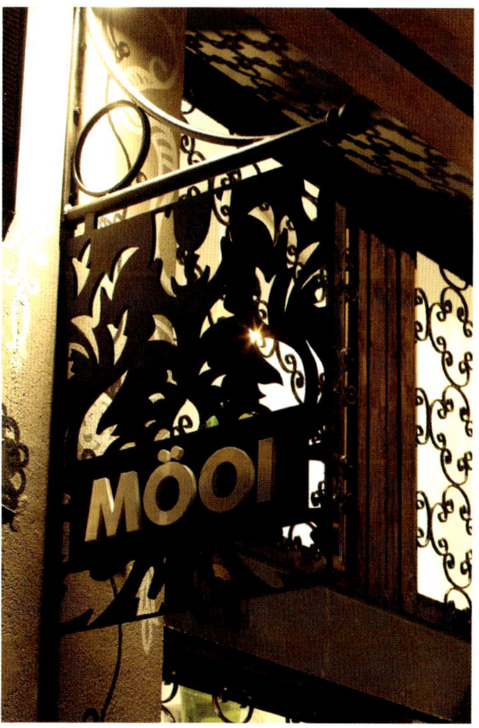
MÖOI

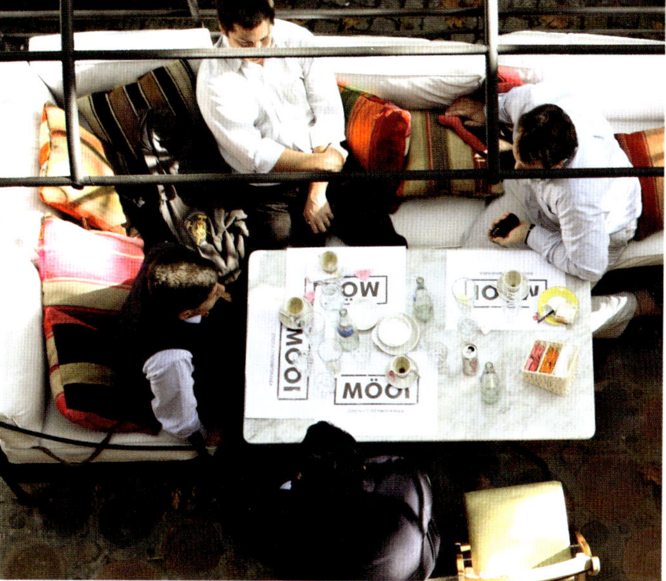
MÖOI

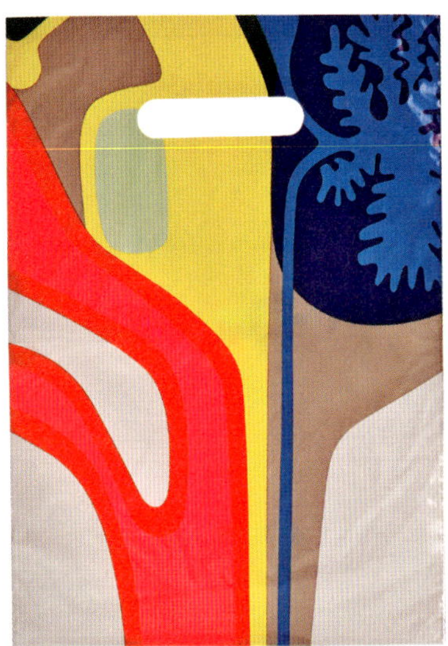

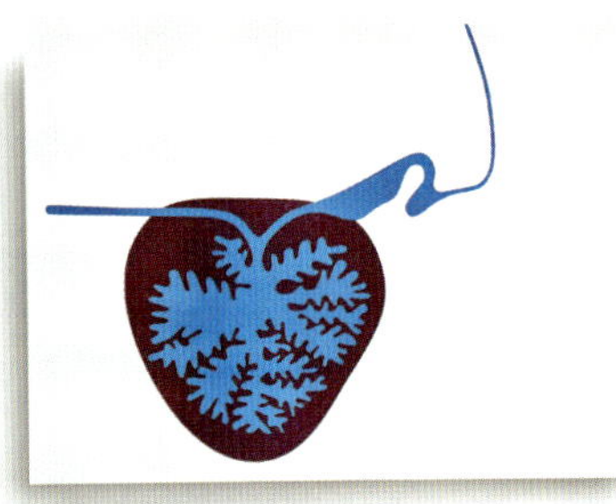

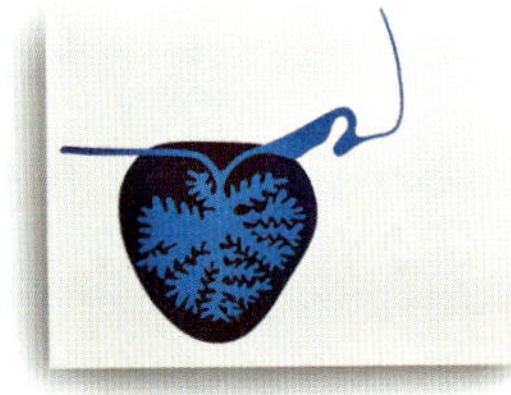

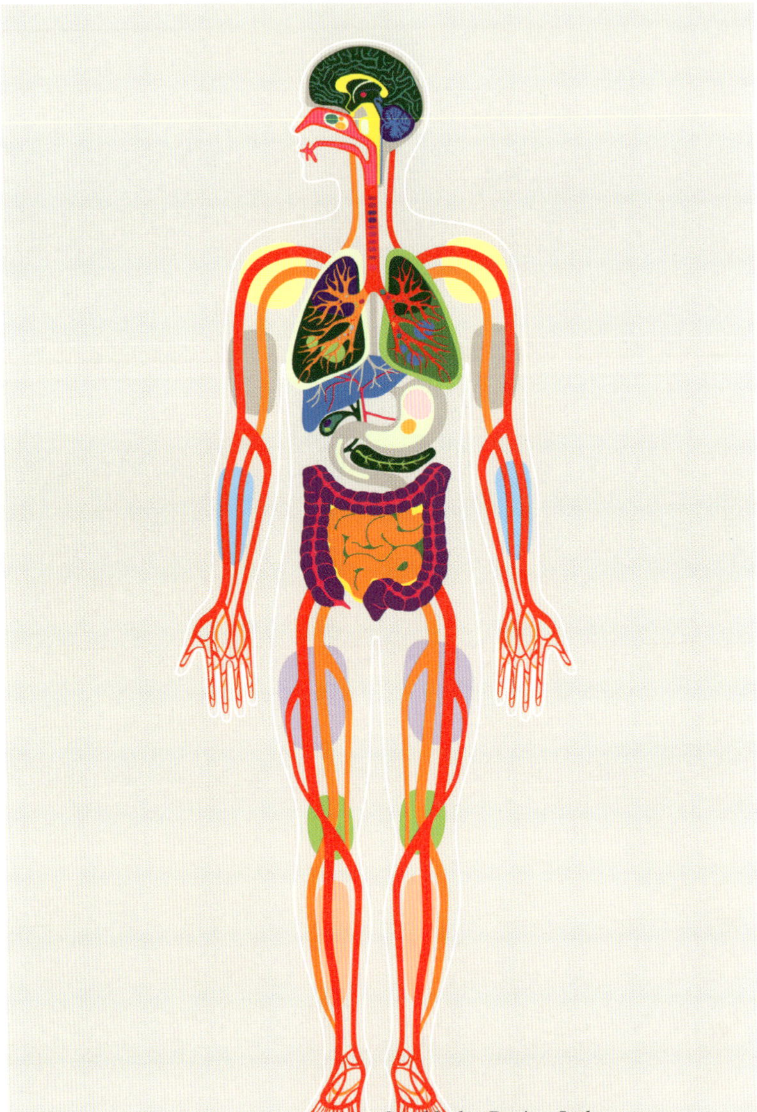

Stockholm Design Lab

Vårdapoteket

A broad, vibrant palette and graphic illustrations celebrates the miracle of the human body while distinguishing Vårdapoteket from other typical clinics and pharmacies in the Swedish scene. Human organs characterised by anatomical and botanical illustrations are set to establish a stronger link with its customers than happy family imagery.

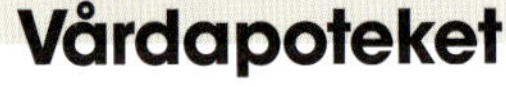

Illustration: Kari Moden
Interior: Urban Design Architects
Client: Vårdapoteket

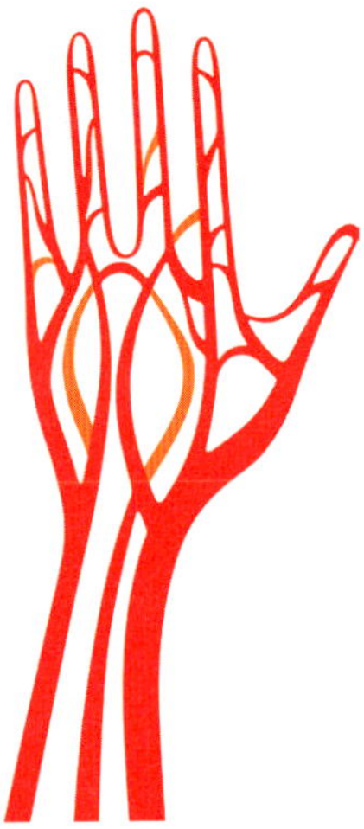

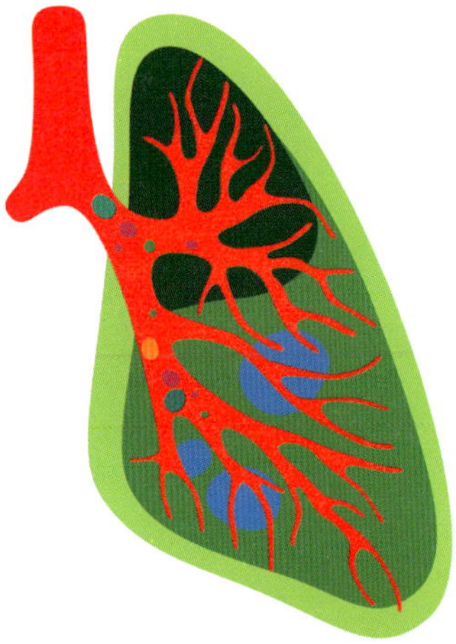

Stockholm Design Lab

Vårdapoteket

A broad, vibrant palette and graphic illustrations celebrates the miracle of the human body while distinguish-

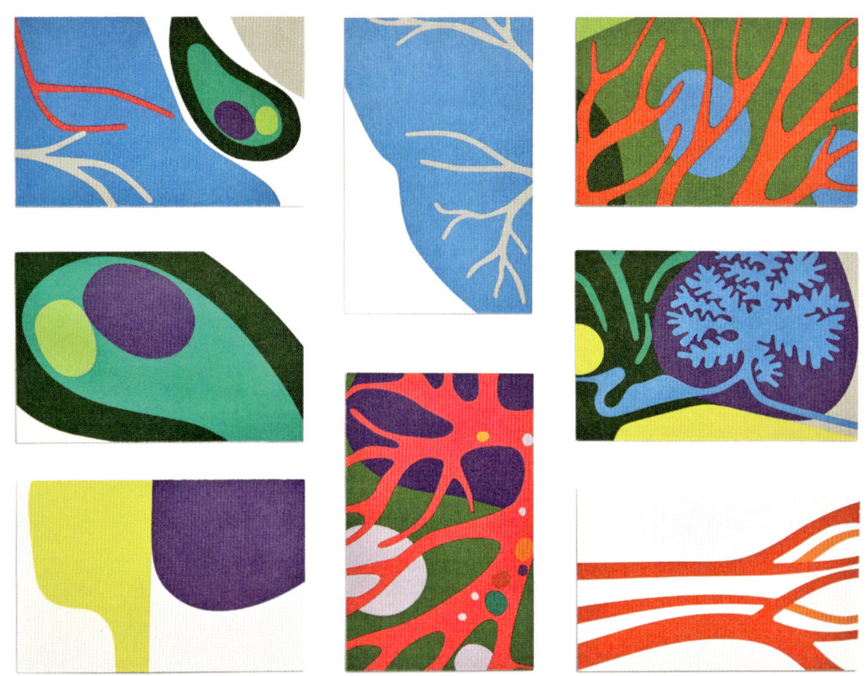

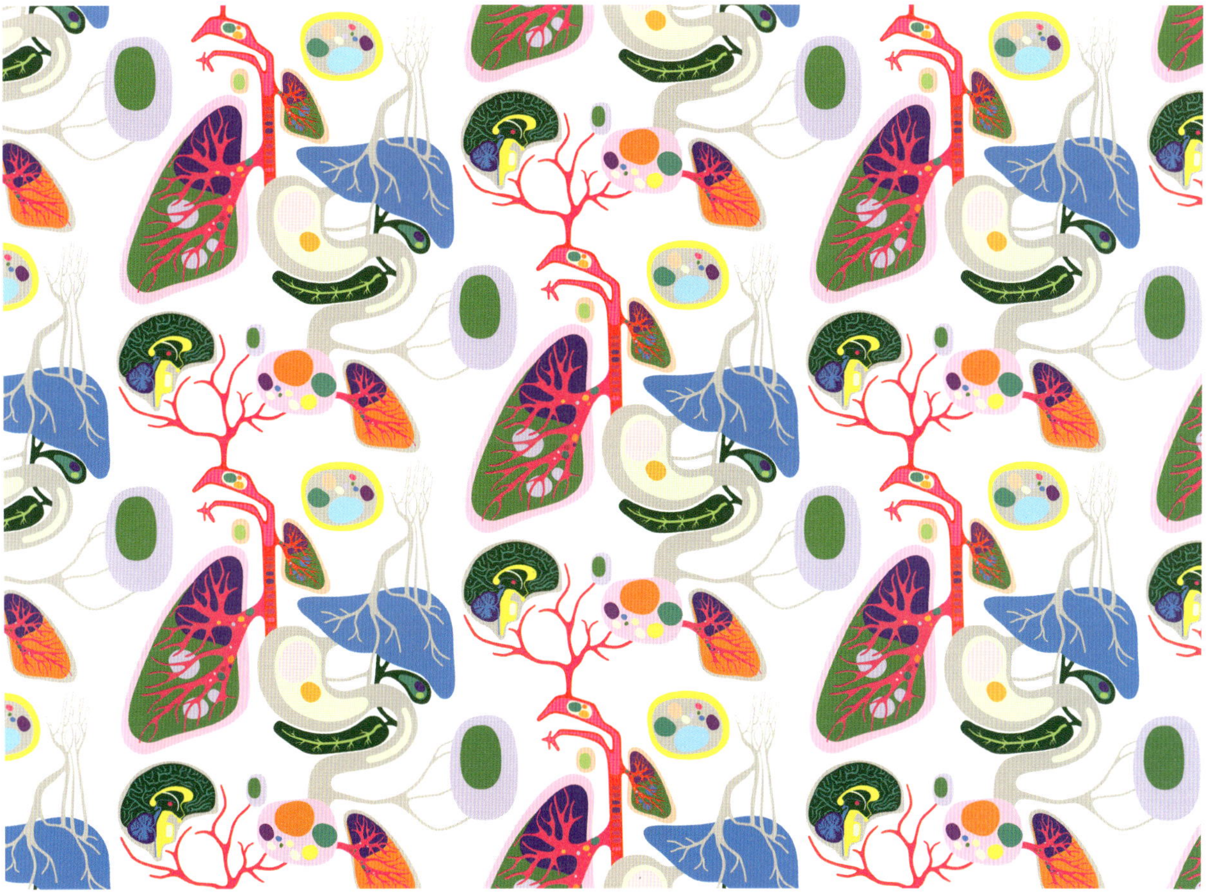

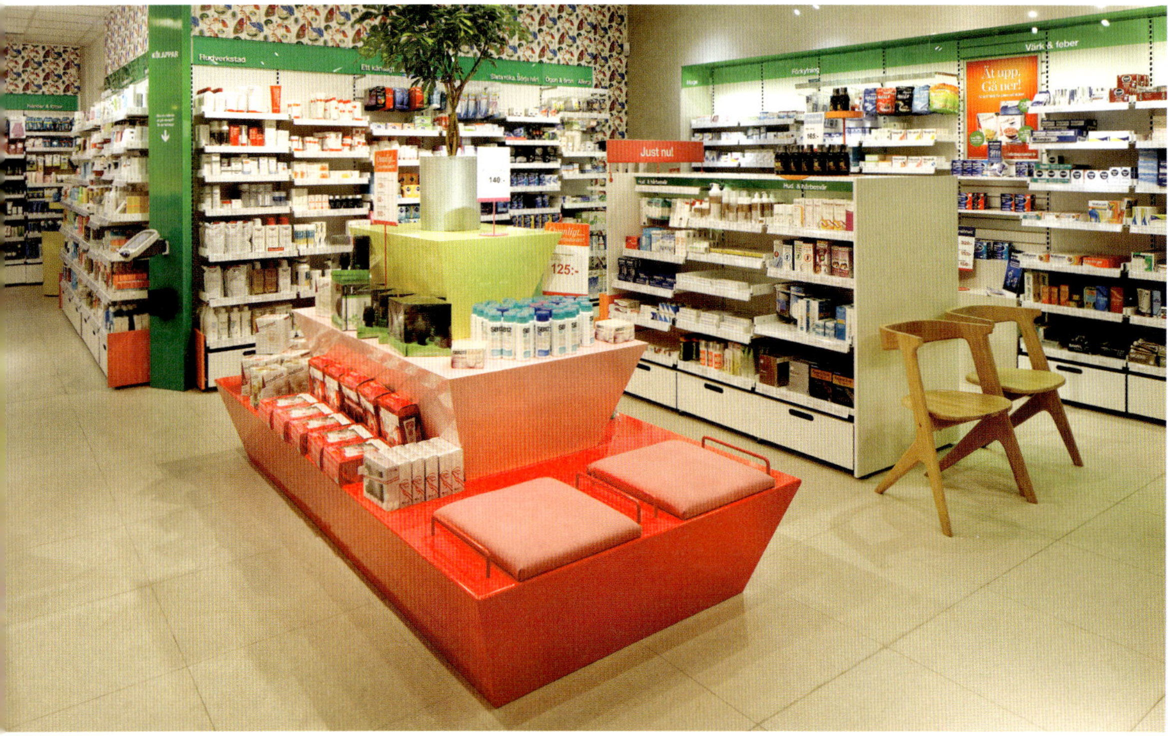

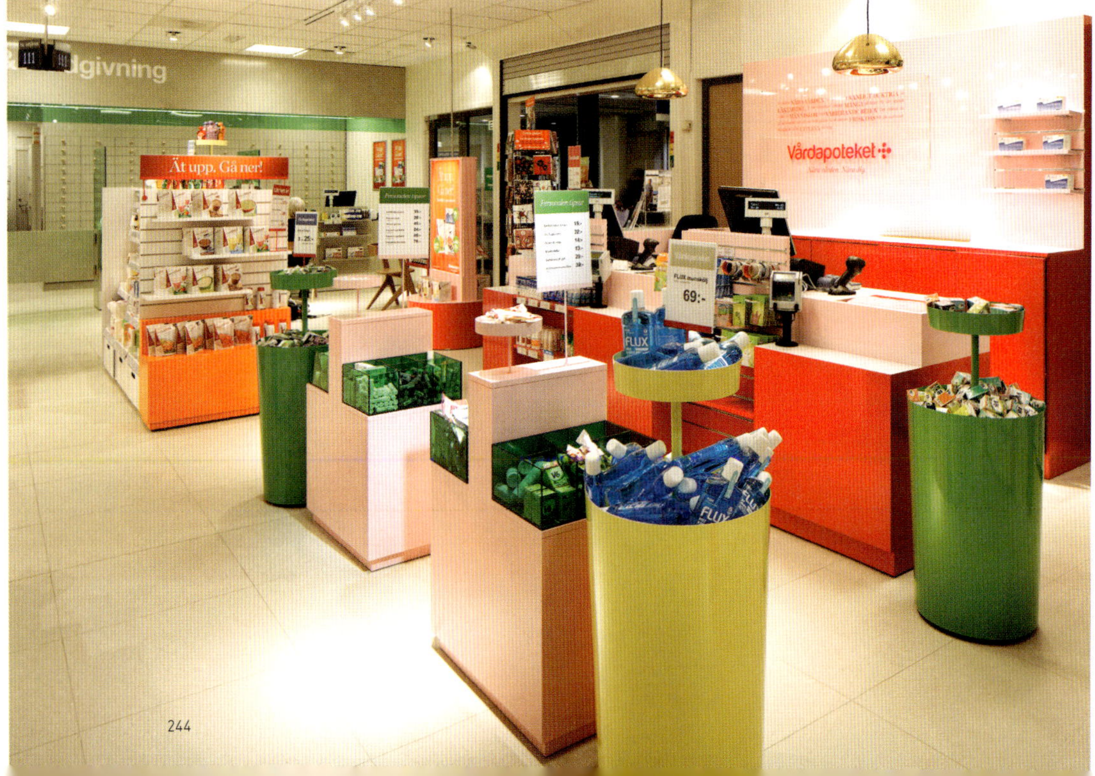
Ät upp. Gå ner!
Vårdapoteket
69:-
FLUX

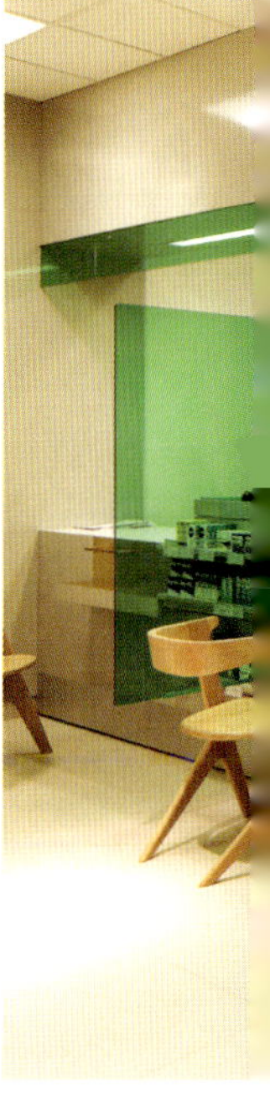

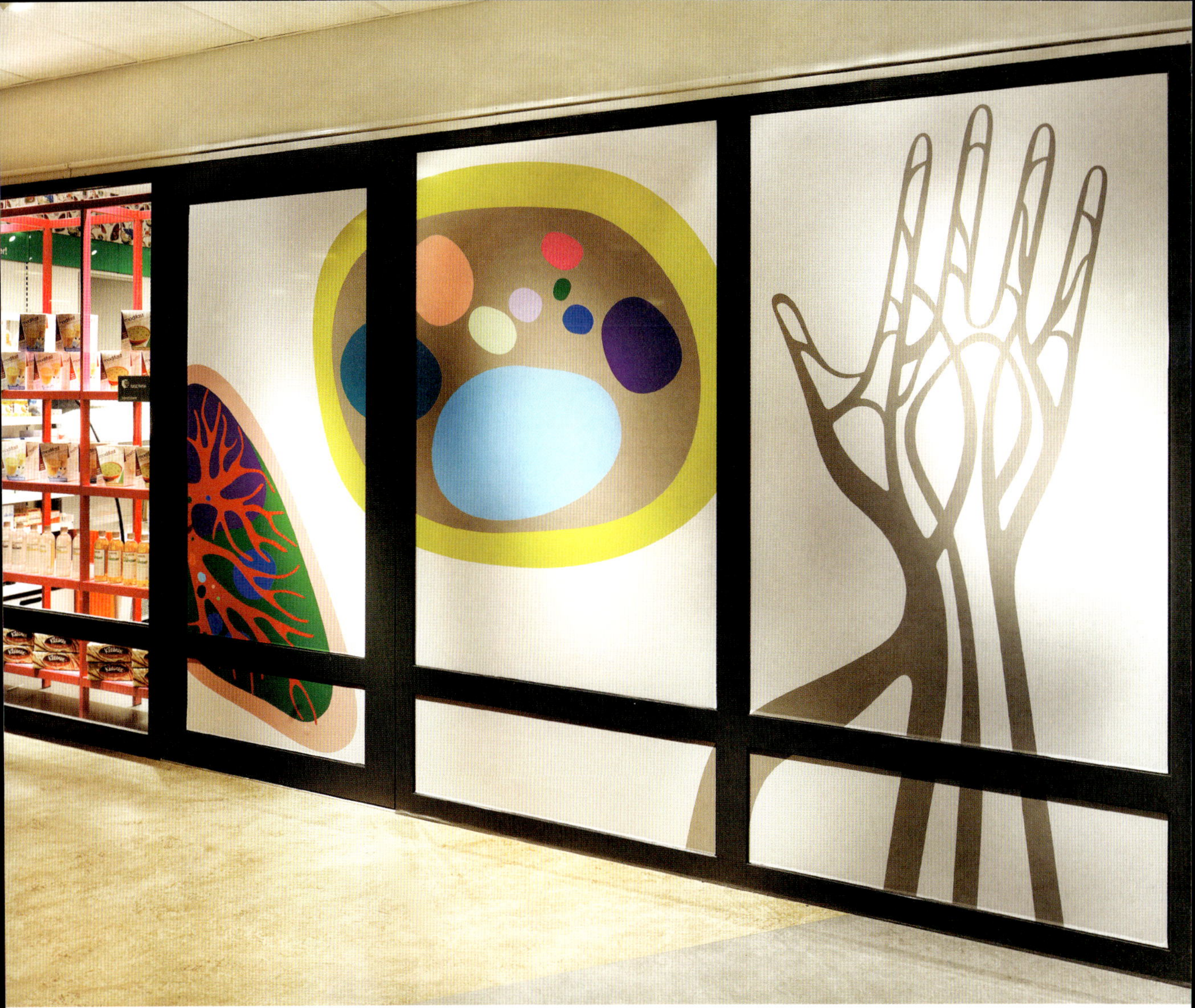

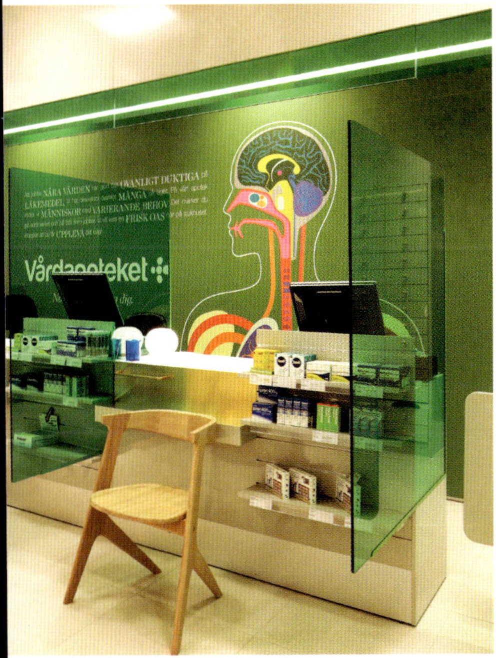
NÄRA VÅRDEN
OVANLIGT DUKTIGA
LÄKEMEDEL
MÅNGA
MÄNNISKOR
VARIERANDE BEHOV
FRISK OAS
UPPLEVA

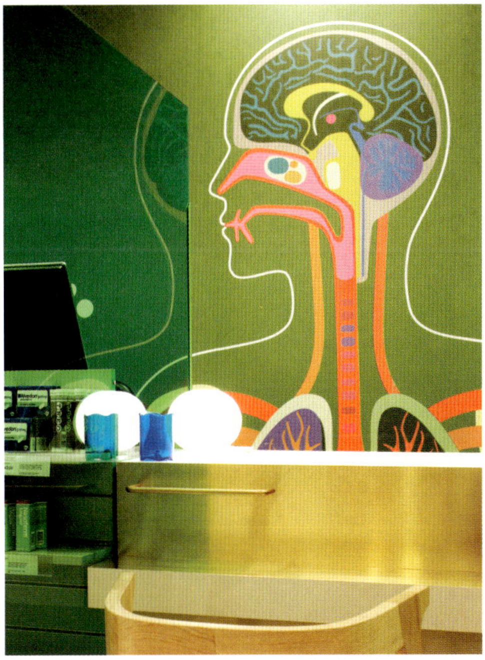

AnAn

Extracting graphic properties from Japanese word characters, gastronomic experience at AnAn is stimulated with a robust geometric pattern running from ceiling to floor throughout the Japanese noodle bar in Germany. Graphic identities echo the architectural space with oriental art and palette to complete its urban look.

Japanese graphics: Keiko Hirasawa, Kentaro 'Ani' Fujimoto, Fuyuki, GWG inc, Maniackers Design, Furi Furi Company, Yamafuji-Zuan, Power Graphixx • Photo: Iwan Baan, Udo Meinel, Mark Raeder
Client: Hosoya Schaefer Architects AG, Autostadt Wolfsburg Germany

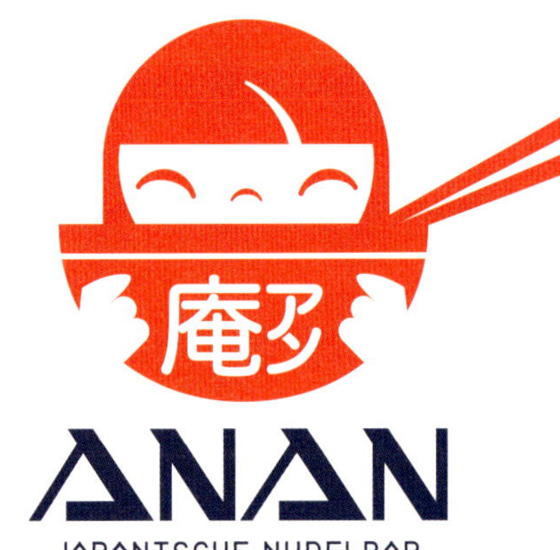

Büro Destruct

AnAn

Extracting graphic properties from Japanese word characters, gastronomic experience at AnAn is stimulated with a robust geometric pattern running from ceiling to floor throughout the Japanese noodle bar in Germany. Graphic identities echo the architectural space with oriental art and palette to complete its urban look.

Japanese graphics: Keiko Hirasawa, Kentaro 'Ani' Fujimoto, Fuyuki, GWG inc, Maniackers Design, Furi Furi Company, Yamafuji-Zuan, Power Graphixx • Photo: Iwan Baan, Udo Meinel, Mark Raeder
Client: Hosoya Schaefer Architects AG, Autostadt Wolfsburg Germany

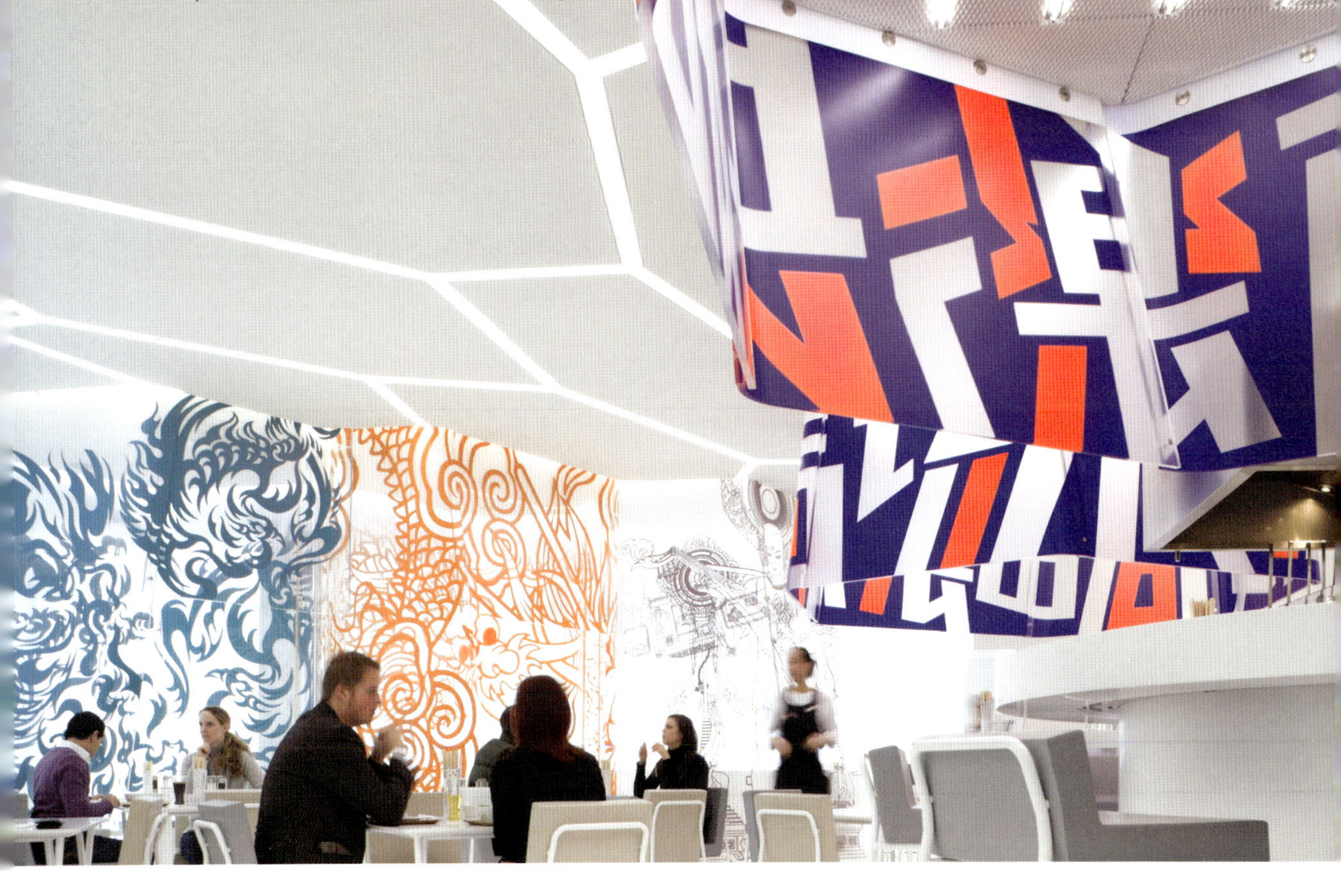

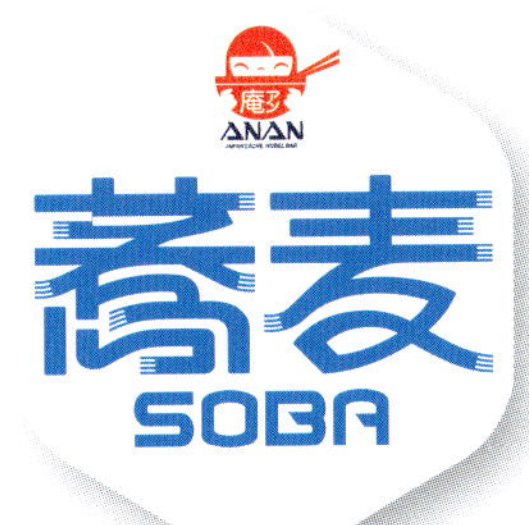
ANAN
蕎麦
SOBA

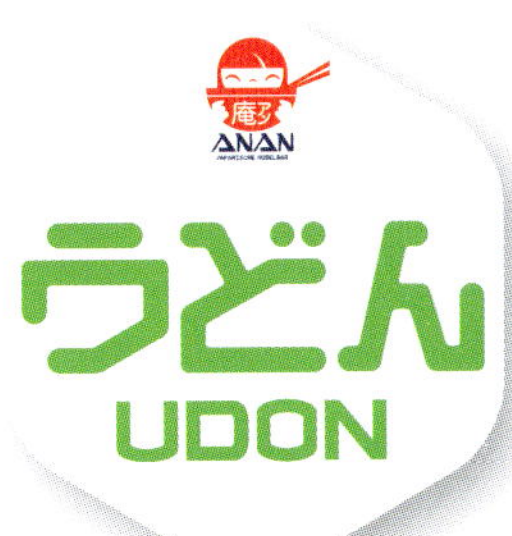
ANAN
うどん
UDON

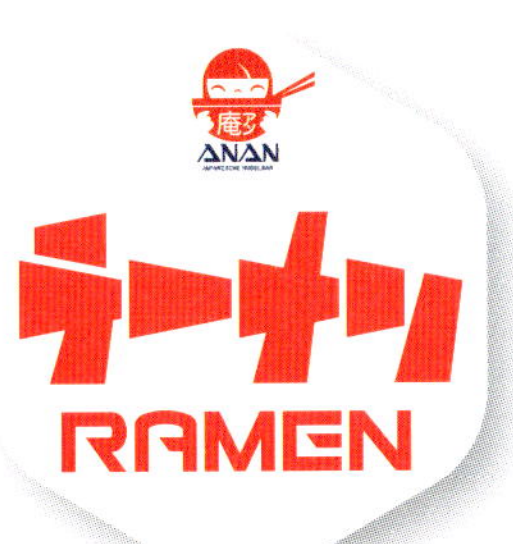
ANAN
ラーメン
RAMEN

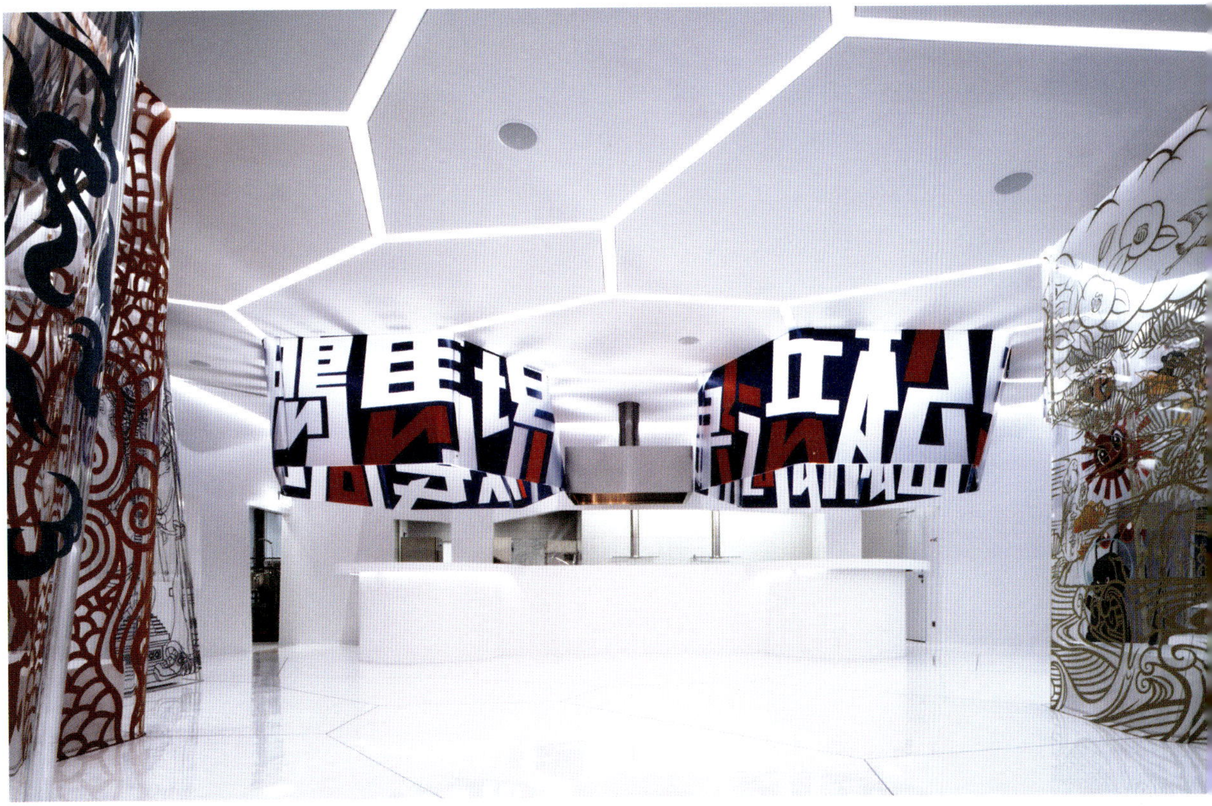

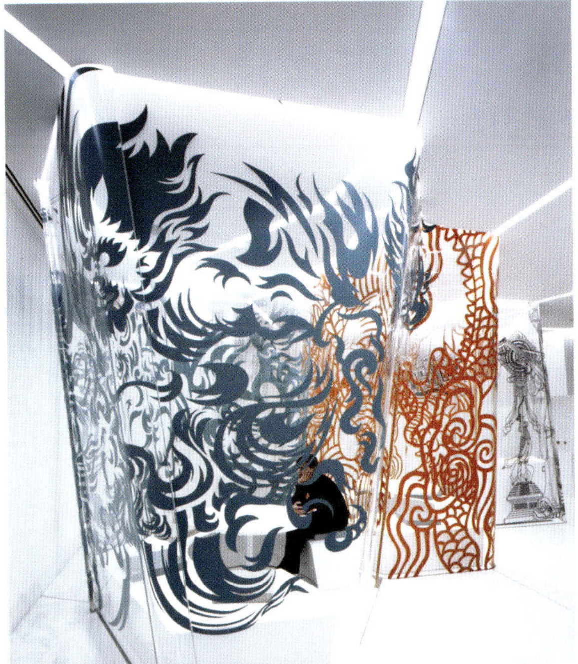

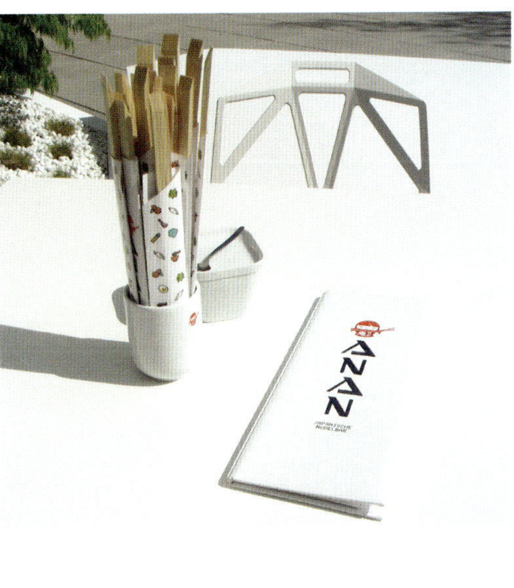
ANAN

De:block

De:block is a nomadic exhibition celebrating Singapore designs. The idea was to stress that good design is much closer to home than people normally think. Correspondingly, the exhibition identity and its collaterals were inspired by everyday items, with an abstract pattern suggestive of the dynamic scene that has been flourishing since the 60s.

Warren Tey

De:block

De:block is a nomadic exhibition celebrating Singapore designs. The idea was to stress that good design is much closer to home than people normally think. Correspondingly, the exhibition identity and its collaterals were inspired by everyday items, with an abstract pattern suggestive of the dynamic scene that has been flourishing since the 60s.

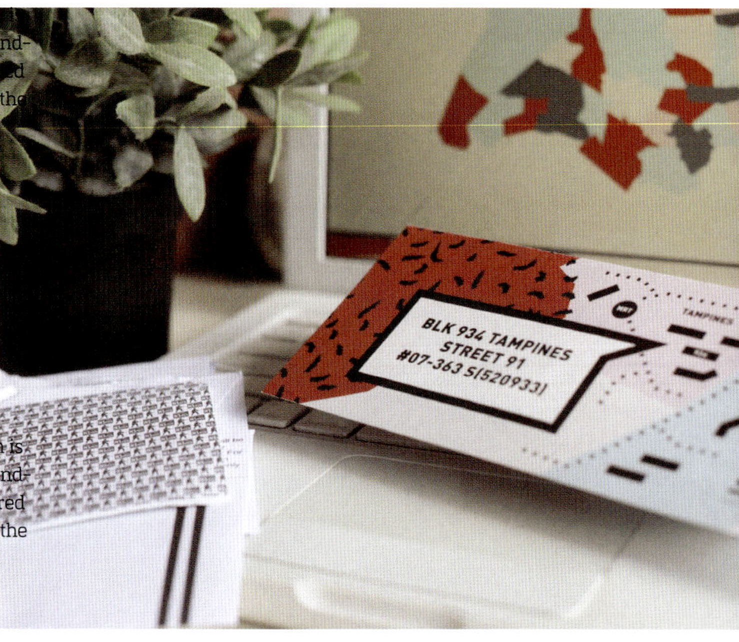

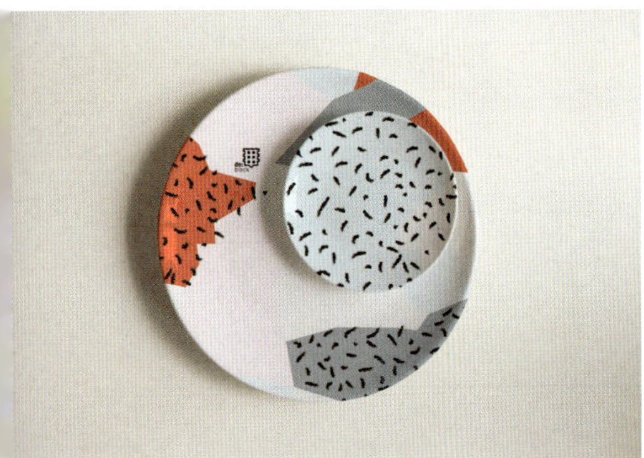

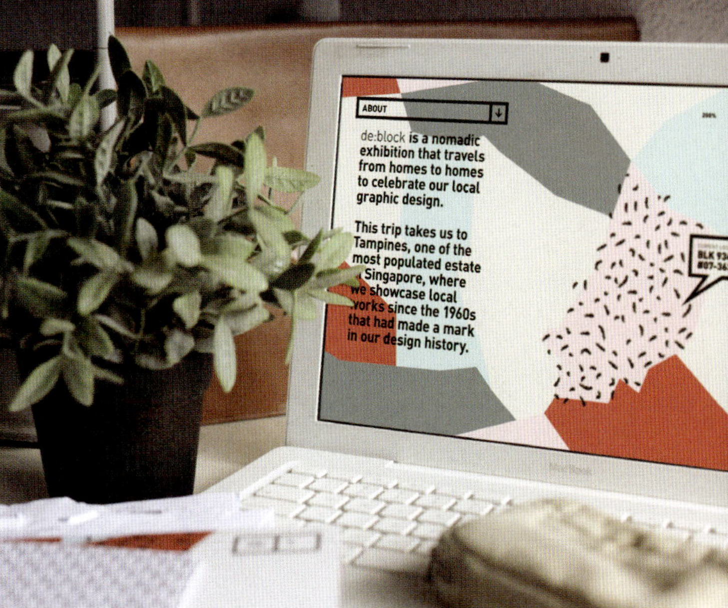

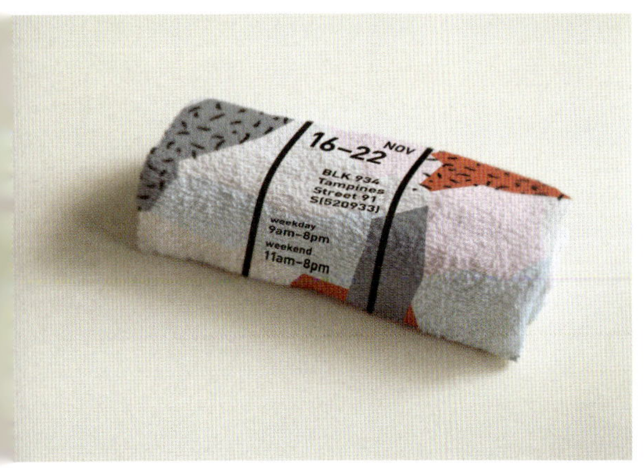

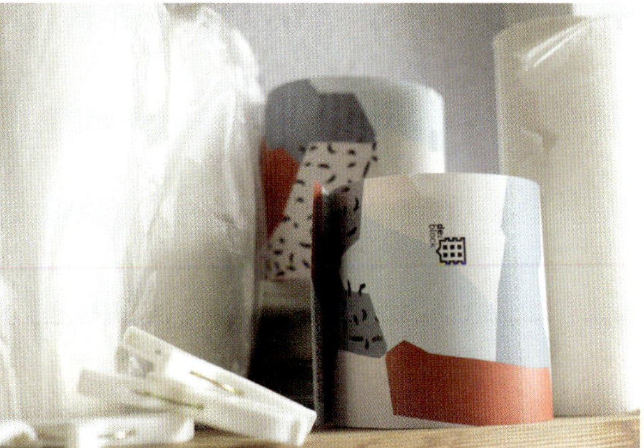

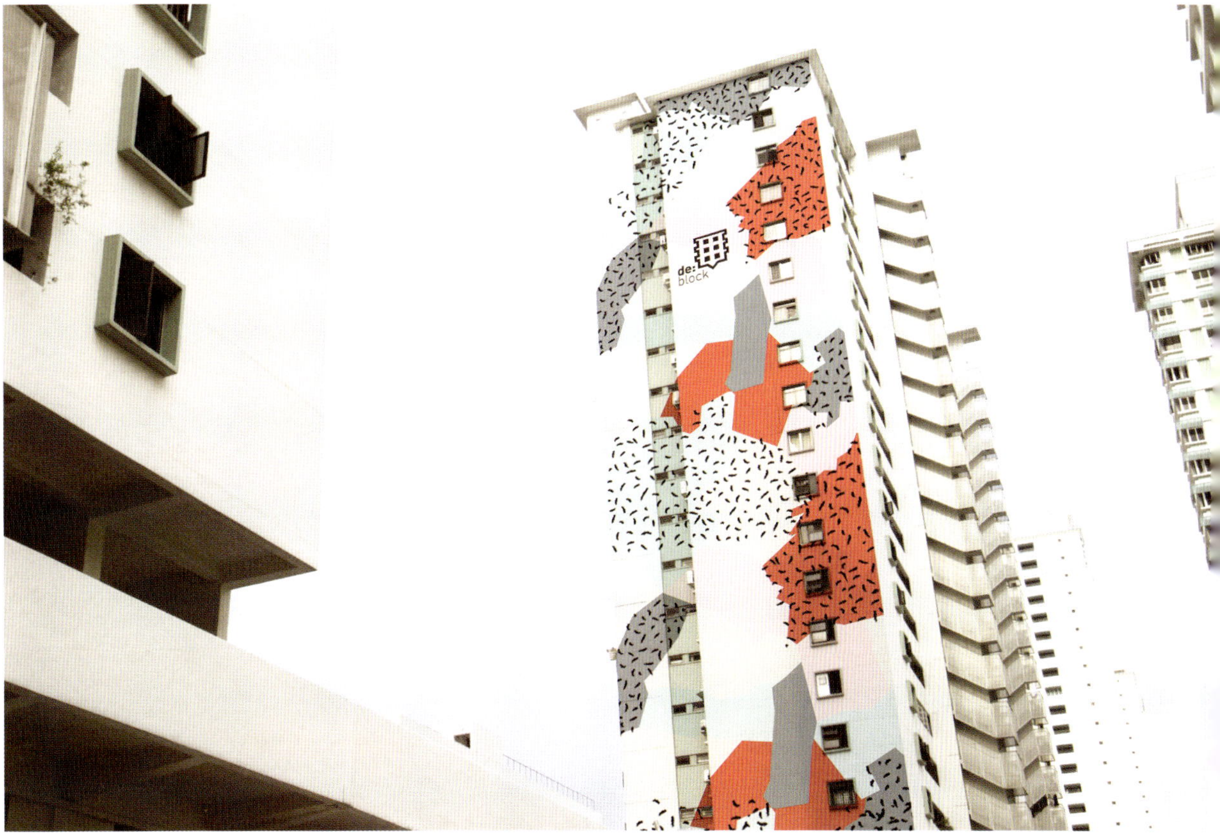

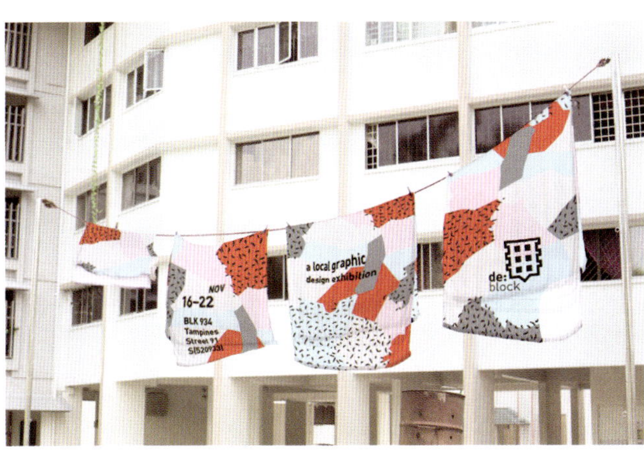
NOV
16–22
BLK 934
Tampines
Street 91
a local graphic
design exhibition
de:
block

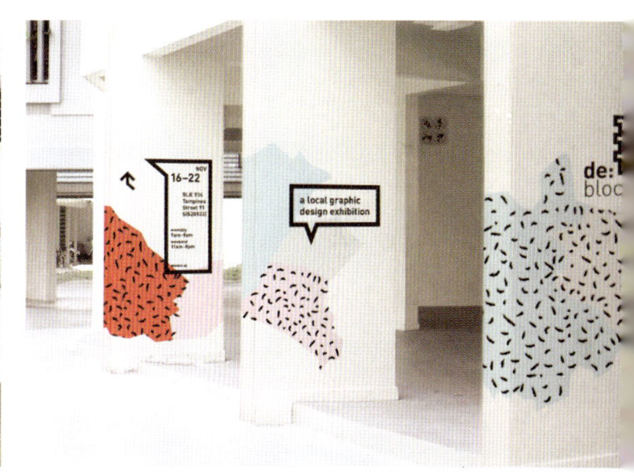
NOV
16–22
a local graphic
design exhibition
de:
bloc

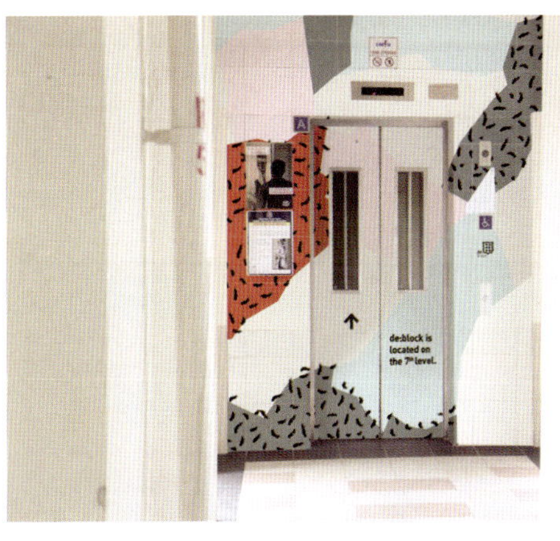
de:block is
located on
the 7th level.

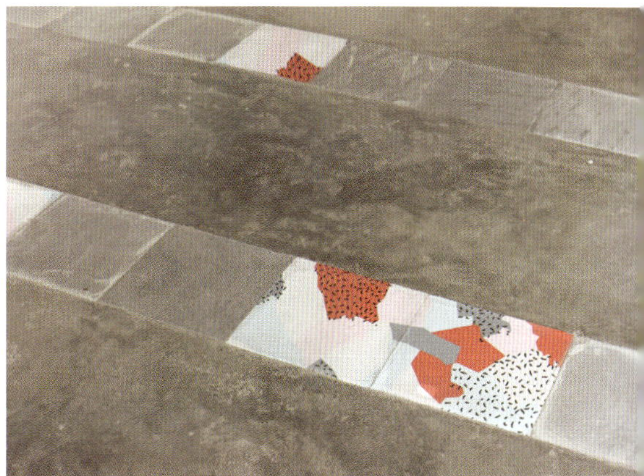

BIO-GRAPHY BIO-GRAPHY BIO-GRAPHY

1983 ASIA, SUSU & YAO

P. 202-205

An Asian design unit founded by Su Su and Yao, specialising in various areas such as branding, character design, packaging, product design, illustration and space design. They had been working in Hong Kong's leading design company Kan & Lau Design Consultants.

Abraham Lule & Kuro Strada

P. 176-177

Lule and Strada are graphic designers based in Querétaro, México. Working across a broad range of fields, they specialises in branding, packaging design and custom lettering; always aiming for an analogue leading method in every project, a strong typography presence is used as the main communicational axis. The duo believes in the artistic approach graphic design can have, without losing its commercial, functional and aesthetic purposes. They like to work with their favourite motto in mind, "Hard work guaranteed run by nice people".

Aleksandrova, Anya

P. 070-071

Aleksandrova is a graphic designer and illustrator from Moscow. She likes to combine design and illustration in her work. She has proudly worked with many clients such as Ginza Project, Sunday Up Market, The Coca-Cola Russia, Time Out Moscow, Akzia Group, HalfBag, and Nebo Gifts Shop, etc.

Bardo

P. 109

Established by Brenda Imboden and Luis Viale, Bardo is a unique design practice that specialises in concept and strategy through creativity in various industries. They are flexible and work under the new paradigm of "no place" through collaboration with experts from different disciplines to enhance the projects.

Besze, Judit

P. 180-181

Based in Hungary, Besze is a freelance graphic desginer who mainly works on branding, graphic design and packaging.

Bielke+Yang

P. 186-189

Bielke+Yang is an Oslo-based graphic design studio led by Christian Bielke and Martin Yang. Their strength lies in identity and communication, for print and web, with projects ranging from concept development, naming, visual profiling, web design to editorial design and packaging design.

Big Horror Athens

P. 126-127

Big Horror Athens is an independent graphic and interactive design studio based in Athens. They design identity systems and multimedia strategies focused on a more fashionable, cultural and passionate way of living. They love typography, clean aesthetics, minimal approaches and clever solutions. The studio was founded in early 2013, by a group of three young people, with many years in the visual communication field (print and interactive).

Bob Studio

P. 066-067, 146-147

Bob is an independent design studio based in Athens and London that works across a wide range of design applications, such as graphic design, typography and illustration. From book, poster, packaging, product and web, to corporate identity and visual communication design.

Booth

P. 164

Booth believes good design is great business. They have experienced with big businesses and start-ups alike, building brands, creating anthems, synthesizing strategies, overhauling websites and making mobile applications.

Büro Destruct

P. 246-247

A Swiss graphic design studio founded in 1994 by Lopetz, MBrunner, HIreber and HGB Fideljus. In line with their motto "Small City – Big Design", the Bern-based studio has been created numbers of excellent art and commercial graphic design projects throughout the 20 years since their establishment.

Calugi, Jonathan

P. 194-197

Each of Jonathan Calugi's work is a take on his quirky childlike doodles with clean minimal lines and simple colours. Some of his recent projects include artist limited series for delonghi, uniqlo and fubon art gallery. The Italy-based illustrator was nominated for Print Magazine's New Visual Artists.

Cheng, Jefferson

P. 068-069

A San Francisco-based designer and illustrator focusing on print, identity, and interactive work with a range of clients, big and small.

Coton Design

P. 076-077

Specialising in logo design, typography, branding, package design and book design, Coton is a studio set up by Japanese graphic designer Hiroko Sakai in Tokyo.

Crosspoint New York, Inc.

P. 082-083

A branch of the successful Korean branding firm Crosspoint, CPNY is a full service branding and design firm founded in NYC in 2007. They strive to create trendsetting brands through creative designing, naming, and strategic consulting. They work closely with clients and collaborators to create award-winning projects and build successful brands. Their strength is in their ability to understand clients and deliver results which both satisfy them and represent them on a personal level, ensuring the best chances for development and success.

BIO-GRAPHY BIO-GRAPHY BIO-GRAPHY

CROWD STUDIO

P. 138-139

CROWD is a Barcelona and London-based studio. They help companies to build and define their brand working from concept to user experience. They are a flexible team that carries out different projects of branding, design, art direction, motion, communication and development of digital experiences.

Designers Anonymous

P. 044-047

Designers Anonymous is the creative agency behind charismatic brands. In a crowded world, they help products, businesses and organisations communicate charismatically to make sure the brands are noticed, understood, admired and remembered.

dn&co.

P. 100-101

dn&co. build brands from the ground up. Strong strategic thinking underpins print, digital, film and exhibition design. An unapologetically modern aesthetic combined with a passion for space and architecture ensure they create work that is original, appropriate and enduring. The studio is based in London.

dolphins// communication design

P. 098-099

dolphins//communication design is a creative business offering design services on visual communication. These services include art direction, design, printing, imaging and web design. The way they approach each project involves a lot of methodical and thorough research, aiming at a creative solution to any communication problem by using prompt and contemporary visual language.

Dung, Kay

P. 032-037

A graduate from Macao Polytechnic Institute, Dung is a Guangzhou-based graphic designer. He was nominated by the 14th Platinum Originality National University Students Graphic Design Competition and the fourth Hiiibrand Awards in 2013. Currently he is represented by Macau creations.

EIGA Design

P. 190-191, 210-213

EIGA is an interdisciplinary design agency. Their role is to spotlight their clients' strengths, aims and values. They use cross-media concepts to convey the brand or company message through a clear and powerful story.

Eskimo Design Studio

P. 216-217

Leading by art director Pavel Emelyanov, Eskimo is one of the most prominent Russian design studios dedicated to the creation of logos, corporate identities, websites and illustrations. A small close-knit team working on the market for over five years, they built up dozens of successful and projects.

Estudio Yeyé

P. 148-151, 226-227, 236-239

Estudio Yeyé is a Mexican design studio based in Chihuahua which specialises in graphic design, photography, publicity and illustration. Their principal goal is simple – To give their clients work that is relevant, innovative and of utmost quality that will help their business to grow.

Ferrandis, Andrea (Kinton)

P.178-179

Andrea Ferrandis is a Spanish graphic designer and industrial designer. Currently she works for the marketing and advertising agency Kinton in Barcelona.

Foxall Studio

P. 095

Founded in 2006 in Istanbul by brothers Andrew and Iain Foxall. Foxall Studio is an art direction agency that creates design and content for fashion, art and design-led brands from their studio in London. Notable projects include designing and art directing the launch issue of Vogue in Turkey, GQ in Brasil and Ponystep and NearEast in London, alongside work for numerous brands including Aquascutum, Bond Street, Bora Aksu, M.A.C, Magnum Photos and Vitra.

FullFill Artplication

P. 222-223

Established in 2008 by like-minded creative souls, they are now one of the leading graphic studios in Indonesia currently serving local and overseas clients. Work done by FullFill can be described in short as impactful, professional and playful. Their strength is in visual exploration to deliver a spot-on communication objective.

Gal Sevi Karniel @ Studio OPEN.Total Brand Experience

P. 220-221

Gal Sevi Karniel is a graphic designer from Tel Aviv, Israel.

Gopaul, Rosie

P. 102-103

Graduated from The Art Institute of Vancouver in 2013 with the Bachelor's degree of Applied Design, Gopaul then had an internship at Rethink Communications and now works as a media designer at Ballistic Arts Media Studios.

Happycentro

P. 064-065, 114-115

Founded in 1998 in Verona, Happycentro has worked for both big and small clients since then. Mixing complexit, order and fatigue is their formula for beauty. In addition to the commissioned work, the team always spends plenty of energy in research and testing on visual art, typography, graphic design, illustration, animation, film direction and music.

Hara Design Institute

P. 108

Hara Design Institute is a design think tank. Led by acclaimed Japanese graphic designer Kenya Hara, they specialises in graphic design, architecture, products, websites, books, exhibitions, hotel direction, urban systems and navigation design.

Huang, Zhong-xing (Park Lane by Splendor)

P. 136-137

Born in Changhua, Taiwan, Huang is a graphic and installation designer. He has been working in the design department at ParkLane by Splendor of CMP, mostly on advertising and graphic design projects.

Il-Ho Jung design, interactive & motion

P. 198-201

Jung is a freelance art director and designer for graphic design, interactive and motion. With joy for design he has developed a broad knowledge of many different disciplines and is always eager to expand it with each new project.

Jullien, Jean

P. 080-081

A French graphic designer living and working in London. Jullien comes from Nantes and did a graphic design degree in Quimper. He graduated from Central Saint Martins in 2008 and from the Royal College of Art in 2010. He works closely with the musician Niwouinwouin. His practice ranges from Illustration to photography, video, costumes, installations, books, posters and clothing to create a coherent yet eclectic body of work. In 2011, Jullien founded Jullien Brothers, a duo specialising in moving images. Besides, he created News of the Times with Yann Le Bec and Gwendal Le Bec.

Kinetic Singapore

P. 228-233

Kinetic is an award-winning creative agency based in Singapore.

Ko. Machiyama

P. 056-061

Graduated from Tokyo Zokei University in 2004, Kotaro Machiyama is a Tokyo-based painter and illustrator who specialising in abstract paintings and fashion illustration.

Kokoro & Moi

P. 038-043

Established by creative director Teemu Suviala and Antti Hinkula in 2001, Kokoro & Moi is a full-service creative agency transforming brands with bold ideas and progressive concepts. They focus on strategy, identity and design.

Kolesnikova, Anastasia

P. 026-031

Kolesnikova is a young designer based in Krasnodar, Russia. She specialises in web and graphic design and works on different kinds of projects ranging from branding identity, logo, printing, illustration, poster and editorial design.

Landini, Federico

P. 194-197

Landini is an Italian self-taught graphic designer focused on identity and type design. Starting from very accurate details he delivers thought-provoking concepts coming from his life experience. A font created using Microsoft Excel '97 and converting his father Fabrizio into Didone style typeface are some of his featured work.

Larios, Enrique

P. 192-193

Larios is a graphic designer based in Guadalajara, Mexico. Specialising in branding, art direction, visual merchandising and advertising design, he is also interested in branding and digital illustration.

Lee, Ken-tsai

P. 048-053

Lee is the assistant professor of Industry and Commercial Design Department and the mastermind of ken-tsai lee design lab at Taiwan TECH, and visual director of Taiwan Designers' Week since 2008. He was selected as the local representative of ADC New York and TDC New York in 2009.

Lim, Sidney

P. 090-091

Born and raised in Singapore, Sidney Lim somehow found his way to London in 2011, where he is currently a graphic design student at Central St. Martin's. Pretty much an open book, he always strives to instil laughter, light-heartedness, and a touch of humour in his work.

Liow, Heng-chun

P. 008-013

A design enthusiast based in Malaysia.

Lo Siento

P. 107, 208-209

Graduating from London College of Communication, London Institute in 2003, Borja Martínez set up the agency in 2004 in Barcelona working in a wide range of projects from packaging, music covers, editorial design, graphic identities for restaurants and film production companies.

Mind Design

P. 162-163

Mind Design is an independent graphic design studio based in East London. The studio was established in 1999 by RCA graduate Holger Jacobs and specialises in the development of visual identities which includes print, web, packaging, signage and interior graphics. Their approach combines hands-on craftmanship, conceptual thinking and most importantly, intuition. Visual ideas are often developed on the basis of research into production processes or the use of unusual materials.

moodley brand identity

P. 020-025

An owner-led, award-winning strategic design agency with offices in Vienna and Graz. Since 1999 moodley has worked together with their customers to develop corporate and product brands which live, breathe and grow. moodley believes that their key contribution is to analize complex requirements and develop simple, smart solutions with emotional appeal – whether corporate start-up, product launch or brand positioning.

BIO-GRAPHY

BIO-GRAPHY BIO-GRAPHY

Mucca Design

P. 120-121

Mucca Design is an award-winning branding design firm based in New York City. Known for the iconic branding behind now-classic culinary NYC destinations such as Balthazar Restaurant, Pastis and Brooklyn Fare, Mucca continues to produce smart and beautiful brands that stand the test of time.

MURA

P. 122-123

MURA is a Taichung-based multidisciplinary branding company.

Nakajima, Ryoji

P. 124-125

Based in Osaka, Japan, Nakajima is a freelance illustrator and painter. Bold lines and simple colours are the distinctive characteristics of his work. He works on a wide range of projects including editorial, publication, products, packaging and promotions.

NHOMADA

P. 142-143, 206-207

Founded by creative director and designer Diego Leyva, NHOMADA a multidisciplinary design studio in Mexico City. They focus on developing branding experiences in all types of media and provide a comprehensive communication service.

Offert, Kinga

P.154-155

Based in Poznań, Poland, Offert is an artist, illustrator and graphic designer. Her passion led her to start up her own constantly evolving label and accompanying shop.

Oh Babushka

P. 218-219

Oh Babushka is a graphic design company that has been crafting original ideas since 2006. They love working closely with makers, individuals, startups and businesses to create beautiful and meaningful design that says things clearly.

ONE & ONE DESIGN

P. 112-113

Located in Beijing, China, ONE & ONE DESIGN focuses on brand integration, brand packaging, VIS design and other design related field.

oraviva! designers

P. 160-161

A Porto-based graphic design studio that develops projects in a wide variety of disciplines such as branding, promotion, editorial design, web design, signage, packaging, motion graphics, illustration and infography. They are known for an emotional approach towards communication, privileging the use of typography, illustration and colour to bring to life strong and meaningful brands.

P.A.R

P. 084-085

Established by Iris Tarraga and Lucía Castro, P.A.R is a graphic design and art direction studio based in Barcelona. They believe in functional design and choosing colour palette and typography precisely for each of their creation. Clear and direct are the significant characteristics of P.A.R, who wants to keep the balance and a sense of harmony in their graphic design.

Perky Bros llc

P. 182-183

Established in 2009, the Nashville-based branding and design office Perky Bros exists to help brands gain clarity, value and distinction through design. They create visual identities, websites, packaging, print materials and any odds and ends necessary to create an authentic experience.

Polyester Studio

P. 214-215

An animation and design studio that creates well-designed character driven stories with enduring concepts full of humour and emotion for cinema, broadcast, online and print media. They are a hands-on, artist-driven shop that strives to give life to an infinity of stories and characters for any medium.

Quintana, Gustavo Emilio

P. 140-141

Based in Guatemala, Quintana is a multidisciplinary designer who works in various design areas such as architecture, interior design, graphic design , industrial design, UI/UX design as well as creative and art direction.

Robot Food

P. 104-105

Specialising in branding, packaging, innovation, creative spaces and web, Robot Food is a Leeds-based design studio founded in 2009.

RONCHAM DESIGN OFFICE

P. 086-087

RONCHAM is a brand design agency based in Pairs, Shanghai and Changzhou. They focus on building brand value that moves their clients' businesses forward. The service includes brand strategy, corporate identity, brand identity, packaging, retail & environmental, etc.

Rossoamaranto

P. 224-225

An agency and brand consultancy founded on a shared principle – the real projects come from ideas. It is also a flexible space that gathers talents from different nature and origin to share ideas, insights and creativity.

Sciencewerk

P. 116-119

Established in 2011, Sciencewerk is an independent design studio based in Indonesia. They are a team of multidisciplinary designers that creates identity design, websites, prints, objects for corporate clients, organisations, individuals, and self-initiative projects. They work collectively in various media with the most interesting people apt in digital to traditional craft.

BIO-GRAPHY BIO-GRAPHY BIO-GRAPHY

SeventhDesign™

P. 240-241

Bruno H. Siriani aka SeventhDesign™ is a graphic designer based in Buenos Aires, Argentina, creating customised and ambitious solutions for national and international clients for almost seven years. With expertise in identity, print, packaging, interactivity and environments, the studio crafts initiatives that integrate multiple disciplines.

Shinsegae Graphic Design

P. 234-235

Founded in 2010, Shinsegae Graphic Design focuses on brand strategy and design, print, package, retail and multimedia design for Shinsegae Department Store in South Korea.

SHISHKI branding agency

P. 134-135

Founded in 2009, SHISHKI is a branding agency for the brave. They are a young and creative team with fresh, non-conventional approach. They have strong principles and proven ready-to-work processes.

Sleep Projects

P. 128-129

Specialising in innovative design projects, Sleep is a multidisciplinary practice. Their portfolio encompasses conceptual design, advertising, art projects, creative direction and spatial design.

Spendowska, Marta

P. 088-089

Working between fine art and commercial art, Spendowska has been collaborating with collectors, fashion, food, beauty brands, ad agencies and magazines since she has moved to the US in 2005. She has also established VERYMARTA to produce a series of watercolour products such as scarves, ceramics, fine art and fashion items. She is represented by a leading international illustration and animation agency Illustration Ltd with offices in London, New York, Hamburg, Paris and Shanghai.

Stockholm Design Lab

P. 242-245

Stockholm Design Lab creates simple, helpful, and remarkable strategic design for global brands and small businesses. SDL has more than 15 years of experience working internationally with a wide variety of projects in all kinds of industries; from airlines, museums, fashion labels, hotels, fast moving consuming goods to retail environments, technology companies, cultural and educational institutions and pharmacies.

Studio AH — HA

P. 168-171

Studio AH – HA is a communication and graphic design studio established in 2011 by Carolina Cantante and Catarina Carreiras. The studio pursues varied creative interests across a variety of mediums, from brand strategy to interior design, naming and identity work, advertising, new media, traditional and fine print, retail and product design, photography and illustration.

Studio Brave

P. 094

Founded in 2002, Studio Brave is a Melbourne-based design studio driven by the creation of unique, distinctive and memorable brand communication. Their guiding vision comes from their name. Brave thinking leads to unexpected outcomes.

Studioahamed

P. 130-133

Studioahamed is a design collective focuses on building connections within creative communities through the means of simplicity and complexity.

Substance

P. 152-153, 165

"Substance" is defined as the most essential and vital part of an idea or experience. It was founded as a multidisciplinary design and brand agency in Paris in 2005. Substance prides itself on providing unique and strategic services including branding, brand strategy, story-telling, interior design, industrial design, packaging design, web design, site showcases, social platform design, media device design, interactive installation design and application design.

Tan, Calvin

P. 156-159

Tan is a Malaysian multidisciplinary graphic designer. He works on a diverse range of projects including branding, packaging, digital art, editorial design, illustration and mixed media.

Tey, Warren

P. 248-249

Tey is a graphic design student from Singapore. He is in his final year in School of Art, Design and Media at Nanyang Technological University. He seeks to challenge and question visual communication in this era.

Tofu

P. 062-063

A young and ambitious creative studio native to Tiong Bahru's vibrant Yong Siak Street, Tofu considers itself an institute for the incubation of ideas. It is a collective of designers, art directors, illustrators, thinkers, collaborators and dreamers, united in their unwavering quest for meaningful communication and the perfection of their craft.

Turner, Vicki

P. 078-079

British Designer, illustrator and maker with a passion for the natural world, Turner works with clients to fix problems and bring stories to life, working in the realms of branding, product, to illustration and continues to develop personal projects through making, drawing and collaboration.

BIO-GRAPHY BIO-GRAPHY BIO-GRAPHY

TYMOTE

P. 092-093

Established in 2008, TYMOTE has been engaging in many different categories of client projects and producing work in the field of graphic design, motion, music and programming. To be the "Pirates of design" is their overarching goal.

viction workshop ltd

P. 166-167

Established as an identity to emphasise the strength of collaborative efforts in the area of visual communication, not only does viction:ary create multiple dimensions for the understanding of design and visual graphics, but also a channel for creative talents to share their truest spirits with people from around the world. Since its establishment under multidisciplinary design house, viction workshop in 2001, viction:ary has built a portfolio of more than 60 publications available worldwide.

Victor Branding Design Corp.,

P. 014-019, 072-075, 090-097, 110-111

Since its estalbishment in 1988, Victor Art Corporation has set a mission in "Your Design Partners" by gathering talents of relevant fields with commitment in branding, visual design, role-shaping, packaging design and advertisement, forming a multi-dimensional professional integration service team.

village®

P. 106

village® is a design company founded by art director and designer Rikako Nagashima in 2014, after working at Hakuhodo Inc. Her work covers a wide range of projects including branding, product design and graphic design.

Vinogradova, Sasha

P. 144-145

Currently living and working in L.A., Vinogradova is a Russian artist and graphic designer. She creates key visuals for movies and programmes for the entertainment industry.

Vissers, Mara

P. 172-175

Currently working for the Persgroep publishers, Vissers is an Amsterdam-based graphic designer. She works closely with the news media including the popular Dutch newspapers de Volkskrant, Trouw and Het Parool. From developing concept to art direction and design, she uses these effective elements to tell every story. She wants to make good design that deliver the right message and feeling through typography, paper, structures, materials, colours, and details, etc.